MRS. SETON

MRS. SETON

*Foundress of
the American Sisters of Charity*

JOSEPH I. DIRVIN, C.M.

NEW CANONIZATION EDITION

FARRAR, STRAUS AND GIROUX
New York

Imprimi potest:
SILVESTER A. TAGGART, C.M.
Visitator Provinciae Orientalis

Nihil obstat:
NICOLAUS FERRARO, S.R.C. Adsessor
Fidei Sub-Promotor Generalis

Roma
3 Martii 1962

Nihil obstat:
JOHN A. GOODWINE, J.C.D.
Censor Librorum

Imprimatur:
† FRANCIS CARDINAL SPELLMAN
Archbishop of New York
New York
June 26, 1962

Contents

Illustrations

Foreword

The great importance of Elizabeth Ann Seton to America has still to be realized. The announcement of her forthcoming canonization by the Church marks the close of a long preliminary process of preparation. Now we look forward hopefully and prayerfully to the full exercise of her influence on our behalf. The potential for our country and our Church of this wise, dynamic woman can be drawn from a careful study of her life, its confluence with civic and ecclesiastical history and its effects both actual and possible. We in New York especially rejoice in the news of her canonization since the history of the Catholic Church in this city almost from its very beginning has been enriched by the memory and by the enduring educational and charitable works of this great daughter of New York.

Elizabeth Ann Seton was but a week old when the First Continental Congress met at Carpenter's Hall in Philadelphia to take the first steps toward independence. She became a charter citizen of the new nation at the age of two. She might be considered the prototype American: her blood lines were Old World—Dutch, French, English, Irish; but her roots were New World: her father was born in Fairfield, Connecticut, and her mother probably on Staten Island, New York. They were blood lines and roots that counted, and bore names like LeConte, Mercier, Van Cortlandt, DePeyster and Bayeux; they were to entwine themselves with names like Roosevelt, Barclay, White, Pell and Craig. It was inevitable that, as a grown woman, she should count the Ogdens and DeLanceys and Hamiltons and Jays and Clintons—and even President George Washington—among her friends and acquaintances.

She was part of the social history of the times, the infant times so important to the future. Her father was the first health officer in New York City, perhaps the first such official in the nation. The Widows' Society in New York, a civic and religious association of charitable women of which she was a founder, was a forerunner of thousands of such efforts across the country today. She gave the young United States schools, orphanages and hospitals at a time when few such institutions existed.

Her coming into fresh prominence on the eve of our beloved country's bicentennial—at a moment when, besides its ever-present political, financial, domestic and international problems, the basic morality of our nation seems at times to have lost its direction—is surely a call to look back, to re-examine our ideals and reaffirm our integrity. There is much to be gained in reviewing an age which produced a Washington, a Jefferson— and an Elizabeth Seton.

Nor can it be accidental that a great woman should come into her own at the height of a campaign for woman's full freedom and total dignity— at the beginning of the International Women's Year. Elizabeth Seton is perduring proof of what woman can and should do.

Her importance to the Church should be clear, but here again there is much to be understood. This is not to gainsay the deep personal devotion to Mother Seton of millions who have sought her intercession and prayed and worked actively for her canonization. Without them it would never have come to pass. But even they must avoid the danger of placing her in her niche and merely going away to parcel out silent moments of their lives to pray to her. Others who have openly doubted the usefulness of her formal canonization have even more to learn.

There is an interesting puzzle of significance in its very delay. The extraordinary sanctity of Mother Seton seems to have been universally accepted when she died in January 1821. Her spiritual director, Father Bruté, who knew it best, instructed her Sisters and family and friends to save every scrap of her writings—and they took him literally: there are extant torn bits of paper with as little as three words on them. Why, then, should so little have been done—except for the 1853 biography of Father Charles I. White—to bring her to the knowledge of the country and of the universal Church until sixty years after her death? It was only in 1882 that James Cardinal Gibbons of Baltimore felt moved to begin the first tentative steps after saying Mass at her tomb. Even this beginning took fifty-four years to complete, and it was not until January 15, 1936, that the Sacred Congregation of Rites was satisfied that "no obstacle exists against taking further steps relative to the Cause." The Cause was formally introduced on February 28, 1940.

It met with formidable technical obstacles. Since there were no living witnesses to her heroic life and virtues, the Congregation initiated an historical process which substituted authenticated writings, her own and those of others, for such witnesses. Although proof of her baptism had been lacking, since Trinity Church and its records had been destroyed when New York was set on fire by the colonial rebels in 1776, direct testimony was discovered written in her own hand in the margin of a page of her copy of *The Following of Christ*.

Actually, once these obstacles were surmounted, the Cause advanced with a certain dispatch, when one considers the enormity and depth of the research and the prudent caution of the Holy See. By 1959 the Sacred Congregation was convinced of the heroicity of her spiritual life and Pope John XXIII accorded her the title of Venerable on December 18 of that year. Two years later, the Congregation declared that God had shown His good pleasure in Mother Seton's glorification by working two miraculous cures through her intercession: the cure of Sister Gertrude Korzendorfer, D.C., of cancer of the head of the pancreas in January 1935 and the cure of Anne Theresa O'Neill of acute leukemia (lymphatic type) at the age of four in 1952. In the midst of a joyful multitude of her spiritual daughters and sons, Pope John beatified Elizabeth Ann Seton on March 17, 1963.

Her canonization now waited a further indication of God's will. In October of that same year, 1963, a Lutheran construction worker named Carl Kalin was allegedly cured of a rare brain disease through Mother Seton's intercession. After eight years of intensive study, the Holy See declared that cure truly miraculous, and Pope Paul VI decreed her canonization on December 12, 1974. Recognition of the importance, even urgency, of her canonization seems to be indicated by the Pope's dispensation from a second miracle ordinarily required by the process.

The canonization of a holy American woman dead for 154 years comes, then, precisely at a time when the American Church like the Church throughout the world faces severe challenges from without and, indeed, at times from within. It comes at a time when many of her faithful members long for reassurance and resolution. In simple words, it comes at a time of great and immediate need.

The instinct of the faithful to look for a God-given leader is unerring. Throughout history, God has raised up saints to meet crises of faith and practice, saints like St. Dominic and St. Francis, St. Teresa of Avila, St. Catherine of Siena, St. Ignatius Loyola, St. Vincent de Paul. What gives special significance to His choice of Elizabeth Ann Seton to meet our crisis—and there is little doubt that He has so spoken through His Church and His Vicar—is that His choices of the past were actually living in the time of crisis.

From all of this, in the providence of God, it is evident that our Church and our country are called to pay special attention to our first native-born saint.

Even a cursory study reveals why. She was the embodiment of the very qualities we are in danger of losing. First and greatest of all, Elizabeth Seton had a solid, unyielding faith: she believed simply and serenely in God, in the teachings of her Church, in the integrity and future of her country. She had unbounded hope and optimism. With faith like this, there was no place for faltering or despair. Her charity embraced all, the loved and the unloved, the liked and the frankly disliked. Everyone found in her compassion and encouragement. Everyone looked to her for stability and peace.

Father Joseph Dirvin's biography is filled with Elizabeth Seton's wisdom and common sense, quoted in her own words and applied in many specific instances to civic, social and spiritual problems relevant to our own times. This new edition at this time is a recognition and an affirmation of her significance and immediacy for the American Church and our beloved country. The fact that it is autobiographical in the sense that Father Dirvin has let her tell her own story unwittingly, by quoting her profusely, makes it an authentic source of the information we all need in order to grasp her importance to us at this present moment.

Father Dirvin has long been a zealous and faithful follower of our new saint. With love and care he has presented this brilliant portrait of a great American woman. He summarizes it all when he describes her as "a woman of hope and unconquerable optimism, a pioneer who stood on the soil of a vast land and felt the first stirrings of its promise. She was truly a pioneer: for she believed in the future greatness of the Church in America just as surely as the breakers of the wilderness and the rail-splitters and the plowers of new farms believed in the vision of a promised land."

Mother Seton's brother-in-law once described her to her grandchildren as "a kind of John the Baptist." It is a very apt and expressive description. She is indeed a bright and shining light. She is indeed a voice crying in our wilderness "to turn the hearts of fathers toward their children and the disobedient back to the wisdom that the virtuous have, preparing for the Lord a people fit for Him."

In Elizabeth Ann Seton, we have a saint for our times.

In Elizabeth Ann Seton, we have a woman of faith, for a time of doubt and uncertainty.

In Elizabeth Ann Seton, we have a woman of love for a time of coldness and division.

In Elizabeth Ann Seton, we have a woman of hope for a time of crisis and discouragement.

Thanks be to God for this saintly daughter of New York, for this valiant woman of God's Church!

TERENCE CARDINAL COOKE
Archbishop of New York

January 30, 1975

Author's Note to New Edition

Since this biography was published in 1962, Mother Seton's life after death has continued to influence the lives of men and women. She has made countless new friends, many of whom have worked tirelessly and prayed enthusiastically for her beatification and canonization. Working within the warm, intimate bonds of what the Church calls the communion of saints—the close-knit family of souls crowned in heaven, safe in purgatory and struggling on earth, all loving and helping one another —she has used her favor with God to solve human, everyday problems, bring health to the sick and salvation and peace to the dying. Nor is this poetic fancy or overblown faith. In three extraordinary instances the Church has definitively said so.

In December 1961 the Church was satisfied, after reams of testimony and years of study, that the cures of Sister Gertrude Korzendorfer, D.C., of cancer of the head of the pancreas in January 1935 and of Anne Theresa O'Neill of acute leukemia (lymphatic type) in 1952 were due to the intercession of Mother Seton and truly miraculous. Pope John XXIII decreed her beatification, which took place in St. Peter's Basilica, Rome, on March 17, 1963.

In October of the same year, a sixty-year-old construction worker named Carl Eric Kalin was allegedly cured of an extremely rare illness diagnosed as "fulminating meningo-encephalitis complicated by primary rubeola (red measles)" in St. Joseph's Hospital, Yonkers, New York.

Mr. Kalin, a Protestant, was admitted to the hospital in critical condition on October 9. His Catholic wife, urged by the Sisters of Charity who conduct the hospital to invoke the intercession of their foundress, Mother Seton, accepted a tiny piece of cloth that had been touched to the remains of the Blessed and pinned it on her husband's hospital gown.

At 6:45 p.m. the patient's condition worsened, and the Sister in charge of the hall, Sister Dominic Rosaire, S.C., sent for the Sister Administrator of the hospital to comfort Mrs. Kalin. When the Sister Administrator arrived, the doctors were working feverishly over the patient. His face had turned a purplish black.

Sister led his wife into an adjoining room, where they began to recite the novena prayers to Blessed Elizabeth Ann Seton for his complete recovery. They had scarcely begun when the attending physician, Dr. Frank Flood, interrupted them with the grave news that Mr. Kalin might not live until midnight.

Sister Dominic Rosaire then went to telephone Sister Marie Clotilde, the assistant mother at Mount St. Vincent, the Sister's motherhouse, to ask for the prayers of the professed Sisters and the novices. Next, Sister Dominic Rosaire placed a first-class relic of Blessed Elizabeth Ann Seton on the patient's head, then fastened it to the wall above the bed.

Mr. Kalin remained in a coma. After a while he began to suffer convulsions, which increased in frequency until they became practically continuous. A neurologist and an anesthesiologist were summoned for a consultation. After a thorough examination they both agreed that, due to massive infection of the brain and the generally poor clinical condition of the patient, death must intervene shortly.

Nevertheless, Mr. Kalin lived through the next few days, his condition remaining, however, extremely critical. The novena to Blessed Elizabeth Ann Seton, begun by the Sisters and Mrs. Kalin on the evening of October 9, continued.

During the night of October 10 a special-duty nurse again applied the first-class relic of Blessed Elizabeth Ann Seton to Mr. Kalin's head and chest. The convulsions ceased immediately, and his high temperature took a dramatic drop; before morning it dropped again, to normal.

He lay for the next three days in a waking condition without the relief of sleep. Finally, on the fifteenth, he fell into a natural sleep from which he did not rouse until noon on the sixteenth. He awakened fully alert and talked in a coherent manner.

On October 17, the last day of the novena to Blessed Elizabeth Ann Seton, he was up and around, and eager to catch up with the news of the outside world. He remembered nothing, of course, of the terrible days he had just passed through.

On November 2, 1963, he left the hospital for home, and in due time returned to full-time work, bearing no trace of his virulent illness. He is now retired and living with his wife in Florida.

The Church ordered an official investigation of the alleged cure which was inaugurated on May 2, 1966. Eight years later she was convinced that God had worked still another miracle through the intercession of Elizabeth Ann Seton, and on December 12, 1974, Pope Paul VI decreed her canonization, which will take place in St. Peter's Basilica on September 14 during the Holy Year of 1975.

The goal I set myself in undertaking this biography was to tell the fascinating life story of Elizabeth Seton exactly as it unfolded, and in a manner agreeable to the widest number of readers.

I had not read far in the great mass of original letters and papers available to the Seton biographer, when it became evident that the best way to achieve this goal was to allow so literate, witty and charming a woman as Mrs. Seton to tell her story herself.

Generous extracts from the thousands of pages written in her own neat, flowing hand have been transferred to the pages of this manuscript in such a way as to form a strong central thread, weaving the myriad strands of a lifetime into a glowing and harmonious whole. Not a word of these extracts has been changed; the finished manuscript has been scrupulously checked and rechecked against the originals. Even awkward, or archaic, or sometimes incorrect, literary usages have been retained. The only editing has consisted of slight changes in punctuation and, in a few instances, spelling, and the adoption of a uniform system of capitalization; and such editing was done after careful study only where considered absolutely necessary.

The same editorial principles have been applied to the letters and jottings of Mrs. Seton's numerous family and friends.

I have hoped, by these methods, to make the most authentic presentation possible of the life and times of a great American woman and universal model of holiness. In the interest of authenticity, also, I have chosen to tell Mrs. Seton's story chronologically, despite the obvious difficulties; for it seems to me essential to the understanding of her personality, character and sanctity, that one realize the problems, the trials, the joys and satisfactions, the sorrows, the consolations, she was experiencing simultaneously.

The use of reference numbers has been avoided in the text, so as not to interrupt the flow of the narrative. The essential sources have, however, been conveniently catalogued by page number; they can be found immediately before the bibliography, to which they are related.

Gratitude should be lasting, and for that reason I should like to repeat my thanks to those who helped and supported the writing of this biography: Pope John XXIII, of happy memory, who in a special audience blessed the work in progress; the late Father Luigi Bisoglio, C.M., and his successor as postulator of Mother Seton's Cause, Father Lucio Giuseppi Lapalorcia, C.M.; the Daughters of Charity of St. Vincent de Paul, who permitted me free and exclusive use of the archives of St. Joseph's Provincial House, Emmitsburg, Maryland, where the great bulk of Seton material is to be found; the staff of the archives of the University of Notre Dame, Notre Dame, Indiana; Father William J. Casey, C.M., who shortened my work by his active research; Father Philip E. Dion, C.M., who was an expert guide to Leghorn, Montenero, Pisa and Florence, all of which figured so intimately in Mrs. Seton's Italian sojourn; Father John P. Cotter, C.M., who helped in the tedious task of compiling the index; Dr. William A. McBrien, who made a critical reading of the manuscript; and many other kind hearts who supported the work with genuine interest and eager assistance.

I wish to record my special indebtedness to the previous biographers of Mother Seton—and to Dr. Annabelle M. Melville in particular—who have plowed the ground, so to speak, and who have done both Mother Seton and myself a great service.

I have reserved until last His Eminence, Terence Cardinal Cooke, Archbishop of New York, who wrote the Foreword to this new Canonization Edition. His joyous reaction to the good news of last December 12 has found its best expression in this personal and official tribute of her birthplace. I tender him my respectful gratitude.

JOSEPH I. DIRVIN, C.M.

Allocutio Pauli Papae VI

Laetamur admodum, Venerabiles Fratres, quod ex latis suffragiis dicimus Beatos Caelites, de quibus agitur, plane a vobis existimari dignos, quibus sanctitatis honores decernantur. Id Nostris quoque votis omnino respondet.

Cum vero omnia jam rite perfecta sint, quae hisce in causis postulantur, statuimus ac decernimus sollemnes ejusmodi caerimonias per Anni Sacri decursum in Vaticana Basilica, Deo juvante, peragere. Ac placet jam nunc dies praestituere, quibus haec sollemnia habebuntur. Scilicet in Sanctorum Caelitum album referemus ... BEATAM ELISABETHAM ANNAM VIDUAM SETON, die quarto decimo mensis Septembris ...

Interea autem, ut haec feliciter eveniant et in Dei gloriam hominumque salutem plurimum conferant, una Nobiscum, Venerabiles Fratres, supplicibus Deo instare precibus ne desistatis.

Allocution of Pope Paul VI

TO THE CARDINALS AND PRELATES IN CONSISTORY, DECEMBER 12, 1974:

Let us rejoice indeed, Venerable Brothers, because We conclude from the voting that the Heavenly Blesseds under discussion seem to you to be certainly worthy of the honors that are the rewards of sanctity. Our own opinion wholeheartedly concurs.

And since everything demanded in these causes has been duly carried out, We proclaim and decree that, with God's help, the proper solemn ceremonies be celebrated in the Vatican Basilica during the Holy Year. It is likewise fitting to assign the dates for these solemnities at this time. We assign for inclusion in the Catalog of Saints in Heaven . . . BLESSED ELIZABETH ANN, WIDOW SETON, on the fourteenth day of the month of September . . .

In the meanwhile, Venerable Brothers, join with Us in begging God without ceasing that these ceremonies may happily take place and may bring great glory to God and salvation to men.

I

American Born

New York, in 1774, was already an old town. Founded in 1614, it had
grown slowly and deliberately in the solid and placid manner of the
Dutch, until the English came and took it. Then it went on growing
with a new bustle and brashness. It had always been cosmopolitan; even
in the days of the Dutch, eighteen languages and dialects could be heard
in its streets. From the beginning it was destined to be a metropolis and
melting pot. Sails and shipping from all over the world dotted its harbor
and crowded its docks; and imports and immigrants arrived every day.
The newest and greenest arrival could see that New York, after 160
years, was gathering momentum to challenge Philadelphia and Boston
and Baltimore.

Though it was confined to the lower tip of Manhattan Island and
could be covered end-to-end in a twenty-minute walk, New York even
in 1774 had its own peculiar look of bustle and congestion; nearly 30,000
people were crammed into that narrow space, 5,000 of them Negroes.

The one threat to its future prosperity was the ferment of revolution.
There had been disaffection for some time. The more thoughtful of
the Colonists rightly felt that Great Britain, whose empire they were
hacking out of the wilderness and building in fresh new cities, was
using them for her own aggrandizement, as a master uses his slaves. The

less thoughtful Colonists were soon to be shown the truth in the clear-cut arguments of Thomas Paine. Annoyance with the mother country was indicated at first only by demonstrations like the Boston Tea Party of December 16, 1773. When demonstrations had no effect, the Colonies grew more determined in their opposition. On September 4, 1774, the first Continental Congress met at Carpenters Hall in Philadelphia to solidify Colonial purpose into a force to be reckoned with. Great Britain refused to recognize the seriousness of the situation and continued to brush away the angry Colonists like so many flies; and the opening of hostilities only wanted the day and the place.

This was the memorable time of the birth of a memorable child, in whose blood ran the best of the past and the highest hopes of the future. Her lineage was of the Old World, but she was of rooted American stock; and before her short life should be over, she would have made her mark on a new nation and on the ancient Church that had come to convert it. But now she was an ordinary baby girl, born to a rising young doctor and his wife in a British colony. The day was the 28th of August, 1774, and the child was the second daughter of Richard Bayley and his wife Catherine Charlton. Her parents named her Elizabeth Ann.

It is not known where she was born, whether within the limits of New York town or not, for it is not known where the Bayleys were living. The first city directory was not issued until some years after. Almost certainly modern New York can claim her, for she was born either in Manhattan, or at her mother's family home on Staten Island, or at a summer place in Newtown, Long Island.

It is remarkable that a child should symbolize so completely a land and its people. By blood and marriage Elizabeth Ann Bayley was connected with the cultures, the religions, the families that had made New York and indeed a great part of the Colonies. Her forbears were French and English and Dutch. She was a direct descendant of the founders of New Rochelle, a lateral descendant of the founders of Pelham. Her kinsfolk were Huguenots and Anglicans; there were even a stray Catholic and a pagan Indian in the background—two-of-a-kind to the bigoted New Yorkers of '74.

Elizabeth's family tree was a Blue Book of the times. There were

Pells and LeContes and Merciers, Van Cortlandts and DePeysters and Roosevelts, Charltons and Barclays and Whites and Craigs.

Her father, Richard Bayley, was the son of William Bayley, who had come to New York from Hoddeston, Hertfordshire, England, in 1726, and of Susanne LeConte, whose great-grandfather, a Huguenot refugee from France via St. Christopher's Island in the West Indies, was one of the founding fathers of New Rochelle. Richard was born at Fairfield, Connecticut, in 1744, but shortly afterwards his parents moved to New Rochelle where they owned a large farm at Mile Square on the border of Yonkers and Eastchester. Here Richard and his younger brother, William LeConte Bayley, were raised. New Rochelle was to be a place of both refuge and delight to Elizabeth during her own childhood.

Richard Bayley was a man of the times, an idealist whose ideals had no higher motive than the worth and dignity of man. He paid scant attention to God: Elizabeth once told a friend that she had heard her father mention God only once, and that on his deathbed. Nominally an Episcopalian, like all the New York gentry of his day, he seems to have been a Deist or some such vague subscriber to religion. There was much of the Founding Fathers in him, much of Jefferson or Franklin.

Intellectually, he was exceptional. As a medical researcher, Bayley had the touch of genius, and his accurate findings in the detection and treatment of croup, diphtheria and yellow fever were uncanny, considering the times and the material he had to work with. For instance, without suspecting the mosquito as a carrier of disease, he instinctively recognized the swamps surrounding New York to be trouble-spots, and fought to have them drained and filled in. He was equally adept as a surgeon, and the great William Hunter himself, under whom he studied in England, praised Bayley's "uncommon dexterity with the knife." In the wake of such praise, it is hardly surprising to find Richard Bayley credited with the first successful amputation of an arm at the shoulder. Despite his eminence in research, medical theory and surgery, Bayley was most of all a general practitioner. He was a completely self-sacrificing physician who gave himself to the poor as much as, or even more than, to the rich. It was while ministering to poor immigrants that he caught typhus and died.

With all this greatness of soul, it is puzzling and regrettable to find

Richard Bayley a failure as a family man. Marriage seems to have been for him a thing of convenience, and he never seems to have grasped his responsibility as a husband and father. He apparently took little thought for either of his wives or his children. His first wife, Elizabeth's mother, was alone for more than half of their eight years of marriage. He and his second wife eventually had a falling-out, and the younger children of this marriage were raised away from him.

Of all his children, Richard Bayley seemed most attached to Elizabeth. Perhaps she best understood him and the love of medicine that drove him so mercilessly. There can be no doubt that Elizabeth and her father were kindred souls, with the same love of life, the same heart for the poor, the same delight in culture and letters. For all his scientific attainments, Richard Bayley was a man of liberal tastes, with a special love for music.

Nothing is known of Elizabeth's mother, Catherine Charlton, except that she was the daughter of the Reverend Richard Charlton, rector of St. Andrew's Episcopal Church, Staten Island, and his wife, Mary Bayeux. The Charltons were from Ireland, though probably of English extraction. After his ordination to the Anglican ministry in England, Richard Charlton was sent as a missionary to the Leeward Islands in the West Indies, then to New Windsor in New York, and finally settled permanently in New York City. When Elizabeth was born, he had been rector of St. Andrew's for nearly thirty years.

This minister-grandfather was especially beloved of his people. He never lost the missionary zeal of his youth and had many conversions to his credit. He was a particular friend to the poor Negro slaves of the gentry; in fact, for a time he was attached to Trinity Church as catechist to all the Negroes of the city. He was an early champion of integration, and instructed his white and Negro converts side by side in the same class. How much of his goodness he passed on to his daughter Catherine we shall never know. It is no small tribute that Elizabeth never forgot her, although she was little more than three years old when her mother died.

Richard Bayley and Catherine Charlton were married on January 9, 1769, in St. John's Episcopal Church, Elizabethtown, New Jersey, by Dr. Charles B. Chandler. Bayley had come to New York four years before to study medicine with his wife's brother, Dr. John Charlton, who was in the flush of a successful career as New York's society doctor. It is strange that Bayley and his bride, both of whom were living on Staten Island (he had been boarding with Pierre LeConte, his mother's cousin), should be married in New Jersey by another minister than the bride's father. Parental displeasure or an elopement are the first reasons to suggest themselves, but these are conjectures.

Shortly after his marriage, it became obvious that medicine was the real love of Richard Bayley's life. Sometime within that first year, so precious to newlyweds, Bayley left for England to study anatomy with the famous surgeon, William Hunter. He did not return for two years. In his absence, his first child, Mary Magdalen, was born; she was more than a year old when he first laid eyes on her. Catherine Bayley called this first daughter after her own sister, Mary Magdalen Charlton, who had married Thomas Dongan, grand-nephew and namesake of the former Governor of New York. (Governor Dongan was a devout Catholic; in fact, his Catholicism was the reason for his removal from office and subsequent flight to his native Ireland.) If his grand-nephew, who married a minister's daughter in a bigoted town, had kept the faith, surely Elizabeth after her conversion would have pointed with pride somewhere in her voluminous correspondence to a Catholic uncle.

Dr. Bayley returned from England in 1771, and for the next four years built up a practice, working with his brother-in-law, Dr. Charlton. His success is underlined by the fact that he shared with Charlton the social distinction of being the first doctor to make calls by carriage. Bayley was off to a good start in his profession. At 30, he was protégé to the town's leading physician; he had tremendous natural talent; he had studied abroad under the most famous of English surgeons; and it did him no harm that he belonged to fashionable society.

According to Episcopalian custom, Elizabeth Ann Bayley was certainly baptized within a month or two of her birth, but there are no official records to prove it. No baptismal record could be found at St. Andrew's, Staten Island, which strongly indicates that she was not baptized there, for her own grandfather was the vicar and a very careful keeper of records. The baptismal entries at Trinity Church, New York, were all destroyed when the church burned in the great fire of 1776. A thorough search of the archives of St. George's Chapel (now a separate parish church) and of St. Paul's Chapel, and even of the archives of the Diocese of London, upon which the American churches depended until 1783, have revealed nothing. However, Elizabeth was a regular communicant of Trinity Church in the years before her conversion, and she could not have been without baptism. She herself wrote on a page of her *Following of Christ:* "Was I not signed with the cross of salvation in Baptism?" There is further proof in the fact, to be discussed later, that the Catholic Church apparently did not require her to submit to conditional baptism when she embraced Catholicism in 1805.

Colonial society was as fond of nicknames as our own, indeed fonder, for each person seems to have had at least two or more. Thus Elizabeth's family and friends shortened her baptismal name to Betty, Betsy, Bette and Bett, and also Eliza.

Elizabeth was only a few months old when her father left home and family once more, early in 1775, for further study with Hunter in England. Whether or not Catherine Bayley wholeheartedly supported her husband's will to improve himself, she could not like what it brought: the loneliness, the anxiety of long months without news, the whole responsibility for her two little girls, the inevitable dependence on family or in-laws in minor crises. Whatever the reason for her not going with him to England, particularly when it meant a separation of a couple of years, it could not have been pleasant to stay at home.

The fact of Richard Bayley's departure at a time when the threats of war were growing louder, points up the eternal optimism of the common citizen. War never comes about suddenly, yet most people refuse to recognize the signs of its coming. It was so with Richard Bayley. He surely would not have left his little family to the dangers of war. Bayley was an honorable man. And, besides, for all his apparent neglect, it need not be concluded that he did not love his wife and little daughters. There are men who love deeply but heedlessly, completely oblivious to the responsibilities of love.

Nevertheless, within weeks of Bayley's departure, the War of the Revolution had begun. In April Paul Revere rode, shouting his warning through the night; the shot heard round the world was fired; at Lexington and Concord and Bunker Hill the embattled farmers stood and fought and died.

Certainly Betty Bayley, who was only a toddler, remembered nothing of these early days of the Revolution, not even the terrible fire which nearly destroyed New York in 1776. With the Declaration of Independence on the 4th of July, the patriots had taken possession of the city, but they were not to hold it for long. It was an uneasy possession at best, for the citizens of power and influence were loyal to the British. In August, General Sir William Howe laid siege to the town, and it fell toward the end of September. In a last desperate attempt to deprive Howe of his prize, the patriots set a fire in a small wooden house on a wharf. In a matter of minutes it had raged out of control, and before the fields bounding the city on the north had stopped its advance ten hours later, the fire had destroyed nearly five hundred buildings. It was in this fire that Trinity Church burned and with it the probable record of Elizabeth Bayley's baptism.

On this night of horror, Richard Bayley was away from his family again. He had returned to New York with the fleet of Admiral Sir Richard Howe, brother to the General, on July 12, 1776. He came home in uniform, enlisted as a surgeon in the British forces. He could have stayed no more than a couple of weeks, for the fleet moved up to Newport, Rhode Island, to engage the ships of the French Comte d'Estaing in an indecisive action, which a violent storm put an end to on August 10.

James Thacher, Bayley's earliest biographer, says that the doctor's enlistment was "a step of necessity rather than inclination . . . for like genius in every clime, Bayley was poor; and the necessity of a lovely wife and beloved children will often dictate a course which sober reason might not approve." Maybe so. Thacher is not to be discounted, for he knew Bayley personally. But this touching portrait of the devoted husband and father is hardly the Richard Bayley of fact. And it must be noted that Thacher was writing in 1829 about a successful and eminent citizen, then dead more than a quarter of a century.

Certain biographers of Elizabeth Bayley Seton have tried to absolve Richard Bayley of blame for his political leanings in the War of Independence. There is nothing to absolve, for there is little to blame. Richard Bayley was a loyalist. He belonged to a loyalist family, to the loyalist stratum of society. There was no stigma attached to this in New York in 1776; it was the side of the majority. Bayley was loyal to the only country he knew, and it is ridiculous to try to make him out a villain because of it. Nor does it clear the air to surmise, as other biographers have done, that Bayley was little interested in politics. With his family connections of Barclays, Jays and Van Cortlandts, Bayley had at least to be conversant with politics. It is significant that, when the war was over, he counted among his friends the new politicians of the era: John Jay, Stephen Van Rensselaer, Alexander Hamilton, and even more significant that these men were Federalists, the conservative element of the new régime.

Certainly it does not add a whit to the glory of Elizabeth Seton to dodge and hedge in an effort to make her a daughter of the American Revolution. She was a child of two when our nation was born. Had she, in her growing-up years, "attached" herself to a cause, presumably it would have been to the cause espoused by her family, just as the modern child mouths without understanding the slogan of his father's political candidate. Nowhere in Elizabeth's writings is there a sentence of political thought. The whole discussion is academic. Elizabeth Bayley Seton was a native American, born on this soil, and after the birth of the nation she was a loyal citizen of the United States, as was her father and each member of her family. And it is America's glory that it was so.

As for Richard Bayley's being poor, Thacher is the only one ever to assert it. Bayley's family was not poor; nor was his wife's family. Money was hardly the reason for his enlistment. He could have earned more as a civilian than as a service doctor; the doctors' fees then were surprisingly comparable to those of modern times; indeed, with the greater basic value of Colonial money, they were probably higher. If enlistment was his only way of getting home, he could have resigned his commission when he landed in New York.

Lieutenant Richard Bayley, surgeon to His Majesty's Troops (he had apparently enlisted with the Army, although he spent much of his time with the Navy), was kept busy at Newport. He was hospital surgeon for Admiral Howe's fleet and for some 5,000 land troops as well. He found time, however, to cultivate a scientific friendship with Michaelis, the famous Hessian doctor; it was in the course of this friendship that Michaelis, for all his fame as a specialist on croup, was forced to give way to the theories of Bayley on the disease, which he found much nearer the truth than his own. There was time for experiment also, and it was here that Bayley began his dissection of cadavers that was to build him a fiendish reputation with the ignorant. In war-torn New York false rumors began to circulate that the young physician was performing cruel and painful experiments on the soldiers.

Letters from home brought Bayley ominous news. Catherine was pregnant again, and things were not going well. Time and again, he was refused leave to go to her and he could do nothing but worry and hope. It must have been for him a winter of bitterness and regret.

In March he was raised to the rank of captain, but whatever spur of necessity or enthusiasm had led him to enlist no longer goaded him. Desperate to get home to his ailing wife, he resigned his commission. To complete his disillusionment with the military life, the commandant refused to give him a penny of pay for his year and a half of service, on the technicality that he had not served his full term of five years.

Richard rushed to Newtown, Long Island, where his wife had gone with their two baby daughters, perhaps to seek the country air, or to take refuge from the devastation left by the fire of the preceding autumn. It is possible that Catherine had relatives there. A century before, in 1671, the town council of Newtown had contracted with a Richard Charlton "to keep a schoole and to instruct ye children and youth there to write and read." Richard arrived in time for the birth of his third daughter— and for the death of his wife. Catherine died on the 8th of May, 1777. They had been married eight years and had been together less than four.

II

Catherine Bayley's death was a blow to Richard. A good and kindly man, he could not but feel remorse at the death of this young woman whom he had neglected. Perhaps he had meant to make it up to her when his studies were over and he was established—people like Richard Bayley always mean well—but now that could not be. She was gone, and he was left with three motherless little girls—Mary was seven, Betty was not yet three; and the baby, whom he called Catherine after the dead mother, was puny and ailing.

With the death of her mother, that strange *pattern* of death that was to weave itself through Elizabeth Bayley's life had begun. In this same year, on the 7th of October, her grandfather, Rev. Mr. Charlton, died at 72, in his rectory on Staten Island, leaving his little granddaughters one-third of his estate.

Richard Bayley looked after his three little girls, probably with the aid of a housekeeper or governess, throughout the traditional year of mourning. Then, on June 16, 1778, he married again. His second wife was Charlotte Amelia Barclay, daughter of Andrew Barclay and Helena Roosevelt, whose father was the founder of the Roosevelt dynasty in America. Bayley was 35 years old, his new bride just two months short of 19. It is reasonable to assume that practicality had no small part in fostering the marriage from Bayley's side. He was a practicing physician, committed to a profession that would take as much of his time as he was willing to give, and his three small daughters needed a mother. Charlotte Barclay probably had more traditional motives. When a single girl of prominent family marries a widower, with three children, it is often for reasons of attraction and love: and Dr. Bayley had good looks, charm, vitality, maturity and professional respect.

Betty Bayley had a new mother, or mother-in-law, as a stepmother was called in Colonial times. Unfortunately, Charlotte Bayley seems never to have been a real mother to the child. There can be no question of her taking care of Betty: washing and dressing her, making her clothes, nursing her through the illnesses of childhood, doing all the things that only a woman can do for a little girl. Indeed, Betty herself recorded, in justice, that her stepmother taught her the first prayers she remembered. But the leaven of love was missing, and Betty, even at four, sensed the lack. Years later she could recall "sitting alone on a step of the door, looking at the clouds, while my little sister Catherine, two years old, lay in her coffin; they asked me: Did I not cry when little Kitty was dead? No, because Kitty is gone up to heaven. I wish I could go, too, with Mama."

It was a strangely precocious reply for a child of four—the date was October of 1778—and stranger still that Betty could recall it so vividly. The plain fact is that Betty was precocious, especially in a religious way. From this time on, she had a predilection for thoughts of death and heaven and eternity. If the child psychologists are right, and a personality is fully formed at five—that is, even before the age of reason—then we may consider Elizabeth Bayley Seton's long-suffering and patience, so opposed to the French vivacity and energy in her, as legacies from her poor lonely mother; and her calm acceptance of trouble as the result of the losses of her first years.

It is hard to say why a true mother-and-daughter relationship never ripened between Charlotte Bayley and Betty, but certainly the stepmother, as the older and wiser, must take the brunt of the blame. After the first strange weeks, any child of three, especially one of Betty's affectionate nature, would have taken willing refuge in a stepmother's arms if she found love there. That she did not is certain. Betty, who was outgoing and friendly and interested in everyone, scarcely ever mentioned her stepmother all her life, and when she did, referred to her with cold courtesy as "Mrs. Bayley." (She once characterized "Mrs. Bayley" in a letter as "a woman of rare and sweet attainments," but this is polite and formal, rather than affectionate, language.) At the age of eight, more than four years after her father's second marriage, Betty was still grieving for her "mother and little Kitty in heaven."

There was certainly no lack of maternal instinct in Charlotte Bayley: she bore her husband seven children. A clue might be found in the mother's natural preference of her own children over the two little girls who were not hers; this suspicion is strengthened by the terms of Dr. Bayley's will, drawn in 1788, which left everything to his "beloved wife, Charlotte Amelia Bayley, and to her heirs and assigns," cutting off his daughters, Mary and Elizabeth, entirely. Charlotte, in turn, in her will divided her husband's estate among her own children, with never a word or a penny for her stepchildren. Natural preference, however, scarcely excuses such lack of feeling toward the children of the man she loved, children whose welfare and upbringing she had willingly accepted.

Richard Bayley, of course, must take his share of the blame. He was a party, at least tacitly, to whatever unhappiness his daughters suffered. The will, executed when Mary and Elizabeth were unmarried and wholly dependent on him, is the completely damning evidence against him— he even left his farm at Mile Square to his mother, who had married again and was well provided for; but for the daughters of his first marriage, nothing.

He did make certain gestures in the right direction. He provided a sound education for Mary and Elizabeth; not just the basic education of the ordinary child, but the extensive, cultural studies necessary to children of position. They were enrolled at a private school known as "Mama Pompelion's." When Betty balked at applying herself to French and music, her father insisted that knowledge of both was proper to a young lady, and she followed his wishes. She was to be grateful for his insistence, for music especially brought her many hours of pleasure and comfort when her world began to dissolve.

Dr. Bayley further relieved the unhappiness of his daughters by sending them for protracted visits to his brother at New Rochelle. Such temporary relief only begged the question, however. These prolonged stays with Uncle William served to point up the anomalous position of Mary and Betty. They were strangers in their father's house, and did not belong in the family group of their half-brothers and half-sisters. There were seven of these: Amelia or Emma, Richard Jr., Andrew, William, Guy Carleton, Mary Fitch and Helen. In a family division, these children, as was natural, would stand on the side of their mother; Mary and Betty were, in a very real sense, another family entirely. Betty wrote at 16: "Family disagreement. Could not guess why when I spoke kindly to relations, they did not speak to me."

This was the agony of Betty Bayley. She was kind, warm, affectionate. She "could not even guess how anyone could be an enemy to another." Such a nature as hers never understands unkindness. Further—and in this fact is the seed of tragedy—such a nature as hers looks for, expects, *needs* a return of the love it freely gives. When instead it is assailed with hatred and dislike, the hurt is terrible indeed. Rebuffed, such a loving soul retreats into aching loneliness. Throughout her childhood and teens, Betty Bayley was lonely. The fact lends a new dimension of pathos to the tale of how, when her father passed in the street making his doctor's calls, she would rush from the middle of class to give him a kiss—a lonely little girl assuring herself of somebody's love.

However, even as a child, Betty was far too sensible to let her troubles rule and ruin her life. Rather she turned them against themselves. Thus she used her enforced loneliness as an occasion for introspection and interior peace. She learned to amuse herself with "the long, long thoughts of youth." Instinctively, she drew closer to God, Whom she came to recognize as the One Changeless Being in a shifting world. Hers was not a unique discovery. It is the discovery of all good souls left to themselves, whether by force of circumstance or by their own free choice, that there is, always and forever, God. It was in God's special plans for Betty Bayley that she was allowed to make the discovery so young.

There is an artless example of her early preoccupation with God. One evening, just at sunset, Betty, who was scarcely six at the time, carried her baby half-sister Emma up to the highest window of the house, and pointing out the reddening sky and the sinking ball of the sun, told the infant that "God lived up in heaven, and good children would go up there," and proceeded "teaching her her prayers." It is a smile-provoking glimpse of the Elizabeth Seton-to-be: the little mother, the little apostle, solemnly instructing a year-old baby!

It was probably a conscious imitation, so dear to children, of the spiritual lessons taught her by Charlotte Bayley, for she goes on in her remembrance:

> My poor mother-in-law, then in great affliction, learnt me the twenty-second Psalm: "The Lord is my Shepherd, the Lord ruleth me. . . . Though I walk in the midst of the shadow of death, I will fear no evil, for Thou art with me;" and all life through it has been the favorite Psalm.

It is good to remember this side of Charlotte Bayley, and to wonder at the expressions "poor" and "then in great affliction." Was it some pain or illness Betty remembered her stepmother suffering, or was Charlotte Bayley beginning to discover her husband's penchant for neglect? The word "poor," especially, is a broad adjective, opening up a wide vista of conjecture, suggesting that perhaps the "poor mother-in-law" had provocation for her strange, apparent bitterness.

In mentioning the early trials of Betty Bayley and her spells of seriousness, however, we must not make the mistake of thinking of her as a little morose old woman at the age of six. She was not that at forty-six, nor would have been such at seventy-six. She was a dark-eyed, dark-curled little sprite who laughed and ran and skipped rope. She had the volatile energy of her French ancestors, and their volatile temper too. As a mother, she was to shake her head over her own little Anna Maria, whose exuberance was an echo of her own, even as Betty's was an echo of her father's. It was only in the quiet moments, when no one was near, that little Betty Bayley's eyes gazed into the distance and her thoughts grew sober and the solitary feeling came.

When she was eight years old, Betty and her sister Mary, who was twelve, went to New Rochelle for the first of their long visits with Uncle William Bayley. There is no proof that the Bayley girls were being "put out to board," but the length of their stay—possibly four years—permits us to wonder.

As for her home at New Rochelle, Betty loved it. William Bayley was very different from his brother. There was more of the British squire than the energetic Frenchman in him. He had done quite well as a merchant, an importer of hardware, in New York until the fire of '76 had put him out of business. He might have rebuilt, had he a merchant's heart, but he was more inclined to the land. In 1781 he bought the 250-acre shore-front farm of his brother-in-law, Joseph Pell, which lay, overlooking Long Island Sound, partly in Pelham and partly in New Rochelle.

It was a curious purchase. Pell had been dispossessed of the property by the New York provincial government in 1779, because of his service in the British Army. By the Patriot's Law, such confiscated property could be purchased by a patriot relative of the original owner. William Bayley was apparently no more of a patriot than his militant brother-in-law; he was, at the very least, a quiescent Tory. Yet through the good offices of his brother Richard (who had himself served in the British Army!) William Bayley was able to make the purchase. While it may have been a sign of the touchy populace's readiness to forgive Dr. Bayley his loyalist sympathies, in view of his professional dedication, kindliness and skill, as some have asserted, it may equally have been a sign of the power and influence of his friends.

Betty could be at ease with her kindly farmer uncle. He was genial and loving, even doting—and he was always there. Little is known of the character of his wife, Sarah Pell Bayley; but it is sufficient to know of her that she accepted her husband's young nieces as her own children. There is a streak of romanticism in the pedigree of this descendant of the John Pell who founded Pelham, New York; she was the granddaughter of an authentic Indian princess and great-granddaughter of the fierce Wampage who slew Ann Hutchinson and her five children.

Besides her uncle and aunt, Betty had her Bayley cousins, who loved her; and there were the LeConte and Mercier and Coutant and Flandreau cousins who literally dotted the countryside. Surely the chief charm of New Rochelle for Mary and Betty Bayley was the sense of belonging that was denied them in New York. Not far behind was the charm of the house and the land. The house, which is lived in even today, was a rambling clapboard Colonial farmhouse, roomy and cheerful. Though surrounded by the trees and fields of the country, it was also a seashore house, with a sweeping view of the great blue Sound and the sails upon it.

Betty gave herself to the paradise of nature, to the land and the sea, with a child's gladness and wonder. She loved everything that grew, everything that moved in the thicket or the grass, or that burrowed in the mud by the water. It was a happy thing for her to run through the fields of daisies and wild mustard, or to trudge barefoot through the sand of the seashore, looking for shells.

"Every little leaf and flower, or animal, insect, shades of clouds, or waving trees," she wrote years later, "[were] objects of vacant unconnected thoughts of God and heaven."

Always God and heaven, even at the age of eight.

Elizabeth had now, she says, a real "pleasure in learning anything pious" and, in the very next breath, "delight in being with old people." Obviously, it was the "old people" who taught her piety. One of these, surely, was Miss Molly B.—Miss Molly Besley—a pious Huguenot relative of both the Bayleys and the LeContes, for within the same paragraph Betty speaks of visiting her.

There is a wonderful rapport between the very young and the very old. It is as if they made an exchange to the benefit of both, the vitality of the one for the wisdom of the other. It is often remarked how an old lady, chatting with a child, will rouse from age and laugh with almost girlish delight; while a little girl, in the company of the elderly, will grow solemn and grave, for all the world "like a little old lady." Even more, a child, seeing the old respected and loved, will learn easily a lifelong lesson of thoughtfulness and care for others. It is very logical to look for the source of Elizabeth Seton's universal compassion for the poor and the sick in New York and Baltimore and Emmitsburg in the reverence shown her older relatives at New Rochelle, such as Miss Molly B., as well as in the example of her dedicated father.

Miss Molly was also the oracle of the French language among the young Bayleys. William Bayley's children spoke fluent French, and there is every reason to suppose that Betty, who was with them so much, gained a certain facility in the tongue. The many translations of French spiritual works made by her during her religious life were hardly the results of the formal lessons her father insisted she take.

During her eighth year Betty learned another lesson of life that contributed, along with her unsettled home life and the company of the old, to her growing seriousness. It was that, not only grownups, but children, too, could be strangely cruel in their behavior. One day some of her little playmates found a bird's nest in a bush, and callously dashed the nearly-hatched eggs to the ground. Betty was horrified at this wantonness, and gathered "the young ones on a leaf, seeing them palpitate, thinking the poor little mother hopping from bough to bough, would come and bring them to life." She "cried because the girls would destroy them, and afterward always loved to play and walk alone." And she goes on in her memories, as if it followed as a matter of course: "Admiration of the clouds. Delight to gaze at them; always with the look for my mother and little Kitty in heaven. Delight to sit alone by the waterside, wandering hours on the shore, humming and gathering shells . . . thoughts of God and heaven."

It was one of the wonders of Elizabeth Bayley Seton that disillusionment never made her cynical or bitter, either as a child or an adolescent or an adult. There were black moods and moments of near-despair, but she always came through them right side up. Nor is it foolish to speak of bitterness in a child, especially a sensitive child like Betty. Even a very young child can learn quickly to cast a wary eye on the world, can nurture the beginnings of a great cynicism. Some of the most pessimistic writing in world literature can be traced to the inequities and hardships of the author's childhood. But Betty Bayley never dwelt needlessly on injustice. While it saddened her, it made her wise with the wisdom of God and man. She turned from it instinctively to pursue her own glad and innocent "thoughts of God and heaven." It is this "instinct" that forces the beholder to see the hand of God, even so early, molding a heroine.

III

The Moods of Youth

In 1786—by her own remembrance—Betty Bayley was "home again at my father's." There is no certainty as to whether she had been at her Uncle Bayley's uninterruptedly for four years, but the phrase strongly suggests it.

Much had happened to New York in those four years. The war was over, and the English were gone. Reprisals and recriminations were the order of the day, as after any conflict, the wilder victors calling for blood, the wiser ones seeking to establish strength in amity and forgiveness.

The English had been led away by General Sir Guy Carleton, the last of the British military governors of the city. Carleton or Lord Dorchester, as he was later known, was a fascinating man. He had been a strong, and wise, Governor General of Canada. It was he who had urged the Quebec Act on George III and his parliament, thus winning the undying gratitude of the French Catholics (who, as Carleton pointed out realistically, outnumbered the English fifty thousand to six hundred in Canada), the equally undying hatred of the bigoted American Colonists, the censure of the Continental Congress—and a place in history, for there can be no doubt that the policy of this Act, respect for the religion and culture of colonial peoples, helped England expand and maintain her empire for one hundred and fifty years.

There seems evidence that Richard Bayley and Guy Carleton were friends, and good friends. A child of Bayley's was called Guy Carleton Bayley; a child of Carleton's was called Richard Bayley Carleton. It is certainly not true, as has been asserted, that Dr. Bayley served the General as staff surgeon, but neither, on the other hand, need it be denied that they were friends. The argument adduced against their being friends: that Guy Carleton Bayley's own mother spelled his name "Charlton" is trifling. Spelling seems not to have been one of the talents of the times—the variant spelling for a single name in Colonial letters is legion. Besides, the boy's sisters, Betty and Mary, always spelled his name "Carlton"—and his son, Archbishop James Roosevelt Bayley, spelled it "Carleton."

One pleasure Betty had in her father's house was the children, her half-brothers and half-sisters. They were all babies at this time: Emma, the oldest, was scarcely seven, and there were four between her and Guy Carleton, who was born in this year 1786. Betty was a born mother, and lavished her care and love on them. It was her custom to sing hymns over their cradles. There is a happy irony in the picture of this little twelve-year-old Protestant girl, who would herself found the first Catholic Sisterhood in America, singing evangelical hymns over the cradle of the father of a future Archbishop of Baltimore! But her greatest pleasure, a pleasure that penetrated her heart and nourished her soul, was in "reading prayers."

When she was thirteen, Betty Bayley had a harrowing experience. Her father, ever eager for new medical discoveries, had set up an anatomical laboratory in the huge pile of the New York Hospital, which lay along the bank of the Hudson on the west side of Broadway, between Duane and Worth Streets. Here under the fascinated eyes of medical students, he resumed the experimental dissection of cadavers begun under Hunter in England and continued at Newport during the war. There were the usual mutterings among the people as to where the corpses came from, the almost certain knowledge that Potter's Field was rifled in the dead of night, and dark and anxious hints that body-snatchers did not hesitate to desecrate family plots in the churchyards. Perhaps it would have stayed in the muttering stage, but the situation was explosive, more explosive than Dr. Bayley knew, and a foolish wiseacre of a student touched it off.

Waving the severed arm of a woman out the window at a group of boys playing in the street, the prankster shouted:

"Here's the arm of your mother that cuffed you soundly more than once!"

By an unfortunate coincidence, one of the boys had just buried his mother and, horrified, ran home to tell his father the fearful sight and terrible words. The father, horrified in his turn, ran to tell neighbors and friends of the fiendish doings over at the hospital; soon an ugly mob, ever-swelling in numbers as the hysteria spread, advanced on the unsuspecting Bayley and his class. Thus began the memorable "Doctors' Riot" of April 13–14, 1788.

The infuriated mob spilled through the rooms of the hospital, smashing retorts and specimen jars, overturning furniture, destroying the patient work of years. The doctors and medical students were able to hide for a time in the unused parts of the rambling old building, but were soon discovered and might have suffered harm but for the intervention of city magistrates. The mob dispersed, but the trouble had been started and worse was to follow, for in the very act of dispersing, the news was carried to every part of the city. All night long, passions seethed and bubbled and in the morning came to a boil when the populace, as if drawn together by a fateful and ominous hand, regrouped.

This mob was more dangerous than the helter-skelter gathering of the day before, for it had a definite purpose: to search the homes of the suspected doctors, including, of course, the home of Dr. Bayley, where Betty and her family sat in dread. Governor George Clinton, John Jay and Alexander Hamilton persuaded the mob to disband by giving them the news that the students guilty of the crude joke had been sent to jail. The crowd seemed mollified and broke up, but only for a time; in the afternoon they reformed in even greater numbers, demanding that the guilty students be handed over to them for punishment.

The authorities refused and Mayor Duane, seeing the violent reaction of the mob, called out the militia. The hysteria grew and, despite the pleas of the Mayor and the magistrates, the mob tried to storm the jail. In the ensuing melee, John Jay was hit with a brickbat and struck to the ground. The excited Mayor was about to give the order to fire, when Baron von Steuben, hero of the Revolution, begged him to wait. The next instant, the doughty Baron himself was on the ground, felled by a stone. In a fury of indignation, he called out:

"Fire, Duane, fire!"

The militia fired, killing five and wounding several of the mob. Now their anger knew no bounds, and they broke up into frenzied bands that ran through the twisting streets of the town, searching for the scattered medical men and crying for their blood.

"A night passed in sweat of terror," Betty recalled it, "saying all the while, 'Our Father. . . .'" A night of terror for a child of thirteen, huddled with her stepmother and her brothers and sisters, awaiting some unspeakable doom! Amazingly enough, they were spared the outrages of the angry mob, but neither Betty nor any of her family would ever forget the night of April 14, 1788.

Entering her teens, Betty Bayley was a lovely girl, small, dark, vivacious, with brown, almost black, curly hair and large dark eyes that grew larger and darker with excitement or interest. Like most girls leaving childhood—and like all intense people—she was given to moods: spurts of almost irrepressible high spirits followed by quiet moments at times earnestly reflective, at times pleasantly melancholy. On one or two occasions these melancholy moods got out of hand and sank to the depths, but Betty was always saved from despair by finding God wherever her thoughts led her, up or down.

Soon after the shattering experience of the Doctors' Riot, Richard Bayley set off once more for England, leaving Charlotte and her brood as he had left Catherine. Betty and her sister Mary went off again to New Rochelle, a rather significant indication of the poor relationship between the girls and their stepmother, for they were at an age when they should have proved most useful to her.

This absence of her father was harder on Betty than any of the others had been, for she never heard from him in all the time he was away, well over a year. No one heard from him, not even his wife, and the fact bears out the streak of irresponsibility in him, most surprising in a man so utterly devoted to the duties of his profession.

The effect on Betty was devastating. She recalled one darkest day in particular, when alone in the fields—she was too proud and loyal, too much mistress of herself to let her relatives see her hurt—she laughed and cried in turns, shaken by gusts of hysteria, not knowing whether her father was alive or dead, but certain that she had lost him and that he had no care or concern for her. But, as always, in the end she came to the rock-solid conclusion that God was her Father, and she opened her heart to receive Him.

This experience, which was but the climax, the peak, or the depth, of what she had known all her life, reveals the generous sweep of Betty Bayley's character. That she could know such parental thoughtlessness, yet never abandon her attachment to and admiration for her father, is a miracle of understanding, especially in a teen-age girl. She, who suffered cruelly from his erratic behavior, did not judge and condemn him. She had grasped one of the essentials of love: to take people as you find them. It was not that she condoned her father's faults; she accepted them for what they were, and loved him in spite of them.

Despite the private griefs, life at New Rochelle continued pleasant for Betty. The Bayley family was a happy family. There were six Bayley cousins: William Jr., was sixteen; Susanne was Betty's own age, fourteen; Joseph was eleven; Richard, nine; Ann was six—she had been born shortly after Betty came for her first extended stay with Uncle William—and John, the baby, was four. In this normal, noisy, lively family, Betty and her cousins Joseph and Susanne were the "older children," while Betty's sister Mary was a grown-up nineteen, and seeing a great deal of young Dr. Wright Post.

It is perhaps inaccurate to speak any longer of Betty as a child. In 1788 fourteen was the age when girls began to pile their hair in curls on top of their heads and to accept invitation to balls. There was no spirit of make-believe about this, no feeling that these were children dressed in their mother's clothes. They were on the threshold of adulthood, and were accepted wherever adults assembled. The span of life was shorter than ours, and the serious business of marrying and raising a family began earlier. Nor was there then any anxiety about early marriages, for eighteenth-century girls were by training more mature and readier to assume the burdens of married life than the modern teen-ager.

Betty Bayley had a normal, healthy interest in boys, the kind of fresh and innocent attraction that enhances the radiance and loveliness of the young girl. Writing words of advice for her daughter Annina years later, she recalled how she had loved dancing, and that she had "never found any effect from it but the most innocent cheerfulness"—except that the time given to it was time spent away from more earnest attention to God, and that pleasant musings on the previous night's ball or the new young man she had danced with proved unfortunate distractions at her prayers, giving rise to passing feelings of guilt. It was a phenomenon she was still puzzling over at 18—"after being at public places, why I could not say my prayers and have good thoughts as if I had been at home."

Nevertheless, it is one of the delightful qualities of Elizabeth Bayley Seton that she shared with the common lot of men and women their attitude toward sex and love and marriage, not only in right thinking but in right practice. It never seriously entered her head, at this time, to choose religious chastity as a way of life. Why should it? It was not counseled by the religion to which she gave her allegiance. It is true that she indulged in "passionate wishes that there were such places in America as I read of in novels, where people could be shut from the world and pray, and be good always. Many thoughts of running away to such a place over the seas, in disguise, working for a living"—but surely the flamboyant romanticism of the growing girl is obvious in these daydreams. Why, while she was dreaming thus, she had begun to pay attention to the courtship of William Seton!

Whether or not she would have considered the religious life and a consecration to chastity had she been a Catholic at this time is another question, but the wholehearted maternalism that was so much a part of her would seem to deny it. In any event, she pursued the standard path, enjoying the company of boys, going on sledding and skating parties in the winter and picnics in the summer, dancing at balls and cotillions. And when, in a few years, she should enter upon marriage, it would not be for reasons of convenience or obedience or security, but for love.

Among the Bayley cousins at New Rochelle, Betty had a favorite. It was the youngest girl, Ann, who was six years her junior. Betty and Ann found a common meeting ground in God. Betty taught the little girl all she knew of Him and, finding her an absorbed pupil, shared with her her own intimate religious thoughts. On this firm basis a close friendship rose, nourished over the years by letters and visits, even after Betty's marriage. It ended sadly with Betty's entrance into the Catholic Church.

Ann Bayley was partner in another friendship, which could not have been as good for her soul—with Theodosia Burr, the famous, talented, ill-starred daughter of Aaron Burr. Burr had personally tutored the beautiful Theodosia to be a paragon of womanhood: a brilliant, intelligent conversationalist to match wits with him; a fireside companion to read to him from the original Greek and Latin of Homer and Terence and Ovid; a hostess of overwhelming charm to enchant the world when he should be president. The dream dissolved with his own disgrace and the tragic death of Theodosia by drowning at sea.

Despite the flow of family life around her and her happy reaching for the joys and pleasures of youth, Betty Bayley still loved to be alone for hours at a time. The long thoughts of childhood grew longer, and her meditations deeper. She pushed through the fields, her long dress brushing the grass and the wildflowers, or walked along the shores of the Sound, her footsteps just eluding the incoming tide. In a sentence evocative of rough water and scudding clouds, she tells of sitting on the rocks by the sea and singing hymns into the wind. More and more, God possessed her. She found Him everywhere.

Elizabeth's great love for the Bible dates from this time. It was a preoccupation that became an integral part of her. Throughout all the rest of her life, as Protestant or Catholic, the Bible was her comfort and her joy. In time of storm, it was her bedrock. She converted her husband, instructed her children, from its pages. Later it was the constant source of her conferences to her Sisters in religion. Whenever she spoke or wrote, the Scriptural accent was evident.

Along with the Bible, she read the religious verse of Thomson and Milton. She speaks of her "delight of sitting in the fields with Thomson, surrounded by lambs and sheep"—an apt illustration, for it was indeed, for her, the age of innocence. Everything amused her, everything transported her: books, stars, cedars, rocks, ice, "drinking the sap of the birch." She had "pleasure in everything, coarse, rough, smooth or easy, always gay."

In this fairy-tale springtime of her life, Betty had a great religious experience. The new-found delight, the fresh-as-dew quality, was still in the words when she wrote of it, years after.

In the year 1789, when my father was in England, one morning in May, in the lightness of a cheerful heart, I jumped in the wagon that was driving to the woods for brush, about a mile from home; the boy who drove it began to cut, and I set off in the woods, soon found an outlet in a meadow; and a chestnut tree with several young ones growing around it, found rich moss under it and a warm sun. Here, then, was a sweet bed—the air still a clear blue vault above—the numberless sounds of spring melody and joy—the sweet clovers and wild flowers I had got by the way, and a heart as innocent as human heart could be, filled even with enthusiastic love to God and admiration of His works . . .

God was my Father, my all. I prayed, sang hymns, cried, laughed, talking to myself of how far He could place me above all sorrow. Then I laid still to enjoy the heavenly peace that came over my soul; and I am sure, in the two hours so enjoyed, grew ten years in the spiritual life. . . .

There seems no doubt that Elizabeth is describing a form of meditation or mental prayer. It is remarkable how she was finding her way so surely in the spiritual life, without ordered spiritual direction. She mentions no Protestant divine as a favorite guide, such as John Henry Hobart was later to be; she does not even speak of attending church—a strange omission by one who loved God beyond her years and was faithful in reporting her most intimate thoughts.

Betty Bayley was not wholly unassisted in her spiritual advance: she had the good thoughts of Thomson and Milton, and she read avidly the pious essays of Blair, a Protestant author of the day. In the main, however, she proceeded under her own direction, or rather under the immediate surveillance of God, Who Himself leads willing souls who do not know the way.

IV

Friendship and Romance

Richard Bayley returned to New York in the fall of 1789 or the spring of 1790. His return was like a signal for events which had tarried in the making to resume. He returned ostensibly to his wife and family, either at 60 King Street or 51 Wall Street (the Bayleys moved from the one address to the other about this time), and the forces of incompatibility began to work once more toward inevitable separation; the separation did not come for at least four years, or Betty would have found a home with her father in the years immediately prior to her marriage.

Dr. Bayley's oldest daughter, Mary Magdalen, married Dr. Wright Post, one of his medical students, in June of 1790. This match must have given Bayley pleasure, for it was a good one. Wright Post was a noble human being; not only was he a competent doctor, but he had a store of wisdom and common sense and was the paragon of domestic virtues which Bayley had never been. Even years later, when the challenge of making a home and raising a family had long since settled into routine, Eliza Sadler, Betty Bayley's dear friend, could exclaim of Wright Post: "Such a husband and father!"

It is true that, in 1788, Post had had a violent exchange with a M. Micheau, a French emigré, and for a while the affair threatened a settlement on the "field of honor." It took to the newspapers instead and became the talk of New York, until it ended with Micheau's departure for England in 1789. It is satisfying to record this touch of fire in Wright Post, and to know, too, that he had the moral restraint to turn back from duelling in a day when duelling was honored. And it was moral restraint; had it been cowardice, Post could never again have raised his head in the spirited society of New York to which he belonged.

Mary Magdalen Bayley, who was 20 at the time of her marriage to Wright Post, was a good, unexceptional woman. She was lovely of face, like her dark-eyed little sister, and had her dark coloring, but here the resemblance ended. They were worlds apart in temperament and personality. Mary had not the French restlessness and energy, the brooding imagination of Betty; nor had she the same will or talent to plumb the more mysterious depths of religion. She was content with the common lot of mortality. Mary lived an ordinary, respectable religious life; she kept an ordinary, respectable house; she raised an ordinary, respectable family. Once, she made a shrewd analysis of herself in a letter to her sister:

> You ask me "if I am good." I am very little so, compared with what you think or practice. I am no otherwise good than in being thankful to God, and trying to act well within the little circle I call my family. I try to circumscribe my wishes within the bound of prudence and propriety, and to act upon that conviction. I make a better wife than I have done, because I find a mutual interest between my husband and myself in loving and feeling the unceasing desire of improving and benefitting our children, persuaded of which, gratitude is ever alive, and I know he thinks it the means by which he can please me the most.
>
> I contribute to . . . institutions of charity and in so doing, I hope, encourage them, but, while I see them well administered, feel no inclination to engage in them. I should then become responsible to others, which I consider a great slavery. You will think this a sorry use of what I might have it in my power to do. It may be so, God be merciful to me! But I feel as if I was urged by an irresistible impulse to steer clear of people and things, as much as I can, so as to avoid interfering with their interests or plans, be they what they may.
>
> I have always had young children at home where, having my affections and time much occupied, I have endeavored to flatter myself that, if I was not in the first capacity for usefulness, I was not out of the way of my duty. I am sensible my understanding and experience befriends me more every

year that passes. While I have that impression, with the capacity for innocent enjoyment, and knowing how useful I am to my children, I rather
wish my lease of life may be long; whatever is the Will of the Almighty.
I hope I may [have] resignation. I have told you all, dear Sis, I have to
say for myself.

There is a basic truth and honesty about the plainness of the talents
and lives of such women as Mary Bayley Post that makes them the salt
of the earth. There is comfort in their homespun philosophy, their
humor, their insight, their shrewdness, their loyalty to life.

With her father's return, Betty, too, left New Rochelle for New
York, and there began for her four of the most humiliating years of her
life. There was no further reason for her to stay at New Rochelle—she
was not her Uncle William's responsibility—but, at the same time, she
was no longer welcome in the home of her father and stepmother. There
is no clue to the nature of the trouble, but there can be little doubt that
it involved Betty directly. It was of this time that she wrote in her journal:
"Family disagreement. Could not guess why when I spoke kindly to relations, they did not speak to me." And again, she told her friend Julia
Scott in 1799 that "my father perseveres in his resolution that I shall
never admit a reconciliation with Mrs. B." Whatever it was all about,
Betty had no home and was forced to accept the hospitality of friends
and friendly relatives. She divided her time between her sister Mary on
John Street and her aunt, Mrs. Thomas Dongan, her dead mother's sister,
on Staten Island.

It is painful to anyone to accept charity, but it is especially painful
for a woman to go begging for security. And it is the supreme martyrdom
for her to make her home perforce with another woman, however
close the ties of blood. Betty Bayley endured this martyrdom throughout
the years 1790–1794.

Yet it was also during these years that she forged the great human
loves of her life. The first was her love for her father. Not that her love
for her father began only in 1790; it had been—because of the early death
of her mother and her consequent loneliness—the sustaining thread of
all her girlhood. But there is a feeling that it was not returned in equal
part until now, when Bayley's own life was disintegrating and he was
made to see Betty's embarrassing situation, for which he was greatly to

blame. Whatever the psychological reasons for the growing bond between father and daughter, there was now great rapport between them. They were after all very much alike, but it seems to have taken the good doctor all these years to discover it.

The rapport was genuine. It was based on mutual understanding and recognition. Betty truly understood, for instance, that Richard Baylay's lack of success as a husband and father was due in great part to his complete absorption in medicine and his compelling desire to serve mankind. She puts her finger on this quite candidly and humorously in the following passage from one of her numerous letters to him:

> Mr. Sitgreaves thinks that men of active genius should never be more than one month in the same place. Who does that apply to? Who is it that could not be made happy by an angel, even if the uniting bond was but a cambric thread? No bonds, no restraints, the air, the ocean, the whole earth—and not even that, *I* believe, would satisfy the restless spirit of the object now present to my mind. Poor Sitgreaves, on the contrary, wants his shelves of books, his segar, the eye of affection inquiring his wish and hastening to fulfil it before it is expressed.

That Betty's diagnosis was accurate is evident from the self-appraisal Dr. Bayley penned his daughter:

> I embrace the opportunity of writing you by the favor of Mr. David Ogden. What is the purpose? A curious question, truly. Shall we be compelled to assign or connect motives to every action of our lives? to every impulse of the mind? to every expression of a heart that feels? I hope not, for surely, in such case, I should be deprived of many little pleasures that a more cautious temper never feels. Calculations, intentions, cautions are entitled to their places. To be always calculating, always cautious, to be always influenced by intention, are motives never to be applied to me.
>
> Major O'Flacharty, in the comedy of the West Indian, takes occasion to express a sentiment to two persons who were *preaching*, as he called it, on the subject of a duel: "Fight first," said he, "and settle your differences afterward."
>
> How applicable to a want of system, how characteristic of someone we are acquainted with! How often have I committed myself in a hurry and had occasion to repent at leisure. On the contrary, the most heartfelt pleasure I have ever felt, has arisen from incautious commitment, nor would I be deprived of the result of such accidental commitment for all the

exclusive enjoyments I have derived from entering into contracts, and all the good bargains I ever made.

Bayley, in his turn, knew that his vivacious little daughter was so much like him that he must caution her to "calm that glowing of your soul, that warm emanation of your chest, for a more temperate climate. Impressions in that case will be less readily admitted, but their effects will last longer." And again he reminded her: "We ought to be cautious how we indulge our propensities for fear of the consequences of habit, which may conduct us far beyond the line of duty."

The correspondence that fed the love of father and daughter became so vital to both that it took on a certain imperiousness. If he were out of the city on business, he expected a letter every day, and made an effort to send as many answers. That Betty's expectations were not less is obvious from her complaint that "one letter from my father in eleven days is rather hard, but I have hopes of the next post producing what to me is of inconceivable value."

They delighted in sharing scraps of philosophy and snippets of news, but, most of all, in just being good-humored and gay with each other. He wrote "on a Tuesday morning in June":

> Thus new objects gives a turn to the mind, a different cast to the temper; again, objects present shakes our mind more forcibly than those more at a distance: thus, we intend one thing today, we are diverted from it tomorrow, the next day new ideas occur and our former intentions are forgotten. This cursed dysentery of the mind has been entailed on both sexes with a remarkable constancy from the time of *Adam and Eve*—apropos why Adam and Eve: great characters are entitled to precedence. *Eve* is said to have surpassed Adam in enterprise, but she is a woman and ill-treated. . . .

On occasion Betty delighted to twit him, in a spirit of inoffensive sauciness:

> Your most welcome letter arrived safe, but not before it was too late to answer it by the next post. It was also without a date, which deprived me of the pleasure of knowing when it was written; but the good intelligence it contained of your health and expected return was as much pleasure as could possibly be afforded by any circumstance, and exhilarated my spirit to so great a degree that Madame Olive, who had passed the day with me, declared that her *chere fille* was *charmante*, and gave me *mille baisers*.

Betty herself has written the perfect epitaph for this great friendship with her father. It is a sentence that might have been written by a Francis de Sales or a Thérèse of Lisieux, or perhaps a poet, and it occurs in a note sent hurriedly to Dr. Bayley in 1801, shortly before he died: "Indeed I am obliged to banish the thoughts of you sometimes, as we do that of heaven when an excessive desire delays us in our progress towards it."

The other permanent friendships dating from this time were friendships in the true and strict sense, that is, they were formed with members of her own sex and were based wholly upon mutual regard and interest and service. Betty Bayley's three closest, lifelong friends were Julia Sitgreaves Scott, Eliza Craig Sadler and Catherine Dupleix. Julia and Eliza were older than Betty, probably two or three years older, and all three were married when Betty first knew them, or were married shortly afterward.

Julia Sitgreaves was from either Philadelphia or Easton, Pennsylvania. Her brother Samuel served in the House of Representatives as a delegate from that state. When Betty first met her, Julia was living in New York where her husband, Lewis Allaire Scott—son of John Morin Scott, the "fiery Son of Liberty"—was serving as the Commonwealth's Secretary of State. The Scotts had two children, Maria and John, both of whom doted on Betty.

Although Julia was older than Betty, Betty was the stronger. Betty herself used the fact in explaining to Eliza Sadler her many attentions to Julia in a time before both realized that possessiveness had nothing to do with friendship or love:

> Julia is a little vain shadow and never interests me but when she is in sickness or sorrow—then I fly to her, hold her in my bosom till the storm is past, and only care enough for her to hold the chain together until it comes round again.

If Betty's rather airy attitude toward Julia was anything more than schoolgirl defensiveness, it quickly made room for a great sturdy union of hearts and minds. They visited constantly—Betty taking jaunts even to Easton and Philadelphia—took long rides on horseback up the bank of the Hudson, shared the immature philosophies of youth. Many years

later, Samuel Waddington Seton, Betty's brother-in-law, was to remember
that they even dressed alike. Julia, in love with life and high society—of
which she was a genuine member—appealed to the lively, carefree French
part of Betty. Her good humor and sociability were to stand her in good
stead in helping her to recover from the frequent ravages of sorrow:
she was married only a few years when her husband died; then followed
in doleful and regular succession the deaths of her brother, her father,
her mother and, finally her dearly loved daughter—in the twenty-first
year of her age and the first of her marriage.

In all these griefs Betty was anxious for Julia "lest the little frame
should sink" under the relentless hammering of fate. But despite chronic
ill-health, Julia outlasted all her troubles and died an old lady in the
1840's.

Eliza Sadler—she seems never to have used "Elizabeth"—was Julia
Scott's opposite among Betty's friends. Eliza was quiet, reserved, dignified:
Betty loved to twit her about her "matron step." She was a woman of
considered judgment and prudence, and throughout life, Betty leaned
upon her for comfort and advice. Despite the fact that the extant correspondence between them is not so voluminous as that between Betty
and Julia, it gives the definite impression that, of all her friends, Betty
loved Eliza Sadler best and that their friendship struck the deepest chord.

For all her sedateness, Eliza Sadler loved the things her wealth bought
her: a handsome home in Cortlandt Street, clothes, a country cottage
on Long Island, the ability to entertain in lavish good taste. Best of
all she loved travel. She had an uncle in Ireland whom she visited
periodically, and a merchant husband forced to cross the sea on business,
and Eliza took full advantage of her opportunities for junkets to England
and the Continent. The Sadler money went to charity, too, for Eliza
had a good heart and was easily persuaded both to give and to serve on
charitable committees.

The third member of Betty Bayley's inner circle was Catherine Dupleix.
Her given name was never used by Betty or anyone else; she was always
Dué or Doux. Like Eliza Sadler, with whom she was also closely bound
in friendship, Dué had Irish roots, probably in Downpatrick. She seems
to have known Julia Scott only slightly, if at all. There was something
Dickensian about Dué; a bit of that "poor lorn creetur," Mrs. Gummidge

—for she too was a sufferer. She was a genuine sufferer for, to begin with, she was not happily married: George Dupleix was a bluff sea captain, perhaps too bluff for the delicate Dué. He was away a great deal on his long voyages and she was left alone in her chronic pains and illnesses which, again, were genuine enough. All in all, she seems to have been miserable much of the time—nor had she any children to distract her from herself.

Dué had, however, much to offer her friends in way of disposition, understanding and sympathy, for she seems to have been a universal favorite: with Dr. Bayley, Sad (Eliza Sadler), the Craigs, Willy Seton (Betty's husband), and the Seton children. In a poetic play on her name, the hearty doctor averred that: "Doux is the break of morn, *doucement* her rising"; then, in a spirit of wicked mischief, "surer than earlier birds." She was a soul of active charity, devoting her time, as well as her money, to the widows and orphans of the town of New York.

Betty's great love of these late teen years, however, was the love of her life—William Magee Seton. It is hard to say when their love began, or even when they met. It is possible that they knew each other in their growing-up years—both the Setons and the Bayleys were well-known families in the small New York society—but the acquaintance would have been slight, for William was six years older than Betty, a great difference in children, and they both spent much of their childhood away from the city.

It is difficult to establish an exact chronology for William Magee Seton. According to the Seton family Bible, he was born in 1768:

> Born 20th April, 1768, 35 minutes after 4 P.M. on board the ship *Edward*, Captain Thomas Miller (long. 68.30, lat. 36). Baptized, 8th of May, at New York.

This date of William's birth at sea, some hundreds of miles off Norfolk, Virginia, is accurate despite the fact that the Rev. Thomas Hall, the Episcopal Chaplain in Leghorn, put down William Magee Seton's age as thirty-seven on his death certificate (information he must have had from Elizabeth herself) because, according to Trinity Church records, his father and mother were married on March 2, 1767. The other dates in William's youth cannot be demonstrated so easily. With his brother

James he was sent to school in England—at Richmond near London—at about the age of ten, remaining there some six years. In a letter written from Pimlico to his Grandmother Seton at Chiswick in approximately 1782, he tells with typical boyish wonder of seeing King George III in the House of Lords "with a crown on his head." He also saw Lord North, the Prime Minister, and thought him by far "the shabbiest of the Lords." He was, besides, somewhat disconcerted to hear the Bishop of Gloucester read prayers "like in a church," but discovered that they "always read prayers before business!"

William Seton returned to New York, probably in 1784, but in 1788 he was back in Europe, to tour, as part of his business education, the principal ports of the Continent—Barcelona, Genoa, Leghorn, among them—and to meet on personal terms the exporters and importers with whom his father's firm dealt. It was in this way that he became fast friends with Filippo Filicchi and his Bostonian wife, Mary Cowper, at Leghorn. Before returning home he went to visit his Grandmother Seton and Lady Cayley, his father's sister, in England. He next made a tour of the manufacturing towns then in the heyday of the Industrial Revolution —Sheffield, Manchester, Liverpool, Birmingham—winding up in London, which he found "very gay":

> There was not a single place of amusement I did not go to, but was much disappointed in not seeing Mrs. Siddons, who is retired from the stage, and Mr. Edwin at last is dead to the great sorrow of all lovers of mirth.

He sailed for New York in the *Montgomery* on July 10, 1790. After a rough voyage of ten weeks he arrived in good time for the marriage of his beautiful sister Maria to Senator John Vining of Delaware on November 24. It was this fall of 1790 or very early in the spring of 1791 that William Magee Seton met Elizabeth Ann Bayley for the first time "in grown-up wise." She was sixteen, he was twenty-two. It was at this time, also, that he wrote the letter to his brother James which Archbishop Seton misquoted—unforgivably, for he had the original—in his biography of his grandmother, and which subsequent biographers have copied. As quoted by the Archbishop, William tells his brother James, who is on business in the West Indies for his father, that "it is currently reported and generally believed that I am to be married to Miss Bayley, but I shall think twice before I commit myself in any direction." The true quote reveals that the passage *does not refer to Betty Bayley at all but to Mary Hoffman!*

> All the girls frequently ask after you, and Eliz. [Aimee(?)] Miss Bayley and Mary Hoffman desire their love. It is currently reported and generally believed that I am to marry the latter but I should think twice before I committed that *faux pas*, and instead of my taste being improved by the variety of Beauty I have seen in my travels, it must be very much depraved indeed, if I could not find a handsomer girl even in New York tho' at the same time I must confess I admire her mental accomplishments very much and was I inclined to matrimony, not all [sic] impossible but what I might fall in love with her, and have no doubt she will make an excellent wife and happy the man who gets her. . . .

Most ironic of all, the "man who got her" was James Seton! James married Mary Gillon Hoffman in March, 1792.

On Sunday, July 17, 1791, Will Seton set sail once more for Europe, bound this time for Leghorn and the Filicchi counting house in the British ship *Eagle*, and accompanied by his brothers James and Henry. It is not known how long he stayed, or whether he returned with James for the latter's wedding. In any event, his courtship of Betty Bayley could not have consumed much more than a year, for they were married at the beginning of 1794.

It is easily understood, judging from externals, why Betty Bayley fell in love with William Magee Seton. He was handsome, charming, mature —with a firsthand knowledge of the great, mysterious world across the waters—he was of the first circle of New York society, and a man of wealth. More important, he was also good-humored, kind, tender, and alive with the energy and zest of youth. He liked a good time, as can be judged from his stay in London in 1789–1790 and from the fact that he was foremost among the social lights of New York: while in Italy he was a frequent opera-goer, was often seen at balls and concerts, and all-in-all made an impact on the social life of Pisa and Florence. He was himself a passable violinist—there is even reason to believe that he once toyed with the thought of making a career of music—and brought the first known Stradivarius to America, having bought the instrument at the dead master's shop in Cremona. (This precious violin was lost on a train by his grandson William, on his way to school at Mount St. Mary's, Emmitsburg, in the year 1850.)

With all his flair for the good things of life, however, Seton had his feet firmly planted on the ground. While enjoying the social whirl he could, at the same time, recognize that New York in 1790 had become "one of the most dissipated places on the Continent." And, at twenty-two, he could be firm in admonishing his brother James, in case certain hints as to his conduct were true, that "gaming is . . . one of the worst of vices, and once it becomes habitual there is no saying where it may end." Although no churchgoer, he possessed the basic human virtues and ideals of that idealistic time, of which an implacable honesty shone most brightly in him. On the debit side, he was probably proud—pride was a trait of the Setons—and petulant, a byproduct of the disease that ravaged and eventually killed him.

Unfortunately, when Betty met William Seton, he was already started in consumption. Although she herself was later to refer to the disease as the "Seton complaint," it was more probably the "Curson complaint," that is, a heritage from William's mother's family. His mother, Rebecca Curson Seton, died young. In 1790, William wrote to James that his stepmother, his mother's sister Anna Maria Curson, would have added some lines, but was afraid of "bringing on the pain in her breast"— the telltale sign. No matter the source of the disease: it is known that three of the thirteen Seton children who reached maturity died of tuberculosis—Rebecca, William Magee and Cecilia—and William Magee apparently passed it on to his own children Anna Maria and Rebecca, and his wife Elizabeth caught it from him; it was still in the family generations later, his grandson Henry and great-grandsons John and William, Henry's sons, dying of it.

The Setons were of an ancient Scottish line tracing back to the lairds who served the Stuarts and beyond. Mary Seton, one of the storied "Four Maries," ladies-in-waiting to the beautiful, luckless Mary Queen of Scots, was an ancestor, and earls and barons and a cardinal are to be found in the family. The New York Setons belonged to the Parbroath branch of the line.

William Seton, the father of William Magee Seton, came to America in 1763. He was born on April 24, 1746, in Scotland, where his mother had gone to visit from the family home in Kirkbridge, Yorkshire, England. In America, he settled for a short time in New Jersey, but soon moved on to New York City, where he married Rebecca Curson on March 2, 1767, in Trinity Church, and also formed with members of his wife's family—notably his father-in-law, Richard Curson—the firm of Seton and Curson, importers and merchants. In 1768, the first Chamber of Commerce of the City of New York was formed in Fraunces Tavern at Broad and Pearl Streets, and William Seton, at only twenty-two years of age, became a charter member.

Seton had five children by this first marriage: three sons besides William Magee, the oldest—James, John, and Henry—and a daughter, Anna Maria. Regretfully, within a few years Rebecca Curson Seton was dead. On November 29, 1776, at Brunswick, New Jersey, Seton married her sister Anna Maria. They were married thus, outside the New York province and before a Presbyterian minister, because their own Episcopal Church disapproved of marriage to a dead wife's sister.

In 1775, just a week after Lexington and Concord, Seton was elected to the Committee of One Hundred deputed by loyalist New York to run the affairs of the city and state in the troublesome days ahead. William Seton was, like Richard Bayley and most professional and mercantile men of the town, loyal to the mother country. His loyalty stood him in good stead, for it brought him rewards. On July 27, 1777, he was appointed assistant warehouse keeper, a strategic job in that it dealt with supplies in a city at war, and in 1779 a notary public. Among the family heirlooms of the Setons there is still preserved his silver notarial seal with the date 1779 and the Seton coat-of-arms. This very seal was used to stamp the last will and testament of Major John André, a friend of Seton's, before he left to meet Benedict Arnold for the betrayal of West Point.

In 1782, the war over, William Seton became assistant to Andrew Elliott, the Chief of Police and Superintendent of the Port of New York. Seton was certainly a man to disprove the old adage that "you can't eat your cake and have it, too." He did! A declared loyalist throughout the war, through sheer character, personality and reputation, he was accepted by the patriots, apparently even without the ritual of penitence

and absolution. The experience gained in the work of the Port was to
serve him enormously in later years when he returned to the commission business. His son, Samuel, reminiscing many years after, says that
his father "struggled through the Revolution." But Samuel was hardly
in a position to know, for he was not born yet, and we have the contrary evidence of a letter written to England in March of 1782 by Captain Ralph Dundas of the Royal Navy, a cousin of Seton's, that his
kinsman "was liked and esteemed by everyone and not spending less
than six guineas a day"—a substantial sum for a man who had just
ceased struggling!   •

Not that William Seton did not deserve every shilling of it. He was
a princely man, magnanimous, honorable and just. He loved his family
with the genial pride and benevolence of a great lord. Under the date
of July, 1791, he happily made the following notation:

> On Saturday the 16th, my dear Mrs. Seton, who was on Long Island
> for her health, came in to see all the children, and we sat down to dinner,
> the whole family met together, viz., our two selves; my daughter Mrs.
> Vining and her husband; my sons William, James, John, Henry, Samuel
> and Edward; my daughters Eliza, Rebecca, Mary, Charlotte and Harriet—
> in all fifteen.

Only Cecilia, not yet born, was missing from this intimate family
gathering of William Seton's five children, of his first marriage, and
seven children of his second. Before the meal ended, Seton and his
wife, moved with tender gratitude, drank a toast to "the Omnipotent
Being Who had helped us raise such a family, none of whom ever gave
us trouble." And Seton repaid the filial goodness of his children by a
prodigal openhandedness. "Let all come to my strong box while I am
alive, and when I am gone you will take care of each other," he would
say.

He had the same kind generosity toward his fellow men; he was truly
the father of the orphan and the friend of the poor in New York. He
was public-spirited in the best sense: eager for the good of country,
whether England or the United States of America. In short, he was a
man beloved.

Hector St. John de Crèvecoeur, the famous Colonial essayist, included
William Seton in his short-lived venture of running a French packet

service and also dedicated the French edition of the *Letters of an American Farmer* to him. He might well, for when Crèvecoeur returned to New York in 1782 as French Consul, Seton was at the dock to break the news as gently as possible that his home was burned down, his wife dead, and his children captured by Indians (they were later recovered), and to support him in his dreadful sorrow.

William Seton's house was always open to a host of friends, and the ornate sedan chairs of the Jays, the Livingstons, and the Hamiltons stopped frequently at his door; Charles Maurice de Talleyrand-Périgord, Prince de Bénévent, apostate bishop and wily diplomat, was an intimate of the houschold during his years in New York.

Seton's shining hour came in 1784 with his appointment as Cashier of the Bank of New York, the state's first such institution. It was easily the most influential position William Seton ever held. The Bank, which was situated in the Walton House at 67 St. George's Square, played an important part in the finances of the state and the nation. Through it, Seton became the good friend and trusted financial advisor and collaborator of Alexander Hamilton. The first board of directors included, besides Hamilton, John Vanderbilt and Isaac Roosevelt. Seton was able to bring his son William Magee Seton in as Clerk of Discount in 1786, when the boy was only eighteen, and to have his friend Charles Wilkes, who had come to America under Seton's protection, succeed him as Cashier when he resigned that post in 1794. Wilkes later rose to the post of President of the bank.

This was the family background of the man Betty Bayley fell in love with. There can be little doubt that she was courted with dash and élan —Will Seton was that kind of young man. And Betty's bubbling, laughing nature would have sprung to instant life at such an approach.

The New York of these years was ablaze with pleasure and merriment. His Excellency, the President of the United States and his Lady were in residence, and this added great excitement to the life of the city. Although Mr. Washington was a man of simple tastes, the people, used to monarchy, even though it lay across the water, did not quite know how to act in a Republic. There was a definite New York aristocracy, without titles, and its members gave the city a glitter of its own. Beside official functions, a galaxy of assemblies, cotillions and parties of every kind filled the social calendar. Grant Thorburn, the city's first florist, did a thriving business supplying swains with bouquets for their sweethearts from his attractive shop on Liberty Street where birds in cages sang among the flowers. The fur wraps worn by these same winsome ladies came from John Jacob Astor's store nearby.

Betty Bayley was a part of all this. She loved dancing, and was probably very good at it, for she was a girl of grace, tiny of frame—she was scarcely five feet tall—and fleet of foot.

Then there was the theatre. The John Street Theatre, the first theatre built by a professional company in America, stood on Nassau Street between John Street and Maiden Lane. Erected in 1754, it was New York's only theatre until the Park Theatre was built in 1798. Here Will and Betty may well have seen Royall Tyler's *The Contrast*, America's first comedy of manners, written as a vehicle for Thomas Wignall, the matinee idol of the day; or *The Fatal Deception* or *Darby's Return* by the famous William Dunlap. Betty went often to the theatre. She loved the world of the mind and its outpouring in poetry and prose and drama. Playgoing was one of the pleasures she reproached herself for in later years because of "the effect on my passions, and the extravagant ideas I imbibed from it." But there is more of the exaggerated anxiety of the mother and the complete abnegation of the saint, than there is of objectivity in the words of warning she addressed to her daughter Catherine.

> The passions represented in a theatre are in quite a different form from their reality. We know that they are the secret springs of the human heart and the source of all our evils, yet on the stage it would appear that the spirit of dominion, pride, resentment, vengeance, etc., proceed from greatness of soul and the elevation of a noble mind, while a veil is thrown over the corruption of the heart. . . .

In 1792 and 1793 Betty had no such philosophic scruples. She was frankly gay and happy. She was worldly, perhaps, but worldly in an innocent way. The later tears of shame were occasioned by a later conscience, by a relentless, probing conscience that had at length put all worldliness away, even the innocent kind, and had turned wholly to God.

The happiness of her courtship years was, in fact, a kind of wonderful, fairy-tale ending tacked on the years that had gone before, the years of loneliness and insecurity. She had reached the nadir of misery in 1791. It was probably no new ill or trouble, just an intensification, a heaping up, of the old—the family quarrel, the temporizing of her father, the hateful dependence on relatives for a roof and a place at table. She recorded it cryptically: "Alas, alas, alas! *Tears of blood*—My God!—horrid subversion of every good promise of God in the boldest presumption—God had created me—I was very miserable. He was too good to condemn so poor a creature made of dust, driven by misery this the wretched reasoning—Laudanum—the praise and thanks of excessive joy not to have done the horrid deed the thousand promises of Eternal gratitude." And writing, on February 19, 1811, to her brother-in-law Henry Seton, who had asked her whether it was wrong of him to regret having been saved from shipwreck, Elizabeth told him of "the moment twenty years ago in which I asked myself the same question, dictated by that anguish of soul which can find no relief." There is no denying the blunt suggestiveness of these statements. It is possible that the thought of suicide crossed her mind—the most horrible and preposterous thoughts cross the most innocent minds—but she could not have entertained it long or seriously: it would have been out of character for her who had come to rely on God so entirely. In fact, the exceptional agony of this experience may be taken as a gauge of her spirituality. It is eternally true that God fits the burden to the back. Considering the intensity of Betty's trial in the light of this truth, she can be judged to have climbed high toward heaven.

Whatever had come in that black night, Will Seton had exorcised it. There was nothing ahead now but the brightness of a new, long day. Like all lovers, Betty and Will had a language of their own, silly, even ludicrous, but a necessary code to exclude every other person in the world from penetrating the wondrousness of their discovery of each other. *My dearest love. My little girl. My dear little owny bony. My dearest Will. My darling. Your own. Your E.*

There are just six notes left of the many Betty must have dispatched by houseboy, urging him to hurry by her final push at the front door. They are short, to-the-point messages, but richly overlaid with every emotion; yearning, trust, archness, teasing, anxiety—in a word, devoted love.

Your Eliza is well, and would be perfectly happy if she could enjoy the society of her friend. I have wished very much to see you, and knew that indisposition only could have prevented my wish. Tomorrow I will wait in anxious expectation. Believe me,

Your Own

My dearest Will,

I have resolved to do my duty and go to see Mrs. Dwight this afternoon, and, if the weather remains clear, it is my intention to pass an hour with Mrs. Wilkes in the evening, where you may have the honor of seeing me, if you please.

Your E.B.

My dearest Will,

Mrs. Sadler is not going to the concert, and wishes very much to see us there this evening. Do not be too late.

Your E.B.

Your Eliza's eye is very ugly, but not very painful; but it will prevent the possibility of my going out. Therefore, you must devote a great deal of your time to me. Come as early as possible. We shall dine at One today, as Post is going out of town.

Your E.B.

An unavoidable something obliges Mrs. Sadler to drink tea with Mrs. Constable. If you are anxious to see your Eliza, you will find her at Mrs. Atkinson's at the piano.

Your Own

The final one has an anxious tone, and seems to hint that the time has come for Will to have a serious talk with Dr. Bayley:

My father dined with us and has gone I don't know where. I do not think you will meet him until the evening. Your *apology* is already made by one who is most earnestly interested in his good opinion of you. Your *E.* will be in Wall Street by five o'clock, and you shall then know more on the subject.

Of course, it all ended happily; everything was in their favor. Dr. Bayley may have paused worriedly at the thought of Will's cough and the frequent "pains in the breast," but he was a philosophic man, and apparently decided to let things work themselves out for themselves.

William Magee Seton and Elizabeth Ann Bayley were married in the home of the bride's sister Mrs. Wright Post on Sunday evening, January

25, 1794, by the Right Reverend Samuel Provoost, Rector of Trinity Church and first Bishop of the Protestant Episcopal Diocese of New York.

Will was twenty-five and Betty was nineteen, and they were very much in love.

V

The World and Heaven Too

William Magee Seton brought his bride to his father's house at 61 Stone Street. It was probably a temporary arrangement until their own house should be ready, but it cannot have displeased the patriarchal nature of the older Seton. It must have been a strange experience for Betty, who had been visiting friends and relatives in a lonely round for so long, to become suddenly part of a large family. There were at least eight Seton children still at home.

There was a daughterly quality in Betty, for she charmed her father-in-law as completely as she had charmed her father. He bestowed upon her a touching mark of his affection and trust by showing her intimate family letters:

> You are the first of my children to whom I have submitted a perusal of them, and I request you will return them to me unsullied by the eye of impertinent curiosity. Let no one look at them. The parental affection I ever felt for my dear William, your husband, you will find strongly marked in every letter. This will give you pleasure, but when I add that this affection has increased ever since, I think every page where I mention him will be doubly dear to you. That you may long, very long enjoy every blessing together is the sincere prayer of your affectionate and fond father.

Betty and Will were supremely happy. That this happiness was rooted in an unassailable love, and not mere physical attraction, was more and more evident with time, for it never abated, even in calamity.

The July after their marriage, Will had to go to Philadelphia on business—usually a wretched journey of two days in a stagecoach that was no more than two benches on four wheels. He wrote to his "darling little girl" twice on the way, from Newark and Trenton, and was rewarded by finding a long letter from her on his arrival, and one the next day. He had been surprised, and delighted, to find, on opening his traveling bag in Newark that she had packed her picture with his clothes, a gesture of love and a shrewd one. Throughout the trip, by his own account, the picture of his "Cara Sposa," was a chief conversation piece, and Will faithfully delivered her in writing every compliment it evoked. The inspired young husband would not have noticed the amused, or bored, glances exchanged as he waxed too eloquent too long! His letter of July 27, 1794, begins with an apostrophe to the portrait:

> This is Sunday morning, and my little girl's dear William [is] as usual employed at writing, instead of being at his devotions; to tell the truth, it was my intention to go to church, but it still rains as if there had not been any for a twelvemonth, therefore, I thought I could not employ myself better than in conversing à *la distance* with my darling little wife, whose picture I have now before me and would not have been without it for the world.
>
> I often ask it many questions, but it does not smile, and I always fancy it "beckoning me to return." I can imagine nothing but anxiety and regret and yet it looks gay. Oh! that tomorrow was come, that might bring me nearer to that little heart, which I am sure must beat to receive its master.

In this same year of 1794, William Seton Sr. had resigned as Cashier of the Bank of New York and gone into partnership with a Mr. Maitland of London, apparently a kinsman. Both William Jr. and James joined their father in this new venture into the commission business he knew so well. The firm of Seton, Maitland and Company was among the largest and most prosperous in New York and its ships criss-crossed the seas between the American capital and London, Hamburg, Leghorn, Barcelona, and Malaga and St. Eustatius, St. Croix and Martinique in the West Indies.

These were affluent years for the Setons, and youth, love, and a respectable luxury made life a kind of paradise. Will and Betty reached the very heart of this paradise in the fall of 1794 when, almost simultaneously, they learned that Betty was pregnant and they moved into their new home. This first home was located at 27 Wall Street, a fashionable address just a few doors from the Alexander Hamiltons and the newlyweds must have had their fill of pleasure and pride in furnishing it (Duncan Phyffe's store was right around the corner from the Setons), planning the colors of the rooms, selecting materials and patterns, and in doing all those mysterious things that are ritual for young, newly-married home-owners. The exquisite happiness of that autumn was still vibrant years later in the pages of Elizabeth's *Dear Remembrances:* "My own home at 20—the world—that and heaven too—quite impossible!"

It is significant that, hard upon this cry of delight, in the very next sentence, she asks whether she must foreswear heaven to keep what she has:

So every moment clouded with that fear: "My God, if I enjoy this, I lose You"—yet no true thought of who I would lose, rather fear of hell and (of being) shut out from heaven.

This is the fear of the soul pursued by the Hound of Heaven: "Lest, having Him, I must have naught beside." It is indicative either of remarkable spiritual growth or of a special divine election. Despite her protestations that she feared only "the loss of heaven and the pains of hell," the fear that she recorded at this time was a higher fear, a true horror of losing God Himself. It is the fear of one teetering on the brink of total abandonment to God. It is the fear of one who has been given to see the desirability of God and sense the ineffable loss of turning away, and who wonders at the cost. Nor is the decision in such a crisis instantaneous. The crisis may last, the soul thus dawdling on the brink, for years. It was to be so, in fact, with Betty Seton, who, despite an ever-growing piety and active charity, had to be purified by suffering before she would cast the balance and fall headlong into the arms of God.

Betty gave birth to her first child in the house on Wall Street on May 3, 1795. As Julia Scott had predicted, it was a girl. Betty had been writing a letter to Julia when the infant announced its imminent arrival, and the young father, flushed with pride and happiness, finished the letter with the glad news. Julia, almost as excited as Will, answered immediately, chattering away of her eagerness to see the little creature, of how lovely it must be, was Betty able to nurse it—the thousand snippets of information young mothers must share. Nor did she forget to tease Will about his "impartial" description of his daughter. A month later, June 4, 1795, the baby was carried to Trinity Church to be christened Anna Maria, probably in compliment to the elder Setons, for it was Will's stepmother's name. Betty's father, Will's sister Rebecca and Mrs. Mary Fitch, an intimate family friend, were the godparents.

With the arrival of Anna Maria the trinity of life was complete and the little family settled down to an earnest domesticity. The following February, Betty was writing with a smug and knowing smile to Eliza Sadler, who was in Europe:

> Really, Mrs. Sad, *il facto:* you go to balls on Sunday night, you depraved creature! And what balls or amusements can compensate [for] that quiet, calm tranquillity which Sunday, and particularly Sunday evening, affords—with husband shaking his slippers by a good coal fire and a volume of Blair opened on the table. But avast! I am an American savage, I suppose, and should not mention these dull insipidities to a *lady* in the largest metropolis in the world, who can go to see blond peringues on Sunday evening and, I suppose, jump among the gayest. And, after all, my Sad, the effects of their manner may be as useful as ours and, as I think, the first point of religion is cheerfulness and harmony, they who have these in view are certainly right.

She goes on, with something of the sententious patriotism then arising in American breasts, to spurn things Continental and to aver that "your boulevards, I dare say . . . are very inferior to the pure air, fine prospect and gliding current of our Battery." What, however, had put to rest forever her once eager desire to travel were husband and hearth. As she wrote her letter: "William is playing *Rosy, Dimpled Boy, Pauvre Madelon, Return Enraptured Hours* and *Carmignol,* all as fast as the violin can sound them." And as for that paragon of children, Anna Maria Seton:

> Respecting a certain pair of eyes, they are much nearer to black than any other color which, with a very small nose and mouth, dimpled cheek

and chin, rosy face, and never-ceasing animation and expression, forms an object rather too interesting for my pen. Her grandfather B will tell you that he sees more sense, expression, intelligence and inquiry in that little face than any other in the world, that he can converse more with her than any woman in New York—in short—she is her mother's own daughter and, you may be sure, her father's pride and treasure. . . .

The letter concludes with a passage that hints at the loneliness of the past and ends with a sigh of gratitude for the present:

So some little beings are born to be treasured, while others are treated with less attention by those who give them being than they receive from their liveliness. But it is all right, and often those who want the fostering indulgent bosom of a parent to lean on, get cheerful through the world, whilst the child of hope will have its prospects darkened by unthought of disappointments. And so we go—there is a Providence which never slumbers or sleeps—but as my husband begins to gap, the clock strikes ten, and my fingers are cold.

In May, Will took Betty on a jaunt southward, leaving little Anna with the Setons for safekeeping. When they arrived in Philadelphia, Betty decided to prolong her visit with Julia Scott, who was living with her sister Mrs. James Cox on South Second Street, while Will went on to visit the Vinings at Wilmington. On their return to New York, they managed to dodge an invitation from John and Mary Wilkes (John was a brother of Charles Wilkes who succeeded William Seton Sr. as bank cashier) to spend the summer with them, and took a place of their own on Long Island, near the Narrows—present-day Bay Ridge. It was a perfect summer. Betty enjoyed her return to country life as never before. There were no visitors to interrupt her, no social demands. She had her baby all to herself; her sister Mary had a cottage nearby; her father ran over frequently in his boat to see her; and "my Will comes three times a week, and when the moon shines every evening."

The boat Dr. Bayley used was an official one, for he had just recently been appointed the first Health Officer of New York, and he used it to travel back and forth between the city and Bedloes Island, which was the official quarantine station of the port; immigrants and travelers had to be screened there for disease before landing at the city proper.

Dr. Charles McKnight was the first medical officer of the Port of New York, appointed by Governor Clinton in 1784, but Bayley was the first to hold the office with the name of Health Officer, with expanded duties and powers. One of McKnight's biographers has asserted that "he was unrivalled as a surgeon, except for Dr. Richard Bayley." Bayley's career and his humanitarianism advanced swiftly, hand-in-hand; in fact, one fed the other. Shortly after his return from Europe in 1790 he had helped organize the New York Dispensary for the benefit of the city's poor. In 1792 he became the first Professor of Anatomy at Columbia, serving on the faculty with his son-in-law, Wright Post, who held the chair of surgery. After 1793, the two exchanged courses. In 1794 Bayley helped reorganize the Medical Society, with his brother-in-law, Dr. Charlton, as head. His special work in the Society was the investigation of the causes of epidemics, which research he pursued with Dr. Samuel Bard and Dr. Tillary. His deductions were brilliant and penetrating. Arthur C. Jacobson wrote of him in the *Medical Times* of 1923:

> Croup, at the time Dr. Bayley lived, had a fifty per cent mortality. Dr. Bayley's contributions to the study of croup led to a very noticeable reduction in its mortality. He proved yellow fever to be infectious and understood thoroughly the conditions under which it throve: rains, heat, stagnant water, filth, new-made ground, low levels, and meteorological factors like extension from the source in the direction of prevailing winds. He showed how to deal with this local origin in truly modern fashion, as by drainage and filling in. He proclaimed the disease a murderer of our own creating. Without taking the mosquito into direct account he nonetheless developed measures of defense that were effectual because they eliminated the pest. For his work in pathology Bayley received full credit from the French, so that we may class him as a figure of international note in his day. In the study of fevers and croup he was very far ahead of his time.

His learned opinions, however, fell on deaf ears in the spring of 1795, when he petitioned the city officials to take more stringent steps to prevent the spread of yellow fever. Had he been listened to, perhaps the terrible scourge of the summer and fall might never have struck. Seven hundred people died of the disease that year. Jacobson says well that the doctor's celebrated "fiery temper" might sometimes be put to his credit as righteous anger.

Despite the horrors which surrounded him, Dr. Bayley found time for his favorite daughter. In fact, conversation with her by frequent, almost daily, letters or visits, became his only diversion. He continued to educate her with his Franklinesque commentaries on life and their appeal to reason. He must have been proud of her, for Betty was maturing, learning life at firsthand, even though a bit awkwardly, as was natural. She thought for instance, with the inflexible dogmatism of youth, that cold reason could rule all, if only the effort were made; yet it was the emotional pangs of worry and fright that were enlarging her heart and her understanding. On August 11, 1796, she wrote to Eliza Sadler:

> My Sad, every hour I pass shows me the instability of every expectation which is not founded on reason. I have learnt to commune with my own heart, and I try to govern it by reflection, and yet that heart grows every day more tender and softened, which in great measure I attribute to the state of my William's health, that health on which my every hope of happiness depends, and which continues me either [in] the most perfect *human* felicity or sinks me in the lowest depths of sorrow. That health certainly does not mend, and I often think very much decreases, and although it is my fixed principle both as a Christian and a reasonable being never to dwell on thoughts of future events which do not depend on myself, yet I never view the setting sun or take a solitary walk but melancholy tries to seize me; and if I did not fly to my little treasure and make her call "Papa" and kiss me a thousand times, I should forget myself.
>
> This disposition is also increased by the expectation of another precious sharer of my lot, whether it be happy or the reverse. Therefore, my Sad, I have become a looker-up, which is certainly the only remedy for my description of sorrow.

The taint was on the rose; Will's health was worsening, and Betty, with characteristic candor, faced the fact. But for this one threat to her happiness, the marriage would have been idyllic. It served to strengthen what she already knew—that nothing on earth could be perfect; and to "look up" toward God became the panacea for every ill, and her constant devotion.

The second "little sharer of my lot" was born on November 24, 1796, and Will Seton had what every father wants—a son. The boy was christened William in Trinity on Christmas Eve, with his Grandfather Bayley, Mary Post and Joseph Covachichi, a family friend, as sponsors. This child was to be the favorite of his mother in later years, and like so many earthly favorites, would give her the greatest happiness and greatest sorrow.

Dr. Bayley's appointment as Health Officer had given him sweeping authority to put into effect some of his accurate theories for controlling yellow fever. However, it was necessary for him to travel to Albany every winter to seek funds and further legal support from the legislature. It was no mean trip. By stagecoach, which was Bayley's usual mode of travel, it took three days, riding from five in the morning until ten at night. Once the coach, attempting to pass a sleigh between Hudson and Kinderhook, slid off the road and down an embankment, turning upside down. No one was hurt, as Dr. Bayley hastened to assure his daughter before she would hear of the accident from someone else.

Often on his appearance before the lawmakers and politicians, the crusading Doctor had to defend himself. It was so in February of 1797, when Betty sent a note to warn him that "the soap boilers and tallow chandlers talk of petitioning the legislature for the removal of the Health Officer." Dr. Bayley's strong hand was being felt by some of the chief offenders (in Bayley's estimation and in truth) against the public health, who soiled the streets with slop and waste and poisoned the air with stinking odors. Bayley enjoyed his yearly trips to Albany. They were, in a real sense, vacations from the daily rounds of his practice and administrative duties, as his daughter recognized:

> Should you be in your retirement, unoccupied by the cares and solicitudes that generally accompany you, a letter from your daughter will be very acceptable; if otherwise, it will be read in haste, and the idea "Bett is a goose" will pass your mind. I send it to take its chance, hoping, as the children say, it may find you well, as I am the same.

He especially enjoyed the company of the great. He always stayed with the Lieutenant Governor, Stephen Van Rensselaer, at Watervliet, and later at Albany, where he hobnobbed with General Philip Schuyler, Alexander Hamilton and Gouverneur Morris, and found "those attentions and formalities he is so fond of receiving"—as Betty knowingly remarked to Julia Scott. He was able also to indulge in some intellectual by-play, which he was far too busy for in New York. He found Hamilton and Morris "men of superior sense and . . . great brilliancy of wit."

I esteem it a high good fortune to be on a footing of communication, of feeling, and sentiment with them. We exchange civilities and opinions with all that freedom and latitude that cautious men never admit. Liberal construction is our motto. We sting, we smile, we admit, without any personal application.

The correspondence between Betty and her father was the more extensive when they were thus separated by so many traveling miles, and a goodly portion of their extant letters belong to the weeks when he was at the state capital. In one of these letters, she tells him humorously: "It is currently reported that you are gone to New London to inquire the origin of 'the fever' and that you are to proceed to Boston and see your children, but I hope you will very soon return and convince the ladies who chatter on the subject that the origin is not the object of your pursuit, but the remedy." Of course, Betty could not know that the empty-headed chatterers were more right than she and, if the origin were discovered, the remedy would follow more swiftly. She concludes the letter with a passage that suggests that she has not lost her earlier hunger for solitude and divine union:

> I have passed one of the most elegant evenings of my life. It is now eleven o'clock, and since seven I have never quitted my seat, and scarcely changed my posture. Part of my family are asleep, and part abroad. I have been reading of the "High and Lofty One Who Inhabits Eternity," and selecting such passages as I wish to transmit to my daughter. How the world lessens and recedes; how calm and peaceable are hours spent in such solitude. They are marked down for useful purposes, and their memory remains. I close my evening employment with "orisons for thee." Peace be with my father!

Will Seton was busy that winter, fulfilling his position as one of the acknowledged social leaders of New York. He was one of four managers or hosts of a brilliant Commemoration Ball, held on February 22, to honor the birthday of New York's, and the nation's, first citizen—George Washington, President of the United States; and he held the same position for a gala City Assembly. His fellow-managers of these formal affairs were James Farquhar, James Scott, Aquila Giles, Jacob Morton, J. R. Livingston and William Armstrong. It is not hard to imagine the striking picture the handsome young manager made in his powdered wig and silk brocaded coat and knee breeches, with his beautiful wife on his arm, her hair piled in ringlets and caught with jewels, her lustrous gown of intricate folds and lace sweeping the floor.

The following June, Betty was on Long Island again for the summer, this time nearer New York. She described her location for Eliza Sadler, who was still in Europe:

> You may probably recollect a house of Mrs. Livingston's on the East River opposite the Battery and facing Governor's Island. Sister Post divides the house with us, and the pleasure of receiving our husbands together in the evenings, the company and protection we are to each other when they are detained from us, counter-balances every inconvenience which a union of families always occasions. We have yet received nothing but pleasure and comfort from our establishment, and the offering of fresh bread, butter and coffee to the dear, well-beloved father of us after a fatiguing sail in his Health Officer employment is a satisfaction of which you can well form an estimate.

Mary and Betty had their sisterly differences, but they were minor. One morning at breakfast, Mary reacted to the rumor that Sad was "enjoying the *agréments de Paris,*" and in one continual round of amusement, with the remark, "Then you see what your gentle, sentimental friend has come to!"—and Betty rose to a stiff and dignified defense: that it was typical of her friend to "submit to all matters of necessity with a good grace," and that she would probably never see Paris again and was right to enjoy it when she could.

Little Anna created another domestic disturbance with her ungovernable temper, which she took from nobody strange—Betty herself had a famous temper, and Grandfather Bayley has been described as "a real Tartar." Sympathetically enough, the good Doctor recommended that the little offender be conquered "by gentleness," but Mary and Wright Post recommended whipping, which Betty found "an unnatural resource, and the last I shall have recourse to"—and Will Seton, like a wise husband and most fathers of daughters, left the problem to Betty.

Betty missed Sad terribly that summer, and wrote to her constantly, both from a yearning to communicate with her friend and in an effort to elicit a letter—she had not heard directly from the European tourist in so long that she was seriously worried, although she knew that the mail could be at fault.

In one letter, she confided her great grief to Sad over the mortal illness of her friend Catherine Cooper, who was "dying in the most melancholy manner, unconscious of the change she is making of this world for the next." This is one of the earliest examples of Elizabeth's preoccupation with what was to become the center of her life—the thought of eternity. Under the press of this thought Elizabeth's soul took its particular shape and form: everything temporal became dull and ugly, everything eternal glittered and shone; the mere thought of anyone she loved forgetting for a moment the eternal destiny caused her agony; and, on the contrary, to see such a one living in the light and hope of eternity, brought her exalted joy.

In August the baby William became so ill that his Grandfather Bayley thought he could not recover. The young mother was terrified at this first encounter with serious illness in her children. So great was her anguish that she half-wished God had not given her the privilege of motherhood.

"What is there in the uncertainty of human happiness," she cried out, "to repay the agonizing convulsion of those twenty-four hours in which I witnessed his sufferings?"

It was only the beginning. The illnesses and deaths of those she loved were to be the constant, purifying cross of her life for, like all who love truly, she suffered more in the sufferings of those she loved than if she suffered their torments herself.

Here we are upon one of the great characteristic glories of Elizabeth Seton: her devotion to friends. Friendship was to her, as it should be, a sort of sacrament. It was her delight, her support, a sinew of her sanctity. It was temperamentally necessary to her. She was no more meant to live and strive alone than man is meant to be a hermit. She humbly admitted it to Eliza Sadler, that summer of 1797, leaving herself open and vulnerable in the process with entire trust:

> You speak of me as independent of you. Do you not know that there is not an hour of my life in which I do not want either the advice or soothings of friendship?

Her whole life bore out how right she was. In more or less degree, her minister, John Henry Hobart; her "Soul's Sister," Rebecca Seton; Eliza Sadler; Julia Scott; Dué; the blessed bishops, Carroll and Cheverus; the incomparable Antonio Filicchi; Simon Bruté and a host of others, were her staffs of life and stepping-stones to holiness. It is hard to imagine her unique spiritual perfection with any of them missing. In the plan of God, each had his or her mite or magnitude to contribute.

Friendship, however, cannot be one-sided. Dependence begets dependence, giving begets giving, trust begets trust, in ever-widening circles that break on the shores of God's love. And this leaning upon her friends made Elizabeth, in her turn, the great friend. Her heart was never closed, her pen never still, her hands never idle. She was a perfect wife, mother, sister, daughter, religious superior, because she was the perfect friend. Friendship is the common denominator of all love, and no one understood it better than Elizabeth Seton.

In the fall of 1797, Betty devoted herself for the first time to the public service of her fellow man. With other prominent New York matrons, she rallied behind Mrs. Isabella Marshall Graham, a devout Protestant Scotswoman, to form an association for the aid of the widow and the orphan, which they called the Widows' Society in New York. Several of her dearest friends were in the group: Dué, Sarah Startin, who was Betty's godmother, and—when she returned from Europe— Eliza Sadler. It was a society with a host of modern counterparts: a high-minded civic and religious organization of charitable women. It had Christian motivation: it was a way for these good women to recognize that their comfortable means came from God by offering to share their plenty with those who were in want. It even had something in common with so famous a Catholic group as St. Vincent de Paul's Ladies of Charity, for the members of the Widows' Society not only gave of their wealth and strove to induce others to give, but visited the poor, taking them food and clothing they had sewn with their own hands. Characteristically, Betty entered wholeheartedly into the work, accepting the office of treasurer of the society, a post she held until 1804.

Betty was, therefore, a clubwoman in the best sense of the word.

Her type is easily recognized and readily admired: were she a Catholic living in a modern parish, she would be foremost among the workers, giving card parties to clear the church debt, ringing doorbells for the Catholic Charities Appeal, filling baskets for the poor at Christmas. It is interesting to report, for the information of those who have a horror of bingo and games of chance run to aid the church that, as treasurer of the Widows' Society, Betty was one of the officials who petitioned the legislature to allow them to raise $15,000 for their good works by a lottery. Vincent de Paul also had resorted to a lottery in 1655 to obtain funds for the foundlings.

And there can be no doubt, the ladies of the Widows' Society, while pursuing their charitable ends, found a great deal of enjoyment in one another's company over a cup of tea or a glass of Madeira.

With the New Year of 1798, Betty learned that she was carrying another child. The knowledge was almost her last piece of good news, for it was fated to be a year of turmoil and sorrow. The trouble began almost imperceptibly, as trouble so often does. Betty's father-in-law slipped on the ice and fell; although he injured himself badly, no one was unduly upset: he would get over it. Yet as winter waned and spring came, he began to ail.

In February Dr. Bayley wrote Betty from Albany, upset and worried over her brother Richard who had gone, through the good offices of the Setons, to learn the exporting business in the Filicchis' counting house at Leghorn (Livorno) in Italy.

Then, in March, Julia Scott's husband died. Betty went to her at once and was her strength throughout the dreadful days of her grief.

I have not left her night or day during the excess of her sorrows [she wrote Eliza Sadler], and such scenes of terror I have gone through as you nor no one can imagine. 'Tis past. Little Julia goes to Philadelphia next week where she is to fix her residence, as her family connections are all there. And I am once more home, ten thousand times more delighted with it than before, from witnessing the horrors of the separation and derangement in that of my friend. My precious children stick to me like little burrs, they are so fearful of losing me again; the moment I shake one off one side, another clings on the opposite: nor can I write one word without some sweet interruption.

Poor Julia was never to forget the devotion of her friend. From this moment their friendship took on new stature and, with her removal to Philadelphia, there began a correspondence of admirable and moving intimacy that was to end only with Elizabeth's death. Julia was gladly to become, in her turn, the support of Elizabeth throughout the poverty of later years.

It is touching to see how Betty continued to sustain her bereft friend with letters full of sympathy, tenderness, understanding, and just the right dash of humor and news to distract her from her grief. There is news of all the friends Julia left behind, of the doings in New York, of Betty's own comings and goings. There is an especially vivid description of a night out in April:

> I went through all the storm with my sister to the theatre for a frolic. We came out in a violent thunder gust and got in our hack, with carriages before, behind and aside. The coachman quarreled: first one wheel would crack, then another; and we passed a full half-hour in this embarrassment. You know how much I like such situations. But my Guardian Angel landed me safe in Wall Street without one single hysteric.

Occasionally there is a ripple of wit. Speaking of a mutual acquaintance who was a sort of grimly determined Pollyanna, Betty wrote: "Heaven defend me from her threatenings, which are that she would make me love her in the course of one twelve-month at furthest."

And of Miss Chippy Jay, of the famous family, who seems to have been a general nuisance:

> Miss G. will tell you . . . about our fears for poor Chippy. A person has returned from a vessel . . . taken by a Privateer, which he (the Privateer) left in chase of another vessel . . . supposed to be the one she is in. How queer it would be if, after all the figitations, she would be returned to us . . . Oh, Oh, Oh!

And again, teasing Julia who apparently, like it or not, had the unpopular Miss Chippy as a houseguest at the time: "I wish you joy of Miss Chippy. Pray get her a husband if you can."

What gives these thrusts flavor is their utter lack of malice. Read in context, they have a rueful good humor, softened by real compassion for the follies of the silly ladies.

As spring deepened, the dear father of the Setons grew worse. His accident had stirred some malign forces of disease in his body, and the great man weakened steadily. His family was plunged into gloom at the threat of losing not only a beloved parent but also the bestower of their prosperity, for, as is so often the case when a man is everything to those who depend on him, there was no one to take his place. Will Seton was especially stricken, and it caused Betty immeasurable anguish that even she could not console him. "His disposition," she told Julia, "is of that kind which does not admit of the soothings of sympathy, but wraps its grief in the stillness of despair. . . ." Nor did it help matters that business was falling off, due to the unwarranted piracy of French raiding ships.

Betty herself was very unwell, so much so that she dwelt on the possibility of death, and not without a certain yearning. It was probably the illness attendant on her pregnancy that threatened her, for she was to be in great extremity at the hour of delivery; there seems no indication of consumption in her at this time. Only "reason and all the best affections of this world" (both the children were ill and crying for her attentions) prevented her from giving up the will to live.

When the great fearful blow fell, Betty was well enough to meet it. After ᵥrallying sufficiently to raise the hopes of his children, William Seton relapsed and died on the 9th of June. The Setons were not alone in their grief: more than 500 people bore his body to Trinity church-yard—a memorable tribute from a city with a population not exceeding 30,000. An impressive obituary appeared in the press:

> Never addicted to vice of any kind, nor to pride nor to ostentation, his heart was replete with every virtue. A real friend, and a friend of mankind, his whole life was marked uniformly by sincerity of heart, dignity of manners and active liberality of mind. But, alas, he is no more! The destitute orphan is deprived of its kindest patron, the helpless widow and the unfortunate of their best friend, his afflicted children of an indulgent parent, and the community of a citizen who in early life gained and never lost their confidence and approbation, their affection and esteem, and one they will never cease to lament.

Betty stated the effect of his loss upon his family truly and succinctly, in a letter to Mr. Seton's sister Lady Cayley: "With him we have lost

Dr. Richard Bayley,
father of Mrs. Seton.

William Seton Sr.
her father-in-law.

Photo of Gilbert Stuart portrait by M. Bruce Harlan

Mr. and Mrs. William Magee Seton about the time of their marriage.

Husband and wife at a later period.

The author at the grave of William Magee Seton in Leghorn, Italy.

"HERE LIES [SIC] THE REMAINS OF WILLIAM MAGEE SETON, MERCHANT OF NEW YORK, WHO DEPARTED THIS LIFE AT PISA THE 27TH DAY OF DECEMBER, 1803."

every hope of fortune, prosperity and comfort and shall feel his loss irreparably. . . . [We], his children, . . . were accustomed constantly to receive his dearest affection and to look up to him as the soul of our existence."

VI

Toil and Trouble

The elder Seton's death had a far more profound effect on Will and Betty Seton than the sincere platitudes concerning his worth and importance could indicate. It changed their way of life completely. Will, as the oldest son, was expected by the Seton code to succeed his father as family patriarch. The older Setons—James, John, Henry, Anna Maria, and Eliza—were married and able to shift for themselves, but there were seven still at home of whom the oldest, Rebecca, was eighteen, and the youngest, Cecilia, was eight. Will and Betty had, therefore, quite literally inherited a large family. Betty admitted candidly that "for me, who so dearly loves quiet and a small family, to become at once the mother of six children . . . is a very great change." Obviously, the new mother, herself not yet twenty-four, could not bring herself to regard Rebecca Seton as a daughter and, in fact, these two were to become such fast friends that they were more sisters than flesh and blood could make them.

It was essential that Betty give up her happy little home on Wall Street, which was too small for her new brood, and move to the Seton home on Stone Street. Due to Betty's imminent lying-in, the change could not be made at once. A makeshift arrangement was agreed upon for the summer, the two youngest boys, Edward and Samuel, going to a private school conducted by a clergyman in Connecticut, and the rest being given into the care of their sister Eliza Maitland, who moved into Cragdon, her late father's summer home at Bloomingdale—located in the vicinity of present-day Seventy-eighth Street and Third Avenue.

Betty has described the two young Seton boys as having "a marked elegance and grace in their appearance and manners that distinguished them from any boys of the age I ever saw, and a sweetness of disposition unequaled." Their father always called them his "little pillars," and never sat down to table but that he had one on each side of him.

With everything else it became necessary for Betty, despite her condition, to be a full-time business secretary to her husband. It was a task she assumed more gladly than any other, because her heart ached for him:

> My poor William has kept me constantly employed in copying his letters and assisting him to arrange his papers, for he has no friend or confidant now on earth but his little wife. His attachment to his father was so particularly affectionate and uniform, that his loss is one of the most severe afflictions to him that could possibly have happened. Most men have the resource in an event of this kind either of particular friends or habits to dissipate sorrow. But my husband has neither, for he has been so long accustomed to leave my society only for his father's, and his father's for mine, that all now centers in the survivor.

When the baby came on the twentieth of July, Betty was so run-down that both mother and child nearly died. Dr. Bayley worked frantically over them, and saved the baby only by breathing directly into his mouth to get the tiny lungs working. It was most fitting that this boy, to whom his grandfather had literally given the breath of life, should be named Richard Bayley Seton at his christening in Trinity Church on August 20, 1798. Dr. Bayley, Mary Post and Joseph Covachichi were the sponsors.

Betty had not yet recovered her strength and the use of her eyes which had been temporarily afflicted—she thought from the severe pangs of delivery, but more probably from the continual letter writing and the general debility of her health—when she and Will were hastily summoned to Cragdon, where little Anna Maria had fallen seriously ill. The child scarcely passed from danger when the distracted parents had to rush the baby Richard back to the city and medical care. To make matters worse, New York was in the grip of another wave of yellow fever, and Betty held her breath in terror for the safety of her husband, her child and her father, who was moving with his customary zeal among the infected populace. Her account of the danger, to Julia, was graphic:

> You are, I am sure, very anxious for your friends in New York in this season of horrors; and I believe we are the only ones who remain. Poor Seton is chained, and where he is, there am I also. Our little darlings are out of town with Mrs. Maitland, and so are all the family occasionally. But our neighborhood is entirely deserted. We are all perfectly well; how long we shall be so, heaven only knows, for several have died in this street, one person three doors off. I have not seen my father for a whole week until last evening; and then he told me that he spent every hour in the hospitals and the lazaretto.

The plague made it impossible to move into Stone Street, which was in the heart of the infected area, and Betty and Will finally went out to Bloomingdale to take over their charges. Here, away from the disease-ridden town, what she had feared most happened. Still trembling at the narrow escape from tragedy, she wrote Julia:

> My William, my husband, my ALL, was . . . ill with the prevailing fever. He happily has had but a slight attack, but sufficient to terrify me for the consequences, particularly as our being at Bloomingdale prevented my father attending him. He is now most happily entirely restored, and is going to stay some time from the city, which is in a state truly deplorable. My sister and brother Post have also both been attacked, but are on the recovery and gone to Long Island. My father resides entirely at Bellevue Hospital.

It was indeed a nightmare time. The fever raged unabated into October, and all Betty's fears returned. Her father still slept the few night-hours' rest he allowed himself at Bellevue, and he grew daily more exhausted from his attentions to the sick and the dying. Will, with true courage, insisted on resuming his daily trips to New York, driven by the responsibility of keeping his beloved father's business working and the necessity of feeding the large family given into his care. Betty, despite a plague of boils and a recurrence of the semi-blindness she had suffered in the summer, would have gone back to the city to be near them, but her father would not permit it. Nor did living conditions at Cragdon compensate for her worries and ailments.

"You may imagine," she commented with her wry touch to Julia, "that eighteen in [the] family, in a house containing only five small rooms, is rather more than *enough*." Yet it was characteristic of the growing piety of Betty that, in the midst of all this turbulence, she should sit down in a snatched moment of quiet and pen a long prayer which began: "Almighty Giver of all mercies, Father of all, Who knows my heart and pities its weakness and errors, Thou knowest the desire of my soul is to do Thy Will . . ."

Her spiritual life at this time contained the seeds of the magnificent asceticism of later years, but they were only seeds. Her sallies toward God had an earnest awkwardness, like the bumbling baby who tries to pull himself erect by grabbing a convenient chair. For example, she wrote:

> I resign the present and the future to Him Who is the Author and Conductor of both. But most certainly I have no enjoyment so great that would induce me to remain here one moment longer, if it depended on me to make the change. Even as the mother of my children, I would not stay if I were sure they would not be deprived of the protection of their father.

And again:

> I am jogging on old style, trying to accomplish every duty, and *hoping* for the reward; without *that* in view, heaven knows this life would be a scene of confusion and vexation *to me*, who neither values it nor desires it. I always thought, and ever shall, *that husbands can be consoled*, [and] children sometimes prosper as well without as with parents; and, at all events, life has such varieties of disappointments that they may as well proceed from one cause as another.

Knowing Betty Seton, there can be no doubting the subjective sincerity of these lines; but they have a ring of unreality. One is puzzled as to whether she is more discouraged with the vicissitudes of life, than she is enamored of the joys of paradise; then realizes it is more an uncertainty of approach, as if she knew the detachment God expected of her, but did not know quite how to achieve it. At any rate, it is out of character. There is, for instance, the unconvincing denial of the fierce maternalism that was so much a part of her personality, both physical and spiritual, especially in later years when she was bounding in great leaps to perfection and it was obvious that her motherhood was an integral part of that perfection.

By the end of October, things were returning to normal. The fever waned, and preparations were made for the return to the ravaged city. Back in the home of her former happiness in Wall Street, where she had to pack her belongings for the move to the Seton house, Betty's spirits brightened. She found a restored gladness in the blazing fire of the familiar hearth, and in welcoming her weary father to sit by it. She ran her fingers over the keys of her piano with the tenderness of caressing a long-loved face. She was almost gay as she prepared the house on Stone Street, supervising the painting and papering that would drive away any lurking vestiges of the terrible plague. The lilt was in the summons she sent Rebecca Seton, to gather up the Seton girls at Bloomingdale and bring them home.

Just disposition was made of her late father-in-law's effects, as Betty reported to Lady Cayley in England:

> My husband, with the advice of his friends and the general consent of the family, sold the greater part of the furniture, as most of it had been in use since my father's [Seton] first marriage, and our keeping it might have created disputes, besides which we have abundance of our own, all new when we were first married. Those things that were not sold were valued by competent judges and the plate was divided.

By the end of November, the lines of a new way of life had been drawn. The two oldest girls, Charlotte and Mary, fourteen and twelve respectively, were at Miss Hay's boarding school at Brunswick, New Jersey. Betty undertook to teach the younger ones, Harriet and Cecilia, at home, for she felt that sending them to school "through snow and wet will give me more trouble than keeping them at home." Besides she herself enjoyed the new role of teacher. It was well that she did, for teaching was one day to be her only means of livelihood. The homely little classroom on Stone Street had even greater significance, for it was in a rudimentary sense the forerunner of every Catholic classroom in the United States.

The little school could hardly have been conducted on rigid lines, for the needs and distractions of the toddlers Anna Maria and William and the baby Richard scarcely honored the hours from ten to two, when lessons were in progress.

Of course, Betty had Rebecca Seton to help her, as well as the family servant, Mammy Huler. While Betty nowhere mentions slaves, their presence must be taken for granted: slaves were common to every prosperous household in the city—Betty's father and Uncle Bayley certainly owned slaves—and there is no reason to suppose the Seton family was the exception.

Betty was enchanted with Rebecca; indeed, as has been said, they were enchanted with each other. It had not always been so, for at first Betty had maintained toward Rebecca that polite wariness which women, and particularly sisters-in-law, hide behind till they have completed their cool appraisal of each other. And her original appraisal of Rebecca had had a touch of snobbery, for she had found her "an uninformed girl, with many good qualities very much neglected." However, thrown together with Rebecca in the family crisis, Betty recognized her former judgment to be completely rash. Rebecca was rather "the most truly amiable, estimable young woman I ever knew. Her virtues are such as would ornament any station, and does honor to the memory of my poor father [Seton], who was her only director in everything."

This observation is indeed a deep compliment to the elder Seton, for Rebecca was a rarely spiritual soul. She was sensitive, pure and sweet in the most unsentimental sense of the words. She and Betty were twin spirits, for it was their identical ardent aim, not merely to save their souls, but to get as close to God as possible. Betty named her most accurately her "Soul's Sister," for she was simply, uniquely that; no other woman in Betty's lifetime ever usurped her place. The sublime beauty of their love lay in the fact that, unlike most worthy friendships that begin with natural attraction or kindred likes and proceed to the things of the spirit, this bond was forged from the first in the realm of the spirit and soared ever higher.

Unfortunately, Rebecca had the family taint, consumption, and it was obvious that her life would be short. She was destined, before she died, to run far with Betty in the paths of holiness.

It was about this time that the domestic difficulties of Dr. Bayley and his wife apparently reached a point of no return. Indeed, it is probable that he had already separated from his family; veiled references in Betty's correspondence during the early months of 1799 indicate that some such upheaval had occurred. Dr. Bayley himself, writing in February from

Albany, where he had gone to settle the matter of a new quarantine station for the Port of New York, informed Betty of what the future might hold:

> Staten Island? Yes, it's more than probable. What then? Why, private considerations must be made, or ought to be made, to yield to the more interesting ones, the public welfare. . . . I love to think on the oddity of my life. What would afford the most inconsolable affliction to another person, that which would afford an aching heart to most people, seems to me as a matter of amusement. Dear, heady temper, go on! Hail to the period when I shall be at rest.

And Betty wrote cryptically to Julia Scott, in March:

> My father, in addition to his former uneasiness, has new sources of distress which make me tremble. Two of my brothers have already shown the most unquestionable marks of unsteady dispositions. We cannot wonder; but this is a sacred subject, and appears to have affected him above all other evils.

Emma, Betty's oldest half-sister, who had become engaged to William Craig in the fall of '98, was caught in the family crossfire, and seems to have suffered great humiliation in planning her wedding. Craig was either a brother or first cousin—certainly a close relative—of Eliza Sadler. When Mrs. Sadler finally returned to New York from abroad in January, 1799, Betty wrote Julia Scott:

> My poor sister Emma is released from her terrible doubts and anxieties, and I suppose the wedding will now take place as soon as she pleases. For myself, I cannot but reflect on the perverseness of human affairs; for Mrs. S.'s arrival, once so much my earnest wish, is now converted into I could almost say a misfortune, except as far as respects her personal safety; for my father perseveres in his resolution that I shall never admit a reconciliation with Mrs. B. [her stepmother]. And, in that case, my intercourse with Mrs. Sadler will be so much mixed with vexation, and our difference will be a source of so much mortification to her, that I can never visit her without expecting to meet those I do not wish to meet, and would now rather wish to avoid what was once so great a pleasure.

Two months later, she confirmed the expected news that the legislature had given her father permission to build his health station near Tomkinsville on Staten Island, and added: "He is building a *hospital* and dwelling house, but I fear not to receive his family. Emma's marriage will be; but when is uncertain." And, apparently in an effort to smooth things over for her sister during these days that should have been the happiest of Emma's life, Betty discreetly asked her father to "think of Emma, and if it is not indispensable to offer her the air of Staten Island." Whether he did or not, we do not know, but Helen, his youngest daughter, was with him there, at least occasionally.

In the end, the wedding took place on June 19, 1799, and Betty was there. She had informed Julia that, "notwithstanding all difficulties, I shall be present, and forget the past as far as possible." She was rewarded for her decision, for everything went off without incident.

It is unfortunate, from the viewpoint of history, that Betty and her family practiced a proper reticence before the world concerning the internal difficulties that left their scars on Betty's life. The piecing together of incidents makes for an unsatisfactory patchwork, but a patchwork that gives a definite picture of a family split and scattered by the violence of selfish passion.

All through the spring of 1799, in the house on Stone Street, the pattern of upset and sickness continued. First one child was ill, then another, then all together. Rebecca suffered two dreadful spells, and kept Will and Betty on the edge of anxiety. The boys came home from Connecticut on a spring holiday, followed by the girls, from New Jersey; and, in true boarding school fashion, each brought home companions to visit till the house was bulging with children. To add to the melee, it was found necessary to vaccinate the infant Richard, who immediately came down with a mild case of smallpox and had to be quarantined in the nursery and the two servants with him, so that Betty was "obliged to set my own table, and do all the work of a servant man, except cleaning knives."

Wistfully, Betty looked to the summer. Will was dickering for a place outside the city, and there were hopes that Julia would come on from Philadelphia for a long visit, but the dream dissolved in an exasperating legal tangle. After Will had purchased the lease, and altered the house to suit the needs of his family, the sheriffs decided there was no clear title to the property and put it up for sale. Will was so angry that he dropped the whole matter and, although Betty thought he might change his mind and follow the purchase through, he apparently did not; for she had to settle for a short stay with the children at the Sadler summer home on Long Island. Here the children ran on the beach and, Betty told Rebecca, "Ricksy is absolutely rosy and, whenever he goes out, he lifts up his little hands to the trees and says, 'Do . . . Do . . .' with such delight and astonishment, and, when the wind blows in his face, shuts his little eyes and laughs as he used to when you flew at him." But all too soon the Setons had to vacate the house, to allow Emma and William Craig to spend their honeymoon there, and go on to the five small rooms of Cragdon. Even this was to be preferred to the noise and heat and recurrent summer fever of the city.

Rebecca left New York early in June to visit her sister Anna Maria Vining, wife of the Senator, at Dover, Delaware, taking little Cecilia with her. It was thought that the visit and the change of air—Colonial doctors were very partial to change of air—might revive her health. Charlotte and Mary Seton had taken Harriet back to boarding school with them and, with the boys also returned to school, Betty was relatively free for awhile and at peace to enjoy her own family. Julia, who had come on from Philadelphia to visit friends in Flatbush, stopped by to see her, and the two friends melted into each other's arms.

Betty basked in this restoration of happy times, strolling in the fields and woods she loved, picking strawberries, carrying home bunches of wildflowers. The evenings, too, were like old times, for she had the leisure to sit at the piano and play to her heart's content.

The only shadow was a two-weeks' trip which Will took to Baltimore to see his grandfather Curson. Betty's heart grew cold the moment it was first broached. She began to miss him, even in prospect, and to worry about a thousand things: his precarious health, the yellow fever in Philadelphia which he must pass through, the results of his meeting with his grandfather—for it was not a vacation jaunt entirely, but an attempt to avert the financial ruin which was upon them. It was a great comfort to her that Sad came to stay with her while Will was gone.

Sad had brought Betty a new—and dangerous—friend from Europe: Jean Jacques Rousseau in his several works, especially *Emile*. Betty found a kindred temperament in this romanticist whose sentimental ideas are responsible for much of the intellectual muddle of today's world. With her characteristic ardor, she succumbed completely to the enchantment of his brilliant, multicolored style. Her devotion was extravagant: he became, in her letters, "Dear J. Jacques," and she even signed his initials with a cross. He excited her sensibilities in a way which helps us understand how so shallow a thinker could have such lasting influence over the minds of men:

> Your J.J. has awakened many ideas which had long since been at rest [she told Sad]. Indeed, he is the writer I shall always refer to in a season of sorrow, for he makes me forget myself whilst reading, but leaves the most consoling impression on every thought. I hope we shall often enjoy his society together.

That excitement is the proper word for Rousseau's effect on Betty is evident from the following passage:

> Every half hour I can catch goes to Emilius' three volumes. I have read with delight, and were I to express half my thoughts about it—particularly respecting his religious ideas—I should lose that circumspection I have so long limited myself to, and be E.A.B. instead of *E.A.S.* Dear J.J., I am yours.

She even admits him to her most sacred circle, as when she urges Sad to come to Bloomingdale, that summer of 1799:

> My William continues his determination of going to Baltimore. I cannot be left alone, and if dear *J. Jacques* and you are my company, I shall have a reproach to make myself I never felt before, that of being satisfied in his absence.

It is understandable why Betty Seton fell under the influence of this prophet of the emotions. To begin with, despite her frequent assertions that reason guided her, she never seemed quite comfortable in its thrall —possibly because she was aware that the followers of Reason ultimately rejected God. On the other hand, she could respond to Rousseau when he said that religion was an emanation of the heart, for that was where she felt it. Nor would she be overtroubled at his Deism, for Deism was all about her. She need not subscribe to it, for the Episcopal Church to which she belonged had a wide roof sheltering the adherents of many contradictory views, and just as she could choose the doctrines she liked and remain in its communion, so she could dote on the ideas of Rousseau that appealed to her and pass over quickly those that did not. As for his teaching on democracy, she lived in a society based on the will of the populace, and she had not the political astuteness to recognize where the Constitution of the United States and her "dear J.J." parted company.

It is possible that, unsophisticated as she was religiously, living in a welter of vague religious beliefs, theories and feelings, the poison of Rousseau affected her less than it affected men raised in a strict religious system like Catholicism. She was immune to his poison because so much of it was in her already. In the long run, however, it was her innocence that saved her from lasting contagion. Like a child picking wildflowers in a swampland, she reached toward Rousseau for certain blooms with which to adorn her love for God. She was wholly unconscious of the dangerous quicksand and God, Whom she trusted with all her heart, prevented her from falling into it.

When, years later, her eyes were finally opened, she shuddered with uncontrollable horror at her near escape from spiritual death:

> I, too, have felt their fatal influence, and once they [the writings of Rousseau] composed my *Sunday* devotion. Dazzled by the glare of seductive eloquences, how many nights of repose and days of deceitful pleasure have I passed in the charm of their deceptions! Mrs. W is gone—hopeless and convinced there is no mercy for her. I remain, the daily subject of that boundless mercy, the mists of night and darkness dispersed, and, if even at the eleventh hour, yet permitted to share in the Vineyard and gather the fruits of Eternal Life.

VII

Disaster

It was well that Betty had enjoyed the summer in the intimacy of her little family and the peace of the countryside and the restoration of her friends, for the autumn brought fresh calamity and terror. It seemed as if God were determined that she should not mistake the utter vanity of earthly things. Yellow fever was again at the throat of New York, and every day brought news to Betty at Cragdon of the death of another friend or acquaintance. And with each piece of melancholy news, her fears for her husband increased.

> My William goes every day to town [she wrote Rebecca], and is more ex-
> posed than many who have lost their lives. That he should escape depends
> on that Mercy which has never yet failed, and which I have reason to bless
> every hour of my life. If he does not, the greatest probability is that you
> and I will never meet again, for never can I survive the scene.

It is characteristic of her that, in the midst of her own anxiety, she could think of others. Eliza Maitland had had a hard summer of illness in her family, and Betty wrote her, urging her to shut up her house and bring the family to Cragdon until all should recover.

It was characteristic of her, too, that despite everything, she could indulge in a bit of gentle raillery at the obtuseness of an unbidden guest. "Mrs. Scott is gone to Long Island for a week," she informed Sad, "and Mr. Stone, fearful that the time Mr. Seton and myself were to pass together should be tedious, has kindly taken her room until she returns."

Julia went home in November, and the Setons returned to New York. But not to peace. Almost at once, little Dick fell ill and his life was in danger for weeks. The greatest affliction by far, however, was the collapse of the Seton fortune. There were many reasons for it. The raiding of the Seton-Maitland merchantmen by the cynical French had been going on for months. Now came disastrous failures of the firm's interests in Hamburg and London. And Will Seton, for all his integrity and prudence, was not the businessman his father had been.

The first shock of the catastrophe was such that Betty had "to use every exertion to keep my poor William Magee alive." His panic can be imagined: he was the support, not only of his wife and children, but of his brothers and sisters as well. Moreover, he was a man of honor, and the thought of having lost the money and goods entrusted to him and to the reliability of the firm, drove him almost to despair. Just before Christmas, of all times, Betty was forced to tell Rebecca the dire news:

> that Maitland has stopped payment in London, and that we are obliged to do the same here. It is a cruel event to William; for, although he has every consolation a man can have under such circumstances, that it is not from his own imprudence and that no part of the blame is attached to him, you may imagine the distress and perplexity it occasions to all. James has been almost crazy, but, on examination, finds less cause of apprehension than he imagined, and it is the general decision of all William's friends and the Directors of the Banks, who have been consulted, that he must absolutely suspend payments. . . . If we were a melancholy family last winter, we are something worse, this; and heaven only knows when our troubles are to end.

The financial ruin did not depress Betty, but the sufferings of her "dear Hub" was a knife in her heart. He swung from hope to the deepest gloom. One minute he felt he could work things out; the next he saw only "State Prison and poverty." It was a catch-in-the-throat holiday season. Betty spent Christmas Day with her father and sister, while Will stayed at home in Stone Street with the children. He was apparently sunk in some mood of stubbornness or melancholy for, as Betty explained to Rebecca, "I had promised to go, and nothing could persuade him to go or to let me stay. He insisted in the most positive manner and I went 'like a wretch,' for so I felt." New Year's was passed in a spirit of false heartiness, the husband and wife each trying to prevent the other from dwelling on past holidays, lest the little enjoyment they still possessed should dissipate in remembrance. But Betty concluded that "it was not the most unpleasant New Year's Day I ever passed, for where there is affection and hope there is a great [deal]."

The point of no return came with the foundering of a Seton ship carrying a heavy and valuable cargo from Amsterdam to New York. Even yet Will could have saved his own assets from the wreckage, for so great was the confidence in his integrity that he had three offers of money in any amount he wished. He refused these generous gestures, preferring to wait until the term of his partnership with Maitland should expire in June.

Actually, Will did not know all the facts of his firm's embarrassment nor the extent of the damage, for the news from Maitland was curt and vague; he thought, therefore, that the prudent thing was to wait and see. In an attempt to get firsthand information, he dispatched Mr. Stone to Leghorn and Abraham Ogden to London. Ogden—whose brother, Gouverneur Ogden, Charlotte Seton was to marry—had been a tower of strength throughout the whole tragedy. Betty fervently informed Rebecca that he "has been more than ten brothers to my William. Night and day, Sunday or weekday, he is always busy for him. . . . Never, in no change or length of life, can his attentions be forgotten."

As a loyal wife, Betty was indignant that Maitland should inform them only "that the creditors have attached *all* the property, and that his mind is in such a state that he can say no more; without considering— while he is indulging his sensibilities—William does not know if he has a right to bread for his family!" It did nothing to soothe her wifely feelings, either, to know that, while her husband was determined "to give up everything, even his furniture," to satisfy just debts, his brother James —who was also in the firm—had bought an imposing three-story house in Greenwich Street; and she remarked tartly to Rebecca: "Thank heavens we are not all sinking!"

She kept Julia Scott posted concerning the unhappy march of events, especially as they affected Will, and, in March, wrote sadly and with some bitterness:

> My knowing all the whys and wherefores makes me a better companion for him; and I am now his only one. Stone, Ogden, and everybody, is gone, and I am most truly his all. The plot thickens, dear friend: not one line of explanation from Maitland, but *Seton's* bills, and all those endorsed by him, refused and returned, give an appearance not very flattering, and makes the future prospect so serious that even *I* cannot bear to dwell on it.

It was indeed the time of the cross and, with everything else, Betty was expecting a fourth child in June. It can be imagined what the ceaseless worry and work did for her condition. She was nearly beside herself. Her children had outgrown all their clothes, and she had to make everything new for them; a dozen shirts had to be mended and made to do for Will and the Seton boys away at school; she had not turned a stitch on the layette for the new baby; the daily household chores came round relentlessly; and, the day finished, she sat wearily writing business letters until one and two in the morning. It was her consolation and comfort to unburden her heart to the faithful friend in Philadelphia:

> Ah, Julia dear, you little know, nor would I wish you to know, what the present state of your friend's mind is nor the paleness of her face, with pain in the back all day and in the side at night, neither of which I have been one hour without for the last two months. . . . I trust in heaven that the storm will go over, but, really, at present it is hard times.

One of the most touching human qualities of Elizabeth Seton was her willingness to share her troubles with her friends. It was not an indulgence in self-pity or complaint, but a recognition of the ritual of friendship. It was what friends were for—to listen and to sympathize and, if possible, to help. She had no false pride; she understood her own weakness and need and, when her turn came, she repaid the favor in kind.

A significant plateau had been reached in the Setons' struggle out of their personal hell—the resignation of Will Seton to anything that should come; and there can be do doubt that Betty's heroic support had helped him reach it. It was not a spiritual resignation—he was not ready for that—but it was resignation, all the same, the resignation of a good man who had come to recognize hard facts of life that could not be wished away. Betty was able to write to Rebecca about him that "never did mortal bear misfortune and all the aggravated distress which accompanies it with so much firmness and patience as my husband does." It made all the difference: despite the fact that Will was forced to make over all his holdings to his friends in trust, despite the fact that every penny of income had ceased and that at least one creditor had instituted a legal suit against him, a certain peace descended on the Seton house.

They still had no definite knowledge of the firm's standing—an inexplicable situation, when it is considered that Seton was the senior partner—but they knew where they stood, which was perilously close to poverty. Faced with the knowledge and freed of false hopes, they could make decisions: to retrench their way of living, to withdraw from a society in which they could no longer pay their way, and to inform the Seton children old enough to understand, of the change in their station. This last was the hardest of all, but Betty undertook it bravely, writing to Mary and Charlotte at Brunswick to tell them, for the first time, what had happened at home. As is so often the case when unpleasantness is squarely met, the reaction was not at all so dire as expected. Mary Seton replied promptly "such an answer as would do your heart good," Betty noted to Rebecca with relief. This show of strength in Mary was to encourage Betty to be firm with Rebecca's protests when, in August, the young girl wished not to return to school, but to take her rightful place beside Rebecca and pull her load:

> Mary wishes very much to be with you, and it is right she should be. You must, my dear Rebecca, exert yourself and not indulge her sensibility, for it is necessary for her future comfort in life that her mind should be strengthened. Try to teach her to look at the events of life as they are, guided by a just and merciful Protector who orders every occurrence in its time and place, and often by these trials and disappointments strives to turn the soul to Him Who is the Source and Comforter of the afflicted.

It is hard to realize that the writer of these wise words, the valiant woman who was standing up against the elemental scourgings of fate, was herself but a girl twenty-five years old.

During that ruinous winter of 1800, Dr. Bayley had made his annual pilgrimage to Albany, and it seemed a respite for Betty in the midst of her worries to resume the playful correspondence with her father that delighted them both. No mention was made of her troubles, either by her or by him. It was as if the letters belonged to a happier time.

He returned to New York in mid-March, to discover that the enemies of his plans to clean up the city against a recurrence of the fever had not been idle. Almost at once he dispatched a letter to Stephen Van Rensselaer to inform him humorously, but in dead earnest, that:

> . . . numerous tinkers, tailors, coopers, shoemakers and soothsayers have forwarded a petition to Albany (I know not to whom directed) to remove the Health Officer, etc., etc., etc. The applicants are the most violent of the Democratic Junto—*Sic res geritur*—it would be very flattering to your very humble servant, if he would be made acquainted as speedily as possible with the state of the petition.

Bayley's powerful friends apparently agreed with the French physician Dr. Delmas, who had pronounced an essay of Bayley's on yellow fever "the best thing written on the subject," and its author "the best friend of humanity and . . . [to] be considered by the Americans their best advisor." At any rate, the truculent petition was never heard of again.

In May, to the vast satisfaction of her sister-in-law, Rebecca Seton returned to New York. She had been gone nearly a year and the fabric of their lives had come unravelled, but they were able to pick up the familiar threads because their hearts were constant. The two friends were soon "snug at [their] work on the sofa," catching up on the thousand things that had happened to both in the months of separation.

The immediate problem concerned where Betty was to go for her confinement. Will had been forced to let Cragdon go. Dr. Bayley had been trying to set his daughter up for the summer in a house on Long Island, but the only one he could find was woefully inadequate to the family needs. At length it was decided that she and Will and the children should go to the Health Establishment on Staten Island until the baby was born, Rebecca remaining at Stone Street with Mary, who had stayed behind when the children went back to school.

On May 24, Dr. Bayley conveyed his grandchildren to Staten Island, and immediately wrote their mother to assure her that they had had a merry hour-and-a-quarter's sail in the schooner, except for a momentary fear of the ship's pitch and roll on the part of Dick. Richard Bayley was, by his own account, immensely enjoying his role of the happy grandfather and added, in the high good humor of his mood, that "nothing on this globe, or on the waters which it contains, was wanted or wished for on my part, two persons excepted—and, what is not less extraordinary, *they are females*." Betty, of course, was one; the other was Dué, who was too ill to make the trip.

With the children off her hands, Betty was able to rest and build up her strength. When she joined the impatient little brood a couple of weeks later, she was ready for her ordeal. The child was born on the 28th of June; it was a girl, and Betty named her Catherine Charlton, after her own mother. It was to be feared, after all Betty had endured, that the birth would have brought the brush with death that had attended Richard's coming into the world; but so amazing was the little mother's resilience, that within eight days she was up and lavishing those attentions on Will and her father that "servants . . . can never give."

Whether or not the wily grandfather had it settled in his mind when he brought the Setons to Staten Island, he now began to protest that, after four weeks' enjoyment, he could not give up the habit of "being a Christian" and "domesticated." Unquestionably he *was* enjoying the domesticity he had almost forgotten in the busy years since his own family life had been disrupted. Any argument about the matter was purely perfunctory, and Betty wrote happily to Julia on July 26:

> The decision is that we remain all summer, and certainly, was there a choice of all creation, I could not wish a pleasanter situation or more delightful rooms with the addition of an upper balcony that commands a view fifty miles beyond the Hook. Seton passes four days of the week with me, and my father very seldom quits the house but to visit vessels.
>
> The boys are indescribably fine fellows: Richard is a miracle of sweet expression and grace, with a size of person and limbs very unusual for his age; William is still more like his grandfather Seton and as sturdy and saucy as ever; Anna continues "little Anna," very healthy but delicately small for five years old, and with the same manner of drawing back and looking downwards, or, rather, sideways, that you see in country children. Her disposition is very much improved and her capacity, I think, uncommon, though I am sorry to say her mother has not been able to attend to it as it deserves; but I am just making a serious beginning. And as to our sweet babe, I think you would wish to be its nurse as well as its godmother, for a more peaceable, serene little being you cannot imagine. Seton may well admire her, for she

sleeps continually and makes none of those crooked faces children of a month old generally do. You will begin to say, as father does, that we are "all wonders". . .

The placid leisure and happiness of this letter reflects that summer of 1800 which, if it was not golden, was at least gilded. The weather was fine, the air sweet, the flowers blooming, the children well. Betty loved to walk, with the tiny Kit in her arms, up and down the length of the "piazza" facing the sea, sometimes even in the half-dark of the dawn, while the rest of the house was asleep. There were lazy afternoons, when she sat reading on a favorite rock beyond a cornfield, the baby asleep on her lap and the children playing all about her. How she loved the cloudless skies, the gentle breezes, the rustling leaves, of such days!

Dr. Bayley enjoyed tramping off to the woods with his gun; and Will, rowing in the Bay. On occasion, the Sadlers and the Craigs would ferry over for dinner. Only Rebecca could not come as often as Betty wished: Eliza Maitland was having her troubles, and Rebecca, on Betty's insistence, was with her as much as could be. Eliza's husband, James, was a drinker and a ne'er-do-well and she had it hard, struggling to raise her large family.

In the evenings, the tinkling of the piano floated on the warm night air, harmonizing with the chirping of the crickets and the strident calling of the katydids. Betty assured Dué, who was on the high seas bound for Ireland, that "every evening we sing *The Sailor Boy* and 'May some protecting angel near still hover round our Dué's head' forms the chorus."

It was not only the peace of the country and the well-being of her children that brought Betty contentment. Will's resignation to his misfortunes had become a habit of mind. Betty told Julia Scott that "his creditors in Europe (or rather Maitland) have allowed him two years to settle the [debt], but in that time nothing is coming in. He seems, fortunately, to have made up his mind, and says but little about his affairs. What he feels is another thing." Betty and Rebecca, even though separated by the wide sweep of the Bay, had resumed their spiritual colloquies by means of frequent notes. They shared pious thoughts, offered spiritual advice and urged each other to holiness especially by the total acceptance of God's Will. They set prearranged times when both would be at their devotions, so that distance might dissolve in a meeting of souls.

Everyone's hopes were lifted with the arrival, in August, of the *Northern Liberties*, one of Will's ships. Excitement ran high ahead of it for days: lookouts were posted, eager eyes scanned the horizon and a number of false alarms anticipated the actual arrival. When the glad day came, there was such a welcome as the lonely settlers of the land must have given the annual ships from home. Betty shared as much of the excitement as she could with Rebecca:

> Your dear heart has beat with joy at the arrival of our *Liberties*, and you may be sure we have had a scene of pleasure such as does not often come; and one that you would have enjoyed as much as I did, except the pouring fifty bowls of tea a day, three days running, has hurt the sinews of my arm a little.

Despite the celebration, however, the coming of the ship changed the Seton fortunes very little. It had all been a sort of wistful make-believe of the prosperity of former days.

Having passed so pleasant a summer, through the kindness of her father, it can be imagined how Betty's gorge rose when rumors reached her that the gossips of Manhattan were criticizing him for opening his home to her, while he neglected his wife and the children of his second marriage. She confined herself to venting her indignation in a letter to Eliza Sadler:

> My father cannot do more than he does to prove his regret for the past . . . Father is more than busy and has many vexations, but he says he "can never rest in this world, and it may as well be one thing as another is the melancholy truth." And all that can be done is to soothe—cruel would the person be who even wished to deprive me of this power. But we must hope there is no such being.

The last week in October, Bayley regretfully watched his beloved summer boarders depart. In a sense they were leaving a world of enchantment for the world of reality, and the cold justice of this world was waiting to deal with them the moment they landed on the shores of Manhattan. Will Seton was given the choice of declaring himself a bankrupt or of going to prison. Either choice was a humbling blow. Had he been responsible only for himself, with no one depending on him, it was in his nature to have chosen prison, for it was against his ideals of honesty to settle for less than he owed. But with a multitude of hungry mouths to feed, it was inevitable that he accept bankruptcy. Privately, however, he vowed never to rest until he had paid every penny of debt. He could not know the impossible task he set himself, or the little time he had left to achieve it, but it was, all the same, a magnificent vow, worthy of the proud name of Seton.

Whether it was a new strength born of this determination or the old stoicism he had acquired, this final blow seems not to have felled him. He remained calm and patient in mind and demeanor, and even his health bloomed. Betty could say to Julia Scott: "Do not be uneasy about my Seton. I have him safe and all to myself." He even weathered a quarrel with his old friend Covachichi, who had stood for three of his children; the quarrel was so bitter as to end in a lawsuit and Covachichi's departure, Betty thought "most probably never to return." But return he did, and the quarrel died.

Betty had one day of grace in the bitter weeks of November: Kit's christening day. She wrote of it with delight to Julia:

> This day, dear friend, the nineteenth [of] November, little angel Kate was carried to church and christened Catherine, after my mother. Her sponsors (you will laugh when I tell you she had five) were Sister Post; Mrs. Dupleix, who sent her an elegant christening suit from Ireland, with a particular request that she might stand for her, that is by proxy; myself, for you (surely you will allow a good representative); and my father and Mr. Curson godfathers. The sweet creature mistook Mr. Beach for my father, as he had spectacles on, and when he threw the cold water in her face, looked up at him and laughed so drolly that I could hardly keep from laughing and crying both.

The christening relieved Betty of an uneasiness that had been with her since she had decided to defer the ceremony until the family returned to town. It had been against her inclination to do so, she told Julia at the time, "for I think the covenant should be entered into as soon as possible, and is much too sacred to be trusted to accident." The other Seton children had been baptized within a month of their birth; Kit was five months old when she was carried to the font.

The sad effects of the petition of bankruptcy descended on the Setons just at Christmastime. Betty was matter-of-fact about the humiliation, but there were, deep within her, unshed tears like the eddies concealed beneath the surface of a pool. These secret tears were behind the date of her letter to Julia written from "New York, Stone Street (for the last time), December 7, 1800."

They were behind such over-light banter as "Let me know the amount of your market bills. I engage I shall supply my large family for less than you can your small one. The excellence of the provision is another thing— all depends with me on the temper with which I enjoy it." They were behind the sincere affirmation: "I think the greatest happiness of this life is to be released from the cares and formalities of what is called the world. My world is my *family*, and all the change to me will be that I can devote myself unmolested to my treasure. Seton can never be more a slave than he has been, and for the present season, while the cloud hangs heaviest, I trust where my trust has never yet failed." It was all a sort of whistling in the dark, but no one has ever said that complete resignation to the Will of God was incompatible with a recognition of the human need to keep one's spirits up.

In mid-December, Mr. Garret Kittlet, the receiver of bankruptcy, arrived to begin the poignant proceedings by taking an inventory of furniture, books, plate—everything, right down to the children's clothing. And Betty, with her indomitable bravery, assisted him in drawing up the list. The official entry of the bankruptcy officials supposedly protected the Setons from the importunities of the sheriffs set on them by impatient creditors; but, even so, during the holy days of Christmas, Betty had to keep a constant watch on the door, scrutinizing every man who put his hand to the knocker before admitting him, lest he be a writ-server. It was exacted of Will to make the final symbolic gesture of defeat, the handing over of the key to his counting house. This done, he had nothing more to say about the affairs of Seton, Maitland and Company.

VIII

A Fervent Protestant

Betty's reference, in her December letter to Julia Scott, that it was the last she would write from Stone Street, had been premature. The Setons were allowed to stay on in the paternal home until May. A change was made in the disposition of the elder Seton's children, however. Possibly because of slender funds, only the two boys and Harriet went to boarding school that winter; Charlotte and Mary went to live with James Seton; and Rebecca and Cecilia stayed at Stone Street.

Cecilia, of course, had to be instructed, and once more Betty opened the little home school. Classes began at ten o'clock and Cecilia, as the oldest, pursued the standard subjects of "grammar, reading, writing, spelling of large and small words, marking, sewing and figures." Her teacher was especially struck by the rare combination of mildness and assiduity in her. Anna, who was not yet six, followed Cecil's curriculum in so far as her fledgling mentality would let her. Even four-year-old Bill and Dick, who was two-and-a-half, were part of the school circle and recited "their lessons: little pieces, names of the United States, divisions of the globe, some of the commandments." It was a charming scene of peace and love.

In February, Betty handed over her school work to Rebecca, while she went to nurse Mary Wilkes, John Wilkes's wife, in her last illness. Her agony lasted ten days, during which Betty left the Wilkes house on Williams Street only to run home at intervals to feed Kit. Dr. Bayley had delayed his trip to Albany to attend the dying woman, but finally had to leave before the end. John Wilkes was never to forget the kindness of the father and daughter, and was to come to Betty's aid when she most needed friends.

When Betty was at home again, Rebecca went off to stay with her sister Eliza, who was about to bear another child. Finances were even worse in the Maitland home than they were at the Setons, and Will, out of his little, sent money to Rebecca to pay the baker and the milkman. Kit was about to cut her teeth, and became so ill with a sore throat and constriction of the chest that she seemed for a time to flutter on the doorsill of heaven. Through it all, Betty was "the old knot of oak," as Will called her affectionately.

But this crisis, too, passed, and soon the house was happy again with its morning schoolwork and, in the afternoon and evening, the comfort for Betty of Will and her father at home and the thousand trivial things of happy family life. The secret smile of content is almost visible in her description of the domestic scene:

> The piano and [a] cribbage party pass them over very cheerfully when there are no particular interruptions. Seton is now poking the fire, scolding me for writing nonsense to Julia, puzzling himself about his dream last night, wondering what he should do if he was a single man, and says he believes his best plan is a voyage to the East Indies.

Dué had sailed for home, and everyone looked for her in a feast of anticipation, conjecturing the weather and the danger from privateers, counting the weeks and then the days. Like the watched pot that never boils, she seemed to be coming all spring.

The big news of these months was a young clergyman named John Henry Hobart. He was responsible for a significant development that was occurring in Betty's religious life. It represented an advance in that it was a shift from the broad fields of eclectic religiosity to a more or less defined road of spiritual order and system. Until now, Betty's basically religious temperament had selected the spiritual doctrines and practices that appealed to her; there had been no one to distinguish for her the true from the false, the good from the worthless.

Without in any way belittling the marvelous strides she had made—
we must never forget that God had plans for this woman and had kept
His eye upon her—it must be confessed that, over the years, Betty had
amassed an amazing hodgepodge of belief and observance. Thus she
wore a Catholic crucifix, looked kindly on the life of the cloister, sub-
scribed to the doctrine of angels, liked Methodist hymns, the quietism
of the Quakers and the emotionalism of Rousseau, read general Protestant works, practiced meditation, was inclined to the narrow Calvinism
of her ancestors in the matter of sin and punishment, and attended the
Episcopal Church. In a word, she had gotten along spiritually the best
way she could. Now, for the first time, she had found someone, not so
much to direct her, but someone she could follow after in the spiritual
life.

John Henry Hobart was, at twenty-five, the youngest of the curates
assisting Dr. Benjamin Moore at Trinity Church; the other two curates
were Abraham Beach and Cave Jones. Hobart had come to Trinity in
December and, almost at once, had electrified the parish with his preaching. He was fiery, wholly in earnest, and his words had the substance of
definite belief and personal piety. He inspired a like enthusiasm in his
hearers, and Betty and Rebecca rallied to his zeal. He had a special appeal
for women, an appeal that had nothing to do with form or figure, since
he was short, disproportioned and wore thick spectacles. It was rather
that, young and earnest as he was, he touched their female hearts. Nor
did it lessen his appeal to them that he was happily married (to Mary
Goodin Chandler, daughter of the Tory minister who had witnessed the
marriage of Betty's father and mother); indeed, coupled with the fact
that he had an ill and aged mother to whom he was warmly devoted and
about whom he worried much, it raised in the breasts of the Episcopalian
matrons of New York a fierce, maternal pride. He was a sort of shining
knight, the ideal husband, brother, son and friend.

Betty Seton fell completely under his charm. It is important to understand why, since attempts have been made, because of her romantic
temperament and ardent enthusiasms, to explain it in sensuous terms.
It would be foolish to discount the sensuous entirely (and the word is
used in its generic natural and innocent meaning), for God made man and
woman attractive to each other and this attractiveness cannot be excluded

from any department of life. Some of the greatest saints, St. Vincent de Paul and St. Francis de Sales among them, had a special power over women.

The attraction of Henry Hobart for Elizabeth Seton was, however, primarily an attraction of the soul. It was the same kind of attraction that drew her to Rebecca Seton. Elizabeth Seton was in love with God. Love of God is not something to be hugged to the breast in secret; it is something to be shared, as God Himself shared it in creation and redemption. Yet Betty's little world was made up of people with whom she could not share it, people who either did not understand or did not care. It was one of her constant cries to Rebecca that "Willy does not understand." He did not indeed—not until Betty's perseverance and the coming of death had opened his eyes. Her father did not understand. Julia and Sad did not understand.

Rebecca Seton did; and so did Henry Hobart. It was like the parting of clouds and the piercing of the sun for Betty to sit in her pew at Trinity Church and hear him put into words what she felt in her inmost soul. Her warm, affectionate nature responded, and the response of kindred souls is love. Where the attraction is spiritual, as it was in this case, the love is spiritual. As a wise judge of her virtue, answering her critics in the Process for her Beatification, pointed out: "She left Henry Hobart for Catholicism." This was proof positive of the spirituality of their relationship. When Elizabeth was convinced of the error of Hobart's spirituality, their relationship died. Conclusively. She barely mentioned his name again in her lifetime.

Now, in 1801, the goodness and zeal of Henry Hobart exalted her and Rebecca. They sat, eyes shining, at Sunday service, sensitive to the least nuance of his voice. They treasured his words as lessons not to be lost. They lived from one Sunday to the next. If they were disappointed when the preacher was some lesser being, such as Mr. Beach or Mr. Jones or even Rector Moore, they were absolutely disconsolate when they were prevented from going to service at all. This, too, is significant; it was church, not the preacher, not even Mr. Hobart, that was their ultimate end. For example, Betty sent a note to Rebecca one Saturday in March:

> My spirits are heavy. Willy says so much about my going tomorrow, and that we shall not without a carriage; that it is madness, the streets almost

impassable, etc.—*you* know *him*—that I think it will be best for *me* to go quietly with him and, if the weather is not really a storm, come to you *after.* You must not lose if *I* must.

Along with their unremitting work for the Widows' Society, they took up eagerly all Hobart's projects of charity. They gave so much of themselves to the poor and the sick and the dying that their friends named them Protestant Sisters of Charity. The term must have originated with some French emigré, or been taken from the pages of a romance, for a nun in New York was as rare a thing as a mermaid. The museum in Greenwich Street had a wax figure of a nun, and it was one of its greatest curiosities.

Hobart became a household saint in the Seton home. He and his wife were frequent visitors, and became part of their circle of friends. Friends they remained for Will, nothing more; he responded to the ministry of Henry Hobart as he responded to any other clergyman: by paying his courteous, dutiful respects. The children, of course, like the natural mimics children are, imitated their mother's enthusiasm, and Betty confided to Rebecca:

> Bill called out, as he opened his eyes this morning: "Dear Henry Hubbard, I wish you would preach for me." Just those words. They woke me from my sleep and occasioned a long, heavy sigh, not unaccountable nor yet accountable. The anxious presage and hope, that He might teach the wisher to be a preacher—oh, what a thought!

Betty began to display, at this time, a certain zeal for proselytizing which was distinctly evangelical. There are constant sighs in her notes to Rebecca over the blindness of one or other of their friends who could not recognize the "treasure" they shared. She reminded Bec of her obligation to attempt the conversion of Eliza Maitland, who was seriously ill. Her own efforts with Will were discreet enough, for she knew him; when she did speak, he would brush her aside with a laugh or a plea that he was "too busy." But she upset Eliza Sadler with a birthday note, advising her of the necessity to prepare for death, and hastened to soften her words:

> My own dear Eliza, I fear you did not understand sufficiently my meaning in the use of those little prayers I gave you—which was to impress on your mind the necessity of preparing for a blessed death. This does not

require a sadness or painful exercise of mind; on the contrary, considering through faith and hope in the merits of Our divine Redeemer, we are His children and the purchase of His Blood, we more naturally anticipate with joy that [event]. . . .

I have observed, dear, that any good resolutions or exercises begun on the period of our birth are more seriously impressed, and chose this for you at this time, as reflecting on a birthday on earth more easily transfers our thoughts to the birthday of our future existence. And it is very useful to make use of that day from year to year to examine our soul's *account in full*, on the progress we have made in approaching that heavenly example of perfection.

She minced no words in scolding Rebecca for departing from a pact they had made for the good of their souls, to withdraw from the world in a kind of retreat on Sacrament Sunday, the day on which they approached the communion table.

The misfortune of the afternoon will, I hope, be a lesson for life to my darling sister, that you should never violate the strict rule, not to leave home on any persuasion on Sacrament Sunday, and to say openly to whoever may request it that it is your rule. It can never be a breach of civility or seem unkind . . . if you say it with a firmness of one who has been at His table who refreshes and strengthens the soul in well-doing. I have often asked myself the question: why should anyone be more earnest and prevailing with me for a trifle or a thing of no consequence in itself, than I am in maintaining the thing I know to be right and that touches the interest of my soul's peace?

Here again, there is an unmistakable showing forth of the apostolic gifts of later years: the concern with spiritual advancement, the scorn for human respect, the talent for direction, even the seasoning of prudence. But, understandably, there is not yet the sure touch; and Betty's earnestness must have made her friends and acquaintances as uncomfortable as it mortified her when she remembered it, in her Catholic years. There can be no question, however, that it was progress, since it was a determined groping toward Christ's system of doctrine and sacraments.

The final door was shut on their former life when the Setons moved to the Battery in May. The sources of Will's income at this time are obscure; but the new address, 8 State Street, was not unfashionable, and the graceful, three-story house, with its balconies, was imposing and substantial. The house still stands and has been remodeled interiorly as Our Lady of the Rosary Catholic Church. In 1801, the house next door belonged to Carey Ludlow, and was a boarding house, which may indicate that the neighborhood was a step lower in the social class than residential Wall Street.

The situation was ideal, for the Seton house was at the geographical tip of Manhattan Island and commanded a panoramic view of the rivers and the bay, bounded by Long Island on the left, New Jersey on the right and Staten Island straight ahead. There was always something to see: the water was alive with ships, the quays gay with sails; cargo vessels from exotic ports moved slowly in and out, and the smaller schooner-ferries leaned to the wind and waves. The Battery was the promenade of the town, and smartly dressed men and women strolled arm-in-arm across its expanse, leisurely avoiding the bustling carriages and sedan chairs. It was a favorite walking-place for young Washington Irving, and Betty may have seen the seventeen-year-old squire lazing along, lost in the pages of a book. In the evening, lights and music added to the scene when Joseph Corré, enterprising owner of Columbia Gardens, a refreshment oasis, dispensed violins and voices with his ice cream at fifty cents a head.

The Battery became a playground for Cecilia, Anna and the boys, but they had special orders not to stray outside the gate of the park. The sea air and the sights delighted them, and they were completely happy in their new surroundings. The adult hearts were not always so happy, for unlike children, adults cannot ignore the sadness of life. Little Kit continued ill and kept her parents anxious. Will moved back and forth between hope and despair, a condition due as much to the lassitude of his disease as to the state of his fortunes. Betty had the portion of all wives, of understanding and putting up with him. "Willy is all aback about something," she confided one morning to Rebecca, "we are all shortly to go to the *Black River*, and I dare not talk of money. He owes me ten dollars, and says he can't pay me." But, before the note was finished, she assured Bec that "the sun shines again." Mrs. Livingston, one of Betty's prominent friends from the Widows' Society, died that May, and Betty sorrowed to Rebecca: "Oh, Rebecca, she was good and amiable, and the trial is now past!"

One of her greatest sorrows was the almost continual absence of Rebecca. Separation from her friends was a trial Betty was to know all her life, but the years never made it easier. To accept it became her constant act of mortification, and she sweetened it by looking ahead to the eternity where separations would be no more.

The Setons went to Staten Island the first week in June, but without Rebecca and without Will, who was about to set off for Baltimore. The minute they landed, the children were "all whoops and hollers" and ran for the fields and haystacks. Betty could not follow her heart and join them, for she had to unpack, supervise the setting up of the six bedsteads they had brought with them, and write a hurried scrawl to Rebecca not to forget the mattress which had been left airing in the yard. But everything was in order by six o'clock and "just as we were going to tea, a great punch bowl of garden strawberries from Mrs. Vandezer crowned the feast. . . . How the heart did melt before Him, the Giver of all!"

Betty was always worried when Will traveled. Before he had left the city, she sent him a domestic note that was also the truest of love letters:

> My love: I send your toothbrush and comb, which I forgot this morning, and also to remind you of the box of silver and the bread basket in my press, which will not lock. Is it possible that I am not to see you again for so long a time? Heaven protect you and return you again in safety. Your darlings have enjoyed this cool day and are merry as birds. They cannot understand that Papa is not to come, nor tomorrow, nor next day, nor the day after— that is for their mother to feel. . . . Dear, dear William, farewell!

Will wrote from Baltimore with like affection, but in the male manner:

> It is needless to say how much I long to enjoy the view with you, and although we are in the midst of plenty and elegance, I long to come home to commence business in earnest, for this idle life will never do; and I fear the jaunt of little utility in point of business, unless I should determine to establish here, for which my grandfather is very anxious; but I shall enter on nothing decisive until I see you yourself, with my friends at N.Y.

How these lines must have cut Betty's heart, revealing as they do the aching of the old wound of his failure! The "plenty and elegance" and the importunities of his grandfather could only remind him cruelly of what had been. After relaying family news—that all the "grandees" of Baltimore were calling on his aunt, Elizabeth Curson Farquhar, who had apparently made the trip with him; and that, as a result, they were committed for dinners and parties every evening, one at the home of "Mrs. Carroll of Mount Clare"—Will returned to what was eating away at him:

> I cannot imagine what Richard (Bayley) could have written your father; he has nothing to do with the creditors in England that I know of; and, at any rate, I hope no blame can be attached to Filicchi or myself. It has, however, given me some uneasiness, and my grandfather has a letter this morning from Maitland, who mentions me and my friends in a very important manner: it only shows, however, the man to be an idiot and influenced by passion, but I don't mean to pass it over in silence.

He went to see Jack and his wife at Summer Hill, their home in Alexandria, and took in the new federal city of Washington on the way back. He was impressed, and thought "the buildings really excel anything I had an idea of. They are more numerous than could be expected, but you see nothing in the streets but cows and pigs. It is a journey from one house to another."

Not long after Betty had gone to Staten Island, Julia Scott visited New York, but the two friends did not meet, for Julia vowed that "she would die of terror if she crossed the Bay," and Betty could not leave the children to come to her. In bidding her farewell and a safe return to Philadelphia, Betty charged her "to send me a kiss by my husband—one, mind, no more; or you will be putting notions in the man's head. He will be with you next Thursday, I suppose, and with me, who will make your one many by all the rules of multiplication, next Saturday, I hope."

In the long run, Betty conceded, it was just as well that Julia had not come, for she would have swooned at the scenes of desolation and suffering that were a daily occurrence at the Quarantine Station: "but to me who possesses a frame of fibres strong and nerves well strung, it is but a passing scene of nature's sufferings, which when closed will lead to happier scenes." Boatloads of immigrants, ill of the yellow fever and of being confined in the filthy holds of the vessels without light or air or even food for the entire voyage, were being landed every day. They were a people sinned against, and the owners of the vessels were at least as callously guilty as the superintendents of modern concentration camps.

Most of the poor immigrants were Irish, and Betty was moved to tears at their faith, as they stumbled from the ships and fell to their knees, kissing the ground and praying aloud in thanksgiving that the frightful voyage was over. Their numbers were so great that tents and shacks and every possible temporary shelter were erected to house the sick and dying.

It was a veritable hell of sickness, and it was to last most of the summer. Betty's daily notes to Rebecca were full of the horror, and her heart ached to soothe the poor sufferers, but her father would not permit her past the extra white railing he had erected to protect his beloved family from contagion. Betty wrote, late one night:

> Rebecca, I cannot sleep. The dying and the dead possess my mind. Babies perishing at the empty breast of the expiring mother. And this is not fancy, but the scene that surrounds me. Father says such was never known before, that there is actually twelve children that must die for mere want of sustenance, unable to take more than the breast and, from the wretchedness of their parents, deprived of it, as they have lain ill for many days in the ship without food, air or changing. *Merciful Father!* Oh, how readily would I give them each a turn of *Kit's* treasure if in my choice! But, Rebecca, they have a Provider in heaven Who will smooth the pangs of the suffering innocent.
>
> Father goes up early in the morning to procure all possible comforts for the sufferers . . . My side window is open, and wherever I look there are lights. Tents are pitched over the yard of the convalescent house, and a large one . . . joined to the dead house.

Through it all, Dr. Bayley was father and friend to these poor outcasts thrown up on a foreign shore. He and his young assistant, Dr. Joseph Bayley (no relation), worked from three in the morning until long after the sun had set. Betty would watch for his infrequent visits to the house, ready to drop everything to bring him a moment's comfort. He loved to snatch a half-hour away from the fetid sick wards, to sit and relax while his daughter played his favorite airs; but after the first few bars, he would fall asleep from exhaustion. Writing to thank Sad for a new batch of music, Betty told her:

> Father is very much interested by *Alone*. And how you could think I would not like the Scotch song, I don't know, for it has been hummed all day long these six weeks, and I am very glad to have the music. If you

should ever meet with *Kate of Aberdeen*, send it, for my father loved it formerly, and it might now amuse.

Despite the pesthouse atmosphere of the Quarantine Station, life within the white paling went on exactly as in the lazier summer before. Betty could be only a silent watcher, disturbed and touched, of the dreadful scene. Friends came and went: Emma Craig; Miss Shipton; Wright Post, who brought a colleague, Dr. Miller, with him and dined on "elegant black fish and chicken pie." The children recited their lessons with the same regularity as at home, with now and then a break in the order for a sail to Sandy Hook and an all-day picnic. The little mother had time to sew against the needs of the winter, and to spend two hours a day at her Bible.

Absence from Rebecca, and from church and Henry Hobart, were Betty's chief privations. Absence made the heart fonder, and knitted more firmly the sacred ties. The frequent fervent notes breathed with longing: "Give H. H. a look and a sigh for me such as you will for yourself. . . . Remember to tell me the text."—"There is no distance for souls, and mine has surely been with yours most faithfully. St. Paul's steeple, Rebecca and H. H. were thought of—thought did not dwell with them; the sweet day of sacred rest is not for me." It added to her yearning, that she could clearly see the house on the Battery across the Bay and knew, from the open shutters or flickering lights, when Rebecca was there.

Toward the end of June, Betty was requited, for Rebecca finally came to spend some days, and then, in quick succession, Willy and the long-awaited Dué. But relief was tainted with worry, for both showed signs of strain and illness. Will, she thought, "looked more indisposed than I have ever before seen him." Dué, while she suffered from real physical ailments, was unhappy at home, too. Isolated phrases from Betty's letters taken alone are unsatisfactory in explaining the difficulty, but gathered together they tell some sort of story, however vague. Sentences like "Dupleix has had a losing voyage, which makes all crooked," and "Think! Poor Dué is not allowed to wear her cross—at least a badge of it, for inwardly it is weighty enough," seem to point the finger of suspicion at Captain Dupleix as the villain.

On the other hand, there are times when both Betty and Sad seem on the verge of losing patience with Dué's whimpering. It may have been basically a real mismating, for the delicate, suffering Doux, with her invalid moods, seemed hardly the wife for the strongly masculine sea captain. In later years the Captain was a faithful correspondent and friend to Betty, who had always liked him; and by that time he and his wife had achieved domestic harmony. During this summer, however, Dué was wretched, and Betty summed up her feelings about her friend in a letter to Rebecca:

> I saw poor *Du*, in my sleep, in her green gown and hair all falling, laying on a litter pale and motionless. Happy would it be for her, but Him above knows best.

Will picked up for a time, and during that time, life was sweet. Betty hastened to convey the sweetness to Rebecca: "My father was here part of the day yesterday, and the rest of it was peace and WILLY—Shakespeare amused him all the evening"; and again: "A walk on the fort with my Willy and the spyglass. Could it be imagined that *all* the scene changes when he is here?" But soon the devil of discouragement was at him again and Betty wrote, with some bitterness:

> Willy is now soured and worried and says I must not come home till October—he is not as tired as I am of this strange way of living: meeting but once a week, and then wearied and out of spirits. Father says I shall go as soon as I please [after] the 15th of September, but *Willy's* please must be *my* please.

Nothing came of the proposed move to Baltimore, even though Will had considered it seriously and Betty, whatever her unrecorded views, had been ready to go if he wished it, since "where he is, is my present home, and our God is everywhere."

Upon her return from Ireland, Dué, who had always been of a pious bent, was taken into the sacred communion which Betty and Rebecca shared. Rebecca was shy at first about sharing her spiritual life with someone she did not know very well, but Betty reassured her: "You may safely, my love, share the affection you bear me with her, as one united by the same link to Him who is our Common Friend and

Guardian; and do it freely, my darling, without reserve or fear such as we feel in affections formed only for this world." Thus began a sort of "religious community"—insofar as there were devotional practices and united spirituality—of which Henry Hobart was the unofficial chaplain and spiritual director; and it is worthy of note, in the light of future years, that Betty became, quite naturally, the leader or "superioress." The others looked unconsciously to her for leadership, and she, just as unconsciously, gave it. What is more, her words of advice and comfort spoke with authority. It was a trait, a talent, that would develop steadily until it reached mature growth in the convent at Emmitsburg.

It was the greatest consolation to Betty that her father, at fifty-seven, stood up so well under the arduous duties of the Quarantine Station. That a man of his years—in 1801, a man of fifty-seven was old—should be able to take the punishment of sixteen hours' work every day, surrounded by contagion, on a few hours of sleep, was truly incredible.

Betty wrote to Sad on the 20th of July: "Father complains for several days past, but never seriously—heaven avert that!" It was the first, faint gropings of death, and the next evening, without knowing it—indeed, with Will and the uncertainty of their future in mind—she girded her soul for the trial in one of the written meditations that were her outlets and her strength:

> The cup which Our Father has given us, shall we not drink it? Blessed Savior, by the bitterness of Thy pains we may estimate the force of Thy love. We are sure of Thy kindness and compassion. Thou wouldst not willingly call on us to suffer; Thou hast declared unto us that all things shall work together for our good, if we are faithful to Thee. Therefore, if Thou so ordainest it: welcome, disappointments and poverty; welcome, sickness and pain; welcome, even shame and contempt and calumny! If this be a rough and thorny path, it is the one which Thou hast gone before us. Where we see Thy footsteps, we cannot repine. Meanwhile, Thou wilt support us with the consolations of Thy grace; even here Thou canst compensate us for any temporal sufferings by the possession of that peace which the world can neither give nor take away.

On Monday, August 10, just before tea, Dr. Bayley sat at the dining-room window, lost in the beauty of the evening, and the harbor scene spread out before him. There was an especially fine sunset, enhanced by a bright, clean rainbow arching over the Bay. The shipping was dense: the merchantmen lying at anchor, the smaller craft darting among them like water bugs, and the cries of the pilots chiming across the water. This was the time of day Richard Bayley enjoyed most, and he called repeatedly to Betty to watch the changing colors thrown on the clover fields by the setting sun. He nursed a cooling drink while he sat, and when Betty came with Kit in her arms to join him at the window, he amused himself by feeding the baby from his glass with a spoon and making her say "Papa."

This was the contented, happy scene Betty always remembered.

Tea over, she sat down at the piano and went through the whole repertory of his favorites. He himself sang two German hymns and *The Soldier's Adieu* "with such earnestness and energy of manner that even the servants observed how much more cheerful he was than any evening before, this summer." He went to bed at ten o'clock.

An Irish immigrant ship had arrived late the afternoon before. The Health Officer had directed the crew and passengers, many of whom were gravely ill, to leave their baggage on board and go, for the night, to the buildings and tents assigned to them. In the confusion of landing, his orders had been misunderstood; and when Bayley visited the station at dawn, he found everyone—crew, passengers, the well and the ill, the dying and the dead, men, women and children—all jammed into one unventilated room, and their baggage with them. Forgetting his usual caution, he strode impetuously into the disease-packed air of the pesthole, and almost at once he was stricken with severe stomach cramps and a blinding headache. When Betty came down to breakfast at sunrise, the servant told her that her father had come in very sick; but, as he was able to sit at table and drink his tea, she was not alarmed. He said nothing, but that was his usual way at breakfast.

Shortly after he left to go back to his duties, she glanced out the window and saw him sitting on a log on the wharf, the hot sun beating down on his bare head. He looked so distressed and bewildered that Betty's heart lurched with dread and, crying wildly, she sent the servant with an umbrella to bring him in. At the door, he looked at her dazedly and mumbled that his "legs gave way under him." With the help of the servant she got him to bed, and he immediately lapsed into the ravings of delirium. The long agony had begun.

Betty had hold of herself by now, and took over with her usual energy and dispatch. She sent for young Dr. Bayley and scribbled off messages to Will and to Mary Post. Presumably she sent word to Charlotte Bayley and her children, too, for it would not have been like her to ignore them or hold a grudge at such a time; they apparently did not come, for Betty made no mention of them: she spoke, in a detailed letter to Julia Scott, only in a general way of "relatives" at the funeral.

A great pathos hovered over the last days of this vital, dedicated man, a poignant mixture of docility and restlessness, of fright and a calm recognition that his end was come. As soon as the first wave of delirium had passed, he lamented to Betty: "All the horrors are coming, my child; I feel them all." And, as a doctor who had seen them so often, he knew fully what they were.

From the first he would not let Betty leave him, and frequently held on to her hand, literally for life. Day and night she sat by his bed, till her head beat with pain and exhaustion. Anna and Bill went to stay at the Posts through the crisis. Mary Post came back and forth across the Bay until the end approached, when she stayed on with Betty, by his side. Dr. Post was in constant attendance, and on Friday, August 14, went to New York to fetch Dr. Tillary in a desperate attempt to save him, but though Tillary, too, remained, it was futile.

Betty related to Julia the piteous words of his suffering:

> He looked earnestly in my face, the third day: "*the hand of heaven is in it—all will not do*," and often wished it was later in the day. [He] complained it was hard work and repeatedly called, "My Christ Jesus, have mercy on me." Once in the night he said: "Cover me warm; I have covered many. Poor little children, I would cover you more, but it can't always be as we would wish."

Wasted with anxiety and the ordeal of seeing her dear loved one, the only parent she had known, convulsed in pain, unable to soften a pang of it, Betty leaned heavily on the Lord. "Oh, my Rebecca," she cried in a hurried note, "if I did not in this hour know Who to look to, how could it be borne!" She was frightened, too, about her father's salvation, and at length decided on an awesome bargain. Going out onto the piazza, in the dead of night, with Kit in her arms, she looked up to heaven and offered the life of the sleeping child in exchange for her father's soul.

Finally, on Monday, August 17, at two-thirty in the afternoon, the end came. It was as Richard Bayley would have wished. Although he had struggled in agony for an hour and a half, he suddenly relaxed in calm and peace, and reached out for Betty's hand; and, holding to the child he had loved above all others, he turned on his side and died.

Betty decided to bury him with her mother in St. Andrew's Churchyard at Richmond—a further indication of her stepmother's absence—but the parish of Richmond would not let the body be carried through the Island, because Bayley had died of the plague. Sorrowfully, plans were made to bury him in a corner of the yard near the house, where the children were accustomed to play. The grave was already dug when, "as if the mercy of my heavenly Father directed it," Betty wrote, "we thought of taking him in his barge . . . which could go within half a mile of the churchyard." At the landing, Joseph Bayley and Darby, her father's faithful boatman, placed the coffin on a lorry, and the final, short journey of Dr. Richard Bayley was made over the twisting hill road, two wagons full of relatives and friends following.

Dr. Richard Channing Moore, the rector of St. Andrew's, read the burial service, and young Bayley and Darby lowered the remains into the earth, close by the church wall, "the sexton nor none of the people daring to approach." It was a hurried, heartrending farewell to a great man, who had served the City of New York and mankind so well, and who deserved at least as impressive a funeral as William Seton of Stone Street.

Back at the Quarantine cottage, preparations were made for the removal to New York. Summer had come to a sad, abrupt end, and within a week, the little family had left forever the house and fields and haystacks and clover that had made up their garden spot of happiness. Before leaving, Betty sat down to write a thank-you note to Dr. Moore:

> I cannot leave the Island without offering to Mr. Moore the acknowledgments of a grateful heart for the blessing and comfort he has procured for us in the bitter hours of heavy affliction. You have, dear sir, placed the remains of my dear father in a sacred resting place, and the only remaining wish I have is, that a small space may be reserved on each side of

him for his two eldest children. This request is not the impulse of unrestrained sorrow, but of a heart that knows where its home is to be, and feels the greatest consolation in the hope that it may be permitted to repose by its dear parent.

Elizabeth Seton was to have a more famous and even more sacred resting place; but Mary Post is buried alongside her father and mother in St. Andrew's, and after her burial in 1856, the remains of her husband, Wright Post, who had died in 1828, were brought there, too, from St. Peter's Churchyard in Pelham.

The trial past, Betty confided to Julia Scott that it was not so much a marvel that she had lived through it, but that she lived at all. But she banished her tears to her heart, and set about facing the unpromising future. As she said to Rebecca, in telling her of friends who had come to condole with her: "I believe they think me an unfeeling wretch, not to answer one tear; but, no matter. My tears are dry. They are left with all the agonies that occasioned them, on the garret floor at Staten Island."

IX

"I Rise Up Early and Late Take Rest"

The mills of God were grinding. They had been grinding with pro-
verbial slowness almost from the day Elizabeth Seton was born; but of
late years they had increased the rhythm of their turning. A pattern
began to emerge, the pattern of Job. It had always been there: in the
loss of her mother, the neglect of her stepmother, the irresponsibility
of her father—the periodic unhappiness of her childhood and adolescence. But now, with the death of her father-in-law, her father, and
with the wiping out of the Setons' worldly possessions, the pattern grew
ever clearer. And ever stronger came her reply: "The Lord has given,
the Lord has taken away; blessed be the Name of the Lord!"

Back in town, there was no let-up of trouble. Since her father's death,
Betty confided to Julia Scott, she had "suffered so much with the nerves
of my teeth and temples that I have been really stupefied." The remedy
was almost worse than the suffering, for she told Rebecca: "Woffendale
has just been hauling at my poor tooth and broke it off short, the three
prongs remaining for life, I suppose." And she finished, with her characteristic writing-off of trouble past, "Well, that is done."

Her father's death drew Betty even closer, if possible, to Will who
was her "only remaining earthly protector." She shared the awe of this
new intimacy with Rebecca: "You know, Rebecca, how I used to wish

to go [*i.e.*, to die]; now I dare not: my William seems as if his life and mine were one." That he was "far from well" deepened her devotion to "my own William," and her letters and notes swelled with the happiness of helping him bear his many crosses, physical and financial—"not domestic!" as she pertly reminded Julia. She contentedly closed one note:

> Last night I wrote two sheets as full as I could crowd them to Aunt Cayley *to please my Will.* . . . *As you and I understand each other,* I may show you the within description to her. With what rapid pleasure the pen run it over—the praise of those we love, how sweet!

Betty had promised Mrs. Scott that "I am going to be well when I get a little rest from my summer fatigues"; but such rest was not for her. No sooner was the family back in New York than the yellow fever struck the city again with fury. One of the best of her friends went down before it—Sad's husband, Henry. Henry Sadler was a happy, good-humored man, and the delight of the little Setons; his frequent visits, or even the anticipation of them, set Anna and Bill and Dick wild with joy. In giving Julia the sorrowful news of his passing, Betty assured her that "I have borne *my part* in the melancholy scene." To make matters worse, Sad had sunk into a state of lifelessness at the shock, and Betty feared a recurrence of the paralytic stroke that had crippled her friend temporarily the year before. It consoled Betty that she was "as seems my lot to be, her only earthly support."

While the very sound of the word yellow fever drove the blood from her heart, yet she had grown so used to the disease that she was unwilling to have it deprive her of the church services of Henry Hobart or the companionship of her "Soul's Sister." She wrote to Rebecca on the 14th of October:

> The terror of our fellow citizens seems to be so awakened that I do not believe you ought to come to town, as prudence says; *but I say,* "Come, dear, 'let us keep the feast' with sincerity and truth."

Julia Scott was a wretched letter-writer. Time and again, Betty had to remind her that she had had no news for months, and was worried. The lady from Philadelphia was especially recalcitrant this fall and winter, and Will got it into his head, whether with reason or not, that he had offended her, which gave Betty occasion for a great deal of merriment and good-natured joshing. She wrote to Julia with mock-seriousness at the end of October:

> How Seton is to get out of his scrape with you, I cannot [see]. . . . You must not be hard with him. He sends you a kiss and says you shall have two when he sees you again, if you forgive him. He is in love with you, your house, and all that belongs to you.

And she signed the letter: "Eliza, the wife of W. M. Seton." She kept the family joke going by writing, in January, that "Seton has been constantly dreaming of you, and as a kiss has often been realized to his imagination—which he thinks an unpropitious sign—he fears you are *still* angry with him, and begs you for pity's sake to let the offences of the old year pass with it"; and she added wickedly, "and his little wife begs you for remembrance sake to write that you are neither sick nor sorry. . . ." Julia answered in the same bantering vein, calling for a truce, and Betty wrote as one who has the last word:

> The peace has almost [finished] poor Seton. He is delighted with your claim, especially as he thinks I am likely to go very soon. Next September is the time I appoint for relinquishment; but if it is true, as we have heard from an intimate acquaintance and relative of yours, that YOU ARE TO BE MARRIED, I do not know what you will do with the budget!

As if the Setons did not have enough troubles of their own, they shouldered an even greater share of poor Eliza Maitland's. Betty took the youngest child, with his wet nurse, for the winter. Then, in February, the ne'er-do-well husband went to jail; and Will, from sheer necessity of brotherly affection, was forced to feed the Maitland household, "six in number . . . from our own storeroom and everyday marketing, as no other part of the family will keep them from starving, or even in firewood." These words are a damning indictment of the selfish Setons and, while they presage a golden crown for Will, they also bear witness to the eternal truth that it is always the poor, out of their little, who give to those who are poorer still.

Mammy Huler, the Seton servant, began to sink under the weight of her years, and Betty nursed her and waited on her as the faithful old soul had for so long nursed and waited on her and her children.

Despite the increase of her responsibilities, Betty continued to play the role of the valiant woman of the Scriptures to the hilt of her energies. Everything went on according to schedule. None of the children, from Cecilia down, went out to school; Betty taught them all. The relief of her widows continued, too; and Betty remained an officer of the Society. She begged from door to door of the town for the poor derelict objects of her charity, and had occasion to thank the good Julia—who, despite her worldliness, was a princely giver—for swelling the Society's funds. To accomplish everything, Betty admitted to her, " 'I rise up early and late take rest,' you may be sure. Never before after twelve, and oftener one. Such is the allotment, and as everybody has their *pride* of some sort, I cannot deny that this is mine." It was a shrewd recognition on her part, but, like all good people, while she never lost sight of even her harmless faults, she failed to comprehend the height and the depth of the virtue over and under all. The artless description of one of her days was a truer picture:

> I have cut out my two *suits* today and partly made one. Heard all the lessons, too, and had a two hours' visit from my widow Veley—no work, no wood, child sick, etc.—and should I complain, with a bright fire within, bright, bright *moon* over my shoulder, and the darlings all well, hallooing and dancing?—I have played for them this half hour.

Will, too, had his courage, but it was of a different kind. Stubbornly, he held on to the barren hope of recouping his losses. Stubbornly, he continued to hold his head high in the society whose prices he could no longer pay. Not all of his prominent friends had deserted him, as not all of Betty's had deserted her, and he received invitations to dine out with fair frequency. Rarely could she accompany him, since she could not or would not leave the children. The fact of her staying behind —and the simple incident of an evening—pointed up the divergence of their outlook. Handsome as ever in his silk evening suit and powdered wig, he stooped to kiss her good-bye, lamenting that she must spend the evening alone. She assured him that she had a companion, a pious work called *Peaceful Soul*. He merely laughed.

To be fair to Will, there was a certain priggishness to Betty's piety at this period; but it was not her fault: it was the self-consciousness of Protestantism, and she sincerely knew nothing else. Her sincerity, in fact—her show of deeds, her practical living, her sense of fun—saved her from the specious religiosity that is insufferable to sinner and saint alike.

The Rev. Hobart went to Philadelphia in February, and Betty gave him a letter of introduction to Julia Scott, which set forth with honesty and complete satisfaction the spirituality of the bond that united them:

> There are various kinds of attachments in this world: some of affection without the soothing confidence of trust and esteem united, some of esteem for virtues which we can neither approach nor assimilate to our own natures, and some, the unbounded veneration, affection, esteem and tribute of "the heart sincere." The bearer of this letter possesses *in full* the reality of the last description in *my* heart, and, in fact, I can give no stronger proof of the affection and esteem I bear you, than in expressing to you what I believe another would pervert or ridicule.
>
> The soother and comforter of the troubled soul is a kind of friend not often met with. The convincing, pious and singular turn of mind and argument possessed by this most amiable being has made him—without even having the least consciousness that he is so—the friend most my friend in this world, and one of those who, after my Adored Creator, I expect to receive the largest share of happiness from in the next.

The tartness of the next paragraph was an admirable indication that the writer's head was not befuddled with sentimentality:

> Well, surely, this is not for Miss Chip's eyes, nor anything else I write; for I am quite out of patience with her follies and flatteries, and hope with you she will at least have the merit of lessening your housekeeping troubles!

Apparently, poor Miss Chippy Jay had not improved.

As the earth warmed to spring, Betty became aware that she would bear another child in the summer. She became aware, too, under the tutelage of Henry Hobart, of new frontiers of the spirit awaiting her approach and, in May, she made a significant advance toward them:

> This blessed day, Sunday, 23rd May 1802, my soul was first sensibly conceived of the blessing and practicability of an entire surrender of itself and all its faculties to God. It has been *the Lord's Day* indeed to me, though many, many temptations to forget my heavenly possession *in His constant Presence* has pressed upon me. But—blessed be my gracious Shepherd!—in this last hour of *His Day* I am at rest within His fold, sweetly refreshed with the waters of comfort which have flowed through the soul of

his ministering servant, our blessed teacher. Glory to my God for this unspeakable blessing! Glory to my God for the means of grace and the hopes of glory which He so mercifully bestows on His unworthy servant! O Lord, before Thee I must ever be unworthy until covered with the robe of righteousness by my beloved Redeemer. He shall fit me to behold the vision of Thy glory.

For the first time since they were married, there was no summer home, no summer holiday, for the Setons that year, but they had the room of the Battery and the air of the Bay. At the beginning of August, her confinement near, Betty was depressed. She hid it from her family, but confided to Rebecca that "my soul is very, very, very sick; I call to my Physician every moment, from the bottom of my heart, but find no peace." It was a passing thing—due perhaps to the unaccountable melancholy and anxious thoughts of a mother at such a time—for, on August 16, she was once more happy and at peace.

It is interesting to note that she had attended church the previous day, just five days from the birth of her baby; hiding away through the months of pregnancy apparently came in with the other pruderies of Victorianism. Despite her own peace, however, she was impatient with Will's spiritual blindness, for she told Rebecca:

> Our H.H. was at St. Mark's instead of St. Paul's; and Willy says those who heard him said he was a great contrast to the gentleman we had, who had given them, in the morning, a schism sermon. Surely H.H. knew nothing of schism yesterday! Willy regretted very much he did not hear him. Regrets are idle things.

The children, with the exception of Kit, were sent to Rebecca at Maitlands' until Betty's confinement should be over, and she confided lightly to Bec that they were looking forward to the treat of hearing Henry Hobart preach: "They are all singing 'Going to Hobe's.' It can't be wrong to let them go. . . . Ask him if he is to be at St. Paul's or Trinity tomorrow." Dué was with Betty, until all should be over. The young mother-to-be was in a wonderfully lighthearted mood, and even the remembrance of her father's anniversary did nothing to chill it: she only entrusted her remembrance to Rebecca: "Dear, dear Rebecca —the 17th of August last year, about this time, three o'clock in the *afternoon"*; and then, in her sensible way: "never mind, someone will be *thinking of us* in a few years."

On the 19th, she sat down to write Julia a long letter, but she never finished it. The new baby interrupted—as Anna had interrupted a letter to Julia in 1795; and Will finished the letter now as he had finished it then:

> Thus far, my very amiable little friend, did our dear Eliza write last night at 11 o'clock; and this morning at twelve, I have the satisfaction to tell you, she was safely delivered of [a] girl. . . . The mother is as well as she usually is on such occasions; *better* than could be expected, for we had neither *Doctor* or *anything of the kind* till a quarter of an hour after the young lady made her first appearance.

Julia must have smiled at his male blitheness in passing off the well-being of his wife—Betty had almost died with Richard! Will had his share of husbandly obtuseness: one day when Betty was out, for example, a messenger boy brought a hat to the door for which he was to collect two dollars; Will, not recalling that Betty had mentioned such a purchase, sent it back, much to her exasperation.

The new baby was christened Rebecca on September 29, but whether in compliment to Betty's "Soul's Sister" or to Will's dead mother is not clear; probably the latter, for Rebecca Seton did not stand for the baby. Eliza Sadler and Will himself were the godparents.

When she was up and around, Betty reaffirmed her dedication to God by writing in her spiritual journal: "Sunday, 12th September, three weeks and two days after the birth of my *Rebecca*, I renewed my covenant that I would strive with myself and use every earnest endeavor to serve my dear Redeemer and to give myself wholly unto Him." The next day, she gave the resolution specific and practical application: "Began a new life—resumed the occupations and duties which fill up the part He has assigned me." She took advantage of preparing the bedside table for a dying parishioner of Trinity to receive the sacrament, for a written reminder of what the sacrament meant to her: "the seal of that Covenant which I trust will not be broken in life nor in death, in time nor in eternity." It is interesting how close she came here to the Catholic concept of the Blessed Sacrament as a pledge of eternal life.

So great was her devotion to the Episcopalian remembrance of the Last Supper that her teeth chattered against the cup of wine in an ecstasy of trembling awe when she received; and after the service she and Dué would ask the sexton for the remnants of the sacramental wine, that they might renew their devotion in receiving again.

Ever pressing her role as missionary, she found an apt pupil in Cecilia Seton, now twelve years old; and a little packet of religious sayings and admonitions "to Cecilia B. Seton from her own sister, E.A.S.," dated 19th of November, 1802, is preserved. Among them is a charming verse, but whether it is Betty's own or something she copied—she had some talent for verse—is not clear:

> As a little child relies
> On a care beyond his own,
> Knows he's neither strong nor wise,
> Fears to stir a step alone;
> Let me thus with Thee abide,
> As my Father, Guard and Guide.

Just at this time, she wrote to Julia Scott to explain a lapse in her correspondence:

> How many reproaches my heart makes me when I think of you. So many years I have called you dear friend, and shall your dear friend be insincere to you? Dear Julia, then I will tell you the plain truth, that my habits both of soul and body are changed, that I feel all the habits of society and connections of this life have taken a new form, and are only interesting or endearing as they point the view to the next. We will never differ on this point; I know your side is the strongest, and that you might use many and powerful arguments to prove the necessity of submission to the manners of the world and the received opinions which guide even the good and wise. Well, my dear friend, that blessed influence which alone can renovate the heart, I pray (and pray with my whole soul) may, before it is too late, convince you of the truth. . . . Now then, dear friend, I explain to you why I have not as much pleasure in writing to you as I formerly had, why it appears to you (though erroneously) that I do not love you sincerely. Dear Julia, let it not be so always. But I know you will love me the better for saying it is so now.

It was not so always. After this letter, which must have hurt Julia as much as it bewildered her, there were few notes between the two friends; but eventually the correspondence was renewed, and lasted unchecked throughout Betty's life.

Betty had managed the conversion of Mammy Huler over the long months of the old servant's last illness, and on a Sunday in October, "Parson Linn" came to baptize her, Betty having spent the Saturday in giving her proximate instruction for the great event. Not many days after, Mammy died, "without a struggle or groan, as a child composed to rest in the arms of its parents, sure of awakening secure."

There is no record of how the Seton household passed that winter and spring of 1802–1803, but in early summer, Betty and the children went to enjoy the country at Sad's cottage on Long Island; and Sad returned the visit by coming to stay with Betty on the Battery while Will made a short trip to Philadelphia. His health was miserable now, and Betty could see the beginning of the end. But she was given a great consolation in finally winning him to her religious way. Whether his awakening was a gradual thing is uncertain, but it would seem the culmination came that summer of 1803, probably in August. Her excitement was evident in two notes to Rebecca: "Willy says he *will dine at home* tomorrow, with a significant smile. I shall be too happy if he means to keep his promise, *freely* and without any persuasion from me." —and—"Since a *quarter* before three I have been, oh, how happy! Come, come, 'Soul's Sister,' *let us bless the day together—one body, one spirit, one hope, one God—*the Father of *all!* I think our Willy will go—he has not left me for five minutes since yesterday's dinner, and has had *Nelson* in his hands very often. If he does, what a dinner will *today's* be to me!"

When her "happy day" came, Betty's soul breathed a great sigh of content and, when Henry Hobart came to rejoice with her, she wrote Rebecca:

> I told him the last twenty-four hours were the happiest I had ever seen or could ever expect, as the most earnest wish of my heart was fulfilled. Dear Rebecca, if you had known how sweet last evening was—Willy's heart seemed to be nearer to me for being nearer to His God. From absolute weariness of body I fell asleep at *eleven,* and left him with *Nelson* in his hand.

Betty and Will now had the support they needed for the terrible ordeal ahead. Will was so far gone in tuberculosis that no remedy could help him, and in desperation he, or Betty, or both, decided on a ocean trip to visit his friends the Filicchis in Leghorn. It was apparently a spur-of-the-moment attempt to ward off death, for no mention of it was made in Betty's correspondence until the summer was nearly gone. Betty was resolved he should not, could not, go alone; and with happy inspiration, she hit on taking Anna, who was now eight, with them—she would be grateful for the company of the child in the lonely days ahead. Will was suffering in earnest and could do nothing to make preparation for the voyage, so he went with the children to stay at the Posts while Betty weaned Rebecca who—to make matters worse—was ill, and broke up housekeeping, distributing the furniture among her friends for safekeeping. It is interesting to note that her own favorite pieces—her writing desk, her piano and a picture of Christ—went to the Hobarts. With her great common sense, she began to prepare Anna for responsibility, writing to her to "take good care of Papa while he is with you, and do all you can to please him."

Friends and relatives thought the scheme was mad, but that made no difference to Betty, since it was a scheme to help Will, and she confided to Sad: "You know that I go *fearless*, for you know where, and how strong, is my trust." She had no illusions about the outcome, as she frankly admitted to Julia: "My Seton's decline is so rapid that there can be no hope of his recovery." She did not, however, discount the intervening mercy of God.

Hardest of all for the loving husband and wife was to parcel out the children: Bill and Dick and Kate to Rebecca Seton, who was at the Maitlands; the baby Rebecca, who continued sick even as the ship sailed, to Wright and Mary Post; and the Seton girls—Will's sisters—to their brother James and his wife. A series of poignant notes to the children, written while the ship was picking its way through the harbor, bore the agony of Betty's farewell:

My dear William: You know how dearly your own mother loves you, and how much I wish to see you good. I hope you are so, particularly to dear Godmother (Rebecca). I am glad that you go to school and learn so fast, for that will please dear Papa, who sends you much love and many kisses, and so does dear Anna, and your own mother.

My own Richard: Your dear mother loves you more than she can tell, and hopes you will be a good boy and mind what your dear Godmother says to you. And she will do everything to make you happy. If you love me, do not plague your sweet Kate, for that would make dear Mamma very unhappy. Remember, my Dick, to pray for us every night and morning; and your dear mother and father will pray to God to bless you and make you a good boy. Papa and sister send you a kiss.

The poignancy of these notes is increased by the large, careful letters formed for a child's eyes, and the occasional lurch of the words from the pitching of the ship.

The letter to Cecilia was entirely spiritual, and showed the advance she had made in the way of God under Betty's instruction:

Although I leave you in the hands of your dearest friends, and under the protecting care of our dear and Heavenly Father, still my heart would dictate to you many anxious requests respecting your habitual observance of that heavenly Christian life you have so early begun; and in order to persevere in this, your first attention must be to make to yourself a few particular rules, which you must not suffer anything on earth to divert you from, as they relate immediately to your sacred duty to God; and, if you find that there are any obstacles in your way—and, doubtless, you will find many, as every Christian does in the fulfillment of their duty—still persevere with yet more earnestness, and rejoice to bear your share in the Cross, which is our passport and seal to the kingdom of our Redeemer. Nor will your steadiness of conduct ever injure you even in the minds of those who act differently from you, for all who love you will respect and esteem you the more for persevering in what you know to be your duty.

Betty was realistic enough to face the possibility that she might never return; she understood the dangers of the crossing, both from the sea itself and from privateers on even French and English warships. She wrote, therefore, to all her friends, with the finality of penning a last will and testament, assuring them of her love both in this world and the next. Before boarding the ship, she had gone with the children on a last pilgrimage to Staten Island. She "walked through the Quarantine garden and trod that wharf's every plank of which *his* feet had been on, sailed over the Bay in *his* boat alone, with Darby at the sail and

William, who used to go with him to get snipes, at the helm." She
visited young Dr. Joseph Bayley, and stood for an hour in the room
where her father had died.

The Setons sailed on October 2. The ship was *The Shepherdess*, and
the captain's name was O'Brien; his wife and eighteen-month-old child
sailed with him. Will took passage as a British citizen and carried a
passport signed by Thomas Barclay, "His Britanic Majesty's Consul
General for the Eastern States of America." The fact has raised some
question as to whether he was indeed—and his wife, Elizabeth Ann,
too—a British citizen; but it is rather obvious that the passport was a
safe-conduct rather than a declaration of allegiance, for it asked in part
that "Commanders of His Majesty's ships of war and Masters of private
armed vessels . . . not only . . . permit them to proceed without molestation or detention, but . . . render them every comfort and aid they
may stand in need of." It must be remembered that these were days
of lawlessness on the seas, as well as the days of the dread Barbary
pirates and of William Bainbridge and Stephen Decatur and "the
shores of Tripoli." The citizenship laws of the time were so vague and
the legal distinctions so involved, that it would serve no good to consider them here. Suffice it to say, for our purpose, that no legitimate
doubt can be cast on the American citizenship of Elizabeth Ann Seton,
foundress of the Sisters of Charity in the United States and pioneer of
American Catholic education.

Will and Betty also carried a letter of introduction to Joseph Jaudens,
Intendente of Mallorca, from James Barry, a merchant friend of Will's,
who would be one of Betty's staunchest Catholic friends in the days
following her conversion.

The actual leave-taking was hard. Rebecca and Harriet Seton brought
the children to the Battery to see their parents pass on their way to
the New York Quarantine, but after waving excitedly, the little ones
began to cry. Will was so choked with tears that he fell into a spasm
of coughing, and Betty scarcely dared upset him further by waving her
"dear red handkerchief." She did not fail to take a long, last look at
the "dear study windows" of Hobart's house. Her spiritual guide had
sent her two religious notes of consolation and farewell. Their turgid
prose was so purple and pompous, that it is little wonder that Betty, in

later years, became embarrassed at the thought of the pietism of this time
—however much it prepared her for the advent of the truth.

The farewells past, everything began to look better, except that little
Anna, normally enough, became violently seasick. Will's pain left him
and his spirits lifted; Betty was cheerful and of "ravenous appetite." The
O'Briens turned out to be kind and friendly, and the steward hovered
over the little group like a family servant. Will's brother Henry left the
ship with the pilot at the harbor lighthouse, and the crossing began.
Will and Betty gave themselves up to the mystery of the sea, the
spanking cleanness of the salt air and the grandeur of the rising and the
setting sun.

Hidden away in her mother's heart was Betty's last cry to Sad: "Take
my darlings often in your arms!"

X

The Lazaretto

The voyage of the *Shepherdess* to Leghorn took nearly, seven weeks. The ship followed the southern route through the Azores to Gibraltar and the Mediterranean. Today's luxury liners make the passage in eight days.

The lovely dark bulks of the "Western Isles" rising up out of the sea on either side as the ship passed through the channel were a welcome sight to the travelers, after the weeks of watery wastes and brilliant sun. The islands meant, besides, hourly expectation of meeting another vessel bound for New York, to carry home the letters written to family and friends in the leisurely days behind. The days had been uneventful for the most part, and Betty had had her longest rest in years. She spent the time reading, instructing Anna in the lessons of the Scriptures, chatting with Will. He had improved considerably, and that made everything right, bringing even a flicker of hope to Elizabeth. Only for a short period did he give way to the petulance of the invalid: when Anna caught whooping cough from the captain's child, and the constant crying and coughing of the children irritated him.

With so much time to herself, it was natural for Betty to indulge her delight in writing down her thoughts, and she began to keep a detailed journal for Rebecca. The great gray mass of Gibraltar caused her to dream that she was painfully climbing a steep and forbidding slope; she had nearly reached the summit, when a voice spoke in her dream: "Never mind, take courage," it said. "There is a beautiful green hill on the other side, and on it an angel waits for you." It was only a dream, but vivid enough to be noted down and wondered about.

A week before the voyage ended, Betty set Anna crying by telling her that "we offended God every day." The child wanted to know whether God put down in His book our bad actions as well as our good ones. The incident triggered an examen and a resolution in Betty's soul:

> Considering the *infirmity* and corrupt nature which would overpower the spirit of grace, and the enormity of the offence to which the least indulgence of them would lead me—in the anguish of my soul, shuddering to offend my adored Lord, I have this day solemnly engaged that, through the strength of His Holy Spirit, I will not again expose that corrupt and infirm nature to the smallest temptation I can avoid; and, therefore, if my Heavenly Father will once more *reunite us all*, that I will make a daily sacrifice of every *wish*, even the *most innocent*, lest they should betray me to deviation from the solemn and sacred vow I have now made.

It is painful to watch her struggling in the dark bonds of the religion of fear, making the most desperate and difficult promises in an effort to escape to the peace and freedom which is the habitat of the holy soul.

A few nights later, a fearsome storm broke just about midnight. Betty tried to shut out the roaring of the wind, the crash of the waves and the groaning of the ship's timbers by earnest reading and long prayer; but her knees trembled as she knelt on the pitching floor, and, in bed, she could not sleep. In the darkness, a little voice, Anna's, murmured drowsily, "Come hither, all ye weary souls," and—the role of protector reversed—Betty crawled into the child's arms and fell at once into a deep sleep.

The storm past, the ship made headway, up past the great bulk of Corsica, birthplace of the Little Corporal who was terrorizing Europe, and the small dot of Elba, where he would be incarcerated after his downfall, up into the Ligurian Sea and the prosperous port of Livorno or Leghorn. The Angelus bells were ringing, as if in welcome to the tired travelers, as the *Shepherdess* moved into the quiet waters of the harbor on the 18th of November. The white and brown houses of the old Tuscan town nestled at the foot of Montenero were a glad sight to the eyes of Betty and Will and Anna; and they went to bed thankful that they had arrived safe and longing for the good things of tomorrow: the meeting with the Filicchis, the reunion with Betty's brother Carleton. God was good to give them this one happy night.

The unexpected horrors that began with the next day are almost un-believable. But they happened. Betty was there, and endured them. For that reason, it is best to have the story of them from her own pen:

19th Nov., 1803—10 o'clock at night.—How eagerly would you listen to the voice that should offer to tell you where your dear sister is now— your *Soul's Sister.* Yet you could not rest in your bed if you saw her as she is, sitting in one corner of an immense prison, bolted in—a single window, double-grated with iron, through which, if I should want anything, I am to call a sentinel with a cocked hat and long-rifled gun—that is, that he may not receive the dreadful infection we are supposed to have brought with us from New York.

To commence from where I left off last night: I went to sleep and dreamed I was in the middle aisle of Trinity Church, singing with all my soul the hymn at our dear Sacrament. So much comfort made me more than satisfied; and when I heard in the morning a boat was alongside of our ship, I flew on deck and would have thrown myself in the arms of dear Carleton, but he retired from me, and a guard, who I saw for the first time, said, "Don't touch."

It was now explained that our ship was the first to bring the news of the yellow fever in New York, which our want of a bill of health discovered; our ship must go out in the *roads,* and my poor William, being sick, must go with his baggage to the *lazaretto.*

At this moment, the band of music that always welcomes strangers, came under our cabin window playing "Hail Columbia" and all those little tunes that set the darlings singing and dancing at home. Mrs. O'Brien and the rest were almost wild with joy; while I was glad to hide in my berth the full heart of sorrow, which seemed as if it must break. You cannot have an idea of the looks of my William, who seemed as if he could not live over the day.

Presently appeared a boat with fourteen oars, and we entered into another fastened to it. The *lazaretto* being some miles from the town [it was at shore but further down the coast], we were rowed out to sea again and, after an hour's ride over the waves, the chains which cross the entrance of the canal which leads to this place were let down at the signal of several successive bells and, after another rowing between walls as high as our second-story windows, and the quarreling and hallooing of the watermen where we should be landed, the boat stopped. Another succession of bells brought down one guard after another, and, in about half an hour, *Monsieur le Capitaine* who, after much consultation and whispering with his lieutenant, said we might come out; upon which everyone retreated, and a guard pointed the way with his bayonet we were to go.

An order from the Commandant was sent from our boat to the *Capitano*, which was received on the end of a stick, and they were obliged to light a fire to smoke it before it could be read. My books always go with me, and they were carefully put up, but must all be looked over and the papers in the little secretary examined. . . .

Poor little Anna! how she trembled! and William tottered along as if every moment he must fall which, had he done, no one dared for their lives to touch him.

We were directed to go opposite to the window of the *Capitano's* house, in which sat Mrs. P(hilip) F(ilicchi) [she was an American—Mary Cowper of Boston]. Compliments and kind looks without number. A fence was between us but, I fear, did not hide my fatigue both of soul and body. . . .

At length we were shown the door we should enter—No. 6, up twenty stone steps—a room with high arched ceilings, like St. Paul's, brick floor and naked walls.

The *Capitano* sent three warm eggs, a bottle of wine and some slices of bread. William's mattress was soon spread, and he upon it. He could not touch wine or eggs. Our little syrups, currant jelly, drinks, etc., which he must have every half hour on board ship—where were they? I had heard the *lazaretto* was the very place for comfort for the sick, and brought nothing.

Soon found there was a little closet on which my knees found rest and, after emptying my heart and washing the bricks with my tears, returned to my poor William and found him and Anna both in want of a preacher. Dear puss, she soon found a rope that had tied her box, and began jumping away to warm herself, for the coldness of the walls and the bricks made us shiver. At sunset, dinner came from the kind F(ilicchis) with other necessaries; we went to the grate again to see them.

And now, on the ship-mattresses spread on this cool floor, my William and Anna are sound asleep; and I trust that God, who has given him strength to go through a day of such exertion, will carry us on. He is our all indeed. My eyes smart so much with crying, wind and fatigue, that I must close them and lift up my heart.

Sleep won't come very easily. If you had seen little Anna's arms clasped round my neck at her prayers, while the tears rolled a stream, how you would love her! I read her to sleep, little pieces of trust in God. She said,

"Mamma, if papa should die here—"

"But God will be with us."

God is with us, and if sufferings abound in us, His consolations also greatly abound, and far exceed an utterance. If the wind (for it is said there were never such storms at this season) that now almost puts out my light and blows on my William through every crevice, and over our chimney like loud thunder, could come from any but His command; or if the circumstances that have placed us in so forlorn a situation were not guided by His hand—miserable indeed would be our case. Within this hour he has had a violent fit of coughing so as to bring up blood, which agitates and distresses him through all his endeavors to hide it. What shall we say? This is the hour of trial. The Lord supports and strengthens us in it. . . .

20th, Sunday morning.—The matin bells awakened my soul to its most painful regrets and filled it with an agony of sorrow which would not at first find relief even in prayer. In the little closet—from whence there is a view of the open sea and the beatings of the waves against the high rocks at the entrance of this prison, which throws them violently back and raises the white foam as high as its walls—I first came to my senses and reflected that I was offending my only Friend and Resource in my misery, and voluntarily shutting out from my soul the only consolation it could receive. Pleading for mercy and strength brought peace and, with a cheerful countenance, I asked William what we should do for breakfast.

The doors were unbarred, and a bottle of milk set down in the entrance of the room, poor Philippo [a servant] fearing to come too near. Little Anne and William ate it with bread, and I walked the floor with a crust and glass of wine.

William could not sit up. His ague came on, and my soul's agony with it. My husband on the cold bricks without fire, shivering and groaning, lifting his dim eyes and sorrowful with a fixed gaze in my face, while his tears ran on his pillow, without one word. Anne rubbed one hand, I the other, 'till his fever came on.

The *Capitano* brought us news that our time was lessened five days, told me to be satisfied with the dispensations of God, etc., and was answered by such a succession of *sobs* that he soon departed. Mr. F(ilicchi) now came to comfort my William; and when he went away, we said as much of our blessed service as William could go through. I then was obliged to lay my head down.

Dinner was sent from town, and a servant to stay with us during our quarantine: Louis, an old man, very little, gray hairs and blue eyes which changed their expressions from joy to sorrow, as if they would console and still enliven. . . . He looked up with lifted hands in some prayer that God would comfort me, and so I was comforted when I did not look at my poor

William; but to see him as he then was was worse than to see him dead. . . .

My William, wearied out, was soon asleep. Ann with a flood of tears, said her prayers and soon forgot her sorrows; and it seemed as if opening my prayer-book and bending my knees was the signal for my soul to find rest. It was *nine* o'clock with us—*three* at home. . . . After prayers, read my little book of Dearth's Sermons, and became far more happy than I had been wretched. Went to bed at *twelve*. Got up twice to prayers, and to help my poor William.

Monday—Awoke with the same rest and comfort with which I had laid down, gave my William his warm milk, and began to consider our situation—though so unfavorable to his complaint—as one of the steps in the dispensations of that Almighty Will which could alone choose aught for us. And, therefore, set Ann to work and myself to the dear Scriptures, as usual, laying close to the dear shiverer to keep him from the ague.

Our *Capitano* came with his guards and put up a very neat bed and curtains sent by F(ilicchi), and fixed the *benches* on which Ann and I were to lie, took down our names: *Signore Gulielmo*, *Signora Elizabeth* and *Signora Anna Maria*. The voice of kindness which again entreated me *to look up* to *le bon Dieu* made me look up to the speaker; and in our *Capitano* I found every expression of a benevolent heart. His great cocked hat being off, I found it had hid his gray hairs and a kind and affectionate countenance.

"I had a wife; I loved her—I loved her. Oh! she gave me a daughter which she commended to my care, and died."

He clasped his hands and looked up, and then at my William.

"If God calls, what can we do? *et quez voulez-vous, Signora?*"

I began to love my *Capitano*.

Read, and jumped the rope to warm me. Looked round our prison and found that its situation was beautiful. Comforted my William all I could, rubbing his hands, and wiping his tears and giving words to his soul, which was too weak to pray for itself. Heard Ann read, while I watched the setting sun in a cloud. After both were asleep, read, prayed, wept, and prayed again, until eleven, at no loss to know the hours. Night and day four bells strike every hour, and ring every quarter.

Tuesday.—My William was better, and very much encouraged by his doctor, Tutilli, who was very kind to him. Also our *Capitano*, who now seemed to understand me a little, again repeated.

"I loved my wife—I loved her, and she died; *et que voulez-vous, Signora?*"

Talked with the F(ilicchis) at the grate, and with great difficulty got my William up the stairs again, nursed him, read to him and heard Ann read; and made the most of our troubles. Our Louis brought us an elegant bouquet—jessamines, geraniums, pinks, etc. He makes excellent soup; cooks all with charcoal in little earthen pots. No sunset—heavy gale, which, if anything could move our walls, would certainly bring them down. The roaring of the sea sounds like thunder. . . .

Wednesday.—Not only willing to take my cross, but kissed it, too. And, whilst glorying in our consolations, my poor William was taken with an ague which was almost too much for him. He told me, as he had often done before, that it was too late, his strength was going from him every hour, and he should go gradually, but not long. *This to me;* to his *friends* quite cheerful. He was not able to go to them; they were admitted to our door— must not touch the least thing near us—and a point of our *Capitano's* stick warded my William off when in eager conversation he would go too near. It reminded me of going *to see the lions.* [She was thinking of a small zoo outside New York.] . . . Ann and I sung *Advent hymns* with a low voice. Oh! after all was asleep, said our dear service alone—William had not been able in the day. Found heavenly consolation; forgot prisons, bolts and sorrow, and would have rejoiced to have sung with St. Paul and Silas.

Thursday.—I find my present opportunity a treasure, and my confinement of body a liberty of soul, which I may never again enjoy while they are united. Every moment not spent with my *dear books,* or in my nursing duty, is a loss. Ann is so happy with her rag-baby and little presents, it is a pleasure to see her. Our *Capitano* brought us news that other five days were granted, and the 19th of December we were free. Poor William says with a groan,

"I believe before then."

We pray and cry together until fatigue overpowers him, and then he says he is willing to go. Cheering up is useless; he seems easier after venting his sorrow, and always gets quiet sleep after his struggle. A heavy storm of wind which drives the sprays from the sea against our window adds to his melancholy. If I could forget my God one moment at these times, I should go mad; but *He* hushes all. "Be still and know that I am God your Father."

Dear home, dearest sisters, my little ones—well—either protected by God in this world or in heaven. It is a sweet thought to dwell on, that all those I most tenderly love, *love* God; and if we do not meet again *here, there* we shall be separated *no more.* If I have lost them *now,* there gain is infinite and eternal. How often I tell my William:

"When you awake in *that* world, you will find that nothing could tempt you to return to *this.* You will see that your care over your wife and little ones was like a hand only, to hold the cup, which God Himself will give if He takes you." . . .

Friday.—A day of bodily pain, but peace with God. Kneeled on our mats round the table and said our dear service. The storm of wind so great. Carleton was admitted at the foot of the stairs and from the top I conversed with him, which is always a great pleasure, as he seems to me next to an angel.

Ventured to remind my poor William that it was our darling William's birthday, which cost him many tears. He also cried over our dear Harriet's profile—indeed, he is so weak that even a thought of *home* makes him shed tears.

How gracious is our *Lord* who strengthens my poor soul! *Consider*, my husband, who left *his* all to seek a milder climate, confined in this place of high and damped walls; exposed to cold and wind which penetrates to the very bones; without fire except the kitchen charcoal which oppresses his breast so much as to nearly convulse him. No little syrup, nor softener of the cough. Milk and bark, Iceland moss and opium pills (which he takes quietly as a duty, without seeming even to hope) is all I can offer him from day to day. When nature fails and I can no longer look up with cheerfulness, I hide my head on the chair by his bedside, and he thinks I am praying; and pray I do, for prayer is all my comfort—without it, I should be of little service to him. Night and day he calls me "*his life, his soul, his dearest, his all.*"

Our *Capitano* came this afternoon, and seeing poor William in a high fever, said:

"In this room what sufferings have I seen! *There* lay an Armenian, begging a knife to end the struggle of death. There, where the *Signora's* bed is, in the frenzy of fever, a Frenchman insisted on shooting himself, and died in agonies."

Little billets of paper pasted on the doors mark how many days different persons have stayed, and the shutter is all over notched—ten, twenty, thirty, forty days. I do not mark ours, trusting they are marked above. He only knows best. Dear, dear William, I can sometimes inspire him for a few minutes to feel that it would be sweet to die. He always says,

"My *Father* and my God, Thy will be done." . . .

Tuesday, 29th, Nov.— . . . After breakfast, read our Psalms and the 35th chapter of Isaiah to my W. with so much delight that it made us all merry. He read, at little Anne's request, the last chapter of Revelations, but the tones of his voice no heart can stand.

A storm of wind still, and very cold. William, with a blanket over his shoulder, creeps to the old man's fire. Ann jumps the rope, and *Maty* [herself] hops on one foot five or six times the length of the room without stopping—laugh at me, my sister, but it is very good exercise, and warms sooner than a fire when there is a warm heart to set it in motion.

Sung hymns, read promises to William shivering under the bedclothes;
and felt that God is with us, and that He is our All. The fever comes hot,
the bed shakes even with his breathing—my God, my Father!

St. Andrew's, 30th Nov., 1803.— . . . At William's bedside, we have
said our daily service; he thought it would stop his shiverings. My William's
soul is so humble, it will hardly embrace that faith, its only resource. At
any time, whom have me but our Redeemer? But when the spirit is on the
brink of departure, it must cling to Him with increased force, or where is it?
Dear William, it is not from the impulse of terror you turn to your God.
You tried and wished to serve Him long before this trial came. Why, then,
will you not consider Him as the Father Who knows all the different means
and dispositions of His children, and will graciously receive those who come
to Him by that way which He has appointed? You say your only hope is in
Christ; what other hope do we need? He says that the first effects he ever
felt from the calls of the Gospel, he experienced from our dear H(obart)'s
pressing the question in one of his sermons: "What avails gaining the whole
world and losing your own soul?" The reflections he made when he returned home were, "I toil and toil, and what is it? What I gain destroys
me daily, soul and body. I live without God in the world, and shall die
miserably." Mr. F.D., with whom he had not been in habits of business,
offered to join him in an adventure; it succeeded far beyond their expectations. Mr. F.D. said, when they wound it up: "One thing, you know, I have
been long in business—began with very little—have built a house and have
enough to build another. I have generally succeeded in my undertakings
and attribute all to this: that, whether they are great or small, I always ask
a blessing of God, and look to that blessing for success." William says, "I
was struck with shame and sorrow that I had been a heathen before God."
These he called his two warnings, which awakened his soul, and speaks of
them always with tears. Oh, the promises he makes, if it please God to spare
him!

2nd December.—Enjoyed the morn and daybreak. Read the commentary
on the 104th Psalm, and sung hymns in bed till ten. A hard frost in the
night. Endeavored to make a fire in my room with brush, but was smoked
out. . . . Patience! Anna sick; William tired out. . . .

Dec. 4th.— . . . Our *lazaretto* captain has sent us andirons, small wood,
etc., and I have decked the chimney with a curtain, so as to make the
smoke bearable. Have had an anxious day between father and Anne. She
was very ill for some hours. . . .

12 Dec.—A week has passed, my dear sister, without even one little
memorandum of the pen. The first day of it, that dear day in which I always

find my blessing, was passed in interrupted prayers, anxiety and watching. Monday, 5th, was early awakened by my poor William in great suffering. Sent for the Doctor Tutilli, who, as soon as he saw him, told him he was not wanted, but I must send for him who would minister to his soul. In this moment I stood alone as to this world. My William looked in silent agony at me, and I at him, each fearing to weaken the other's strength. At the moment, he drew himself towards me and said,

"I breathe out my soul with you."

The exertion he made assisted nature's remaining strength, and he threw a quantity from his lungs which had threatened to stop their motion, and so doing, experienced so great a revolution, that in a few hours afterwards, he seemed nearly the same as when first we entered the *lazaretto.*

Oh, that day! It was spent close by his bedside on my little mat. He slumbered the most of every hour. And did I not pray? and did I not praise? No inquiring visitor disturbed the solemn silence; no breakfast or dinner to interrupt the rest. Carleton came at sunset. Mrs. F(ilicchi), they thought, was dying; he thought his poor brother so. And then came our *Capitano* with so much offered kindness.

He was shocked at the tranquility of my poor William, and distressed at the thought that I was alone with him; for the doctor had told him that, notwithstanding his present relief, if the expectoration from the lungs did not return, he might be gone in a few hours. "Would I have some one in the room?" "Oh, no! What had I to fear?" And what *had* I to fear? I laid down as if to rest, that he might not be uneasy. Listened all night: sometimes by the fire, sometimes laying down, sometimes thought the breathing stopped, and sometimes alarmed by its heaviness, and kissed his poor face to feel if it was cold. Well, was I alone? Dear, indulgent *Father!* Could I be alone while clinging fast to Thee in continual prayer of thanksgiving . . .?

At daylight, the wished-for change took place. Mr. Hall [the Protestant minister in Leghorn] came in the morning with Mr. F(ilicchi) and the *Capitano*—went away with the promise to come again—and the intervening days and evenings have been spent in constant attention to the *main* concern. . . . Have . . . (when I could only keep awake by writing, according to the old custom) busied myself in writing the *first sermon* for my dear *little Dick.* William goes on *gently,* but keeps me busy. Anne is a treasure. She was reading yesterday that John was imprisoned.

"Yes, Papa, Herod imprisoned him, and Miss Herodias gave him liberty."

"No, my dear, she had him beheaded."

"Well, Papa, she released him from prison and sent him to God."

Child after my own heart!

Tuesday 13th.—Five days more, and our quarantine is ended. Lodgings are engaged at Pisa, on the borders of the Arno. My heart used to be very

full of poetical visions about this famous river, but it has no room for visions
now. One only vision is before it.

No one ever saw my William without giving him the quality of an
amiable man, but to see that character exalted to the peaceful, humble
Christian, waiting the Will of God with a patience that seems more than
human, and a firm faith which would do honor to the most distinguished
piety, is a happiness allowed only to the poor little mother who is separated
from all other happiness connected with this scene of things.

No sufferings, nor weakness, nor distress (and from these he is never free
in any degree) can prevent his following me daily in prayer, the Psalms and
generally large readings of the Scriptures. If he is a little better, he enlarges
his attention. If worse, he is more eager not to lose a moment; and, except
the day which we thought his last, he has never failed one day in this course
since our entrance in these stone walls, the 19th [of] November.

He very often says *this* is the period of his life which, if he lives or dies,
he will always consider as blessed, the only time which he has not lost.

Not the smallest murmur—"oh!" and lifting up of the eyes, is the strongest expression I have yet heard from him in the rapid progress of his complaint, which has reduced him almost to nothing, and from its nature
gives him no release from irritation in violent coughing, chills, oppressions,
weakness. . . . [He] often talks of his darlings, but most, of meeting, one
family, in heaven. . . .

When I thank God for my creation and preservation, it is with a warmth
of feeling I never could know until now: to wait on *Him* in my William's
soul and body; to console and soothe those hours of affliction and pain,
watching and weariness which, next to God, I alone could do, to strike up
the cheerful notes of hope and Christian triumph, which from his partial
love he hears with the more enjoyment from me, because to me he attributes
the greatest share of them; to hear him, in pronouncing the name of his
Redeemer, declare that I first taught him the sweetness of the sound—
oh, if I was in the dungeon of this *lazaretto*, I should bless and praise my
God for these days of retirement and abstraction from the world, which
have afforded leisure and opportunity for so blessed a work.

14th Dec.—Said my dear prayers alone while William was asleep. Did
not dare to remind him of them, for weakness and pain quite overpower
him. Rain and storm, as indeed we have had almost every day of the
twenty-six we have been here.

The dampness about us would be thought dangerous for a person in
health—and my William's sufferings—oh! well I know that God is *above*,
Capitano, you need not always point your silent look and finger there; if I
thought our condition the providence of *man*, instead of the "*weeping
Magdalen*"—as you so graciously call me—you would find me a lioness, will-

ing to burn your *lazaretto* about your ears, if it was possible, that I might carry off my poor prisoner to breathe the air of heaven in some more seasonable place. To keep a poor soul who comes to your country for his life, thirty days shut up in damp walls, smoke and wind from all corners, blowing even the curtain round his bed (and his bones almost through) and now the shadow of death, trembling if he only stands a few minutes! He is to go to Pisa for his health—this day his prospects are very far from Pisa—but oh, my heavenly Father! I know that these contradictory events are permitted and guided by Thy Wisdom, which only is *light.* . . .

Thursday.— . . . William says he feels like a person brought to the light after many years of darkness, when he heard the Scriptures as the law of God and, therefore, sacred, but not discerning what part he had in them or feeling that they were the fountain of *eternal life.*

Friday night.—A heavy day. Part of our *service together*, part alone. They have bolted us in tonight, expecting to find my William gone tomorrow. But he rests quietly, and God is with us.

Saturday and Sunday.—Melancholy days of combat with nature's weakness; and the courage of hope which pictured our removal from the *lazaretto* to Pisa.

The courage and the hope were rewarded. December 19 was the day of release, and Will was still alive. Betty rose at daybreak and made all ready for their return to the world. At eleven, the bolts were drawn and the Setons were free.

Two men made a seat with their crossed hands, and thus carried Will to the Filicchi coach. He held tight to Betty's hand for strength and life as the little group made its way through the knot of onlookers clucking their sympathy and murmuring "Poverino!" Betty was in an agony of apprehension, but she had not counted on the softness of the Italian air; despite the fact that it was December, it was much warmer and milder than it had been in the cold, damp *lazaretto*.

The road to Pisa was heavy with mud from the rains, but despite the jolting of the carriage, Will picked up noticeably during the fifteen-mile journey, looking about him fondly at the ancient yellow earth and the exquisite slender cypresses. Their spirits caught a mellowness from the soft gray and golden brown of the houses and *palazzi*, from the wonder of the Leaning Tower, as they entered the old town and wheeled over the narrow cobbled streets and across the stone bridges spanning the canals and the storied Arno—hardly, in its dark muddiness, the romantic river of Betty's dreams.

The Filicchis had engaged lodgings for them in a fashionable old house conducted by Madame De Tot on the bank of the Arno. Close by was the medieval Chapel of the Thorn, built to house one of the sacred relics of Christ's passion and a favorite stopping place for Pisan sailors on their way to sea. The house was exactly what Will loved—rich, elegant, tasteful—and he enjoyed that day and the next, talking about his life, home and the children, the joys of eternity. Carleton, who was to stay with his sister and brother-in-law four days, rounded out the happiness of the little group, giving Will the news of Leghorn, and catching up on the happenings of New York since he had left it five years before.

The happiness was a last, gracious favor from God. On the night of the twentieth, Betty had scarcely fixed her pillow for the night, when Will called to her urgently. His last agony had begun.

There was a decided change in him the next day. A heavy languor oppressed his mind and body—but the Seton stubbornness was not dead. He got it into his head that he would go for a ride in the carriage, and nothing would dissuade him, even though the physician, a Dr. Cartelach, whispered to Betty that the attempt might kill him. He was "carried down in a chair; and, supported in my trembling arms with pillows, we rode. Oh, my Father, well did You strengthen me in that hour! In five minutes we were forced to return; and to get him out of the coach and in the chair up the stairs and on the bed—words can never tell—"

Two days later, Will was so much better that he insisted on trying the carriage again. This time he was equal to it, and so enjoyed seeing the remembered sights of former years that Betty, in bewilderment, almost concluded that riding was good for him.

But the next day, Christmas Eve, told the tale. Will sank so rapidly that he felt he could not last till morning. Nevertheless, he was cheerful, and spoke lovingly of the children and of the goodness of God in giving him time to reflect. A little laudanum helped him sleep until midnight. When he awoke, he expressed concern that Betty had taken no rest.

"No, love," she answered, "for the sweetest reflections keep me awake.

Christmas day is began. The day of Our dear Redeemer's birth here, you know, is the day that opened to us the door of everlasting life."

"Yes," he said, "and how I wish we could have the sacrament!"

"Well, we must do all we can."

Betty put a little wine in a glass and "said different parts of Psalms and prayers which I had marked, hoping for a happy moment; and we took the cup of Thanksgiving, setting aside the sorrow of time in the view of eternity." Resourceful woman!

Will, too, had his resourcefulness. Captain O'Brien paid him a visit that Christmas Day, and Will took the opportunity to place Betty in his charge that he might see her home safely. He did it with such serenity and such calm that her blood ran cold as the finality of the act came home to her. He was completely resigned now, and even eager to die:

Monday.—Was so impatient to be gone that I could scarcely persuade him to wet his lips, but continued calling his Redeemer to pardon and release him. As he always would have his door shut, I had no interruption. Carleton kept Anna out of the way; and every promise in the Scriptures and prayer I could remember I continually repeated to him, which seemed to be his only relief. When I stopped to give him anything:

"Why do you do it? What do I want? I want to be in heaven. Pray, pray for my soul."

He said he felt so comfortable an assurance that his Redeemer would receive him that he saw his dear little Tat [Rebecca] smiling before him; and told Anna:

"Oh, if your father could take you with him!"

And, at midnight, when the cold sweat came on, [he] would reach out both his arms, and said repeatedly.

"You promised me you would go. Come, come, fly!"

At four, the hard struggle ceased. Nature sank into a settled sob:

"My dear wife—and little ones"—"My Christ Jesus, have mercy and receive me," was all I could distinguish; and again, repeated, "My Christ Jesus," until a quarter past seven, when the dear soul took its flight to the Blessed Exchange it so much longed for.

I often asked him, when he could not speak,

"You feel, my love, that you are going to your Redeemer?" and he motioned "yes" with a look of peace. At a quarter past seven on Tuesday morning, 27th December, his soul was released—and mine from a struggle next to death.

Though the struggle was over, she could not yet rest, despite the fact that she had not slept for a week and had had but one meal since the day before. By Tuscan law the dead had to be buried within twenty-four hours, since there were no methods of preserving corpses. However, if Will's body could be gotten to the Protestant cemetery at Leghorn and placed in the charnel house there before sunset, the technicality of the law would be covered and the burial could be deferred until a reasonable hour next morning. In the meantime, much had to be done; and, as the household was in mortal terror of catching what Will had died of, Betty had to do it alone. At the last moment, two women of courage came forward and, with their assistance, she washed Will's corpse and prepared it for burial. "Oh! Oh! Oh! what a day," she exclaimed to Rebecca. "Close his eyes, lay him out, ride a journey, be obliged to see a dozen people in my room till night—and at night crowded with the whole sense of my situation."

At eleven o'clock on the morning of December 28, Betty and Anna, accompanied by the Filicchis and all the English and American colony of Leghorn, stood in the lovely little English cemetery while Mr. Thomas Hall read the Episcopalian burial service, and Will—just thirty-five—was lowered into the earth.

A flat marble slab—cracked in several places by the merciless bombings of World War II—marks his resting place. The epitaph reads simply: "Here lies the remains of William Magee Seton, Merchant of New York, who departed this life at Pisa, the 27th day of December, 1803."

XI

Leghorn and Florence

A part of Betty's life was over, over with such finality that she would never again be able to take it up. It was not just that Will was gone; her whole way of life was gone. While he lived, there was always the chance that he might somehow restore his family to its place in affluent society. That this was ever in his mind is evident from the fixation he had on his deathbed that a London lottery ticket taken out in Betty's name had won the grand prize, and that he had received word from his brother James to the effect that all his bills were paid. Neither was true; but Betty wisely did not contradict him, that he might die in peace.

Even Betty did not realize the change that had set in, for she could not know, on that sad last Wednesday of December, what the Providence of God had in store for her over the next few months: if lack of money and a husband to earn it would alter her pattern of living, a change of religious belief would destroy it entirely.

As she rode the short distance from the cemetery to the Filicchi palace, her "poor, high heart was in the clouds, roving after my William's soul and repeating: 'My God, you are my God; and so I am now alone in the world with You and my little ones. But you are my Father, and doubly theirs.'" Although surrounded by every anxious kindness, she longed to be alone; and, after she had received the sympathy calls of Mr. Hall and her *Capitano*—ever the comic opera character "with a black crape on the hat and arm, and such a look of sorrow"—Betty closed the door of her room and cried her heart out.

It was the house of Antonio Filicchi that gave Elizabeth hospitality. Antonio was the younger of two remarkable brothers. He was thirty-nine years old when Elizabeth first knew him, having been born in Gubbio on August 22, 1764. His culture was equal to his noble birth, and his piety equal to both. After elementary education in Gubbio, he had studied philosophy at Pisa and law at Rome, finishing with a doctorate in both civil and canon jurisprudence. He had stayed on in Rome for a time, practicing law with Monsignor (later Cardinal) Riganti, before joining his brother Filippo in the import-export business at Leghorn. In 1794, he married Amabilia Baragazzi, whom he loved tenderly and called fondly his "piccinina"—"little one"—and who bore him seven children. His high birth, wealth and legal knowledge made him of service to his country; and he went on official missions for the Grand Duke of Tuscany to Milan in 1798, and to Paris in 1812. He received numerous civil decorations and, at his death in 1847, was a Cavalier of St. Stephen and a Patrician of Gubbio.

Filippo Filicchi was a year older than his brother. He went into the commission business early in life, but the fact does not argue a lack of education, for he was versed in Latin, Spanish, English and French. He spent the years 1785–1786 in the United States, establishing business contacts and meeting the leading men of the day: Washington, Jefferson, Madison, John Adams and Bishop Carroll. He was in America again in 1787–1788; and it was through his friendship with William Seton Sr., that young William Magee Seton returned with him to Italy in 1788. Filippo was back in the United States the following year to marry Mary Cowper of Boston. President Washington named him American Consul General at Leghorn on December 10, 1794, and he held the post until November, 1798. He died in 1816.

The goodness of these two men and their families was so extraordinary that even eight-year-old Anna perceived it. "Oh, Mama," she exclaimed, "how many friends God has provided for us in this strange land! for they are our friends before they know us." Antonio laid his heart on his sleeve at once. "Your dear William was the early friend of my youth," he told Elizabeth. "You are now come in his room."

It must be understood from the first that this friendship of the Filicchis was not based alone upon kindness and pity, but upon the qualities of heart and soul they found in the widow of William Seton. It speaks volumes for the force of her personality—compounded as it was of charity, kindness, patience and long-suffering, plus a natural common sense, wit and breeding—that she captivated everyone she met. The O'Briens, the ship's steward, the common seamen, the *Capitano*, the Filicchis—husbands and wives and children—all fell under her spell. She received exceptional treatment and deference from all because she was an exceptional person. It was the fame of her heroism in the *lazaretto* spread abroad in the town that brought the citizens of Leghorn to see her depart with her dying husband, before they had even seen her face. It was her astonishing courage and capability throughout William's last agony and death that caused the neighbors of Pisa to declare that "if she was not a heretic, she would be a saint."

Antonio and Filippo Filicchi were especially struck by the beauty of her soul. She was, indeed, a beautiful woman; and they were men: but there is an inner beauty that pales and dominates the physical beauty of form and figure—"the beauty of the King's daughter is from within" —and it was this spiritual loveliness that captured their hearts, especially the heart of Antonio. Whoever does not grasp this essential fact will sadly misconstrue the warm and affectionate friendship that quickly developed between Antonio and Elizabeth. Theirs was truly a friendship founded on the rock of religion and growing in religious strength through the years. Proof is in Antonio's eager campaign—begun scarcely a day after Will's burial—to bring Elizabeth's promising holiness within the pale of the true Faith. On January 3, 1804, she was already writing to Rebecca:

> I am hard pushed by these charitable Romans, who wish that so much goodness should be improved by conversion, which to effect they have even taken the trouble to bring me their best-informed priest, Abbé Plunkett, who is an Irishman; but they find me so willing to hear their enlightened conversation that, consequently—as learned people like to hear themselves

best—I have little to say; and as yet keep friends with all as the best comment on my profession.

Despite her lightness of tone, it is significant that she listened and was not offended—and Hobart had warned her of "the splendid and sumptuous worship of Italy." It is significant, too, that the Filicchis were well-bred people, who would not have harassed a guest in Elizabeth's sorrowful plight with rude and unwanted proselytizing. Yet, on January 9, Antonio was writing to her, at Florence, the following warm and courteous letter:

> Pardon me, my beloved sister, virtuous friend and companion of the worthy friend who is now, I hope, in heaven, if I trouble you with these few lines. In your absence I seek for alleviation to my afflicted feelings, and I expect indulgence from your goodness. I did desire your Carleton to remember me warmly to you in the enclosed letter of his; but the sweet idea of receiving and possessing a direct answer with your name under it, encouraged me to a direct application.
>
> Your dear William was the early friend of my youth. You are now come in his room. Your soul is even dearer to Antonio, and will be so forever. May the good Almighty God enlighten your mind and strengthen your heart to see and follow in religion the surest, true way to the eternal blessings. I shall call for you, I must meet you, in Paradise, if it is decreed that the vast plains of the ocean shall soon be betwixt us.
>
> Don't discontinue, meanwhile, to pray, to knock at the door. I am confident that Our Redeemer will not be deaf to the humble prayers of so dear a creature. My Piccinina Amabilia will join her hands most happily; and if your little lovely Ann will promise not to be any more angry with me, my innocent Patrick will pray also for her. Your most affectionate and respectful friend, brother and servant,
>
> Antonio Filicchi

Special note should be made of the language of this first letter written by Antonio Filicchi to a woman who, but a few days before, was a stranger: it is every bit as ardent and forthright as any in the long years of their correspondence. That it was concerned with the spiritual cannot be denied. It is a rare exposition of the text: "The truth shall make you free." There can be no constraint in the things of the spirit.

In considering Elizabeth's reaction to the immediate attempts to convert her, it must be allowed that her natural courtesy would incline her to give kind hosts, whom she expected to leave very shortly, a hearing; but it must also be allowed that the sensitive spirituality of Antonio had discovered in her a soul that would respond swiftly to the truth. Thus was born the extraordinary holy friendship that Bishop, later Cardinal Giuseppe Pecci of Gubbio was to liken to the bond that united St. Francis de Sales and St. Jane Frances de Chantal.

When the first wave of her grief had passed, Elizabeth sat down to write a string of letters—to Rebecca, to Mary Post, to Eliza Sadler, her uncle John Charlton and John Wilkes—telling them the sad news. She asked Rebecca to get in touch with the rest, especially Henry Hobart, her brother Barclay, Joseph Bayley, Aunt Farquhar and the Seton girls.

The Filicchis were anxious to distract her from thoughts of the terrible days past, and Amabilia took her and Anna on a visit to Florence. She could have had little heart for sightseeing at such a time, but once in Florence, that loveliest of cities caught her up in its enchantment. Instinctively, she recognized the exquisite churches as the soul of its charm. No dint of modern dress or modern buildings can destroy the medieval joyousness of Florence; nowhere in the world could Elizabeth Seton have been better introduced to what the Catholic soul can achieve.

Ironically enough, the first Catholic Church that she ever in her life mentioned entering was *La Santissima Annunziata*, the most Italian and the least Florentine in the city. Here indeed was the sumptuousness Henry Hobart had warned her against. But she liked it:

> Passing through a curtain, my eye was struck with hundreds of persons kneeling; but the gloom of the chapel, which is lighted only by the wax tapers on the altar and a small window at the top darkened with green silk, made every object at first appear very indistinct, while that kind of soft and distant music which lifts the mind to a foretaste of heavenly pleasures called up in an instant every dear and tender idea of my soul; and forgetting Mrs. F., companions, and all the surrounding scene, I sank on my knees in the first place I found vacant, and shed a torrent of tears at the recollection of how long I had been a stranger in the house of my God, and the accumulated sorrow that had separated me from it. I need not tell you that I said our dear service with my whole soul, as far as in its agitation I could recollect.
>
> When the organ ceased, and Mass was over, we walked round the chapel. The elegance of ceilings in carved gold, altars loaded with gold, silver and other precious ornaments, pictures of every sacred subject, and the dome a continued representation of different parts of Scripture—all this can never be conceived by description; nor my delight in seeing old men and women,

young women and all sorts of people kneeling promiscuously about the altar, as inattentive to us and other passengers as if we were not there.

It is a strange fact that she, who had been used to the bare and elegant simplicity of Trinity Church and St. Paul's, was most drawn to the splendid in church architecture. The classic, muted glories of *S. Maria Novella, S. Firenze* and the interior of the *Duomo*, she more or less passed over. But the grandeur of *S. Lorenzo* and the Medici Chapel struck her with the same force as the *Annunziata*. Coupled with her irritation at the golden singing of the famous tenor, Davide, at the opera, it leads one to suspect that her taste was that of the ordinary person rather than of the artist. In fact, after summing up the treasures of the Pitti palace as forming "a pattern of elegance and taste," she added: "So say the connoisseurs. For me, I am no judge, as Ombrosi says." It is a curious and unexpected lack in an otherwise refined and sensitive mind.

She wrote of *S. Lorenzo:*

A sensation of delight struck me so forcibly that as I approached the great altar, formed all of the most precious stones and marbles that could be produced, 'My soul doth magnify the Lord, my spirit rejoices in God my Savior,' came in my mind with a fervor which absorbed every other feeling. It recalled the ideas of the offerings of David and Solomon to the Lord, when the rich and valuable productions of nature and art were devoted to His holy temple and sanctified to His service.

Annexed to this is the chapel of marble, the beauty and work and richness of which might be supposed the production of more than mortal means, if its unfinished dome did not discover its imperfection. It is the tomb of the Medici family. Monuments of granite, lapis, golden crowns set with precious stones, the polish of the whole which reflects the different monuments as a mirror, and the awful black Cosmo's who are represented on the top of the monuments as large as life, with their crowns and sceptres, made my poor weak head turn and, I believe, if it had been possible that I should have been alone there, it would never have turned back again.

Everywhere she went, though distracted from her loss, she could not forget it, or her children so far away. The vistas of the Boboli gardens reminded her of advanced spring in New York, and she thought of her dear ones there, and had to close her eyes and feign sleep to keep back the tears. The memory of Will was a constant ache within her, for on the long voyage he had described ecstatically the wonderful things they would see together—and now she was seeing them alone. She had gone to hear Giacamo Davide only because Will had been so anxious she should; and it is touching that, because Will had wanted to take her, she tried to be pleased, but could not. She wrote of her visit to the Uffizi gallery:

> As my curiosity had been greatly excited by my Seton's descriptions, and the French having made great depradations, it did not equal my expectations. The *chef-d'oeuvre* of D. [Donatello?], a head scarcely to be distinguished from life, the Redeemer about twelve years of age—a Madonna . . . Madam LeBrun, a French painter, and the Baptist very young, were those that attracted me most. The statues in bronze were beautiful, but [I], being only an American, could not look very straight at them. . . . The sacred representations were sufficient to engage and interest all my attention and, as the French had not been covetous of those, I had the advantage of my companions—but felt the void of him who would have pointed out the beauties of every object too much to enjoy any perfectly—*"alone but half enjoyed."*

It is a delight to come upon her shrewd recognition of American puritanism in her comment on the statues of the Uffizi, and her sensible attempt to reject prudery. She found the same reaction in herself at the Museum of Physical and Natural History, or *Specola:*

> This morning I have indeed enjoyed, in the anatomical museum and cabinet of natural history. The "work of the Almighty hand" in every object—the anatomical rooms displaying nature in every division of the human frame—is almost too much for human nature to support. Mine shrank from it; but, recalling the idea of my God in all I saw, though so humiliating and painful in the view, still it was congenial to every feeling of my soul. . . . If I was allowed to choose an enjoyment from the whole theatre of human nature, it would be to go over those two hours again with my dear Brother Post [as] my companion.

It was understandable that Elizabeth should be taken with a painting of the Descent from the Cross—which Monsignor Bardi, a native of the region, identifies as one in the Church of *S. Maria Novella.*

> A picture of the Descent from the Cross, nearly as large as life, engaged my whole soul—Mary at the foot of it expressed well that the iron had entered into hers, and the shades of death over her agonized countenance so strongly contrasted the heavenly peace of the dear Redeemer that it

seems as if His pains had fallen on her. How hard it was to leave that picture, and how often, even in the few hours' interval since I have seen it, I shut my eyes and recall it in imagination!

When Elizabeth and Anna were alone, they needed no longer pretend. On the evening of January 8, she wrote:

> When we said our dear service together, she [Anna] burst into tears, as she has always done since we say it alone. She says, "My dear Papa is praising God in heaven, and I ought not to cry for him, but I believe it is human nature, is it not, Mamma?"
>
> I think of what David said: "I shall go to him, he cannot return to me." Her conversation is dearer to me, and preferable to any I can have this side of the grave. It is one of the greatest mercies that I was permitted to bring her, for many reasons.

Elizabeth had many things on her mind, especially concerning her children and their future. Apparently she had not heard from home, and, therefore, did not know that Rebecca Seton had suffered another serious attack but had recovered; nor that her own little Rebecca was completely well again. The baby especially preyed on her mind, because Will, in his last agony, had thought he saw the child waiting for him in paradise; and she asked Rebecca: "Is she, too, in heaven? Thy Will be done. How do I know how many are gone? Thy Will be done. It is my Father's."

The tension building inside her increased when she returned to Leghorn and discovered that Captain O'Brien was not prepared to sail at the end of January, and that there would be a month's delay.

The Catholic churches of Florence, with their almost sensible suggestion of a Presence, had taken hold of Elizabeth, despite her continued air of superior amusement at the efforts of the Filicchis to convert her. In a later letter to Rebecca, she was to express her delight in the simple fact that the churches were always open:

> How often you and I used to give the sigh, and you would press your arm in mine of a Sunday evening and say, "No more until next Sunday," as we turned from the church door which closed on us (unless a prayer day was given out in the week). Well, here they go to church at four every morning, if they please. And you know how we were laughed at for running from one church to the other, *Sacrament Sundays*, that we might receive

as often as we could. Well, here people that love God and live a good, regular life, can go (though many do not [do] it), yet they can go every day.

When Amabilia told her, at Mass on Candlemas Day, that Christ was really present on the altar, she put her face in her hands and cried. This was the way to her soul—her hunger for the Bread of Life; and it led directly to her conversion.

Filippo was a graver man than his ardent brother, and he challenged her squarely on her obligation to seek the truth he had begun to unfold to her.

"Oh, my, sir," she asked him, rather archly, "if there is but one Faith, and nobody pleases God without it, where are all the good people who die out of it?"

Matter-of-factly he answered: "I don't know. That depends on what light of Faith they had received. But I know where people go who can know the right Faith if they pray for it and inquire for it, and yet do neither."

"Much as to say, sir, you want me to pray and inquire, and be of your Faith?" she pressed, still smiling.

"Pray and inquire, that is all I ask you," was the unmoving reply.

She did not brush aside his warning, for she wrote Rebecca:

So, dearest Bec, I am laughing with God when I try to be serious and say daily, as the good gentleman told me, in old Mr. Pope's words: *"If I am right, O teach my heart still in the right to stay; if I am wrong, Thy grace impart to find the better way."* Not that I can think there is a better way than I know—but every one must be respected in their own.

She was not to laugh long.

The new sailing date gave some weeks of leisure for a return visit with Amabilia to Florence. They came back to Leghorn in time for Elizabeth to accompany the Filicchi family on a pilgrimage to the shrine of *La Madonna del Grazie* on Montenero. This shrine, the most famous in Tuscany, held a special place in the affection of the Filicchis, for their family had long been among its most fervent clients and choicest benefactors; and a few years before, in the time of the Directory, the Vallombrosian monks who were its guardians had hidden Filippo there from the French. The monastery was old, dating from the fourteenth century, and some of its buildings were spectacularly carved out of the volcanic rock of the mountainside. After a long, almost perpendicular ascent, pilgrims were rewarded in the temporal sphere with a breathtaking panorama of the Port of Leghorn, the wide blue reaches of the Mediterranean and the distant, snow-crowned Alps.

Elizabeth and her friends attended Mass in the monastery church, where the gem-encrusted picture of the Virgin was enshrined above the high altar. According to pious tradition, this painting of the Mother and Child, dishonored and despoiled of its ornaments in its former sanctuary on the Grecian isle of Negroponte, was miraculously transported to Tuscany, where a poor shepherd found it and, by the Virgin's command, brought it to Montenero. During the Mass, at the sacred moment of elevation, a young English tourist leaned toward Elizabeth, and said in a loud, rude whisper: "This is what they call their *Real Presence*."

Elizabeth was shocked; but her shock was a grace from God, opening the floodgates of her soul and forcing her to look at doubts and questions she had scarcely known were there:

> My very heart trembled with shame and sorrow for his unfeeling interruption of their sacred adoration; for all around was dead silence, and many were prostrated. Involuntarily I bent from him to the pavement, and thought secretly on the word of St. Paul, with starting tears, "They discern not the Lord's Body"; and the next thought was, how should they eat and drink their very damnation for not *discerning* it, if indeed it is not *there*? Yet how should it be *there*? And how did *He* breathe my soul in me? And how, and how a hundred other things I know nothing about?
>
> I am a *mother*, so the mother's thought came also. How was my God a little babe in the first stage of His mortal existence *in Mary*? But I lost these thoughts in my babes at home, which I daily long for more and more.

On February 18, 1804, the mother and daughter were on board the *Shepherdess* in the care of Captain O'Brien. The Filicchis had seen them off with gifts, and all the money and passports and letters of recommendation they would need for any emergency of the voyage. They were not yet out of the harbor when a sudden storm in the night dashed the *Shepherdess* against another ship, and the Captain was obliged to put back to the wharf for repairs.

Shaken by the experience and by disappointment, little Anna broke down and confessed to her mother that she was ill. She was ill indeed; and Elizabeth's heart sank as she noted the child's burning cheeks and dull eyes, and the telltale rash on her body. Dr. Tutilli pronounced it scarlet fever, and warned that she must not be allowed to sail at the risk of her life. Elizabeth, in her discouragement and desire to get home, would have taken the risk, trusting to the mercy of God; but the Captain would not let them aboard, because of the delay it would cause him in the quarantine station at Barcelona. Elizabeth had no course but to give way; yet she could not hide her despondency from Rebecca: "the hand of God is all I must see . . . but it pinches the soul."

There were times during the next three weeks when she thought Anna must die, but the child came safely through. Then Elizabeth herself came down with the disease. The tenderness of the Filicchis during this new trial undoubtedly softened Elizabeth's heart toward Catholicism, as the love of the early Christians for one another softened the harder hearts of the pagan Romans. "Oh, my! the patience and more than human kindness of these dear Filicchis for us!" she exclaimed. "You would say it was Our Savior Himself they received in His poor and sick strangers."

Certainly, the added weeks allowed the essential element of time for reflection on truths which had found tenuous root in her heart; and more and more her defenses crumbled. She was too honest to turn away long from overwhelming evidence and conviction; and, characteristically, she immediately put down her new religious experiences for Rebecca, that this dear disciple, this "Soul's Sister," might ponder them, too.

How happy would we be, if we believed what these dear souls believe: that they *possess* God in the Sacrament, and that He remains in their churches and is carried to them when they are sick! Oh, my! when they carry the Blessed Sacrament under my window, while I feel the full loneliness and sadness of my case, I cannot stop the tears at the thought: My God! how happy would I be, even so far away from all so dear, if I could find You in the church as they do (for there is a chapel in the very house of Mr. F.) how many things I would say to You of the sorrows of my heart and the sins of my life!

The other day, in a moment of excessive distress, I fell on my knees without thinking when the Blessed Sacrament passed by, and cried in an agony to God *to bless me*, if He was *there*—that my whole soul desired only Him.

A little prayer-book of Mrs. F.'s was on the table, and I opened a little prayer of St. Bernard to the Blessed Virgin, begging her to be our *Mother;* and I said to her, with such a certainty that God would surely refuse nothing to *His Mother,* and that she could not help loving and pitying the poor souls He died for, that I felt really I had a Mother—which you know my foolish heart so often lamented to have lost in early days.

From the first remembrance of infancy, I have looked, in all the plays of childhood and wildness of youth, to the clouds for my mother; and at that moment it seemed as if I had found more than her, even in tenderness and pity of a mother. So I cried myself to sleep on her heart.

She was greatly stirred and astonished at how sincerely her Catholic friends practiced what they preached. Through them, for example, she learned the lesson of the cross and the significance of suffering.

This evening, standing by the window, the moon shining full on Filicchi's countenance, he raised his eyes to heaven and showed me how to make the sign of the cross. Dearest Rebecca, I was cold with the awful impression my first making it gave me. The sign of the cross of Christ on me! Deepest thoughts came with it of I know not what earnest desires to be closely united with Him who died on it. . . .

Why, Rebecca, they believe all we do and suffer—if we offer it for our sins—serves to expiate them. You may remember when I asked Mr. H[obart] what was meant by fasting in our prayer book—as I found myself on Ash Wednesday morning saying so foolishly to God, "I turn to you in fasting, weeping, and mourning," and I had come to church with a hearty breakfast of buckwheat cakes and coffee, and full of life and spirits, with little thought of my sins—you may remember what he said about its being old *customs,* etc. Well, the dear Mrs. F., who I am with, never eats, this season of Lent, till after the clock strikes three. Then the family assembles. And she says she offers her weakness and pain of fasting for her sins, united with Our Savior's sufferings. I like that very much.

God leaves nothing to chance, and His plans for Elizabeth Seton were becoming clearer every day. She was a good Protestant when she came to Italy, but it seems evident, from her instinctive reaching out toward the symbols and doctrines of the Catholic Church, that she was also *anima naturaliter Catholica*—a soul naturally Catholic. Thus it is interesting to see how she was drawn to the Catholic practices of daily Mass, of visits to the Blessed Sacrament, of fasting and of making the sign of the cross. It is interesting to note her reaction to the cynical un-

Photos by The Lane Studio, Gettysburg, Pa.

Mr. and Mrs. Antonio Filicchi, close friends of Mrs. Seton, who were instrumental in her conversion. From sketches in the possession of the Filicchi family. *Below:* Antonio Filicchi at a later period.

Filippo Filicchi.

Palazzo Filicchi, home of Antonio Filicchi in Leghorn, where Mrs. Seton stayed. It is now a school for girls, conducted by the Venerini Sisters.

View of Leghorn and surrounding country, as seen from Montenero.

Left: Shrine of the *Madonna del Grazie* at Montenero.

Right: High altar in the Medici Chapel, Florence, which particularly impressed Mrs. Seton.

St. Catherine's Church, Leghorn, where Mrs. Seton attended her last Mass before sailing to America.

The high altar of St. Catherine's.

belief of her co-religionist in the church of Montenero: "Involuntarily I bent from him to the pavement"—the attitude of adoration; and her reaction at the window of the Filicchi palace: "I fell on my knees, without thinking, when the Blessed Sacrament passed by." It is particularly interesting, in the light of her role in the history of the Catholic Church in America, that her soul responded from the beginning to the doctrines of the Real Presence and the universal Motherhood of Mary—doctrines that are the keystones of American Catholic devotion.

It might also be said that, having made tentative gestures toward these, she could not turn back. She had, in a way, committed herself— even though she had yet to pass through a sort of "dark night of the soul" before the final submission, as she was prepared for the consideration of these doctrines by a sort of "dark night of the senses" in the *lazaretto*.

At any rate, when the time arrived at last to take passage for America on April 8, Elizabeth had come to some kind of terms with the truth. During the long weeks of Anna's and her own illnesses, Filippo and Antonio had swept aside her prejudices and instructed her anew by means of books and earnest conversation. She read Francis de Sales' *Introduction to a Devout Life*, a polemical work called *Unerring Authority of the Catholic Church*, Bossuet's *Exposition of the Catholic Doctrine*, and an orderly marshalling of proofs of the Church's divinity written out in Filippo's hand and prepared with the assistance of his friend Father Pecci. This manuscript was especially telling, since it made many of its points from the Bible and from the Episcopalians' own *Book of Common Prayer*.

Elizabeth's exact position regarding Catholicism when she left Italy is hard to establish, since we must depend entirely on her writings; and words, like statistics, have a knack for meaning whatever their interpreter wants them to mean. It is certain that she went through no formal ceremony of abjuration or reception into the Church at this time. Some biographers have assumed that it was merely a question of there being no time for this; but to take such a stand is to cast in a bad light her year of hesitation in New York. Elizabeth Seton was too honest not to embrace the Faith as soon as she *believed*: and there can be no doubt about the sincerity of her confusion after her return to America. It seems safer to state that she was *intellectually convinced*, and seeking the gift of Faith when she sailed from Italy. The distinction is difficult for those raised in the Faith from infancy; but Faith is a gift to be bestowed by God, and He bestows it at His own good pleasure. Aside from the theology of the question, there are many examples—notably that of Cardinal Newman, who had to wait for years after he was convinced of the Catholic position to say *I believe.*

There is an abundance of evidence that Elizabeth was convinced at this time. Thus she wrote of Filippo: "Oh, Filicchi, you shall not *witness against me.* May God bless you forever, and may you shine as the "stars of glory" for what you have done for me!" The reference to the Book of Daniel, Chapter XII, Verse 3, is unmistakable: "They that instruct many to justice (shall shine) as stars for all eternity." She penned a note of gratitude to God: "I must always love to retrospect Thy wonderful dispensations: to be sent so many thousands of miles on so hopeless an errand; to be constantly supported and accompanied by Thy consoling mercy through scenes of trial which nature alone must have sunk under; to be brought to the light of Thy truth, notwithstanding every affection of my heart and power of my will was opposed to it."

That Elizabeth was yearning for what the Faith would bring her is evident from her reflections on her last Mass in Leghorn:

> Oh, my soul, how solemn was that offering! For a blessing on our voyage, for my dear ones, my sisters and all so dear to me—and, more than all, for the souls of my dear husband and father—earnestly our desires ascended with the blessed sacrifice, that they might find acceptance through Him who gave Himself for us. Earnestly we desired to be united with Him, and would gladly encounter all the sorrows before us, to be partakers of that blessed Body and Blood. Oh, my God, spare and pity me.

Positive indication that she did not yet have what she yearned for seems to be apparent in a further sentence in which she dwells upon the sacred parting of Antonio and Amabilia:

> My Savior! My God! Antonio and his wife—their separation in God and Communion! Poor I, *not.* But did I not beg Him to give me their Faith, and promise Him *all* in return for such a gift? Little Ann and I had only strange tears of joy and grief.

Anna, young as she was, had taken on her mother's new habit of soul, and pestered her with eager questions: "Ma, is there no Catholics in America? Ma, won't we go to the Catholic Church when we go home?"

There is a curious entry in Elizabeth's *Dear Remembrances* about her last morning in Leghorn: ". . . kneeling in a little confessional perceived not the ear was waiting for me, 'till the friar came out to ask Mrs. F[ilicchi] 'why I did not begin.' " That there can be no question here of a regular confession is evident from the fact that she was not received into the Catholic Church until the following year; and something that she wrote to Amabilia on that occasion merely emphasizes it. "So delighted now to prepare for this good confession,"—she recorded on March 14, 1805—"which, bad as I am, I would be ready to make on the housetop, to insure the good *absolution* I hope for after it. And then to set out on a new life, a new existence itself."

On April 8, 1804, at Leghorn, she could only have wanted to open her heart to the Dominican priest or seek his advice.

The opportunity for New York came by means of Captain John Blagge and his ship, the *Pyamingo*. The Filicchis immediately considered the personal dangers of the voyage, apart from the dangers that attended any voyage of the times. Blagge was a young man of whom they knew nothing, and Elizabeth was a beautiful young widow. From the first it was evident that she could not go alone. There is some indication that Amabilia herself first suggested that Antonio make the trip with Elizabeth, but the final decision was a family decision: their business interests in America and Canada would be served, Elizabeth and Anna protected, and the good work begun in Elizabeth's soul finished in the weeks of passage. Apparently, Filippo could not see his way clear to go, and so the choice fell upon Antonio.

Elizabeth did not have to busy herself with a multitude of preparations: she had been ready for months. She had only to make her farewells to Will, and went alone, for the purpose, to his grave. She "wept plentifully over it," she told Rebecca, "with the unrestrained affection which the last sufferings of his life, added to the remembrance of former years, had made almost more than human. When you read my daily memorandums since I left home, you will feel what my love has been and acknowledge that God alone could support it by His assistance through such proofs as have been required of it." Many years later, she recalled: "It seemed that I loved him more than any one could love on earth."

Elizabeth's thoughts turned naturally to home and what she should find there, but Filippo silenced her spoken fears with sarcastic amusement: "My little sister, God the *Almighty* is laughing at you. He takes care of little birds and makes the lilies grow, and you fear He will not take care of you. I tell you He will take care of you."

On the morning of departure, Antonio knocked on Elizabeth's door at four-thirty to rouse her for Mass. The sky was hung with stars and the wind was fair. Downstairs, Amabilia embraced her tearfully and told her that she would not go to the wharf, but would part with her dear Antonio at Mass.

Here is a beautiful example of the mystery of love. That trust on which alone true love can build was the presiding virtue of Amabilia's heart. Cynics might smile at the wife thus sending forth her husband on a lonely voyage with a lovely girl; but such cynics have not loved as Antonio and Amabilia loved each other. Even the cynics must fall silent at the final tryst sealed with the Body and Blood of Our Lord Jesus Christ.

It was only a three-minute walk to the Church of S. *Caterina*. As the little party entered the odd, octagonal-shaped church, looming like a medieval fortress in the darkness, the winding canal with the starshine upon it for its moat, a cannon sounded from the *Pyamingo* as signal that she would hoist her anchor two hours hence.

Elizabeth had been apprehensive about the parting of husband and wife, and she rejoiced in her heart when "her dear brother passed the struggle like a man and a Christian—dear, manly soul, it appeared to me, in the 'image of God.'" Filippo and Carleton Bayley were waiting at the Health Office, with their letters for America. Filippo's last words were both farewell and solemn conjuration:

"I meet you the day of Judgment."

At eight o'clock, Elizabeth was

quietly seated with little Ann and dear Antonio on the quarter-deck. The anchor weighed, sails hoisted and dear "Yo, yo!" resounding on all sides, brought to remembrance the 2nd of October, 1803, with a force as strong as could be borne. Most dear Seton, where are you now? I lose sight of the shore that contains your dear ashes; and your soul is in that region of immensity where I cannot find you.

But the broken heart turned in a trice to the Only One who could mend it, and restore her to him she had lost: "My Father and My God, while I live, let me praise Thee; while I have my being, let me serve and adore Thee!"

XII

A Cross Instead of a Weathercock

The voyage to America took fifty-six days. Throughout the first week, the ship skirted the shore of the Mediterranean, and Elizabeth was awed at the majesty of the distant Alps and Pyrenees. Some excitement developed when the wind dropped as they approached Valencia and the little *Pyamingo* was becalmed amid the towering warships of Lord Nelson's fleet which, months in advance, was spoiling for the Battle of Trafalgar. The routine boarding of the *Pyamingo* by parties from the seventy-four gun *Excellent* and the *Belle Isle* struck terror into Elizabeth's womanly soul, and she cried to the Lord: "Oh, my God, if I should die in the midst of so much sin and so little penitence! how terrible it will be to fall into Thy hands!"

The cry was undoubtedly called forth by the remembrance of her past sins, which her new knowledge of the Catholic doctrine of sacramental forgiveness and insistence on penance, had agitated. There was also a nearer reason in the humiliating temptations nature had made her prone to since leaving Leghorn.

There was a twofold reason for these temptations, the one natural, the other supernatural. Elizabeth and Antonio were woman and man: the fact that their affection was solidly grounded on God and the things of God did not in any way destroy the normal attractions of human nature. Indeed, the spirituality of their relationship directly provoked the assaults of the Devil: in his eye, they were enemies to be destroyed before they could work effectively for God. The greatness of Elizabeth's soul made it a special target for Satan; and God permitted it to undergo the process of purification that He has always permitted in molding His greatest saints—like St. Anthony of the Desert or St. Thomas Aquinas.

Let it be stated immediately that both Elizabeth and Antonio came through this distasteful trial clean and untouched. It is understandable that she should be terrified and should echo, in the candid pages of her *Journal*, the piteous cry of Peter on the water: "Lord, save me!" Souls more spiritually sophisticated than she had been terrified before her. St. Catherine of Siena, after three days and nights of enduring images loathsome and attractive at once, had reproached her divine Master for absenting Himself throughout the trial that had nearly engulfed her soul; and, in awe and wondering, heard His reply that He had always been there in the inviolate center of her heart. Elizabeth's only mistake was that, in the turmoil of temptation, she confused her own part in it, blaming herself for things she could not help and did not want. But, in the end, she acknowledged with humble gratitude: "The Lord is my Refuge; my God is the strength of my confidence. If the Lord had not helped me, it had not failed that my soul had been put to silence. But when I said my foot had slipped, thy mercy, O Lord, held me up."

Considering, in the plan of God, the exceptional union of Elizabeth and Antonio and the great good it was to accomplish for the American Church, this trial, perhaps, had to come; and never again did it recur to constrain their relations and obstruct God's work. Elizabeth recorded joyfully—and secretly, not for Antonio's eyes—"Most dear Antonio, a thousand times endeared to me by the struggles of your soul, Our Lord is with us!" The glorious victory was an effective answer to the weak excuse of selfish souls, that "this thing is bigger than both of us."

The storm subsided as quickly as it had struck, and Elizabeth's religious instruction continued. She and Antonio discussed in thorough fashion the tenets of the Catholic Church. She read carefully, under his supervision; and found particular enjoyment in Alban Butler's *Lives of the Saints*. They fasted and prayed together and celebrated with special devotions the greater feasts as they occurred.

Elizabeth understood more clearly now where it was all leading, and the consequences; and she began to prepare for the dismay and opposition she knew she must meet in New York. She was particularly disturbed about the effect her new leanings would have on Henry Hobart. No one wants to hurt a friend, especially one like Hobart, who had done Elizabeth much good. With her delicate thoughtfulness, she drafted an explanatory letter that he might read in quiet and leisure, away from the heat of verbal discussion and recrimination:

> As I approach to you, I tremble; and while the dashing of the waves and their incessant motion picture to me the allotment which God has given me, the tears fall fast thro' my fingers at the insupportable thought of being separated from you. And yet, my dear H., you will not be severe: you will respect my sincerity; and tho' you will think me in an error and even reprehensible in changing my religion, I know that heavenly Christian charity will plead for me in your affection.
>
> You have certainly, without my knowing it, been dearer to me than God; for Whom, my reason, my judgment and my conviction used their combined force against the value of your esteem. The combat was in vain, until I considered that yourself would no longer oppose or desire so severe a struggle, which was destroying my mortal life—and more than that— my peace with God.
>
> Still, if you will not be my brother, if your dear friendship and esteem must be the price of my fidelity to what I believe to be the truth, I cannot doubt the mercy of God who, by depriving me of my dearest tie on earth, will certainly draw me nearer to Him—and this I feel confidently from experience of the past and the truth of His promise, which can never fail.

June 4, 1804, was a day of smiles and tears. Elizabeth's family and friends were at dockside to welcome her home, and for some minutes there was a pandemonium of joy. She was shaken with tears to find all four children well; the sight of little Rebecca was an unexpected boon, for Elizabeth had almost convinced herself that the child was dead. It was only when the first flurry of excited squeals had subsided and she was presenting Antonio, that she missed Rebecca Seton. In the midst of her happiness, she had to be told that her Soul's Sister had been dying for weeks; indeed, it seemed that she had been hanging on to life by the sheer power of her will, waiting for Elizabeth to come.

Life never waited for Elizabeth. There were no moments to rest in the possession of what she had. From the ship and the glad welcome, she went to the sickbed. It was as if she had never been away.

Head crammed with new ideas, heart reaching out to new beliefs, no funds, no livelihood—Elizabeth knew that her former life was over, but she had counted on Rebecca as the only one who would understand, *really* understand, to the point of joining Elizabeth in her stand. It was the whole reason for the *Leghorn Journal*.

> The dear, faithful, tender friend of my soul through every varied scene of many years of trial, gone—only the shadow remaining, and that in a few days must pass away! The home of plenty and comfort, the society of sisters united by prayers and divine affections, the evening hymns, the daily readings, the sunset contemplations, the service of holy days together, the kiss of peace, the widows' visits—all, all gone forever!
>
> And is poverty and sorrow the only exchange? My husband, my sisters, my home, my comforts—poverty and sorrow. Well, with God's blessing, you, too, shall be changed into dearest friends.

It is an index of Elizabeth's advance over the past few months that, where before she had lamented the cold deathbeds of those who had not her Protestant fervor, she now trembled for Rebecca who had not Catholic consolations. As she told Amabilia,

> The impressions of your example and the different scenes I passed through in Leghorn are far from being effaced from my mind, which indeed could not—even in the most painful moments of attendance on my beloved Rebecca—help the strong comparison of a sick and dying bed in your happy country, where the poor sufferer is soothed and strengthened at once by every help of religion; where the one you call *Father* of your soul attends and watches it in the weakness and trials of parting nature with the same care you and I watch our little infant's body in its first struggles and wants on its entrance into life.
>
> Dearest Rebecca—how many looks of silent distress have we exchanged about the last passage, this exchange of time for eternity! To be sure, her uncommon piety and innocence and sweet confidence in God are my full consolation; but I mean to say that a departing soul has so many trials and temptations that, for my part, I go through a sort of agony never to be described—even while, to keep up their hope and courage, I appear to them most cheerful.

Poor Rebecca was too weak to do more than repeat, gasping, the words of Ruth to Noemi: "Your people are my people; your God, my God."

The weeks of June were complicated ones. Elizabeth's immediate needs were food and lodging for her children, and she could find them only in the charity of others. Wright Post, John Wilkes and her godmother, Sarah Startin, pooled their resources to give her this charity. It is a humiliating thing—and was doubly so for her who had fallen from such social eminence—to eat the bread of another and to live in another's house. That much of it was owed her in justice—Post was indebted to her father for launching his medical career, and Wilkes to the senior Seton for setting him up in business and to Dr. Bayley and Elizabeth herself for their attentions to his dying wife—did little to cut the bitterness of it. Yet, it does justice to her humility that Elizabeth always accepted charity gracefully. Perhaps it was a lesson she had learned from her poor widows; and, in the present case, she could console herself that it was a temporary arrangement until Rebecca should be out of her babyhood, and that the future promised her independence.

The state of her religious convictions did not help matters. Elizabeth was not one to accept help under false colors. She announced at once, therefore, that she was thinking of becoming a Catholic. The shock of such an announcement to genteel society in New York of 1804 was appalling. The city was frankly bigoted. It had an unofficial "state religion" —Episcopalianism; other Protestant sects were tolerated with varying degrees of scorn and pity. But *Romanism!*—*Romans* were the shiftless, scrubby immigrants who attended the shabby little church on Barclay Street.

Elizabeth could not have been taken seriously at first. Her friends would consider, understandingly, that she had been through a nightmare of suffering and, when at her lowest ebb, had been set upon by kind, well-meaning foreigners—she would come to her senses soon enough. Amusingly, kind, well-meaning people did exactly what they accused the Filicchis of doing: tried to draw her to their own persuasions. Thus, "one of the most excellent women [she] ever knew," a member of the Church of Scotland—probably Mrs. Graham—urged her: "*Oh, do, dear soul, come and hear our J. Mason, and I am sure you will join us.*" And a Quaker friend coaxed: "*Betsy, I tell thee, thee had best come with us.*" Another "faithful old friend," an Anabaptist, lamented tearfully: "*Oh, could you be regenerated! Could you know our experiences and enjoy with us* our *heavenly banquet!*" And even her old Methodist servant, Mary, groaned and "contemplated" over Elizabeth's soul because it had "*no convictions.*"

It spoke well of the basic sense of justice in her benefactors that, however distasteful her religious leanings, they nevertheless held out helping hands. But time would make a difference. Post, to his credit, remained constant her whole lifetime; but John Wilkes slipped away gladly when the opportunity offered, and Mrs. Startin eventually washed her hands of her godchild.

With the funds offered her, Elizabeth made do very well. She took "a small neat house about a half-mile from town, where,"—she told Julia Scott—"we occupy the upper room, and will let the lower floor as soon as I can find a tenant." This house was probably one on Moore Street, east of Greenwich Street. She reported to John Wilkes, who was in Albany at the time, that his brother Charles "was quite pleased with my little home and my darlings, whom he found eating their bread and milk with a very good appetite." She assured Julia, in advance, that there was no need of help from her: "I spend much less than even those friends imagine; and delight in the opportunity of bringing up my children without those pretentions and indulgences that ruin so many."

The announcement of her new religious interests did more harm to Elizabeth's peace of mind than to her livelihood. Everyone, it seemed, rushed to dissuade her, for diverse reasons; her true friends, to save her from folly; some of her in-laws, to save the family from disgrace; and Henry Hobart, from sincere religious horror and a measure of ministerial pique. Hobart's first approach was solicitous and affectionate, and Elizabeth could smile at the naïveté of such questions as "how can I ever think of leaving the church in which I was baptized?" and "how can you believe there are as many gods as there are millions of altars and tens of millions of blessed hosts all over the world?" This was not the best that Mr. Hobart could do; it was just that he had underestimated the strength and knowledge of his opponent. A lawyer once remarked of him: "The Church needs no abler representatives. . . . He is the most parliamentary speaker I ever met with: he is equally prompt, logical and practical. I never saw that man thrown off his center."

When this redoubtable fighter brought his artillery to bear on Eliza-

beth, she could smile no longer. The heaviest broadside was a book—
Dissertation on the Prophecies by Thomas Newton—which churned
up the waters of her soul. They were not to subside for many long,
anguished months. Actually, the book did her a service, in that it cut off
for all time a possible haven of retreat. All her life she had thought that
"everybody would be saved who meant well." Now, she found that her
own sectaries did not hold so easy a doctrine. "It grieves my very soul,"
she told Amabilia, "to see that Protestants as well as your (as I thought,
hard and severe principles) see the thing so differently; since this book
so valued by them sends all followers of the Pope to the bottomless Pit."
And she consoled herself with a bit of wry humor: "It appears by the
account made of them from the Apostle's time, that a greater part of the
world must be already there, at that rate."

While the battle for Elizabeth's soul was being joined, Rebecca Seton
was slipping away. The end came over the second weekend in July. She
suffered extremely on Friday evening, then fell into a coma, and Elizabeth thought that all was over. She rallied, however, recovered her
senses and seemed easy and free from pain. On Sunday morning, at sunrise, she exclaimed at the beauty of the day:

"Oh, my sister," she whispered to Elizabeth, "that this might be my
day of rest. Shut the windows, and I will sleep."

Elizabeth raised her head, to make her easier, and in that moment
she died. It was a grievous loss, to be measured only by the depth of
their friendship, and the outpourings of Elizabeth's most secret and
intimate thoughts in the *Leghorn Journal* gives the awesome glimpse into
that depth. Elizabeth suffered her loss, and kissed the hand of God. She
confided to Julia Scott that, left to herself, she would gladly exchange the
world for "a cave or a desert"—"But," she finished simply, "God has
given me a great deal to do, and I have always and hope always to prefer
His Will to every wish of my own."

Four days later, another, more famous death shook New York: the
death of Alexander Hamilton at the hands of Aaron Burr. The two,
while outwardly friendly to each other, had long been bitter political
enemies. Burr was an ambitious man whose plans and hopes had been
agonizingly thwarted; in the national election of 1800, the votes of the
federal electors for Burr and Jefferson had been tied for thirty-six ballots,

until Hamilton's deciding vote was finally given to Jefferson for President and Burr for Vice President. Then, Jefferson's purchase of the Louisiana Territory in 1803 had thrown terror into the New England Federalists, because they saw in this vast new region a threat to their political control of the nation. In their desperation, they hatched a wild scheme: Vice President Burr was to run for Governor of New York and, when he had won the election, was to lead the state and other Northern states into secession. Hamilton gave the scheme away, asserting that Burr was a "dangerous man and one who ought not to be trusted with the reins of government." A duel was inevitable, and Hamilton was fatally wounded. The great Founding Father lingered all night and all the next morning, but at two o'clock in the afternoon of July 12, the bells of the city began to toll the news of his death.

Elizabeth was talking to Charles Wilkes in her little home at the time, and she observed "that he was really so affected . . . that he could scarcely command himself." Charles Wilkes and his brother John were old friends of Hamilton, from the days when the three of them had worked with William Seton Sr. to establish the Bank of New York. The impressive state funeral was held on Saturday, and Wright Post and James Seton's brother-in-law, Josiah Ogden Hoffman, walked among the mourners.

Newton's *Prophecies* and other books supplied by Mr. Hobart did their work of unsettling Elizabeth's mind, and when she read them alternately with the Catholic works that contradicted them—notably Robert Manning's *England's Conversion and Reformation Compared*, which Antonio had secured for her from Father Matthew O'Brien on landing—she entered into a tortured maze that was all turnings and no direction. Yet she did not lose confidence in God, Who seemed more her Father and All than He had ever been before. With true humility, she looked upon her sins as the spawners of the clouds that covered her soul, and made the Penitential Psalms her cry for light. It was, perhaps, Elizabeth's salvation at this critical moment that little Anna, who had not to struggle with the complexities of religious conviction, brought the Blessed Virgin to her mother's mind.

> Anna coaxes me, when we are at our evening prayers, to say [the] Hail Mary, and all say, "Oh, do, Ma, teach it to us!" Even little Bec tries to

lisp it, though she can scarcely speak; and I ask my Savior why should we not say it. If anyone is in heaven, *His Mother* must be there. Are the angels, then, who are so often represented as being so interested for us on earth, more compassionate or more exalted than she is? Oh, no, no. Mary our Mother, that cannot be. So I beg her with the tenderness and confidence of her child to pity us and guide us to the true faith, if we are not in it, and *if we are*, to obtain peace for my poor soul, that I may be a good mother to my poor darlings. For I know, if God should leave me to myself after all my sins, He would be justified; and since I read these books, my head is quite bewildered about the few that are saved. So I kiss her picture you [Amabilia] gave me, and beg her to be a Mother to us.

When Elizabeth left Italy, Filippo had given her a letter of introduction to the Right Reverend John Carroll, Bishop of Baltimore, which was at that time the only American See. The elder Filicchi had counted on Bishop Carroll to guide Mrs. Seton into the Church. But another piece of his advice, given in the spirit of fair play that accorded so well with Elizabeth's own way of acting—to inform Mr. Hobart and her intimates of her intentions—had militated against this first, excellent counsel. Filippo had not appreciated fully enough Elizabeth's partiality for Hobart, or Hobart's intelligence, or Elizabeth's lack of readiness to take the final step. The result was that Elizabeth, after hearing her dear minister, held off contacting Bishop Carroll. Two things decided this course: the minister's proof to her satisfaction that the Episcopal Church was as true a church as the Catholic, and his suggestion that she let all controversy rest until her mind was settled and quiet. Hobart, after all, knew Elizabeth much better than either of the Filicchis did, and he understood how eagerly her agitated and exhausted soul would reach out for rest. From the *psychological* viewpoint, it was excellent advice; nor need anyone impugn the sincerity of his motives. It is easy to think ill of the "enemy," but it is much fairer to try to understand his point of view.

Antonio, who had stayed on in New York, impatient for the outcome, was too hurt and angry to make the attempt. On the 26th of July, he wrote Elizabeth a letter that was alternately raging and tender. From the first word, there was no mistaking his indignation or his wounded feelings, there was no sparing of his "dear sister" for failing to keep her promise of writing to Carroll, there was no hiding of his scorn for her vacillation. But, just as evident was the magnitude and constancy of his friendship, giving him the right to speak, and softening the harshness of his language. He made an uncompromising act of faith in her sincerity, whatever she did; and, to remove all danger of Elizabeth's penury influencing her spiritual decisions, he placed his fortune and that of his brother at her command.

Antonio informed Elizabeth, in this letter, that he had written to Bishop Carroll, since she had not, and had enclosed a copy of the letter she had prepared for the Bishop—not as a communication from her to Carroll, but as a concise history of her case in her own words. He enclosed to the Bishop also the manuscript Henry Hobart had prepared in answer to the one Filippo and his friend Father Pecci had given her. Antonio assured Carroll that, although he was long overdue in making a projected business trip to Boston, he would wait in New York for the Bishop's reply. Weeks passed, and it did not come. Antonio could not know that the Bishop was out of town, visiting his sisters at Rock Creek, and he wrote again urgently, pleading that the salvation of six souls— that of Mrs. Seton and her five children—waited on the Bishop's answer. This time the answer came immediately, arriving the day before Antonio was to leave for Boston. He hastened with it to Elizabeth. It is not known what Carroll wrote, but Elizabeth reported to Antonio in Boston, on August 30:

> The Bishop's letter has been held to my heart on my knees, beseeching God to enlighten me to see the truth unmixed with doubts and hesitations. I read the promises given to St. Peter and the Sixth Chapter [of St.] John every day, and then ask God, can I offend Him by believing those express words? I read my dear *St. Francis*, and ask if it is possible that I shall dare to think differently from him, or seek heaven any other way. I have read your *England's Reformation*, and find its evidence too conclusive to admit of any reply.
>
> God will not forsake me, Antonio. I know that He will unite me to His flock; and, although now my Faith is unsettled, I am assured that He will not disappoint my hope which is fixed on His own word, that He will not despise the humble, contrite heart. . . .

She was in a truly terrible state. Her soul was paralyzed. It could not move either forward or backward. Every new argument solidified the Catholic position, but did not impel her an inch toward action or belief.

She stayed away from Protestant worship when she could, without comment, excuse herself; and when she went, had no interest in it.

> Antonio . . . would not have been well-pleased to see me in St. Paul's Church today, [she admitted to Amabilia] but peace, and persuasion about proprieties, etc., over-prevailed. Yet, I got in a side pew which turned my face towards the Catholic Church in the next street, and found myself twenty times speaking to the Blessed Sacrament *there*, instead of looking at the naked altar where I was, or minding the routine of prayers. Tears plenty and sighs as silent and deep as when I first entered your blessed church of [the] Annunciation in Florence; all turning to the one only desire, to see the way most pleasing to my God—whichever that way is!

By September, Henry Hobart was completely out of patience with her, and flatly dismissed the whole question with the statement that the Catholic Church was corrupt and the Episcopal Church had returned to the primitive doctrine. He finished by asking crossly: "What more would you have when you act according to your best judgment?"

Elizabeth answered, that her judgment would be enough for this world, "but I fear in the next to meet *another* question."

She did not dare show him the Bishop's letter. They parted painfully; and, considering her attachment for this hero of her soul, it must have cost a great deal to tell Antonio that "Mr. H. and all the other *Misters* have left me to my contemplations, or rather, to my 'best judgment,' I suppose"—and she added with her usual spark—"but I rather hope to God." There is no mistaking the bitterness.

It seems certain now that Elizabeth was passing through a trial that had nothing to do with controversy. Indeed, the thought suggested itself to her then; for she told Antonio: "Really, it would seem that the evil spirit has taken his place so near my soul that nothing good can enter in it, without being mixed with his suggestions." It was a trial similar to that of Vincent de Paul who, for four years, could not form the words of an act of faith; or a trial like those of so many saints who could not, at times, pray. As summer passed into fall, Elizabeth largely turned away from Protestant arguments and objections. She constantly bolstered her courage by reviewing the Catholic convictions she clung to. But it was precisely when she did, that the doubts and uncertainties and scruples rained upon her soul in fury. Thus she told Antonio:

I fell on my face before God (remember I tell you all) and appealed to Him as my righteous Judge, if hardness of heart, or unwillingness to be taught or any human reasons, stood between me and the truth; if I would not rejoice to cast my sorrows in the bosom of the Blessed Mary, to entreat the influence of all His blessed saints and angels, to pray for precious souls even more than for myself, and account myself happy in dying for His sacred truth—if once my soul could know it was pleasing to Him.

I remembered how much these exercises had comforted and delighted me at Leghorn, and recalled all the reasons which had then convinced me of their truth—and immediately a cloud of doubts and replies raised a contest in this poor soul, and I could only cry out for mercy to a sinner. . . .

and

After reading the life of St. Mary Magdalen, I thought: "Come, my soul, let us turn from all these suggestions of one side or the other, and quietly resolve to go to that church which has at least the multitude of the wise and good on its side"; and began to consider the first step I must take. The first step—is it not to declare I believe all that is taught by the Council of Trent?—and if I said that, would not the Searcher of Hearts know my falsehood and insincerity? Could you say that you would be satisfied with His bread and believe the cup, which He equally commanded, unnecessary? Could you believe that the prayers and litanies addressed to Our Blessed Lady were acceptable to God, though not commanded in Scripture, etc., etc.?

Filippo wrote her long, grave, wise, courteous letters, going to every length to clear up specific points of perplexity; but he, too, saw it was not a question of controversy or conviction.

"What must I do, my dear Filicchi?" I hear you say. Pray, pray incessantly, pray with fervor and confidence. Be sincere in your wish to know the truth, and firm in your resolution to follow it. Never think of the consequences for what relates to your situation and family affairs. There is a Providence. Let, therefore, prayer be your only advisor—abandon all others if you believe one. You cannot ask without something be given you; you cannot knock and find the door always shut; you cannot seek never to find. Sincerity, confidence and perseverance in prayer; calmness and tranquility of mind; courage and resolution in heart; a perfect resignation to Providence —you cannot fail to succeed. Avoid the labyrinth of controversies. They will not make you wiser.

He tried to stop the panic whirling of her fears and anxieties:

> I was in hopes you would have retained the maxim that Our Savior wishes our salvation more than we can wish it ourselves. Your anxiety, therefore, is unreasonable, and your trouble a temptation. You pray to your Father, to your Creator and to your Savior—and you tremble. You do not know His goodness. These were not the sentiments that accompanied the prodigal child nor Mary Magdalen. St. Paul fallen from his horse and called by Him whom he knew not, did not trouble himself. He calmly said: "What will You have me do?" It is only in calm and tranquility that we may do some good. It is only our enemy delights in trouble, and trouble is his element. He knows that he cannot catch fish in clear water. You are perplexed, uncertain; pray, pray constantly and with fervor, but calmly. If you trouble yourself for being troubled, you will never find peace.

Despite her confusion, Elizabeth probably saw her real situation more clearly than anyone did. Piteously she wandered on the edges of the Catholic crowd, standing wistfully on tiptoe to try to get a true glimpse of what was at the center. She visited a poor Catholic man who was sick, and came away consoled and satisfied. Passing St. Peter's on Barclay Street, she dragged her feet, lingering to read the inscriptions on the tombstones as an excuse to stay, yearning to go inside, and falling down, kiss the steps of the altar:

> Every day to visit my Savior there and pour out my soul before Him is the supreme desire. But, oh! Antonio, my most dear brother, should I ever dare to bring there a doubtful, distracted mind, a confusion of fears and hesitations, trembling before God in anguish and terror lest it should offend Him whom only it desires to please?
>
> In the sure confidence of your mind, you must smile at your poor sister's expressions as the effusions of a heated imagination; but, oh! my soul is at stake, and the dear ones of my soul must partake my error in going or staying. Far different is my situation from those who are uninstructed, but my hard case is to have a head turned with instruction, without the light in my soul to direct it where to rest.

These months of Elizabeth's conversion, of her leaving the comfortable old house for the new, constituted one of the great trials of Christian history. Its like is hard to find, except in the lives of God's greatest saints. She suffered excruciating anguish of spirit, rejected with contempt by Protestants, blamed by Catholics, in terror of her own secret thoughts, seemingly unnoticed by God, the hem of Whose robe, nevertheless, she never let go. Such suffering of soul was bound to take its toll of her body. She lost weight until she was scarcely more than a skeleton. She cried incessantly. Her little children tried to comfort her with their caresses and their continual, soothing sounds—"Poor Mamma!"—and these failing, they carefully watched their behavior lest they add to her distress.

It did not help that those she respected most judged her to be the unworthy cause of her own suffering. Her "most dear Filippo" scored her "imagination . . . rendered so sensible by constant stretch" and her "great propensity to melancholy": and he told her bluntly: "In a spiritual concern, you have followed only worldly prudence, that prudence which the Gospel calls folly. You have acted as if you had thought that God was not to be obeyed without the consent and advice of your friends. You have met with the punishment you deserved." The revered Carroll, Christ's Shepherd in America, warned Antonio that she

> ought to consider whether the tears she sheds and the prayers she offers to heaven are purely for God's sake and arise solely from compunction for sin, and are unmixed with any alloy of worldly respects or inordinate solicitude for the attainment of some worldly purpose.
>
> . . . A fear arises in my mind that God discovers in her some lurking imperfection, and defers the final grace of her conversion till her soul be entirely purified of its irregular attachments.

The Bishop was nearer the truth than Filippo; and his considered and cautious advice certainly comes nearer to putting the finger on the source of Elizabeth's trouble, thereby pointing out the probable cause of the prolonged agony: the trial was great because it was a struggle for a great soul. Even Carroll could not, at that time, know how great a soul. We, in our day, do.

Elizabeth lived a cloistered existence in her little cottage, not so much because it was somewhat out of town, but rather because of her "strange" religious predilections. She was beginning to feel what it would be like to be a Catholic. Not that she minded. She had a real attraction for solitude; and, besides, most of those who mattered to her still came when they could: the Posts, Harriet and Cecilia, Sad—who thought Elizabeth's new ideas bizzare and unnecessary, and Julia Scott—who took the tack that her friend was free to believe as she wished, Dué and Richard

Bayley. James Seton and the two Wilkeses came to bring her letters from Antonio. Strangest of all, upon Elizabeth's return her stepmother had completely reversed herself and now showed her every attention and kindness.

Julia, with her usual largeness of heart, offered to adopt Anna, in order to relieve Elizabeth of part of her burden and give the child the advantages her mother could no longer afford. There are indications that the offer was seriously weighed for a time—Elizabeth worried about an education for the growing girl—but, in the end she refused it, cherishing nonetheless her friend's kind heart.

The little widow was far from idle. She held school each day for her children (the care of Will's young brothers and sisters, now that he was dead, devolved on the elder Setons). She gathered her five around the fire and told them the stories of David and Daniel and Judith. She taught them hymns. They said their prayers together. In the evening, Elizabeth played the piano, and the children sang and danced. At bedtime she laid her hand on each head in blessing, and made the sign of the cross on each little brow. The whole order of day was so popular that the neighbors' children clamored to hear the stories and sing the hymns and learn the prayers.

In September three of the children came down with whooping cough and Elizabeth was exhausted with nursing them night and day. Then Mary, the old mammy, fell sick, and for nearly three months Elizabeth had to do the servant's duties as well as her own—the cooking and washing and cleaning and making fires—besides giving Mary the tender care that eventually brought some improvement. As winter came on the snow piled in huge drifts, cutting the little family off from the town. With all her added labors and the strain of her religious trial, Elizabeth contracted a severe cold, and suffered increasing chest pains. It was, perhaps, the beginning of the dread consumption.

All her spare time Elizabeth gave to her Bible and her books. Over and over she read à Kempis and Francis de Sales and the *Lives of the Saints*. And she prayed, prayed, prayed, for light.

When Antonio had set out for Boston, he was to stay for some weeks, then move on to Canada, and return to New York in the fall. The Canadian trip was put off because of a delay in procuring a passport; but his business in the New England Hub grew complicated, and he found himself making side trips to Salem, Massachusetts, and Portland, Maine, and eventually fighting a lawsuit for Filippo. The upshot was that he was away all fall and winter.

Elizabeth worried about him. She knew his goodness, but she knew his florid and winning nature, too, and the thousand temptations that could assail a lonely man whose wife and children were half a world away. She fully earned the title of "sister" he had bestowed upon her, by her constant, anxious queries and solicitudes:

> When thought goes to you, Antonio, and imagines you in the promiscuous company you must meet, without any solid gratification, fatigued by your excursions, wandering in your fancy, etc.—oh! how I pray that the Holy Spirit may not leave you, and that your dear angel may even *pinch* you at the hour of prayer rather than suffer you to neglect them.

Woman that she was, she divined immediately what he, probably from embarrassment, had failed to tell her: that he was taking English lessons from a young lady, and teaching her Italian in return—and Elizabeth teased him about it:

> Your letters . . . are so free from mistakes and so perfectly well expressed that I shall imagine you have found some kind directress to supply the deficiency of her you left behind you. She may be more happy in many respects, and worthier of so distinguished a favor, but certainly can never excel in truth or affection; and, when you return, must yield her claim to a more ancient pretension.

He answered with a small boy's sheepishness:

> I am giving (you rightly guessed) some Italian *leçon* in exchange for English ones, to a very genteel, good and *pretty handsome* young Miss, first daughter of this Mrs. Stoughton. She is one of the new converts to the Roman Catholic religion from the Presbyterian communion since three years.

And he did not fail to let her know—with a man's studied casualness— that he was safe and living in God's grace:

> For my part, I must acknowledge the effect of your good prayers for me, as never I was so less bad in my life as I think I am now since I left New York. Last Tuesday, my wedding day from ten or eleven years ago, sacred to the Guardian Angels, I went to church to confess.

The relationship of Elizabeth and Antonio was one of extraordinary beauty: rare and delicate, strong and ardent, human and supernatural, innocent and prudent, all at once. As true friends, they did not hide their need for each other. For example, Elizabeth confessed to him: "I begin now wishfully to watch for J. Seton's chair every evening, hoping that he will bring me a letter from you. This you may think childish, dear Antonio; but remember, you have not a *female heart*, and mine is most truly and fondly attached to you—as you have proved when I have been most contradictory and troublesome to you, fearing too much not to possess your invaluable affection." And he, in turn, lectured her on one occasion: "Most cruel and yet beloved sister . . . I have called twenty times for your letters at the post office, scolding the very twenty times the Post Officer for his cold answer: 'No letters for you.' Do you keep your letters to be delivered to me by your own hand, as with equal cruelty you did already at Florence?"

Their mutual need was quite understandable and legitimate. Both were completely alone. No one but Antonio understood Elizabeth's crisis; no one but Elizabeth understood Antonio's loneliness. He was her perfect confidant because, after his first sharp letter from Boston, he never blamed her hesitation, never hurried her. She could pour out to him the fears and anxieties festering within her, and receive in return the only needed advice: to keep doggedly at her prayers.

When Elizabeth finally accepted John Wilkes's plan for her to take in twenty boarders, after vainly holding off her decision against Antonio's return, Antonio was dubious about its success, not because she had failed to consult him, but because he was afraid it might interfere with the great business of her conversion. Perhaps the key to his ability to bring her comfort was his natural acceptance of her sincerity and his calm assumption that, eventually, she would come to the Church in peace. It was precisely the vote of confidence she needed.

On her side, Elizabeth was Antonio's perfect support. He expressed it best when he told her that her letters were "a lesson for language and style, a pattern of friendly expressions, a living example and excitement to virtue and godliness, a true blessing in my present wandering, wearisome life."

The friendship was prudently guarded, for both were aware that human nature bore watching. Antonio employed the rather elementary precaution of suggesting, and even commanding, from time to time, that Elizabeth refrain from writing him. She laughed at such tactics, because she was infinitely wiser. It was not alone that she recognized more clearly than he their need for a mutual exchange, or that she knew him better than he knew himself and had a truer estimate of his basic holiness and piety. It was that she took the surer, more positive way of constantly immersing their affection in the Heart of God. Her letters are dotted with such proof as the following:

> I could cry out now, as my poor Seton used to: "Antonio, Antonio, Antonio"; but call back the thought, and my soul cries out: "Jesus, Jesus, Jesus!" There it finds rest and heavenly peace, and is hushed by that dear sound as my little babe is quieted by my cradle song. . . . Jonathan loved David as his own soul, and if I was your brother, Antonio, I would never leave you for one hour. But, as it is, I try rather to turn every affection to God, well knowing that there alone their utmost exercise cannot be misapplied, and most ardent hopes can never be disappointed.

The language of the Filicchi-Seton correspondence is frankly affectionate, warm and ardent. It could not be otherwise. They were affectionate, warm and ardent souls. Antonio had a sunny, volatile, Latin temperament. And what letters of Elizabeth's to any intimate friend, male or female, do not reveal her romantic, tender heart? People cannot shuck their personalities to satisfy suspicious minds. A myriad justifications spring to the defense of these great spiritual friends. Their letters could be placed side by side with the enthusiastic outpourings of the greatest saints: of Augustine, Jerome, Bernard, Vincent de Paul, Francis de Sales, Jane Francis de Chantal, Louise de Marillac, Joan of Arc, Therese of Lisieux—to say nothing of the divine Song of Solomon. When argument is exhausted, however, one must return inevitably to the awesome, beautiful contemplation of two noble souls whose constant message to each other was: "Be good, be holy"; whose love was planted, watered and brought to perfect bloom by God.

There can be no doubt that, now in the waning months of 1804, it was providential that even Antonio, who had awakened the vision of truth in Elizabeth, be away from her while she sought its reality. It was God's

Will that she work out her salvation alone. This was evident from the fact that, despite the efforts of Antonio or herself, no outside help could be found for her other than what she had already. Bishop Carroll was ill, and Antonio's pleas to him went unanswered. Elizabeth tried several times to contact Father Matthew O'Brien, but could not. Even more, she mistakenly thought he was the only priest in New York—there were also Father William O'Brien, Father John Byrne and Father Vrennay; but she did not know it. There might have been a multitude of spiritual guides, and none of them could have helped her except by advising her to do what only she could do—to fight off the onslaughts of the Evil One, to ride out the storm in prayer and patience.

She sank to the bottom of the slough of despair in early January, and propelling herself upwards from its mire in terror, she broke through the surface of a calm sea and saw, with gladness, the blue sky overhead and the Sun of God's Truth enthroned in it.

It is significant that she described the denouement in detail for Amabilia Filicchi. This lovely, quiet woman has been too often deprived of her great part in Elizabeth's conversion. It was Amabilia who led her first into a Catholic church, Amabilia who taught her the realities behind the symbols of Catholicism, Amabilia who gave her Antonio. Elizabeth herself did not deny to Amabilia the glory that belonged to her. Give credit though she justly did to Antonio and Filippo, yet Elizabeth kept the intimate *Journal* of her conversion for Amabilia, as she kept the *Leghorn Journal* for Rebecca Seton. For Amabilia's eyes, then, she first put down the story of how family and friends, attempting to dissuade her from her course, had caused anxiety and doubts to spring up in her soul; of how for months she could not "cast the balance"; and of how, at last, she came to peace. The moment of victory is best savored in Elizabeth's own words:

> Would you believe, Amabilia, in a desperation of heart I went last Sunday to St. George's Church. The wants and necessities of my soul were so pressing that I looked straight up to God and I told Him: "Since I cannot see the way to please You whom alone I wish to please, everything is indifferent to me; and until You do show me the way You mean me to walk in, I will trudge on in the path You suffered me to be born in, and go even to the very Sacrament where I once used to find You." So away I went.

. . . But, if I left the house a Protestant, I returned to it a Catholic, I think; since I determined to go no more to the Protestants, being much more troubled than ever I thought I could be, while I remembered GOD IS MY GOD.

But so it was, that [at] the bowing of my heart before the Bishop to receive his absolution—which is given publicly and universally to all in the church—I had not the least faith in his prayer, and looked for an apostolic loosing from my sins, which by the books Mr. H. had given me to read, I find they do not claim or admit. Then, trembling to communion, half-dead with the inward struggle when they said the BODY AND BLOOD OF CHRIST. Oh! Amabilia, no words for my trial! And I remember in my old prayer-book of former edition, when I was a child, it was not as now: said to be *spiritually* taken and received.*

However, to get thoughts away, I took the *Daily Exercise* of good Abbé Plunkett to read the prayers after communion; but finding every word addressed to Our dear Savior as really present and conversing with it, I became half crazy—and for the first time could not bear the sweet caresses of the darlings or bless their little dinner. O my God, that day!

But it finished calmly at last—abandoning all to God—and a renewed confidence in the Blessed Virgin, whose mild and peaceful look reproached my bold excesses and reminded me to fix my mind above with better hopes. Now they tell me: take care, *I am a mother*, and my children I must answer for in judgment, whatever faith I lead them to. That being so—and I so unconscious, for I little thought 'till told by Mr. H. that their faith could be so full of consequence to them or me—I WILL GO PEACEABLY AND FIRMLY TO THE CATHOLIC CHURCH: for if Faith is so important to our salvation, I will seek it where true Faith first began, seek it among those who received it from GOD HIMSELF.

The controversies on it I am quite incapable of deciding; and as the strictest Protestant allows salvation to a good Catholic, to the Catholics I will go and try to be a good one. May God accept my intention, and pity me. . . .

Come then, my little ones, we will go to judgment together, and present Our Lord His own words; and if He says, "You fools, I did not mean that," we will say, "Since You said You would be *always* even to the end of ages,

---

* Elizabeth's recollection was most accurate. In 1783 the American Anglicans took the official name "Protestant Episcopal Church." At the new church's first General Convention held in Philadelphia in 1789, the Anglican Book of Common Prayer was revised. Among the significant revisions: the sentence, "the Body and Blood of Christ . . . are verily and indeed taken and received by the faithful in the Lord's Supper," was changed to "spiritually taken and received." The old wording explains Elizabeth's intense devotion to the Anglican sacrament and her eagerness to accept the uncompromising Roman Catholic belief in the Real Presence.

be with this church you built with Your Blood—if You ever left it, it is Your *word* which misled us. Therefore, please to pardon Your poor fools for Your own word's sake."

I am between laughing and crying all the while, Amabilia—yet not frightened, for on God Himself I pin my faith; and wait only the coming of your Antonio, whom I look for next week from Boston, to go valiantly and boldly to the standard of the Catholics and trust all to God. It is His affair *now*.

After this manifesto of decision—delivered about the middle of January—there was, naturally enough, some last-minute fear, some last-minute holding back, but it was the hesitation on the threshold. Only a proferred hand was needed to bring her inside, and the privilege of extending such was given to Father John Cheverus of Boston.

Back in October, Antonio had told her about the "learned and eloquent Cheverus." When Antonio returned in February, he and Elizabeth both sat down to state her situation to this holy, zealous priest, begging his advice and comfort that he might have "the merit of determining and perfecting the work."

She did not wait for his reply before making the first, tentative steps, for her heart was high and happy. On Ash Wednesday, February 27, 1805, she noted in Amabilia's *Journal*:

A day of days for me, Amabilia. I have been where?—to the Church of St. Peter with the cross on the top instead of a weathercock! That is mischievous—but I mean I have been to what is called here among so many churches *the Catholic Church.*

When I turned the corner of the street it is in—"Here, my God, I go," said I, *"heart all to You."* Entering it, how the heart died away as it were in silence before the little tabernacle and the great Crucifixion over it. "Ah, my God, here let me rest," said I—and down the head on the bosom and the knees on the bench.

If I could have thought of anything but God, there was enough, I suppose, to have astonished a stranger by the hurrying over one another of this off-scoured congregation; but as I came only to visit *His Majesty,* I knew not what it meant till afterwards—that it was a day they receive ashes, the beginning of Lent; and the droll but most venerable Irish priest, who seems just come there, talked of death so familiarly that he delighted and revived me.

The church was, of course, St. Peter's on Barclay Street, and the "droll but most venerable Irish priest" either Father Matthew O'Brien or Father John Byrne. The pastor was the Dominican Father William O'Brien, who had been appointed in 1787, the year after the church's founding. At the time of Elizabeth's conversion he was more or less an invalid and was—or at least had been for a time—a patient of her uncle's, Dr. John Charlton.

The Crucifixion by the Mexican artist Josè Maria Vallejo, which so moved Elizabeth, still hangs over the main altar of the present church. It had a like effect on Mary Post when she first saw it, on March 15, 1810. She told her sister:

> I went yesterday to a concert of sacred music in St. Peter's Church, which took place in order to obtain money towards defraying the expense of building St. Patrick's—which is to be placed on the spot enclosed for burial near where you lived when you first returned from Italy. The music did not answer my expectations, but I would have gone much farther to see the picture over the altar; although I must say I found it painful to see such a sight for the first time under the observation of such an assemblage of people. It came fully to my mind what you once told me, that you had passed almost a whole day there. It is easy to guess your employment under such an influence.

Mary's prudish reaction to Our divine Lord's unclothed state was similar to the reaction of Elizabeth herself before the statues in the Uffizi Gallery. Years later, Elizabeth was to confide to Father Gabriel Bruté that Mary, in trying to draw her away from her progress toward St. Peter's, had one day whispered to her: "They say, my sister, there is a great picture of Our Savior ALL NAKED—!" And Elizabeth continued: "Dearest G., it is a fact that a most pious, better-informed woman than my sister or poor Betsy Seton found me kneeling before my Crucifixion, and shrank back with horror, seeing a naked picture." Even puritanism, however, could not prevent Vallejo's masterpiece from smiting Mary Post's soul.

Cheverus answered Elizabeth and Antonio on March 4, and on the receipt of it Elizabeth immediately made her Catholic submission. It was such a letter as to dissipate the last faint wisps of hesitation from her soul:

Your conscience whispers sometimes that you are too partial to the Catholic side, and unwilling to pass to the other side when your ideas seem to lead you to it. But it appears to me, that if at times you have doubts, anxieties, you are never for a moment a strong Protestant, although you are often—you say—a good Catholic; and I believe you are always a good Catholic. The doubts which arise in your mind do not destroy your faith; they only disturb your mind.

Who in this life, my dear Madam, is perfectly free from such troubles? "We see as through a glass in an obscure manner," we stand like Israelites at the foot of the holy mountain, but in spite of dark clouds and the noise of thunder, we perceive some rays of the glory of the Lord and we hear His divine Voice.

I would, therefore, advise your joining the Catholic Church as soon as possible, and when doubts arise, say only: "I believe, O Lord, help Thou my unbelief."

From the moment of reading this letter, Elizabeth enshrined Father Cheverus in a special niche in her heart. Even from so far away, his gaze had pierced her soul. How well he had probed it is evident from the secret confidence she made Father Bruté in 1816:

I tell you a secret hidden almost from my own soul—it is so delicate—*that* my hatred of opposition, troublesome inquiries, etc., brought me in the Church more than conviction. How often I argued to my fearful, uncertain heart: at all events Catholics must be as safe as any other religion; they say none are safe but themselves—*perhaps it is true*. If not, at all events I shall be [as] safe with them as any other. It is the way of suffering and the cross; for me, that is another point of security.

The force of Filippo's advice had at length come home to her. Months ago he had asked her:

Do you expect ever to be able to understand all the subaltern questions that may arise? If you are sick, you send for a doctor. Do you pretend to question him on every point of his medical science before you submit yourself to his prescriptions? You are satisfied to know he is one of the best doctors in the place.

Our prudence in temporal concerns may well be followed in our spiritual ones. The study of religion cannot, ought not, to be complicated. You know that Jesus Christ has established a Church that cannot err, cannot fail and, of course, cannot be subject to variation. . . . If you find it, submit yourself to her decisions without further inquiries. . . . Your submission will be reasonable even on those points you may not understand, because it is reasonable to trust in the word of a Church which is the column of firmness and truth.

And submit herself she did, on March 14, 1805, in the presence of Father Matthew O'Brien and Antonio Filicchi. The stress of months was gone, and she was once again her old, gay self, almost fey in her carefree happiness.

> After all were gone, I was called to the little room next the altar, and there professed to believe what the *Council of Trent* believes and teaches; laughing with my heart to my Savior, who saw that I knew not what the Council of Trent believed—only that it believed what the Church of God declared to be its belief, and consequently is now *my belief*. For as to going a-walking any more about what all the different people believe, I cannot, being quite tired out—and I came up light at heart and cool of head the first time these many long months—but not without begging Our Lord to wrap my heart deep in that opened side so well described in the beautiful Crucifixion, or lock it up in His little tabernacle, where I shall now rest forever.
>
> Oh, Amabilia, the endearments of this day with the children, and the play of the heart with God while keeping up their little farces with them!

The question has long been agitated as to whether Elizabeth was baptized conditionally upon her reception into the Catholic Church. Her first biographer, Father Charles White, stated categorically that she was. Father Charles Souvay, C.M., late Superior General of the Vincentian Fathers and the Daughters of Charity, studied the question thoroughly and came to the conclusion that her re-baptism was merely possible, not probable. His conclusion is sound. Bishop Carroll and Father Cheverus both believed in the validity of Episcopalian baptism, as conferred at that time. Carroll, in fact, warned his priests to investigate the Protestant baptisms of converts carefully, lest they incur the ecclesiastical penalties laid down for clerics who should confer the sacraments needlessly. There is no record of conditional baptism for Elizabeth in the archives of St. Peter's, Barclay Street. But, when every scientific argument has been turned and carefully examined, the most convincing argument of all still remains with Elizabeth herself. She never mentioned Catholic baptism for herself, or her children, or later for Cecilia or Harriet Seton. It is impossible to imagine her, who habitually noted down the minutest details of her life even to verbosity, omitting anything so important, had it occurred.

Once a Catholic, Elizabeth set about preparing for the consolation of her first confession. She had none of the fear of it understandably common in most adult converts.

> So delighted now to prepare for this good confession which, bad as I am, I would be ready to make on the housetop to insure the good *absolution* I hope for, after it. And then to set out [on] a new life, a new existence itself. No great difficulty for me to be ready for it, for truly my life has been well culled over in bitterness of soul, these months of sorrow past.

And on March 20, she exclaimed with joy over her day of release:

> It is done! Easy enough: the kindest, most respectable confessor is this Mr. O'[Brien], with the compassion and yet firmness in this work of mercy which I would have expected from Our Lord Himself. Our Lord Himself I saw in him, both in his and my part of this venerable Sacrament. For, oh, Amabilia, how awful those words of unloosing after thirty years' bondage! I felt as if my chains fell, as those of St. Peter at the touch of the divine Messenger. My God, what new scenes for my soul!

She waited now for the heavenly feast, the reality of the Divine Food whetting the appetite of her soul as the most desired of Protestant communions could never have done. This was her lodestone, the reward she had never lost sight of in the darkest shades of confusion. She went each morning to Mass with the shining eyes of a child who presses his nose against a shop window filled with the most fabulous sweets.

> ANNUNCIATION DAY, I shall be made one with Him who said, "Unless you eat My Flesh and drink My Blood you can have no part with Me." I count the days and hours. Yet a few more of hope and expectation, and then— How bright the sun, these morning walks of preparation! Deep snow or smooth ice, all to me the same. I see nothing but the little bright cross on St. Peter's steeple. The children are wild with their pleasure of going with me in their turn.
>
> 25TH MARCH
>
> At last, Amabilia, at last, GOD IS MINE AND I AM HIS! Now, let all go its round—I Have Received Him. The awful impressions of the evening before, fears of not having done all to prepare, and yet, even the transports of confidence and hope in His Goodness. MY GOD! To the last breath of life will I not remember this night of watching for morning dawn; the fearful.

beating heart so pressing to be gone; the long walk to town; but every step counted, nearer that street, then nearer that tabernacle, then nearer the moment He would enter the poor, poor little dwelling so all His own— and when He did, the first thought I remember was: "Let God arise, let His enemies be scattered!"—for it seemed to me my King had come to take His throne, and instead of the humble, tender welcome I had expected to give Him, it was but a triumph of joy and gladness that the deliverer was come and my defense and shield and strength and salvation made mine for this world and the next.

On, on she rushed in her natural exurberance: "Now, then, all the excesses of my heart found their play and danced with more fervor— no, must not say that—but perhaps, almost with as much as the royal prophet's before his ark. For I was far richer than he, and more honored than he ever could be. Now, the point is for the fruits. So far, truly I feel all the powers of my soul held fast by Him who came with so much majesty to take possession of His little poor kingdom."

The greatest joy of all was that she could receive Him again, and again, and again—as long as her life should last; and she began at once to prepare for "an Easter Communion . . . in my green pastures, amidst the refreshing fountains for which I thirsted truly."

XIII

"Poor, Deluded Mrs. Seton"

Elizabeth Seton had indeed done violence to herself in becoming a Catholic in New York in 1805.

It is an awesome thing to contemplate how the splendid Church of Medieval and Renaissance Christendom had come to Manhattan Island, shabby and mean and soiled. By far the greatest part of the congregation on Barclay Street was composed of poor immigrants, Irish, French and German; and it is no reflection on their piety and faith to record that they had as little of manners and polish as they had of money. They stayed in their squalor through no fault of their own; they were kept there by social convention and even by law—John Jay's odious "Naturalization" law, which insisted that no one could hold political office unless he renounced allegiance even to foreign ecclesiastical rulers.

Be the blame where it may, it was a distasteful thing for a gentlewoman like Elizabeth Seton to become identified with these despised and "off-scoured" people. She remembered her distaste vividly more than ten years later, in relating to Father Bruté, with her gift for mimicry, a conversation she had had with Wright and Mary Post:

> My brother Post once asked me so simply:
> "Sister Seton, they say you go to the Catholic Church. What is the difference?"

"*It is the first Church, my brother, the old Church, the Apostles begun,*" (answered the poor, trembling Betsy Seton, dreading always to be pushed on the subject she could only feel, but never express to these coolest reasoners).

"*Church of the Apostles,*" said my brother, "*Why, is not every church from the Apostles?*"

Sister Post interrupted:

"Well, Apostles or no Apostles, let me be anything in the world but a Roman Catholic—a Methodist, Quaker, anything! A Quaker, indeed, I should like extremely; they are so nice and orderly and their dress so becoming. But Catholics—! Dirty, filthy, red-faced—the church a horrid place of spits and pushing—ragged, etc., etc."

And Elizabeth added, sadly: "Alas, I found it all that indeed."

Some of the priests were little more genteel than their parishioners. Writing to Antonio in Philadelphia on April 6, 1805, she contrasted them to what he had said of the gentle Cheverus "and his manner of instruction."

It requires indeed a mind superior to all externals to find its real enjoyment here. A stranger has assisted, the last week, but certainly is not my acquisition in that respect. I am forced to keep my eyes always on my book, even when not using it. Never mind, these things are but secondary, as your dear eloquence has taught me; but it is my weakness to be too much influenced by them.

Aside from thus lowering her social standing, Elizabeth's conversion further estranged her from her family and friends. They remained on speaking terms, but a subtle though distinct change had taken place, and their patronizing airs infuriated her, as she confided to Julia Scott: "I could go almost mad at the view of the conduct of every friend I have here, except yourself. It would really seem that, in their estimation, I am a child not to be trusted with its daily bread, lest it should waste it."

Though grace had overlaid her natural spiritedness, it could rumble dangerously like a suppressed volcano when patronizing passed on to criticism. "I tell them instantly, with a cold, decided countenance, that the time of reasoning and opinions is past," she told Antonio, "nor can I be so ungrateful to God, after the powerful conviction He has so graciously given me, as to speak one moment on the subject, as it would certainly offend Him." Surely there was nothing more to talk about after that! Dué, too, was kept busy defending her friend to the "kind ladies" who wept over "the poor, deluded Mrs. Seton," but hers was a friend's defense: "She always tells them how happy she is that anything in this world can *comfort* and *console* me."

John Wilkes reproached her sharply but courteously for offending her "Uncle [Charlton] and other friends," but offered no insult to her religion; he agreed, in fact, that *"the evidences of the Christian religion were all on that side,"* and finished by assuring Elizabeth that her "sentiments made no difference to him." Mary Post was not happy over the change, but learned to live with it and never lessened her love.

Saddest of all was the break with her beloved Henry Hobart. She did not linger over it, but reported simply to Antonio: "Saturday last I had a very painful conversation (certainly for the last time, with Mr. H.), but was repaid fully and a thousand times on Sunday morning by my dear Master at Communion, and my Faith, if possible, more strengthened and decided than if it had not been attacked." And with these words she closed the book of her greatest Protestant enthusiasm forever.

Elizabeth's half-brother Carleton displayed a knowledge of the world far beyond his nineteen years, when he wrote her from Leghorn:

> I shall say nothing to you about your change of faith, as you must know best what you do. I can only assure you that it will not diminish in the least the sincere affection I have always had for you and yours. What troubles me most is that I fear it will serve for a cloak to those who could not otherwise have refused them, to withdraw those little assistances which your present situation necessarily requires.

Elizabeth was introduced to Catholic ceremonies at a puzzling time for a new convert. It was Passiontide, and the Holy Week ceremonies completely mystified her, except when she discerned in them "the Divine Sacrifice, so commanding and yet already so familiar for all my wants and necessities. That speaks for itself, and I am all at home in it." Her other familiar landmark was the *Pange Lingua* of Holy Thursday with its closing verses beginning *Tantum Ergo*, "that lovely hymn to the Blessed Sacrament." The words perfectly suited the mood of her conversion and set her off on one of her beautiful written meditations for Amabilia:

"Faith for all defects supplies, and sense is lost in mystery"—"Here the faithful rest secure, while God can vouch, and Faith insure." But you would sometimes enjoy, through mischief, if you could just know the foolish things that pass my brain after so much wonderful knowledge as I have been taking in it, about idol worshipping, etc., etc.,—even in the sacred moments of the Elevation, my heart will say, half-serious, "Dare I worship You, Adored Savior?" But He has proved to me well enough *there* what He is, and I can say with even more transports than St. Thomas, "My Lord and My God!" Truly, it is a greater mystery how souls for whom He has done such *incomprehensible things* should shut themselves out by incredulity from his best of all gifts, this Divine Sacrifice and Holy Eucharist —refusing to believe in spiritual and heavenly order of things *that* W*ord* which spoke and created the whole natural order, recreating through succession of ages for the body, and yet He cannot be believed to recreate for the soul. I see more mystery in this blindness of redeemed souls than in any of the mysteries proposed in His Church. With what grateful and unspeakable joy and reverence I adore the daily renewed virtue of that Word by which we posses Him in our blessed Mass and Communion!

John Wilkes' scheme for Elizabeth to board his own motherless sons and the sons of his brother Charles, plus a dozen or so others, was put off until May and finally abandoned altogether. Filicchi, aware of the Protestant atmosphere of New York and of the cooling of Elizabeth's connections toward her, made the suggestion that she take her children back to Italy to live. He urged it strongly upon her, as she told Amabilia:

Much he says of my bringing all the children to your Gubbio to find peace and abundance. But I have a long life of sins to expiate, and since I hope always to find the morning *Mass in America*, it matters little what can happen through the few successive days I may have to live, for my health is pitiful. Yet, we will see. Perhaps Our Lord will pity my little ones. At all events, happen now what will, I rest with God. The tabernacle and Communion! So now I can pass the Valley of Death itself.

She had already told Julia Scott that she had made up her mind not to accept Antonio's "fascinating schemes" for the present, "though I do not see my duty to my dear ones in a clear view, either way." She had long perceived the problem—even before Antonio—of bringing up her children as Catholics among Protestant relatives, and of their remaining in the Church should she die while they were small; for, on January 24 she had written to Antonio:

You speak so highly of the Catholic priests of Boston. Perhaps it would be best you should give a short history of your dear sister to the one you esteem most, as I may one day find the benefit of your doing so; for it is plain, that if the gracious God should bless me so as really to unite me to your Communion—though I might persevere through every obstacle myself, I could never separate my children from the influence of my connections, and must try every way for the best.

There were reasons far beyond her later position in a religious society for giving Elizabeth the name of "Mother." The word was more than a title; it was an affirmation. She was essentially a mother. Everyone felt it: the poor, the sick and dying in New York; her intimate friends; the orphaned Setons; her future pupils in Emmitsburg. It was, perhaps, the charm that drew good men to her. There was much of the devotion and dependence of sons in the affection of Antonio Filicchi, of Simon Gabriel Bruté and a host of college students, seminarians and priests at Mount St. Mary's—and even of her husband, her own dear William. It should not be surprising, then, that at every turning of her life, her first thought should be for her children. It was the desire of her children's salvation, as well as her own, that brought her into the Church. It would be the good of her children that would influence her move to Baltimore, and even the final version of the rule for her Sisterhood.

And it was this paramount responsibility for her children that led her now to ponder various plans for her future livelihood.

The collapse of the Wilkes plan caused her to cast about for a house, because the house she had lived in since her return to America was an integral part of it. An alternate came her way almost immediately, and she hastened to submit it to Antonio for his counsel:

Mrs. Dupleix . . . has suggested an idea of which I wish your opinion. A Mr. White, an English gentleman of very respectable character and a complete scholar, but in reduced circumstances, is endeavoring to establish a school for young ladies and perhaps boys also, in which his wife will assist. He has seen my children, and is interested for us. He has offered to teach them, and receive me as an assistant in his school, in case it succeeds—in which there is every prospect—as he is well recommended, and a school such as he proposes is very much wanted, I should have a good prospect for the education of my boys.

Antonio answered at once, approving the new plan, and suggesting that she might want to consult Fathers O'Brien and Cheverus, and John Wilkes. With her usual dispatch, she had been ahead of him, and already had the business-like approval of Wilkes and Wright Post, and the permission of Father O'Brien to say—in the face of Protestant fears —that her "principles and duties in this instance were separate, except the former were called for."

The priest's advice is as valid today for Catholic teachers in public school, who are in the same position as Elizabeth Seton was then. In commenting on it, Antonio remarked with wise practicality: "In such country as America in particular this mutual forbearance is quite to the advantage of the true cause of Catholicism, since the proportion of its inhabitants and its schools and institutions are so much against us."

This statement of policy was necessitated by the activities of Henry Hobart. No sooner had word gotten around that Elizabeth was considering the school venture, than the rumors flew that Mr. and Mrs. White were Roman Catholics and that Mrs. Seton joined herself in their plan to advance the principles of her new religion. Hobart had already warned Elizabeth that he felt it his duty to alert the parish against "the falsity and danger of [her] principles." She had quite agreed that, "if he thought it his duty, he must act in conformity to it," and had affirmed that she, for her part, would do the same. Now poor Hobart, like Lewis Carroll's knight, who "galloped off in all directions at once," warned the populace of the plot to pervert their children. To his credit, however, when Dué and Sad went to him and explained that the Whites were Protestants and "Mrs. Seton's only intention was to obtain bread for her children, and to be at peace with all the world instead of making discord between parents and children," Hobart immediately offered to make amends by using his influence to advance the school.

No sooner was Antonio's vote in, than Elizabeth entered into an agreement with the Whites. Her profits were to be one-third of the proceeds, including the education of her children. She had been partially freed from her household duties for the project by the generosity of Julia Scott, who had offered her $300—of which she took only half, and with it hired a woman to relieve her of "the dreaded burden of patching and darning."

In the midst of her attempts to settle down to a steady way of life, Elizabeth did not neglect her correspondence. She wrote to Father Cheverus, announcing her reception into the Church and thanking him for his part in it; she set out for his inspection her pattern of spiritual reading and begged him to suggest additions or changes. His reply is lost, but it sent Elizabeth into raptures of satisfaction. She passed it on to Antonio under the impulse that makes friends anxious to share their treasures:

> Judging your heart by my own, you will be pleased that I enclose you Cheverus' letter, which I beg you will keep as gold until we meet again. I cannot part with it without reading it many times; and while my soul is lifted in thankfulness and joy for its privilege of asking and receiving advice and being numbered among the friends of so exalted a being as your Cheverus, its sensibilities are increased and every power brought in action in the remembrance that it is to my Brother, Protector, Friend, Benefactor, that I owe this. . . .

She continued to fulfill her duties as a true and loyal sister to Antonio by writing to him as frequently as possible while he was delayed by business in Philadelphia, where she had sent him armed with a letter to Julia introducing him as "very much the gentleman, but too different a character to engage acceptance on first acquaintance." Her letters were a pleasing contrast to the Boston correspondence; they were uniformly gay and happy, revealing as nothing else could her new sunniness of soul. She teased Antonio unmercifully by refusing to let him forget the Boston instructress he had been too shy to mention: "Do you meet any elegant friends in Philadelphia?" she asked him. "Any pupils for the Italian language? Any sirens? God preserve you! I pray that your good angel may have no cause to turn from you, and that you may be faithful to all his admonitions." She opened her very heart to him, sharing each spiritual discovery and reward, and even revealing with unconscious simplicity the purity and delicacy of her soul:

> From circumstances of particular impressions on my mind, I have been obliged to watch it so carefully and keep so near the Fountain Head, that I have been three times to Communion since you left me, not to influence my faith, but to keep peace in my soul, which without this heavenly resource would be agitated and discomposed by the frequent assaults which,

in my immediate situation, are naturally made on my feelings. The counsel and excellent directions of O'B also, if even I was sensible of them before, strengthen me and, being sometimes enforced by command, give a determination to my actions which is now indispensable. . . . Sometimes I am really afraid to go to him, having so little or nothing to say; for though there is a cloud of imperfection surrounding every moment of my life, yet, for those things that have a name, my soul would be too happy in being so free from them, if it did not dread the hour of temptation, knowing too well its fraility to even hope such a state should last.

On one occasion, when she had missed writing her usual weekly letter and he had complained, she answered with true female exasperation at the smugness of his injured male dignity:

You are, to be sure, a counsellor of the first order, and open your cause as a plaintiff, when I thought, opening your letter: *let me see Antonio's defense.* But you men, when once convinced of your consequence, are saucy mortals—that is well known. Three weeks today since you left your sister without any direction to you, in a state of utter uncertainty if your neck was broke or not, or perhaps you had not stole a march on me and gone to the Northward instead of to the Southward—and then you very modestly commence an accusation, in answer to a letter containing a most humble and earnest address to your charity and compassion!

When he told her, on May 21, that a court action he had instituted would not be tried until October, and that consequently, "my sweet Piccinina must wait longer for me than she expected. I shall pass a second winter in America, and cannot help it"—Elizabeth was glad she had written to Amabilia of Antonio's longing for her and his dear children:

Oh, how you would be pleased to see him so well, so handsome, so delighted with your sweet picture as scarcely to permit anyone to hold it in their hands—and certainly the expression of it is just such as you would have wished; tender and sorrowful, as if lamenting your separation. He feels it so—and speaks as tenderly to it as if you were present. He also talks of his Patrick as if he had seen him but yesterday. . . .

It was well that God had given Elizabeth these springtime weeks of happiness, for her accustomed course of trouble and sorrow was soon to resume. In the time of sunshine she had run quickly in God's way under the direction of Father Matthew O'Brien, whom she liked and trusted. He admitted her to Communion every Sunday, and introduced

her to the Society of the Holy Sacrament, whose rules he felt would
help her toward the perfection she sought.

In May Elizabeth moved to her new home, which was to serve also
for the schoolhouse. It delighted her that it was in the next street to
St. Peter's. Unfortunately, the school was doomed from the start: by
July there were still only three pupils beside the White and Seton children. Elizabeth herself was a sort of Jonas, for all protestations to the
contrary, this strange gentlewoman—turned Catholic—was not to be
trusted in the eyes of fashionable New Yorkers. Then the old mammy
fell sick again, and tiny Rebecca became so ill that it was thought she
must surely die. All the added work and worry, plus her teaching duties,
took their toll of Elizabeth, and she was soon so weak that the least
exertion left her faint and giddy. Mrs. Startin prescribed a glass of wine
a day, and the tonic helped to restore her. Perhaps the greatest reason
for the school's failure, however, was the lack of administrative ability
in Mr. White. A school of his had already failed in Albany; and Antonio,
who had stopped off in New York in July on his way to Canada, had
scarcely left the city when White informed Elizabeth that he could not
pay his share of the quarter's rent, due two days hence.

With the announcement, things moved fast; for Elizabeth had to get
out of the house before the landlord should attach the furniture and
all her effects. The Posts came to the rescue, and Wright Post hustled
the family off to his country seat in Greenwich. Then, as now, Greenwich
was called the Village, and the Post house was on Blessing Street (now
Bleeker Street) near Waverly Place.

Elizabeth was more or less disgruntled during her stay with her sister
and brother-in-law, which lasted until November. Because of the distance
from town, she was deprived of Mass and the Sacraments, even on Sunday. Then there arose a difficulty over the Catholic law of abstinence,
which, at that time, was commanded for Friday and Saturday of each
week. Elizabeth explained, rather petulantly, to Antonio: "My sister
procures fish with so great expense and difficulty (really as if for the
greatest stranger!) that my bread-and-water spirit is ashamed to partake
of it." The problem was easily disposed of by a dispensation from Father
O'Brien, "which, however," Elizabeth avowed, "shall never be used but
to keep peace."

She bridled, too, at suggestions for her future which she reported sarcastically to Antonio: "Some proposals have been made me of keeping a *tea* store or china shop, or small school for *little* children (too young, I suppose, to be taught the "Hail Mary.") In short, Tonino, they do not know what to do with me, *but God does*; and when His blessed time is come, we shall know."

On the opposite side—the Posts or their many friends who were in and out constantly plagued Elizabeth with unwelcome discussions of her religion, and even urged her to "hear some of their fine preachers"; and she was really alarmed for her children because of "the ridicule they are forced to hear of our holy religion and the mockery of the Church and ministers—besides their minds being poisoned with bad principles of every kind which I cannot always check or control." The latter accusation could hardly have been meant for the Posts, but probably for unruly playmates.

Elizabeth was aware that she was not entirely in the right. She begged Antonio not to give her "the scolding I know I deserve." She recognized the healthfulness of the country situation both for herself and the children; indeed, it may well have saved their lives, for the yellow fever struck the city hard almost immediately after they had left it. She appreciated the goodness of the Posts, and she confessed to Julia, after the ordeal was over, that part of her dissatisfaction was due to this very goodness: "It seemed as if there was no escape from the inconveniences and trouble I was necessitated to give the family of my brother P. The more kind they were to me, the more painful was my sense of it." Surely much of her unhappiness could be laid at the door of nature, dragged down by illness and discouragement.

Elizabeth had sought advice in her predicament from a new director, whom Cheverus had recommended to her—Father Jean Tisserant. Little is known of Tisserant except that he was an emigré priest from the Diocese of Bourges. He had come to Wethersfield, Connecticut, via England, in 1798; and when Elizabeth first met him, was on his way to take up religious duties in Elizabethtown, New Jersey. Cheverus, in his letter of introduction, assured Elizabeth that, "if you want advice upon any particular subject, Mr. Tisserant is both learned and pious." Throughout the ensuing year, Father Tisserant became Elizabeth's principal spiritual adviser. His advice in September of 1805 was prudent and to-the-point:

> Do not let the ardent zeal for whatever can contribute to the glory of God and the edification of your neighbor—which, with so much pleasure, I have observed in your words and actions—make our holy religion appear to those you live with more rigid than it really is in things that are only of counsel or of ecclesiastical institution; and, in which, consequently, a person can be dispensed by the proper authority whenever there is sufficient reason.

Elizabeth had apparently showed Tisserant's letter to Sad, who added her own sharp words of advice. Knowing both Mary and Elizabeth as she did, she understood that the problem was basically one of personalities, for the Bayley sisters had always had their disagreements.

> Does your sister and her husband really desire your remaining with them? [she asked Elizabeth]. Of this I think there can be little doubt, however some inequalities of temper may seem to contradict it. Were this not the case, I am inclined to rely upon the good judgment of P[ost] that he would find means of putting an end to such domestic inquietudes. Perhaps not even *I* have it in my power to conceive how hard (in your situation) such inequalities are to submit to. But let us only repeat with that respected teacher of the truth, that the harder they are to bear, the greater will be your reward if you bear them as a cross at the foot of which feelings of worldly considerations must be sacrificed when we resolve to do all for the glory of God. Now this can only be done from a conviction that your duty is to remain where you are, or rather that you are placed there by the divine Will. . . . Ask yourself if, at any time past that you can recollect, your sister appeared happier than she does at present. You might be enabled by such retrospections to remove from your mind some of the scruples you feel respecting her quiet. For my part, I am inclined to believe that you may be an instrument in God's hand to do her much good.

Elizabeth's already strained relations with the Setons were further stretched by the quickening interest in Catholicism of Cecilia and Harriet Seton, and their cousin Eliza Farquhar. Cecilia was undoubtedly the moving spirit of this little group, both as the bravest and the most spiritual. She had advanced wonderfully in piety even as a child, and a religious bond had already bound her to Elizabeth before the Italian voyage. Now, at fifteen, she was ready to take a place such as Rebecca had filled in Elizabeth's heart.

It is not hard to understand the eager interest of Cecilia and Harriet. Elizabeth had been their true mother in the years following the death of William Seton Sr., and they adored her. In the simple directness of their youthful logic, whatever she did must be right.

As the months went on, Harriet and Eliza Farquhar quailed and retreated before the growing force of family displeasure. Eventually, young Eliza abandoned the field altogether. But Cecilia was made of sterner stuff. Behind the facade of her frail beauty and the languor of advanced consumption, there lurked the streak of Seton stubbornness.

Cecilia was living with her brother James in his home, "The Wilderness," on the banks of the Hudson at present-day Forty-third Street. The house was on a peninsula of land that became an island when tides of rising water cut it off from the "mainland." Because of the distance from town and the family's increasing determination to keep Cecilia from her Catholic sister-in-law, the two had recourse to constant notes sent back and forth, usually through the good offices of young Sam Seton, whom they affectionately and conspiratorially referred to as "Much loved." Sam was a jolly youth, and his good-natured pranks and practical jokes were sunshine in Cecilia's exile.

Although Elizabeth herself was only a convert of a few months, she showed remarkable ability to direct Cecilia's soul. It was more than a mere development of the capacity for spiritual leadership which had caused Rebecca Seton and Catherine Dupleix to look up to her. Then she had been dealing with elementary beliefs and practices that were almost self-evident; now she was a member of a Church that regarded spiritual development as a science governed by laws that were founded upon unalterable doctrine. She could not recommend even to Protestant Cecilia practices that seemed good and holy and fitted to advance the soul that used them. Elizabeth had, of course, competent spiritual guides to instruct her; but what is noteworthy is how quickly she assimilated their teaching, so thoroughly as to be able to pass it on to someone else, clothed in her own words. Certainly in the following exhortation to Cecilia, she spoke confidently, "as one having authority":

> We must pray literally without ceasing—without ceasing; in every occurrence and employment of our lives. You know I mean that prayer of the heart which is independent of place or situation, or which is, rather,

a habit of lifting up the heart to God, as in a constant communication with Him.

As, for instance, when you go to your studies, you look up to Him with sweet complacency, and think: O Lord! how worthless is this knowledge, if it were not for the enlightening my mind and improving it to Thy service; or for being more useful to my fellow-creatures, and enabled to fill the part Thy Providence may appoint me.

When going into society or mixing with company, appeal to Him Who sees your heart, and knows how much rather you would devote every hour to Him; but say: "Dear Lord! you have placed me here, and I must yield to them whom You have placed me in subjection to—O keep my heart from all that would separate me from Thee."

When you are excited to impatience, think for a moment how much more reason God has to be angry with you, than you can have for anger against any human being; and yet how constant is His patience and forbearance.

And in every disappointment, great or small, let your dear heart fly direct to Him, your dear Savior, throwing yourself in His arms for refuge against every pain and sorrow. He never will leave you or forsake you.

It is a marvel of concise direction! In these short paragraphs Elizabeth gave Cecilia a way of life that, properly followed and built upon, could lead her to salvation and even perfection.

Elizabeth and Cecilia found a warm friend and champion in Father Michael Hurley, O.S.A., who came to St. Peter's as an assistant in July, 1805, from old St. Augustine's in Philadelphia. He was a serious and determined young priest of twenty-five when he began his New York ministry; and, from a habit of speech, Elizabeth and Cecilia, with their penchant for mischievous nicknames, called him "Whyso," and later "St. Michael" or "St. M." They bestowed on him the kind of reverent and enthusiastic worship Elizabeth had once held for Henry Hobart.

It may have been through Father Hurley that Elizabeth became enamored of the works of the Augustinian Thomas of Jesus, to whom she mistakenly gave the title of saint. She confided to Cecilia that "Blessed Father Thomas has taken the place of all other reading and almost other prayers, for his works are a continual prayer." She avowed that "these Augustinians have certainly a very sweet spirit," and expressed her satisfaction that the great St. Augustine was her "patron saint in the chronological order," since she had been born on his feast day, August 28.

Elizabeth was dealt a "heavy blow" by the death of her half-sister Emma Craig in childbirth on July 22, 1805. She had been closer to Emma than to her other half-sisters, especially after Emma's marriage to William Craig in 1799 which had occasioned so much family upset. The reconciliation with her stepmother had brought Elizabeth yet more into the family circle and she, who was a family person, rejoiced in knowing her sisters Mary and Helen better. She helped nurse Emma in this last illness, and confessed to Julia that "sitting up with her and seeing her struggles was almost too much."

The renewed bond with her sisters was indeed providential, for Mrs. Bayley herself took sick in August and died on the 1st of September, leaving the two teen-age girls almost bereft. It was an "indescribable satisfaction" for Elizabeth to attend her stepmother also in her last hours, thus sealing off forever the unhappiness and rancor of former years. Mary Cowper Filicchi added a touch of pathos to the scene by asking—in a letter to Elizabeth dated September 27—to be remembered to "your amiable mother, Mrs. Bayley."

A matter that pressed on Elizabeth's mind these months was the education of her boys William and Richard, who were now nine and seven respectively. She recognized the need for male influence over them —in May she had confessed to Julia Scott that "my saucy boys almost master me"—and when Antonio Filicchi offered to pay for their schooling she accepted the offer gladly.

The choice of a school was thoroughly studied. The recently re-established Society of Jesus conducted Georgetown College or Academy at George Town, Maryland, and the Sulpician Fathers, St. Mary's Seminary and College, at Baltimore, Maryland. There was also a Sulpician Seminary and College at Montreal. Without having investigated the relative merits of the schools, Antonio at first favored sending the boys to Baltimore; but Father Tisserant suggested Montreal, and when Antonio had seen the installation there, in the summer of 1805, he swung to Tisserant's view. In fact, he was so favorably impressed that he made application for the young Setons and advised Elizabeth—even though the college could not take them for at least a year—to prepare them to "appear well-bred" and to "know how to write and read well, at least." He may have been merely paraphrasing the school's entrance require-

ments; but Antonio knew the Seton boys, and his words seem, therefore, to suggest that he did not think them ready to take their places
among the young gentlemen they would meet at Montreal.

Whether or not he had hit home, Elizabeth wrote to him at Boston
that "your idea of the Canada seminary frightens me"; and she added:
"I have a little secret to communicate to you when we meet (a sweet
dream of imagination) which, if you meet my opinion and views, could
render the Baltimore plan every way most preferable." This was an historic sentence, for it seems most probable that Elizabeth's "little secret"
was the germ of the idea that led to the establishment of the first Catholic day school in America, or the first native sisterhood, or both. Some
months later, when Filicchi had been told the secret, he referred to it
only as "your . . . dreams for your future old age."

The letter which first mentioned Elizabeth's "secret" was written on
October 11, 1805, and contained a paragraph revealing her inimitable
talent for giving memorable advice in a lighthearted and offhanded way:

> Do tell me when you have news from Leghorn what your dear Amabilia
> says of your long absence, and all the etceteras you know I would be so
> glad to hear. Also, say something to me of your dear friends in Boston,
> whether your calender of SAINTS is increased, if you have any new SCHOLARS,
> and if the old ones improve—and above all things, dear Tonino, if you try
> earnestly to "be good," which is my greatest interest.
>
> You remember the first letter you ever wrote me, you said your soul
> would call for me in Paradise; and now I declare I believe St. Peter would
> let me pass as soon as you—though I am at the eleventh hour—and per-
> haps listen to my entreaty not to shut the gate till Antonio enters. This
> sauciness is not a specimen of my humility, but to make you put on your
> consideration cap and not to be too sure because you have been always an
> Israelite; and of all things, do not trust to the prayers of others so much.
> You know you are without excuse, if you do not practice the good you have
> successfully taught.

Antonio answered on the 22nd, bidding her not to be frightened about
the Canadian scheme, since he had made no solid engagement; and,
like the true lover, he proudly displayed—in answer to Elizabeth's question about his wife's feelings—Amabilia's wholehearted trust in him:

> She is so good as to write me with great deal of delicate sentiment that,
> knowing my heart and principles, she will not, she thinks needless, to say

a word to me to shorten it [his absence]—as much as it may be in my power. She bids me only not to expose myself to unnecessary dangers; and confides that my health is to myself, to her, to the family, the most important, the essential, point of all speculations.

The days of Elizabeth's exile in Greenwich were ended in November, when John Wilkes revived his old plan for her to board students attending the school conducted by Mr. William Harris, Episcopalian Minister at St. Mark's-in-the-Bouwerie. In asking Antonio's consent to the plan, she told him the Wilkes brothers were "not sure that Mr. *Harris* (the School Master) will be associated with a Catholic, nor that *parents* will commit their children to my care, to live with me. I heard these suggestions with humility and secret gladness that I might bear the reproaches of *His* Name, and said I would do *anything* honest for a living." However, Mr. Harris proved to be broadminded, and Elizabeth soon rejoiced at being in her own home again—"on Stuyvestant Lane, Bowery, near St. Mark's Church." On the feast of St. Nicholas, December 6, she wrote with supreme content to Julia Scott:

> I hope this happy season will find you . . . as happy as it does me. Scarcely can that happiness be realized which has given me again a home; three dollars a week for each boy, with washing and mending paid for, will help at least to make us less a burden. And the pleasure of doing something for my darlings makes every labor easy. They already have their comfortable clothing, in anticipation of your love and care. . . . The one hundred dollars is laid by safely. It is a store for necessity. Anna will attend an excellent dancing master at Mrs. Farquhar's (who is our near neighbor) on the strength of it: not for the steps, but to obtain a little polish and to please Aunt Scott.

The work was not easy. Elizabeth had more than a dozen children committed to her care, "to board, wash and mend for." Even though she had "a good old woman" to help her, she found herself falling asleep at night prayers from the long day of activity that began at dawn. Nevertheless, although she still had most of her substance through the charity of John Wilkes, Wright Post, Mrs. Startin, Julia Scott and Antonio, she was indeed pulling her share of the load; and, best of all, was once more mistress of her own household.

XIV

The Preparation of a Soul

At the turn of the year, Cecilia Seton's always precarious health failed
suddenly. Her illness posed a perplexing and delicate problem for Elizabeth—aside from the anxiety of losing her. Knowing the child's soul as
she did, Elizabeth knew that she was well on her way to the Catholic
Church. At the same time, she was aware of the Setons' displeasure at
Cecilia's interest, and their all-too-well-founded suspicions that Elizabeth
favored it. So far, they had not forbidden her the sickroom; but Elizabeth was certain that, the minute she mentioned the Catholic faith to
the girl, she would be permanently excluded—and all would be lost.
What to do? It was a knotty problem for a new Catholic; indeed, it
was a knotty problem for the competent Cheverus—as he humbly admitted—but he gave just the right advice, in a letter of the 26th of
January, 1806.

> I must tell you first, that your conscience ought to be free from
> scruples about the past, since you have done in regard to your interesting
> sister everything which you thought discretion and prudence could allow.
> In her present situation, is it your duty to go farther? I am at a loss myself
> how to give an answer to this question . . .
> Neither the obstacles you mention, nor the sickly state of the dear child,
> permit to instruct her in points of controversy. What you have told her 'till

now, appears to me nearly sufficient. I would recall to her when op-portunities should offer, the amiable and pious wish of living one day in a convent, and there to become a member of the Church . . .

The most embarrassing circumstance will be when you will see her near the period of the fatal disorder. Then perhaps you will be near her oftener and alone. Let the love of Our Adorable Savior in His Sacrament and on the cross be the subject of your discourse. You might also men-tion the anointing of the sick in St. James, and if she desires it and it can be done, procure to her the blessing of receiving the last Sacraments. Could they be hardhearted enough to refuse such a request and at such a time? . . .

Your beloved sister has been made by Baptism a member of the Church. Wilfull error, I have reason to think, has never separated her from that sacred body. Her *singular innocence of mind and ardent piety* have also, very likely, preserved her from offending God in any grievous manner; and I hope in consequence that, even if she cannot receive the Sacraments, she will be a member of the triumphant Church in heaven.

The reference to Cecilia's expressed desire for the convent indicates how she "thought with the Church," and how closely her footsteps had followed the path that had carried Elizabeth there. The letter might, indeed, have been written for Elizabeth in the latter days of her sojourn in Leghorn.

Cecilia recovered, however, and hurried to make up time in coming to a full knowledge of the truth.

Despite her worries for Cecilia, Elizabeth's new-found contentment persisted, as she told Julia on January 20: "This season finds me so much more comfortable and happier in every respect than the last, that your dear heart would rejoice if it could witness the change." A deep peace lay in this letter and Elizabeth gave the reason for it in a laconic para-graph that summed up an era of her life:

You asked me long ago about my religious principles. I am gently, quietly and silently a good Catholic. The rubs, etc., are all past. No one ap-pears to know it except by showing redoubled kindness—*only* a few knotty hearts that must talk of something, and the worse they say is: "So much trouble has turned her brain." Well, I kiss my crucifix, which I have loved for so many years, and say they are only mistaken.

So we go, dear Julia, traveling on. Take care, Miss, where you stop.

The letter was delivered by Antonio, who was on his way to Baltimore to try the legal suit that had kept him in America an extra year. This infinitely kind man had promised to investigate Georgetown and St. Mary's as possible schools for the Seton boys while he was in Maryland, and had further relieved their mother's mind by promising them places in his counting house at Leghorn when they should be old enough. It was typical of him that, before he left New York, he thoughtfully sent Elizabeth one hundred dollars and Milner's *Letters to a Prebendary*. He and Filippo, besides, never ceased to remind her that she and her children could make a home with them in Italy, whenever she wished.

Elizabeth was finding all manner of good and loyal friends to replace the old ones she had lost. Despite the weighty business of his office, Bishop John Carroll himself joined Father Tisserant and Father Cheverus as a more or less regular correspondent. One Sunday morning at St. Peter's she met James Barry and his wife, Joanna—the same Barry who had known Will and so graciously given him a letter of introduction when the Setons sailed for Leghorn. The friendship that developed with the little widow was a boon to the Barrys, who had just buried their daughter Mary in January. Father Francis Matignon, Pastor of Holy Cross Church in Boston and Cheverus' dearly loved colleague, also became at this time one of Elizabeth's cherished correspondents and friends —though she was never to meet him face to face. Matignon, born in Paris in 1753, came to America in 1792 with Father Maréchal, the future Archbishop of Baltimore, and Father Richard, the only Catholic priest ever to serve in the Congress of the United States. Matignon was Boston's first priest, and was to serve the city for twenty-six years.

Elizabeth had, therefore, no lack of advisers; nor did she ever fail, especially in the critical moments of her life, to consult them. It was this humble prudence of hers that gave her work the solidity that guaranteed its permanence and expansion.

Elizabeth's health was poor that spring. She was a tiny, bird-like creature, and had a bird's quick energy and rapid metabolism. It was almost natural that she should collapse from time to time, so that nature might have some little period of rest to restore the ravages to her frame. The fact that constant heavy trials and the inexorable development of tuberculosis piled ever-increasing burdens on her temperament made it practically a miracle of divine grace that she survived to do her life's work.

Her weakness and her duties to her boarders prevented her going to church on Ash Wednesday and, continuing throughout Lent, prevented her from keeping the penitential season as she would have liked; however, as happens so often, her resignation and acceptance of disappointment brought Elizabeth blessings of their own in the deathless good advices of Father Tisserant. On March 9 he wrote her:

> You tell me that you were prevented from going to church on Ash Wednesday. . . . Your Lent has commenced with a sacrifice and with the mortification of the will, and with good resolutions which I hope God will bless. Strengthen them by the practice of what the Church enjoins at this holy time. But do not exaggerate things. Remember what you have to do as a mother and in the employment which you have undertaken. . . .
>
> You did well to reject the thoughts that tended to disturb the peace of mind which you enjoyed at the beginning of Lent. The recollection of our past faults ought not to beget disquietude. A mental calm that springs from a principle of pride or presumption, or leads to the neglect of duty, is indeed to be feared; but yours, accompanied as it is by a sense of your former sins, and with a constant disposition to do all you can in the future for love of Our divine Master . . . is, in my opinion, the result of . . . filial confidence. . . .
>
> It will give me pleasure to learn that you are accustoming yourself to banish those vague anxieties which sometimes haunt your mind. . . . The habit of dismissing them will give you more control over your imagination, and will contribute to your perfection as well as to your happiness.

As Lent drew to an end and the Church's cries to penance grew more insistent, Tisserant warned her lest she think the message meant for her, and commanded her to put off to a later time, when she should be stronger, the penitential practices she was eager to perform. With great wisdom, he substituted for her devotion on Good Friday a practice that was wholly spiritual:

> Cast yourself in the arms of an expiring Savior. Give yourself to Him, and dwell upon the confidence and consolation which this great mystery should inspire. You have told me that the Heart of Jesus was your refuge. Let it be so always. Retired within that asylum, what have you to fear? and what can appear to you burdensome or painful?

In consequence of acceding faithfully to the direction of Father Tisserant, Elizabeth could assure Antonio that her weakened condition was not due to irresponsible mortification: "The kind protestors say it is only the consequence of keeping Lent, but that is not the truth, as really every precaution has been taken—but God knows and will direct it."

Because of her distance from town, Elizabeth made a day of it, the Sundays she could go to St. Peter's. She would attend an early Mass, then have breakfast at Sad's or Dué's or the Barrys', or even with Father Byrne or Father Hurley; and return to hear more Masses. She would take her dinner with some friend, also, and go back to church for Vespers. Sunday was often her day for confession and spiritual direction, although she sometimes met with disappointment because the priests were busy with their other duties.

On April 18, Antonio wrote that he had been to Washington, Alexandria and Mount Vernon; and had been received by Bishop Carroll and Bishop Leonard Neale, his coadjutor, who was also at this time President of Georgetown. "I have visited both the colleges," Antonio told her. "I have taken all the proper information. I shall keep my word with you, and when in New York, we shall consult together and resolve for the best. My preference, meanwhile, is decidedly for Montreal." He was desirous, too, that Tisserant, Cheverus and Matignon should join in the discussion and final decision.

But, for some reason—perhaps her "secret"—Elizabeth was, and had been, set on Baltimore; and, like a woman, had blithely gone about the business of getting her way. In the January letter that Antonio had carried to Julia Scott, Elizabeth had told Julia that her boys would "go to the college at Baltimore immediately, if he [Antonio] can obtain them a situation." Such could certainly not have been his intention, to judge from this letter of April 16, unless his inspection of the schools had altered this original purpose—for the schools did not, apparently, particularly impress him. As a matter of fact, Bishop Carroll was having his hands full with both Georgetown and St. Mary's at this time: the Jesuit college could not assemble an adequate staff of instructors, and the Sulpician school was suffering from the anti-French prejudices of Federalist Maryland; to add to the trouble, both schools were fostering a bitter rivalry toward each other.

Almost as if she had not read Antonio's letter—which she had—Elizabeth answered, weighing the balance for Georgetown. She cited as her reasons, that Bishop Carroll favored Georgetown (naturally enough, since it was the child of his brain) and had offered to pay two hundred dollars toward the boys' expenses the two years they could be placed there; Father Tisserant went along, and so did Mr. Barry—and it also appealed to Elizabeth that the Barrys had a home near the college. That she, so to speak, "put a thumb on the scale" by adding the weight of a very partial letter from a Mr. Kelly, who was an instructor at Georgetown, showed what her choice was. Nevertheless, she must not be denied the credit of sincerity—albeit the sincerity of a woman whose mind was made up—in her protestation that "I very unwillingly and only in obedience to Mr. Tisserant make these observations to you, well knowing that you only can be a proper judge of what is right; and it would make me very unhappy to add voluntarily in any way to the trouble you already have for your poor sister."

Antonio gave way gracefully to the majority opinion for Georgetown, but reminded Elizabeth that Montreal should be kept in mind for the future, "when I trust your boys will be more prepared and more susceptible of a more refined education."

As it turned out, Elizabeth was right and Antonio was wrong—in the sense that, had the Seton boys gone at this time to Montreal, Mother Seton, her spiritual daughters and her work for Catholic education might have been lost to America. Although the thought of going with her family to Montreal was to come up again, the fact of her boys' being at Georgetown and the friendships she made because of it were certainly strands pulling her to Baltimore when the moment of decision came.

Within the week William and Richard Seton set off in the care of James Barry for Philadelphia, whence, after stopping to greet Mrs. Scott and Antonio, who was on his way back to New York, they proceeded to Baltimore. It was a time of partings for Elizabeth, because Antonio and Father Tisserant, too, were preparing to sail for Europe. Before they left, however, she had a joyful surprise in the arrival of Bishop Carroll in New York.

With her usual ardor, Elizabeth had already conceived an enthusiastic respect and affection for Carroll, and loved to study the portrait of him in the possession of the Barrys. To meet face-to-face this kind, saintly patrician, her father in God, was an overwhelming experience for the intense little widow; but her delight increased almost to ecstasy when the Bishop proposed to give her a week's instruction and spiritual direction in preparation for the Sacrament of Confirmation. She dashed off a letter to Father Tisserant, asking him to be her sponsor, but it arrived too late, and Father Hurley was proxy for him when the ceremony took place on Pentecost itself, May 26, 1806.

She chose the name of Mary which, she told Antonio in excited happiness, "added . . . to the *Ann Elizabeth* . . . present the three most endearing ideas in the world, and contain the memento of the mysteries of salvation." Carroll was pleased with her choice and always henceforth directed his letters to "Mrs. M. E. A. Seton"; Elizabeth herself began to sign much of her correspondence in this manner.

It was well for Elizabeth she had received the sacramental strength of the Holy Spirit, for in July a storm of religious hatred broke about her head that made the former coldness and insults seem smiles of approbation. It was a storm she had to meet alone, for Tisserant had sailed on June 9, and Antonio shortly afterward. The conversion of Cecilia Seton was the cause of it.

Although Cecilia made her home with her brother James, she was visiting her sister Charlotte, who was married to Gouverneur Ogden, when the crisis came. She was quite candid about her intentions, and served notice of them days in advance. Thus the Ogdens and the Setons had absolutely no grounds for the later accusation that she had deceived them.

It was necessary to remember that Cecilia was only sixteen years old and in the grip of a fatal disease, in order to understand the full horror of the terrible trial she suffered in the family counterattack. Ruthlessly, they levelled on this frail girl their heaviest artillery. It was painful enough to their sensibilities when one bearing their proud name had become a despised Roman; but Elizabeth was, after all, only a sister-in-law: Cecilia was a *Seton*, their own sister.

The threats they made were worthy of an ogre in a fairy tale; Cecilia would be sent away to the West Indies in a ship, then standing in the harbor ready to sail; Elizabeth would be destroyed and her children turned out to beg their bread; Ogden, a member of the New York Legislature, would prevail upon that august body to banish Elizabeth from the state. Charlotte Ogden and Mary Hoffman Seton turned into veritable hellcats and struck viciously.

There can be no doubt that Elizabeth had encouraged Cecilia's aspirations—she could not conscientiously discourage her from seeking the truth—but she in no way acted dishonorably; and there is poetic justice in the fact that the proof the Setons advanced for Elizabeth's complicity was wholly invalid. Mary Hoffman Seton had deliberately searched Cecilia's bureau and discovered Catholic literature, which Elizabeth was immediately accused of supplying, although Cecilia stoutly maintained that she had bought the books herself.

There is a momentary temptation to smile at the extravagance with which the Setons threatened Cecilia, but the aroused family was in earnest and said just the monstrous things that might be expected to terrify a child of sixteen. They finally locked her in her room for several days to think over whether she would precipitate such dire retribution upon the sister-in-law she so tenderly loved. It is always cowardly to strike at a person through a loved one, but its effectiveness cannot be denied.

It was not effective with Cecilia. She was too brave, she knew too well Elizabeth's mettle, she loved and trusted God too much, to be deterred. On the morning she was to be disowned and turned out-of-doors, the young girl showed that she, too, had her pride; she departed of her own accord, leaving a note that stated her position with determined dignity:

My dear Charlotte: In consequence of a firm resolution to adhere to the Catholic Faith, I left your house this morning; and can only repeat that, if in the exercise of *that* faith my family will again receive me, my wish is to return and give them every proof of my affection by redoubled care to please them and submission to their wishes in every point consistent with my duty to *Him* Who claims my first obedience. Under these circumstances, whatever is the Providence of Almighty God for me, I must receive it with entire resignation and confidence in His protection—but in every case must be your affectionate sister, Cecilia.

She went to the only refuge she knew, to the home and arms of Elizabeth. Three days later, on June 20, 1806, she knelt before Father Michael Hurley and made her submission to the Roman Catholic Church.

Charlotte and Mary called a family meeting, and issued the ultimatum that, should Cecilia persevere in her mad course, they would consider themselves bound never to speak to her again, nor to allow her over their thresholds. A month later, Cecilia stated her intention so to persevere, in a letter to Mrs. James Seton: "I am fixed, and firmly fixed; and nothing but death can break the bonds."

Elizabeth was pilloried all over the town. Everyone, it seemed, condemned her perfidy. Her Uncle John Charlton and her godmother, Mrs. Startin, cut her out of their wills. It was the loss of a huge sum of money to one who could well use it: both Charlton and Mrs. Startin were enormously wealthy, and had announced Elizabeth as their sole heir. Her name was treated with such contemptuous laughter at every fashionable dinner table that her boarders, taking the cue from their parents, became impudent and unruly, and to add to the indignity, the same parents turned around and reproached Elizabeth for not being able to handle their children! Henry Hobart took the trouble to visit everyone who knew her and warned them about communicating with her or supporting any endeavor she might attempt. Even Dué broke with her in disgust. This was a harder blow even than the betrayal of their long, intimate friendship, for Dué had shown such eager interest in Catholic teaching that Elizabeth had held great hopes for her.

It seems hardly too much to say that the wave of anti-Catholic feeling generated by Cecilia's conversion and Elizabeth's part in it ultimately contributed to the riot at St. Peter's on Christmas Eve of that year, when a mob of raucous men gathered in front of the church to heckle the worshippers. They were dispersed by a member of City Council and Andrew Morris, a friend of Elizabeth's and the first Catholic officeholder in New York City.

As they were to do years later, at the time of the Know-Nothings, the Irish next day formed a cordon to defend their church. A wild fight followed, in which the poor Councilman was killed and several wounded. The sad peace of that Christmas Day was restored only when Mayor DeWitt Clinton himself appeared on the scene and issued a proclamation that the Catholics were to be no more molested.

Elizabeth was cast down when she wrote in August to Antonio of the new persecution. Despite the heart plunged in the Heart of Christ, and the arms flung wide to embrace the cross, it was not easy for one who had danced at the President's Ball to be spurned like a dog. It was not her own fate that worried her, though, but the future of her children. Anna had only just awakened to the companionship of her aunts and her cousins—those same relatives who now breathed such venomous hatred What was to become of Anna, what was to become of Kit and little Rebecca—should their mother die and leave them to the charity of their Protestant kinsfolk? More and more, Elizabeth saw that she must get out of New York. "If you were now here, my dear brother," she pondered wistfully, "I think you would exert your friendship for us and obtain the so long desired refuge of a place in the Order of St. Francis for your converts." The reference is obscure—it may be that Elizabeth had been impressed by a convent of Poor Clares in Italy—but the yearning for the peace of the religious life is unmistakable. Her "secret" again.

In the midst of abuse and calumny, Elizabeth did not fail to receive from her true friends the support and encouragement she needed. "If blessed be those that are in tears, you, my poor, beloved sister, are blessed indeed," Antonio consoled her from London. "Courage and perseverance. . . . Pity, pray for your persecutors. Your forbearance, your fortitude, your charity, your piety will put them to blush at last. If not, God and I are your protectors; of whom shouldst *thou* be afraid?" Bishop Carroll took up this same theme of perseverance and the effect it must have on others; and Dr. Matignon wrote:

> Your perseverance and the help of grace will finish in you the work which God has commenced, and will render you, I trust, the means of effecting the conversion of many others. You already experience much consolation in the step taken by your dear sister, who has been led not less by your example than by the maladies and afflictions dispensed from Heaven, to embrace with so much fervor the only way to eternal life.

She found a special consolation in Anna's First Communion, which seemed to her the child's coming-of-age. "When you return, it will no longer be my little Anna, but my friend and companion," Elizabeth told the little girl. Anna had gone to stay with friends in town, that she might be near Father Hurley, who was giving her a week's instruction and spiritual preparation. Elizabeth added her own encouragement and advice in a note luminous with love:

My darling daughter: You must not be uneasy at not seeing me either yesterday or today. Tomorrow I hope to hold you to my heart, which prays for you incessantly that God may give you grace to use well the precious hours of this week; and, I repeat, you have it in your power to make me the happiest of mothers and to be my sweet comfort through every sorrow, or to occasion the heaviest affliction to my poor soul that it can meet with in this world.

And as your example will have the greatest influence on your dear little sisters also, and you do not know how soon you may be in the place of their mother to them, your doing your duty faithfully is of the greatest consequence, besides what you owe to God and your own soul. . . .

Remember that Mr. Hurley is now in the place of God to you. Receive his instructions as from heaven, as no doubt the dear Savior has appointed them as the means of bringing you there.

Antonio backed up his words of spiritual comfort to Elizabeth with an indignant letter addressed to John Murray and Sons, New York, guaranteeing that she should not suffer material want because of persecution.

Gentlemen: Christian religion founded in charity is so well understood by some of your neighbors, as to allow themselves the privilege of substituting vexation and persecution to the consolation and relief due to virtue in distress. I refer to my most respected convert, my virtuous, unfortunate friend, Mrs. W. M. Seton, as the persecuted person. The persecutors are her relations, her pretended friends; and religion, in the shocking inconsistency of their brains, is the pretense for vexation. I profess and I will evince, thank God, for better principles.

In addition to the order left with you on my departure from America, you are requested to furnish Mrs. Seton with whatever farther sum she might at any time call for to support herself and family. Perhaps she might resolve to seek for tranquility or retirement with us poor Roman Catholic fools, and we shall not be at [a] loss to find an asylum for them all at Gubbio or somewhere else. In that case, I would beg of you, my worthy friends, to lend her the necessary assistance. . . .

He enclosed this letter to Elizabeth, that she might understand what her resources were; and it is a tribute to her spirit of charity that she would not deliver the letter because it formally accused her persecutors. Antonio, however, knowing her virtuous heart, had wisely sent a duplicate direct to Murray.

While she accepted gratefully all the comforting words that came her way, she found her peace in the firm direction of Cheverus and Matignon who, she told Antonio, "opposed every wish of quitting so uncomfortable a situation—though certainly I never explained it in its extent to them—and I rest satisfied that, in obeying them, I shall do the Will of God which is the only object." It was this peace that caused her to exclaim:

> Upon my word, it is very pleasant to have the name of being persecuted, and yet enjoy the sweetest favors; to be poor and wretched, and yet to be rich and happy; neglected and forsaken, yet cherished and tenderly indulged by God's most favored servants and friends!

It is rather worthy of note that Elizabeth was silent, so far as posterity is concerned, about Antonio Filicchi's departure from New York. Once he had sailed, she never saw him again; yet, contrary to custom, she seems not to have written a line concerning the actual moment of parting, almost as if it were too sacred to write about, even to closest friends. She did not have to; anyone could easily imagine how it wrenched her heart and soul. And yet, she had perfected an attitude toward absent friends that thwarted distance: she loved her friends in God, from the depths of her soul, and spiritual love has nothing to do with place or time. It was always Elizabeth's lot that those she loved best were, for the most part, never near her; but she met them constantly just the same, in thought, in prayer and especially in the Mass and Holy Communion. And she never let go the certainty that she would be reunited with them in heaven, never to have to part with them again. Nor was it merely words, nor a device to soothe, but a bright reality.

Although she never lost the recollection of "the last kind look of my dear Tonino," Elizabeth constantly looked forward to the day of eternal meeting. She prayed unceasingly for it, and she recorded the reason for her holy anticipation in a memorable passage written for Antonio's eyes alone:

> Do you remember when you carried the poor little wandering sheep to the fold, and led it to the feet of its tender Shepherd? Whose warning voice first said: "My sister, you are in the broad way and not in the right one"? Antonio's. Who begged me to seek the right one? Antonio. Who led me kindly, gently, in it? Antonio. And when deceived and turning back, whose tender, persevering charity withheld my erring steps and strengthened

my fainting heart? Antonio's. And who is my unfailing friend, protector, benefactor? Antonio! Antonio! Commissioned from on high, the messenger of peace, the instrument of mercy. My God, My God, My God reward him! The widow's pleading voice, the orphan's innocent hands are lifted to You to bless him. They rejoice in *his* love, oh! grant him the eternal joy of Yours!

For his part, Antonio let Elizabeth know that obligation was not all on her side. When he wrote to give her the glad news that he had finally arrived safely in Leghorn, he told her in detail of a narrow escape he had had on Mount Cenis in the Alps when, through lack of a light to guide them, he and the other coach passengers were in imminent danger of plunging over a precipice, and were saved by the providential appearance of a shepherd carrying a lantern. Antonio attributed this escape without qualification to the prayers of Elizabeth.

> I looked immediately on you as my principal intercessor, and you must have had certainly a great share in my delivery. What wonder, then, in my readiness to be serviceable to you! Through your good example they find me now a better Christian than I was; and through you my mercantile concerns are blessed by God with an uninterrupted success. I shall not, therefore, be so fool as to desert your cause. Pray only Our divine Redeemer to extend His mercy towards me to the most important welfare in our next life. If I have been happy enough to be the instrument of introducing you to the gates of the true Church of Christ here below, keep me fast by you when called upstairs.

Meanwhile, the plan of God for Elizabeth Seton and the American Church began, almost imperceptibly, to get on. Pieces of this divine plan were already evident when Antonio left: Elizabeth's own desire for the religious life which, she confessed to Bishop Carroll that November, she had dreamed about since leaving Leghorn; her apprenticeship in teaching and the care of children; and her anxiety to remove her own children from the reach of their Protestant relatives. Now, Father William Valentine Dubourg began to put the pieces together in his energetic, practical way.

Dubourg was born in 1766 at Cape Français on the Island of San Domingo. He went to France for his education and remained there to study for the priesthood at St. Sulpice. The French Revolution drove him to America, via Spain, where he joined the Sulpician Community.

In 1799 he helped found St. Mary's, and was President of that institution when Elizabeth first met him in New York in November, 1806.

As Father Dubourg distributed Communion in St. Peter's, he was struck by the extraordinary fervor of a little woman in widow's weeds who wept as she received her Lord. He rightly guessed that this was Mrs. Seton, of whose trials and holiness he had heard in Baltimore, but checked with one of the parish priests when he sat down to breakfast afterwards. He had no sooner been assured of her identity, when there was a knock at the door and Mrs. Seton herself entered. The two were soon engrossed in an historic conversation over a cup of coffee.

Dubourg was the type of man who came immediately to the point. He asked Elizabeth her plans for the future; and she found herself telling this stranger of her dreams for some form of convent life in Montreal, where she might teach, when her boys should be finished at Georgetown —and she emphasized that this had been the ultimate wish of Antonio Filicchi. Dubourg concurred in the idea at once, and said he saw no difficulty in realizing it immediately. Other biographers have reported that he broached at this time the suggestion that she carry out her holy intentions in Baltimore; but Elizabeth certainly made no mention of Baltimore in the letters she sent off at once to Bishop Carroll and Antonio Filicchi. As a matter of fact, in Antonio's letter she said expressly that Dubourg "would have sent me to Montreal in a moment." It seems rather that the Baltimore plan evolved soon afterwards, in Boston, where Dubourg consulted with Cheverus and Matignon.

Assuredly, when Dubourg returned from Boston, the Baltimore alternative was definitely in the air; and Elizabeth's two priest friends in the New England capital wrote letters that glowed with the halo of true prophecy. Cheverus urged a change to Baltimore as better for her family and for the progress of religion in America. Matignon was even more specific: "You are destined, I think, for some great good in the United States," he told her, "and here you should remain in preference to any other location."

Both Bostonians, however, urged caution and a patient willingness to wait for the manifestation of God's Will. As Matignon put it: "God has His moments which we must not seek to anticipate, and a prudent delay only brings to maturity the good desires which He awakens within us."

Because of illness, Bishop Carroll did not communicate his views of the plan for six months, but he then informed Elizabeth that, although Father Dobourg had not discussed it with him, and he did not, therefore, know any particulars, "it is enough for me to know that it has the concurrence of Dr. Matignon and Mr. Cheverus."

And so, Elizabeth was happy that winter of 1806–1807. To begin with, her health was good, her boys were safe at Georgetown, her beloved Cecilia was with her, and the little girls were growing into the companions every woman wants in her daughters. Anna particularly pleased her; for, she told Julia, she was "almost as much a woman as her mother," and added with a mother's proud candor, "[but] much more discreet and considerate." What gave the greatest lift to her spirits, however, were the unexpected fires of hope Father Dubourg had lit in her heart. Even as a Protestant child reading ridiculous romances, the peace of the cloister had had a fascination for her. It had taken a firmer hold with the advent of Catholic reality, but remained still only a more vivid dream. But now, a wise, practical churchman had assured her that it was possible of attainment—and that greatest of God's servants, her dear Cheverus, had agreed with him! Was it any wonder she was so happy?

The mere possibility was enough for Elizabeth. She was indeed a dreamer, but she never confused dreams with realities. If the reality was to come, God would bring it—Cheverus and Matignon had said so, and she was content. This willingness to wait was, perhaps, the reason why she seemed scarcely to notice that her advisers had all swung their thoughts to Baltimore, while she, in a strange reversal, went back to thinking Antonio's thoughts of Montreal.

To add to Elizabeth's happiness even the breach with the Setons was healed—at least in so far as Cecilia was concerned—as winter passed into spring. It came about as a sort of legacy from Eliza Maitland. In March, poor Eliza, who had ailed so long and suffered so meekly the indignity of a worthless husband, entered upon her last illness. She asked for Elizabeth, who had always befriended her, and for Cecilia. The family granted her dying request or, as Elizabeth put it dryly to Antonio, "our services were willingly accepted to share the burden. No doubt, they would have been more acceptable, if they could have made us mute for the time, but it passed off very well." Elizabeth went at night, "like the bird of wisdom, you know," and Cecilia in the day, two or three times a week. When the end came, Elizabeth was alone with the poor woman and "closed her dying eyes."

Writing to Julia, Elizabeth took the occasion of Eliza Maitland's passing to urge on her fashionable friend warnings of eternity—as, in fact, she did in nearly every letter to Julia over a period of sixteen years.

Julia, my precious friend, this dear Eliza did not love the world. She had a bitter portion in it; and you would say a life passed in the slavery of poverty and secluded from those allurements which commonly endear us to the present scene would have ensured her at least a peaceful death. Some nights before her last, in an interval of ease, she conversed with me and observed herself that such had been her situation, but added:

"How is it, that until we are just going, we never think of the necessary dispositions to meet death?"

I made some consolatory reflections to her; but, although she said but little on the subject during her illness . . . her fears and dread continued to the last.

Oh, Julia, Julia, Julia! "The last, last, last sad silence." The soul departing without hope. Its views, its interests centered in a world it is hurried from. No Father's sheltering arms, no heavenly Home of joy. My Julia, Julia, Julia! Eternity—a word of transport, or of agony. Your friend, your own, your true, your dear friend begs you, supplicates you, in the Name of GOD—think of it. Oh! if she should see your precious soul torn, dragged an unwilling victim—what a thought of horror!

Do not be angry with me, dearest friend. Say not the entreaty is from a heart torn with misfortune or depressed by melancholy. Not so! Never was a more cheerful or contented heart than your friend's, absolutely reposed in the bosom of the tenderest of Fathers.

Frequently, in answer to urgings such as these, Julia would protest that Elizabeth did not credit her sufficiently with the seriousness toward religion which she assuredly felt. She had a point. Elizabeth was always prone to impatience with the ignorance and placidity of Protestants, to measure their piety with the unfair yardstick of her own zeal and deep holiness. Julia had not a quick mind, nor was religion her chief interest by any means; but she did the best she knew how, and God surely rewarded her strong suits of loyalty, kindness and generosity. Nor can the constant, impassioned pleas of her holy, beloved friend have fallen on totally deaf ears.

In spite of themselves, the Setons were impressed by the "sweet, submissive manner and prudent behavior" of Cecilia, when they met her at Eliza Maitland's bedside, and one and all invited her to forget the past and come to visit them. Elizabeth, however, was someone else again. They were polite to her, and she herself acted "as if I had seen them but yesterday"; but she was realistic enough to recognize that, once Eliza was dead, "I probably shall see them no more."

In April, Mary Hoffman Seton, James's wife, asked Cecilia to come to live with them and help her with the children. Elizabeth lamented her going, but did nothing to dissuade her. "My precious, merry little *Cis* is gone, and I may truly say I am lost," she told Julia. "Anna's disposition is so different. She knows how to put her cheek to mine and mix a silent tear; but to turn that tear to a smile is only the province of sweet *Celia*." In June, Mary died unexpectedly, and the weight of James' household and eight children fell upon Cecilia's frail shoulders. The melting affection of Elizabeth's heart was strongly underscored by Mary's death; for despite the contempt and hatred the dead woman had shown her, Elizabeth was deeply moved:

> The most painful, cruelly painful circumstance and circumstances of poor Mary Seton's death (Mrs. James Seton) has been more sensibly felt by myself (though apparently the person least interested) than can be imagined [she told Julia]; and once more completely covered every power and faculty of my mind with the veil of sorrow. So many painful combinations never before united in the death of any one of the many I have been so nearly connected with, nor deprived my soul of those cheering, consoling reflections which have always accompanied its deepest afflictions.

The truth was that resentment could not live in the sanctified air of Elizabeth's soul. It might flicker rarely and momentarily on her lips, but it went no deeper. At this period, she had reached the haven where past differences were completely forgotten. She confided to Julia "that I have never felt myself bound to my dear little sister Post any time half as much as the present." Dué had gotten over her pique—at a fortunate time for Elizabeth, for both Dué and Sad were about to sail for

Ireland, and it would not have been pleasant to watch Dué go, hostile and silent.

Elizabeth's own half-sisters, Helen and Mary Bayley, were on affectionate terms with her. Harriet Seton was still loving, but subdued for fear of her family. Only Charlotte Ogden remained cold; but she and Elizabeth had never been deeply attached. His wife gone, and Cecilia reconciled to him, James Seton made the reconciliation complete by seeking out Elizabeth. She described his man's way of going about it for Sad:

> James walked in my room the other morning and took me in his arms like one of the children, asked some questions about a bundle at the Customs House, and seemed to have met me every day of the twelve months I have not seen him. I like that. So all the world should do.

In the early summer of 1807 Father Hurley was recalled to Philadelphia as Pastor of St Augustine's. His loss was hard on Elizabeth, but harder on Cecilia, whose true spiritual father he was. He left at a time when she needed him most; for no sooner had she taken over her brother's household than the children's governess began to spread rumors that she was poisoning the mind of her oldest niece Emma with Catholic principles, and the old gossipings and accusations rose like a swarm of gnats from a swamp.

Moreover, Cecilia was back in the old world she had been so happy to leave. As her brother's hostess, she had to pour tea for his visitors, preside at his dinner table, take a hand at cards, accompany him to the houses of family and friends—and she despised it all, particularly as she was defenseless before pitying smiles, patronizing airs and open controversy. It was an agony to her to hear her beloved Faith openly ridiculed and insulted. The kindest of her guests and hostesses merely stared at her with rounded eyes, as if she were something out of a sideshow. Her lot, in a sense, was much harder than Elizabeth's had been, for Elizabeth had been able to stay quietly in her own little house, away from the acrimony and mortification.

There is testimony to the turmoil of Cecilia's day in the fact that many of the notes to Elizabeth which were her only consolation were dashed off late at night or in the early morning. These were also the only times

when she could sink exhausted into the comfort of her prayers and
spiritual books. It was easy to understand her prophetic cry: "Oh,
sister, if we . . . could but go to some corner of the earth and devote our
whole time to God!" Or her piteous question addressed to Elizabeth
when St. M. had departed, as to whom she should go now for confession
and direction.

Elizabeth had chosen for herself Father Louis Sibourd, who had come
to replace Father William O'Brien as Pastor of St. Peter's—and Cecilia
followed her lead. Elizabeth's progress under Father Sibourd was firm
and lasting. He permitted her to approach the Holy Table three times a
week, if circumstances would let her, and dispensed plain and substantial
advice. "Begin again today," he told her, for example. "What is lost must
not cause dejection. What you have gained will be lost, if you do not
begin again as if nothing had been done." Her soul was running ever more
swiftly in the way of perfection. Her *Spiritual Journal* extending over
the summer and fall glowed with a gentle rapture and a sureness of approach that increased with each entry.

> Renewed the *entire* sacrifice fervently. Yielded *all*, and offered every
> nerve, fibre and power of soul and body to sickness, death at any and every
> appointment of His Blessed Will.

She rightly built her holiness out of the things of her daily life. Thus,
her children became for her signposts to goodness, in a humble extension
of the Scriptural observation that "a little child shall lead them":

> Beloved Kate, I will take you, then, for my pattern, and try to please
> Him as you to please me. To grieve with a like tenderness when I displease
> *Him*, to obey and mind His voice as you do mine. To do my work as
> neatly and exactly as you do yours, grieve to lose sight of Him for a moment,
> fly with joy to meet Him, fear He should go and leave me even when I sleep
> —this is the lesson of love you set me. And when I have seemed to be
> angry, without petulance or obstinacy you silently and steadily try to ac-
> complish my wish. I will say: "Dearest Lord, give me grace to copy well this
> lovely image of my duty to Thee."

> Received the longing Desire of my soul . . . and my dearest Anna, too.
> The bands of nature and grace all twined together. The parent offers the
> child, the child the parent, and both are united in the source of their being,
> and rest together on redeeming love.

She knew discouragement—and the means of routing it:

> The heart down—discouraged at the constant failure in good resolution; so soon disturbed by trifles; so little interior recollection and forgetfulness of His constant presence. The reproaches of disobedience to the little ones much more applicable to myself. So many Communions and confessions with so little fruit often suggest the idea of lessening them—to fly from the fountain while in danger of dying from thirst! But, in a moment, He lifts up the soul from the dust.

Like an obedient daughter, she knitted her sanctity on the loom of the Church's liturgy. Every season, every feast, every saint commemorated, had its proper lesson, and she learned it so well that she made it a personal instruction applicable to herself alone. Through all, however, ran the golden thread of the Eucharist. ["If] as [is] certainly true, . . . that bread naturally taken removes my hunger," she cried out, "so this Heavenly Bread of Angels removes my pain, my cares—warms, cheers, soothes, contents and renews my whole being!"

It all had its effect—as Antonio and Carroll and Matignon had said it would—and the people of New York began to exclaim in amazement at the tranquility and contentment of the Widow Seton who had been through so many trials. It had not been easy, of course, as she confided to Filippo Filicchi:

> My daily object is to keep close to your first advice (with St. Francis) to take every event gently and quietly, and oppose good nature and cheerfulness to every contradiction; which succeeds so well that now it is an acknowledged opinion that Mrs. William Seton is in a very happy situation; and Mr. Wilkes says, speaking of *his* possessions: "Yet Providence does not do so much for me as for you, as it makes you happy and contented in every situation." Yet indeed—for how can he build who has not the rock for his foundation? But Mrs. William Seton is obliged to watch every moment to keep up the reality of this appearance. You know, Filicchi, what it costs to be always humble and satisfied.

Elizabeth's will to be happy had its physical effect, too, as she told Antonio: "When I eat and drink and laugh, I am as well and gay as at fifteen." Despite her many trials, she also had many blessings; she knew it, and was grateful.

She had sufficient money for her needs: when her boarders were at their peak, they brought her $1300 a year; John Wilkes paid her rent; Julia Scott sent regular remittances which Elizabeth protested were so much more than she needed that she had to "put it at interest"; Antonio, with Bishop Carroll, paid for her boys at Georgetown, in addition to the unlimited funds Antonio positively commanded her to call on. Only Wright Post and Mrs. Startin, who gave her a last hundred dollars before turning away forever, had reneged on their promised aid. Elizabeth commented that her brother-in-law was not one to advance money unless it were needed, but Antonio, with a man's view, remarked that he was probably "short of cash."

She was blessed in her children also. The boys were doing well in their studies and the authorities were more than satisfied with their conduct. Anna had developed into a mother's pride of loveliness, and advanced rapidly in reading, writing, geography, French—anything, in fact, she attempted; Elizabeth was especially delighted that she was more adept at the piano than herself. Kit was an affectionate child, of quicker brain than the others; unfortunately, her health was in a state of decline, or rather, of suspension between well-being and actual sickness—but Elizabeth considered it the greatest blessing, if she should relinquish her to God in her state of innocence. Rebecca had a singular sweetness of disposition; it did not matter that she was plain of feature compared to all the others—everyone doted on her.

But, with everything, it was apparent that God was only marking time in His plans for Elizabeth. Dubourg had felt it. Cheverus and Matignon had put it into words. Since her conversion Elizabeth had been preparing—without knowing it, for she could not see herself as important as others made out—for a great work. The time had been almost a sort of novitiate, for she had listened to the voices of her directors, had borne her trials and temptations, and had advanced remarkably in the love of God. Now—again without her knowing it—the time of preparation was nearly over: her days in New York were numbered. And the beginning of achievement came about, as so many of God's plans do, by circumstance.

The bigotry set afoot by Cecilia's conversion the year before had dealt a deadly blow to Elizabeth's boarding establishment, but it had taken all this time to make its full effect felt. By November of 1807, the number of her boarders was down to ten; then dwindled to seven, then five. She was concerned lest her part in the project was harming Mr. Harris as it had harmed Mr. White in 1805; but he assured her that she had no blame in the matter, and that he had every intention of continuing his school for three more years, and would need her boarding facilities. He was apparently something of a fighter, and Elizabeth resigned herself to carry on, even though she was disturbed at the bad effect her rude boarders might have upon her little girls, and despite the call of her "dream" tugging at her heart. Most of all, she feared to anticipate the Will of God, or to turn from duty, however unpleasant—as she told Antonio:

> I repeat to you, Antonio (as you may be anxious on the subject) these are my happiest days. Sometimes the harassed mind, wearied with continual contradiction to all it would most covet—solitude! silence! peace!—sighs for a change; but five minutes' recollection procures an immediate act of resignation, convinced that this is the day of salvation for me. And if, like a coward, I should run away from the field of battle, I am sure the very peace I seek would fly from me, and the state of penance sanctified by the Will of God would be again wished for as the safest and surest road.

These were indeed the words of a "proficient" in the spiritual life.

Elizabeth missed her boys sorely, and by February of 1808 could no longer hold off asking Bishop Carroll if they might not be allowed to come home for a visit. The opportunity of sending them presented itself when Father Dubourg went North to help with the Lenten services at St. Peter's; and her mother's heart overflowed with the happiness of having all her five children together for the first time in nearly two years.

In April, the reduced number of boarders forced her to move into a smaller house, at less than half the rent. What the next move would be, she did not know. At precisely this point, the Will of God manifested itself.

With no other motive than to unburden her heart to a friend, Elizabeth told Father Dubourg the depressing state of things: the parents of the handful of boarders remaining were dissatisfied, some with her for taking a smaller house, some with Harris for giving their sons too much freedom; all but two would go to College in the fall, and there would not be enough income to pay the baker and the house rent. In an instant,

Dubourg suggested the solution, and she knew that he spoke with the voice of God, as she hastened to assure Julia Scott:

> So sweet is the Providence that overrules us—at this very moment of solicitude for our destination when the present means fails, Mr. Dubourg . . . has offered to give me a formal grant of a lot of ground situated close to the College, which is out of the town and in a very healthy situation; and procure me immediately the charge of a half-dozen girls, and as many more as I can manage. Added to this, he will take my boys in the College and the entire charge of them for a very small consideration, in order that Filicchi's money may assist me in another way.

Elizabeth protested her lack of talents for the enterprise, but Dubourg brushed her protests aside; and when he left with her boys for Baltimore, at the beginning of May, she was determined to accept his offer, if her friends and advisers should agree. The previous fall she had reluctantly let go her own preference for Montreal, when Filippo Filicchi had joined his voice to the voices of Cheverus, Matignon and Dubourg, urging her to remain in America. True, she had, even afterwards, broached the subject once more to Bishop Carroll, but the exchange had been half-hearted and altered nothing. She was sure Wright Post and John Wilkes would approve this new project, since it would relieve them from the burden of her support, and she was right. Her director, Father Sibourd, urged her to accept it; and when John Cheverus wrote from Boston that he and Dr. Matignon "infinitely prefer it to your project of retreat in Montreal," her decision was fixed.

Elizabeth had once written, half-jokingly, to Julia, when her boarders were failing: "I can . . . decamp; you know my encumbrances are not weighty." How true it was can be measured by the speed with which she "decamped" for Baltimore. Dubourg had given her two or three months to make ready, but scarcely three weeks after deciding to go, she was on her way.

There was nothing or no one in New York to hold her, except Cecilia, and it was arranged that she should follow Elizabeth when James and his children no longer had need of her. Elizabeth had thought for a while of urging an obscure claim to her Uncle Charlton's will, in order to build a house on her lot in Baltimore and deed it to her children for their future protection; but she abandoned the idea when Dubourg told her it would be better to lease a newly built house at $250 a year, until the new school was established and the Filicchis had been consulted as to its future. James Barry was dead, and his wife had sailed for Madeira with their dying daughter. Harriet Seton was in misery, both because of her thwarted desire to enter the Church and her ill-starred engagement to Elizabeth's irresponsible brother Barclay, who had long ago sailed for the West Indies and had not returned—but Elizabeth could do nothing to help her.

There was a last-minute hesitation as to whether she would travel by sea or overland through Philadelphia. Julia's mother was dying, and Elizabeth—even in this moment of personal joy—wanted to do what she could to help her dear and faithful friend. She sent a hurried note, asking Julia to make the decision: "*Could the presence of YOUR OWN friend relieve you from a moment's sorrow? . . . Be sincere . . . as* they tell me it will be much less expense to go by water."

Whether or not she had Julia's answer, Elizabeth sailed from New York on the *Grand Sachem* on June 9, 1808. She stayed the last night in Sad's house on Cortlandt Street, where she had known so many joys and sorrows. In Sad's absence, William Craig did everything to make her and the children comfortable, and to send them away with only the happiest memories. The next morning, Craig, Wright Post and James Seton saw them off.

Despite all, leaving New York was a heavy parting for Elizabeth. The city had been often cruel to her, and she was right to obey the injunction of Christ: "Whosoever shall not receive you, nor hear you, going forth from thence, shake off the dust from your feet for a testimony to them." But she was also right to weep over the city, as Christ had wept over His faithless City of Jerusalem; for New York was *her* city, the city of her birth, of her friendships, of her happy marriage, and most of all of her conversion: and she would one day joyfully return it good for evil by coming home to stay in her spiritual daughters who brought it, and bring it still, the things that are to its peace.

Now, however, on the 9th of June, 1808, she had to endure the heavy parting, and she turned to Sad to share it with her:

I saw once more the windows of State Street, passed the Quarantine, and so near the shore as to see every part of it. Oh, my Lord—in that hour! Can a heart swell so high and not burst? . . .

My Eliza, think of me, when you pass it again, battering the waves of my changeable life. Yet would I change one shade or trial of it—that would be madness, and working in the dark. Oh, no—the dear, dear, dear adored Will be done through every moment of it! And may it control, regulate and perfect us; and when all is over, how we will rejoice that it was done!

XV

Baltimore

The *Grand Sachem* was scarcely past the lighthouse, thirty miles from
New York, when Elizabeth was writing happily to Cecilia: "All the
fatigue and weariness of mind and body past—the firmament of heaven
so bright, the cheering sea breeze, and merry sailors, would drive old
care away indeed . . . !" As usual, her beauty and charm had immediately
won the good will and service of the whole ship for herself and her
children; and—also as usual—she regarded all the attention with a sort
of innocent amazement and delight.

"Everyone is so kind!" she told Cecilia. "A very mild, modest young
man came down before we had been a half hour on board, and said:
'Madam, my name is James Cork. Call on me at all times. I will help you
in everything.' " A Mrs. Smith and her daughter brought out almonds
and raisins to coax the children from their fear of the sea and the dreadful
spasms of sickness it brought on.

Kit and Rebecca responded philosophically: they played and ate until
the rolling of the ship made them ill, then went sound asleep. Poor
Anna was beyond help: she was miserably sick the whole time, and
scarcely had a minute's merciful sleep.

It was often a rough voyage, and Elizabeth prepared herself constantly
for death. The seven days seemed endless to the children, and they grew

restless, "sometimes begging to go back to Cicil, sometimes stretching their sight towards land where they look for Willy and Dicksey— Mother's heart, in firm and steadfast confidence, looking straight up- wards."

With the news that they were almost there, however, the little family grew lighthearted, and Elizabeth recorded the change of mood:

> After rolling and dashing all night . . . with both little dear ones in my narrow berth, the hand held over to Ann who sleeps beneath me—praying every ten minutes and offering a life so justly forfeited—here we were flying up the Chesapeake. A fairer wind and lighter hearts never went through it, I believe. The girls are singing, and eating almonds and raisins —sending ships overboard to New York.

The journey's end brought more serious thoughts to Elizabeth:

> Tomorrow, do I go among strangers? No. Has an anxious thought or fear passed my mind? No. Can I be disappointed? No. One sweet Sacrifice will reunite my soul with all who offer it. Doubt and fear fly from the breast inhabited by *Him*. There can be no disappointment where the soul's only desire and expectation is to meet *His* Adored Will and fulfill it.

It was her only reason for coming to Baltimore: to fulfill the Will of God—she could not know then in how wonderful and lasting a way— and it was significant that she should yearn for the Mass and the Holy Eucharist as the starting point.

At eleven o'clock on Wednesday evening, June 15, 1808, the *Grand Sachem* berthed at the Baltimore wharf; but the passengers could not leave the ship until they had entered their baggage at the Customs House the next day. Soon after nine on Thursday morning, the feast of Corpus Christi, the travellers were on their way by carriage to St. Mary's in the pouring rain. There had been no delegation to meet them, because "Father Dubourg's Chapel"—the chapel designed by Maximilian Gode- froy for St. Mary's Seminary—was being consecrated that very morning.

Elizabeth Seton's entrance into the Catholic life of the city—and of the United States—was as dramatic as if it had been staged. The Pontifical Mass had begun when the black-clad little widow arrived at the door of the Chapel with her wide-eyed children. She was met with a triumphant peal from the organ and the "bursting of the choir"; and

—as if meant for her ear alone—the beloved voice of Father Hurley, her St. M., raised in the *Kyrie*. So ravished was she by the unexpected brilliance of sight and sound that she could only grope, in trying to describe it later for Cecilia: "Human nature could scarcely bear it—your imagination can never conceive the splendor, the glory of the scene—all I have told you of Florence is a shadow." Her response was instinctive and profound: she was "prostrate in an instant."

When Mass was over Elizabeth found herself in a welter of greetings, and the babble of happy and excited voices beat all around her—the Bishop's, Father Hurley's, Father Dubourg's, his sister's, and so many others. The children stared and smiled shyly, bewildered by it all. They had never seen such a universal display of kindness and affection. They were actually *wanted* here—and all these people were *Catholics* like themselves.

Elizabeth was enchanted with her "new-built" house. Though she described the home on Paca Street rather proudly to Julia as "a mansion . . . in the French style of folding windows and recesses," she confided to Sad more soberly and truly that it was "upon a small scale . . . but really comfortable in every respect." First impressions are often the truest, and what endeared Elizabeth most to her dwelling, she told Cecilia straight off, was that it was "almost joining the chapel" where there was "Mass from daylight to eight. . . . Vespers and Benediction every evening." She repeated these advantages, in almost the same words, for Dué and Sad. They made it, in her eyes, a mansion indeed.

On the day of Elizabeth's joyful arrival at St. Mary's, Harriet Seton wrote, in bitter contrast, a despairing note from New York. She was nursing Cecilia, who had been ill since Elizabeth left, and braving the wrath of the Ogdens to do it. Her heart was sunk in gloom at the dim prospects of her ever becoming a Catholic, or marrying—she was far from sure whether Barclay even loved her. She was entirely miserable and— she well knew—with good reason. The Ogdens and the Hoffmans and the Farquhars had moved swiftly to consolidate their defenses against the further encroachments of Catholicism the moment Elizabeth left New York. Eliza Farquhar was closely watched. Emma Seton was sent away to boarding school, at the expense of her uncles Martin Hoffman and Gouverneur Ogden, to keep her from Cecilia's example and influence.

Every bit of mail between New York and Baltimore was carefully censored, and the children sullenly refused to write under such conditions—except when they were able to smuggle an occasional note to their "dear sister" Elizabeth.

It was in many respects a delightful summer for Elizabeth. Except for two hot weeks in June, the weather was exceptionally pleasant and temperate for Baltimore; and the same kind of soft, mild air blew through Elizabeth's soul.

Many of the city's distinguished families—relatives and friends of Bishop Carroll and Father Dubourg—called to pay their respects and welcome her among them. A former governor of the state, Colonel John Eager Howard, was so charmed with the little widow that he offered her and her family a home in his own mansion, and promised to educate her children as his own; but she gently and gratefully declined.

Strangely enough, Elizabeth never mentioned meeting any of the Cursons—Will's people—who were long residents of the city; probably they had been warned away from her by their cousins in New York. She did see Jack Seton, who had lost his livelihood and was, Elizabeth told Cecilia, "poverty and misery itself." He had been going about among his friends, borrowing a couple of shillings a day to exist; and talked distractedly about going off to try his fortune some place else, leaving his family behind in Alexandria until such time as he could send for them. Henry Seton, too, had fallen upon hard times, and was in a New Haven jail—presumably for pauperism—from which he sent Elizabeth desperate, begging letters, threatening to kill himself if he were not relieved. Elizabeth felt his situation sorely, but felt herself bound "by every tie of duty"—to her children and her school—to refuse him assistance. She did what she could, however, not to leave him forlorn, writing to comfort him and, on the practical side, enjoining Cecilia to let James know how badly off his brother was. At just this time, too, the Setons' good-for-nothing brother-in-law, James Maitland, died, apparently in some horrible way, for Harriet Seton commented to Elizabeth: "What an awful exit it must have been. It makes my blood run cold to think of it."

Besides Cecilia and Harriet, the other New Yorkers who had not cast Elizabeth off, wrote friendly letters assuring her of their good will and interest in her happiness. Wright Post had sub-let her little house in Manhattan for her—at a slight reduction, in order to secure an immediate tenant—and sent on some articles of furniture she had left with him. She heard frequently from George Dupleix, whose duties had forced him to bring his ship to New York before his wife could reach Bristol, England to join him for the voyage. At Elizabeth's direction he had called at Henry Hobart's for a few pieces of furniture that had been in the minister's care since she sailed for Leghorn in 1803, and dispatched them to her at Baltimore. Dupleix's letters were filled with a rough good humor and manly friendliness.

> I received yours, last Monday, with its affectionate enclosure for Dué [he wrote on August 24]. You must know, right or wrong, I opened it and read it several times with much delight. If this is a fault, it is yours for not having wafers [of sealing wax]; but I perceive, now that you are growing rich, you are growing stingy. . . . You saucy Mrs. Seton! This is gun for gun! . . . When I meet with a good New York cheese I will send it to you; in the meantime you will get an English one of a good family, I judge, from the liberty the rats and mice have taken with it.

Elizabeth was especially concerned about a picture of Father Hurley she had left behind, and begged Cecilia several times to have it sent; she was perturbed lest he discover that she did not have it, and importuned Cecilia: "*I am in a handsome scrape indeed: oh, do see about it!*"

She also had a kindly letter from John Wilkes which, she said, surprised her very much. Elizabeth seemed at times to bear a querulous attitude toward Wilkes—and toward Wright Post, too—almost as if the help they gave her was due in strict justice, which it was not. Her attitude was probably caused by the fact that they sometimes felt it necessary to accompany their charity with a disapproving lecture on her religion; but she never seriously denied their goodness to her, nor ceased to be grateful for it.

When Father Hurley had come to Baltimore for the consecration of St. Mary's Chapel, he had brought with him a wealthy Philadelphia convert of his, Samuel Sutherland Cooper, who was intent on the priesthood. The Monday following the consecration Elizabeth traveled to Georgetown with Father Hurley and Cooper to bring her boys back to Baltimore. Cooper, who was thirty-nine, and Elizabeth had been immediately attracted to each other. It was a different attraction from the kind that had drawn her to Henry Hobart or Antonio Filicchi, and she dealt with it peremptorily before it should get out of hand. She explained it in a letter written months later to Julia Scott:

> I met him on my first arrival here. . . . He had then made the resolution of taking Holy Orders and, as you know, I had long since renounced everything like earthly attachments. From the involuntary attraction of certain dispositions to each other, there was, however, an interest and esteem understood. You may be sure, though, I have always considered him as a consecrated being—as he did me—and the only result of this partiality has been the encouragement of each other to persevere in the path which each had chosen.

And, at the end of August, when Cooper entered St. Mary's Seminary to begin his studies for the priesthood, Elizabeth confessed to Cecilia:

> If we had not devoted ourselves to the heavenly spouse before we met, I do not know how the attraction would have terminated; but as it is, I fear him not, nor any other. But such a perfect character is a fit offering to the fountain of all perfection. He has my rosary and little red cross by way of memento of our Georgetown expedition.

Cecilia had met Samuel Cooper when he went to New York in midsummer, and had found him not at all what she expected—he was indeed far from handsome, and of odd, erratic personality—but Elizabeth's only comment was: "I should not wish you to know him as I do."

It was certainly in the plan of God that Elizabeth and Cooper should meet, for he was to play a vital part in the establishment of the Sisters of Charity at Emmitsburg; but that the meeting and the subsequent friendship was handled prudently is evident from the fact that it was never allowed to deepen—for example, no correspondence such as marked Elizabeth's other friendships ever developed. There can be nothing but praise for either Cooper or Elizabeth: when they met, they were free to marry if they chose, but neither of them would allow a normal attraction to interfere with their religious vocations. Nor should it be forgotten that, on Elizabeth's part, the match would have brought her children all the financial security she had ever desired for them.

Meanwhile, Elizabeth was in a glow of satisfaction with her new life. She told Dué happily:

> All those little, dear attentions of human life which I was entirely weaned from are now my daily portion from the family of Mr. Dubourg, whose sister and mother are unwearied in their care of us. The little niceties which I cannot afford are daily sent to us as a part of their family.

Madame Fournier, Father Dubourg's sister, was a kind of fairy godmother. Elizabeth described her for Julia as "a most amiable, affectionate character, and though beyond forty, a very elegant woman. She arranges my affairs for me, such as clothing my dear boys, placing and providing necessary furniture, provisions, etc., with an ease and gaiety of manner as if the favor were all on my side." Elizabeth was also able to hire "a very good servant at four and one-half dollars per month," who did the washing, cleaning and cooking.

Money was no problem for the time being. Elizabeth had brought a tiny fortune with her, she explained to Julia: "I had saved at interest five hundred dollars of your money; the bill you sent made six, and the four of Filicchi's for the last year (you are the only persons I receive from) made me the rich possessor of 1,000 dollars when I arrived here." The fact that she was able to procure everything she needed from the seminary, which bought by the gross, made for a saving of at least one-third on every article purchased.

The children were as delighted as their mother at being together again, and the objects of so much attention and love. Elizabeth described them proudly but sensibly for Julia:

> My boys appear to be the most innocent and well-disposed children that can be imagined for their age. Neither of them appears to me to show any distinct marks of genius, but their progress in their classes is superior to that of most boys of ten and twelve. William will be twelve in November; Anna was thirteen the third of last May. But your little Kate has more talents than either of the three elder, and Rebecca more than all of them together.

Even the children, however, were concerned about their mother's health. She had begun to suffer chronic pain in the breast accompanied by general weakness, and she admitted that her boys and girls were much affected: "Not one of them but anticipates the sorrow of being dispersed." Their insecurity was the direct result of the haphazard and uncertain existence they had been subjected to since the death of their father. Their mother was their only solid hope.

She, for her part, took her illness with serenity. "Sickness does not frighten the secret peace of mind which is founded on a confidence in the divine goodness," she confided to Julia, "and if death succeeds it, I must put a mother's hopes and fears in His hands Who has promised most to the widow and the fatherless." She assured Julia, however, that Dr. Chatard, the eminent French physician of the Seminary, saw "no cause of serious apprehension for the present," and was restoring her strength with a bottle of porter a day.

Elizabeth's spiritual life had become placid, too, and she rejoiced that she was "daily and hourly receiving the most precious consolations, not with the enthusiastic delight . . . I once experienced, but gently, gratefully, offering to resign them in the very moment of enjoyment." She knew that sensible consolations were special favors that she would not have always, and welcomed trials as coming from the Father whose "mercies are endless." She only prayed with deep humility and distrust of self, that they would come from without rather than from within for, as she knew from hard experience, "that, and that alone is real anguish."

She had a new spiritual director who captivated her soul with his own holiness, a Sulpician named Father Pierre Babade. She called him her "patriarch," but for all the venerability bestowed on him by his white hairs, he was only forty-eight when Elizabeth first knew him. His temperament was like hers, romantic, poetic and tender; and like all souls that have disciplined such a temperament, he burned, as it were, with a pure white flame of divine love. Elizabeth was later to tell Bishop Carroll that Father Babade was "the only one of nine different priests I have confessed to of necessity to whom I ever yet had opened my heart." He showed her, as no one else had, the consolation and comfort and tenderness of Holy Mother Church, the very qualities that would appeal most to her maternal heart. He allowed her to receive her Eucharistic Lord every day, at a time when such spiritual generosity was far from common. He taught her the religious practices that he himself loved, and she urged one of them upon Cecilia:

The Angelus bell rings morning, noon and night—at half-past 5 in the morning precisely, again a quarter before 2 in the day, and a quarter before 8 at night. Meet your own soul's sister in the sweet salutation. I say it with particular attention, and always on the knees, because there is a particular indulgence annexed to it; which indulgence, and every other I can gain—after the example of our *most dear patriarch*—I offer to God *for the departed.*

The school she had come to Baltimore to institute, the first tentative step toward her incomparable contribution to American Catholic elementary education, began slowly enough; and she did not hasten it. She was well used, now, to waiting on the Will of God. Only four days after her arrival in the city, she stated her position simply for Dué: "My prospect of an establishment I leave to God Almighty." Elizabeth's school was to teach the science of the world in the light of eternity, for she heartily concurred with Father Dubourg that:

There are in the country, and perhaps too many, mixed schools, in which ornamental accomplishments are the only objects of education; we have none that I know where their acquisition is connected with, and made subservient to, *pious* instruction—and such a one you certainly wish yours to be.

She did indeed, but not unless God wished it also, and not until He had shown His hand. She stressed the uniqueness of her purpose when she wrote Antonio Filicchi in the first months that, as time went on and she had to build on the lot provided her, she would need his financial help, and begged him to state the specific sum she could call upon. On August 20, she wrote him for the third time:

[The letters] written you since I am in Baltimore are committed to the charge of angels. If you do not receive them, sad will be my disappointment —but the Will of Almighty God be done! So much of my, or rather the *scheme* of these revered gentlemen, depends on your concurrence and support that I dare not form a wish. Every morning at the Divine Sacrifice, I offer (as I know they do also) the whole success to Him Whose blessed Will alone can sanctify and make it fruitful.

And she finished with a striking sentence of abnegation which was at the same time a solemn prophecy:

For my part, I shall naturally look for disappointments, and have always found them so conducive to the soul's advancement, that if we succeed in forming the purposed establishment I shall look upon it as a sure mark that Almighty God intends an extensive benefit without calculating my particular interest, which is always best advanced in poverty and in tears.

When summer vacation time was over, and the little school on Paca Street began, Elizabeth had seven pupils: four boarders and her own three girls. Bill and Dick had moved across the yard to stay at the College. Her little class, she admitted, was as much as she could manage in her state of weakness; but it was also in line with her plan, which was to accept no more than eight boarders during the first year or two, and no day scholars.

Elizabeth set out her terms for board and tuition in a letter to Julia Scott: "Two hundred dollars per year. Extra accomplishments which require the assistance of masters, as music, drawing, etc., are paid separately. The masters engaged in the service of the college attend at my house on the most moderate terms, though they are the best that can be procured."

An order of day was quickly adopted: "In the chapel at six until eight, school at nine, dine at one, school at three, chapel at six-and-a-half, examination of conscience and Rosary." The curriculum included reading, writing, arithmetic, English and French, and plain and fancy needlework. By December Elizabeth's pupils had increased to ten, and she found that "from half-past five in the morning until nine at night every moment is full—no space even to be troubled." Father Babade took charge of the religious instruction of the children, and was constantly in and out of the school. A special devotional exercise consisted in reading aloud the story of the Lord's Passion every Friday.

Elizabeth herself, in her new role as schoolmistress, found it necessary to do some "postgraduate" work; she saw, of course, the funny side of it, and described it for Julia:

What would amuse you, my darling friend, would be to see your old lady at five in the afternoon (as soon as school is over) seated gravely with a slate and pencil, with a master of arithmetic stuffing her brains with dollars, cents, and fractions, and actually going over the studies both in grammar and figures which are suited to the scholar better than the mistress.

She knew that Julia would chuckle particularly over the scene, since shortly before, she had complained of getting old, and Elizabeth had commented mischievously: "You are older than myself, and as I am full thirty-five, I wish you joy!"

The school was only part of Elizabeth's projected "establishment"; the other and more important part was the foundation of a religious Sisterhood. It seems quite obvious that this was part of the Baltimore plan from the beginning. Not that Elizabeth had proposed herself as foundress; her "dream" of the religious life had been much humbler: to live in a convent and make herself "useful as an assistant in teaching."

Father Dubourg, however—and his clerical friends of Baltimore and Boston—apparently had thoughts, however vague and undefined, of a religious community developing from the Paca Street School, for Elizabeth wrote to Antonio Filicchi on July 8, 1808, less than a month after she had arrived in Baltimore: "It is proposed to . . . begin on a small plan admitting of enlargement if necessary, in the hope and expectation that there will not be wanting ladies to join in forming a permanent institution." The rapid development of the permanent institution and religious Sisterhood further indicated that it was intended all along.

On October 3, in a letter to Julia, Elizabeth called herself "your poor little Nun." On October 6 she wrote the following memorable news to Cecilia:

> It is expected I shall be the mother of many daughters. A letter received from Philadelphia where my blessed father, our patriarch, now is on a visit, tells me he has found two of the sweetest young women, who were going to Spain to seek a refuge from the world—though they are both Americans, *Cecilia* and *May*—and now wait until my house is opened for them: next spring, we hope. He applies to me the Psalm in our Vespers: *The barren woman shall be the joyful mother of children*, and tells me to repeat it continually, which you must do with me, my darling.

There can be no mistaking the import of these words. The two young women from Philadelphia intent on the religious life were Cecilia O'Conway and Maria Murphy, who was the niece of Matthew Carey, the famous publisher.

Indeed, Elizabeth herself seemed to have a confidence, often expressed, that God would bring about this ultimate achievement of a

Sisterhood; but she left the matter in the hands of her priest-advisers, not in the Quietistic sense, but as one who knew that God would speak to her through them. In so doing she was acting precisely as St. Vincent de Paul—who was to be the soul of her community, although she did not know it yet—had acted nearly two hundred years before. Vincent had always allowed prudent advice and circumstance to unite in revealing the Will of God to him. Elizabeth Seton did the same. She was waiting now for the full revelation, which was unfolding with startling swiftness.

She told her sister, Mary Post, of the plans her "Revered Gentlemen" had in mind for her at the same time that she informed Cecilia; and Mary answered, agitated and bewildered, on October 27: "To my too worldly mind it seems almost incredible, surrounded as you are by dear little children, that you can familiarize yourself to the contemplation of any change that must incur the necessity of separation from them." Mary's reaction was most understandable: she knew that Elizabeth was at least as intensely maternal as herself; she knew also, even as a Protestant, that it was not the practice for mothers to take their children into the convent with them. Unwittingly she hit upon the reason why Elizabeth could even think about the convent in her present situation: "It can only be that you have a perfect reliance on the care of Him Who is the ruler of all things," she said. "Submission to His Will and faith in His protection—that is the foundation of your peace." She was right; this was the foundation of Elizabeth's peace: But, as regarded her desire for the way of religion, Elizabeth submitted herself and had faith and perfect reliance upon God to find a way to achieve it which would include her children. Never, at this time or any other, did Elizabeth consider the abandonment of the little ones God had given her.

After discussing Elizabeth's momentous plans, Mary gave her the family news: her new baby, Emily, was the image of Elizabeth; their brothers Richard and William were in love; Carleton had begun practice as a country doctor on Long Island. As for Barclay, Elizabeth knew from Harriet's mournful letters that he was leading a roistering and dissipated life on the Island of Jamaica, and breaking Harriet's heart.

Julia Scott, as usual, was thinking of new ways to help her friend, and

Elizabeth was delighted when she proposed sending her clothes she no longer wore; "but do not send the best," Elizabeth warned her, "nor fear that anything can be useless. All turns to account with me, particularly anything of John's for my boys. Their clothes are my heaviest expense." Of course, Julia paid no attention to her, and Elizabeth was soon describing for her the excitement at Paca Street when an enormous box arrived from Philadelphia:

> Anna's spirits are so even and independent that you would hardly believe she was in a transport at the sight of the white beaver hat especially, as Miss Dubourg has one exactly like it. . . . Rebecca wears the brown one and Kitty had a brown one also presented to her accidently; and so everybody is pleased, and mother enjoys it as much as they do.
>
> Dear, dear Julia, many things you have sent were of too much value for such children; but care will not be wanting, and they are much more useful to us than you would perhaps imagine, as I am obliged to be more attentive to appearance here than in New York—not myself, but the family. Poor little self is always dressed for the grave, which must ever be my dearest anticipation; though not in the sense you take it, darling.

She finished the letter with a beautiful tribute to her friend, and a graceful lesson in the art of receiving:

> Oh, my dear, dear Julia, when I think of . . . you, my first, last and most faithful friend, my friend who has borne so many years with all my negligences and who is unchangeable through so many changes, I would wish to lay at your feet to be your servant. . . . But such is the divine order, that the good must be received on my part, and not bestowed; and I must be content with that dispensation which heightens His favors by conveying them through a hand so dear and beloved.

There had been a moment in September when it looked like Cecilia might come at once to Baltimore, and Elizabeth had written her an excited welcome—but the excitement had been premature. The happy moment had been precipitated by the discovery that a "housekeeper" whom James Seton had hired to help Cecilia, held a rather more intimate position in his house—and Father Sibourd, in indignation, was on the point of ordering Cecilia to remove herself from such a sordid situation; but when the repentant James sent the woman away, Sibourd said Cecilia might stay, with the understanding that she was to leave immediately at the first whisper of any future scandal.

Poor Cecilia's chances of ever reaching Baltimore were considerably weakened by the appearance in New York, that October, of Father Anthony Kohlmann, S.J. Although the news had taken some time to reach America, the Holy See, on April 8, 1808, had raised Baltimore to the rank of an Archdiocese, naming Carroll Archbishop and Metropolitan, and creating the four suffragan sees of Boston, New York, Philadelphia and Bardstown, Kentucky. The new Bishops-elect were John Cheverus for Boston (Dr. Matignon had humbly begged off); Richard Luke Concanen, an Irish Dominican, for New York; Michael Egan, O.F.M., for Philadelphia; and the Sulpician Benedict Joseph Flaget for Bardstown. Concanen, who was in Italy at the time, had wisely asked that a Vicar General be appointed for New York until he should arrive, and Carroll had selected Anthony Kohlmann.

Kohlmann's acceptance of the post was a great relief to Archbishop Carroll, who had had all kinds of trouble with New York. The old Pastor, William O'Brien, had never gotten along with his younger assistant and namesake, and the two scarcely saw each other. Then Matthew O'Brien and John Byrne, both of them Elizabeth's former directors and friends, fell from grace and became drinking cronies and the scandal of the city. Father Kohlmann came to New York to reform and reorganize it in preparation for the installment of its Bishop; but when Concanen died in Naples on his way to America, June 19, 1810, Kohlmann was forced to stay on as administrator of the new See until 1815. Among the Vicar General's immediate plans for New York was a school for Catholic children, and he looked to Cecilia Seton to teach in it. It would be several months before she could get him to change his mind and allow her to join Elizabeth.

As if Cecilia had not trouble enough with the delays that kept her in New York, one of the town's young blades was attracted to her and began calling frequently at The Wilderness under the guise of taking Italian lessons. As soon as she was aware of his real intentions which, while not dishonorable, were not to her liking, she was terrified lest Elizabeth hear rumors of her "beau" and think she had abandoned her thoughts of the religious life. She wrote earnestly asking Elizabeth what she should do. Elizabeth considered, indeed, that a seventeen-year-old girl might naturally be pleased at these new-found attentions and told her flatly that, if she still intended giving herself to God, she must in fairness to her admirer put an immediate stop to his visits. Cecilia had already done so by the time her sister-in-law's letter arrived, and was able to ask with youthful dignity: "Did you, then, think your Cecil could trifle with another's happiness?"

On December 7, 1808, Cecilia O'Conway arrived at Paca Street in the company of her father, who told Mrs. Seton that he had brought his daughter to offer her to God. Miss O'Conway stayed to assist Elizabeth in her schoolwork until such time as they should enter upon a formal religious life. She had the undoubted honor, therefore, of being the first of Mother Seton's daughters and "Philadelphia's first nun." Elizabeth was glad to have Cecilia O'Conway with her, for increasing calls were being made on her house and time, and she had been on the point of sending for Cecilia Seton. At Archbishop Carroll's recommendation, Catholic parents were asking that their children be given religious instruction at the school on Paca Street, and Elizabeth was admitting small bands of girls to make a week's preparation for First Holy Communion under the direction of Father Babade. She described for Cecilia Seton the simple, fervent ceremony at which one of these little classes received their Lord for the first time:

> Imagine six of us, the girls all in white, as modest as angels, receiving from the hand of our blessed Father B[abade] *Our Adored Lord.* He had been all the week preparing them, and every night our little chapel has resounded with love and adoration. This morning, in the subterraneous Chapel of the Blessed Virgin, in the very depth of solitude . . . he celebrated the Adorable Sacrifice and dispensed the Sacred Passover. His tears fell fast over his precious hands while he gave it, and we had liberty to sob aloud, unwitnessed by any, as no one had an idea of our going there.

Fortunately, Elizabeth was well again. The pain in the breast and the weakness were gone. She ascribed it to the fact that "winter has always been my cheerful season; and here I am sheltered from all cold and changes of weather, wet walks, etc."

She had gotten it into her head that, just as God had called her to the Church through the Filicchis, so, too, he would call her to the religious life through them. She had already written three letters to Antonio and one to Filippo, informing them of the work begun in Baltimore and of the hopes she had from it, but had received no reply. Actually, Antonio had received her letters of July 8 and August 20 and had answered them on November 30, expressing his joy at seeing her "out of New York" and "among true Christians," and directing her to draw one thousand dollars on Murray for her establishment—and to ask for more, if she needed it. However, due to the war between England and Napoleon and to the American Embargo Act, Europe was effectively sealed off from the United States, and Elizabeth did not receive this letter for a year; she discovered at that time that Filippo was very ill.

She wrote Antonio again, on January 16, 1809, telling him expressly that she looked for God to speak to her through him:

> The subject of my last [letter] to you . . . so nearly concerns all my hopes and expectations for this world, which is to do something—if ever so little —towards promoting our dear and holy Faith that I am sure you would give me some encouragement, if you had any opportunity; or your reasons for not encouraging our plan (if indeed it is the Will of God that it shall not be realized). It has long since been committed to Him; but I cannot help begging always in Communion while my heart is turned toward Livorno: "Oh, dear Lord, put in their hearts whatever is your Holy Will for me."

After humbly relating certain signs by which God had already shown His favor, especially the high esteem in which the Catholics of the city held her little school and the growing number of young women who wanted to dedicate their lives to it as religious teachers, she returned again to her chief reason for writing: "not to make any formal request, but only, by showing you the situation in which Our Lord has placed us, give you the necessary intelligence to direct you in doing His Will for me. Whether it is His pleasure to advance or retard my views, His dear, adored, blessed Will be done! I have none; and if He but continues to give me Himself, I am blind to everything else."

Five days later she was writing to Filippo in a vein of suppressed excitement, but also with the utmost simplicity:

> Mr. Dubourg always says: "Patience, my child; trust in Providence." But this morning at Communion, submitting all my desires and actions in entire abandonment to *His* Will, the thought crossed my mind: *Ask Filicchi to build for you. The property can always be his.* Be sure, thinking of it at such a moment shows how much it is the earnest desire. Indeed, it is as

much wished as I can wish anything which is not already evidenced to be the Will of Our Lord. . . .

She went on to assure Filippo solemnly and vehemently that she did not seek her own gratification. What could she expect, after all? "Neither rest, repose or exemption from poverty. I long since made the vow, which as a religious I could only renew." And she cried out ardently to him in conclusion: "So do, do, dear Filicchi, hold me up and keep your little candle in the candlestick. But, hush! Our Lord will direct all. Whatever you say or do I shall consider as His Voice and Will."

"The Spirit breatheth where He will," and while Elizabeth's ears were straining for a word of reply from Leghorn, God spoke—almost in the miraculous accents of Sinai—from close by her. Apparently, the wondrous event had been set on foot a couple of months before, but its culmination came after January 21, when Elizabeth had dispatched her letter to Filippo. It is recorded by Father Dubourg, in a letter written to Abbé Henri Élèves on July 15, 1828; and aside from minor inconsistencies, which the passage of twenty years could explain, must be taken at face value:

> Some years ago God called in an extraordinary manner another soul chosen to accomplish His designs, Mother Seton of New York. . . . This lady felt a strong desire for the religious life which she regarded as the manifest work of God. But she was not encouraged by her director, who represented to her as a serious impediment the tender age of her five children.
>
> She came, however, to reside in Baltimore, and was there brought in contact with a priest who was much occupied with religious establishment. Mr. Cooper had then been a year in the seminary: both addressed themselves to this priest.
>
> In her frequent conferences with her director, Mrs. Seton learned that he had thought for a long time of establishing the Daughters of Charity in America; and as the duties of this institute would be compatible with the cares of her family, this virtuous lady expressed a most ardent desire of seeing it commenced and of being herself admitted into it.
>
> An insurmountable obstacle stood in the way of this project; this was the absolute want of pecuniary resources to lay the foundation of this new Society. They resolved to pray jointly to God to remove this obstacle.
>
> One morning, in the year 1808, Mrs. Seton called upon her director and told him, at the risk of being considered a visionary, she felt obliged to

disclose to him *what Our Lord, in a clear and intelligible voice, said to her after Communion:* "Go," said He to her, "address yourself to Mr. Cooper; he will give you what is ncessary to commence the establishment."

"What you tell me is possible," replied the priest, "but I have strong reasons for prohibiting you from following what may only be the sport of your imagination. If it is God Who has spoken to you, He will make His Will known also to Mr. Cooper; and you may rest assured that he will be docile to the Voice." She withdrew, satisfied.

On the evening of the same day, the director received a visit from Mr. Cooper, who began by expressing his astonishment that nothing had yet been done in favor of the female sex, "which," said he, "has so powerful an influence in regard to morals and religion."

On the reply of the director that, for fifteen years, he had been revolving such a project in his mind, and that certain pious persons in Baltimore were offering daily prayers for the same good work: "What, then, prevents you?" asked Mr. Cooper.

"The want of means," answered the priest, "for an establishment of this kind cannot be undertaken without funds."

"Oh, well," said Mr. Cooper, "I have ten thousand dollars which I can give you for this purpose."

Struck at the coincidence of these two communications, the priest inquired if he had seen Mrs. Seton that day, or if he had ever spoken to her upon the subject.

"Never," said he. "But do you think of entrusting Mrs. Seton with this affair?"

The director answered:

"You may be sure, sir, that I could not do better. She is here for that purpose, and I will relate to you what she told me this morning. Compare her statement with the offer you have made, and bear in mind that, although you have been coming to confession to me for a year, this is the first time we have alluded to the subject which I believed far from your thoughts."

"God be blessed!" exclaimed Mr. Cooper; and he added: "What you tell me is nothing new."

Nevertheless, the priest did not consider it well to accept the offer for two entire months, that the donor might have ample time for reflection. And when, at the end of this period, he presented himself with the money, he said:

"Sir, this establishment will be made at Emmitsburg, a village eighteen leagues from Baltimore; and thence it will extend throughout the United States."

At the mention of Emmitsburg the priest expressed some surprise and incredulity; but Mr. Cooper, while asserting that he wished to exert no influence in regard to locality, nor in the direction of the work, repeated in a confident tone that it would be at Emmitsburg.

In fact, the prediction was verified some time after, contrary to all the former convictions of this ecclesiastic and those of the foundress; and what is still more astonishing, in spite of the strongest opposition of the venerable Archbishop Carroll, who yielded at last to the force of circumstances. You know how God has blessed and propagated it throughout the land.

This account of how Samuel Sutherland Cooper became a divinely directed benefactor of Mother Seton's community differs noticeably from the circumstances set forth by Father White in his biography of the foundress; but since it came from the pen of a man who was directly involved in the negotiations, it must be preferred to White.

With this new turning of the tide, Elizabeth wrote at once to Filippo, on February 8, 1809, to acquaint him with her new prospects and to enlist his aid at the suggestion of, or at least in consultation with, Father Dubourg and Mr. Cooper.

> You will think, I fear, that the poor little woman's brain is turned who writes you so often on the same subject; but it is not a matter of choice on my part, as it is my indispensable duty to let you know every particular of a circumstance which has arisen since I wrote you last week. . . .
>
> Some time ago I mentioned to you the conversion of a man of family and fortune in Philadelphia. His conversion is as solid as it was extraordinary; and as the person is soon to receive tonsure in our seminary, in making the disposition of his fortune he has consulted our Reverend Mr. Dubourg, the president of the college, on a plan of establishing an institution for the advancement of Catholic female children in habits of religion, and giving them an education suited to that purpose. He also desires extremely to extend the plan to the reception of the aged, and also uneducated persons, who may be employed in spinning, knitting, etc., so as to found a manufactory on a small scale which may be beneficial to the poor.
>
> You see I am bound to let you know this disposition of Providence, that you may yourself judge how far you may concur with it . . .
>
> In my former letter I asked you if you could not secure your own property and build something for this purpose on the lot . . .
>
> If you should resolve to do so, the gentleman interested will furnish the necessary expenditures for setting us off and supporting those persons or children who at first will not be able to support themselves.
>
> Dr. Matignon will appoint a director for the establishment, which, if you

knew how many good and excellent souls are sighing for [it], would soon obtain an interest in your breast so ardently desiring the glory of God.

But all is in His hands. If I had a choice, and my will would decide in a moment, I would remain silent in His hands. Oh, how sweet it is, there to rest in perfect confidence! Yet, in every daily Mass and at Communion I beg Him to prepare your heart, and our dear Antonio's, to dispose of me and mine in any way which may please Him. You are our Father in Him; through your hands we received the new and precious being which is indeed true life.

Elizabeth revealed in this letter to Filippo a further startling fact: that Dr. Matignon had suggested Cooper's plan to Elizabeth long before Cooper himself had ever thought of it. It is no wonder that everyone concerned in the matter was profoundly convinced that the hand of God was writing on the wall!

While the business of establishing her community was thus absorbing her mind, Elizabeth encountered a private problem that shook her mother's soul. Anna Maria, who was not yet fourteen, had fallen in love. The news stunned Elizabeth, for she had not been the least bit aware of what was happening. It was not that she had been so naïve as not to look for such a thing; she had been a lovely, susceptible young girl herself, and for that reason had kept more than half an eye on her daughter. As she told Eliza Sadler, in discussing the affair: "I have no reproach to make myself, for it is impossible a child could be more strictly watched or carefully advised than my Annina"—(she had begun to call her after the Italian manner). More than once she had remarked to Julia how Anna had matured physically beyond her years, and as long ago as the summer of 1807 had confided that "the greatest difficulty I have to encounter is the loveliness of my Anna. She is indeed a being formed to please." Since coming to Baltimore, Anna literally had not been out of her sight—that was what astonished and puzzled Elizabeth so much about this infatuation.

As the facts emerged, Anna had been attracted to the young man, and he to her, without either of them ever having spoken a word to each other. His name was Charles DuPavillon, he was a student at St. Mary's College, and the two had been smitten in chapel, of all places! The romance had been carried on by means of secret looks and glances and the exchange of notes and tokens through Bill and Dick, who were too young to have any more sense. It was the secretiveness, the failure of Anna Maria to confide in her, that wounded Elizabeth more than anything else; yet, it was probably this very secretiveness that added just the right dash of romance for the young people.

DuPavillon must have been several years older than Annina, for he received his college degree from St. Mary's in 1810. He was from the Island of Guadeloupe in the West Indies, and was a young man of independent wealth; his only family was his widowed mother. In his romantic entanglement with Anna he displayed good sense, honesty and integrity. He it was who insisted on Anna's telling her mother, both because he was afraid the two boys would be found out as go-betweens and get in trouble with the college authorities, and because he was anxious to have Elizabeth's consent to their attachment. Elizabeth frankly admitted that Anna would never otherwise have brought it out into the open, due to her natural reserve.

Julia Scott, as a worldly-wise woman, sent her friend some very sensible advice. After reminding Elizabeth that she was taking the matter much too seriously, she went on:

> An attachment formed at so early an age is not likely to leave any durable impression on the mind, tho' felt with violence at the time; and as you were so fortunate to discover it immediately, I did not apprehend any ill consequence, nor should you view poor Anna's conduct too severely. I believe we expect too much from human nature if we hope *unlimited* confidence from our children; and Anna was too young, and had been too little in society, to be aware of the impropriety of receiving and answering a letter from a young man.

Julia was not on the scene, however, and neither knew Anna well nor how profoundly the attachment to DuPavillon had taken root in her heart. Elizabeth countered Julia's well-meaning letter by asking: "Are you not happy, most happy, in your Maria? But she never had the milk of an *inflammable* mother, as poor Ann had."

After the first shock, Elizabeth hid her feelings, even from her closest friends, and allowed only her pity for Annina to show through. Thus she told Julia:

It seems as if the moment she was made sensible of the uneasiness and sorrow she occasioned me, the terror and alarm of her mind banished every fancy and imagination which had blinded her; and she became docile and attentive to my will, as if it was not opposed to her own. Poor, dear child, I do not know how she can be so patient; as I well remember, at her age I should not have been—neither seeing nor hearing from the dearly beloved.

To Eliza Sadler, who had returned to New York, she even pretended to approve of the romance: "I knew more of him [DuPavillon] than she [Anna] did herself, thro' my *soul's friend* (Father Babade) who is also his, and had always wished Anna might be so fortunate as to gain his affection in the way she has, which seems to be solid and sincere."

She opened her true sentiments, however, to Dué, the following year when the attachment still persisted:

> My Annina—that is the pinch—my Annina: so young, so lovely, so innocent, absorbed in all the romance of youthful passion. As I have told you, she gave her heart without my knowledge; and afterwards what could a doting and unhappy mother do but take the part of friend and confidante, dissembling my distress and resolving that—if there was no remedy—to help her at least by my love and pity?

Now, however, at the beginning of 1809, Elizabeth took firm and prudent action. She allowed the lovers to meet once, in her presence, and there the matter was threshed out. Elizabeth pointed out that Annina was obviously too young to enter into a formal engagement, and laid down certain rules of conduct. The young people were to have no further communication for the time being. Since Elizabeth's removal to Emmitsburg was under consideration, and Anna would go with her, Elizabeth agreed that Charles might write to Anna there, but always enclose the letters unsealed to herself. The two youngsters humbly agreed, and the matter rested there.

Talk of establishing the new community at Emmitsburg rather than at Baltimore must have begun in earnest soon after Elizabeth had written her second letter to Filippo, for on February 29 she confided to a friend, Rose Stubbs of New York, that her community was about to be formed and that "we are going to begin our novitiate in a beautiful country place in the mountains." Things were moving swiftly indeed. On March 2, when she wrote Julia Scott the news of the proposed expansion of her work, she said that Cooper had actually begun to look for a site in Emmitsburg:

> As you have so long shared all my pains, my dearest, how much pleasure it will give you to know that Providence has disposed for me a plan after my own heart. A benevolent gentleman of this place has formed a scheme of establishing a manufactory for the use of the poor, and includes in his intention the education of children rich and poor. He is about purchasing a place at Emmitsburg, some distance from Baltimore, not very considerable, and has offered me the department of taking care of the children who may be presented, or rather of being the mother of the family.
>
> This pleases me for many reasons. In the first place, I shall live in the mountains; in the next, I shall see no more of the world than if I was out of it, and have every object centered in my own family, both of provision, employment, etc. . . .
>
> Such is the prospect, dearest; but whether it is to be accomplished or not is the question. I am quite at my ease on the subject, caring very little how I am disposed of, the remainder of my life, if only I may persevere in acting the mother's part with fidelity.
>
> The care of teaching will be off my hands, tho' not the superintendence, and I do not hesitate to embrace the offer of going to the country, as no doubt it will be a means of prolonging my days for my dear ones; and probably be an effectual means of extricating Anna from the effects of her imprudence. For if *young D.* is hereafter true to his attachment, he may easily claim her; if not, her happiness depends on seeing him no more.

She concluded by asking Julia whether she could lend "three thousand or two thousand dollars on the best security in either Philadelphia or Baltimore, to be refunded in a year," toward the inauguration of the scheme. For once, Julia could not help her, for she had her capital invested at the moment in the building of a new house. Furthermore, she was upset at the news of the proposed change, since it was the giving up of "a certainty for an uncertainty, and establishment secure and respectable and in which you are protected and already known—at the very critical point of time, too, when its advantages must increase—for one which *may* be more agreeable." Julia was anxious, also, as to the effect of the move socially and educationally upon Elizabeth's children; but most of all—good, dear friend that she was—she was worried about its effect on Elizabeth. What would Elizabeth do, if it should not succeed? What would be the effect on her peace of mind and soul?

You are to be the superintendent of the female part of the establishment, the mother of probably a very large family, rich and poor, a heterogeneous mixture which will only increase your difficulties and render your duties more arduous. The whole arrangement, care, provision and responsibility devolve on you. My dearest friend, you will be overwhelmed; no peaceful hours, no peaceful moments, will you know. Anxiety and solicitude will cloud your days. Were you only an assistant, you would be much better off, for then your duties would be clear and distinct; but burdened with the weight of responsibility, you will be distracted with fears, and uncertain whether you do right or wrong.

You are too little acquainted with the ways of the world to be aware of the difficulties attending the care of a large establishment; nor can I point them all out to you, tho' my mind is deeply, I had almost said horribly, impressed with them.

It was an eloquent and persuasive letter, conceived in love, and Elizabeth answered it on March 23, trying to soothe Julia's fears. In doing so, she painted a far rosier picture of the conveniences at Emmitsburg and of her own lack of responsibility than the facts warranted. Elizabeth was definitely to be the Mother Superior, with all the responsibility that post involved, even though she would be under the guidance and rule of Father Dubourg (since January, Dr. Matignon had apparently relinquished his role, and the Sulpicians had taken over the directorship of the proposed community).

Archbishop Carroll had hesitated at first to commit the post of Superioress to Elizabeth, because of her children, but at length determined to give the unique arrangement a trial. The question of the children was to be much more carefully considered when the time came to adopt formal rules for the Sisterhood.

Two days after writing her *apologia* to Julia, on March 25, 1809, the feast of the Annunciation of Our Lady, Elizabeth Seton pronounced vows of poverty, chastity and obedience—binding for one year—in the presence of Archbishop Carroll. It was a dedication she had long wished to make, and a transport in her letter to Julia had shown what her mind was in making it—"to speak the joy of my soul at the prospect of being able to assist the poor, visit the sick, comfort the sorrowful, clothe little innocents and teach them to love God!—there I must stop!" St. Vincent de Paul had not yet been mentioned in connection with the Sisterhood,

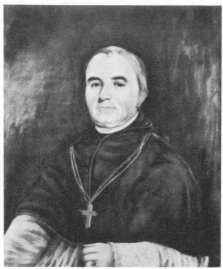

Upper left: Bishop Louis William Valentine Dubourg; *right*: Bishop John Dubois. *Lower left*: Bishop Simon Gabriel Bruté de Rémur; *right*: Bishop John Lefebvre de Cheverus.

Photos by The Lane Studio

An early photograph of the house on Paca Street, Baltimore, where Mother Seton opened her first Catholic school and where the Sisterhood was formed.

The Stone House, first residence of Mother Seton and Sisters at St. Joseph's, Emmitsburg, from an early photograph before modern restoration.

Interior of the Stone House.

Photos by The Lane Studio

The White House at St. Joseph's in Mother Seton's time, from an old painting.

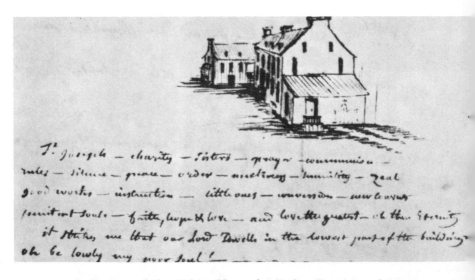

A drawing of the White House by Father Bruté in a letter to Mother Seton.

but these were decidedly Vincentian ideals. Indeed, Elizabeth had performed these corporal works of mercy all her life—even as a little girl —but what increased lustre they took on when sealed by God in the taking of a *vow* to do them!

From this day on, Elizabeth became known as *Mother* Seton. She wrote happily to Cecilia:

> My dearest, the scene before me is heavenly. . . . The tender title of *Mother* salutes me everywhere, even from lips that have never said to me the common salutation among strangers. They give me the silent little squeeze in the chapel, for here no one speaks as in New York.

The Eastertime, that spring, was a season of rapture for her: she had reached at last that high, shining meadow of religious peace she had seen near the summit of the mountain in her dream off the coast of Gibraltar in 1803. She tried to conjure up some sensible image of it for Cecilia Seton:

> Imagine twenty priests all with the devotion of saints, clothed in white, accompanied by the whole troop of the young seminarians in surplices also, all in order surrounding the Blessed Sacrament exposed, singing the hymn of the Resurrection. When they come to the words, "Peace be to all here," it seems as if Our Lord is again acting over the scene that passed with the assembled disciples. Hush!

The word had gone out that the mystic wedding feast was prepared, and spotless young souls hurried to join the consecrated little Mother in going forth to meet the Bridegroom. "I can give you no just idea," she told Cecilia breathlessly, "of the precious souls who are daily uniting under my banner, which is the cross of Christ." Cecilia O'Conway was already there, and Maria Murphy, who had come from Philadelphia in Holy Week; Susan Clossy, the first New York recruit, came on May 24; and Mary Ann Butler, another Philadelphian, on June 1. Ellen Thompson, of Emmitsburg, wrote for admission, and her description of herself was the best testimonial she could have given. "I am but a child," she wrote Elizabeth on the 2nd of May, "I only begin to crawl in the ways of God; and that interior spirit which detaches us from everything which is not God and makes the true spouse of Christ, I have to acquire yet. I wish to do it; it is all I can say yet."

Elizabeth was pleased to see that even the aristocracy of Baltimore was attracted by the growing band of Sisters. Louisa Caton, she told Cecilia Seton, was "panting for the moment of our departure, and has no peace but in my arms. . . . She refuses the most splendid matches, to unite herself to Our Lord." Louisa was a granddaughter of Charles Carroll of Carrollton and a cousin to Archbishop Carroll. Unfortunately, the Catons were a worldly family; and Julia Scott, an old family friend, had warned Elizabeth that Emily Caton, who formed with her sisters Louisa and Mary a beauteous trio known as the "Three American Graces," was not a fit companion for Anna Maria Seton. Elizabeth had acknowledged that even the Catons were unhappy over Emily's conduct; "but what can be expected," Elizabeth asked, "from a warm heart and lively imagination nourished only by romances?" Louisa's yearning for the convent was apparently a romantic fancy, too, for—to Elizabeth's disappointment—she allowed her family to talk her out of it, and later married Sir Felton Bathurst, aide to the Duke of Wellington.

Louisa's loss, however, could not affect the glorious band of generous souls that was forming, and on April 13, Bishop-elect Cheverus, with exalted vision, hailed the prodigy that had come about in a scant nine months.

> I see already numerous choirs of virgins following you to the altar [he exclaimed to Elizabeth]. I see your holy order diffusing itself in the different parts of the United States, spreading everywhere the good odor of Jesus Christ and teaching by their angelical lives and pious instructions how to serve God in purity and holiness. I have no doubt, my beloved and venerable sister, that He Who has begun this good work will bring it to perfection.

Only Cecilia Seton was missing from the scene of general joy. It had been a very unhappy year for the poor girl. She had endured uncomplainingly the burdens and heats of the day, the frowns and viciousness of her family; and now it seemed that the Master of the vineyard was going to deny her even her denarius. For it was her director, Father Anthony Kohlmann, who was effectively barring the way to Emmitsburg. He was determined upon his school, and upon having Cecilia teach in it. She had written Elizabeth despairingly in March:

Mr. Kohlmann seems more and more averse than ever to my leaving New York. He has gone so far as tell me I cannot go unless in opposition to his advice and the Will of God; that in Baltimore I can do no good, but here I can do much for the glory of God.

It was a tremendous test of her faith, but she met it nobly. To add to her anguish, James was very displeased at the notion of the school, but at length consented to have it operate in his house, in order that he might retain the good services of his sister. Mr. Redmond, another clerical adviser, would not even let Cecilia carry through a proposed visit to Elizabeth, telling her that it was "foolish to think of it," and that it would be "a great *self-indulgence.*" Obviously, the priests of New York were taking no chances of losing her. The greatest irony of all was that the hostile Ogdens and Farquhars were urging Cecilia to join Elizabeth and asking her why she did not—she was, of course, an embarrassment and a threat to them in New York.

Elizabeth had kept Archbishop Carroll informed of Cecilia's situation, and found him a champion of Cecilia's desire to leave New York. The Archbishop promised to write Father Kohlmann his views of the matter, and although he did not do so at once, his expressed intention was enough to make Father Kohlmann's advice to Cecilia undergo gradual and subtle changes. The priest told her vaguely in the middle of March that, if it was the Will of God, she should go, but he thought it better to put off her departure until the fall when James' oldest girl would have returned from school and assumed the care of the children. A week later, he conceded that Cecilia had a vocation to the religious state, but as Mrs. Seton could begin the new community without her, she must not hurry.

At length Archbishop Carroll spoke his mind, and Cecilia made ready to leave New York at once, despite the fact that James had just moved into town, and her own health was failing fast. Sam Seton was to escort her to Baltimore, and Harriet would come, too, but just for a visit, as Barclay had at last made a definite promise of coming to New York during the summer to marry her and take her back with him to Jamaica.

The little group left New York on June 1 and arrived at Paca Street on June 12.

Cecilia was not in time to assume the religious habit with the first band of Sisters. On the very day that she had been carried to the ship, shaking with the ague of her disease—June 1, 1809—Elizabeth, Cecilia O'Conway, Maria Murphy, Susan Clossy and Mary Ann Butler put on the formal religious habit for the first time. It was not really a change of dress for Elizabeth, for she had worn substantially the same attire since her husband's death in Leghorn. The habit was, in effect, the standard widow's weeds worn in Italy: a black dress with short shoulder cape, and a white muslin cap with crimped border tied under the chin by means of a black crepe band. A rosary was draped from the leather belt that served for a cincture.

Elizabeth's beads, given to her by Madame Fournier, are preserved at Emmitsburg. They are black, and quite large. A cross hangs from them engraved with the words "*Caritas Christi urget nos*"—"The Charity of Christ urges us on," which was the motto given by St. Vincent de Paul to his Daughters of Charity; and also the words: "*Pauperes evangelizantur*"—"The poor must have the Gospel preached to them," the motto chosen by St. Vincent for his priests, the Vincentian Fathers. Attached to the cross is a silver ring engraved with the words: "*Cor unum—anima una*"—"One heart—one soul." It is not known whether any or all of these texts were etched at the time the beads were first worn, or later, when the Vincentian rule had been adopted.

It may have been on this eternally memorable evening of the first putting on of the religious habit that the following moving scene occurred. Archbishop Carroll and certain unidentified priests—almost certainly Dubourg and Babade among them—had been discussing with Elizabeth and her new Sisters the foundation of their community and its future when an awesome sense of her major role in the plans of God, and of her consequent obligations, smote Elizabeth's soul. She cried uncontrollably for some minutes, then fell on her knees in abject humility and confessed before them all the most shameful and regrettable faults and sins she had committed since the time she was a little girl. She finished by raising her hands to heaven and sobbing out her unworthiness:

"My gracious God! You know my unfitness for this task. I, who by my sins have so often crucified You, I blush with shame and confusion.

How can I teach others, who know so little myself, and am so miserable and imperfect?"

The next morning—June 2, 1809—the feast of Corpus Christi—the public caught its first glimpse of the five Sisters dressed in their religious garb, when they attended Mass and received Holy Communion in St. Mary's Chapel. Elizabeth could not have helped recalling this same feast one year before, and the wonderful things that had happened in between.

XVI

Emmitsburg

The state of Cecilia Seton's health hastened Elizabeth's plans to leave for Emmitsburg. In May she had told Julia Scott that she and her little band of Sisters intended to leave Baltimore by "the middle of next month, as my house is then to be given up." When the middle of June came, however, the Sisters' new home in the Maryland mountains was not quite ready to receive them; but poor Cecilia was so desperately ill that Dr. Chatard insisted on getting her into the mountain air as quickly as possible. It was arranged, therefore, that Father John Dubois, the Pastor of Emmitsburg and the surrounding district, should move out of his house on the lower slope of St. Mary's Mountain, leaving it to the Sisters until their own home should be ready.

Accordingly, on Wednesday, June 21, 1809, the feast of St. Aloysius, the historic trek began. Elizabeth, Sister Maria Murphy, Cecilia, Harriet and Annina were the pioneers; and while they were not going far westward—only some fifty miles—they were as truly pioneers as if they meant to push beyond the Cumberland Gap or the Great Divide. For, at the end of their short, rough, exhausting journey, they intended to found a spiritual settlement that would shelter countless thousands in the future and nurture millions more.

They traveled slowly, even for those days—because of the heat and

the cowpath of a road and their own limited stamina, but mostly because of the invalid Cecilia—and it would be Saturday, the fourth day,
before they reached their destination. Their route was much the same
as it is today: over the gentle hills and the flat fields, through Reisterstown
and Westminster and Taneytown. From Westminster Elizabeth dispatched a letter, factual but cheerful, to Father Dubourg:

> We are so far safe, tho' our progress is so much slower than you expected.
> Your turnpike road is, to be sure, a very rough one, and we were obliged
> to walk the horses all the way; and have walked ourselves all except Cecilia,
> nearly half the time—this morning, four miles and a half before breakfast.
> The dear patient was greatly amused at the procession, and all the natives
> astonished as we went before the carriage. The dogs and pigs came out to
> meet us, and the geese stretched their necks in mute demand to know if we
> were any of their sort, to which we gave assent.

It was not gratitude or friendship alone that prompted Elizabeth to
keep Dubourg thus informed; if he was not already the formal superior
or director of the community, he was its active adviser at the time. As
early as May Father Charles Nagot, Superior of the Sulpicians in America,
had been designated as director of the Sisters, and plans were laid for
him to live near them at Emmitsburg, but his years—he was seventy-
five—and failing health made this impractical; and by the beginning of
August Duboug was *de jure* and *de facto* the Sisters' director.

As the women left Westminster, walking beside their broad-wheeled,
canvas-covered wain—the Conestoga wagon of the Prairies—they came
upon immediate signs of mountainous terrain ahead. The hills grew
steeper, creeks ran through the floors of the narrowing dells and rocks
cropped out of the hunched-up earth. Soon the first, long blue ridge of
the Catoctin Mountains appeared, and then another and another until
the horizon was a glorious wall of green and blue with intricate pockets
and folds still in shadow. As the travelers neared Emmitsburg, St. Mary's
Mountain rose up over all. How good it would be to know Elizabeth's
thoughts when her eyes first saw and blessed this noble mound!—for
she was to love it almost as part of her being, and referred to it always
as "my mountain"; and the lovely valley lying at its feet as "my valley."
The use of the personal pronoun was not pride of possession but an
affirmation of kinship: from the time she was a little girl nature had

led her to praise God just as it praised Him. "All ye works of the Lord, bless the Lord . . . O ye mountains and hills, bless the Lord; praise and exalt Him above all forever."

The village of Emmitsburg was strung out along two roads which crossed each other. It was founded in 1786 on a tract of land belonging originally to Charles Carroll of Annapolis, the father of the signer of the Declaration of Independence. For this reason, the first settlers considered calling it Carrollstown, but finally decided on Emmitstown, which soon became Emmitsburg. The Church, named for St. Joseph, was built in 1793. It had in its time such distinguished pastors as John Dubois, third Bishop of New York, and Simon Gabriel Bruté, first Bishop of Vincennes, and after a succession of Sulpician and secular pastors, passed into the hands of the Vincentian Fathers in 1850.

When Mother Seton first came to Emmitsburg, the village had several hundred inhabitants, mainly Irish, Germans and Negroes, slave and free. Approximately half the villagers were Catholic, the rest mainly Lutherans and Presbyterians with a smattering of Episcopalians, Quakers and Methodists.

When the little band of tired women had arrived at the crossroads, they turned left onto the road running toward the southeast. After half a mile they came to the beginning of their new property, but passed on to Mount St. Mary's College where Father Dubois awaited them.

Dubois was born in Paris on August 24, 1764, and became a priest in 1787. Driven from France by the Revolution, he sailed for America, arriving at Norfolk, Virginia, in July, 1791, armed with letters from his friend, Marquis de Lafayette, for the first families of Virginia: the Randolphs, the Lees, the Beverlys, and for James Monroe and Patrick Henry. He stayed for a time with Monroe, and took lessons in English from the orator of the American Revolution. Undoubtedly it was the friendship of such distinguished men that allowed him, after obtaining the necessary faculties from Bishop Carroll, to minister to Catholics in the bigoted city of Richmond, and even to offer Mass in the capitol itself. In 1794 Carroll appointed him pastor of Frederickstown in Maryland. It was, like most other American parishes of the time, a mission outpost; and from the church he built in Frederickstown, Dubois rode out on horseback to care for his flock scattered over Western Maryland, Virginia and lower Pennsylvania.

Emmitsburg was one of his regular stops. The little village now had two churches: in addition to St. Joseph's in the town itself, there was St. Mary's, a log structure at the foot of the mountain which, according to local legend, William Elder had named for the Mother of God in 1734. The village had a resident pastor, too, Father Matthew Ryan, who was there as early as 1796; but, from wisps of evidence, he seems to have been a strange, even scandalous character. He died in 1817 and is buried in the graveyard alongside St. Joseph's; but it was Dubois, not he, who was pastor when Mother Seton arrived in 1809.

In 1805 the Catholics of Emmitsburg built a two-room house of rough-hewn logs which Dubois moved into permanently after the willing parishioners had constructed a new St. Mary's Church of brick a little above it on the lower rise of the mountain in 1807. Here in 1808 he opened a school for boys which became a junior seminary to prepare students for St. Mary's in Baltimore, when Dubois entered the Society of St. Sulpice in 1809. In a short time, however, Mount St. Mary's College was functioning as the seminary and college it is today.

The month Elizabeth Seton spent in Father Dubois' house was like the days in paradise before Adam and Eve were driven forth to earn their bread in sweat and sorrow. To begin with, the religious life she had so long desired was hers, and God allowed her this time to delight in it before the heavy trials, almost the rule-of-thumb for religious foundations, should begin. Then, her beloved Cecilia was with her at long last, and only death would separate them now. Even more, Cecilia's health had picked up so amazingly that death and separation were pushed hopefully into the background. Harriet Seton was showing signs of coming to a decision about the Catholic Church; Annina was away from Baltimore and DuPavillon; in a few days, Kate and Rebecca arrived to complete their mother's contentment.

Elizabeth was especially enchanted with the countryside, and well she might be, for it is one of the most beautiful spots in all the Southland. "We are half in the sky," she exclaimed to Matthias O'Conway, the father of Sister Cecilia, "the height of our situation is almost incredible."

It was not so happy a time for Harriet Seton. She had been thoroughly miserable when she came to Baltimore. Her health was excellent, but her spirits were down, due both to the embarrassment the faithless Barclay was causing her by his callous absence in Jamaica, and to the struggle in her soul between the desire to be a Catholic and the fear of being cast off by family and friends. She was the classic, tragic heroine of romance, beautiful but sad, young but unhappy. Wandering through the primitive wildness of wood and meadow, wrestling with her destiny, she might have been mistaken for Guinevere or Deirdre of the Sorrows.

Her destiny, however, was not to be one of long repining. Two factors precipitated the crisis that brought her peace, happiness and eternal salvation. The first was her friendship for Father Babade. Although Harriet had known him only the nine days she spent in Baltimore, a deep understanding had developed between the two. It was truly amazing, the magnetic power this white-haired poet and mystic had over the souls of good women. His love for God, emotional and enthusiastic, was exactly the kind of love a woman would understand.

Certainly the romantic Harriet, in the throes of an unhappy love affair on the one hand, and a fearful, yet sincere, seeking for God on the other, found him just the director she needed, a man of kindly sympathy, but also the man of ardent action. His sensitive heart could feel her pain, but his burning devotion could impel her to push past it to the comfort and consolation of God. He bombarded her with letters, warm, glowing, spiritual—as all his letters were—urging her to find the solution to her troubles in submission to God. She answered in kind, pouring out her heart.

The second factor forcing Harriet to a decision was a letter from Barclay. It played into the hands of God and Father Babade, for it showed how shallow, thoughtless and cruel her so-called lover was. It stated quite baldly that he might not return to marry her for at least eight or ten years; nor did it even hint that she might come out to Jamaica and marry him there. Indeed its whole tone was so rude and offensive that it could have been written only by a boor. Barclay actually related the tale of a young man who had left his mistress lovely and youthful and, after long separation, returned to find her withered and old, and then went on to ask the astonishingly beautiful Harriet whether her bloom had faded!

Elizabeth, relaying the news in her brother's outrageous letter to Julia Scott, reported that Harriet was "so shocked with a proposal which so evidently shows his indifference to her, that it seems to disgust her with everything of the kind."

Certainly, it drove her to consider what was best for herself, whether Barclay should ever return to claim her or not. After this fresh wound to her honor, she could not face the fashionable world of New York in the coming winter social season. Indeed, the more she thought about it, she told Elizabeth, she could no longer bear the thoughts of taking up her life again with the Ogdens or any of the relatives who had so persecuted her for the Catholic leanings. Closer and closer she drew to the determination never to return to New York, but to stay with Elizabeth and Cecilia who loved her truly.

Despite her clearing thoughts, however, despite the kind advice of Père Babade, she could not take the step that would unite her completely with her Catholic loved ones. Every day she would walk with Elizabeth and Cecilia up the mountainside, but when they had come to the little church, and the two had gone inside to make a visit, she stayed back, wandering in the woods or sitting upon a rock, lost in the agony of her indecision.

At length, one evening, coming out of church, Elizabeth found the poor girl in tears.

"Why, O why, cannot I go into the church with you?" she sobbed.

"And why not, if you wish it?" Elizabeth kindly replied.

Harriet thus began to attend Mass and evening devotions each day. Not long after, on the eve of the feast of St. Mary Magdalen, her patroness (her full name was Harriet Magdalen Seton, and Babade and certain of the Sisters always called her by this second name), the crisis came. A few days before, Father Babade had written that he would offer Mass for her in Baltimore on her name day; it had also been arranged for Father Dubois to do the same at Emmitsburg. Deeply moved, Harriet left the log house on the evening of Friday, July 21, between ten and eleven o'clock, to seek the solitude of St. Mary's Church. Elizabeth has left a description of her

> stealing up to the church by the light of a full moon, in deepest silence. her arms crossed upon her breast, and the moon's reflection full on her pale

but celestial countenance. I saw the falling tears of love and adoration, while we said, first *Miserere* and then *Te Deum*, which from her childhood had been our family prayers.

Descending the mountain, she burst forth the full heart: "It is done, my sister, I am a Catholic. The cross of Our Dearest is the desire of my soul. I will never rest till He is mine."

Her resolution so emotionally taken faltered in the ensuing days, and even when she had taken hold of it again she still refused—in her "weak and uninformed faith," as Elizabeth called it—to open her heart and soul to any but Father Babade. But when she had heard that both Archbishop Carroll and Father Dubourg had summoned Babade, who was on a missionary journey to Philadelphia, Germantown, and Burlington, New Jersey, to receive her into the Church, Harriet became strong in faith and resolution, and awaited his coming with a holy impatience.

Harriet's acceptance of the Church was not the only spiritual joy for Elizabeth during this wonderful month of July 1809. Even in the temporary home of the new community, its number increased. Sally Thompson, of Emmitsburg, joined the Sisters; and Elizabeth knew that, when the permanent move to their own property down the road should take place shortly, her sister, Ellen Thompson—who had written such an artless, humble letter of application—would be with them. In the meantime, laborers were putting the finishing touches to the stone cottage which was the only building on the Fleming farm purchased by Mr. Cooper, and the Sisters were happily scrubbing and sweeping in preparation for moving day.

Just before Elizabeth left Baltimore, she had welcomed the first two Baltimoreans to ask admission into the sisterhood: Catherine Mullen and Rose White.

Rose Landry White was easily the most important of all Elizabeth's first companions, for she was to serve as her assistant and her successor. Like Elizabeth, she was a widow. The story of her marriage was romantic in a bizarre sort of way. Her husband, a sea captain, was a friend of her father's, and presumably of an age with him. According to the story, the two men had sat on the piazza of the Landry home admiring Rose's extraordinary beauty and grace as she skipped home from school. Turning to his friend, White made the request for her hand: "Keep her for me," he said. Bishop Carroll married the pair, and is reported to have remarked laughingly to Rose after the ceremony:

"It is well for you, my child, that I did not examine the register. Had I done so, I would not have performed that ceremony, since you are only fourteen."

It is, of course, possible that some lesser cleric had made the arrangements for the marriage—which met the canonical requirements for age —without Carroll's entering into them; but it is difficult to imagine the wise old Bishop, in so small a community, not knowing that he was assisting at the marriage of a child-bride. Of such stuff are legends made.

The Whites were blessed with a daughter and a son, who were left to the young wife's upbringing when Captain White was lost at sea. Rose fell under the influence of Father John Baptist David, who converted her to a holier life and to works of charity. She was twenty-five when she joined Mrs. Seton in June, 1809. Her little girl had died soon after the father, and the boy—like the Seton boys—attended Mount St. Mary's during the early years of the Sisterhood. Due perhaps to Mrs. White's being a few years older than the other Sisters and to her experience with the world, Elizabeth left her in charge in Baltimore when she herself set out for Emmitsburg.

In the last week of July Sister Rose led the remaining Sisters to their Promised Land. The group included Sisters Cecilia O'Conway, Mary Ann Butler, Susan Clossy and Catherine Mullen; William and Richard Seton; and two pupils who had attended the Paca Street School, Julia La Britton and Isabella O'Conway. It is not known how long their journey took, but Sister Rose, when she composed her *Journal* some years later, remembered certain incidents that have passed into the folklore of the community—for example, that the Seton boys slept in the wagon at night to guard the baggage; and Sister Cecilia O'Conway recalled that they whiled away the tedious lumbering hours by regaling themselves with the droll stories of St. Teresa's travels.

On the last evening of the trip they stopped at a rather rundown inn, "where," Sister Rose wrote, "we had but poor accommodations. We asked for supper but told them, as it was Friday, not to prepare any meat. When we went to table, there was plenty of chicken on the table. Sister Kitty remarked we had told them not to prepare any meat. 'Oh,' said the woman who waited on the table, 'chicken is not meat.' We smiled and made our supper on bread and butter, tea and eggs."

The next morning the travelers started off without breakfast, and before long Sister Susan fell violently ill. When they stopped for their meal, which served for breakfast and lunch, they managed to procure some remedies for her; but these did little good, and when they reached Emmitsburg that afternoon, the doctor had to be sent for. There was something oddly prophetic about this, for the early years of the Sisterhood were one long history of illness and death, and the doctor made many a call after this one. As for Sister Susan, her illness was a passing thing and she lived longer than Elizabeth.

The American Sisters of Charity mark July 31, the feast of St. Ignatius Loyola, as the anniversary of their permanent establishment in their own home at Emmitsburg. The date is accurate enough, if the few days preceding are considered as days of preparation, for Sister Rose states positively in her *Journal* that Mother Seton and the first band of Sisters waited in welcome for the second group at the farmhouse on Saturday afternoon, which was July 29. The first Sisters, therefore, must have moved into the farmhouse or Stone House, as it has always been called, on Friday, July 28—as Father Bruté recorded in a chronology he compiled, although he is not always reliable in the matter of details—or Saturday, July 29. Saturday and Sunday would have been so taken up with "getting settled" and putting things in order that it would have been difficult to follow a regular order of day. Therefore, it is easy to understand why Elizabeth and her Sisters, and consequently tradition, would have dated the establishment at Emmitsburg from Monday, July 31, as, probably, the day on which they first began to live the religious life there.

It is not so easy to establish how the community came to be designated in the early years as "Sisters of St. Joseph" or "Sisters of Charity of St. Joseph"; or whether, in fact, the designation was actually "of St. Joseph's"—both forms appear in early correspondence and memoranda. Father White, in his usually correct biography of Mrs. Seton, states that Elizabeth herself chose the title because she wanted to place the Sisters and all the works of the community under the patronage of the Foster Father of Jesus. His explanation must be accepted with some skepticism, however, simply because it comes as a surprise: there is no indication in all Elizabeth's previous letters, or in her spiritual jottings —which is more to the point—that she had a special devotion to St. Joseph at the time. Had she, on the other hand, desired to dedicate her community to the Blessed Sacrament, the all-consuming devotion of her life, it would be easily understandable. If, therefore, the community was indeed consecrated to St. Joseph by its title, it is more believable to attribute the suggestion for such a consecration to Father Dubourg or one of the Sulpicians, just as nearly every other suggestion for the foundation came from them.

There is a strong possibility, however, that the title came merely from the location of the Sisterhood, that the valley in which they settled was St. Joseph's Valley—as it has been ever after—taking its name from St. Joseph's Church in a reversal of the way St. Mary's took its name, from its situation at the base of St. Mary's Mountain. At any rate, it seems evident that the title of the sisterhood was meant as a temporary and convenient one against the day when the young community should become in some way affiliated with the French community of St. Vincent de Paul, as Father Dubourg and Father Babade and other Sulpicians intended.

The nine new arrivals, added to the eleven already there—Sister Ellen Thompson had come—immediately overtaxed the facilities of the Stone House. The house had only two rooms on the ground floor, and two more in the garret. The Sisters laid their mattresses on the floor, for there were no bedsteads. Father Dubourg, who had come from Baltimore to be on hand when they arrived, had to go to the village for cups and saucers before supper could be served that Saturday evening; and he gave them his first piece of practical advice: to start cultivating carrots at once, to be used as a substitute for coffee. This "carrot coffee" became the Sisters' daily drink, morning and evening.

On Sunday the little community rose early in order to go to confession and attend Mass at St. Joseph's Church. They approached the Holy Table together, thus sealing their religious beginning in the divine Bond of Charity given by God to mankind. After breakfast, they returned for High Mass, Mother Seton and two others staying behind.

The first officers of the community were announced that day. These officers seem to have been appointed, either by Father Dubourg or by Mother Seton with his concurrence, rather than elected. Sister Rose was to be Mother's assistant; Sister Kitty, housekeeper; Sister Cecilia Seton, secretary and school Sister; and Sister Sally, procuratrix or treasurer. Sister Sally's appointment was dictated by practicality, for she was, it will be remembered, a native of Emmitsburg, and knew both the merchants and their wares.

It is to be noted that these first Sisters of St. Joseph kept their baptismal names in religion, and—probably because there were already two of the same name, Cecilia O'Conway and Cecilia Seton—their family names as well, for the purpose of positive identification. Thus, the Daughters of Charity's practice of retaining the family name was adopted in the American community from the first. Elizabeth's given name was never used, but only her family name; she was always referred to as Mother Seton or Mrs. Seton. What is especially heartwarming, however, is that these early Sisters even used their nicknames—Sister Sally, Sister Kitty, Sister Sus; and Elizabeth herself usually dropped the title "Sister," calling them, as a mother would call her children, Kitty, Sus, Sally, Rose. It is all a happy indication of the easy informality that helped make them a true family.

Not that such informality implied disorder. Elizabeth had always had a talent for organization. The pattern of devotions laid out by her for Rebecca Seton and Dué; the efficient running of the large and complicated Seton household; the roster of lessons and prayers and stories and singing in her own little home were all examples of that talent. And so, at Emmitsburg, even in these first days when the community was, as it were, still adrift, order prevailed.

The immediate appointment of officers has already been noted; a religious order of day was practiced immediately, too. The Sisters rose at five o'clock, and said their morning prayers and made a meditation before going to Mass. At first they had to go out to Mass, either to the village church or to St. Mary's, for Father Dubois was the only priest in the vicinity until Father Charles Duhamel became resident pastor of Emmitsburg in the autumn of 1809. In either case it was a long enough walk, especially in bad weather, and the Sisters adopted the custom of reciting the joyful mysteries of the Rosary on their way to church, and the sorrowful mysteries on their way back.

Breakfast over, they assembled at nine o'clock for an Act of Adoration of the Sacred Heart, then went about their duties until a quarter to twelve, when they had an examen of conscience, short visit to the Blessed Sacrament—which was reserved in a tiny alcove of the house—and the reading of the New Testament. At dinner other portions of Scripture were read. Recreation followed, and, at two o'clock, the Sisters met again before the Blessed Sacrament for the reading of the *Imitation of Christ* and another short visit. They worked until five, then made a longer visit in their little chapel and recited the glorious mysteries of the Rosary. The *Spiritual Combat* was read during supper, after which the Sisters enjoyed another recreation period until eight-thirty, when they listened to one of their number read from a spiritual book, said their night prayers and retired.

It was a full, well-balanced day, even during these summer months before the opening of school. There were a thousand small tasks to take the place of school work: the routine cleaning, sewing, cultivating the little garden, bringing the overgrown property back to some semblance of discipline. Doing the wash was an all-day affair. There was no water for the purpose in or near the house; only a spring of drinking water outside. So the Sisters gathered up the soiled clothes and went off, carrying the heavy wash tubs, to the banks of Toms Creek, several hundred yards down the hill that fell away from the house in the back. Sister Rose described it laconically but graphically enough:

> Our washing place was at the creek where we took our clothes early in the morning and remained all day. Not a plank to stand on, not a covering but the tree under which we placed our tubs. And if rain came on, we would have to bring up our clothes all wet and heavy. No accommodations, no water to work with at the house. We continued till winter in this way.

That final sentence recalled simply and without complaint what must have been a minor ordeal of suffering and hardship; icy water, raw, rough hands, biting winds—and several of these women, at least, had been gently born and used to comfortable and even luxurious living.

Since the Stone House was crowded from the first, as has been said, the building of a larger structure, to serve as school and convent both, was begun almost at once. The foundations were dug quickly, on a site about two hundred yards up a slight rise in front of the Stone House, and a little closer to the front road, and the skeleton began to rise. The carpenters worked swiftly, for they were eager to get the walls and roof up before the cold weather set in in earnest. The project brought new excitement into the life of Father Dubois, for he loved building. He had already supervised the building of a church in Frederickstown and the first college "halls" at the Mount—nor was he above putting his hand and back to work—and he was to go on building all his life. Elizabeth was forever joking about this passion of his, but never to him; she knew how serious about it he was, and how deeply he would be offended.

Father Dubourg had returned from Baltimore after a few days and prepared the little alcove to serve for a chapel by installing a small altar and hanging a door that could be closed when the Sisters were not using the corner for their devotion. He also gave them a copy of *Christian Perfection* which, Sister Rose remembered, they had never seen before, and a bell to summon them to exercises. Then he announced their first retreat, which he would open on August 10.

The retreat was a unique event for the Sisters; none of them, Elizabeth included, had ever made one before. At its close, Father Dubourg instructed them to write out their resolutions, each in her own hand, without having spoken about them, to anyone. It was a wise stroke. He was able to assess, by carefully studying the sheet each Sister brought him, the extent of her education, and especially the growth and needs of her soul.

In these first days the spiritual approach of the little band of Sisters to their director should have been in a spirit of free and open and joyous intimacy; but, unfortunately Elizabeth was forced, in these first days of August, to dissemble her true feelings toward him, for she had already written to Archbishop Carroll to protest Dubourg's first action of consequence.

After Dubourg had gone back to Baltimore on July 31, Elizabeth received a letter from him forbidding the Sisters to have any more to do with Father Babade. The letter came as a shock to the Sisters. It is easy to say that they should not have taken it so hard, that they were religious women, that all spiritual writers warn against excessive attachment to a particular confessor; but this is to assume too much—it was not an excessive attachment in this case—and to forget that these were simple, well-meaning girls and women who were, for the most part, almost totally ignorant of the rules of the spiritual life. Elizabeth had more experience than any of them, but she could hardly be called, at this time, an expert in ordered spirituality. She and her dismayed Sisters—with the exception of Rose and Kitty, who had come to the community too late to know Father Babade—only were aware of the frightening fact that, with a stroke of the pen, they had been deprived of the one confessor to whom they had truly opened their hearts, of the one director who had known how to appreciate their faltering steps and to inspire them with the enthusiasm that would quicken their pace on the road to perfection. Elizabeth understood this, for she was a wise mother and a courageous one, who had the spirit to fight for her children.

Her letter to the Archbishop, written on August 6, was as humble and dependent as that of a child who has been put upon by some adult and has appealed to his father for support; it had also the straightforwardness and something of the bewildered outrage of such a child. She began by assuring the Archbishop that

> Mr. Dubois, who is all kindness and charity to us, we begin to get accustomed to, and we also have the consolation of observing in some degree the system which is hereafter to govern us; and, no doubt, the goodness of Our Lord will support us thro' all our weakness and infirmities.

Then she came to the point at once:

> Yet, as you are truly our Father, it cannot be right to conceal from you that both myself and Sisters have been greatly chagrined by a letter received from our Superior soon after I came here, which required of me not only to give up a correspondence with the person in whom I have most confidence, and to whom I am indebted for my greatest spiritual advantage; but also to eradicate as far as possible from the minds of the Sisters that confidence and attachment they all have for him.

Elizabeth was particularly incensed over the talebearing—by whom? Rose? Kitty? Father Dubois? It had to be one of the three—which had certainly influenced Dubourg's high-handed decree; and she disposed of the accusations with thoroughness:

There has been some very busy persons making exaggerations to our Superior about my writing large packages to Father Babade, which packages —sent only twice—I truly explained to him contained letters from Cecilia, Harriet, my Anna, Maria Burke (and my little girls who are fondly attached to him and used to write to him constantly when in Baltimore); and the packages he twice sent us contained the life of Clotilda of France and the manner of regular meditation and mental prayer, which I have never followed in a manner necessary for a community.

She exposed her motive for appealing to the Archbishop with unaffected honesty; it was not for her own relief, but for that of her Sisters:

Accustomed as I am almost habitually to sacrifice everything I most value in this life, I should have acquiesced quietly, tho' my heart was torn to pieces. But the others could not bear it in the same way; and the idea, so difficult to conceal, that our Superior was acting like a tyrant, the reserve we all felt to the excellent Mr. Dubois, knowing that he and the Superior had but one soul—all this, my dear Sir, has been the source of a thousand temptations, and the enemy of all good has tried us hard, you may be sure.

It is astonishing that this letter should have been written by a convert of little more than four years, placed at the head of a scarcely formed community; it has all the verve of a veteran mother general who knows that the rights of her subjects have been violated and that she has all Canon law behind her. For Father Dubourg was definitely in the wrong; he had no license to interfere with the internal freedom of conscience of the Sisters. It is difficult to see how he could have made such a mistake, but the possibility of jealousy cannot be overlooked. Despite his obvious dedication and piety, he was not immune to the weaknesses of fallen man. He himself admitted to Elizabeth in later years that he possessed "a sensibility perhaps too great for my own happiness."

Father Babade was idolized by the Sisters. They may have been too loud in his praise, as women are apt to be, but they had good reason for their adulation. He was a holy, sincere, understanding, disinterested confessor and director.

How qualified he was to direct these first Sisters of Charity is evidenced from the uncompromising advice he gave Sister Maria Burke on June 13, 1809.

When I look at you with cool unprejudiced eyes, I cannot find in you that lovely countenance I wish in you. You look sad, stern and rough. Your air and look seems to me calculated for cooling the warmest hearts and shutting them to that open confidence to which you would be easily entitled; and indeed, such an appearance does not at all become a member of such a society as that to which merciful God has incorporated you. Such a disposition seems to me very improper in a community destined by Providence to the practice of charity works, and to render amiable the true and only true religion among those who do not know it or are prejudiced against it.

I request you to weigh in the balance of the Lord this consideration. You are not called to be an anchorite, to live alone by yourself; you are called to live a common life in a religious community. Then you must both find your own happiness in the community and contribute for your part to the happiness of the community.

Each of your Sisters, after the generous sacrifice she has made in renouncing at once the world, the flesh and the blood and, in a word, everything, must, of course, expect to find in the community that hundredfold, that compensation promised her below by Our Lord as a pledge of the eternal reward that awaits us in a better future world. Then you must all love each other and render you amiable to each other; you must console and comfort each other by the most sincere and tender reciprocal love. Each one ought to share in the fate of her Sisters, in her joys and sorrows, in her troubles and in her peace, in her toils and her rest and recreation.

Then, my dear child, if you separate yourself of your Sisters in her plays and recreation to indulge in self-repose in intemperate contemplation, you deprive the community of what it is entitled to. . . . I already know that you are now less liked and cherished than before. You are, it is true, very much esteemed and respected; but I wish for you less respect and more love, because I wish for you what is less dangerous for you and more profitable to others.

Moreover, he used the power he had over their souls with circumspection. There is no least evidence to give the lie to his firm insistence that he had never interfered, or wished to interfere, in the external affairs of the community.

But such a man can be a thorn in the sides of his confreres—and there were more Sulpicians than Dubourg who were in favor of cutting him off from the Sisters; indeed, they may well have harried Dubourg into making his move, a thing not unheard of in community life. It is not easy to hear another perpetually praised, nor to be continually passed over in his favor.

At any rate, once Dubourg's prohibition got around, the fat was in the fire. Not that the Archbishop abused Elizabeth's confidence—that was a sacred matter between them—but Babade and the Sisters knew of it, of course, and that was enough. Immediately everyone took sides, or rather, the Sulpicians in general took sides against Babade and the Sisters. Where the Archbishop stood cannot be clearly determined. He seems at times to have had the habit of procrastination until things settled themselves, or at least of not showing his hand too readily. He may have been extremely cautious in this matter as, it will be seen, he was in the matter of the permanent rule, because the Sulpician General in France had once almost recalled his priests from America, and Carroll had had to plead to keep them.

His reply to Elizabeth, however, was apparently ambigious enough to give her the heart to write again, even more urgently, in a letter that seemed to sense his desire to remain neutral but refused to let him be so.

Our Superior has written to us the welcome news that we may expect our Father Babade here in a short time, but mentioned that he did not know if you would give him permission to hear the Sisters. How many times since have I begged Our Lord to direct me what to do! On one hand, I know it may displease you if I say any more on the subject; and on the other side, my dear girls are continually begging me: "O dear Mother, do write to the Bishop. He is a Father to us and will not deny your request." But I have put them off until the last few days.

My Cecilia is again sick and blistered and her pains being accompanied by particular depression of spirits, the only consolation I can give her is the promise of writing you, to beg in her name and the names of four other Sisters who desire the comfort and feel the necessity as she does of unfolding their souls to him, that you will allow them the privilege which will ensure their contentment and peace.

For my part, I assure you that, if it is not granted to me, you will leave a soul so dear to you in a cloud of uneasiness which can be dissipated in no other way. It would seem as if Our Lord has inspired this confidence in my soul and in those of many others round me for my severe and most painful trial, circumstanced as I am. His ever blessed, adorable Will be done; but as He permits us to desire, and express that desire to you as our Father, you will not be displeased with me for again troubling you on a subject on which you seemed already to have made known your intentions.

The unhappy situation was harder on Elizabeth than just the loss of Father Babade's direction. It brought her the agony of spiritual desolation, as if God were asking her to be a victim for her Sisters' peace. She laid it simply before the Archbishop.

Added to all, it pleased Our Lord to withdraw from me all comfort in devotion, and deprive me in a manner of the light of His countenance at the very time the foot of the cross was my only refuge. Now, I am going straight on by Faith; but, if I were to indulge myself, instead of rejoicing in the delightful prospect of serving and honoring God in a situation I have so long earnestly desired, death and the grave would be my only anticipation; but you know your child too well to believe any such indulgence is allowed. On the contrary, I abandon myself to God continually, and invite all my dear companions to do the same.

She had come a long way from the time when, covered with the shades of despair, she had thought of suicide. This trial of divine abandonment, and the exterior trial of Father Dubourg's displeasure, were only the beginning of the many sufferings she would have to undergo in order to bring her community to lasting life. They were as necessary to her spiritual motherhood as the pangs of childbirth to physical motherhood. Very little is gotten for nothing, either in this world or the world of the spirit.

In the meantime, piqued by the resistance of Babade and the Sisters to his wishes and the uproar their resistance had caused, William Dubourg resigned as Superior of the Sisterhood. It was another mark of that extreme sensitiveness he recognized in himself but, like most sensitive people, could not help. Elizabeth was immediately filled with remorse. Although, by her own admission, she had always been in awe of Dubourg, she had a solid admiration for his gifts, and had certainly not wanted to be rid of him; she had only wanted to defend the souls of her daughters. Furthermore, she was deeply sorry to have hurt this man to whom she owed great gratitude, for it was he who had rescued her from the conflicts of New York and made it possible for her to have, at last, her "dream": the convent. At once she wrote him an abject letter:

My Father, the pleadings of so weak a creature does not merit your attention, I know, yet once more be patient with one you have borne with so long. It seems but a dream that things are as they are, that you have given your children to a Father-in-law while their real Father still lives and loves them with a Parent's tenderness. And why? The mother is worthless. Pity them, pity her; try her once more and if she ever even vexes you again, quit her and them forever.

It was a shrewd letter, a coaxing letter, a woman's letter. It was completely sincere—Elizabeth was greatly upset—but it said to this man who was acting like a little boy: "Forget what has happened, and do for us what you set out to do. It has nothing to do, in the long run, with your overall stewardship. We need you." And it said all this without giving an inch, for Elizabeth wrote her second letter, already quoted, to Archbishop Carroll afterward.

Had Elizabeth known the manner of man who would succeed Dubourg—the father-in-law or stepfather referred to in the letter—she would have been much more than upset, she would have been dismayed. That man was John Baptist David, an energetic man of positive ideas which could not be gainsaid. He and Elizabeth clashed from the first; and had he stayed on beyond the two years of his Superiorship, the young community might very well have been wrecked.

Externally, life was not so grim. The Sisters and the children alike were enjoying the novelty of their mountain home, and Elizabeth would not let the miasmas in her soul poison their fresh air and sunshine. Anna received rambling, schoolgirl letters full of small talk from her young Aunt Mary Bayley, Elizabeth's half-sister, and her cousin Catherine Post, who were at Miss Hays' school in Brunswick. Mary was to play Pleyel's *Concertante* at a school concert, and was properly frightened and proud at the prospect. Elizabeth herself was able to write charming, friendly notes such as the one to George Weis, in Baltimore, in which she did not forget to tell George and his good wife that the little dog they had given the Sisters as a going-away gift "races after every priest he sees, and is faithless to his master and mistress both; but he is so handsome and lively, that we cannot help loving him, as well as for her sake that gave him—but not as we love the pigeons, for everybody takes care of them, and there is no such thing to be seen here as a tame pigeon."

The day was drawing near when Father Babade should come to receive Harriet into the Church, and everyone shared in her excitement. She herself sent off letters telling him in detail the state of soul he would find her in. On the 30th of August she confided to him that "for five days have I been on the tip-toe of expectation, looking with the greatest eagerness at every black coat I see flying in the road."

Babade received Harriet into the Church according to plan—he arrived back in Baltimore from his mission trip on September 16 and Harriet made her First Communion on September 24, the feast of Our Lady of Mercy—but, strangely enough, there is no mention, either by Harriet or by Elizabeth, about his coming to Emmitsburg. There is extant, however, a poem dated September 24, 1809, which he composed to commemorate Harriet's great day.

Most disappointing is the lack of any evidence as to who won the controversy between the Sisters and their first Superior, whether or not Carroll gave way and granted faculties to Babade to hear the Sisters' confessions. There is a hint that he did not; for Dubois, anxious to heal the rift, offered to ask for Babade as his assistant at Emmitsburg, but warned him that he might not be able to direct the Sisters in the confessional at first, if the Archbishop should withhold faculties from him. Babade prudently refused this kind offer, preferring to keep aloof from the squabble and to give no least appearance of connivance, until his superiors had spoken.

This time of turmoil was so dangerous to the infant community that it was a mark of God's Will for its future that it did not collapse. Dubourg's resignation had done nothing to settle matters. Elizabeth was still trying in every possible way to get him back. She appealed to Carroll, Nagot and Dubourg himself. She was so far successful with Dubourg, who probably regretted his hasty action, that he assured her he wished "to be with you tho' absent, share in every distress, be edified in every good action, assist in every doubt"; and he promised to ask Nagot to restore him to his former post. It was this preeminent authority of the Sulpician superior that complicated the situation and made it almost a foregone conclusion that Elizabeth would lose out in the end. Today, a newly formed Sisterhood would come without question under the authority of the bishop of the diocese; but the bishop's authority was not so clear then, and this fact may explain why Archbishop Carroll did not speak out decisively and at once. There seemed to be the presumption that, since the Sulpicians had been active in forming the Sisterhood, they were, therefore, its legitimate superiors, and even the Archbishop was hesitant about disagreeing, even though he did not like it.

In the meantime David's appointment hung suspended, or at least his use of it, and for all practical purposes the Sisters were without a superior; although Father Dubois ministered to their spiritual needs.

Outwardly, the little world of the Valley moved on. On September 20 Elizabeth wrote Julia Scott, bringing her up to date on the news:

> You will hear a thousand reports of nonsense about our community, which I beg you not to mind. The truth is, we have the best ingredients of happiness—order, peace and solitude. There are only sixteen now in family; a steward, who supplies all outdoor wants, a housekeeper, who regulates within, a superintendent of the workroom, and my dear Cecilia (who takes charge of my children and two dear little girls I brought from Baltimore) take all fatigue and care off my hands, as much as if I was a child myself.
>
> I am a name to keep up regularity and to say there is a head to the house. The chief work I do is to walk about with my knitting in my hands (we supply, or are to supply, by knitting and spinning, the college and two seminaries of Mr. Dubourg with stocks and cloth), give my opinion, see that everyone is in their place, write letters, read and give good advice.

Elizabeth made it sound like she was a retired chairman of the board; she was, in fact, more like a corporation manager. Especially in the time of flux the weight of the Sisterhood's present and future lay on her shoulders, and she admitted, at least, that those shoulders were frail enough. Even to this glum news, however, she gave a touch of brightness.

> If I am not strong in health, it is because my constitution is broken. Air, exercise, good food, indolence and content ought to strengthen me. But so long a combat as I have gone thro' will leave its vestiges. Yet there is no settled complaint of any kind.

Elizabeth did not cover over with cunning embroidery her worry about Anna. "If you had her," she told Julia, "she would be a source of perpetual uneasiness to you, for as she grows up and looses herself from that blind obedience exacted from a child under thirteen, she takes many varieties of temper, which makes her disposition so unequal that, until she is more matured and experience teaches her some necessary lessons, it is very difficult to make her happy. The great error, now past and irreparable, on my part is to have made her my friend and companion too soon." The poor mother need not have blamed herself; if indeed a grown-up role had been asked of Anna too soon, it had been the death of her father, the horrors of the *lazaretto* and the poverty and persecution of New York that had made the demand.

Nevertheless, Elizabeth had her children with her—the boys were at Mount St. Mary's and joined the family circle every Wednesday—and she had her religious life; and it was good. Even the heavy trials were good, for they were sloughing away her imperfections. She could write, therefore, to reassure this dear friend, the truest sentence that ever came from her pen: "If you knew half the real good your friend possesses, while the world thinks she is deprived of everything worth having, you would . . . allow that she has truly and really the best of it."

XVII

Sisters of Charity

Archbishop Carroll made his first visit to the Sisters of St. Joseph's Valley on October 20, 1809. Although as a missionary bishop he was enured to Colonial travel, the trip must have meant special hardship for a seventy-four-year-old man. It was worth it, nonetheless, both to him—to see with his own proud eyes the beginnings of the first native American Sisterhood, and to the Sisters—to be able, with their own pride, to show their revered father what they had begun. Donning his mitre and his pontifical robes, he sat before the altar in the little alcove and confirmed Harriet and Annina. Inevitably he would have discussed with Elizabeth the resignation of Father Dubourg; but nothing seems to have been settled, for, after his return to Baltimore, she wrote him on November 2, begging him to bring about the restoration of their superior.

She made a good point in arguing that, if Father David went to Kentucky with Bishop-elect Flaget, as the rumors had it, the Sisters would have had three superiors in the space of a year—which was certainly not in their best interests. She could not know that the rumors were premature, for it was not at all certain that Flaget would be going to Bardstown; he had humbly protested to Rome his appointment as bishop, and was preparing to sail for Europe to thwart it in person. But always she returned to the feeling of personal guilt and her desire to atone for the offense she had committed: "Since it is our first Superior I have offended, to him I ought to be permitted to make the reparation."

She had done much soul-searching and, as is characteristic of the saints, the deeper she probed, the more she blamed her own wrongdoing; for, the larger loomed the so-called petty faults of anger and indignation and self-will:

> The truth is, I have been made a Mother before being initiated, and that must excuse all. To you I attempt no justification—you know all. Being a convert, and very much left to my own devotion, how gratefully attached must I be to the one who has shown unceasing care for my soul and done everything to enlighten it and discover to it the full consolation of our holy Faith. In my place, my dear Father, you would have experienced my trial, but you would at once have offered it up to God. I am late in seeing the necessity of this measure, but not too late, I hope, since it is never too late with Our good Lord, and He can dispose every heart to accommodation.
>
> You will see how good a child I am going to be. Quite a little child. And perhaps you will have often to give me the food of little children yet, but I will do my best as I have promised you in every case. That I am sure of your prayers for my advancement is one of my greatest comforts.

It was an admirable letter, but she was flagellating herself needlessly. With her cool head she must have known that she had done the only thing she could do. She might well have offered up her own pain at Father Babade's loss, but she could not have offered up her Sisters' pain, simply because it was not hers to offer. As their mother, she had no choice but to fight for justice to be shown them.

And, as even the gentle Christ has pointed out in the gentlest of His sermons, those who fight for justice are persecuted for justice's sake. Elizabeth's "persecution" was the refusal of Father Nagot to set aside David's appointment—despite her letter, Carroll had left the decision to him—and the sting of Nagot's words. "The yoke of the Lord," he told her sternly, "is as sweet as self-will is restless and miserable, so long as one does not know how to conceal it and sacrifice it, and obey in silence." One of the hardest trials the soul can suffer is to be misunderstood by good men. Had Nagot seen the letter Elizabeth addressed to the Archbishop on December 14, he would have known how unnecessary his reprimand was:

I have had a great many hard trials, my Father, since you were here; but you, of course, will congratulate me on them, as this fire of tribulation is no doubt meant to consume the many imperfections and bad dispositions Our Lord finds in me. Indeed, it has at times burnt so deep that the anguish could not be concealed; but by degrees custom reconciles pain itself, and I determine, dry and hard as my daily bread is, to take it with as good a grace as possible. When I carry it before Our Lord, sometimes He makes me laugh at myself and asks me what other kind I would choose in the valley of tears than that which Himself and all His followers made use of.

October brought Elizabeth one great consolation, a letter from Antonio. It had worried her that she had not heard from him in a year and a half, but the combination of Napoleon's blockade and the American Embargo Act had made a wall too formidable to breach. Her anxiety had increased when John Murray of New York had informed her some months before that no further Filicchi funds were available for her to draw on—a fact she could not understand, since reliable report had it that the Filicchi firm had recently increased its ample assets by $100,000.00. The Filicchis had been, in fact, highly prosperous ever since they had befriended Elizabeth, a coincidence which Antonio never failed to note or to lay to the goodness and prayers of his "dear sister."

But now she knew that her beloved Antonio was well and happy, that Filippo, though ailing, was still alive; and that they approved the foundation she had made. They showed their approval in a practical way by authorizing Elizabeth to draw an extra thousand dollars from Murray for its advancement. The sum would come in handy, with the new building going up.

Elizabeth hastened to answer Antonio's letter with their old camaraderie:

You will laugh when I tell you that your wicked little sister is placed at the head of a community of saints, ten of the most pious souls you could wish, considering that some of them are young and all under thirty. Six more postulants are daily waiting till we move in a larger place to receive them, and we might be a very large family if I received half who desire to come; but your Reverend Mother is obliged to be very cautious for fear we should not have the means of earning our living during the winter. Yet, as Sisters of Charity, we should fear nothing.

She assured him that Filippo had been mightily prayed for, and that he himself had a large place in all her Communions, "but one in every week entirely yours. What else can I do, my more than brother, in return for your unfailing goodness to your poor sister?" Unfortunately, she could not send this letter until the following May, when a Father Zocchi, who had been laboring as pastor in Taneytown, returned to his native Italy and took it with him.

Despite the occasional boons from heaven, like Antonio's letter and Harriet's conversion and Carroll's visit to the Valley, Elizabeth's trials increased as the autumn burned itself out and the cold winter succeeded it. Her son William took seriously sick toward the end of October, and despite the fact that he was moved to the Stone House and tenderly cared for, he grew steadily worse. Finally, all hope was abandoned and his shroud was made; then, almost imperceptibly, he began to get better. Cecilia's first false strength had dissipated itself and she now declined swiftly. The shock of all shocks, however, was the unexpected illness and death of Harriet.

She had always been inclined to sick headaches and biliousness, but they were considered normal illnesses; she was generally strong and healthy, with no sign of the family consumption in her. It seems to have been a kind of brain fever that seized upon her in the last week of November. She lingered four weeks in great suffering, and died just before Christmas. Throughout the four days and nights that preceded her death, she sang hymns and muttered and sobbed in complete delirium. Seeing the Sisters approach Communion—her bed lay close to the sacred alcove—she sat up, staring wildly about her, and complained so piteously at being shut out from her Lord that everyone was reduced to tears. Father Dubois administered the Sacrament of Extreme Unction on December 21, and at two o'clock the next morning she was gone. Cecilia, who was lying desperately ill beside her, leaned over to kiss the cold brow and praise God for giving peace at last to this beautiful, restless, unhappy girl.

It is to be hoped that some shame smote the hard hearts in New York when the news of her death reached them. The years had not changed them. No sooner had she informed them, first of her determination to remain on in Emmitsburg, and then of her conversion, than they had begun to revile her by mail quite as mercilessly as they had reviled Elizabeth and Cecilia face to face. It was worse, in a way, for the hateful written words had a power to wound every time they were read; and Harriet must have read them again and again, in some horrible, compelling fascination, for she did not destroy them. They are there still to witness against the persecutors, dead and gone for more than a century —her aunt, the redoubtable matriarch, Elizabeth Farquhar; her own sister Charlotte; her brother-in-law, the important member of the New York Legislature, Gouverneur Ogden. The approach of each was different, but the venom was the same. Aunt Farquhar prompously defended "dear Barclay," berated poor Harriet for not going to Jamaica to join him—she had not been asked!—and pleaded the martyrdom of her own ill-health as an inducement for the unhappy girl to return to New York. Charlotte was cold and waspish. Ogden declaimed like a penny politician, winding up his long, rambling letter with this ridiculous peroration:

> Reflect for a moment, then, on your situation, supposing the hand of death has laid Mrs. S. and Cecilia in the grave. What is it? Unfriended and deserted by relations, you will find yourself immured in the gloomy recesses of your mountains, dependent on the scanty provision of the Sisterhood and perhaps under the control of another, less indulgent superior. Really, I should pity you; but to this, methinks, with jargon of a convent, I hear you say: "My religion will support me under every trial." Believe me, then, there are *useless* trials never intended or imposed by Our heavenly Father but, on the contrary, militating against His express commands.
>
> Besides, let me also remark that the establishments at Baltimore and St. Joseph's are novel things in the United States, and would not have been permitted by the populace in any other place than in the democratic, Frenchified State of Maryland. The religion they profess is uncongenial to the habits, manners and nature of Americans; and ere long I predict from many causes the demolition of every building in that state in any wise resembling a convent or Catholic hospital.

Maria Monk on a soapbox!

Death delights in ironies. It was Cecilia who was supposed to die, not Harriet. The shroud had been made for William; Harriet used it. Harriet had, with supreme lightness of heart, selected the site for the community cemetery; hers was the first grave. Elizabeth had led her household on a tour of the property one day, and it was indeed in her practical mind to select a burying ground. They came to a little wood of tall trees with stretches of grass and moss between. Harriet took a last bite of the apple she was eating and, tossing the core against a large oak tree, laughingly indicated the spot where it fell to the ground as the place where she should be buried. There she lies today, at the foot of the same oak, surrounded by the Sisters and schoolgirls who have lived and died in the Valley throughout the past one hundred and fifty years.

While Harriet had never formally joined the sisterhood, she had followed all the daily exercises; and her death had a solemn effect on the Sisters, as if it were the first community death. Anna was deeply moved for more personal reasons: Harriet had been her friend; and at fourteen, death is a bewildering thing. Elizabeth, however, while showing little, was more stricken than all. Her sister Mary Post and Julia Scott knew she would be, and were anxious for her. Harriet had been more than sister-in-law to Elizabeth; from the age of ten she had been her child—and a mother's grief cried out in the quiet words she addressed to Julia: "Here I go like iron or rock, day after day, *as He pleases and how He pleases*; but, to be sure, when my turn comes I shall be very glad."

As might be expected in the drafty little cottage—snow actually sifted into the garret and partially covered the Sisters sleeping there— sickness was a commonplace that winter. Harriet was scarcely dead when Anna and Sister Susan and a new postulant, Sister Martina Quinn, fell seriously ill. Save for the coming of the newborn King, it was scarcely a merry Christmas, with the smell of death on the house. Elizabeth took her turn in the makeshift infirmary, and she confessed to Archbishop Carroll in the middle of January that "I really began to think we were all going"; but by March she had returned to her usual optimism and was assuring Julia that the reports of wholesale sickness had been exaggerated. Perhaps they had been, but also, the community had grown hardened to illness by then. Getting used to trouble can take much of the ache out of it. It is appalling to read of the hardships at St. Joseph's that winter of 1809–10, which were indeed very real; but there comes a point of numbness, almost of indifference—such a point as Macbeth reached when he received the news of his wife's suicide with the flat remark: "I have supp'd full with horrors." Thus the Sisters, enured to their hard lot, may well have taken it in easier stride than it normally demanded.

Some hardships have been embroidered by time, such as the tradition which holds that the Sisters' first Christmas dinner consisted solely of smoked herrings and molasses; as a matter of record, the community account book states that, on December 24, 1809, the Sisters purchased, besides five dozen herrings, "19 lbs. beef, 13 lbs. lard, two turkeys, 1 goose. . . ."

The scourge of sickness was, in a way, the least of Elizabeth's troubles. Even the loss of Father Babade and the resignation of Father Dubourg were slight in comparison with the trial that now engulfed her and her community. Once Father Nagot had definitely confirmed Father David as the new Superior of the Sisterhood, David took complete charge, not only of the spiritual concerns and the temporalities which Dubourg had helped administer, but of everything in sight. It was evident from the first that this stern, unyielding disciplinarian was going to run the community unaided and that Elizabeth's role and that of her council was to be merely the carrying out of his orders. Needless to say, she did not like it; nor did she intend to suffer it without a struggle.

John Baptist Mary David was born in Nantes, France, in 1761. After his ordination in 1785 he joined the Sulpicians and taught philosophy and theology in their seminaries until the French Revolution forced him to leave the country. He came to America in 1792, where he taught at St. Mary's, Baltimore, and Georgetown and labored on the Maryland missions.

Immediately upon his confirmation as Superior of the sisterhood, David began to lay plans for the establishment of the school at Emmitsburg. Not only were the Sisters' wishes not consulted, they knew nothing of the matter until they received the first peremptory commands. Elizabeth wrote in protest to Father Dubourg, begging him to represent to his confrere the limitations of his authority. Dubourg answered on December 28, assuring her that he had "communicated to the Reverend Superior your ideas concerning the school, and many reflections of mine concerning the latitude he should allow you to direct with your own council what is to be done in your house, consulting only when you feel at loss." It was in vain, for on the same day David wrote Elizabeth that he was formulating the regulations for the school and would submit them to his brother-Sulpicians for approbation, and only then would he send them to her "for revision." As for the community, he admonished her loftily: "take care, dear Mother, to establish very strict regulations."

The effect of the Superior's rigidity was to freeze Elizabeth, despite herself, into a like rigidity of resistance, as she explained to Archbishop Carroll with her usual candor on January 25, 1810:

St. Joseph's House is almost ready. In a very short time we expect to be settled in it. You know our rules have hitherto been very imperfectly observed, but now the moment approaches when *order must be the foundation of all the good we can hope to do.* And, as so much depends on the Mother of the community, I beg you to take her first in hand, for I must candidly tell you she is all in the wrong—*not from discontent with the place* I am in, since every corner of the world is the same to me if I may but serve Our Lord, nor *with the intention of our institution,* for I long to be in the fullest exercise of it.

But circumstances have all so combined as to create in my mind a confusion and want of confidence in my Superiors which is indescribable. If my own happiness was only in question, I should say: "How good is the cross for me; this is my opportunity to ground myself in patience and perseverance"; and *my reluctance to speak* on a subject which I know will give you uneasiness is so great that I would certainly be silent. But as the good Our Almighty God may intend to do by means of this community may be very much impeded by the present state of things, it is absolutely necessary you, as the head of it and to whom, of course, the spirit of discernment for its good is given, should be made acquainted with it before the evil is irreparable.

Sincerely I promise you, and really *I have endeavored, to do everything in my power* to bend myself to meet the last appointed Superior in every way; but after continual reflection on the *necessity of absolute conformity with* him and *constant prayer* to Our Lord to help me, yet the *heart is closed:* and when the pen should freely give him the necessary detail and information he requires, it stops; and *he remains now as uninformed in the essential points* as if he had nothing to do with us.

An *unconquerable reluctance and diffidence takes place of those dispositions* which ought to influence every action; and with every desire to serve God and these excellent beings who surround me, I remain motionless and inactive. It is for you, my most revered Father, to decide if this is temptation, or what it is. . . .

If you think proper to make known the contents of this to the holy

Mr. Nagot, you will do so. But if, after consideration of every circumstance, you still think things must remain as they are—whatever you dictate I will abide by through every difficulty.

There could be no better exposition of Elizabeth's habitual realism. She saw clearly how vital the questions of authority and of rapport between the Superior and the Mother were to the well-being of the community; and, at the same time, she humbly opened her soul for the Archbishop's inspection, that he might decide whether she was at fault. Surely this letter establishes, right from the beginning, that the long series of disagreements with Father David in the year and a half ahead, would not be, on Elizabeth's part, a personal vendetta.

The Archbishop did not answer until March. His letter was disappointing in one way, for he did nothing to clear the air or to define the provinces of Superior and Mother; he merely told Elizabeth that he had heard Father David was to go to Emmitsburg soon, and that she should "make every effort . . . to meet him." In another way it was a striking letter, for Carroll made graphically clear his conviction that Elizabeth was to be an immolation for the sisterhood's success. Humanly speaking, Elizabeth was being unfairly tried, but Carroll told her in effect to ignore the unfairness and to eat the strong meat that made saints.

> Let it be your only concern to progress more and more towards the union of your soul with God, and an entire disengagement from the things of the earth. It would be a triumph for heterodoxy and irreligion, and—what is of much more consequence—the disappointment of pious and admiring Catholics, should anything happen to shake the stability of your holy establishment.
>
> It is not to flatter or nourish pride, the seeds of which are sown in every heart, that I declare an opinion and belief that its ultimate success under God depends on your sacrificing yourself, notwithstanding all the uneasiness and disgust you may experience, and continuing in your place of Superior.

It was the kind of uncompromising advice Our Lady gave to King Alfred in Chesterton's *Ballad of the White Horse*:

> I tell you naught for your comfort,
> Yea, naught for your desire,
> Save that the sky grows darker yet
> And the sea rises higher.

Elizabeth, to her everlasting credit, took the advice. Although she was never to abandon her struggle with David when she thought he was wrong—which was most of the time—she never acted out of pride of place, but in the defense of the rights of the community; and while she called on Carroll again and again to sustain her, she did not leave her post.

Carroll's letter had actually helped Elizabeth's sky grow darker by revealing another mix-up. Samuel Cooper was quarreling with the Sulpicians over the way the Emmitsburg property he had bought for the Sisters was vested—it was in the joint names of Cooper, Dubourg and Dubois—but the Archbishop warned her to stay out of it, for her own peace of mind. "You have surely heard of the apprehensions entertained of the soundness and stability of Mr. Cooper's mind," he wrote, "which, however, in its perfect state is a strong and magnanimous one; but you will occasionally observe its workings and consult other counsellors as well as, and even more than, him."

Elizabeth had mentioned in her letter to Carroll that St. Joseph's House, as the new building was known, was nearly ready. It was hardly the precise word; the building would not be ready for months. What she should have said was that the Sisters were going to move in anyway; and that, so desperate was she for its facilities, she was thinking of it as finished indeed. Thus, only the day before, she had written to a friend in Roscommon, New York, Rose Stubbs, "we have an elegant little chapel; thirty cells, holding a bed, chair and table each; a large infirmary; a very spacious refectory; besides parlor, schoolroom, my room, working room, etc." The modest building must have seemed huge to her from the vantage point of her little cottage.

The arrival of two more postulants had overtaxed the cottage completely, and Elizabeth decided that some of the Sisters must make a trial of sleeping in one of the more advanced rooms of the new house. Rose, Kitty and Susan were selected, and moved their few belongings up to the cold, cavernous shell. They encountered inconveniences they had not dreamed of: with no way of telling time, they would rise at one, two or three in the morning, and hurry down to the Stone House for meditation; on rainy days they could not traverse the sea of mud between the two buildings, but one of them would have to struggle through to bring back food. They had their spinning wheels with them, and on such days they would sit at them all day, pedaling away furiously to keep warm.

About this time the future shape of the community began to emerge. Although the term "Sisters of Charity" was already in use, Elizabeth's first reference to the French community of St. Vincent appeared in a letter to Eliza Sadler written on January 9, 1810: "If you recollect the system of the Sisters of Charity before and since the Revolution in France, you will know the rule of our community in a word, which amounts only to that regularity necessary for order and no more." And, in her January letter to Rose Stubbs, she wrote: "Our community increases very fast, and no doubt will do a great deal of good in the care of the sick and instruction of children, which is our chief business. The rule is so easy that it is scarcely more than any regular religious person would do, even in the world."

It is certain that, from the beginning, the intention was to pattern the community after that of St. Vincent; and it is just as certain that the intention originated with the Sulpicians and not with Mother Seton. It was an intention easily arrived at. The works Elizabeth envisioned for her community were the works of Sisters of Charity; to any European, and especially to a Frenchman, Sisters of Charity meant only one thing: the Daughters of Charity of St. Vincent de Paul. It is not remarkable, therefore, that the thoughts of Dubourg had turned at once to the French community as at least a model for the American Sisterhood. Nor should it be forgotten that the ties between the Sulpicians and St. Vincent's priests and Sisters had always been close—the Sulpician Founder, Jean Jacques Olier, had been St. Vincent's disciple—or that Dubourg had nourished for fifteen years the dream of establishing St. Vincent's Daughters in America.

The interest in the French community took a more positive turn, however, with the superiorship of Father David. David wanted to unite the American Sisters with the Paris Motherhouse at once. When Bishop-elect Flaget left for France in the autumn of 1810, he was instructed to bring a copy of the French rules and constitutions back with him. Further instructions, given at that time or while he was in Europe, asked him to arrange for French Daughters of Charity to come to America to teach the Emmitsburg Sisters the spirit and the letter of St. Vincent's rule and, presumably, consolidate the union with Paris.

It is to be noted that, thus far, the future of Mother Seton's Sisters had been planned exclusively by the priests of St. Sulpice. With David now the prime mover, it can be stated with fair certainty that Elizabeth had little or nothing to do with the arrangements. Not that she did not, at this point, approve. She was very conscious of her own ignorance of the technicalities surrounding the establishment of a religious community, and was quite content to leave them in the hands of her more experienced directors—provided the ends of the institute she envisioned were attained. This is evident from a letter addressed to Carroll on September 5, 1811, after the French rules had arrived: "The rules proposed are nearly such as we had in the original manuscript of the Sisters in France. I never had a thought discordant with them, as far as my poor power may go in fulfilling them." She even seemed ready to step aside, should her responsibility to her children conflict with the regulations of the French rules. "The constitutions proposed have been discussed by our Reverend Director, and I find he makes some observations on my situation relative to them; but surely an individual is not to be considered where a public good is in question; and you know I would gladly make every sacrifice you think consistent with my first and inseparable obligations as a mother."

The question of the union with France, involving as it did Elizabeth and her children, was to get very complicated. Now, in January of 1810, however, Elizabeth could not forsee this, and was quite content not only to pattern her rule after the French rule, but even to have the first steps taken toward union. At least, there is no evidence that she protested either move. She was well occupied in struggling with David's encroachments and her inability to communicate with him.

Despite the great spiritual forces stirring in Elizabeth's soul and in the heart of the community, the small surface things of life continued to engage her attention. As she told Sad, who had just returned from Ireland: "Our mountain seems the limits of the world to us, but beyond them, dearest Eliza, you know I have many most dear interests." A former pupil of the Paca Street School, Marie Renedaut, informing Anna of another former schoolgirl's wedding, remarked in high glee that the groom, "a few days before the wedding . . . fell out of a gig and sprained his leg, but the thoughts of marriage cured him"; but she did not forget a more serious message for Elizabeth: "Tell Mater that Mama, Rebecca and myself visit the almshouse almost every week. . . . I know it will give her some satisfaction." James Seton's daughter Agnes, who had been interested in the Church, sent a pathetic little thank-you note for the gift of a gold crucifix, promising to wear it always. Mary Post relayed the news that their half-sister Helen Bayley and Sam Craig were forming an attachment, but Elizabeth was not to let on—it was a secret.

At home Elizabeth was keeping a watchful eye on her children. On March 9 she addressed a reproving note to Kate or Josephine as they also called her. This writing of notes to one another in the same house was a family custom, begun by Elizabeth herself when Anna was a toddler.

> My poor Josephine: The fault of quarreling you have so often confessed and declared you would not do so again, that it hurts my very heart to find you have been guilty of it. But your Lord is the one you have most offended, my poor child. To Him, Who is so good to you, you are most ungrateful. You cannot go next Sunday; but if you have no marks or cross between now and next Wednesday, I will once more present your poor little soul to Him as a lamb the wolf is trying to tear from His dear arms. Tell Rebecca I did not think she would so soon forget her good promises; but I beg Our dear Lord, and Our sweet Mother to give you both pardon for all your faults, through the Precious Blood which washes sins away. Your poor Mother.

It seems a hard punishment, to deprive the child of Holy Communion, for she was hardly in mortal sin; but Elizabeth, surely, saw no theological problem. She lived in an age when the vestiges of Jansenism still kept even advanced souls away from the daily reception of the Eucharist. Her severity toward an easy approach to the sacraments is the one disappointment encountered in the wide, warm, sunny spirituality of Mother Seton. It flowed certainly from her own profound love of the Blessed Sacrament, from the white-hot purity of soul she demanded of herself in approaching the Holy Table; but it came, too, from her firm conviction that there were more sacrilegious Communions than were suspected, and that even children, sometimes on the occasion of their First Communion, were guilty of them. It is a horrible thought, but who is to say that one so spiritually sensitive as she, was wrong, particularly when the children of her day were so much older than modern children at the time of First Communion?

Elizabeth's conscience in the matter was formed, also, by her directors. Thus, Father Dubourg had written her on July 13, 1809:

> I have often reflected on the danger of frequent regular Communions in a community. That danger must strike you as it does me. Repeat them very often to our Daughters, that the rule does not *prescribe* any number of Communions in the week, but only *restricts* them to three, leaving it to the prudence of the Director to permit whom he thinks fit to approach so frequently or render Communions more rare with certain individuals. Nothing should so often be inculcated as the dispositions necessary for very frequent Communion, and the assurance that the Superiors will never judge of the merits of a Sister from her approaching oftener or more seldom, but from the fruits she derives from it.
>
> The extraordinary fourth Communion in the week should be limited to the feasts of Our Savior and Blessed Lady, and three or four of the patrons, such as St. Joseph, St. Vincent de Paul, St. Aloysius and St. Francis de Sales. This limitation will set a greater value on that favor, and excite a greater devotion on those days.

A strange thought, surely, to us who follow the daily invitation of Pope St. Pius X, but it was the accepted thinking of the day and the people who lived then must be judged in the light of it. And, in fairness to Father Dubourg's concern about regular Communion, it must be remembered that the Sisters had often but one priest available to confess to.

Elizabeth needed the day-to-day happenings, the bits of news, the problems to be dealt with, the press of business, the carefree recreations, to keep her balance; for Father David was contemplating another move which would literally divide the little community before it had been permanently formed. It was seriously proposed to send Elizabeth to Baltimore with a few Sisters, and to replace her at Emmitsburg with Sister Rose White. The rise of the plan and how close it came to fruition are difficult to determine, simply because there was so much secrecy about it: Elizabeth knew very little, and even the Archbishop scarcely more; while David, after the first shocked reaction to the news, kept his counsel.

The background can be reconstructed with fair accuracy. David had small confidence in Elizabeth because of her conflict with Dubourg and her open antagonism to his own way of acting. Rose, on the other hand, was his spiritual protégé. There were broad enough hints about dissension in the community, not an open rift, but an unspoken difference of opinion. Rumors of Rose's possible elevation were enough to cause the dissension without the already accomplished division of the little group into two camps: Father Babade's partisans, and Sister Rose and Sister Kitty—with perhaps a few latecomers—who had no interest in Babade and who rejoiced in David's appointment as Superior. In a community of only fifteen women this division could have had very serious consequences; it is a tribute to their spirituality that it did not.

Nevertheless, Father David was playing with fire. It is hard not to hold him responsible for the plan of separation, for it was raised only after his assumption of office and was abandoned abruptly when he resigned. It is true that Elizabeth told Antonio Filicchi, in a letter of May 10, 1810, that "our blessed Bishop intends removing a detachment of us to Baltimore"; but this could have been a prudent, official way of putting it, since Carroll's consent was necessary to such a move, or due to Elizabeth's lack of knowledge of the facts. Even though Carroll admitted later that he had once thought kindly of the proposal, because of the relief from responsibility and conflict it would bring Elizabeth, the whole tenor of his letters resisting it demonstrated that the plan could not have originated with him.

On February 20, 1810, the Sisters moved into St. Joseph's House. The physical adjustment did not take long, for their belongings were few. All were conscious of the importance of the day and marked it with as much solemnity as they could muster. A procession formed at the cottage, and Father Dubois led the way up the slight slope, carrying the Blessed Sacrament and followed by Elizabeth and her daughters and the schoolchildren. Even Cecilia took part in the holy little parade, being carried on a litter.

February 22—appropriately enough the feast of St. Peter, first father of the Church, and the birthday of George Washington, first father of the country—was of equal importance, for on that day three children from the village were admitted to the school. These three neighborhood children were the first tiny seeds of the vast American parochial school system. This is no place to investigate how the huge Catholic educational complex evolved from this nebulous beginning, nor to deal with the doubts raised as to whether it did so evolve. The simplest approach is the best. These children were parishioners of Father Duhamel, however vaguely defined the limits of his parish. As such they must be considered the pioneer pupils of the Emmitsburg parish school which descends from Mother Seton's day school in an unbroken line. They were, therefore, the first pupils of a parish school in America, forming the primary cell of the modern parochial school system. To Elizabeth Seton belongs, then, the honor that has traditionally been bestowed on her of being the foundress of the parochial schools in America. This does not mean that she worked out a "system" of such schools, but only that she established the first one. Nor was it something that just happened; she fully intended it. On December 28, 1809, Father Dubourg had assured her that, "far from objecting to your plan of opening a day school at St. Joseph's, Mr. David and myself beg it should be done without loss of time."

On March 19, 1810, the feast of St. Joseph, patron of the house and school, Father Dubois sang the first High Mass in the unfinished building. It was a gala day for Elizabeth. That it was celebrated in primitive, even spartan, surroundings did nothing to lessen its glory. "So poor was the little altar," one of the Sisters remembered, "that its chief ornaments were a framed portrait of Our dear Redeemer which Mother had brought with her from New York, her own little silver candlesticks, some wild laurel, paper flowers, etc.—yet what a happy, happy company, far from the busy, bustling scenes of a miserable, faithless world!" *That* was Elizabeth's joy: the delight in one more milestone passed in the pursuance of her dream.

The inconveniences of the first months in St. Joseph's House—it was not finished until the early fall—were at times almost brutal. When the Sisters attacked the chips and shavings lying in untidy heaps about the yard, they stirred up a horde of fleas that plagued them unmercifully. Fleas also infested the hair used in making plaster, and as this hair had been stored in the attic where the Sisters all slept on the floor, they spent many a miserable night "carrying our mattresses from one place to another to find rest." Withal, they were so bitten that their skin was purple. As the plastering progressed they were forced to move from room to room, and at one point they were living in the entrance hall. A make-shift kitchen was built onto one end of the house, but it gave way one night in a violent storm of wind and rain that blew down the chimney, put out the fire, and sent Sister Rose scurrying into the house with the half-cooked supper.

Much has been said of the Sisters' poverty, which was real enough, but it was not destitution. The fare was plain, to be sure; the account book for 1810 lists purchases of flour, bacon, mackerel, codfish, whitefish, and even "5 lbs. tea—3½ lbs. coffee"—nothing in great quantities, except for the flour; but Elizabeth makes mention in her letters of butter and eggs and milk, and by the beginning of 1811 a small farm was flourishing inhabited by "young calves, pigs, chickens, etc." In March, 1810, the odd Mr. Cooper brought from Philadelphia "for Cecilia a barrel of honey, one of treacle which we make great use of, a box of Smyrna figs, one of raisins, one of prunes and seventy or eighty yards of pelice flannel, besides pieces upon pieces of India chemise muslin." She told Julia Scott: "He will never let us want what he can give. We never see him, or even thank him for his pure benevolence. Many strange be-ings there are in this world, dearest."

Every Sunday the Sisters went up to the Mount for Mass. Sister Rose recalled that

> there was no bridge nor road. . . . When the water was . . . low we would walk over the creek on the stones, climb the fences and often lose our way through the thick woods. We would carry our dinners in a sack, and often fry our meat at the Mount and take it from the frying pan and place it on a piece of bread—without knife or fork; eat standing, and take a good drink of water, and go up to . . . Vespers.

If they were caught in the rain, they had an especially dreary trip home.

> At this time we never wore a shawl, much less had an umbrella. . . . When we come to the creek, we would meet a horse which Father Dubois would send from the Mount to take us across. And the oldest Sister would remain standing in the rain by the old oak tree until all had passed over; then, in her turn, she would be taken and borne—(some) times continue her ride to the farmhouse door of our home. Our shoes would be heavy with mud, and our clothes so wet that we would have to change. We

continued this Sunday going to church for many years, both winter and summer.

The Sunday repasts were eaten in a lovely woodland spot of rocks and moss and wildflowers and gurgling stream called the "grotto." Elizabeth would extend the grace before meals by reciting the Canticle of the Three Children from the Book of Daniel. Her sense of fitness saw a special efficacy in saying here this beautiful prayer that called on all nature to bless the Lord.

She described in her own way one of these "grotto" Sundays, for Eliza Sadler:

> Yesterday we all—about twenty Sisters and children—dined, that is, ate our cold ham and cream pies, in our grotto in the mountain where we go on Sunday for the Divine Office. Richard joined his mother's side, and love with every mouthful, handing the cup of water from the cool stream with as much grace as an angel. But William contented himself with a wave of his hat and a (promise of seeing me) afterwards; and going home, he followed in a part of the wood where he would be unobserved, and gave such expressions of love and tenderness as can come only from the soul— but always unobserved, and never forfeiting his character of being a man.
>
> They are two beings as different as sun and moon, but William most interests poor Mother. In the afternoon catechism he was asked if his business in this world was to make money and gain reputation or to serve God and to use all his endeavors to please Him. "My business is to do both, Sir," answered William with the tone of decision.

Elizabeth's boys, who were now thirteen and eleven respectively, were beginning to excite her interest; and it was but natural for a widow to watch for the first hints of manhood in her sons. She confided happily to Dué, who was still in Ireland:

> Without partiality—they are two as sweet fellows in looks, manners and disposition as poor Mother's heart could wish. Richard always Mother's boy! All his desire centers in a farm, that he may never quit her. William is the boy of hopes and fears. Reading some lines in an almanac the other day of the whistling of a sea boy in the main-top shrouds, "That's your sorts," he cried, "I'm your man!"—and always talks of roving the world; but yet has great ideas of being a gentleman in everything, without knowing that a gentleman without a penny is but a name. However, as his gentleman notions makes him a fine fellow, keeps him from meanness and cowardice, I trust it will all turn out well; for a more loving and tender

heart cannot be imagined—tho' the talents of neither of them are distinguished, which does not disappoint me, knowing well they often ruin their owners.

It was a curious mixture of fondness, shrewdness and sober wisdom. As the years went on Elizabeth's pride in her sons would be more and more tinged with anxiety over their irresponsibility and lack of that deep-seated piety that was her life. William's "dualism" expressed in his answer to the catechism question and his gentleman's instincts were telltale signs.

With early spring it was evident that Cecilia was going fast. On March 26 Elizabeth wrote Julia an unusually nostalgic letter that was full of her impending loss. She was preparing herself.

> For my part, I find so much contentment in this love (of God) that I am obliged to put on my consideration cap to find out how anyone can raise their eyes to the light of heaven and be insensible to it. I remember when Anna was six months old and everything smiled around me—venerating the virtues of my Seton and sincerely attached to him, accustomed to the daily visits and devoted love of my father, and possessed of all I estimated as essential to happiness—alone with this babe in the see-saw of motherly love, frequently the tears used to start and often overflow; and I would say to myself while retrospecting the favors of heaven: "All these, these and heaven, too?"
>
> Sometimes falling on my knees with the sleeping suckling in my arms, I would offer her and all my dear possessions—husband, father, home—and entreat the Bountiful Giver to separate me from all, if indeed I could not possess my portion here—and with Him, too.
>
> Nor do I remember any part of my life, after being settled in it, that I have not constantly been in the same sentiment, always looking beyond the bounds of time and desiring to quit the gift for the Giver.

She went on to talk of Harriet's going, then got to the point of it all:

> Cecilia will very soon follow her—I think in a very few months, more probably weeks. What can I say? They are both far dearer to me than myself. We part, nature groans; for me it is an anguish that threatens dissolution—not in convulsive sighs, but the soul is aghast, petrified. After ten minutes it returns to its usual motion, and all goes on as if nothing had happened. This same effect has followed the death of all so dear. Why? Faith lifts the staggering soul on one side, Hope supports it on the other. Experience says it must be, and love says—let it be. And so goes your friend thro' her passing career. It will not last long, that is all she is sure of.

Was there ever a clearer picture of self?—her own confessor could not have summed up her spirituality so simply: the desire for eternity. Was there ever a more graphic picture of grief, a more lasting affirmation of love?

It was quickly put to the test. By the beginning of April Cecilia's condition was so grave that Dr. Chatard and Archbishop Carroll both urged Elizabeth to take the last desperate step of bringing her to Baltimore. There, at least, she would have expert medical care and the ineffable comfort of her dear Father Babade to soothe her last days. And so Elizabeth set out on what was to be her final visit to Baltimore, or to any place else in the great world outside her Valley. She took along Anna, Cecilia's dear companion, and Sister Susan. They stayed at the home of George Weis for three weeks, through Holy Week and Easter; and there, on April 29, Cecilia died.

They were days of turmoil for Elizabeth—the night-hour watches with Cecilia, the bewildering parade of acquaintances and friends who had found out she was there, the knowledge that Charles DuPavillon was about to sail for home and that she must keep a vigilant eye on Anna during the tender days before he went—and over on Paca Street, David and his confreres were deciding her fate: indeed, the letter announcing her imminent removal from office was waiting for her when she got back to Emmitsburg with Cecilia's body. Cecilia! Not alone her "dear, dear sister," her child, but the first of her religious daughters to be called to heaven. Many a Sister of Charity since has been carried back from Baltimore to be laid in the "little sacred wood"; but it shall always be remembered that Sister Cecilia was the first, and that their first Mother had brought her.

Elizabeth and Susan were so unstrung with grief and nerves and exhaustion and the relentless, pounding rain on the trip home that, when Mr. Cloriviére, a cleric from the Mount, met the little cortege at Westminster, they were in a state of true hysteria, laughing and chattering as if they were returning from a picnic; they could not even meet the gaze of the shocked young man, but kept turning away with suppressed giggles.

It was all very well for Elizabeth to say that the danger point of her grief was passed in ten minutes; but the ache of loss remained for months

and years. She talked of Cecilia incessantly, the thoughts of her breaking through the most unrelated conversation. "The children are good as
angels," she reported to Julia at the end of May, "the boys very regular
and assiduous. No dear, dear Cicil—no soul meeting soul when the sun
sinks behind the mountain. But— But— But—!"

Elizabeth had been forced to leave Anna behind in Baltimore at the
home of the Robert Barrys, because there was no room for her in the
wagon that took Cecilia back to Emmitsburg for burial. She did not like
to leave her, for DuPavillon was still in Baltimore; and it was with a false
assurance that she told Sad that Anna's "modesty and reserve is really
angelic," and that Mrs. Barry was "a European, and will and does keep
her always under her own eye." In reality, Elizabeth was terrified lest "my
dear one . . . be led into those indiscretions which, tho' apparently trifling
at the time, yet must hurt the purity of a heart innocent as hers." Her terror increased when she overheard Louise Caton coax Anna: "Come, Anna,
stay with us. We will get a much better match for you. You don't
know the enchantment of cockades and epaulets!" However, the crowded
wagon and the chance for drawing lessons, which Anna had seized upon
as an excuse to stay near her beloved, compelled the poor mother to
depart without her; but only after the strictest instructions: Anna must
not be alone with Charles, she must submit all notes to Mrs. Barry, she
must not go to the Catons.

When all was over, and Charles had sorrowfully departed with the
promise of returning in ten months to claim his bride, Anna grew restless. The truth was that she was unhappy. She was beginning to see
that she had, in a way, burned all her bridges. She had promised herself, and must in honor keep her promise; and she began to realize,
with a hint of panic, that she had committed herself to the great unknown. She saw now, too, that she had lost touch with her mother;
that despite all the kindness and understanding and willingness to be
of service, her mother did not approve of her romance. Completely bored
and miserable, she wrote Elizabeth almost every day, begging to come
home; but, in her eagerness to have what she wanted, she had engaged
herself to the Barrys and to the drawing master and to classes in the
winter. On the 4th of June she was driven to the humble admission:

"I am as unhappy here, almost, as I used to be at the Mountain. I wish very much to be with you. I do not even like the idea of being here in the winter, but what can I do? I must submit to everything. You see I am in a dilemma; therefore, to you I look to free me."

No parent could withstand such remorse and pleading trust, and, finally, Elizabeth sent for her. But the mother could not draw the great sigh of relief until July, when she wrote thankfully to Julia:

> Her Alexis has made out to convey two letters to her already, expressive of the romance of his age. But never could I have believed (having once been Betsey Bayley) what he says in both of them, that she had never given him the least proof of her affection: "Anna, you always refused me, and I respected your delicacy; but at the last moment—when I left you, perhaps for a watery grave—could you continue to refuse one single kiss? One only proof that I was dear to you? The remembrance that you persisted in doing so is a continual cloud of sorrow." This language is trifling—but to me the music of heaven—that my darling should have had the virtue and purity of an angel in the first dawn of youthful and ardent affection (for she certainly is not without passion) is a joy to her Mother, which a Mother only can know.

Anna wrote joyfully on June 10 that Mrs. Caton would escort her to Emmitsburg at the beginning of July; and she confided to Elizabeth: "The Bishop told me the other day, tho' as in secrecy and you will keep it such, that you would probably be down in the fall again and, still more probable, not go back. At least, he said you would be down before October with a few—I hope he means Father's (Babade's)— children. Yet, dearest mother, let me come to you; the thing is uncertain yet."

Uncertain was the word. As has been said, when Elizabeth returned to Emmitsburg, she had found David's letter proposing to install Sister Rose as Mother, and instructing Elizabeth to prepare the Sisters "by a special letter" for the change. Fortunately, Rose was away at the time, and Elizabeth wrote to her Superior immediately that she would "wait for further directions before announcing to the Sisters the change that is intended in my situation, as in Rose's absence no one else would be willing to take the place of Mother without your immediate order." Her wise decision to wait may have saved the community, for even after

Rose's return, nothing further was heard of the proposal until Anna's letter arrived. On hearing Anna's news, Elizabeth wrote at once to the Archbishop, humbly assuring him of her disinterestedness and proving it by making the offer of five hundred dollars she had in Emmitsburg and five hundred more placed with Robert Barry in Baltimore, if the prelate should "find either of these sums some little help in promoting any plan Our Adored may please to suggest—or if He pleases us to remain here quietly, *so be it.*"

In her admirable resignation to news that, humanly speaking, must have wrenched her heart, Elizabeth was able to go along outwardly as if the foundations of her life's work were not being shaken. It had been a hard year, so far, with trial piled on trial, and her health had inevitably suffered; but she painted an idyllic picture for Dué:

> My health is excellent, *considering.* These good souls who call me Mother feed me like a pig with fresh eggs, milk and butter, coffee and cream, good vegetables, home bread, etc., etc., and oblige me to live a thousand times easier and better than I ever did. Never do the least kind of work of any kind. To walk round with knitting in hand, and give the look of encouragement or reproof, thro' the house and school is my chief business.

Dué, who knew her, could not have been fooled—just as Julia, or Sad or Mary Post were never fooled. They could not envision the energetic Elizabeth in a rocking chair. Nor could they, of course, appreciate her tasks as a religious superior: the vigilance, the spiritual direction, the conferences, the correspondence, the temporal affairs, the administration of the school—there were already forty to fifty pupils; but they knew she was not a guest at a summer resort.

Most important of all, in the midst of her greatest afflictions, Elizabeth never forgot how to laugh. She shared with Anna the uproar she caused at supper when she choked on the pepper, and passed on Sister Cecilia O'Conway's news that Anna was "the grandmother of twelve chickens." She even accepted, because there was no malice in it, the Sisters' jokes about their Director's "strict rules and regulations."

Elizabeth had *balance,* a superior common sense, divine and human, that put everything in its place unerringly, tidily. It was the secret of her unbroken happiness, which is to say, of her unbroken virtue. She knew when to speak and when to be silent, when to fight and when to submit. She had the pride to stand up for what was right, and the humbleness to accept the human fact that she might falter. Thus she told Matthias O'Conway with simplicity: "You will laugh at me when I tell you I have seen more real affliction and sorrow here in the ten months since our removal than in all the thirty-five years of my past life, which was all marked by affliction. You will laugh, I repeat, because you well know that the fruit will not be lost—or, at least, I hope not; though, indeed, sometimes I tremble."

In July, Sister Rose went to Baltimore on business that had to do, probably, with the entrance of her son into Mount St. Mary's; but the rumors swirled again that David was about to act on his proposal to replace Elizabeth. Wanting to know where she stood, Mrs. Seton wrote at once to the Archbishop, asking bluntly if the rumors were true. He could not tell her; for he did not know; but his letter was a comfort:

Since my last to you not a syllable has been said by Mr. David or any members of Mr. Nagot's council called *Directeurs*, concerning a change in your house: if any be intended, I must hear of it very soon.

The proposal, if renewed, will not create any uneasiness on your account. You have gone through many trials in overcoming the obstructions, interior and exterior, which were interposed to your change of religion. To these, other difficulties equally or more painful succeeded; but it has still pleased God to reserve another which must naturally disappoint your expectations more than any preceding one. That is, you are destined to be tried by disapprobation and humiliation where you expected to meet confidence and tranquillity. This was wanting, perhaps, to perfect your other sacrifices, and to operate in your heart a perfect disengagement from human things and expectations—even the consolations of religious retirement.

Mr. Dubois has, without doubt, earlier information than me of the views of Messrs. Dubourg or David; but still, their good sense must and will cause hesitation before they resolve finally to assign to Sister Rose the government of the monastery and limit you to the school.

* * *

It would be, in my opinion, a fatal change to the prosperity of the Sisterhood, and prove ultimately detrimental to any project of your removal to Baltimore. If this event were to take place after your relinquishment of your present station, it would by many be attributed to your disgust, and, consequently, [be] of prejudice to the situation. Therefore, if it should be again proposed to me, it is my determination to resist the proposal till Mr. David has finished his visitation and made his report.

Here, evidently, was question of another proposal: to make Elizabeth headmistress of the school under Rose as Mother Superior. The good gentlemen of Baltimore, like those of New York before them, seemed not to know what to do with Elizabeth—except that they were determined to remove her from office! But, as she had told Antonio formerly, God would know what to do with her.

The rumors continued to blow about on the summer breeze, and they set Elizabeth thinking, and her thoughts were of her children. When she was preparing to come to Emmitsburg the year before, she had hurried over Carroll's doubts as to whether it was possible for her to assume the double role of spiritual and physical motherhood, and whether the isolation of the country was to her children's best interests. Now she weighed the doubts more precisely. Had the matter of her children been advanced as a reason for changing her to Baltimore? Did the approaching consideration of a permanent rule, and her own uncertain connection with it, make her take a longer look at her children's place in the scheme of things? No one knows; but Annina and Bill and Dick and Kate and Rebecca were very much in her thoughts that summer. On July 20, she told Julia:

> The thought of living out of our valley would seem impossible if I belonged to myself; but the dear ones have their first claim, which must ever remain inviolate. Consequently, if at any time the duties I am engaged in should interfere with those I owe to them, I have solemnly engaged with our good Bishop Carroll, as well as my own conscience, to give the darlings their right, and to prefer their advantage in everything.

And she finished, rather ruefully: "As it is, they are as you yourself would wish them to be, except a certain polish, which nothing belonging to me ever had or will have."

She pursued the same train of thought—and in almost the same words—when writing to Eliza Sadler on August 3, at the same time giving her a glimpse, in rare revelation, of what the Valley meant to her and how hard it would be for her to leave it:

I have told you my present situation is of all I could imagine in this world most congenial to my views, sentiments and disposition. The liberty of solitude, a country life, and plenty without the trouble or care of providing, would tie me to the Valley for the remainder of days if I belonged to myself; but the claim of the dear ones must ever remain inviolate. Consequently, if at any time the duties I am engaged in should be inconsistent with my duty to them, the one must give place to the other. It was the only condition on which our good and blessed Bishop Carroll would permit me, or rather consent to, my coming here. All these things are in the hand of the Chief Shepherd. I am at peace. A lazy, sleepy soul, give me but quiet, and all is given; yet that quiet is in the midst of fifty children all day, except the early part of morning and a part of the afternoon. But *quiet it is.*

Order and regularity cannot be skipped over here, and I am in the full possession of that principle which in the world passed either for hypocrisy or a species of it. You know, that manner of looking upon twenty people in the room with a look of affection and interest, showing an interest for all and a concern in all their concerns.

You know I am as a mother encompassed by many children of different dispositions, not all equally amiable or congenial; but bound to love, instruct and provide for the happiness of all, to give the example of cheerfulness, peace, resignation, and consider individuals more as proceeding from the same origin and tending to the same end than in the different shades of merit or demerit.

I assure you the little woman is quite a somebody, and perhaps you are the only one of all who ever knew her who could justly appreciate her means of happiness.

On August 9 she told George Weis: "Everything here is again suspended and I am casting about to prepare for beginning the world again with my poor Annina, Josephine and Rebecca; as we have many reasons to expect from many things past, lately, that our situation is more unsettled than ever." As always, she rose above her weariness of soul: "His Adorable Will be done during the few remaining days of my tiresome journey which, being made with so many tears and sown so thick with crosses, will certainly be concluded with joy and crowned with eternal rest." She finished with one of those arresting calls to perfection which were so characteristic of her: "Look up! The highest there were lowest here. . . . Now, my friend, we are in the true and sure way of salvation for that long, long eternity before us; if only we keep courage we will go to heaven on horseback instead of idling and creeping along. . . . George, George, be a man! but a supernatural man crucified in Christ."

The following week Flaget arrived back from France. His efforts to prevent his elevation as bishop had failed: Rome had made up its mind months before not to listen to his protests, as his Superior General, Father Emery, had informed him with the greeting, "My Lord, you should be in your diocese." But he had not failed in his quest of St. Vincent's rule. Moreover, the Superior of the Daughters of Charity had apparently looked favorably upon the proposal of taking the American Sisters into his family, and had designated Sister Marie Bizeray, Sister Augustine Chauvin and Sister Woirin to go to America. Probably, Flaget carried Sister Bizeray's warm, friendly letter with him.

My dear Sisters: As it is not yet in my power to leave France, I write for the purpose of proving to you that you are the object of my thoughts. I hope I shall have the pleasure of seeing you in a few months, as the good God Who calls you to our holy state, and has inspired me as well as several of my companions with the desire of being useful to you, will not fail to prepare the way for our departure. That all-powerful God Who made choice of poor fishermen, weak and ignorant men, to become the foundations of His Church, is pleased also in our days to employ the most feeble instruments, for the greater glory of His Name, to found an establishment that will be agreeable to Him, since it has for its object the service of His suffering members. Oh how beautiful is that calling which enables us to walk in the footsteps of Our divine Savior, to practice the virtues which He practiced, and to offer ourselves as a sacrifice to Him as He offered Himself for us! What gratitude, what love, do we not owe to that tender Father for having chosen us for so sublime a vocation!

Let us thank Him, dear Sisters, and pray Him for each other, that He will grant us the grace of corresponding faithfully to this inestimable privilege. Let us have recourse to the Blessed Virgin, to St. Vincent de Paul, our father, to Mademoiselle LeGras, our blessed mother, that they may obtain this happiness for their cherished daughters. There can be no doubt of our being dear to them, since we love them and desire to be subject to them.

As Monseigneur Flaget will have made known to you the dispositions which his zeal and holy interest for you have awakened among us, I will conclude, dear Sisters, soon to be companions, by assuring you of the sincere and entire devotedness and respect of

Your very humble sister,
Marie Bizeray

As summer waned, Elizabeth had much on her mind: the discussion of the rule, the coming of the French Sisters, the growth of the school and the sisterhood—three more candidates, sent by Father David, had arrived in July: Angela Brady, Fanny Jordan and Julia Shirk—and the see-saw condition of her status. She had, besides, "the entire charge of the religious instruction of all the country round," and saw to it that every opportunity to visit the sick was embraced though "the villages round us are not very extensive." With it all, there was constant sickness in the house. The dread consumption was firmly entrenched among the Sisters, and they were as helpless to rout it as the modern world is to eradicate cancer, even more helpless, since it leaped like fire from victim to victim. It is melancholy to read on the long row of stones by Harriet's oak tree the record of those young lives of the first years, eaten away before they could ripen.

But Elizabeth continued to shrug off her burdens and hide her worries. The letters sent out of the Valley took nothing with them but the air and the sunshine. Thus, in a letter of October 23 she bantered with Julia, chiding her "lazy" friend, who had not written for months:

> Twice I have begged you to say, "*I am alive*"; but either you are very cross, angry, troubled or MARRIED. Yet, in every case your own friend must cry: "Dear, dear, dear, dearest!" I would take any pain for you but the *last mentioned*; that admits not of proxy. . . . But I had better count the parti-colored leaves of the mountains and woods than guess at half the *perhaps* of a *lady*. What poor mortals they are; and when lady and fashion —spelling in all *fashionable lady*—are put together, who can detail the whys and wherefores she may find for not writing to a country friend, a poor body stowed in a corner, with a fool's mark upon her, too? But, my well-beloved, I hope before the frost benumbs your little dear fingers you will be pleased to address one word of remembrance to your woodland friend. You may direct to Madame Goose, if you think proper, tacking the name of Mr. Dubois who will know to which of his flock it belongs.

She then went on to tease the Philadelphia matron about age, but with a certain poignancy: "If I guess right, you are advancing a little.

Dearest, dearest little Glorianna, you must, must, at last be old! To be sure, I expect my nose and chin will soon look like nutcrackers—but yours turns up, I remember. We ought to have some little pickininnies in the corner."

In November Elizabeth was given a great joy. The Papal Bulls, elevating Carroll and Cheverus, Flaget and Egan, had at last arrived in America, and the Archbishop proceeded to consecrate his three suffragans. The fourth, the Dominican Richard Concanen, had died at Naples on June 19, as he was about to embark for his See of New York; his death caused Father Kohlmann to continue as administrator of the diocese until Bishop John Connolly, O.P., arrived on November 14, 1815. The Archbishop consecrated the Bishop of Philadelphia, Michael Egan, O.F.M., on October 28, and John Cheverus, the Bishop of Boston, on November 1. Both these consecrations took place in St. Peter's Pro-Cathedral; but Benedict Flaget's consecration as Bishop of Bardstown, on November 4, was held in St. Patrick's Church, Fell's Point, of which Father Francis Moranvillé was pastor. Cheverus preached on this latter occasion, hailing Carroll, the first Metropolitan in the United States, as "the Elias of the New Law, the father of the clergy, the conductor of the car of Israel in the New World: *Pater mi, Pater mi, currus Israel et auriga ejus.*"

On November 21, Elizabeth was called to the parlor of St. Joseph's House and found two strange clergymen. The one said simply, "I am Cheverus."

Cheverus! The "learned and eloquent Cheverus" of Antonio! The "dear Cheverus" who had given her the final push into the Church. The "blessed Cheverus" who had been her friend and adviser in every change and contingency of the past five years. She had never seen his face, probably never a picture of it; but on hearing the name she fell to her knees, kissed the purple ring and remained there, weeping, unable to speak for a full five minutes. Only then could she give attention to his companion, Bishop Egan. We do not know what Cheverus and Elizabeth talked of in the two days he spent in the Valley, but it was the intimate, exalted talk of friends. Knowing what the new Bishop meant to her, Father Dubois suggested that she try to get the prelate to extend his stay. "Exert all your insinuating eloquence upon the old Bishop," Dubois urged her. (Cheverus was forty-two at the time!) But whether or not Elizabeth tried to detain him, the Bishop of Boston would not stay.

She made him agree, however, to call on Eliza Sadler when he passed through New York, and sent with him an excited letter of introduction. "It will please you to see our blessed Cheverus," she promised Sad, "because he carries your *friend* and the darlings in his very heart, and we love him with a sentiment not easily described. . . . Look at his purple ring and remember how often we kissed it."

Sad was impressed. "I was above stairs when the Bishop called," she related for Elizabeth. "He sent up the letter, and as soon as I cast my eyes on the name, I ran down without opening it. Yet, the *ring* excited something of the sensation you wished, for it is too beautiful not to attract the eye; and in looking on it, the idea that it had fixed yours, or at least the dear young ones, was present while I conversed with your *revered friend*. There is all that ease and simplicity I so much admire in so dignified a character." So impressed was she that she went with a Catholic friend to St. Peter's on Barclay Street to see the Bishop confer Confirmation, and to hear him preach in English and French.

John Cheverus had humbly sought to warn Elizabeth in 1808 that "whenever you see me, one of the heroes of your evening stories will shrink into a little, ordinary man." She had not found him so at all. He was what she expected, what she *knew*, only intensified by the glance of his eye and the tone of his voice and the gesture of his hand. The Bishop, for his part, had seen at last not only the valiant, holy little woman, but the successful foundress, and his approval of the well-grounded religious community he observed is most satisfying to hear. "I almost envy their [the Sisters'] happiness and yours," he wrote Elizabeth. "I hope their pious example has not been lost upon me." And he reported to Archbishop Carroll that he had visited the "holy mountain" and been "very much edified."

With the consecration of Bishop Flaget, it became definite that Father David would go to Kentucky with him; and at the banquet given for all the new prelates in November, Father Nagot had resigned as

Superior of the Sulpicians in favor of Father John Mary Tessier. The Archbishop had hastened to give Elizabeth the news, knowing that she would welcome it as a sign that the storms buffeting her would soon be over. But the sign was a premature one, a mere lull, a break in the clouds.

XVIII

The Rule

Bishop Faget decided not to go to his See in Kentucky until the following May. Father David, therefore, continued in office, doing nothing either to relinquish his hold on the Sisterhood or to pave the way for his successor. It is unbelievable that, in these "lame duck" months of his rule, he should continue to press plans that must have a lasting effect, for better or worse, on the community; but he did, and in such a positive, even impatient, way that, it must be concluded, he looked on the radical change he proposed as vital to the community's welfare. He talked openly about it now—not to Elizabeth, who was most concerned, but to a dinner companion! This dinner companion was a Baltimore friend of Elizabeth's, Margaret George.

Miss George began a letter on Christmas Day, expressing her alarm at the state of Elizabeth's health and reminding her that "no one could or would supply your loss"—especially to the Seton children; but on the 27th, she got down to the news. David was not considering the establishment of a religious community in Kentucky. It was too early for that, he thought. But he *was* going to try to establish one in Baltimore, before he left. "You know who would be *superior*," the girl commented drily. Rose White. And such a community would not teach; it would care for the sick.

It was no wonder that Elizabeth was bewildered. The gentlemen in Baltimore, it seemed, could not make up their minds. First, Elizabeth was to be transferred to that city; then, she was to stay at Emmitsburg, but under Sister Rose as Superior; now Rose was to come to Baltimore, but not as head of a school, but of a hospital! And to compound the confusion, Father Babade told Margaret George that the Archbishop was on the point of sending for Elizabeth!

The New Year of 1811 came in ominously enough. To the unsettling news from Baltimore was added a cryptic note from Babade concerning Anna. "No letter from Charles," he wrote. "Such was the case with dear Harriet before her deliverance. Such a disappointment contributed not a little to hasten and accomplish her true and eternal gratification." The wise priest suspected that DuPavillon would not return; and his comparison of Anna's lot with Harriet's was wholly prophetic.

Most alarming of all, however, was the serious decline in Elizabeth's physical condition. What is more, for the first time she named her illness for what it was, "our family enemy"—tuberculosis. She wrote quite frankly to Julia on February 1:

> My spirits and peace are the same as when I last wrote, but the health of the body a good deal altered. Tho' always wrapped in a coating coat, with a lamb's wool shawl and worsted stockings, some cold has penetrated to the breast; and without cough or expectoration or acute pain, it keeps an almost continual slow fever on me.
>
> Your first thought will be that comfort and good nourishment are wanting; but you will believe the sacred assurance that I have both: not only as I wish, but even as your tender heart would wish for me—have had fire in my chamber night and day all the winter, chicken broth, new eggs warm from the nest, little knick-knacks of many kinds, as every good Sister in the house is continually contriving something for me, and the advice of the best French physician in Baltimore, Doctor Chatard, who is my particular friend.

A few days later she gave Dué, who had returned from Ireland in the fall, the same grim news: "Since I wrote you, my peace and quiet is the same and even increased, as has always been my case when the body grows weaker; and mine weakens every day, notwithstanding what I think even an excessive care, such as going to bed with the children, rising with them two hours later than the community, having fire always in my chamber, a little nice something at my meals, and the boundless attention of many kind hearts who are always watching to hinder my lifting a finger except to knit or reel a ball of yarn."

The disturbing factor was not so much Elizabeth's acknowledgment that she was ill, but her submission to the special attentions of the Sisters and acceptance of a mitigation of the rule. Her illness must have been so marked as to terrify everyone; and for the Sisters, and for her children, she allowed herself to be "pampered," especially at this time when the future of both was being threatened by her Superior's plans. No one who has not lived the common life can know what it cost her to depart from it in the matters of diet and sleep, particularly since, as Mother, she was expected to be a model for all. And she was a model, even now, for she was showing her Sisters an example of obedience and humility in time of sickness. It can be a very great pride to follow the rule when one is not able.

Julia Scott was so alarmed that, overcoming her dislike of the pen, she answered Elizabeth's letter at once, with a host of do's and dont's of her own:

> You are, then, ill; but seek to persuade me that you have every comfort requisite for your situation. Do not deceive me, my friend. . . . You say you have the best advice. Is it not that you do not leave your room during the winter months? . . . And a change of air which your physician will surely prescribe as the best medicine in the disease you apprehend will give me the happiness of receiving you in my house, my arms and my heart. This visit would be a mutual comfort to us. Your plans and views for your children would be laid open to me much better than in any other manner, and perhaps I should have the satisfaction to relieve your mind of some of its anxiety for beings so dear.

Elizabeth tried to still her friend's fears with an infusion of her own confidence in God: "As to my health, you must, must leave it to the dearest, kindest, best of Fathers. He will let me stay with the darlings many years yet, I hope." With the suggestion that Elizabeth come to visit her, however, Julia had touched a chord. All this winter and spring the ailing little woman reached out to her friends and lived in the happy past she had shared with them. "I could not but smile to myself the other night, in an hour of silence and quiet," she told Julia, "to find I was but seventeen, and passing thro' memorable scenes with you at Easton as really as if I could *really* see and hear you." And she assured Sad: "Aunt Sadler and Uncle Craig is one of the unfailing sources of the children's remembrances. William will tell everything his Uncle Craig ever said to him, every kind indulgence. They can tell every article of your room upstairs: where the sofa stood on which you sat, the little bird, wooden cow, the white dog, etc.; and all ends with a sigh which goes round and commonly finishes with a silent kiss for Mother."

This unusual nostalgia took the special form of a very human wish to see the ones she loved best in the world. "I have a strong hope that you will take into your mind to come to see us in the spring," she confided to Julia in February; and in March: "I cannot give up the hope that you will one day come here. . . . You know I always stick to hope to the last." And in May, her invitation to Sad was truly a pleading: "Give me at least the *hope* that you will sometime or other come to the Mountain. If I had worlds, I would give them, to show Sister, Dué and yourself the beauty of its shades in the setting sun, the waving of the wheat fields, our woods covered with flowers, and the quiet, contented look of our habitation. . . . Come, dear Eliza; at least, try to come—say at least you will try to come. What is the atom of distance in this world, if only you can find the opportunity?"

She was not ashamed of her longing. She did not think to reproach herself for it. She had a firm grasp of the truth that "the nearer a soul is truly united to God, the more its sensibilities are increased to every being of His creation: much more to those whom it is bound to love by the tenderest and most endearing ties."

Elizabeth's funds were as low as her health; and she applied to Julia as the bountiful lady had always commanded her to do. "As I am obliged to be a lady, and have many wants," she wrote jokingly, "you shall do as I would delight to do to you, dearest, and supply them, at least the extra ones. . . . A trifle, ten or twenty dollars, will serve the present time. . . . Yet I feel hurt, dearest, as if it is taking advantage of your goodness to ask what I do. But my doctor's bill for William and dearest Harriet and C[ecilia] took all in the purse, and more than I expected."

Julia considered the request "a proof of your friendship most dear to my heart. . . . I should have acted in the same manner towards you; but," she scolded, "I do not think I should have written the postscript. I am half angry with you for it. I enclose what has long been due to you." Only the truest of friends could give so gracefully.

Harriet had been dead a whole year, but one night Sister Cecilia O'Conway startled the house with a dream she had of her. Elizabeth recounted it for George Weis—"a dream of very singular kind of our Maddelene, telling her that Cicil was above with the Virgins and Martyrs, but that she was suffering inexpressibly for sins at New York, and will suffer till next October except Masses are offered for her continually. True or not, it has awakened the prayers of the whole house for her."

And then, Elizabeth had a letter from her brother Barclay, of all people, grieving for Harriet in the most artificial and extravagant language. It was a comic piece, hinting darkly at Elizabeth's "power over the mind of her I loved," yet grandly assuring her that he felt for her "a brother's love still," and requesting the "melancholy satisfaction to be informed of her illness, many particulars of which from your own pen will be consoling to my mind, and particularly as I have had so few." Elizabeth answered the preposterous gentleman quietly and evenly, giving him what he asked, but not failing to remind him, by quotes from his own letters to Harriet, of the insults he had offered the luckless girl.

Margaret George had told Elizabeth that the Archbishop would send for her, but it was Rose who was summoned, in February, and by Father David. The summons came ostensibly because Rose was ill—"I should have reproached myself," the Superior wrote, "had I not in this instance complied with the Doctor's and the Archbishop's requests"; but it is worthy of remark that Elizabeth herself was ill, as has been said. In fact, David's real purpose seems to have been revealed by his impatience when the weather delayed Rose's journey to Baltimore, and he began to send letter on top of letter urging "her coming at any risk."

It is wonderful, indeed, that the importance David gave to Sister Rose should not before now have caused an open breach in the Sisterhood. On March 16 Elizabeth told the Archbishop: "Rose's virtues are truly valued by me and by us all, but from the time she knew she was proposed as Mother of this house in my place . . . her conduct has undergone an entire change, and has been very unfavorable to her happiness and ours." Now, however, with Rose's call to Baltimore and the crescendo of new rumors, relations between the two women showed definite strain; although Elizabeth assured the prelate, "Our reserve is of the mind, not of the heart; her affectionate kindness to my children binds me by gratitude independent of our spiritual connection."

Archbishop Carroll wrote immediately to relieve Elizabeth's mind, pointing out that her authority in office stemmed, "I presume . . . partly [from] the choice of your Sisters, and partly [from] the approbation of the Superior." He assured her that he had "not heard for a long time the slightest mention of a proposed change in the government of St. Joseph's; nor of settling our dear Rose here with, and at the head of, a colony from your house." Besides, he went on with an almost bland innocence, he had seen Rose and "her candor is such that she would undoubtedly communicate with me on the subject, if she had ever heard of it." Then he finished on the note of dogged conviction he had stressed from the beginning:

> She [Rose] assuredly is liable to failings, for who is without them? But if any thought of placing her at the head of a colony from St. Joseph's, they must have persuaded themselves of the practicability of governing it more by the efficacious influence of a good heart than by the dictates of reason, deliberation and experience. If you should ever be permitted to resign your maternal charge over your community, I would rejoice on your own individual account, but my hope for the continuance of the establishment would be very much weakened, and all your friends would feel their anxiety for your lovely children highly increased.

The suspicion grows that, with exquisite diplomacy, John Carroll preserved the *status quo* of Elizabeth and the community—indeed, in all probability, its very life. With his usual benignity, he listened graciously to both sides, but he had made up his mind early that Elizabeth must stay; and no matter the interest and sympathy he showed other proposals, he never said "yes" to them, and his "yes" was essential. The bald fact is, that in a year and a half of trying, the dictatorial Father David had not got his way.

It was all over now. The plans for a change in authority were dead. But David was determined on having a last fling at leaving his mark on the community before going to Kentucky. He proposed to conduct a retreat at St. Joseph's. Elizabeth bristled, and flew into action. She dispatched a note to the Archbishop, asking him to refuse his permission for the retreat, and a scathing reply to David. Of what earthly use was a retreat now, she demanded, unless it were followed by an acceptance and application of the rules which were under discussion? And to what purpose whould they discuss the rules with him, since he was leaving, and the superior who followed him might think very differently and "subject us to new changes and uncertainty?"

It was a flare-up of the all-but-forgotten Bayley temper. She was quite right and logical, of course, although anger as much as logic had dictated the letter. She was not fighting now for any great principle, but against what she could only consider with disgust as senseless, a great waste of time and words. The weight of accumulated wrongs she had suffered from this high-handed man, the worries and anxieties, had snapped her control for the moment—and she was miserably ill.

Years later, when she sent a copy of this letter to Father Bruté, that he might know all her heart, Elizabeth wrote on the back of it: "Could you think your poor, poor Mother ever guilty of such impertinence? O Our Jesus, pity the ignorance and blindness of such a moment!" The retreat was not held—whether from the wise intervention of the Archbishop, or because David retreated before the aroused Mother, is not known; but the man of storms left quietly for Bardstown with Bishop Flaget on May 12, and Rose returned to Emmitsburg. She had been, after all, only a pawn; and the quiet silence under which she hid any disappointment she might have felt, taking up again her post as assistant and her old affection for Elizabeth as if nothing had happened, is proof enough that she was of the spiritual stature to succeed her when the time came.

The day that David left Baltimore with Flaget, Elizabeth wrote humbly to Archbishop Carroll:

Now, after two years' trial, experience has too well proved how illy I am qualified to meet the views of the Reverend Gentlemen who have the government of this house, who require a pliancy of character I would for some reasons wish to possess, and may eventually be the fruit of divine grace, but as yet is far from being attained.

She was being hard on herself again. She had fought courageously for what she thought was right, and was worthy of praise, not reproach. John Carroll, who had observed all, had no word or act of condemnation for the brave little Mother.

Things were to be better. The "Reverend Gentlemen" whose views she could not meet, the Sulpician Directors in Baltimore, now met hers. Their new head, Father Tessier, perhaps made the difference. At any rate, they named as Superior of the Sisters the man she would have chosen herself—John Dubois. Elizabeth told Carroll on May 12 that Dubois had always been her preference for two reasons: "being on the spot, he sees things in a different point of view from those who are distant," and "he always and invariably has recommended me to refer constantly to you, which is not only in the order of Providence, but the only safety I can find for the peace of my mind." When Dubois took formal charge is impossible to say, but he was certainly in command at the end of the summer, and was to be so for the remainder of Elizabeth's life.

The past continued to haunt Elizabeth. Mary Post wrote in June to tell her that their dear Uncle Bayley had died suddenly. What a flood of happy memories of New Rochelle the news must have released!—for, at such a time, people remember only what was happy. Elizabeth and Mary both had lost all touch with their uncle's family, possibly over Elizabeth's conversion, and they had not even been informed of his death; Mary had heard it from a neighbor. It was a sad close to a bright relationship; but such is so often the way with families.

Elizabeth was experiencing a piercing sadness at home. True to Father Babade's premonition, Charles DuPavillon had thrown over Annina. At least, the fickle young man had had the honesty to tell her that he had chosen a bride in Guadeloupe; hers would not be the long-drawn-out ordeal of false promises and expectations her Aunt Harriet had suffered. Elizabeth relayed the humiliating news to Julia Scott in a letter that did not hide her indignation and contempt: "The young DuPavillon, to whom she gave her foolish little heart, found on his return to his family and possessions someone who nabbed him on the spot and saved him the trouble of disposing them for his return to my darling. Well, so much the better."

She went on to report that Anna had taken the news "with a rational and patient conclusion that it cannot but be a good escape to lose a heart which does not know its own constancy." A wise sentiment, but a bit too glib for a fifteen-year-old girl. The voice may indeed have been the voice of Annina, but there is a suspicion that the words were her poor mother's.

The child's feelings toward Charles, however immature and romantic, were real enough. After her last, bittersweet days with him in Baltimore she had withdrawn into an inscrutable silence which her mother had prudently refrained from probing. Elizabeth had told Julia in October:

> Anna, as quiet as puss in the corner, keeps her sensibilities all in order. Has no letters since I wrote you, takes the matter coolly, gathers nuts, dries fruits, shares in all the amusements of the boarders of the house, and seems to have resigned all to Him Who knows best.

The girl had definitely refused to be separated by the sea from her mother—that is why Charles had returned to Guadeloupe without her; and, there can be little doubt, as Elizabeth said, that she "had long since felt the imprudence of connecting herself so soon and with so little experience." But now, at the start of the summer, she was simply a jilted girl—and must have been shamed, hurt and heartbroken with the intensity that the first heartbreak of life brings.

However, Annina had had taste enough of the world to turn from it and give her whole heart to religion, applying as a candidate for her mother's sisterhood. In this action, too, there was the immature need of youth to dramatize itself. Already, at the beginning of July, she was writing to girl friends in Baltimore: "I have some hopes yet that after you have seen a little of the world, and experienced its nothingness, you will come and end your days with Sister Annina of St. Joseph's"; and "when you are tired of the world, I have some hopes you will come and join your Nun, though I am so unworthy of the name."

It seemed, almost, the classic procedure of sentimental novels, the flight to the convent to hide disappointment in love; but, like her affection for Charles, it was real. Soon, in the moment of sober, mature truth that her mortal illness brought, she would abandon the last vestige of playacting and worry lest "everyone will think in Baltimore my illness is occasioned by disappointment, that is, mortification; but Our dear Lord knows how much I have thanked Him for my escape. He knows how I dreaded being obliged to fulfill my foolish promises."

That month of July Elizabeth first met the man who was to be truly the friend of her life and who would refine her soul to a golden perfection. His name was Simon Gabriel Bruté de Remur, and he was at the time thirty-two years old and just two years a priest.

Father Bruté had had a colorful life to date. Born at Rennes in 1779 of well-to-do and prominent parents, he had lived through the Days of Terror untouched despite his loyalty to the Church. Indeed, he had taken an active part, with his widowed mother, in harboring hunted priests in the family printing shop or in the living quarters above it. He had watched martyrdoms in the square outside his home; perhaps he had seen the Vincentian martyr of Rennes, Blessed René Rogue, die by the guillotine on March 3, 1792. When the uneasy peace of Napoleon had come to France, he had studied medicine and graduated as a physician in 1803. He had not practiced his profession long, however, before he realized that what he wanted more than anything else was to be a priest. He studied at St. Sulpice in Paris and was ordained in 1808, joining the Sulpicians soon afterward. He was put teaching theology in which he was especially skilled; but when Flaget returned to America in 1810, Bruté volunteered to go with him, because the zeal of the missionary was uppermost in his heart.

It was a short visit Simon Gabriel Bruté made to the Valley in 1811, probably no more than two months; but during that time he ministered in some way to the Sisters, sufficient for a soul as spiritually keen as Elizabeth's to appreciate his great purity of heart. His English was ludicrously broken, but fortunately Elizabeth spoke fluent French; and with this common language for a bridge, she began to teach him the language of his adopted land by going over with him, phrase by phrase, the *Imitation of Christ*. He was never, all his life, comfortable in English, probably because his mind was so swift and vivid, and the hard-earned words never quite kept up with the tumbling thoughts.

The zero hour was approaching when the permanent rules of Mother Seton's Institute would be adopted. They had been discussed and re-discussed since Flaget had brought the rule of the Daughters of Charity of St. Vincent de Paul from France the year before.

The official rule of the American Institute, when adopted, would not be a revolution but a completion. From the first days in Baltimore the Sisters had lived according to the spirit of St. Vincent's rule. Even when the official copy had come from Paris, and Elizabeth had read it carefully, she had "not a thought discordant" with it.

The period of discussion—which was not unduly lengthy when the slow communication system of the times is considered—was not concerned, therefore, with the bulk of St. Vincent's prescriptions; these could be, and were, accepted quite easily. It was obvious that there would have to be a shift in emphasis on the ends of the French rule. The American community embraced all the Vincentian ends, but its cornerstone was education; the cornerstone of St. Vincent's community was the ministry to the poor and the sick, although he included teaching as part of that ministry.

Time was to prove this shift of emphasis almost academic, for within Elizabeth's lifetime the Emmitsburg Sisters would establish orphanages in Philadelphia and New York. Nor was the fact that they received paying boarders an impassible barrier to identification with the French community, since the income was needed both for livelihood and to finance their works of charity.

The great question was: should the Emmitsburg community be one with the French community, or should it, while adopting the spirit and the letter of Paris, be separate? Three important matters hinged on the answer: the government of the community, the status of Mother Seton and the fate of her children. Besides Mother Seton herself, the decision was in the hands of the Sulpicians and of Archbishop Carroll; in fact, their part was paramount, for they were her lawful superiors and she must abide by their choice—and, even should she demur, surely enough Sisters would be found to ratify it.

The key to Mother Seton's opinion was her children. Nothing is more clear than her constant assertion that their welfare came first. She would never abandon her responsibility to them, nor delegate it to any guardian, as she had told Mrs. Dupleix on February 11, 1811, in unmistakable words: "By the law of the Church I so much love, I could never take an obligation which interfered with my duties to them, except I had an independent provision and guardian for them, which the whole world could not supply to my judgment of a mother's duty."

The question of her children was one of those she raised in a letter of May 13, 1811, to Archbishop Carroll: "How can they [the French Sisters who were expected] allow me the uncontrolled privileges of a mother to my five darlings?" The other questions she asked the Archbishop were pertinent: "What authority would the Mother they bring have over our Sisters (while I am present) but the very rule she is to give them? And how could it be known that they would consent to the different modifications of their rule which are indispensible if adopted by us? What support can we procure to this house but from our Boarders, and how can the reception of Boarders sufficient to maintain it accord with their statutes?"—these questions were pertinent, but they might have been susceptible to compromise; to Elizabeth's mind, the question of her children admitted of no compromise. It should be remarked here that, oddly enough, evidence is entirely lacking of any direct attempt, either by letter or by personal courier, to have these points of doubt cleared up by Paris.

Elizabeth's role in the question of union with France may be summed up thus: there is no evidence, as has been said earlier, that she inaugurated the idea of union—the idea came almost certainly from the Sulpicians; and David in particular; on the other hand, there is no evidence that she did not approve of it, in the beginning—in fact, there can be strong presumption that she did.

In the famous letter of July 15, 1828, to Abbé Henri Élèves, alluded to in former pages, Father Dubourg wrote: "In her frequent conferences with her Director, Mrs. Seton learned that he had thought for a long time of establishing the Daughters of Charity in America; and as the duties of this institute would be compatible with the cares of her family, this virtuous lady expressed a most ardent desire of seeing it commenced and of being herself admitted into it."

And had Elizabeth disapproved, she would certainly have fought the idea, as she fought the prohibition concerning Father Babade. When she understood more clearly what such a union might entail, she raised certain questions, chief of which was the question of her future relationship with her children. It is difficult to conjecture whether, or how much, the questions she raised affected her approval of the union. Certainly it can be presumed that, as Foundress, she had a maternal love for the Sisterhood and would not wish to depart from it—for, be it noted, it was not alone a question of whether she might continue as Mother Superior and retain her authority over her children, but of whether she might remain in the community under such a condition.

Yet, it is certain that she was ready to obey the final decision of the Archbishop and her other lawfully constituted superiors, even as she had been ready to obey them in the matter of Sister Rose's accession. She expressed this readiness most beautifully to George Weis: "Here I stand with hands and eyes both lifted to wait the Adorable Will. The only word I have to say to every question is: *I am a mother.* Whatever providence awaits me consistent with that plea, I say Amen to it." Nor must it be forgotten that, on the very eve of Archbishop Carroll's first tentative approval of the new rules, September 5, 1811, Elizabeth urged: "Surely an individual is not to be considered where a public good is in question." Her willingness to step aside for the good of the community, if the Archbishop thought proper, could not be clearer, whether there was to be union with France or an independent establishment. What she thought in her human heart, what she *wished*, is impossible to say; and, in a very true sense, is irrelevant: she *willed* whatever God, speaking through her superiors, willed.

That she embraced wholeheartedly the spirit of St. Vincent, there can be no doubt. She governed the community by his spirit from the beginning, and later, by his rule. She urged him and Mlle. LeGras—St. Louis de Marillac, Foundress with him of the Daughters of Charity— upon her Sisters as patrons and exemplars. She translated their lives from the French for community use. That her community considered itself of the family of the Daughters of Charity is evident from the *Council Minutes* during Mother Seton's lifetime and immediately after her death, which repeatedly refer to them as "our European Sisters," and invoke precedents, sought from them by letter, in applying the rule. In one instance the *Minutes* expressly state the wish of the community "to conform to the original rule of St. Vincent as far as we know it."

In 1850 the Emmitsburg community effected the union with France. The action had been prophesied and approved by the Mother of God when she appeared to St. Catherine Labouré, a novice Daughter of Charity and the Seer of the Miraculous Medal, on the night of July 18–19, 1830. "When the rule will have been restored in vigor, a community will ask to be united to your community. Such is not customary, but I love them; God will bless those who take them in; they will enjoy great peace," Our Lady had said. In 1846 a number of Sisters on mission from Emmitsburg in the Diocese of New York had separated from the Emmitsburg Motherhouse to form the Sisters of Charity of St. Vincent de Paul of New York; the Sisters of Charity of St. Vincent de Paul, Halifax, and the Sisters of Charity of St. Elizabeth, Convent, New Jersey, were formed from the New York group in 1856 and 1859 respectively. In 1852 Sisters on mission from Emmitsburg in the Archdiocese of Cincinnati, formed an independent community, the Sisters of Charity of Cincinnati, Ohio; and from this group, in 1870, was formed the Mother Seton Sisters of Charity, Greensburg, Pennsylvania.

It is futile to conjecture whether Elizabeth Seton would have approved either the union with Paris or the separations from Emmitsburg. She was dead many years when they occurred. No one can say what another person would surely do in a given set of circumstances. Elizabeth herself, had she lived beyond 1821, could not have said what she would do in 1846 or 1852.

The Sulpician opinions in the original question of the union are easier to establish. John David was in favor of the union; in fact, it was his idea. This was the scholarly conclusion of Father Charles Souvay, C.M., who was an expert on the matter; and certainly Elizabeth's letter of May 13, 1811, to Carroll supports the view. Benedict Flaget carried out David's instructions to procure an official copy of the French rules; he also arranged for Sister Bizeray and her companions to come to America—both facts are vouched for in Mother Rose's *Journal*. It can be presumed that William Dubourg and Pierre Babade were in favor of union, since both of them were connected with the establishment of the community in Baltimore, which was apparently, from Father Dubourg's letter of July 15, 1828, intended as a foundation of the Daughters of Charity in America. The Director mentioned in the letter was Dubourg himself. Charles Nagot, too, may be presumed to have looked kindly on the idea of union with France, because he seems to have approved generally of the actions of David, whom he had appointed Superior of the Sisterhood.

John Dubois, on the other hand, was against a union with the French Sisters at this time; Bishop Cheverus wrote to Elizabeth on January 4, 1811: "I concur in opinion with Mr. Dubois about the propriety of your establishment remaining independent from the Sisters of Charity and continuing to be merely a house of education for young females." Dubois, evidently, considered the union only as inopportune in 1811, for, when he began to feel the press of his many duties he expressed a different sentiment in a letter of April 18, 1816 to Father Anthony Garnier:

> I desire more than anything else in this world to be free of the care of the Sisters, but I see no other hope than that of uniting them to some other society to take care of them. If the Reverend Superior approves, I will try to enter into correspondence on this subject with the Superior of the Fathers of the Mission, formerly Lazarists, to see if it were not possible to form a union between the Sisters here and those in France.

Even Bishop Flaget seemed to have second thoughts about the projected union which he had helped along, for he wrote to Simon Bruté on October 17, 1811:

> I dread the arrival of the religious women who are to come from Bordeaux. . . . Their hopes will be frustrated, they will be unhappy, be it at Baltimore or Emmitsburg. If there were yet time to turn them back, I would be of the opinion it should be done. I would wish at least that they be informed in detail of the spirit which reigns in the house at Emmitsburg, of the slight hope of serving in hospitals, and if they wish to come after that, we would not have to reproach ourselves.

This letter, however, may be considered not so much as evidence that Flaget had changed his mind, but as a realistic recognition that, with the accession of Dubois, who opposed the union, the French Sisters would find the picture changed.

As for Archbishop Carroll, while he allowed steps toward union to be taken, he seems never to have been inclined to it, personally. That he was as concerned as Elizabeth over her children's future is evident from his numerous letters already quoted; he had even hesitated about her assuming the role of Mother at Emmitsburg for this reason.

It is just as clear from these letters that he had become increasingly convinced that it was vital to the welfare of the community that she continue as its head—a position which the union seemed to threaten. And, it is safe to say that, as the ordinary of the diocese, he was not anxious for the government of the community to pass into external hands: he had even disliked the control exercised by the Sulpicians, as is obvious from his letter of September 11, 1811, to Mother Seton, tentatively approving the new constitutions: "I am rejoiced . . . to know that the idea of any other connection than that of charity is abandoned between the daughters of St. Joseph's and the Society of St. Sulpice"; and in the same letter he had stated previously: "It affords me great pleasure to learn that all the material points, on which a difference of opinion was thought to exist, have been given up by Messrs. de Sulpice in their last deliberations. If they had not, I do not think that I should have approved the constitutions." In any event, Carroll's satisfaction when the union did not come off was unmistakable in a jotting written on September 17, 1814:

> At the very institution of Emmitsburg, though it was strongly contended for its being entirely conformable to and the same with the Institute of St. Vincent de Paul, yet this proposal was soon and wisely abandoned for causes which arose out of distance, different manners and habits of the two countries, France and the United States.

In the end, the permanent rules and constitutions of Mother Seton's Sisters of Charity were approved by Archbishop John Carroll on September 11, 1811, and confirmed by him, after Elizabeth and the Sisters had discussed and voted on them, on January 17, 1812. Thus, the idea of union with France was abandoned for the time.

What caused such an abandonment? The attitudes and opinions of the persons involved, certainly. Then, the failure of the French Sisters to arrive in America: had they been present to demonstrate their way of life and to clarify the points of doubt, the final decision might conceivably have been different. Some have contested the full validity of the traditional reason for their failure to come—governmental refusal—suggesting that the difficulties raised in Baltimore and Emmitsburg may have held them back after their way was cleared; but Flaget's letter of October 17, written after Carroll had approved the new rules, assumed that the Sisters had not been informed of the difficulties. There is absolutely no evidence that they had.

Rose White's statement in her *Journal* that "Bishop Flaget had the promise of Sisters to accompany him to America, and the money was provided to pay their passage, and it was then he secured for us the rules, constitutions, etc.; but the Government under Bonaparte interfered, and the Sisters were not at liberty to leave France"—must be taken at face value. Nothing was ever heard of the Sisters again. Their detention in Europe must be regarded as an act of man that was permitted to fit into the plans of Providence.

The differences of milieu between established European civilization and the exigencies of American frontier culture has been advanced as another reason for the failure of the union. These differences certainly influenced the final decision of the Sulpicians and the Archbishop, as is evident from Carroll's jotting quoted above. Be it noted again, however, that no apparent effort was made to bridge over these differences by compromise. It seems prudent to state that they were more formidable in appearance than in actuality. After all, the Daughters of Charity were laboring at that time not only in France and the rest of Europe, but also in mission lands, where they encountered conditions no more normal or standard in regard to their rule than they would have encountered in America. The rule lent itself to accommodation in these lands, and surely could have so lent itself in the United States.

The reasons for the abandonment lay, in the last analysis, in the men who made the decision. John David favored the union; John Dubois opposed it. David was no longer Superior of the Sisters when the final decision was made; Dubois was—and he had an ally in Archbishop Carroll. As for Mother Seton's opinion *now* in the closing months of 1811: Carroll, Dubois—and Cheverus—were her friends, and they were all against the union at this time. Carroll especially she looked upon as her father, and always presented everything to him for his opinion, advice

and decision. She did not fight his decision and the decision of her
Sulpician superiors now; she formally approved of it, as did all the
Sisters but one. What she thought in her inmost heart—who knows?

The kindly old Archbishop knew that his first approval of the rule
in September, 1811, would bring great peace to Elizabeth's soul. "It
will be like freeing you from a state in which it was difficult to walk
straight, as you had no certain way in which to proceed," he told her.
Although he had seemed to be silent at times in the past when Elizabeth had cried out to him, he now disposed firmly and lovingly of the
controversies that had most tried her. The Babade affair should never
happen again. "I am exceedingly anxious," the old man wrote, "that
every allowance shall be made not only to the Sisters generally, but to
each one in particular, which can serve to give quiet to their consciences,
provided that this be done without endangering the harmony of the
community; and, therefore, it must become a matter of regulation."

Nor should any future clerical superior attempt to wield the autocratic
power David had assumed. The prelate made it quite clear that "no one
of that body [the Society of St. Sulpice] but your immediate Superior,
residing near you, will have any share in the government or concerns of
the Sisters, except (on very rare and uncommon occasions) the Superior
of the Seminary of Baltimore, but not his Society. This, however, is to
be understood so as not to exclude the essential superintendence and
control of Archbishop over every community in his Diocese." And the
Superior himself was not to rule, but to advise and help; for it was
Carroll's express wish "to confine the administration of your own affairs,
and the internal and domestic government, as much as possible, to your
own institutions once adopted, and within your own walls. Your Superior
or confessor need be informed or consulted in matters where the Mother
and her Council need his advice."

He ruled on Elizabeth's own situation in the manner of a wise, indulgent and grateful father: "Your own particular situation required special consideration on account of your dear children. It seemed to me that
only general principles for your and your family's case should be now
established, grounded on justice and gratitude; and that any special
considerations should be deferred to the period when the circumstances
may require them. At present too many persons would be consulted, and

amongst them some who are incompetent to judge; and even they who are most competent might find their most equitable provisions rendered useless by the changes produced in a few years."

In the glow of quiet good sense and benignity diffused by the Archbishop's letter, Elizabeth settled down to a thorough study of the final draft of the rule with her Sisters and Father Dubois.

XIX

"O Annina, Child of My Soul!"

Archbishop Carroll had been indeed prophetic when he told Elizabeth that the ultimate success of the Sisterhood would depend upon her own success in self-sacrifice. Throughout the months the all-important rule was under final discussion she endured the most agonizing personal trials.

She had confided to Dué in February her suspicions concerning her children's health. "I believe they have their inheritance," she had said, "except Annina, who for six months back is a picture of health—as they all are in color and brightness; but it is a deception of beauty and requires perpetual care." Now, in October, Anna and Bill both were proving her fears all too well-founded. At the moment Bill was the worse. Elizabeth was frantic with worry; she could not leave Anna, or the Sisters, and had to resign her firstborn son to the competent hands of Sister Susan, who was infirmarian at the Mount.

Bill's life hung in the balance for weeks, with his poor mother catching only an occasional glimpse of him, and wondering each time whether it would be the last. Then she herself developed a painful plague of boils such as she used to experience in New York. Yet, through it all, she was what her dear Will had always fondly called her, "the old knot of oak," but spiritually seasoned now. "I tell you *He* loves us," she declared to

Madame Chatard on November 6, "and I never had more tranquillity than during these exterior pains. Exterior—for my children are good, and, if they are taken, will go but a little while before and, no doubt, smooth the way I must follow. Our Sisters have been all in the infirmary by turns, but the daily work never stops, and *Notre Seigneur* is so good as to leave always enough to answer the bell." On December 8 Mary Post wrote to console her. She was herself essentially a mother and knew what her sister suffered, that children "so wind themselves round one's heart as to almost make one wonder how existence could be supportable without them."

Elizabeth was sure by now that Anna was going the sad way of Cecilia, even though she remarked hopefully to Julia Scott that "she may not be as ill as I imagine, for never was anyone easier frightened, after so many hard trials." The child was not entirely bedridden yet, and Elizabeth snatched every moment she could to amuse and encourage her with cheerful companionship. The two rode horseback together in the clear, cold days of early winter. Both knew what was to come, and they used the little pleasures God had given them to keep their spirits up. Anna was "very cheerful and lively," and the smile never left the mother's face. Gently she rallied *"dearest Sad and Dué dear,"* who "do not see our Mountain and bright skies; they do not hear our spinning wheels, nor hear the recreation bell, nor see the merry fry when running out of school, nor mount the old country horses to trot away the rheumatism. Anna and Mother try it with great success."

Then she turned to the long-known secret of her content: "Dearest Eliza, how many pains, how many comforts, but ten of these for one at least—ungrateful!—I should say a hundred at least to a single pain. What is sorrow when the heart is at rest? When it is still, and looks at the All-Wise and All-Merciful thro' every cloud?"

The mother and daughter had much to talk about on their country rides: the fast-growing love of God in Anna's heart; the coming separation—yes, they talked of that, for the mother was a realist and eternity her only reality, and the child had learned well this truth that made all bearable—and the glad news that William was better. They chatted, too, about the things the women of a family love to share: the news from Mary Post that her baby had been weaned and cried piteously now when he saw his mother from the new vantage point of the nursery trundle bed, that she sorely missed her daughter Catherine off at school, that Barclay Bayley had died suddenly in Jamaica—Mary had left it to Elizabeth to draw the moral: "I leave you, my dear, to make your own comment on the wonderful dispensations of Providence."

They talked, too, of Dué who, enjoying an unusual spell of good health, had found her misery in an imaginary fear that she had offended Elizabeth, since she had received no letters for a long while; but especially they talked of Dué's soul, which was hesitating tearfully on the doorstep of the Church. " 'Tis right, my friend," she had said humbly, "that I should thus be tried on all sides; perhaps it is the only way to bring me to truth. I pray for that, my friend, with all the sincerity of my heart; and yet I am still what I was when I left you, between both ways."

The change in Annina's condition, the swift plummeting downward, came at Christmas. So many of Elizabeth's sorrows reached their climax at this happiest season of the year! The holy night itself was a night of watching, made holier still by the First Communion of some of the children. Elizabeth, going to call the house at half-past eleven, found most of it awake and waiting. "Gratitude and love resounded in a moment thro' all the dormitories from young and old," she told Father Babade. "Even dear Annina, laying in her cold sweat and fever, joined the loud chorus."

The sustained, holy cheerfulness of this sixteen-year-old girl, who was entering on her long agony, was truly a marvel. Never was it made clearer that time had nothing to do with holiness. In a scant nine months the vivacious, pretty girl—always innocent and good and pious—had attained what looked very like heroic sanctity. Her progress, like the Magdalen's, was fired by penance and sorrow for sin. Her sins, however, were not the sins of the Magdalen's, but the little pamperings of the flesh; the fond half-turnings to the world, the quarrels and fits of impatience, the prayers half-attended to, the impulsive breaking of silence, but to her they were enormities—the sure sign that she had passed beyond simple goodness to the company of God's wholehearted few.

Once she had taken up the religious life, she did so in earnest. When her mother—now her religious mother, too—admonished her "for the little care of her health: rising at the first bell and being on the watch to ring it the moment the clock struck, washing at the pump in the severest weather, often eating what sickened her stomach"—

" 'Ah, dear Mother,' she replied, coloring deeply as if she was wounding humility, 'if Our Lord called me up to meditate, was I wrong to go? If I washed at the pump, did not others more delicate do it? If I ate what I did not like, was it not proper, since it was but a common Christian act to control my appetite?' "

Perhaps what the girl had done was not wise, but it was the simple approach of youth to the challenge of mortification.

Annina's sufferings were excrutiating. The consumption not only devoured her lungs but apparently spread to the bones, which protruded at places. Her whole body throbbed with pain, and her nerves were so drawn that she could not at times focus her eyes. A seton—horrible pun on her name!—which was a cord introduced under the skin and pulled each day to keep a passage open for drainage, festered her side and added to her suffering. She accepted it eagerly: "Let me pay my penance for so often drawing in my waist to look small and imitate the looks of my companions," she said, "let the ribs draw now with pain for having drawn with vanity."

Elizabeth kept a detailed diary of Annina's ordeal, as she had of Will's in the *lazaretto*. It is an unflinching saga of pain, graphic in description as the old Acts of the Martyrs. Only the great love and pity coursing through it save it from being macabre and horrible. How a mother could have written it, or read it over afterward, is a mystery. But the age was a strong-minded and earthy one, and even spiritual doctrine was often taught in the grim accents of Louis of Granada. Only a soul so nurtured could call in the little boarders—as Annina did—and displaying the horror of her wasted, discolored body, remind them that they, too, would come to grips with death.

And who, after all, are more right, more honest: the soft ones of today, reveling in the frank, gamey language of stage and screen and novel, yet drawing back from the first touch of discomfort, or the heroic young girl who suffered so gladly and the brave little mother who recorded it?

The picture was not all stark, however, but mellowed by a great pathos and compassion. The mother and daughter drew closer in a most sacred union that strove valiantly to shut out the merely human: Elizabeth gently but firmly pressing Annina to the fullest, holiest exploitation of her pains, Annina rebuking Elizabeth when the mother could not hold back her tears.

On January 30, 1812, Father Dubois anointed the dying girl. "The desire for the Holy Oil seemed almost to disturb her," Elizabeth wrote, "but Our Dearest was so good as to hasten our wish. The Reverend Superior arrived. What a moment for her! He must wait for a book, and she kept her eyes on a crucifix when the pouring sweat and agony of pain would permit. When it came, she presented her hands the moment they were wanted, with such a look of joy!!! Oh, happy, happy Mother in that hour and moment!" Elizabeth shared the moment with Sad, for she knew her friend would understand what it meant to her to see her child "receive the last Sacraments with my sentiments of them."

On the next day, January 31, Annina was formally received into the Sisterhood by Father Dubois. "Dear Mother," she confided happily, "I could not but be amused to hear Mr. Dubois say so much about consecration, having been accustomed long before my illness to perform this act, and since continually repeating it. But now it is to be done that I may become a Sister, and be numbered among the children of Blessed St. Vincent." Some weeks later Elizabeth told her that Father Bruté had written to say how pleased he was that she was now a Sister of Charity. The girl's answer was simple and noble: "Yes," she said, "I somehow had to check a rising wish to live ever since that day."

Annina was thus the first Sister to be accepted into the community after the formal ratification of the rules and constitutions, which took place on January 17, 1812. The changes from the original rule of St. Vincent were very slight. Elizabeth was permitted to retain dominion over her children and their worldly goods, while holding the post of Mother Superior; she was also pronounced eligible for reelection to office even beyond the two terms provided by the constitutions. Education was named as an end of the Institute, and the admission of boarders was provided for. Otherwise, the American and the French rules were identical.

The great step taken, Elizabeth wrote in awe: "Eternity! Mother! What a celestial commission entrusted! Mother of the Daughters of Charity, by whom so much is to do also for God through their short life!"

The Sisters entered a retreat conducted by Father Dubois on February 2, the feast of the Purification: there they were informed that the rules would be tried for a year, and at the end of this period the Sisters would be admitted to vows.

On this same feast of the Purification Elizabeth wrote with a kind of exaltation:

> At the feet of our sweet, happy Mother Mary, listening to dear old Simeon doting on the darling Babe—offering the precious sufferer in my arms when He entered our chamber—and oh, to hold them both up to the Eternal Father! The child offering the mother, the mother the child. The sweet half-hour of love and peace with Jesus between us, as she sits on her bed of pain and I kneel beside her. Covering her when she laid down and giving her the usual cross on the forehead—she said, with the most endearing smile:
>
> "Yet a little while you see me, again a little while you shall not see me, because I go to my Father."
>
> Then, as if she feared it was too much to use such sacred words, added: "So says my dear Lord."
>
> In her sleep she cried out:
>
> "Oh, eternity, eternity!"

Distance dulls the apprehension of trouble, and despite the frankness with which Elizabeth had described Annina's condition, neither Julia Scott nor Mary Post realized how close to death she was. Both wrote letters urging Elizabeth to let the girl come to them for the benefits of change of air and surroundings. Julia wrote an unusually humorous letter, no doubt to cheer up both mother and daughter.

> What do you do with yourself in the mountains, my dear friend, such severe weather as we have lately had? As to me, whose likeness to a frozen turnip I daresay you well remember, I have been perfectly congealed, my limbs stiffened and faculties all benumbed notwithstanding I was within a yard of a good fire all the time. For, indeed, I could not bear to remove from it, and kept constantly turning around, like a joint of meat on the spit, lest the neglected side might freeze whilst the other was scorching. This statement is to serve as an apology for not having written to you for some weeks.

The imminent separation from Annina had swung Elizabeth's thoughts the more strongly to the eternity where she would be united with all she loved forever, and had set her to importuning Julia again to think of her soul. She saw her friend "surrounded by circles, smiling and bowing, dissipating care. My Julia, should I ever have the pleasure of seeing you in a tabbed-cap and gray-gown, with eyes and *heart* directed upwards—hush! hush!—I should take my turn at dancing then, and one of my greatest cares would be dissipated—for how can I love, and with so much reason love you, and not think of you in the long, long, long life to come?"

The good-natured Julia protested once more her serious thoughts on the subject:

> Your imagination, I find, still pictures your friend young and gay and fond of company. But you are mistaken indeed, my Eliza. What will you say when I assure you I have not passed five evenings in company—I mean in what is commonly called parties—this winter? I would you could view me at this moment, with a huge pair of spectacles on my nose—without which I can neither read nor write for more than a few minutes. And as to a tab cap, dearest, that I have worn for some months, for there is nothing more fashionable; and, besides, I have grown out of all shape, and am as *broad* as long. Company indeed! If they will but let me sit quietly by the fire, it is all I wish.

"Shall I ever, my Eliza, my best friend, shall I ever have the joy of beholding you again make one of my fireside circle?" Julia finished plaintively. ". . . And yet we are within two hundred miles of each other. That abominable mountain road! You might as well be in Kentucky as where you are—but so it must be."

Mary had good news indeed, that she was coming to see her sister in May; and there were the family doings which Mary never failed to keep Elizabeth abreast of: their brother Richard was off with a cargo to Gibraltar, William to Liverpool, and Carleton at Harlem with "his intended," Grace Roosevelt. Helen was staying at the Posts, "apparently satisfied with having stolen one heart"—Sam Craig's—"and Mary is with [William] Craig, catching all!"

Surely the letters served their purpose of distracting the mother and daughter from their misery for the moment—but the end was inexorably upon them. It came on March 12, 1812. Bruté arrived from Baltimore in time to comfort the dying child, and to leave her for the altar, where he offered the Holy Sacrifice for her happy passing. Annina called after him repeatedly that "she prays for all, all her dear Sisters, Seminary, and all," as he had suggested. It was indeed the moment of the Passion for Elizabeth, who knelt bravely, holding high the crucifix for her child to see, until, led away by the Sisters, she went to stay before the Blessed Sacrament while Annina died.

The very night before, leaning on her mother's knee, the gasping girl had scrawled a last "Consecration at the Foot of the Cross":

> Amiable and adorable Savior, at the foot of Your cross I come to consecrate myself to You forever. . . . O dear Jesus, I offer Thee all my sufferings, little as they now are, and will accept with resignation—Oh, by Thy grace let me say with love!—whatever You will please to send in future. I offer in union with Your blessed merits all the sufferings I ever suffered: those which I endured at a time I did not know how to unite them to Yours, those I have experienced during this last sickness—I offer more particularly to Your glory, and in expiation of the offenses and grievous sins committed during my life. O my Jesus, pardon the impatiences, ill humors and numberless other faults. . . .

St. Joseph's was a house of sorrow, for Annina had been loved by all: the Sisters, the boarders—all. Elizabeth was absolutely wooden in her grief, and moved like one who had lost contact with reality. When her boys arrived from the Mountain, however, she stopped their violent sobbing with a word. "You are men, and Mother looks for support from you," she said.

Annina was buried the next afternoon at one o'clock—the third to be laid in the "little sacred wood," and the third Seton. It was an unusually poignant procession, as the funeral processions of the young always are, with the girls all in white except for the members of Annina's "community" or spiritual class, who wore black shawls; the Sisters, the four remaining Seton children—and the little mother. When the graveside prayers were said, and all had turned away in solemn, uneasy silence, one tear was seen to glisten on her cheek; only this, and the slow, strong, almost fierce, words: "Father, Thy Will be done!"

The words had fought their way up from the calm depths of her soul where the storm of her daughter's death had driven her—that beautiful daughter who was her firstborn, her friend and companion, her support in the *lazaretto* and the empty days that had followed, her spur to the

Church, her comfort in persecution, that daughter who had almost broken her heart but had so fully mended it. The death of Annina desolated Elizabeth as no death before ever had, as no death after ever would. Her Superior and Director, Father Dubois, was awed and disturbed by the force of the desolation, so much so that he did a shocking thing: he wrote about it to Father Bruté, discussing its impact on Elizabeth and other intimate details of her spiritual life that no director had a right to reveal to anyone. But reveal them he did, and they now stand revealed. In the same wrongful way he was to talk about what he considered faults of poverty in her, in a letter written after her death to Mother Rose. To Bruté he said now, on May 7, 1812:

> I fear that the terrible trial she suffered at the death of Annina was intended to put an end to or to curb the exaggerated pleasure she took in praising her; to banish the excessive fear she felt lest her daughter say or do something too human when in the presence of others. The excuse was her fear of scandal, but I am afraid there was something else besides that. A hundred times I wanted to probe this wound; but it is only lately that I dared to touch it.

And he finished in a tone of caution: "When I speak to you of the trial in connection with Annina, and its probable cause, do not touch this chord as I do now—that would drive the poor mother to despair."

Elizabeth herself told George Weis: "For three months after Nina was taken I was so often expecting to lose my senses, and my head was so disordered, that unless for the daily duties always before me, I did not know much what I did or what I left undone." A week after the funeral Elizabeth could write to Julia "a very few words only from the solitary heart of the Mother who left her darling in the woods with Harriet and Cicil. . . . I am well, just going to the Mountain for a walk. PEACE!" By the beginning of May, however, the floodgates burst, and she emptied her heart to Sad in a healing stream of remembrance:

> The remembrance of my lovely one now forces itself in every moment: her singular modesty and grace of action, the lifting her eyes from the ground to cast the rays of her very soul into mine—which was often her only expression of her desires or wishes, and now I am so happy to think I never contradicted any of them—her rational and pure sentiments set down in so many ways, the neatness and order of all her little affairs, and ingenious way of uniting economy and elegance in her plain and simple

dress—this was always a delight to poor Mother, but now an *admiration;* and it appears to me I never saw or shall see anything to be compared to her.

Poor, poor Mother, let her talk to you, Eliza.

If you could have seen at the moment, when kneeling at the foot of her bed to rub her cold, cold feet a day or two before—she saw the tears, and without being able to hide her own, tho' smiling at the same time, she repeated the so-often-asked question:

"Can it be for me? Should you not rejoice? It will be but a moment, and reunited for Eternity. A happy eternity with my Mother—what a thought!"

These were her very words. And when in death's agony her quivering lips could with difficulty utter one word, feeling a tear fall on her face, she smiled and said with great effort: *"Laugh, Mother, Jesus!"*—at intervals, as she could not put two words together. . . .

Poor Mother must say no more now; only pray, Eliza, that she may be strengthened. . . . You believe me when I say with my whole soul, "His Will be done forever!"

Eternity was Anna's darling word. I find it written in everything that belonged to her: music, books, copies, the walls of her little chamber, everywhere that word.

It was a severe, a long-lasting grief—she would talk of Annina until she died, for no mother ever forgets a dead child—but it was a grief of the heart only, never a grief of the soul. Natural grief, grief at times beyond human control, is one thing; resignation is something else again— and Elizabeth was resigned from the first moment of her darling's illness. With her usual penetration, she knew how to make the distinction: "The separation from my angel has left so new and deep an impression on my mind, that if I was not obliged to live in these dear ones [her remaining children], I should unconsciously die in her; unconsciously— for never by a free act of the mind will I ever regret His Will." She knew that her Adored had said: "Father, if it be possible, let this chalice pass from Me," but had added, "nevertheless, not My Will but Thine be done"; and even, "My God, My God, why hast Thou forsaken Me?"—but He had also said, "Father, into Thy Hands I commend My Spirit."

Mary came to the Valley with her husband, Wright Post, in May, as she had promised. It was a short visit, but a joyous one, for the two sisters had not seen each other in four years. There was much to talk about, much to weep over together; and the tears came on Mary's face one evening as she sat in the infirmary on the bed where her niece had died and listened to the little children sing a hymn they called the *Hymn of Anna.*

Mary was captivated with the Sisterhood. She wrote to Elizabeth the minute she got home:

> I left you, dear Sister, with sensations I cannot describe. It seemed to me as if I must have crossed the threshold of existence. . . . I left you giving the spring to action, and consistency to visions of the soul, that might sometimes occupy good minds in a perspective contemplation. It seemed to me that I had actually seen an order of beings who had nothing to do with the ordinary cares of this life, and were so far admitted to the society of the blessed as to take pleasure in the same employments, while they were at the same time exempt from the solicitude for, from having ceased to have a value for what usually occupy the attention of mortals.

Elizabeth's brother-in-law, too, was "deeply impressed." Riding home in the stage, the husband and wife had suddenly realized that they had been so deep in another world that they, the most devoted of parents, had scarcely given their children a thought! And the visit had finally scotched the fears of Elizabeth's friends that she was living in squalor and destitution. Had Mary come even a year before, she might have carried a different tale back to New York, but now she was able to tell everyone eagerly of how "elegantly situated" her sister was.

The community of St. Joseph's had come a long way in two years. The finished "White House" was indeed spacious and gleaming, the fields around it green and dotted with wildflowers or under cultivation, the farmyard had a growing colony of cows and pigs and chickens—and everything was kept in its place by neat fences: even the little cemetery was a picture, with its enclosure of white palings and the heaps of fresh flowers the children delighted to keep on the three lonely graves. There were eighteen Sisters, nearly thirty boarders and about twenty day pupils.

Mary Post could not know, however, that all this property had yet to be paid for. At the time of her visit and for many months before—and indeed all during Annina's illness—Elizabeth had serious financial worries, which she had outlined for General Robert Goodloe Harper of Baltimore the previous December:

The promising and amiable perspective of establishing a house of plain and useful education, retired from the extravagance of the world, connected also with the view of providing nurses for the sick and poor, an abode of innocence and refuge of affliction, is, I fear, now disappearing under the pressure of debts contracted at its very foundation.

Having received the pensions of our boarders in advance and with them obliged not only to maintain ourselves but also to discharge the endless demands of carpenters and workmen, we are reduced now to our credit, which is poor indeed. The credit of twenty poor women, who are capable only of earning their daily bread, is but a small stock, particularly when their flour merchant, grocer and butcher are more already in advance than they are willing to afford.

She was at a loss what to do. Father Dubourg had previously suggested that she might write to a number of wealthy Catholics for assistance: "Mrs. Caton, Mrs. Harper, Mrs. Patterson, Mrs. Montgomery . . . the old gentleman (Charles Carroll) and also Mrs. Bonaparte, who being now an imperial princess might perhaps think it suitable to her new dignity to pay for the honor of protecting the Sisters of Charity. . . . Madame de Neuville (wife of the French Ambassador) . . . would, I believe, be gratified at the idea of being one of your foundresses, as she had been in France a great benefactress of your society . . . It may be the means by which He (God) intends to supply you, as it is indeed the one by which St. Vincent de Paul has made all his great foundations."

Elizabeth did not follow this advice to any great extent, although she suggested to Mrs. Harper, who was the daughter of Charles Carroll, to "tell your sweet nieces to look at the price of a shawl or vest and think of the poor family of St. Joseph." She may have thought it more practical to enlist one of the members of fashionable society to beg for her —as St. Vincent had enlisted the Duchesse d'Aiguilon and others—for in her December letter to General Harper she had asked him: "Will a friendly hand assist us, become our guardian protector, plead our cause with the rich and powerful, serve the cause of humanity and be a father to the poor? Would Mrs. Harper be interested for us . . .?"—and perhaps it was through the good offices of the Harpers that several of the ladies mentioned by Dubourg made donations to the sisterhood.

The harried Mother wrote also to Bishop Cheverus to ask him what he thought of her making a personal begging tour through the principal cities of Baltimore, Philadelphia, New York and Boston. The prelate discouraged the proposal because "in the present situation of affairs, very little, I am afraid, would be collected. An application by a circular letter would hardly produce anything, but at least it would not be attended with the same inconveniences. . . ." In the good man's opinion, Catholic America was not yet ready for the methods of collecting funds for charity that have become routine.

Elizabeth could not look to the Filicchis for help: because of the effective sealing off of Europe, she would not even hear from them for several years; and Cheverus felt that, according to the last instructions from Italy, she could draw only on those funds needed for herself and her children. Julia Scott kept up her regular, generous gifts, and some of these, at least, went to the Sisters' support. But, in the end, Elizabeth had to fall back on the tuition of the boarders to find solvency. It was a tribute to her administrative ability—which she always deprecated—that four years after these desperate days of 1812, the institution was on a paying basis.

To arrive at this happy condition, however, Elizabeth had to push into the background her dream of a school only for the poor, and allow her establishment to become an academy for the well-to-do; she had hinted that it would come to this in her letter to Harper. Thus it was that some of the most famous Catholic names of the day appeared on the school roster: Harper, Carroll, Brent, Barry, Chatard, Godefroy.

There were always poor or non-paying pupils, of course; and these were put in a special class called St. Joseph's Class, which did not admit of the extra educational fillips paid for by the boarders. If exceptionally bright pupils were found among the members of St. Joseph's Class, the Sisters would give them private instruction on the side. In any case, the poor were not refused except in hard times when the Sisters had not the funds to receive them.

The school was well run—both Elizabeth and Father Dubois had educational experience—and functioned smoothly even at the start when conditions were primitive. To these two, John Dubois and Mother Seton, must go all the credit for the soundness, quality, and maturity of the system. Elizabeth was, of course, principal or headmistress, and also taught certain classes in history and religion; as time went on she was able to confine herself to her proper duties of administration and supervision. She went the rounds of the classrooms every day, and made a detailed inspection of each class at least once a month, paying special attention to the ability of the teacher and the aptitude and progress of the pupils. On these occasions she would sit in the back of the room, eyes closed, absorbed and thoughtful.

The school Sisters, besides Elizabeth, were Cecilia O'Conway, Fanny Jordan and Margaret George, who had entered the community on February 14, 1811. They were assisted by lay teachers, uniformly competent in their fields. The names of two of these have come down to us: the French teacher, Madame Guérin, whom Father Dubourg had brought from Martinque, and who later joined the community as Sister Madeleine, and Madame Séguin, who was so fine a musician that she gave distinction to the school and was well paid for it.

The curriculum embraced reading, writing, spelling, grammar, geography and arithmetic. Tuition was first set at $100.00, then went quickly to $110.00, then to $125.00. Music, needlework and languages were privately taught at fees ranging from $5.00 to $8.00.

The school day was as long and arduous as that of many modern seminaries. The children rose at a quarter to six, and were in chapel for morning prayers at a quarter after. There was a short study period either before or after Mass, depending upon when the priest arrived, and breakfast was at 7:30. Classes began at eight and continued until 11:30, when the children said the Rosary in common. The recreation time after dinner lasted until three o'clock. The girls then went to their respective classrooms and started the afternoon session with a brief "adoration." There was another recreation period at five, and then study until supper at 7:15. After supper the older girls listened to the reading of a spiritual book, while the younger ones often went right to bed.

Diligence and achievement in study were rewarded in the way of Sisters by the bestowal of holy pictures, statues, medals and books. The lack of these qualities was punished by public disgrace, the names of careless or lazy pupils being read out in the refectory once a week. Stubborn cases were sent to Mother Seton for a lecture and a penance, and the hopeless were sent home.

Discipline was in the hands of Sister Kitty Mullen. She had no easy task, for she had to regulate the behavior of every child in every waking moment, in school or out. She had help, of course, each group of ten children, called a decury, being under the immediate supervision of a Sister prefect or "angel." The more serious faults were reported in writing to Mother Seton at the end of each week, and she did the correcting and punishing.

As a mother, Elizabeth applied the familiar penalties of the home. A favorite one was a spiritual variation of standing-in-the-corner; the culprit would be made to kneel or sit on a bench in front of Mother's prized picture of the Redeemer for a length of time commensurate with the offense; and the spot quickly became every bit as ignominious as a town whipping post or gallows. Thus, Mary Harper, the daughter of General Harper, famous lawyer, orator, congressman and senator, and granddaughter of Charles Carroll, one day snobbishly asked a playmate: "Do you know who I am? I am the daughter of General Robert Goodloe Harper!" Mary soon found herself sitting before the picture until she had come to a humble knowledge that the General's daughter really was no better than anyone else.

On another occasion, Elizabeth used a mother's equally classic refusal of sympathy. A little redheaded girl, who had taken a real envy toward the lovely dark hair of one of the Sisters, tormented the Sister until the nun seized a stick and thwacked her where it would do the most good. The child ran sobbing to Mother, but all the comfort she got was, "Served you right!"

Sometimes Elizabeth used ridicule. Old Sister Martha remembered in 1886 that, as a child in school, she had taken a scissors one day and snipped off her curls. "Look at that child!" Mother Seton exclaimed. "What has she done that for? I believe I will call her Harry, for she's made herself look so much like a boy!" With quick wit Sister Fanny countered, "No, Mother, call her Bob, because she has bobbed herself!" And the name stuck.

The overall complexion of the education at St. Joseph's was, however, moral and spiritual, and this was almost entirely the doing of Mother Seton. Like the goodness of God which must diffuse itself, her essential holiness touched and changed everyone she met. Her school was a Catholic one and in her eyes it was a failure unless it educated its students to lead devout Catholic lives, that is, to see the purpose of human existence in the true focus of eternity. In this sense, no jumble of technicalities and definitions can obscure the fact that St. Joseph's Academy was the archetype of American Catholic elementary education.

Elizabeth's methods of teaching goodness were eminently practical and worthy of study. There was, of course, the most effective method of all, the example of her own sanctity. No child could miss the lessons of her quiet recollection, her absorbed prayer, her shining Communions and—best of all to a child's mind—the obvious happiness these brought her.

The girls knew that she loved them, and they loved her in return: not only for her charm, her gentle playfulness, her smile, her solicitude, but because of what shone from her eyes and lighted all her face. It was this that sent them running to her, that made them desperate for her approbation. It was this that made them think the day perfect that brought them one of her constant little spiritual notes, such as this: "Mother begs Our Lord to bless her dear Eliza that she may be an ever-blooming rose in His paradise. Come under the shawl this morning, and love and bless Our Jesus—your poor, affectionate Mother." It was the maternal tenderness within her that made them always remember her best with her arms flung wide to embrace.

Twice a week Elizabeth gave formal spiritual instructions or conferences to the older girls, and then allowed them to ask questions. Here she showed a perfect balance of matter and method. At the start she quieted any uneasiness they might feel, lest she be trying to smother them with religion: "Your little Mother, my darlings, does not come to teach you how to be good nuns or Sisters of Charity," she would say plainly, "but rather I would wish to fit you for that world in which you are destined to live: to teach you how to be good . . . mothers of families." She did not discourse on virtue to minds so young; rather, she *taught* it, making liberal use of stories, examples and applications.

Setting out to warn her girls of the dangers that lay in frequenting balls, the theatre, the gay world, for example, she began: "The fable says that a butterfly asked an owl what she should do to keep from burning her wings, since she could never come to the candle without singeing them. The owl counselled her to abstain from looking even at the smoke of it." With such a start, it was not hard to draw the moral that occasions of sin must be avoided; and she strengthened her theme by wisely and realistically identifying her hearers with the fable: "You will first burn your wings, poor little moth(s), before you will withdraw from the flame. In all these cases, there is more safety in our fear than in our strength; it is ever easier to abstain from such pleasures than to use them well."

To get across the point that the direction of intention was necessary to spiritual advancement, Elizabeth used the analogy of an artist: "If a painter should draw his lines without proposing any idea to himself, his work would be a blot." And she described the heart properly prepared for Holy Communion as "a crystal vial filled with clear water, in which the least mote of uncleanness may be seen."

All her teaching had the simple directness of the Gospels, and she imitated the Divine Teacher by drawing on things familiar to her hearers for her clear, uncomplicated parables and illustrations.

Elizabeth was vivid in everything she did and said. It is little wonder that anyone who had known her, even in passing, could never forget her. Certainly "her girls" did not. Long after they had left the Valley they kept up a correspondence with their Mother—they always used the religious term in the intimate accents of children—asking her advice: How can I get over this dreadful fear of confession? Would it be wrong to accept the attentions of this young man?—and a host of lesser things. Often it was just for the sheer joy of a chat, a return for the space of a letter to the remembered peace of their school days. And, despite the demands of the rule, the press of duties, the many letters to parents and merchants and superiors that kept the pen in her hand almost continuously, she always found a stray, unused moment for a note in reply.

Annina was not yet dead when Elizabeth's baby, ten-year-old Rebecca, began her long, slow descent to the grave. It started casually enough with a fall on the ice which no one paid much attention to at the time. Rebecca, in fact, hid her pain for two reasons: a child's—she slept in her mother's room and did not want to be taken from it to the infirmary, and a grown-up's—she was unwilling to add to her mother's troubles. But the hip was seriously injured, and Bec aggravated the injury by continuing to walk as straight as possible, despite the increasing pain, so that no one would notice her lameness. By the time her Uncle Wright Post looked at it in May, it was beyond all remedy.

The Posts had gotten in their visit just in time, for war erupted in June. The British, desperate to keep their supremacy of the seas as a balance of power against Napoleon, who held most of Europe, had for years been kidnapping men to man their ships. Between 1804 and 1807 alone they had taken 6,000 men from American ships, and had lately grown so bold as to sail into American ports on their impressment raids. Jefferson had long temporized, attempting to fight physical force with economic measures such as the Embargo Act. The indignation of the country grew, however, and there were repeated demands for the conquest of Canada, to drive the British from "our continent." When young firebrands like Henry Clay and John C. Calhoun came to Congress in 1811, they gave the popular indignation official tongue; and by June 1, 1812, President James Madison had no choice but to send a war message to Capitol Hill. War was declared on June 18.

Almost immediately the City of Baltimore broke out in civil violence. Feeling ran so strong among those who favored the war and those who did not that both factions fell to killing each other in the streets of the gracious old town. Eliza Sadler, who had been visiting in Wilmington and had thought of traveling the remaining distance to see Elizabeth, turned around and went home; thus political passion deprived the two of ever seeing each other again.

Little Rebecca, however, was in Baltimore that dangerous summer. The kind Dué, as soon as she had heard of Bec's trouble, had written Elizabeth of a new method of treatment for such an injury practiced in New York; but Elizabeth was unwilling to subject the child to the long, uncomfortable journey or to spend the money for it without some assurance of success, and wrote to Dr. Chatard for his opinion.

In the meantime, General Harper came to Emmitsburg, and so insisted that Bec return with him to be placed under Dr. Chatard's care—even to taking the child for a trial run in his carriage to the Mountain to see whether she could bear the trip—that Elizabeth had to give way. The poor mother was touched by the solicitude of the Harpers, the Catons and particularly Dr. Chatard. "Oh, lay my heart at his feet!" she wrote to the great man's wife. "The tears begin to flow at the first thought of his goodness to all I have loved." But she commanded: "You will not let her go from under your roof without yourself, at least. Some little companions she loved much when they were here may be troublesome to you, but you will regulate all; and beg your dear Chatard to forbid her being taken abroad, even if able to go. And she will be returned the first opportunity, if he finds there is no remedy. . . . She is poor, you know, and must not mind the wardrobe." Elizabeth did not want the winning little girl spoiled by indulgent people, such as the Catons.

Even the eminent French physician could do nothing, however, for Rebecca; he concurred with Wright Post, saying that the pain would go in time, but that she would be permanently crippled.

On September 28 Gabriel Bruté came to the Mountain to stay on as assistant to Father Dubois, and almost immediately Elizabeth began to relish him as a spiritual director. Thus began the golden age of her soul.

Although so young in the priesthood, Bruté was old in the ways of God. More to the point, he had a glorious spiritual affinity with Elizabeth: both were of the same volatile, enthusiastic, ardent nature, with a religious response that bubbled and boiled like a cauldron long on the fire. It was this affinity that made their relationship almost unique in spiritual history, for they mutually aided each other to God, more in the manner of friends than as director and penitent. In this sense Elizabeth often guided Bruté spiritually as much as he guided her—not, of course, in the official way especially blessed by God, for he had the grace of his office and priesthood, which she had not. They thought and acted and prayed as one soul. He looked upon Elizabeth as a mother: to her he was a brother or a son; eschewing the formal "Mister" of normal clerical address, she freely called him Gabriel or, more often, simply "G."

John Dubois had tried to give Bruté some idea of Elizabeth's soul. In doing so, he had recognized the greatness of it, conceding that "a first-class saint, a St. Francis de Sales," would be needed to understand and direct it adequately. He admitted quite humbly that he could not, and the unfortunate analogy he used bears this out: Elizabeth's soul, he said, was "like gold brocade, rich and heavy . . . hard to handle." If this were so, it was rather because her soul resembled the flag of her free country, whipping in the breeze. Hers was essentially a free soul, for the truth had made it free; and while firmly tied to the pole of standard religious rules, moved freely in the winds of the Spirit— the ardors, the enthusiasms, the spontaneous prayers and ejaculations and acts of devotion.

Gabriel Bruté understood this, because his own soul was so similar, and he gave Elizabeth the space and air she needed. He even blew upon it with his own flashing, almost at times incoherent, spiritual cries and aspirations, and watched with satisfaction as it responded into leaping, straining life.

Elizabeth's joy in Bruté's understanding was unbounded: "Blessed G., I am so in love now with rules," she cried, "that I see the *bit* of the bridle all gold, or the *reins* all of silk. You know my sincerity, since, with the little attraction to your Brother's [Dubois'] government, I even eagerly seek the grace [of the] little cords he entangles me with."

From this time on the story of Elizabeth Seton's soul is the story of a correspondence, an intimate, exalted exchange of notes and jottings dashed off, rather than of formal letters.

Bruté was having an agonizing time of it with the language of America, and Elizabeth renewed her attempts to teach him—attempts they were, for he was never to be wholly successful in substituting English for the chattering French tongue in which he could pour out the turbulence within him. He was beginning manfully to preach in his new language now—"bad preaching as it may be," he conceded—for it was the only way "to force this dreadful English into my backward head." He would bring the bare outlines of his sermons and conferences to Elizabeth, often just the bare thoughts, and she would flesh them out into astoundingly beautiful homilies. The balanced sentences, the formal paragraphs, did not straiten him, for he kindled in the pulpit and his driving sincerity came through to form a memorable bond with his hearers.

Bruté's first sermon to the Sisters was on the occasion of the funeral of Sister Maria Murphy, who died on October 15, and he did well enough. Maria had been Elizabeth's second recruit, and had joined the community over the objections of her mother. She was a good Sister, so gentle that Elizabeth had nicknamed her "my dove," but so burning inwardly with divine love that, when the Viaticum was brought her, she almost fell out of bed to meet her God, crying out in a transport, "O my Jesus, my dear Lord!" Maria was the first of Elizabeth's daughters not bound to her by family ties to die, and it pleased her "to have been, and to be still, *her Mother!* The natural one was *present*, but the spiritual one, who had all her dear little secrets of the soul, was the dearest."

Maria was soon followed by Ellen Thompson, who died the next month, only ten minutes after receiving Holy Communion. "O happy Mother!" Bruté exclaimed to Elizabeth, "Already three of your dear daughters in heaven, not counting the first two, the tender sisters whom your example has already led there. Give, give thanks, and redouble your zeal to follow these celestial souls!"

On October 7 Archbishop Carroll came to the Valley to give Confirmation. Though neither knew it, it was the last time that the Father of the American Church and its Mother were to meet. It was the last time the young Setons would embrace the kindly old man who was as much parent as prelate to them.

In a recent letter Julia Scott had asked the ages of the Seton children and Elizabeth seized the occasion to take stock of her little brood. "The most interesting, endearing of little mortals, our Kitty, is in her thirteenth year . . ." she told her friend. "For the mind's education I think very, very few children can surpass her." Rebecca was "all gaiety and smartness, very sensible, and advanced in everything a child of her age (in her eleventh year) should know, very fond of music and always of late at her piano."

Elizabeth protested her friend's assumption that she was training her children to follow their mother's vocation:

> Dearest Julia, you talk of making nuns like making bread. How can I make my dear ones love the life I love . . .? The truth is, I never look beyond year to year for either myself or them, as you know how much my constitution was long ago impaired; and my children have the most marked symptoms of our family complaint, and look forward themselves with cheerfulness and pleasure to an early reunion where there is no separation—especially the girls.
>
> William and Richard look forward to the world in that kind of a doubt which is unavoidable after the fate of so many of our family. But their chief thought and desire is always to be near Mother. Certainly, before long, they must declare what they intend for their future employment.

I never urge them, as I know their talents are not brilliant; and they may, after some time, be better able to judge for themselves.

It was a hardheaded appraisal, particularly of the prospect of death, and many a mother would not have had the courage to make it; but it agreed with the truth. Earlier Elizabeth had told Sad that her children were so familiar "with death, they have marked out my place next to Nina, and every day some new rose bush or shrub or flower is carried there. Kitty will sometimes kiss me in a transport and ask: "Oh, Mother, won't we be happy when we are there?" Little Bec is more given to tears, and often says: "*If I should be left behind—!*"

Even William, after the burial of Annina, had blurted out: "Now, my Mother, your prayers must be for *me*, that *I, too*—"; but he could not finish. Elizabeth's fears for William were lessened that fall, however, for he and Richard—who were sixteen and fourteen now—had worked for the first time in bringing in the harvest both at the Mount and at St. Joseph's, and it had done them so much good that she told Sad: "All my alarms for William are over." She never worried much about Richard's health, for, unlike the others, he was so big and robust of body that they called him "the giant" and "Daddy Dick."

With all this talk of illness and death, it must not be thought that the family circle was lugubrious. On the contrary, it was unusually joyous and laughing and happy. The brothers and sisters got along well together, and their relationship was even characterized by a great tenderness.

In November Elizabeth assured Sad that "all is well. The dear ones and Mother have just been dining round our old breakfast table on roast pork and stewed apples, like true Yankees. William and Richard as merry and innocent as if they were five years younger. They are on their weekly visit to the Valley, which they truly enjoy." How much this weekly get-together meant to them was apparent from a note of William's, written to Catherine in 1823: "If we could only get into the little breakfast-parlor again . . .!" These two were very much alike, inclined to be quiet and serious, but at the same time fond of people and travel—time was to prove that Kit was Bill's match in roving the world. Bec and Dick, on the other hand, had similar dispositions. She was a merry little madcap, and he so given to fun and nonsense as to be at

times downright foolish. Naturally enough, he was Bec's favorite, and
could easily send her into whoops of laughter.

All was well with the outside circle of Elizabeth's friends and relatives
that autumn, too. Dué had at last taken the step into the Church and,
Sad informed Elizabeth, was showing an astonishing bravery under the
fire of disapproval. "And my Dué dear is really so courageous as to
hold up her head to the world in a case where her poor friend looked
and often felt like a culprit!" exclaimed Elizabeth. "But so it is. Those
who seem strongest are sometimes weakest." Father Anthony Kohlmann
was afraid Dué would meet with her most painful opposition when
Captain Dupleix returned from his latest voyage and found his wife a
Catholic. Whether the priest's uneasiness proved right or not, Dué
persevered, and became one of Kohlmann's best workers and a real
mother to the poor.

Mary Post's biggest news was that their half-brother Richard had
married Catherine White, granddaughter of a British Admiral and a Van
Cortlandt, on October 26 at Kingsbridge, and all the family, except William, had attended—Mary herself, Helen, Mary Fitch Bayley, and Carleton and his fiancee.

A letter came also from Joseph Bayley, her father's friend and protégé,
and Elizabeth recorded that it "lifted my heart to the skies. How foolish
nature loves to be cherished!"

Tucked away in her Valley, Elizabeth scarcely knew there was a war,
except when prices rose to worry her. She complained about the mails,
which ordinarily were "bad indeed," but now were "crazy," and added
with a touch of naïveté, "I have heard that there have been political
quarrels which interrupt the mail." She compared her peaceful life with
Julia's: "Your wheel is always going round, every few weeks some change.
Mine stands almost still, only that, as I grow older, my health is better;
and this fine, clear weather [I] feel as well and as gay as when Betsey Bayley used to race up your steps in Broadway to get a [glimpse] of her Glorianna before a walk out to Brannon's."

But her thoughts were always with Anna and the life ahead. She had
had a harrowing spiritual experience at Anna's grave in September, and
had written it down when the fainting mood was still upon her:

Begging, crying to Mary to behold her Son and plead for us, and to Jesus to behold His Mother—to pity a Mother, a poor, poor Mother so uncertain of reunion.

Then the soul, quieted even by the desolation of the falling leaves around, began to cry out from eternity to eternity: "Thou art God. All shall perish and pass away, but Thou remainest forever." Then the thought of Our Dearest stretched on the cross and His last words coming powerfully— stood up with hands and eyes lifted to the pure heavens, crying our: "Forgive, they know not what they do." Did *she?* Adored! Did she know?

And all the deathbed scene appeared. At this moment, in the silence of all around—a rattling sound rushing towards—along, Annina's grave a snake stretched itself on the dried grass—so large and ugly; and the little gate tied—but nature was able to drag to the place, and strong enough to tie and untie, saying inwardly: "My darling shall not be rooted by the hogs for you!"—then put up the bars, and softly walked away.

Oh, my dear ones, companions of worms and reptiles! And the beautiful soul, WHERE?

That horrible storm was long since past, and she was truly at peace now, the cries of her soul peaceful cries, as the pen flew over the paper on the 25th of January, 1813.

I sit writing by the window, opposite my darling darling's *little* Wood. The white palings appear thro' the trees. Oh, Julia, my Julia, if we may but pass our dear eternity together! Are you good? Do you try to be good? I try with my whole heart. I long so to get above this blue horizon. Oh, my Anna, the child of my soul! All, all dear ones so many years gone before! ETERNAL REUNION!

XX

Mother

1813 was a year of respite and reward—of respite from the incessant shocks and assaults that had battered Elizabeth from the first days in the Valley; and, because she had withstood them so nobly, the reward of witnessing the first perfect fulfillment of the rules and constitutions of the Sisterhood. It was as if the stream of her life, no longer forced to dash over sharp, unyielding rocks, had emerged into a deep, calm pool.

The serenity was in every word of a letter written to Julia Scott on the anniversary of Annina's death: even the agitation for her friend's soul was muted: "Oh, if I could share . . . the peace and contentment of my days and the joyful anticipation of the conclusion of them! Oh, Julia, no lover ever loved, or longed for, the beloved with the ardor of my soul for yours. Perhaps it is a wrong conclusion of mine, from your situation and what I know of the turn of your mind, to think that you have little consideration or value for our dear futurity. Many, many may be your dear thoughts, quite unknown to me, my precious Julia."

The spiritual collaboration with Gabriel Bruté began to produce memorable results. The sermons and instructions, often written out in Elizabeth's hand, are interesting as indices of her soul. It is not always easy to determine what was meant for Bruté's use and what for her own—she, of course, gave conferences and instructions to the Sisters—but their minds and hearts were so much at one that the end results are always reliable mirrors of Elizabeth's soul.

An instruction which Bruté gave on the occasion of First Communion at the Mount, February 2, 1813, is preserved in Elizabeth's writing. It reads in part:

> He who perseveres to the end shall be saved. Piety must be habitual, not by *fits*. It must be persevering, because temptations continue all our life, and *perseverance* alone obtains the crown. Its means are: the Presence of God, good reading, prayer, the Sacraments, good resolutions often renewed, the remembrance of our last ends; and its advantages; habits which secure our predestination, making our life equal, peaceable and consoling, leading to the heavenly crown, where our perseverance will be eternal!!!
> . . . The lesson of perseverance, how necessary on this day—for you a day of anticipated heaven. . . .

There is enough practical material here for an extended retreat.

Thoughts for the feast of the Assumption, 1813—also in Elizabeth's hand—are surely her own, for they are a mother's thoughts.

> Jesus nine months in Mary, feeding on her blood—Oh, Mary! these nine months. Jesus on the breast of Mary, feeding on her milk! How long she must have delayed the weaning of such a child!!!!
> The infancy of Jesus—in her lap—on her knees as on His throne; while the rolling earth, within its sphere, adorned with mountains, trees and flowers, is the throne of Mary and her Blessed Infant, caressing, playing in her arms. O(o), Mary, how weak these words!
> The youth, the obscure life, the public life of Jesus. Mary always, everywhere, in every moment, day and night, conscious she was His Mother! Oh, glorious, happy Mother, even through the sufferings and ignominies of her Son.
> Her full conformity to Him—O(o), virtues of Mary—the constant delight of the Blessed Trinity—she alone giving Them more glory than all heaven together. Mother of God! Mary! Oh the purity of Mary! the humility, patience, love, of Mary!—to imitate at humblest distance.

It is worthy of note that Elizabeth's devotion to the Motherhood of Mary and the filial relationship of Jesus paralleled the like devotions in the spirituality of Louise de Marillac, first Mother of the Daughters of Charity and, like herself, a physical mother and wife and widow. Among Louise's most personal devotions was this adoration of Jesus during His nine months in His Mother's womb—mentioned above by Elizabeth. And Elizabeth once confided to Bruté: "Blessed, it will please your so kind heart to know that this week past or more, our soul's dear Baby has been much more present to me than the beloved babes of former days, when I carried and suckled them. He, the Jesus Babe, so unspeakably near and close, hugged by his poor, silently delighted wild one!"

The great central love of Elizabeth's life was ever, of course, the Holy Eucharist. Bruté, himself very near sainthood, was so impressed by this love that he wrote of it feelingly after her death: "May my heart, my soul, know the grace and prove the grace of the Holy Sacrament of my Jesus as Mother did! Will I ever forget that face, fired with love, melted in tears at His approach in Communion? To the last, exhausted death on that face, as He came—it was still inflamed, and blushed in ardent love, desire inexpressible of eternal union in Him."

Elizabeth's room opened off the chapel, and she never ceased to marvel that God allowed her so close to Him: "I sit or stand opposite His tabernacle all day, and keep the heart to it as the needle to the pole," she confessed in happy wonderment, "—and at night still more, even to folly; since I have little right to be so near to Him."

She apprehended God's Reality in the Blessed Sacrament with extraordinary keenness, and her apprehension never failed to dull the fears of unworthiness that rose in her even while she rushed toward the sacred meeting. Thus she recorded a "most precious Communion, preceded by alarm and thoughts of fear—but all settled in one thought: how He loves and welcomes the poor and desolate. He said, while the soul was preparing: 'See the Blood I shed for you, is at this very hour invoked upon you by your brother [Father Bruté]."

And again: "Watching night and cramped breast made heavy head for Communion. As the tabernacle door opened—the pressing thought: This Bread should not be given to a dog, Lord! Immediately, as the eyes closed, a white old shepherd dog, feeding from the shepherd's hand in the midst of the flock, as I have seen in the fields between Pisa and Florence, came before me. Yes, my Savior, You feed your poor dog, who, at the first sight, can hardly be distinguished from the sheep—but the canine qualities You see!"

It can be imagined what an explosive effect the ardent, realistic holiness of such a soul as Elizabeth's must have had on her Sisters. She herself told Gabriel Bruté that she was "a *torpedo* among them, for they tell the Superior I strike their very joints when I say a word." Due allowance being made for her humility—that she did not talk to Bruté of her maternal tenderness, her essential sympathy and understanding—it is evident that, speaking formally to all the Sisters in a body, she adopted a "no-nonsense" attitude.

She had no patience with doddering or meandering in the spiritual life—patience in such serious matters as salvation or perfection was always her short suit: she had no patience, for example, with the smug assumption of certain Protestants that they would be saved with a minimum of striving, no patience with priests who did not exploit the awesome possibilities of their office to the full. Because of this peremptory readiness to cut to the heart of things, her conferences to her religious daughters were a delight of practicality and sense, couched in the simple, direct, logical words and examples of the teacher

To attain an interior life she told them:

> You must be in right earnest, or you will do little or nothing. . . . What sort of interior life would you lead, if every time the door opens, or if any one passes you, you must look up; if you must hear what is said, though it does not concern you? Or, if you remain silent and in modest attention to your duty, what would be your interior life, if you let your thoughts wander from God? I once heard a silent person say that she was listening to everything around her, and making her Judas reflections on everything that was said and done; and another, that she delighted in silence because she could be thinking of her dear people. But you know better than that.

There is an astonishing similarity here to the plain talk St. Vincent de Paul used in addressing his first daughters; in fact, Elizabeth's formula for perfection was identical with that of St. Catherine Labouré, the future Daughter of Charity and Seer of our Lady who, still a child on her father's farm when Elizabeth was speaking, would be nurtured on Vincent's simplicity. Catherine's formula was: to do what she was supposed to do, as well as she could, and for God. Elizabeth elaborated it for her daughters in this way:

What was the first rule of our dear Savior's life? You know it was to do His Father's Will. Well, then, the first end I propose in our daily work is to do the Will of God; secondly, to do it in the manner He Wills it; and, thirdly, to do it because it is His Will.

I know what His Will is by those who direct me; whatever they bid me do, if it is ever so small in itself, is the Will of God for me. Then do it in the manner He wills it—not sewing an old thing as if it was new, or a new thing as if it was old; not fretting because the oven is too hot, or in a fuss because it is too cold. You understand—not flying and driving because you are hurried, nor creeping like a snail because no one pushes you. Our dear Savior was never in extremes.

The third object is to do this Will because God wills it, that is, to be ready to quit at any moment, and to do anything else we may be called to.

The fundamental practice of all religious life—the constant walking in the Presence of God—was stripped of all verbiage so that the slowest Sister could not miss it: "You will never receive any lively impressions of grace until you overcome . . . dissipation of mind. If you are ever so fervent at your prayers, or desire ever so much to be good, it will be all like putting hartshorn in a bottle and leaving the cork out. What will it be worth? So all the prayers, readings and good talk you love so much will be to little purpose, unless you place a sentinel at the door of your heart and mind. You often lose in ten minutes by your dissipation of mind more than you had gained a whole day by mortification."

At times she would be overcome by the longing of the saints, and would cry out:

How is it that many of us keep the rule as to the letter of it, and also look pious enough—there is no want of good will, nor idleness indulged— and in a house where it would seem so easy to become saints, you would say, what is the matter? Why are we not saints? Why is there so little progress in perfection, or rather, why are so many tepid, heavy, discouraged, and going along more like slaves in a workhouse than children in their own home and the house of their Father? Why?

Because we do not watch over our interior, do not watch the impulse of nature and grace in our actions, nor avoid the occasions of the habitual faults we live in when it is in our power, or keep a good guard on ourselves when it is not.

Frequent indulgences of useless thoughts, inconsiderate words, expressions of natural feelings and changes of temper, all stand at variance with our sweet interior life, and stop the operation of divine grace, too often indeed even to grieving the divine Spirit and sending Him away.

It especially grieved Elizabeth when the young, new candidates did not run as eagerly in the heavenly way as they might. "Young people especially should fight cheerfully," she reminded them, "since Our Lord has so kindly called you in the morning of your days, and not exposed you to the anguish and remorse we feel after so many years of sin. It moves my very soul to see you young ones taken and sheltered by Our dear Lord, and yet you often look ungrateful . . . can you expect to go to heaven for nothing? Did not Our dear Savior track the whole way to it with His tears and Blood?—and yet you start at every little pain."

Ruthless as she might be in pointing out failure, Elizabeth never left her children desolate. "One particular point you must attend to," she told them. "As soon as you have committed a fault, make your quick act of contrition for it, for fear it draw you into another, as one weight pulls another after it. Make your sincere acts of contrition by a loving and sorrowful turn of your heart to Our dear Savior; and, then, instead of pondering your fault, try to think no more about it, only to guard against repeating it, or to say *Paters* and *Aves* in penance for it while you work. Every day must bring its trials; why, then, should we be troubled and surprised?"

And she urged another remedy just as practical:

> The rule given us for securing the heavenly practice of pure intention is to be careful of our morning offering, which seals the whole day; since Fénelon says, that after it is made fully and sincerely, if we should forget to renew it from hour to hour—as good souls commonly do—and not retract it by any act of our will—if no mortal sin comes in the way—our first good offering secures all we do for the day. What a comfort that is!

Reading these clear-cut rules for high holiness, it is difficult to keep in mind that this earnest, assured teacher but a few years back was groping in darkness. Granted that her teaching was not original doctrine —it was the pure teaching of Jesus Christ—that the thoughts and many of the illustrations were culled from the great Catholic divines of the ages, nevertheless, Elizabeth spoke as one having authority: she knew whereof she spoke, for she had a thorough grasp of the complexities of religious thought, to the point where she could put them into the simplest of terms; and the words and accent and turns of phrase were unmistakably hers. She had been, indeed, quick to master the ways of God.

Elizabeth was frank and courageous in admonishing individual Sisters, although it was a duty that she had to force herself to, since it went against her kindly, indulgent grain. Bruté has testified that she was "little inclined [to] preach to others . . . to have as a Superior to instruct, direct, reprove, . . . so impressed that she did poorly, badly, neglectfully, and to the injury of souls." A Sister remarked in passing one day that Elizabeth's writing pens were nothing but stumps.

"Well, my dear one," the Mother countered, "that is to atone for your waste of pens."

When a Sister did not approach Communion with the others, Elizabeth bluntly asked the reason. She had no right to ask; it can only be said in her defense that she may have known that the reason was not a matter of conscience, but it was nonetheless a dangerous and unjustifiable question. Be that as it may, the Sister answered:

"Mother, I felt a little weak, and took a cup of coffee before Mass."

"Ah, my dear child," was the hard reply, "how could you sell your God for a miserable cup of coffee?"

It is not to be thought for a moment that her subjects ever considered Elizabeth a stern or rigid mother. The actions of her whole life, the devotion of her religious daughters, the way they clung to her hand for support at the hour of death, would cry out against such a thought. Bruté said of her, in loving tribute, that she was "a true pattern to her Sisters: their mother for love, their servant for humility, their true superior for prudent guidance, their friend in every pain they felt." Tenderness was her chief characteristic, "Mother" a title truly earned. Gaiety was so natural to her that she once told her "Blessed G." that "reading a picture of judgment to our black caps the other evening, I got laughing, as so often happens when my nerves are weak, and to hide it I said I hope at least in the great rising we will each be able to lay hold of our crucifix that we may hold it up for defense; and all agreed that it was a shame that we have so few in the house that we cannot allow a poor Sister in her coffin that last possession. . . . Our God, when will I be good, and look at death and judgment as I ought?"

Elizabeth never forgot, however, that she once was "Betsey Bayley," which is to say, that she never forgot the Bayley temper she had allowed to die down by dint of heroically neglecting it; she had long ago banked its fires, but she was always conscious of the glowing coals deep under the ash. Humbly she told Father Bruté: "Conscience reproaches aloud —how little charity and delicacy of love I practice in that vile habit of speaking of the faults of others, of the *short, cold, repulsive conduct* to my betters, as all certainly are, and for much of my behavior to you, my visible savior. I would put it out (especially some words of reproach and disappointment the other day) I would put them and it out with my blood!" And she admitted candidly: "I am in one continual watch to keep down my eyebrows and wear the ready smile, if even it sometimes be 'ghastly'!"

Her annoyance at breaches of the rule and her fears lest she be too harsh in her reproofs often troubled her, and she found no peace until Bruté had assured her that the annoyances was righteous and the reproofs merited. Toward the end of her life she wrote him in evident peace: "As to *private* concerns, I have none, unless it be my trials occasionally at the conduct of different Sisters, and that you have forbid me speaking of; and since you think proper, and I am acquitted before God, I am too happy it is so."

So far was she from the cold, relentless rule of the rigorist that she readily admitted to Bruté that it would be "like changing an Ethiopian to pretend to preserve the spirit of detail which the charity and natural disposition of our Superior [Father Dubois] has made the spirit of our community. Long may Our Lord spare him to it, for who could ever be found to *unwind the ball* as he does, and stop to pick out every knot? Too happy I to break the knot and piece it again! And it does seem to blind eyes like mine so far from the spirit of simplicity to be obliged to spell every word and feel the pulse with *your Sisters,* but I will try more and more."

When the rules and constitutions had been promulgated at the retreat held in February, 1812, a year's probation was assigned the Sisters before their admission to vows. For unknown reasons the probation period was extended, and the first pronouncement of vows did not take place until the feast of St. Vincent de Paul, July 19, 1813. The ceremony was preceded by a retreat, during which a letter arrived from Father

Babade, praying that the spirit of St. Vincent would descend upon Elizabeth and all the community.

When the historic day arrived, seventeen Sisters pronounced their vows: Mother Superior, Mary Elizabeth Ann Seton, and Sisters Rose White, Kitty Mullen, Ann Gruber, Elizabeth Boyle, Angela Brady, Cecilia O'Conway, Susan Clossy, Mary Ann Butler, Adele Salva, Louise Rogers, Margaret George, Sally Thompson, Martina Quinn, Fanny Jordan, Theresa Conroy and Julia Shirk. These vows were not perpetual, but were to be renewed each year. After this first vow-taking on St. Vincent's Day, the annual renewal took place on the feast of the Annunciation, March 25, the day established for it by St. Vincent and St. Louise.

The solemnity of the occasion affected Elizabeth with the same fears of inadequacy and unworthiness she had felt when the Sisters first donned the habit in Baltimore; and Sister Cecilia wrote her a remarkably wise and affectionate letter of reproof:

> My beloved Mother, how [you] surprise me by your *alarm* on the duties of a Superior. Precious soul, what is the difference between it and those of a *Christian parent?* Not the common kind of cruel parent who destroy their children by their wicked tenderness, but to know how to vary correction according to different dispositions—always to treat the young, the stranger and the timid with gentleness until their true turn of mind is known. . . .
>
> Spiritual parent must be both attentive to soul and body, attentive to keep the proud and self-willed under *obedience*, the same restrained as a spoiled child, yielding with parental indulgence where neither sin, fault nor breach of rules are in danger. . . .
>
> Be a mild, patient *but firm* MAMMA, and you need not tremble under the burden of superiority. Jesus can never give you a task above your courage, strength or ability. Come, precious darling, don't let uneasiness and fear appear so plain to the weak. You must at least be the MOON, if the sun is too bright and too dignified a character. The more gentle and modest light will suit our valley in the growing fervor of your little company. I do not want you to dart the rays of the great St. Theresa. *Times, places* and circumstances change the order of this life. I will try to *be good.*

Elizabeth kept the letter and wrote on the back of it: "Cecilia's admirable lesson to me." Cecilia did not stop there in her devotion. As late as 1815 Mother Seton was writing to Bruté: "*Cecilia* has taken my soul in hand, and declares *it shall be perfected.* She will do violence to *His* Heart, she says, and every Communion and prayer for that until her Mother is a *true Mother.* She says these things with such awful emphasis, it makes me cold; yet how precious the prayers of such a soul!"

In September Catherine Dupleix came to Emmitsburg. The good woman had made plans for a visit during the winter of 1812 when Annina lay dying. Elizabeth had been so lifted up with the anticipation of seeing her old friend that she told Eliza Sadler: "Every noise, every bark of the dog, makes a look-out for Dué, tho' the very idea is extravagant. . . . It is more happiness than I dare look for in the common course of things."

But Dué had not come. Elizabeth had been disappointed, too, when Sad had gotten as close to her as Wilmington, and had turned back. Therefore, when her sister Mary Post told her in July that Dué was "very unhappy . . . and wishes very much to visit you," Elizabeth refused to let her hopes rise only to be dashed again. When Sad wrote in mid-September, however, that Dué was actually on the point of setting out and hesitated only because her usual diffidence had conjured up preposterous doubts as to whether she would be welcome in the Valley, Elizabeth dispatched an excited letter of assurance: "The very possibility of seeing Dué is like a foretaste of heaven to me and if she is only delayed by the fear of not finding entrance in St. Joseph's House, tell her the front door, the back, the side door, which will lead her in the chapel, and all the windows up and down will open at her approach . . . I have to take a free breath at the thought!"

Elizabeth chattered on happily, giving Dr. Chatard's address in Baltimore where Dué might stay on her journey: "She will find *my bed* there. . . . If the pillows are silk and the counterpane down, she must do penance in advance for the hard ones she will find at St. Joseph's." And so the "weak" Dué made the arduous trip, despite the war and the constant threats of civic violence, and on the night of September 28, 1813, lay asleep behind the curtain in Elizabeth's room.

Strangely enough, when Julia Scott, who had resisted all Elizabeth's blandishments to brave the "abominable mountain road" to Emmitsburg, showed the first signs of a change of heart, Elizabeth put her off. Julia wrote in November that "I hear of so many people who see you that I think my fears must have magnified the danger of getting to you. Should heaven prosper my wishes, I shall yet make the attempt." Elizabeth answered cautiously: "Oh, yes, come, Julia; come and see! . . . You will see so many things so droll to you, your amusement would be quite as great as going to your springs, etc., only that the accommodation in our village is very bad, and you could not probably remain more than one night. It is a tavern, and of the lowest kind, they say. With me, dearest, you could not put up with the inconvenience. My room [is] the worst of the whole community, and at night our poor little darling Rebecca, her good nurse, and Kitty, are all my inmates. But you will see what next summer will say. My Julia, next summer!"

It is interesting that Elizabeth should discourage Julia from enduring the same inconveniences that she had never mentioned in regard to the Posts and Dué. She knew, of course, her society friend's habits and fastidiousness—she had once disuaded her from crossing the Bay to Staten Island, lest the miserable plight of the immigrants turn her stomach—but Elizabeth was always prone to judge her in the light of former years, forgetting, despite Julia's protestations, that age and trouble might have matured her.

The little woman of the Valley had a great surprise in February, 1814, in the form of a letter from her half-sister Helen. Helen had long kept aloof, out of pique because Elizabeth had not answered her former attempts at correspondence, but now she realized that "many and various reasons may have concurred to cause your silence."

She gave Elizabeth her small bits of news: that she was waiting for Sam Craig to return from South America to marry him; that she had moved out of the Posts when young Catherine had come home from boarding school, and was living with Carleton, who had married Grace Roosevelt on November 4, 1813. The newlyweds had intended "making Emmitsburg the honeymoon jaunt . . . but the roads at that time were almost impassable. Grace is quite anxious to become personally known to one so dear to her husband." Their sister Mary Fitch Bayley was living with brother Richard, who had moved to the country "where . . . he will save, if he does not make," for business in New York was at a stalemate due to the war.

The letter shook Elizabeth with a great gust of nostalgia for her family and for New York—she was always proud of her "New York girls" among the boarders—and she broached a half-hearted thought to Sad of sending William to set up in business there. "My greatest anxiety in life is my poor boys," she confessed. "William was seventeen last November 21. Look out for himself he must, part from Mother he must, poor, dear child." William, who was "inclined to follow the drum," was especially restless at the time because his friends, "young Carroll," grandnephew to the Archbishop, had gone to Europe as part of the Peace Commission of Henry Clay, and "young Brent," another of the prelate's grandnephews, had a commission in the Navy. Richard was a different case—"Mother's boy forever, but a lively, crazy one. He told Rebecca, laughing, the other day: 'I dreamt I was a soldier last night, and when I found it was a dream, it seemed I would die with joy!'" Elizabeth finished wryly: "He is nearly a year and half younger than William, and four years younger in mind."

Sad answered this letter sharply, bidding Elizabeth forget New York, and not "try to bring back former times." This, she felt, could only bring heartbreak; Elizabeth was happy in her new life; let her forget the old. It was wise advice, but Sad did not understand wholly how well divine charity had healed Elizabeth's soul.

The mother had said well that the boys were "her greatest anxiety in life." Until the day she died, they would be her greatest personal worry and the worry would be largely unrequited.

It was balanced, however, by her satisfaction in her two girls. She had written in her last birthday note to Catherine Josephine:

Birthday of my Josephine, and Mother's heart rejoices. It will look a little to the uncertainty of her crown, yet the good angel looks so smiling and points to the tabernacle. How can I help hoping my dear one will be safe? But, my darling, you must renew every good resolution, and keep close by your Good Shepherd. You know, the little lamb only stepped aside to crop the spear of grass, and then a little further, and a little further, 'till it could no longer hear the voice of the Shepherd; and then, when entangled in briars and thorns—you know the rest. My dear, dear one, think well of the little lamb. And take care of our dear little lamb, our little limping dear one. Oh, yes, take care and be a good angel to her! Bless, bless you forever!

It was obvious that "the little limping dear one," Rebecca, was going the way of Annina, not as swiftly, perhaps, but just as relentlessly. The family tuberculosis had apparently settled in the weak spot of her injured hip, and was beginning to show its ravages. The mother felt no longer, however, the sharp terror of nature at the thought of separation, she no longer had to beat down rebellion within her, to cling blindly to the hand of God. She had learned well, and now she set about preparing her latest burnt offering with a holy calm—not that she was immune to a mother's tears; but there was now no wildness, no desperation, in them.

Rebecca travelled to Baltimore in April to receive the Sacrament of Confirmation from the trembling old hands of John Carroll; but before she went, she passed Holy Week in the infirmary at the Mount with Sister Susan, probably to prepare under Father Dubois for the Sacrament. The notes Elizabeth sent her daily were evidences of the new intimacy between the mother and daughter, the new peace in Elizabeth's soul.

One, for example, was a note giving Rebecca permission to approach the Communion table:

> My own child of eternity: With the little pen I answer my dear every day dearer little darling, how much I desire she should go and unite still closer to Our Only Beloved. . . . Make your careful preparation of the purest heart you can bring Him, that it may appear to Him like a bright little Star at the bottom of a fountain. O my Rebecca! child of eternity, let peace and love stay with you in your pains, and they will lighten and sweeten them all.

Another was an assurance to Bec's request for her mother's prayers:

> Your poor Mother does pray for you with the cries of a Mother's heart. My soul's darling, bear all your pains with Our Jesus, and commit your precious soul *all to Him*. And you must pray much for me, that at last in our dear eternity we may rest in Him forever.

Nourished on such spiritual sweetmeats, it is not surprising that Rebecca's soul climbed steadily higher up the ladder of holiness while the months and years of her illness dragged painfully on. She wrote her mother on Holy Saturday:

My soul's Mother, I fully expected you here today, but was very much disappointed when I saw the weather was not good; but I see it is our dearest Lord's Will that I should not see you, but I am resigned. . . .

The child who wrote this was not yet twelve! As she went on, she was honest enough about how much she missed her mother, how "Daddy Dick" came in to comfort her, and how at bedtime she "felt heavy enough. I thought to myself: *no Mother tonight to give me holy water, no Mother to kiss.* Then my heart failed a little and the tears had to come, but Sister Suzy knelt down. . . ."

Bec was never cast down long, however, and the next day, Easter Sunday, she was telling her mother with delight: "I fell asleep, and while I was laying there, the brother [Father Bruté] comes in, and when he found me asleep he told Sister Suzy to tell me when I woke that, while I had been so near the grave when Our dear Lord arose, that the stone fell on my leg and gave me the cramp. So, my Mother, I send you the little picture which he drew me. You may be sure it amused me a great deal." Bruté was a clever cartoonist, and constantly illustrated his letters and spiritual notes. He also left many finely drawn pen-and-ink sketches of the Valley and the Sisters' establishment which are valuable records of the early days of the Sisterhood.

Just at the time Rebecca was off to Baltimore for her Confirmation, the community was closing out its books with Father John David. In the *Council Minutes* of the Sisterhood for April 2, 1814, the Sister Secretary noted this item of business:

> Rt. Rev. John David, of Kentucky, in accordance with Rt. Rev. Dr. Flaget, proposed a union of an Establishment in their Diocese with ours. . . .

No sooner had David arrived in Kentucky in 1811 than he had cast about to provide a community of Sisters for the new Diocese of Bardstown. To this end he had begun a rather petulant correspondence with Bruté, badgering him to copy out the rules and constitutions of the Sisters of Charity. Whether Bruté was unwilling to become embroiled, or could not lay his hands on the documents requested, David had no success until 1813, and even then, Bruté sent him only the constitutions.

David went ahead with his plans anyhow, and actually began his foundation on July 12 of that year with a nucleus of six girls. He had, very crossly, corrected Bruté's first impression that he wanted Sisters of Charity for the Kentucky community, but by the summer of 1813 he had changed his mind—he wanted Sister Rose for mother superior; and was greatly chagrined when Dubois would not send her—nor Sister Kitty, nor Sister Fanny, who had been his alternate choices.

Dubois was willing to release a Sister for the important post, but he intended to name her himself. The Sisters, too, in their April 2nd meeting, were quite willing to accede to David's request that his community be joined to theirs, that alterations be made in the constitutions, and even that a separate novitiate be established in Kentucky—with the proviso, however, that the Kentucky novices "should be disposed, in case the Council of the Mother House required it, to come and make *here* their novitiate."

These very liberal concessions, however, did not satisfy David; and when he refused to have the Council in Emmitsburg pass on the qualifications of his novices, the Council very properly refused any union on his terms. The unusually large letters with which the vote of "No" is written in the *Minutes* suggests that Elizabeth and her assistants may well have been at the end of their patience!

Although the case for union dragged on in a three-cornered argument involving Kentucky, John Dubois and the Archbishop, the Sisters took no further official notice of the matter; and the Sisters of Charity of Nazareth, although they largely adopted St. Vincent's rule, were never amalgamated with Emmitsburg. David's last dealings with the Sisterhood at Emmitsburg had been as uproarious and truculent as his first—and met with the same lack of success; and apparently he had bypassed Elizabeth just as completely as before, since there is no extant shred of correspondence between them about the Kentucky project.

Another project proposed at the same time, however, met with instant success. It was one of important and memorable impact, for it concerned the first branch put out by the parent tree, the first foundation of the Sisters outside the Valley; and as the original candidate for the community, Cecilia O'Conway, had come from Philadelphia, it was a happy justice that the bread she had cast upon the waters should first return there. Considering the elation that must have run high in St.

Joseph's House, the *Council Minutes* are most prosaic in recording the great event:

> August 14, 1814. The trustees of the Orphan Asylum of Philadelphia petitioned for three Sisters proposing to give $600 annually for the support of themselves and the orphans. Reverend Mr. Hurley strongly in favor of this first opening of extending the services of the Sisters of Charity—it was agreed to accept this charge. Sister Rose was appointed to go with Sister Susan and Sister Teresa—Sister Betsy was appointed as Assistant in place [of Sister Rose].

The Philadelphia Roman Catholic Society for Education and Maintaining Poor Orphan Children had its first tenuous roots in 1797 as a result of the constant waves of yellow fever which had left many destitute children in their wake. The society was more formally organized at a meeting held in the "little chapel" of Old St. Joseph's Church, Willings Alley, in 1806, and was legally incorporated on December 18, 1807. At that time a building was rented on South Sixth Street, adjoining Holy Trinity Church, and a matron installed. Father Hurley, who was Pastor of St. Augustine's, became a strong supporter of the work of charity. It was he who suggested to the Board of Trustees that they procure the Sisters of Charity to advance the work.

On August 20 the *Minutes* of the Sisters' Council carried further news of the project, just as matter-of-fact as the first, but for all that, unable to hide the heroic courage of these zealous women.

> A letter was read from the Archbishop which seemed for a moment to raise obstacles to the Sisters taking charge of the orphan establishment— yet leaving it in our power to decide these obstacles only presenting personal inconveniences the Sisters generously determined to meet them and begin the good work.
> Another letter to the same purport was read from the Vicar General and one from Reverend Mr. Hurley, the present menacing aspect of public affairs rendering it dangerous and disagreeable to the Sisters—
> Unanimously agreed that no personal inconvenience should prevent Sisters of Charity doing what duty and charity required—

Thus the Sisters brushed aside the second thoughts and misgivings of the men who needed them so badly. The decision made, the good women wasted no time in beginning this first of their works wholly devoted to the poor. It was to them a happy augury for their institute because, while they had earnestly desired from the very beginning to minister to the orphan, they had not dared hope they could begin so soon.

On September 29, 1814, the little band of pioneers set out with Elizabeth's blessing and the gift of "a small half-flannel shawl" each, "the first worn by the Sisters." They traveled overland, by way of Little York and Lancaster due to "the menacing aspect of public affairs," mentioned in the *Minutes*. The city of Washington had been burned in August, including the White House where the vivacious Dolley Madison had distinguished herself for bravery. On September 11 the British Fleet, under Admiral Cockburn, appeared off Baltimore, and the next day General Ross landed troops to besiege the city from the south. During the bombardment of Fort McHenry, on the night of the 13th, amid "the rockets' red glare, the bombs bursting in air," Francis Scott Key had written the words of the national anthem. Although the city beat off the invaders, it was still uneasy and fearful and British warships still prowled the sea outside the harbor, when Sister Rose and her companions left for Philadelphia.

They began their new work as true Sisters of Charity, in humility and poverty. The humility of Rose White, the first American Sister Servant— as St. Vincent called the superiors of his houses of charity—was evident in the little farewell note she sent Archbishop Carroll:

> I think I can see your surprise when you heard of the choice made to send poor Rose to Philadelphia, knowing so well as you do how little capacity I have for any good, and my little judgment for managing—and how much may be spoiled by my being sent as Sister Servant to any city; but God's Will be done, and pray, my dear Father, that I may prove no obstacle to the good in view, nor a scandal to the community.
>
> I am as one stupid and all surprised; I know nothing, and can see nothing, but my ignorance and weakness, which is ever before me. If any good is done, it will be God alone Who will and can do it; as for me, I know nothing but sin, and an unhappy disposition of impatience, which has caused myself and others much pain in this blessed family where I have often rendered myself an unworthy member of it.

The humility and spirit of poverty of all three was evident in the way they begged hospitality on their journey, complaining only of the "fine accommodations" of the hotel they were forced to stop at in Lancaster. The hired carriage they rode in, and even the shoes on their feet, were paid for by the Lady Managers of the asylum, a group of Catholic women of Philadelphia who had banded together under the leadership of Mrs. Rachel Montgomery as an auxiliary to assist the asylum financially.

Sister Rose praised Mrs. Montgomery as a "true mother of charity," and she and the other ladies of the auxiliary proved themselves indeed worthy forerunners of the Vincentian Ladies of Charity who aided the asylum in later years. This was the same Mrs. Montgomery who, as the friend and fellow-convert of Samuel Cooper, had hailed the Sisters at the time of their foundation in Baltimore in 1809 as "estimable characters whose virtues and good examples . . . will illuminate our darkened hemisphere," and had tried unsuccessfully to procure the first flannel for their habits. She was particularly drawn to Mother Seton and still visited her at Emmitsburg.

It was one of the marks of the first American Sisters of Charity that they always saw the amusing side in all they did. Thus Sister Rose has left an arch account of what must have been an exasperating attempt to find the orphanage when they had entered Philadelphia:

Next morning very early we set off for Philadelphia and arrived there in the evening—had to inquire our way as we moved through the streets, as we knew not even in what street we were in. Frequently the driver . . . Mr. Livers would give us the reins to hold, and would get down from his seat, and ask at several houses if they could tell us where St. Joseph's Asylum was. No one seemed to understand him. He became a little tried; and on one of the Sisters asking him if he had any information to guide him,

"Oh, no," said he, "you might as well ask a hog about a holy day, as to ask those people where St. Joseph's Asylum is."

We drove on without knowing where we were going; but our good Angel was with us, for, wearied with going up one street and down another, Mr. Livers stopped and thought he would ask again when, behold!—we were before the door of Trinity Church, which was next to the Asylum.

The carriage having been closed, the housekeeper of the priest, a good Frenchwoman named Justine, approached the carriage thinking it was a corpse brought to be buried. When she lifted the curtain, as if by inspiration she said:

"Are you not from St. Joseph's?"

"Yes, who are you?"

"Rev. Mr. Roelof's housekeeper."

"Will you tell us where the Asylum [is]?"
"Yes, you are at its door. Will you not get out of the carriage?"

The Sisters entered the church, while the woman went in search of Father Hurley, for whom they had a letter. They could not take formal possession of their establishment until October 2, when the woman who had been in charge moved out with all her effects, including most of the furniture.

When the Sisters left Emmitsburg, Father Dubois had escorted them as far as Taneytown, giving "lessons of economy all the way"; but even Dubois could not have envisioned the bottom-of-the-barrel economy they would have to practice. Sister Rose drew the picture of it dryly and well:

> The Asylum was in debt five thousand dollars, the subscriptions for its support few; the embargo made goods double price, and it was often told us to reflect that the sum allowed for support was only six hundred dollars a year. They had no occasion to remind us, for our fears were so great that we would not be able to make out that for three months we never eat bread at dinner, but used potatoes; no sugar in our coffee, which was made of corn. . . . The poor children had not been accustomed to get any sugar in their nursery beverage which was weak coffee and dry bread, sugar being very high. However, Rev. Mr. Hurley, hearing of our not using sugar, commanded us to use it, and some was sent.

It is no wonder that Mother Seton's modern daughters possess extraordinary talent for administration in conducting huge hospitals, schools and orphanages—their talent is a legacy left them by the first, indomitable Sisters of Charity. What Elizabeth did for the solvency of the Motherhouse, Rose did for their first foundation. At the end of only their second year at the Philadelphia asylum, the Board of Trustees was amazed to find that the Sisters had a surplus of $200.00 and by the end of the following year, had liquidated the original debt!

Elizabeth informed Julia Scott, of course, that the Sisters had gone to Philadelphia, and were but a few blocks from her. She especially wanted her to meet Sister Sus:

> My Julia, there is one of the sweetest souls gone to Philadelphia from this house, who has lived in my very heart and been more than an own sister to me ever since I have been here. She even slept always behind my curtain, and has nursed Cecil, Harriet, Anne, William and Rebecca through

all her sufferings with inconceivable tenderness. She has the care of the poor orphans belonging to our Church with our good Sister Rose White, who has the little institution in her care. If you have ever a wish to find a piece of myself, it will be in this dear Susan Clossy. . . .

She also told Julia that William's heart was "all alive for a berth in the Navy, which has been really applied for through Mr. Brent of Washington." Elizabeth was not at all anxious for this, because she thought it dangerous to his soul, and would much rather have seen him settled in some kind of business. William was hot for the service, however, and Elizabeth, not wishing to interfere overmuch in his life, tried to help him attain his desire. She wrote to Archbishop Carroll, who made the application to Brent, his nephew. The kindly old prelate was harried by the upset of the times, but he always had a moment for Elizabeth and her children. "If your dear William was not concerned, even you would scarcely have a line from me at present," he told her wearily. "He is indeed not forgotten by me, and his interests are recommended to those by whom he can be benefited. But truly, since the misfortunes of the City of Washington, and the deplorable condition to which the ignorance and perception of our leaders has brought our national affairs, I see little prospect of William profiting by any appointment he may obtain; yet every attention will be paid."

On the 20th of November Elizabeth transmitted Carroll's message to her son, and bade him not be impatient or sulky at the delay. "My dear one, be indeed a man," she wrote firmly. "Our good God has His times and moments for everything. It is evident that you ought to go; therefore, certainly He will open the door. . . . I know how you feel, and the ardor of your desire; but be a man and a Christian both. God will provide. Trust all to Him and your poor Mother's heart, which begs incessantly for you."

Elizabeth has been accused at times of being too indulgent with her children; but it is an unfair accusation, based probably in part on the highly colored accounts she habitually made of them to her friends, particularly Julia Scott, and Eliza Sadler. Surely, however, a mother can be excused for telling the best and hiding the shortcomings of her children, even from closest friends like these.

Nothing she ever told them was untrue; she even sometimes admitted to them that her children were not geniuses—but she was rarely as frank with them as she was with Antonio Filicchi or Gabriel Bruté. Thus she told Antonio on July 1, 1814, that her boys were "so far, children of exemplary conduct as it relates to common behavior and the simple discharge of pious duties; but they have no striking talents, no remarkable qualifications, nor are their dispositions even unfolded in many points. They can never be brought to express any decided wish but the only desire to please Mother and do what she thinks best." No mother could be more realistic than that! In all her many agonizing efforts for her sons, she never for a moment thought of worldly position but only of their soul's salvation.

On the human side, Elizabeth's problem was that of any widow left to guide teen-age boys alone: as a woman, she did not fully understand their masculine restlessness, their adventurous dreams, their aggressiveness; and as a wise woman, she knew that she did not understand—hence her diffidence, her habit of suggesting and then hastily qualifying the suggestion or withdrawing it entirely, her anguished attempts at objectivity. It was all further complicated by her innate tenderness, her pity for their orphanhood, her realization that they had not had a normal childhood or adolescence, surrounded as they were by religious acrimony, financial insecurity and finally, the bewildering atmosphere of convent life and nuns, and the recognition that their mother was a woman set apart, a religious foundress and mother superior.

The wonder is that Elizabeth had succeeded in making their snatched moments of family life as normal as she had: her air of informality with her Sisters was, in fact, a direct result of her amazingly able attempt to be at the same time a physical and a spiritual mother. In the end, it was Elizabeth's wisdom that saved her from spoiling her children and setting them up for disaster. As she told Bruté, she knew "American parents to be most difficult *in hearing the faults of their children*"; and for Elizabeth Seton, to be forewarned was to be forearmed. If the sons of so great a mother were a disappointment to her, it was assuredly not her fault.

On William's eighteenth birthday, November 25, 1814, Elizabeth's customary birthday note announced the theme that she would improvise upon in all the many letters to him in the years ahead—his soul's salvation.

> You know your *Mother's heart*. It had a dear communication for you, for our *eternity*, my William. Be blessed a thousand, thousand times! Take a few little moments in the church today, in union with your Mother's heart, to place yourself again and again in the hands of God. Do, my dearest one.

For the next few months all her correspondence would be concerned with getting this son she loved so dearly started in the world. As Christmas approached, and still no appointment for the Navy came, Gabriel Bruté made an offer which caused her mother's heart to quicken. He was going to Europe, and would take William with him, to enter the counting house of the Filicchis. There were various reasons for Bruté's trip; he wanted, of course, to see his mother; to bring back his sizable library; to enlist more priests for the American mission; and there was, besides, certain undefined business connected with his recent appointment as President of St. Mary's College in Baltimore.

In this connection, Elizabeth teased him unmercifully: "Mr. Tessier writes in such triumph that his darling was called for even by the superior overseas *on particular business*, and how happy that thy precious pearl was esteemed and confided in equally by *both*. The clearer eye of the Mountain [Dubois] and old microscope of the Valley [herself] must laugh at these doting grandpapas, though so venerable. The darling himself must smile at their poor, blind optics. Our Lord permits; let it pass. *Tu es sacerdos in eternum secundum ordinem Melchisedech*. There the soul's grand triumph—all else but smoke."

William agreed to go. Anything was better than sitting back, watching his friends start out to make their way in the world.

Elizabeth hastened to advise Antonio, in a letter of December 20, that William was coming. She remembered the Filicchi promise made many years before to take her boys into the Leghorn office when they should be old enough. William had tried to find a desk in some American mercantile establishment but, she told Antonio: "No kind of business can be done here in the distracted state of the country."

Womanlike, when she had exhausted the reasons Antonio would understand, she cast herself on Amabilia's maternal heart: "Amabilia

. . . will be as ready to bless with her kindness the poor William as she was his sister and unworthy Mother. She is a mother, and can enter at once into the fears and apprehensions of a heart already overwhelmed with favors and benefits received. Yet I dry off the tears these thoughts must bring with the joyful recollection of the blessings which will be poured on you and your dear family for what you have done and do for us in our necessities."

In January Gabriel Bruté and William left the Valley for Baltimore on the first leg of their journey. The leavetaking can be imagined. Even seven months later the bruises to Elizabeth's heart had not wholly healed, for she confided to Fillipo Filicchi: "If you could know what we have gone through only to decide on this separation from William, for we have been so linked by our particular situation and total division from family connections, that it is like tearing soul from soul—as you will know when you see *into* his disposition, which exteriorly is cold and reserved, but very different in reality." And she added wistfully: "Dear, dear child, if only he could master his bad pride, I believe all the rest would be secure."

William boarded with the Chatards while in Baltimore, and for a time it seemed he might go no further, when the possibility of an opening in the counting house of Luke Tiernan was raised. Richard and Catherine and Rebecca, and for a long moment Elizabeth herself, seized at this straw to hold William near them; but when John Dubois expressed his firm opinion—an opinion shared by Carroll and Cheverus—that William should carry out his original intention, Elizabeth and her son made up their minds that he should go to the Filicchis.

The confused war news kept him waiting more than two months. Peace had already been made at Ghent, but the news had not reached America; it came, in fact, shortly after Andrew Jackson's brilliant but unnecessary victory over the British at New Orleans. The country went wild celebrating this prestigious victory and the peace together. Mary Post described the elaborate celebration in New York, which was apparently starting its career as the ticker-tape town, the city of all the world since the days of ancient Rome that could stage a triumph.

We have had illuminations, fireworks and all demonstration of joy at the return of peace. . . . Our new State House, which is a very beautiful building and said by people of judgment to be equal if not superior to any in Europe, was superbly illuminated. The construction of the building is peculiarly favorable for lighting to advantage and putting up many large and appropriate pictures as transparencies. The cupola was covered with variegated lamps, and moving lights placed in different situations gave it the effect of enchantment.

Even Elizabeth wrote joyfully, but with caution, to William:

> We hear peace is declared. Oh, that it may be so! You have enjoyed the gazettes so much, I know. I cast my eye on General Jackson's name and read it with pleasure, knowing you had read the same more than for the events of the day, for, my dear one, your poor Mother looks only at souls. I see neither American or English, but souls redeemed and lost. But you must. Your case is quite different. Love your country, yet also all countries, my William. See things as they are; passions and excesses you will find everywhere.

The two travellers finally left Baltimore for New York on March 27. Robert Barry, under instructions from Elizabeth, had furnished William with $700.00—$400.00 the Filicchi draft from Murray, the rest of it part of the little insurance policy William's father had taken out in Annina's name—all the ruined merchant had been able to leave his family; a hundred dollars from Julia Scott had gone to buy the young man's clothes. He went armed with something even more useful, however, a classic letter of advice from his mother. It bore solid lessons in economy, courtesy, application, but most of all it was a great cry of the spirit:

> Be not, my dear one, so unhappy as to break willfully any command of Our God, or to omit your prayers on any account. Unite them always to the only merits of Our Jesus and the maternal prayers of Our Mother and His. With them you will always find your own poor, poor Mother's. You cannot even guess the incessant cry of my soul to them for you.
> Don't say Mother has the rest to comfort her. No, no, my William. From the first moment I received you in my arms and to my breast you have been consecrated to God by me, and I have never ceased to beg Him to take you from this world rather than you should offend Him or dishonor your dear soul; and, as you know, my stroke of death would be to know that you have quitted that path of virtue which alone can reunite us forever. Separation, everything else, I can bear—but that, never. Your Mother's heart must break, if that blow falls on it.

William's welcome in New York was very different from the all-but-unnoticed departure of the little widow and her children ten years before. The Sadlers, the Craigs, the Murrays, the Posts, vied with one another to give him a taste of the world's entertainment. The Posts opened their pocketbook with their hearts and supplied him with "shirts, cravats, handkerchiefs and all kinds of underthings"; and his Uncle Post even had a suit made for him at the tailor's. On April 6, Bruté and William sailed in the *Tontine* for Bordeaux.

Back in Emmitsburg, Elizabeth began one of her famous *Journals*, to keep Bruté abreast of the happenings at home while he was gone. The young priest himself had requested it of her; and it is so filled with the gaiety and freedom of their relationship that there is temptation to quote it endlessly.

Father Dubois, she reported, was "in his element," giving the children a retreat: "Almost I laughed out at his opening, telling [them] . . . to be as many little stumps—no, '*chunks*'—of fire put together. *One*, he said, if left *alone*, would soon go out. My eye fell on an old black stump in the corner [herself]—and a big, inward sigh to the live coal far away [Bruté], which used to give us the blaze in a moment."

The Superior had "a moment of vexation on receiving Mr. Bertrand's bill to Mrs. Seton, but I laughed him out of the important affair." A rich old woman had gone out of her mind, and her husband had importuned the Sisters to take care of her at any price. Elizabeth admitted to Bruté that it could be the "beginning of our hospital. . . . You may suppose how many plans of a *building* through the zealous brain of your Brother [Dubois]: '*I* will, *I* will, *I* will!' While I, with hands crossed on Mary's picture and the crucifix under the shawl, bow and assent, and smile— and expect it may be *in Spain*. Yet, it may be the moment." Dubois was, she said, "gay as can be, planning and laying out [the] future—'What *I* will do.' He lives in futurity and I in the past, until the world of realities."

Father Duhamel, who was old and sick, kept Elizabeth and the Sisters highly amused with his salty grumbling. One minute, it was directed at Dubois: "The fellow says, 'Come, old gentleman, ain't you going to get up and say Mass?'—when I am obliged to scream as if I had lancets in my back, if they only go to lift me!" The next minute, it was against

Bruté, as Elizabeth told her "Blessed G." with obvious relish. Duhamel missed Bruté so much, that he grew angry every time he thought of it: "Poor, crazy Bruté, if his neck ain't broke, the Lord help him!" he would say; and in the next breath: "But you are very happy, Ma'am, to have such a gentleman to take care of your son."

And again: "Poor Hickey got a great compliment this morning. An Irishman told him the three priests at the Mountain all put together is not worth one Bruté. Poor creatures, they tell me to my face—now Bruté's gone, all is gone! Some say they will not go to confession till he comes again. Poor, dear, good Bruté! Did you see his letter, Ma'am, *to everybody to save souls?* Poor, crazy Bruté! He says he will be on the high seas—he would be much better *here*, attending his congregation. He could tend six congregations at least. He can do what would kill ten men, if only you give him bread, and two or three horses to ride to death, one after t'other. Poor gentleman, if he was but steady!"

Elizabeth interrupted the old priest's indignant rambling:

"But, Mr. Duhamel, he is sent by the gentleman in Baltimore, by Mr. Tessier."

"Oh, my dear Ma'am, he has turned their heads, too!"

The newly ordained John Hickey had been sent to the Mount by Father Tessier to substitute for Father Bruté. Elizabeth had known him well during his seminary years, and, therefore, felt no constraint toward him. He was a bumbling, bashful, completely inept young man; and Elizabeth got a great deal of mischievous amusement from his agonizing blushes when, in the time-honored custom of mothers superior, she stood by the table making small talk while he tried to choke down his breakfast after saying Mass for the Sisters. She was not amused, however, when Hickey preached a lamentable sermon before a crowded congregation in the parish church, for she stood in awe of the responsibilities of the priesthood. She reported the incident to Bruté:

Gave our Reverend J. Hickey a scolding he will remember. The congregation so crowded yesterday, and so many strangers—to whom he gave a sermon so evidently lazy; and answered this morning:
"I did not trouble myself much about it, Ma'am."
"Oh, sir, that awakens my anger. Do you remember a priest holds the honor of God on his lips. Do you not trouble to spread His fire He wishes

so much enkindled? If you will not study and prepare while young, what when you are old? There is a mother's lesson."

"But, prayer—"

"Yes, prayer—and *preparation*, too."

Blessed soul, God has not given—yet He may give.

Whether the mother's lesson was lost on the young priest, or God had not yet given, Elizabeth was soon regaling Bruté with his latest exploit in the pulpit:

> No one would believe anyone so droll in hesitations—and unconnected—trying to say how the flesh was our enemy, he would detail the senses . . . and coming to the smell, after hems and haws and folding his arms—"the smell—*the smell, my breathren, distracts us!!*" I pray for him more than even for your crazy English, and scold him with all the authority of an *ancient.*

Elizabeth's heart and soul had its fill of anguish that spring of 1815. No sooner had William gone to New York than she received the tragic news that Julia Scott's daughter, Maria, had died unexpectedly at the home of her husband's parents in Copenhagen. Elizabeth's natural desire was to be with her faithful friend in this dark hour, but, as she explained, "we are obliged, each one, to be at our post, or all goes wrong; and our school would suffer without my presence just now. . . . Oh, our Julia, may the God of all mercy bless and comfort you!"

Then, on a Sunday soon after William had sailed, Father Dubois came running from his little house on the Mountain, crying "Mother, Mother," with the dire news that Napoleon had escaped from Elba and France was rising around him. She wrote William on May 21 that some thought the *Tontine* would return: "You can easily suppose what will be our anxiety till we hear from you; but you know my old and confident rule, that *those who most want* the protection of heaven are *surest* of obtaining it. My very soul cleaves to you day and night, and night and day." Her *Journal* for June 13 showed where her true anxiety lay. "Such letters from Baltimore about the late event! Ah, they do not see the heart of Faith so high, with Our God overlooking the clouds of all human events. What is the worst and the worst that can happen to the *dearest*, Death? And what of that? But the poor 'pupil' who may make shipwreck of his dear eternal interest, or the one hand less to hold the chalice—*there the point*, and the *immense interests*."

Confidence in God had always been Elizabeth's devotion, but now it was refined by the positive practice of constant abandonment to the divine Will. For some months past her soul had been plunged into sadness, no self-pitying sadness, but a wise sadness born of the fear of the Lord and the recognition of her own shortcomings. She was indeed passing through yet another room of the soul's mansion, spoken of by her dear St. Teresa, drawing closer to the center, the inner court, and unalloyed union with God. Thus she confided to Bruté the previous autumn:

> Understand, Blessed, and let not your too kind, too patient, heart *in its turn* "be sad." The sadness of mine I cherish as a grace, and do hope to have it to my *last hour*, because it makes me so watchful that I cannot open my lips since St. Raphael's Day without fear. A blessed fear! Would that I had had it these forty years—how short *my account* would be! And be assured that sorrowful mixture which works in every prayer, *sleeping* or waking, and asks our God continually, "Am I indeed in full charity with *all*? Pure, delicate, sincere charity?"—is no work of temptation; because, after the look over the whole and repeated act of contrition (such as poor I can offer) I give up all to Our dear God of mercy and compassion. Besides, it is a community grace, for I have said to our Betsy and Margaret since: "Do you know what you do? Mind—I have agonies of soul for less than that." They both are quite too easy, as well as myself, on this edge of mortal sin. O my God, if He was not my God, I should go crazy in *head* as well as the poor body!

And now, in June, 1815, she broke off in the midst of her bits of news to cry out to him:

> You see I say not a word to you of my poor interior world. The poor little atom in darkness, clouds and continual miseries—going like a machine in the beautiful round of graces—a sad month, the past—but yet another begun in the same stupidity and weariness of soul and body. Communion itself but a moment of more indulgence for this state of torpor and abandonment, *wanting all* and *asking nothing*—for after so much asking and so much granted, to remain still the same unfaithful thing so long! Poor, poor soul, where will it end? *There* the point of *dreadful* uncertainty. I look over to the little Sacred Woods, then up to the clear vault—all is silent. Poor, poor soul!

Nevertheless, even in the midst of this dreadful aridity, when it seemed that God had turned His back on her, when she "searched [her] vacant brain, and not a word,"—the heart continued to "flow and overflow." She knew that the living waters of grace were within her; she did not know, perhaps, that she was betraying the signs of union and contemplation already begun.

The *Tontine* did not return. Before full summer she knew that Bill and Bruté had landed safely in Bordeaux, despite a most dangerous voyage that had staved in the sides of the vessel and forced the captain to lighten his ballast by throwing the cargo overboard. William charmed her by saying that, in the midst of all these perils, "I slept sound, and dreamt of you."

The dangers were not past, however. With the return of Bonaparte, Bruté feared that, as a priest, he might be arrested. He, therefore, left William with a Mr. Preudhomme, whom they had met on the ship; this gentleman, in turn, lodged the boy with his sister Madame de St. Césaire at Marseilles. As an American, William himself was safe from molestation so long as he wore the American cockade and eagle. Mr. Preudhomme thought at first of sending him on to Leghorn in a Sardinian ship, but this plan was abandoned because the Mediterranean was "infested . . . with Algerines, who are in perpetual war with the Sardinians." At this juncture a Mr. Parangue appeared and, when he discovered that William was the son of the William Seton who had been his friend, did everything possible to arrange an overland trip through Nice and Genoa. William made the journey safely, and arrived in Leghorn in early August.

It was a painful arrival for the strange, shy boy, for the Filicchis had not known he was coming; Elizabeth's letters had not reached them, and her courteous plans had gone awry. She had intended William to remain in France until the Filicchis invited him to come to them, but the upheaval of the times had hurried him on to Italy unannounced.

Antonio and his family were not even at home, but on vacation at Lucca. The stiff, gentlemanly Filippo and his wife, Mary, gave the boy a kind welcome, however. They put him out to board with a friend, because Filippo was not well and told Elizabeth frankly that the "several apprentices I successively invited in my family have more or less incommoded us and . . . I am become so fond of quiet and ease that the least trouble vexes me." He tried to twit her in a heavy-handed sort of way, saying he had "almost a mind to scold you for having sent here your son without previous leave; but as that proves that you have had a great confidence in our goodness, I will not say anything, lest you should appeal from my sentence and that I should be condemned to give you thanks in lieu of reproaches."

Filippo's point was well-taken. In the letters Elizabeth had dispatched the moment she heard of William's precipitate journey to Leghorn, she had resorted to a devious simplicity that was unassailable.

> You will have no doubt of the tender love of Our good Master for your poor little American convert [she had told Filippo], since even this so well-advised step, as being approved by our venerable Archbishop, who treats us like darling children; the blessed Bishop of Boston even pressing it; my Reverend Superior here insisting; and, at last, Our God throwing my poor William in your hands without permitting the delay and time for knowing your will to receive him. . . . All this proves indeed I must be a little child and take from the Adorable Hand my little hard crust; for though my delight and pride that you and Antonio as the Providence of God to us have so long supported us, is increased instead of lessened, yet to abuse and take advantage of your goodness to us was far from my intention.

Who could resist such sincere flattery and abject dependence? And to Antonio she wrote: "Scold me if you are angry (but gently). . . ." There was no scolding. Years before Antonio had promised the Seton boys a place in his counting house, and his word was gold. Filippo assured Elizabeth that, if her son had "a mind to improve himself, if he renders himself capable of doing what I must do myself now, if he becomes useful, he will not have occasion to regret your resolution of sending him here. I hope he will, for he seems of a very good disposition and of model behavior. If he walks straight in the way shown to him, if he possesses . . . the principles of Christian morals in which he has been educated, you need not be anxious for him."

Nevertheless, like any good mother, she was anxious. She worried about his clothes: "Our kind Rose has made you pantaloons. I fear so much that something might happen to those you have." She worried about his behavior: "My William, do, do mind economy, order, submission to every wish of the generous friends who are such true friends to us." She worried about his sense of gratitude: "Do write Mr. Bruté a few kind lines, my dear one, *it is proper.* You should: he has been so kind to us; and do love everyone of the Filicchi family for me. . . . A grateful heart is the only return in our power; and your conduct, my dearest one, must express it for us all."

But, most of all, she worried about his soul: "Be sure, as I told you, to remain faithful to your external duties. . . . Write me how often you have been to the sacred tribunal since you left me." This central, spiritual worry became one of the major crosses of her life, filling her with a terror that called across the sea again and again in piteous, poignant cries: "Child of my soul, *be good* and *be happy!* The only thought that frightens me when I feel weak and faint is that I will see you no more in this world. But that is nothing, *if only in the next* . . . O my William, tears will overpower—and my soul cries to our eternity. My dear, dear one, if the world should draw you from Our God, and we not meet there! That thought I cannot stand. I will hope, do hope. My God, who knows a mother's love, sees, and He will pity."

Elizabeth's preoccupation with William's soul was a most mysterious phenomenon. It was so constant as to seem an obsession, a thing far beyond the normal fears of a mother, even so saintly a mother as Elizabeth. But William's later years prove it not to have been vain. He married a Protestant, Emily Prime, and seemed for a time to have grown lax in the Faith. Though he made a good and holy end, and raised a son who became an archbishop and a daughter who became a nun, he was haunted all his life by a pact made with his wife at the time of their marriage, that the boys should be raised Catholic and the girls Protestant. One has a definite feeling that, in some dim way, the intense spiritual sensitivity of his mother felt the future, and feared.

On the human side, Elizabeth's attempts to keep William within the warmth and intimacy of the family circle were peculiarly affecting. She spoke to him lovingly of his long dead father: "You have now seen the dear grave, the counting house he was in at your very age where he gained everyone's good will by his amiable manner and peaceable disposition." Richard, she told him, knowing their brotherly fondness, "is anxiously waiting to know how it is with you"; and, appealing to his sense of pride as the elder, she suggested: "Do, my love, write him at once, and tell him how you regret every moment you lost in improving yourself—as I am sure enough you do, by experience."

As for his sisters and herself, she drew a vivid sketch of their affection: "Imagine your *three* sitting on the little old black trunk, Bec's arm round me and Jos' head on my shoulder, while we read together the greatest delight on earth to us: a *letter from our William*. Bec . . . cries out: 'Dear, dearest love to my Billy. Oh, how I did dream of him last night!' Alas, our dreams are all we have, my Willy."

With her first-born son so far away, it comforted Elizabeth to have her sister Mary, who had seen him in New York, tell her: "He has great resemblance to yourself and his Grandfather Seton—so much to the latter that at first I thought it was only him that he resembled. He reminded me of the story we used to admire so much [at] Mama Pompelion's, where we read of men with girlish modesty and reserve combined with manly strength and fortitude." Mary had sad news when she wrote on June 12. Their brother Richard had been thrown from his carriage by a runaway horse and killed instantly, leaving his wife with one small child and another on the way. The plight of her sister-in-law wrung Elizabeth's tender heart, and she told Eliza Sadler she would have gone to her at once, if she could.

In September she made a last trial of medical science in an attempt to relieve Rebecca's sufferings, sending the little girl to the famous Dr. Physick in Philadelphia. Julia Scott was touchingly eager to take the child into her home, but Rebecca, who knew Aunt Scott only by her letters, preferred the orphanage and the Sisters who were "family" to her. So eager, indeed, was poor Julia that, overcoming her dread of travel, she drove all the way to Emmitsburg in her grand coach-and-four to fetch the child. Through some mix-up or delay of letters, however, Rebecca had already left for Baltimore two hours before. But that was not the worst. Ironically, these two great faithful friends, Julia and Elizabeth, who had not seen each other for thirteen years and who had yearned for the comfort of reunion, now met for exactly one hour; and, as Elizabeth put it, "then away, perhaps to meet no more till eternity." They never did meet again on this earth.

Elizabeth was, all at once, a mother bereft—Dick was in Baltimore on a visit, Bill in Italy, Bec in Philadelphia; only Kit was with her. The little mother's heart spanned the miles to be with Rebecca, and she sent letter after letter to console and sustain her throughout the arduous examinations and treatments she had to endure. Knowing how frightened Bec might be, Elizabeth made herself vividly present to the child by telling her what she did every minute of the day, and reminding her that she must put up with the pain of their separation. "My Rebecca," she wrote soothingly, "we will at last unite in His eternal praise, lost in Him, you and I, closer still than in the nine months so dear when, as I told you, I carried you in my bosom as He in our Virgin Mother's—then, no more separation."

Elizabeth held herself in readiness to set out for Philadelphia if Dr. Physick should deem an operation necessary; but even this great man could do nothing for the ailing little girl, except to devise a wooden brace to help her walk. A tumor had formed on the injured hip now, and it was growing large and soft; but even the increased pain failed to dampen Rebecca's bounce and energy and interest in everything new and strange.

Aunt Scott took her riding, to see the grand sights of the classic city: "to the museum, the Bank of Pennsylvania, Bank of the United States, the water works and I do not know where else." Rebecca's mother had trained her well, however, for she wrote: "What was better than all, Sister Rose took me to the poor house. You must know what a coward I am, as you have experienced me. I do not dare to think of my own sufferings after having seen theirs, though Sister Rose tells me I have seen but the best part of it." One old lady had used up all her tobacco, and the child was happy that she had thought to spend nineteen cents for snuff and tobacco for the inmates. Bec was especially fascinated with an old gypsy queen, Agnes, who had herself hung with "old watch seals, beads and chains." Queen Agnes, who had been cared for by Mrs. Seton years before in the New York hospital, thought Bec "a pretty gal."

In a letter of October 26, Elizabeth amused her daughter with the story of little Miss McCarthy of New York, who had been brought to the Emmitsburg school by her father:

> Poor little soul, she is so grieved at being from him, and so spoilt. She is fat and healthy and strong enough but thinks herself so weakly. You would have laughed to see her. She began to tell me, "Mrs. Seton, if any-

body speaks the least word hard or loud to me, I begin to faint just so" (and she began throwing herself back, shutting her eyes and trembling) "and if I go to learn anything, I get such a headache; and I can hardly ever get out of bed before twelve o'clock." Oh, my! Well, poor darling, she could not eat our cooking, *she was sure*. But no sooner did I give her up to the bell and the rule before [the] little woman, though she looked a little mad at me the first day, began to take it easy. And this morning she walked in my room with an orange in her hand for my acceptance.

November was a month of reunion. Rebecca came home, exhausted but content; a letter arrived from Antonio Filicchi, the first Elizabeth had had from him in three years; and by the end of the month she knew that her blessed Bruté had landed safely in Baltimore. She hastened to answer Antonio's letter, singing anew the hymn of her thanks, this time for his kindness to William:

> I cannot hide from Our God, though from everyone else I must conceal, the perpetual tears and affections of boundless gratitude which overflow my heart when I think of him secure in his *Faith* and your protection. Why I love him so much I cannot account, but own to you, my Antonio, all my weakness. Pity and pray for a mother attached to her children through such peculiar motives as I am to mine. I purify it as much as I can, and Our God knows it is their souls alone I look at.

She would never get over her wonder at God's goodness. The Sisters, she told her Italian brother, treated her "more like the Mother *above* than 'the poor Protestant dog,' as you used to call me, just dragged out of the mud and set on the rock. O Antonio, my brother dear, the ways of Our God how wonderful! See my so good little Sister Post and excellent Mrs. Scott *wrapped* in their blindness, and *I* in the milk and honey of Canaan already, beside the heavenly perspective. . . . We pray for you continually, Antonio. You laugh at the fine bill of exchange; but wait till the great accounts are to be settled. You will find the widow's and orphans' prayers were *counted*."

She had unhappy news for Antonio, too: the old Archbishop was dying, and she dreaded the moment of his loss. "My eyes are blind with writing and tears," she told her young Baltimore friend Ellen Wiseman. "Our blessed Archbishop's situation, tho' we must give and resign him, presses hard on me as well as on thousands, harder on me than you would imagine."

The great Father of the American Church died on the third of December in the eighty-first year of his age. He had used the long years of his stewardship well, had kindled an undying Catholic flame; and not the least of its embers was the little community at Emmitsburg, which he had tended so lovingly.

Bruté came to the Valley as quickly as he could, bringing letters from William and the Filicchis in Europe and from Mary Post and Eliza Sadler in New York. He could not stay long, for he had to hasten back to Baltimore to be installed as President of St. Mary's on December 18. Elizabeth sent teasing letters after him that were at the same time sober essays of direction—and humble confessions of her pain at his loss. "From the last look out of the gate I hastened to the dear bench in the choir," she confessed, "where the clay of the soul's 'beautiful feet' yet remained and left their full blessing of peace." She did not even attempt to conceal the blotch an unwary tear made on the page of her letter:

> In this little life of your Mother, not a moment since I saw you to write a word but the meditation, or a volume would not have been enough to say half the heart that fastens to yours more and more, if possible—but with such freedom of the local circumstance, or position of the moment, that I shall see you go again to fulfill your big *Presidentship* (oh, bad omen, G., I did not know that tear was there)—Well, I will see you go to do *His Will of the present moment* with no other sighs or desires but for its most full and complete *accomplishment*.
>
> Your little silly woman in the fields (most happy name and place for her, my G.) your little woman, silly of our dear silliness of prayers and tears, will now hold closer and closer to *Him* Who will do *all in you*, as He does in my poor little daily part, and try always to bring you (*tut!* there again my candle is so dim I cannot see) . . . try always every moment to bring you the support of a Mother's prayers, her cry to Him for your full fidelity as for our poor William's "deliverance from *evil*." . . .
>
> I am truly silly, going as you know to meet everybody in the grace of the moment, which we can never know till we find the humor and temper of the one we are to meet with—the many mistakes all swallowed and comforted by *intention,* intention, intention, our true peace and security with Our Beloved, as you so often delighted to tell me.

Perhaps the most delightful, and certainly among the wisest, pieces of Elizabeth's advice was the dialogue between "Sam"—as she always

called Satan—and the "good angel," which was a sort of installation gift
to the young college president:

> *Sam*—now we'll catch M. *le President!* First, we will fill his head with
> plans of reformation—every successor improves on his predecessor, to be
> sure! Of course, with the *succession* comes multiplied distractions of
> thought, complaisances, etc.—that alone a fine trap, if there was no other,
> but (oh, joy to the grinner!) we will catch him, too, by endless conversa-
> tions and opinions (to be sure, a president must be *full* of opinions!)
>
> This seraphim's wings shall be clipped; and the modest, retiring, devout
> spirit shall swell and fill and push and insist (oh, be joyful, what a change
> we will see!) and this simple heart, loving now to see but his God in, and
> the salvation of, souls, shall be plunged in the labrynths of science and
> grow fat as a doctor (oh, we will have fun this next year, *1816!*)—short
> thanksgivings, quick preparations, forced offerings. . . .

> *Good Angel*—Well, at least he will have abundant sacrifice of dearest,
> choicest consolations. He will act in full opposition to his own choice. His
> daily bread will be dry and hard. He will be a bond of union and peace
> to his confreres, a *spirit* of purest, ardent piety to worldlings, and an example
> of cheerful and tender forbearance to his pupils—poor, dear G., after a little
> while of subjection and patience to his wild heart, it *shall* be set free from
> the yoke, improved and experienced, to return with new ardor to its more
> simple and heavenly delights.

Elizabeth wrote *finis* to this momentous year of 1815 in a solemn note
to Julia Scott, written on Christmas Eve:

> My Julia dear: I must give you my venerable blessing this last post
> of the year 1815, and repeat to you that all my sad inconsistencies, neglects,
> ingratitudes, etc., have nothing to do with the poor heart that loves and ever
> will love you most tenderly. . . .
>
> Rebecca is *just so*—wild and lively and suffering, making me laugh con-
> tinually about her Philadelphia jaunt, especially her little conversations, and
> the pleasure she had with you. . . .
>
> Sister Rose has sent me so many bills you have paid (amounting to at
> least sixty dollars). How happy you are to be able to do so truly charitable
> an action, and how happy we are that it is from you we receive it . . .
>
> Will you, my Julia dear, love your poor, bad Betsey? You will, you must!
> William is so well pleased with his position at Filicchi's! They are so kind
> to him; so far, so good . . .
>
> Say, "Bless your friend this 1816."

XXI

"The Soul . . . Goes Quietly On"

The start of the year 1816, in which Elizabeth was to lose her second daughter, was in marked contrast to the start of the year 1812, in which she had lost her first. She possessed now a great, deep wisdom of soul, whereas then she had struggled in a welter of confusion and puzzlement.

She had been terrified at the imminent loss of Annina—indeed the whole question of her children, of the apparent conflict between her allegiance to them and her allegiance to the religious life had tormented her. She had been bewildered by the acrimony of good, religious men at war over rules and constitutions; she had been torn between her own will to battle for what she thought right and her desire to remain in the peace of obedience and conformity to God's Will; she had been troubled at her resentment toward directors and her earnest wish to be docile.

The years between had resolved all these far-flung conflicts. Elizabeth had learned the hard but sure way of buffetings and contradictions, softened and given meaning by the luminous direction of Simon Gabriel Bruté.

Most of all, she had learned the lesson that, even within the bounds set by community rules and prescriptions, every soul retains its individuality, and receives individual attention from God—is given specific talents and capabilities, is surrounded with certain circumstances, is confronted with its own peculiar problems and difficulties. She had come to understand the implications of her position, to realize that it was not by accident that Elizabeth Seton, widow and mother of five children, had founded a religious community, and that, therefore, she must expect the trails and confusion that such an apparent dichotomy would inevitably raise. And when she had found the bridge of reconciliation, she had found the secret of peace.

To find the secret was not everything: she had to accommodate herself to it. It was a great frustration to be different from her Sisters, to have to divide herself and her time. It was humiliating not to be able to give herself up as wholeheartedly as they could to the practice of the religious rule she had ordained for them. By God's decree, enunciated through the lips of her directors, Mrs. Seton had been forced to bring a part of the world into the convent with her, and she had to come to terms with both. Some students of her life, not fully understanding this, have criticized her for carrying out her maternal duties sometimes to the apparent detriment of her religious life. She was only doing what was for her the Will of God.

In the description of a sudden summer storm, written to her sister Mary Post during these years of growing wisdom, Elizabeth drew a microcosm of her life. It was all there: her own spiritual striving, her fears of a less worthy past, her Sisters, her children—and finally the peace she had come to possess always:

> The beautiful serenity of last night at nine o'clock, when I was alone with you enjoying the brightest moon and clearest sky that can be imagined, was suddenly darkened over. The whole mountain, which overhung with black, threatening clouds and quick darts of lightning, looked too awful; and I turned to my beautiful moon in her serene majesty over our plain with inconceivable delight, thinking to my God: *the soul that looks only at You goes quietly on, and the black and fearful storm can come so far and no farther. . . .*
> Dropping asleep with my crucifix under my pillow and the Blessed Virgin's picture pressed on the heart, Kit and Rebecca fast asleep near me— think of the contrast, to wake with the sharpest lightnings and loudest thunder succeeding each other so rapidly that they seemed to stop but half a moment between, to give time for a sense of the danger. Every part of the house seemed struck in an instant, and the roarings of the winds and tor-

rents through the mountains so impetuous, that it seemed they must destroy, if the lightnings should spare.

Our God, what a moment! I had no power to rise, or to remember I was a sinner, or give a thought to the horrors of death, or the safety of the children. God my Father in that moment so pressing—and the plunge in eternity the next instant.

O my Mary! How tight I held my little picture as a mark of confidence in her prayers who must be tenderly interested for souls so dearly purchased by her Son, and the crucifix held up as a silent prayer which offered all His merits and sufferings as our only hope—

How you laugh at your poor, half-brained Betsey Seton, but never mind—

The decadence of the storm brought me down from the clouds, and I felt really, I suppose, as one who is drawn back from the door of eternity, after having been half in, and I crept away to the choir window, to see what had become of my little, peaceable Queen, who was wrapped in clouds alternately lightened as they passed over her with so much brightness, they appeared at first sight like balls of light hastening towards us, while she was tak[ing] her quiet course above them, to disappear behind the mountain.

There again I found the soul which fastens on God. Storms or whirlwinds pass by or over it, but cannot stop it one moment. My Mary, dear, how nice it would have been to have died then—if it had been the right time. But since it was not, here I am, very happy to meet all the countenances of terror and wonder this morning, and the repeated appeal of: "O Mother, what a night!"

This same sense of peace lying beneath the surface storms was in a note to Bruté, in which Elizabeth discussed the apparent contradiction that plagues the lives of all souls especially dedicated to God: the seeming misuse of their talents in works that strike them as unnecessary or unsuitable—and often are. Here again was the wise turning to God Who alone can resolve such conflicts in favor of good:

While I say our *Te Deum* in union with your thanksgiving, my heart fills at "O Lord, save Thy people," thinking how things are shared in this world. I see a quiet, moderate, *experienced* man put in the center of a congregation who is not "saved" for want of an active, zealous, driving man, because they must have "fire" cried in their ears; and I see a zealous, driving man without *experience* put in a seminary where he will "save" none, because he cannot wait to gain a heart or unfold a temper, and his zeal, instead of bedewing the plant in the thirsty ground, crushes it under foot. Alas, well if he does not root it out forever!

O Lord, then *"save!"* Save the redeemed of Thy Precious Blood, and send wisdom from above.

"Blessed," I am truly *downhearted* this day, poor leper! Yet, "Glory to the Father, Son and Holy Ghost!" has been my incessant prayer with one hundred meanings. Too sick to do anything but pray.

This basic contentment and peace stood Elizabeth in good stead, for the sadness of life never ceased. "We are all well, your sweet Rebecca excepted, whose tumor is inflamed, very sore and, I believe, near breaking," she wrote Dué. "Poor darling, her fast rolling tears—at times without any other sign—is the whole expression of her pain. Blessed child, she would hide them, if she could, to keep me from suffering."

The poor mother, in her turn, did everything to distract the child. "I sing her our old songs of thirty years ago," she told Julia Scott, "tell her stories, and use all my inventions to pass over her weary hours." She asked Julia to send Rebecca a doll, since "Mother and a doll seems to be her only pleasure in life"; and she confessed, in one of the outbursts of girlishness that never quite left her, "I am extremely fond of (dolls) myself."

In February, Mary Post sent the pathetic news that her oldest son, Edward—the pride of his father—was dead; and, despite Elizabeth's constant annoyance at what she called her sister's lack of religious sense, Mary displayed a calm abandonment to Providence in her grief that could come only from deep religious feeling.

Richard, who had been off in Baltimore with his friend Borman for several months, finally returned home at his mother's insistence; but, having had a taste of the outside world, he began at once to fret and to badger her in his anxiety to be off again, to start his fortune. Elizabeth wrote wearily to William: "I have now just the same old course to take for Richard I once had for you, my darling son—letters after letters to move the Baltimore hearts to receive your brother." Luke Tiernan could not help her, and she turned next "to attack poor Mr. Barry's continued kindness."

She even thought of New York and the Ogden counting house— Abraham Ogden, at least, had been kind to her—but her memories of the rest of the Ogdens, particularly her sister-in-law, Charlotte Seton Ogden, deterred her. "If you knew what I do of the peculiarities of that family, you would never wish him to be there," she admonished William. "From the manner they have behaved to me, I doubt much their receiving a child of mine. You know, it was they who wrote the threatening letter that the house would be burned over my head, calling me siren, etc., etc."

In connection with Elizabeth's efforts to place Richard, it is interesting to observe that she had not wholly shaken herself free of the prejudices of the class into which she had been born: it is obvious that she considered certain types of work eminently more respectable than others. Thus she informed William with evident distaste that his brother might go to "Mr. Elder's, who is a grocer (wholesale, though) . . . I know, too, it will vex you; but he pushes so hard to go—and, really, I see no prospect for him, unless in New York."

She was in her forty-second year, now, and considered herself an old woman. Certainly sickness and trials had ravaged her beauty and preyed on her buoyancy; and she constantly referred to herself humorously as "an old bag of bones" or "an old worn-out thing." She suffered another spell of sickness as the winter of 1816 waned, and Julia Scott wrote in alarm, quoting Sister Rose as the source of her information that Elizabeth was doing too much.

Elizabeth laughed off her friend's concern, pointing out that Rose was "so long away, she does not know home as it is," and citing the elaborate fuss the Sisters made of her. "Their care and attention to save me every trouble would appear even ridiculous to others who, not living with us, do not know the tie of affection which is formed by living in community," she wrote proudly. "Perhaps you have no idea of the order and quiet which takes place in a regular way of life. Everything meets its place and time in such a manner that a thing once done is understood by the simplest person as well as by the most intelligent." And she added with a dry humility that surely did not fool Mrs. Scott: "For my part, you know better than anyone what a fine intelligence I ever had for anything but taking care of No. 1!"

Elizabeth learned in March that William was not receiving the letters she and the girls wrote almost daily, and she cried over his complaints and reproaches. "I cannot help it," she told him. "Absence, separation, all that must be endured. But to think that the one we love most in

the world neglects us—oh, that is hard! Yet, you know me so well, my
son, your heart did justice to its Mother, even when it pained you most.
We send four letters different directions at a time."

In all of them, she returned again and again to her fears for his soul.
"This morning," she wrote on April 5, "I found myself praying for your
confessor—that will make you laugh—so anxious that he should lead
you well. I beg so hard you may be 'an honest man,' as you say, at Easter,
for you know an honest man gives to God his due as well as to man. Is
it not so?"

In commenting upon the turbulence of domestic politics, she gave
William a memorable lesson in reverence for authority:

> There is every prospect of new COMMOTIONS. How you will be shocked
> to see Mr. Jefferson turned to a John Gilpin in the papers! You must
> allow there is something revolting, to see a chief magistrate treated so.
> I do not understand politics or characters, but have a horror to find our
> Government can countenance such a press freedom. The children read it
> to me for fun in our recreation, but my Bayley blood mounted. Do, my
> son, reflect and be moderate in these cases. Always take the side of order.
> It is God's first law, says our true poet.

It was a sparse season for news all around, the mails a complete muddle.
Dué had been writing all winter and spring, yet Elizabeth told Antonio
Filicchi in April that she heard from no one. In May she received a
note by special messenger from Eliza Sadler, in which Sad averred that,
to write by post "seems labor in vain." She gave Elizabeth the welcome news that Dué "had much better health this last winter than I
ever remember her to have had, though she has gone out constantly and
taken little care of herself. She is engaged in an excellent work, trying
to get the girls' schools of St. Peter's and St. Patrick's regulated." It
would seem that hard work and outside interests were the medicine that
benefited the ailing Dué most.

Sad herself was in the midst of establishing a manufactory for the
poor and aged whereby they might more easily provide their own living.
She sent along to Elizabeth a book just off the press, the meditations
of that pious Protestant lady, Mrs. Isabella Graham, whom Elizabeth
had aided in founding the Poor Widows' Society of New York. Mrs.

Graham, dead the year before, had possessed a fine religious mind, and Bruté pronounced her meditations beautiful and profound.

Mary Post, too, made use of a messenger, Mr. McCarthy—he of the spoiled little daughter—to send gifts: "stockings for the girls, muslin for caps for mama and cravats for brother, if sisters will hem them." Mary expressed the hope that Rebecca would suffer less with the coming of the warm weather, but the poor child was beyond such hope. She had had some relief in the spring, when her tumor broke, but only for a time. The agony shooting through her thin little body was so intense that she could neither stand nor lie down, but she had to keep a sitting posture. She sat most of the day and night on her mother's knee, leaning against her, so that in time Elizabeth's left arm lost all sensation, becoming almost atrophied, and her legs grew so stiff that she limped when she walked.

Elizabeth had the sole care of Bec—except for Sister Susan, who had returned from the orphanage in Philadelphia—for Dick and Kit had departed for Baltimore. In May Luke Tiernan had finally agreed to take the young man into his home and business; and Kit, who was an intimate friend of the Tiernan girls followed her brother there in June. Kit was sixteen now, and Elizabeth felt she should begin to see more of the world than the Valley and the Sisters and the boarders. The girl had, besides, a splendid opportunity for advanced drawing and music lessons; she was exceptionally proficient in music, and earned her whole livelihood by teaching piano to the children of St. Joseph's, at a salary of $200.00 a year. Certainly it was a time when the poor mother needed the strength and comfort of her son and daughter, but she refused to be selfish by interfering with their prospects.

Despite her pains, little Bec never let go her high spirits. She sat all day clinging to her mother, babbling a thousand bits of nonsense, or drawing pictures on rice paper, or listening while Elizabeth read "beautiful stories so instructive" from a three-volume set of books for children called *Parents' Assistant,* or delighting in the wild and mischievous notes sent in by her little schoolmates.

While Elizabeth was writing to Willy on July 2, she told him, Bec sat "painting a little picture, and laughing till she cried at the flies plaguing me." Father Bruté, a prodigious walker, was making missionary tours on foot during the summer holiday, and Elizabeth told him that Bec, reading "with full joy the chapter *In Tempore et Eterne* on the *agility* hereafter to be given to her little, poor body, now almost fastened to the seat on the bed, laughed gladly at the thought that, like some Ignatius or Anthony of Padua, you will make your walking journeys with an anticipated *agility* to be perfected in the high eternal regions."

Indeed, as Mother Seton's true spiritual child, Rebecca dwelt happily on the thoughts of her dissolution and the gladsome eternity to follow it. She was not afraid to die; nor did she see any bravery in her lack of fear: it was what she had been born for, to die. "Dearest Mother, you think I am not willing to die, but I am," the little girl once protested. "Indeed I am. All I fear is my sins." Like Annina before her, but in a more lighthearted, unsophisticated way better suited to her thirteen years, the child bounded forward in sanctity during the last terrible months of her illness. On the 29th of June Elizabeth noted to Bruté: "Poor beloved! We examine much together if she is in the good disposition of *the Will*. She is so *sure*—only she says, 'Perhaps I indulge my feelings too much, not staying in bed at night; but I do suffer so in it.' Strange indulgence! Yet do pray for the poor lamb: it has so many little old and even saucy ways of pride, pretension, etc. (Seton maladies)."

This fear of indulging herself at the expense of God's Will bothered Rebecca from time to time. Thus she whispered to Elizabeth on July 20: "I will try again to go to bed, dear Mother (I know I cannot stay) but must take it quietly. We will offer up the pain of getting in and out, and let it take its way."

And yet, it was wholly characteristic of the vibrant little spirit that Rebecca could season the fiercest pang with the salt of fun. Elizabeth noted in the *Journal* she kept of Bec's last months as carefully as she had kept Annina's:

> Bec told so droll a story while my head was wild with fever like her own—both on the same pillow.
> "*What state do you live in,* my son?" said a country schoolmaster to his little scholar.
> "*In a state of sin and misery,*" answered the boy.

And we two laughed like fools at the state we were in: looking beyond at the eternal peace and serenity to come so soon, too, for me, she says.

I tell her, "Can you say with a true heart, 'Thy Will be done!'?"

"Oh, that I can," she answers, brightening with joy, "if *that is enough.*"

Dear, dear darling, how she is wrapped in the very nerves of my soul.

She was indeed. The innocent little scapegrace was more like Elizabeth than any of the other children.

It is hardly surprising that, when Elizabeth, according to her custom, sent a spiritual nosegay for the feast of the Visitation to Juliana White, an alumna of St. Joseph's, it was a death prayer—as if Bec were speaking through her mother's lips:

Oh, my Lord Jesus, who was born for me in a stable, lived for me a life of pain and sorrow, and died for me upon a cross; say for me in the hour of death: "*Father, forgive,*" and to Thy Mother, "*Behold thy Child.*" Say to me, Thyself, "*This day thou shalt be with Me in Paradise.*" O My Savior, leave me not, *forsake me not. I thirst* for Thee, Fountain of Living Water. My days pass quickly along, soon all will be *consummated* for me. *To Thy hands I commend my spirit,* now and forever, Amen.

There were renewed hopes that Dué would make another visit to the Valley that July, but they were not fulfilled. Rebecca looked for her; and when, the week before St. Vincent's Day, Sister Susan remarked that "it is well Mrs. Dupleix did not come this week, as we are all going in retreat," Bec replied with her prompt pertness: "The very reason I would wish she had come: then I would have had her all to myself." Not quite, for Elizabeth could not leave the child for a minute, as she told Kit in Baltimore: "I could take no other retreat but by her side. Most of her time is passed in my arms or on my knee. We wet each other pretty often with tears."

Elizabeth missed Kit and Dick sorely but, while stating the fact of her longing, refused to indulge it:

Lilacs, little blossoms of many kinds and tiny branches from our dear graves are all around me. Our room looks so pinky from morning till night. You would laugh, for I keep close by the cabinet, and pick up my books so carefully that Sister Susy twirls in and out twelve times a day and finds nothing to do. Sisters Agnes and Martha read Chateaubriand every evening to me with wondrous delight, and I with so new delight in him, that I could not help putting some little pages in *your* book. O Kit, my Kit, what is this? It seems—but never mind what it seems. My trinity of earthly love must be in the soul—not in the present enjoyment—as well as the spiritual heaven.

It hurt her that Dick was showing a thoughtless bent, and the note ended sadly: "But no, no letters from Dick. That truly puzzles me most painfully." Thoughtlessness was to be the least of the heartaches he would cause her in her few remaining years.

Kit came home to Emmitsburg at the beginning of September, much to Elizabeth's joy: the girl told Aunt Scott that "Mother wished me to have applied longer with my drawing master . . . but Rebecca's situation was so alarming that I could not be happy from home."

Kit brought significant news from Father Bruté. The first Vincentian missionaries to America had arrived in Baltimore, where they had been Bruté's guests for two weeks. This first band of thirteen was led by the Venerable Felix de Andreis, who may some day be canonized, and included Joseph Rosati, the future first Bishop of St. Louis. They had come at the invitation of Bishop Dubourg of New Orleans and, after pausing at St. Mary's in Baltimore, set off on an exhausting and perilous journey to the West, stopping on the way to visit Flaget and David in Bardstown. Elizabeth wrote to Bruté on September 2 that she had received Holy Communion and "directed those of the Sisters to thanks for the blessed missioners sent to enlighten our savage land." Appropriately, it was "Leper" Sunday, when the parable of Dives and Lazarus was read in the Mass, and Elizabeth took note of the day by heading her letter "St. Lazare"—in St. Vincent's time the Vincentian mother house in Paris had been called St. Lazare, and even today his priests are often called Lazarists. In the years ahead when the community at Emmitsburg should have united with St. Vincent's Daughters of Charity, some of Elizabeth's daughters would pass under the authority of St. Vincent's successor, and under the spiritual direction of these same Lazarists or Vincentian Fathers.

Julia wrote excitedly on September 20 to tell Elizabeth that her son, John Scott, was engaged to marry Miss Mary Emlen of Germantown: "as the affair is but just concluded, I cannot tell you anything of plans or arrangements, tho' you may suppose my brain is very busy in forming them." She sent a parcel containing "an old gown . . . worn by your friend last winter . . . of the gown you can make a petticoat only, but I could not resist the temptation of sending it with the old body on, from the fancy that you would put it on, to try how Julia's things would fit you." Elizabeth did, indeed, put it on, and pirouetted mincingly to the vast amusement of her daughters.

Little Bec was failing fast, and never out of her mother's arms, so that Kit had to act as secretary in dealing with Elizabeth's heavy correspondence. Bec's soul took on the mature stature of the saints in these last days, and her utterances were far older than her fourteen years. On the 17th of October she assured her mother cheerfully: "Now, if Dr. Chatard was to say, 'Rebecca, you will get well,' I would not wish it. Oh, no, no, my dear Savior, I know now the happiness of an early death, and to sin no more. My Mother, there is the point; yet nature and grace has had a hard conflict."

Toward the last her mind began to wander, and she told Elizabeth one morning: "I have been a long while with dear Dick [who was actually in Baltimore] so busy filling up little bags. The last one was almost full and Dick put a big apple in it, but I took it out to examine it before I tied it up, and found a black spot on it. 'Dick,' said I, 'that cannot go in; do you not know the Holy Scriptures say, 'Nothing defiled can enter heaven?' " At other times she would fancy she was winding balls of yarn, or would laugh delightedly at her mother's broken voice singing hymns to soothe her. But always, coming to herself, the dying child would turn to God. "You would never believe the foolish thoughts in my mind," she confessed to her mother on one such occasion, "I am even making little rhymes. My love is so weak, so imperfect. Oh, my Mother, I have been so, so, unfaithful, I have proved it so little!"

The end came on November 3, 1816. The afternoon before, she had told Elizabeth with conviction: "I have just been handing Our Lord my little cup. It is now quite full. He will come for me."

At night [noted Elizabeth in her *Journal*] the Superior came again, promising to stay with her to the last. . . . At last, near four in the morning, she said:

"Let me sit once more on the bed. It will be the last struggle." [Sister] Cecil beside her, Mother's arms lifting her, she sunk between us, but the darling head fell on its well-known heart it loved so well. After she seemed gone for awhile, nature made another push, and she said distinctly: "Ma, the girls talk so loud."

"Think only of your dear Savior now, my darling," I said.

"To be sure, certainly," she answered, and said no more, dropping her head for the last time on her Mother's heart.

The death of Rebecca was not Elizabeth's only grief that autumn. Word had come from William that Filippo Filicchi, too, was gone. Sadly she told Bruté: "If you knew how much *I had counted* on his life, how you would laugh at me. But, God alone! I am too happy to be forced to have no other refuge."

She spoke true. Elizabeth Seton had come at last to the port of full peace. Writing of her reaction to Bec's passing, Father Dubois said:

> The Mother is a miracle of divine favor. Night and day by the child, her health has not appeared to suffer. She held the child in her arms without dropping a tear, all the time of her agony and even eight minutes after she had died. *Mulierem fortem.*

Rebecca's death was surrounded with strange hints of the preternatural. Elizabeth, in informing William of his sister's death, wrote on November 11: "She said often, if it was possible to show herself to you, she would. But one thing she was sure: her Lord would not refuse to let her see you, and, from the heavenly graces He favored her with in this world, we may well think He would deny her nothing."

Mary Post was preoccupied with the same notion of extrasensory manifestation. "How thoroughly the little saint must have investigated the probable events of her translation, to speak of it in the way she did," Mary wrote her sister on December 7. "We have often heard the subject discussed as regarding the probability or not of departed spirits revisiting their former scene of attraction. Could such a belief be admitted, this instance of filial piety might be likely to fully determine that question. When you write, tell me, dear, the exact time of Rebecca's death. Events of importance to us, perhaps, make us notice that connection with them that we should not be impressed by at another time. I certainly had a very remarkable dream about the time it must have taken place; and had a similar dream, and was in company with the same persons, about the time of my Edward's death—persons that you are acquainted with, that I am not."

Elizabeth herself noted an odd, if not remarkable, occurrence in her *Journal*. Her tale began on the eve of Bec's death:

> "Come and see me next night at eleven, for (she told Sister Margaret very gaily, who was speaking of someone going home) I will be home to-morrow."
>
> About a quarter before eleven, kneeling by her [corpse], surrounded by her night watch in the choir, through the opposite window next the chapel door, I saw in the midst of the blackest sky imaginable, and rolling loud thunder and lightning with driving wind rattling everything around us, the purest white cloud, bright as if near the sun. As it advanced rapidly towards the window, I was forced to smile with Cecil, who knew her promise—gazed at it with delight of thousand, dearest imaginations; then dropped in the thought of the Blessed Reality to be received next morning in the white cloud of the sacred veils.

Elizabeth would not console herself with telepathy or superstition or even miracles: the eternity beyond the horizon was enough for her.

Not long after Bec had been laid to rest, Father Bruté, straitened by the arms of his president's chair, tried to assuage his burning zeal for souls by urging the Faith upon Eliza Sadler. He had already, the previous summer, attempted the conversion of Mary Post by mail, and thought it "curious" that Elizabeth should consider the attempt useless.

> Your letter to Sister admirable [she had written], if first the big stone of darkest ignorance and indifference was removed on the point of first necessity—*that there is any true church or false church, right faith or wrong faith*. But Blessed Soul, you, nor anyone who has not been in that ignorance or indifference, can imagine the size and depth of it. And putting myself again a moment in the place of my sister (even with my great advantage of having been passionately attached to religion when a Protestant, which she is not), I imagine I read your letter and, looking up with vacant surprise, would say:
>
> "What does the man mean? Would he say that all who believe in Our Lord are not safe, or if even a poor Turk or savage does not believe, is he to be blamed for it? They make God a merciful Being indeed, if He would condemn souls of His own creation for their parents bringing them in the world on one side of it or the other!" . . .

For ever accustomed to look only to little exterior attractions, as the dress and quiet of the Quakers, a sweet, enthusiastic preaching among the Methodists, a soft, melting music of low voices among Anabaptists, or any other such nonsense, the thought of a right faith or wrong faith, true church or false one, never enters the mind of one among a hundred.

O my God! My heart trembles and faints before Him here in His little sacristy close to His tabernacle, while I ask Him, *"How am I here?—I taken, they left."*

If Bruté thought Elizabeth's reasons curious, the modern priest, faced with the widespread indifference to truth which is a blight on America and the world, does not. She knew, from experience, whereof she spoke; she knew that the impetus of God's grace alone could vault the non-believing soul over its "ignorance and indifference" into the promised land of truth. It was, indeed, this very refusal of the good Protestant to consider the possibility of a true church, that was the essence of Eliza Sadler's reply to Bruté. Sad was not at all offended that he had attempted her conversion—her letter is, in fact, clear proof of her habitual courtesy and intelligence—but she rejected firmly his thesis:

> For the kind motive of your letter I need hardly offer you my acknowledgments. As a Christian professing the faith you do, you cannot be other than a watchful servant of your Master, ever ready to seize occasions of leading sinners into the path you believe necessary to their salvation. Suffer me to assure you that I reverence your piety, and duly appreciate the zeal and benevolence that distinguishes your character.
>
> The truth, however, obliges me to assure you that I feel it impossible to subscribe to the belief that out of your Church there can be no Christians. Ever since I have been capable of reason, I have endeavored humbly to make the law of my Redeemer the rule and guide of my actions, unworthily and unperfectly, but not blindly; and I believe that He Who sees the inmost thoughts will judge of my faith, as He promised to do by all those who believe in His Name: and my constant prayer is that He may enlighten my understanding so as to enable me to obey His divine precepts, and give testimony of the faith I profess.

Elizabeth was having her own troubles in explaining the Church's teaching to a prospective convert, as she related to Bruté in a letter of December 26; and it is interesting to note that, in the intervening years since her own conversion, she seemed to have forgotten the torments once raised in her soul by the intricacies of Christian argument:

Brain and heart burning (this day of St. Stephen, who saw heaven open) with our poor Miss Marcelle's questions on faith. . . . Poor girl! she has to combat the horrid impressions of the deriders and mockers of religion as well as the rest of *her* oppositions. Yet, such good disposition— esteeming herself in this house as a *wretch*, as I did myself in Leghorn. . . . Do, do, do pray for her.

She says she believes Our Redeemer *came*, but *why original sin?* Then, why a God did so much to repair it, etc., etc.?

Tut! My vacant brains were never busy enough about that to mind, even what I have read of it, except to *adore* and skip up to the scene where all will be revealed. She stared when I told her gravely they were *mysteries of love*, as much as when I assured her I was only an *adorer*, too, of the mystery of the Church, the only ark in the world—and all the heathens, savages, sects, etc., were only in my heart for prayer, but never in my brain for what became of them, or to trouble my faith in His wisdom and mercy. The Father most tender, Father of *All*, my immense God—I His atom.

Rebecca's death had released Elizabeth to take up again her full duties as Superioress and principal of the school—not that she had relinquished the reins of government during Bec's illness, but she had not left the child's room for months, and all business, spiritual and temporal, had had necessarily to be transacted there. Now she entered into the affairs of the house with a new vigor, as she told Dué: "Every moment, I may say, of life, someone is looking to me to say or do something: sixty and more children boarders, besides the country children, and treble the Sisters we had when you were here." She assured her friend that she enjoyed "better health and lighter heart" than before, and finished playfully: "You must give me up, as I do myself, into His hands Who has done so much for us both."

Samuel Cooper visited the Valley in November to discuss the incorporation of the Sisterhood, which General Robert Goodloe Harper was sponsoring in the state legislature. In early December Bishop Cheverus came, on purpose to visit Elizabeth, but also to administer Confirmation to the children of St. Joseph's while he was there. Since Archbishop Carroll's death, Cheverus had been considered for Baltimore. Archbishop Neale, who had succeeded to the See, was old and sick; and when Cheverus arrived in November to invest him with the pallium, he asked the Boston prelate to accept the appointment as his coadjutor. It was a popular choice, but Cheverus demurred, and begged Elizabeth to join him in praying "Our Lord to look down on this Diocese and to preserve it and myself from what is intended. The very idea is more than I can bear."

The reservation with which Elizabeth would enter into such a prayer can be imagined, since it would be the ultimate happiness for her to have the "Blessed Cheverus" nearby. In any event, the two dear friends shared a happy 6th and 7th of December; and when Cheverus left, it was the last parting for them in this world.

For some months Elizabeth had suffered increasing anxiety over Richard. He was a basically irresponsible and immature young man. Elizabeth bravely shielded this fact from most of her friends, noting in her letters only the good things said of him, especially the praise of his "innocence" and good humor; but with every post from Baltimore that fall and winter of 1816 her heart sank deeper in dejection over him:

> Richard . . . does not give poor Kit and I as much comfort in a year as one of your letters, though so far away [she told William]. His heart is not turned like yours, my son, and I dread, yet hope, everything. You would not guess half the trials we have had with him in Baltimore through his childish, thoughtless, disposition. Mr. Williamson, Mr. Tiernan's son-in-law, who lives in the house with him, says: "He is a fine young man, but will be lost for want of employment and by company." Not that he keeps any, out of the house, that I ever heard; but there is so much in it— and they send him to wait on this one and that one, and he must be dressed, etc., etc. . . . So, you may guess if I have any other hope but to look up to God, your Father and mine.

Elizabeth had more reason for confiding in William than merely to unburden herself. Her older son himself was growing restless, talking gloomily of his future prospects, and hinting—apparently as a motive for her to call him home—that he "did not think he was giving satisfaction to the Filicchis." The poor, distracted mother tried to quiet him by pointing out the trouble she was having with his brother. The Filicchis, nor anyone else who had seen him in Italy, she assured him, had said any word but in his favor. With a rare burst of candor—she seldom let her children know the extent of her trials—she told this first-born son exactly what her life had been, and was, doubtless hoping that some feeling of manly shame would prompt him to stifle his dissatisfaction:

I never can lament your not having property to set out with, for out of hundreds of young men whom I have happened to know with something before them beginning the world, I never saw one succeed in any comparison with the thousands who have their character to support and bread to earn the first set-out. The destruction of all your grandfather's family has evidently happened through their dependence on their father. He used to delight in saying: "Let all come to my strong box while I am alive, and when I am gone you will take care of each other." You know the result, your dear papa having indeed to take care of brothers and sisters till his children wanted bread at last, if God had not given(n) uncommon friends— And for me you know well how it has been.

But it is all a reason more for you, my son, to keep well with Him Who turns every heart as He pleases, and will bring you forward with honor and credit, if you make Him your Friend. And, if you do not, friends and good prospects are as variable as the seasons. And if you suffer, my beloved, through this painful separation, then I must, who look on this life as a moment and has so many other fears about our eternal settlement. A mother's heart, I can truly say, has one continual agony. You have a hundred ways of forgetting me, but I not for one moment forget you. . . .

You must take courage with me, and push on, and do not let your mind rest on the sad thought of future prospects, since the Providence of God turns out so often quite different from our calculations. . . . You are but twenty, my beloved, too young yet to begin the world if you even had means; so, be patient and trust.

She did not let the matter rest there, but wrote immediately to Antonio Filicchi, on January 12, 1817, begging him "By the dear crucifix at which I look while making the request that you will tell me something about William, and what may be the possible event of his present situation. . . . I do entreat you, dear Antonio, tell me if you are satisfied with him, and intend he shall remain for any length of time with you."

Richard's eye was on further horizons than Baltimore, and he began to express the wish to be with William in Leghorn. Elizabeth, however, had no intention of imposing unduly on the kindness of Antonio; but when it became apparent in February that Dick must leave the Tiernan counting house, because of the expected return of Luke Tiernan's son from Europe, and a projected partnership, she did venture to ask Antonio whether any of his business friends in Europe might take Richard. The habitual slowness of communication, aggravated that winter by the freezing over of American ports, further complicated Elizabeth's tangled web of trouble. Thus, Richard was back in Emmitsburg before the news of Elizabeth's anxiety for him reached William; and William himself had practically resolved to return to America before he had received Elizabeth's letters begging him not to be hasty.

The extent of the mother's devotion and concern showed in a note dashed off to William on St. Valentine's Day:

> My soul's own William: The bitter, freezing North wind is now always rattling, and they write me on every side—New York and Baltimore—that the ice will let no vessel go to you. Yet, my head and heart is so full of you, that though letters for you are waiting at both ports, I must write. If I wake in the night, I think it is your angel wakes me to pray for you. And last night I found myself actually dropping asleep, repeating your name over and over, and appealing to Our Lord with the agony of a mother's love for our long and dear and everlasting reunion.

It is to be hoped that the love of such a mother made the son at least pause to weigh his discontent objectively.

The state of Maryland granted incorporation to the Sisterhood in January, 1817, the corporate title being fixed as "The Sisters of Charity of St. Joseph's," and the ends of the institute defined as "works of piety, charity and usefulness, and especially for the care of the sick, the succor of aged, infirm and necessitous persons, and the education of young females." The document named twenty-two Sisters above the age of twenty-one.

The community was firmly planted now, ecclesiastically and civilly, flourishing in numbers and good works, producing its constant harvest in minds and hearts and souls and, most of all, in the perfecting of its members. Here—scarcely eight years after she began her work—is the retort incontrovertible to those who have caviled over Mother Elizabeth Seton's contribution to spirituality in America, pointing out that the archival evidence for her talents as a mother superior and directress of souls is much sparser than the like evidence for her talents as a mother, a friend, or an administrator.

There are logical reasons for the sparsity of such evidence. Mother Seton's Sisters lived under the same roof with her; she had no need to write them letters of spiritual advice. It was not her custom to write out in full her formal conferences and instructions, but to jot down her thoughts in outline and develop them as she spoke. Even these outlines are lost for the most part to posterity, for it was apparently not her habit to save them; those which remain were preserved by the Sisters and especially by Father Bruté. In this regard, it is significant that the great bulk of original material available to the biographer of Mrs. Seton are letters and writings in her own hand, preserved by those to whom, or for whom, she wrote them; and that the collection of letters received by her from others is much more meagre.

The proof of Elizabeth's success as a spiritual mother is in the admiration of holy adepts such as Carroll and Cheverus and Bruté. It is in the wholehearted devotion of her daughters: she at first took innocent delight in the fact that, on their deathbeds, they clung to her like true children; but with age and deepening holiness she grew flustered and embarrassed at the way they mingled her name with the Name of Jesus in their final aspirations. The ultimate proof, however, is in her impact upon the American Church; in the eleven thousand American Sisters of Charity who give her allegiance; and in their hundreds of schools and orphanages and hospitals and houses of charity.

Indeed, Mother Seton's most distinctive contribution to the science of spirituality were the American qualities she brought it. Her religious direction, despite her French masters, had an American practicality, generosity and informality. Her instructions were simple and down-to-earth. She stressed efficiency in administration and pedagogy, to be achieved through simplicity and directness of approach. She taught hard work as an essential means of salvation and perfection. And all was to be done with open hand, warm heart and friendly smile. She was a woman of hope and unconquerable optimism, a pioneer who stood on the soil of a vast land and felt the first stirrings of its promise. She was truly a pioneer: for she believed in the future greatness of the Church in America just as surely as the breakers of the wilderness and the rail-splitters and the ploughers of new farms believed in the vision of a promised land. Her brother-in-law Sam Seton was not far from the truth when he described her for her grandchildren as "a kind of John the Baptist."

It is worthy of remark that she clung, prophetically and with sure Catholic instinct, to the hand of her who was to be proclaimed Patroness of the United States. "We honor her continually with Our Jesus," she told her Sisters. "His nine months within her—what passed between them—she alone knowing Him—He her only tabernacle. . . . *Mary, full of grace, Mother of Jesus!* Oh, we love and honor Our Jesus when we love and honor her!—a true proof of our blessed Church being the one Jesus best loves. . . ." And she concluded with the all-encompassing reminder: "Mary [is] the first Sister of Charity on earth."

Bruté, in editing this passage in later years, crossed out the word "best" and, with theological precision, substituted the word "only," so that the amended phrase reads: "a true proof of our blessed Church being the one Jesus *only* loves." In so doing, the zealous man called attention to Elizabeth's unwillingness, despite her frequent impatience with "the blindness and ignorance" of her Protestant friends, to place them outside the reach of God's love. She revealed her delicacy of thought in the matter in a letter to Eliza Sadler, written that winter of 1817. The combination of Bruté's letter to Mrs. Sadler aimed at her conversion and Elizabeth's failure to write over a period of months had apparently caused the New York matron to fear that her friend was angry with her. Elizabeth wrote feelingly to assure her that such was not the case.

My poor cheek began to burn the moment I saw the well-known, long-loved writing from your dear hand and, after reading, my quiet heart began to shake at the thought that your first impression at my long silence was so far from the true cause. But I silence it by an appealing look to the dear crucifix—so long the book of my dying Bec—that, so far from religion being a source of coldness or neglect towards you . . . it is that very identical point in your and my little compass of life that brings my thoughts and often liveliest imaginations closest to you—not as you might suppose, ever dear friend, as it relates to our views of faith (for that most delicate and sacred subject I have long since learned to leave to God, except where my duty is explicit), but as it relates to our taste and habits of life: mine being so exactly what you would most fondly delight in, that over and over I have said, and most frequently now say to myself, "If only dear Sad could see it and know it!" For your *matron step* and *quiet look* and independent *intention* are now precisely the rule of my life.

Elizabeth closed with a charming passage that breathed serenity and contentment:

> Since dearest *Bec is* gone . . . and I am free from so many painful cares and able to fulfill so many more duties in the little service of our little world contained in St. Joseph's, everything seems to wear a new color, and life has a charm for me which I often wondered you found in it. So far from the world, surrounded by all the sweets of the country and retirement, an old woman to whom the nearly one hundred souls in our house look for their daily solace of a Mother's smile, incapacitated by my *want of capacity to manage and bustle* from taking any other part but to try and keep off the evil spirits which always would steal in such a multitude, and turn everything to the account of peace and order, writing and translating, my ever darling pastime now as ever, with the knitting always on the same table with the pen to show the visitors they are not unwelcome.

The feast of the Annunciation was a day of exceptional sweetness. "One day of my poor life without a cloud," Elizabeth recorded, "the most singular peace from the Vespers of Mary when, drawing a meditation for our vows, the very soul melted before Him. Then this morning's awaking at 4:30, with the Ave sung to waken the dormitories. Our meditation, office of the Blessed Virgin Mary, preparation, Mass, vows so peaceable. Then all day so, so sweetly, so gently, among all the little duties of *hearing, reading, speaking,* singing Vespers and hymns, and my dear old *Holy Court*—making many extracts." And, as if pinpointing the reason and seed of all this beatitude, she wrote in the margin: "Anniversary of my dear First Communion."

It was evident that Elizabeth had reached a plateau high among the mountains of sanctity. It showed in the tranquility of her daily life, in her letters, in everything she said and did. Even Mary Post sensed it and paid tribute in a remarkably perceptive letter of April 5:

> My dearest sister, with all the difficulties and trials your life has been attended with, I still think you are blessed beyond the usual lot of mortals. I believe in a presiding Providence, and that you have always been its peculiar care is to me most certain. . . . It can be from a well directed and governed spirit alone that you can estimate things as they ought to be estimated. But to have attained that state of mind making you independent of what troubles all the rest of the world who have not obtained it. . . . God grant grace to myself and those who want it, to do as well as you have done.

Mary took great pride in displaying her sister's goodness, and her own recognition of it, to others; and she found an unusual opportunity when Bishop John Henry Hobart and his wife came to call on her one day.

Do not be dissatisfied with me [she begged Elizabeth] if I tell you that, in a late visit from your old friends Bishop and Mrs. Hobart, after many inquiries after you, I showed them your last letter to me. I felt a conviction that the sensible, candid and amiable exposition of your feelings and motives in regard to religious impressions . . . must gratify every good heart —therefore, particularly one that, I believed, knew how to appreciate them. I was not mistaken. The high encomium he bestowed on you convinced me you have his former friendship with increased approbation—admiration, I think more appropriate.

Hobart actually took the letter with him, and when he returned it, assured Mrs. Post that he was "very much indebted" to her "for the opportunity of perusing a letter so interesting as a picture of the most amiable, frank and affectionate heart of the writer." Elizabeth must have smiled to herself, remembering when the good Bishop had said far less kind things of her.

She did not smile, to hear that her *Leghorn Journal*, written only for her "Soul's Sister," Rebecca Seton, had recently been published in Elizabethtown, New Jersey, without either her knowledge or her permission. She was greatly agitated. As a Catholic and religious foundress she feared the unorthodox sentiments of former days, and particularly "the pompous Protestant expressions" she was then fond of.

It is not known with any certainty how the publication came about. Bruté always blamed Hobart for it. "I am sure it is Bishop Hobart who printed the *Journal* of Mother Seton," he insisted. "She had trusted it to him—he took a copy . . . probably makes a private use of it for his devotees, etc. . . . ." Poor Hobart! There was really no evidence to connect him with the publication. Indeed, one feels sorry for him in these later years: he seems genuinely to have admired what Mrs. Seton had become; and George Edmund Ironside, a convert from Episcopalianism, who entered upon a public controversy with him in 1820, charged him with hypocrisy, alleging that "you . . . have more than once expressed your wish to pass the end of your days in the bosom of the *Roman*

Catholic Church." If such a charge was true, Hobart was indeed a man to be pitied.

Kit came across a copy of the printed *Journal* in Baltimore, in May of 1817, and hastened to assure her mother that "there is nothing at all to make you uneasy about. It tells your little story of jumping on the wagon going to the woods, your walking round to look at the parsonage house, all the rest—I believe like the one we have. . . . It is entitled *Memoirs of Mrs. S.*; but I do not think it has those pompous Protestant expressions. Indeed, dearest, I believe any other woman but you would be proud of it. Don't be uneasy. I don't think it will be ever printed here in Baltimore." Charlotte Tiernan was more understanding, and sympathized with Elizabeth's chagrin that "every disinterested person should be acquainted with your private feelings."

The *Journal* was, of course, a beautiful work which the publishers rightly recognized in their flattering, if somewhat inaccurate and sensational, preface to the book:

> There is one fact connected with the voyage [to Italy] that we have not yet related. At the Lazaretto Mrs. S. became a *Catholic!* Her daughter Ann, of which she so feelingly speaks, afterwards took the veil at a convent of which her mother is now *Abbess*, near Baltimore in Maryland. Ann is now dead and, we trust, with her redeemed in heaven. This work was not written with any intention of ever coming to the eye of the public. . . . The only excuse we would offer for proposing to publish it (if an excuse should be asked) is, on a perusal of the manuscript, we were pleased and struck with an idea that it would be *beneficial* if given to the world. We, therefore, have taken the liberty of making it public. Although the author is now buried within the dark walls of a monastery, it is to be hoped all her writings may emerge to the light, for they will be considered an acquisition to the Christian library and precious in the annals of American literature.

It is interesting in this connection that Father White, Mother Seton's first biographer, thought certain of her letters worthy of inclusion in American anthologies; there is, to be sure, much merit in the suggestion.

Easter brought more letters from William, full of his discontent; but Elizabeth detected, also, a new note of maturity. "If I was only of sufficient use to spare one clerk in the counting house," William explained, "I might still, though under every debt of gratitude to Mr. Filicchi, say I earned my bread; but that is far from being the case. . . . Do not

Mother Elizabeth Ann Bayley Seton. (This portrait was painted for the Filicchi family, an engraving of Mother Seton being used for the face, and the habit painted around it.)

Drawing by Father Bruté, showing Mother Seton standing beside
the four graves of Harriet, Cecilia, Annina, and Rebecca Seton.
The words above her head are "ETERNITY! JESUS" and on the book
in her right hand, "THE WILL OF GOD."

Mother Seton on her deathbed, drawn by Father Bruté.

Mother Seton's tomb at Emmitsburg, Maryland.

suppose, dearest mother, I speak through any whimsical or boyish notions, or through any disappointment, for I meet every sort of kindness beyond what I could ever hope; but it is a duty to tell you my heart, which I submit to you for your direction, but determined only to do your will in this case and every other." Elizabeth could scarcely hold out against such reasonableness and filial submission. Indeed, she was proud of her son; and her pride shone in the reply she made him on April 4, 1817:

> Far, indeed, be it from me to hold so dear and generous a son by any tie of duty to me in a situation which does not meet the bent of his wishes. Yet, your own Mother is obliged both by duty and love to entreat you to have yet a little patience, that we may judge for the best with more safety. I wrote Mr. Filicchi earnestly some months ago on the subject of your future prospects in commerce, and twice since most pressingly on the situation of Richard. . . .
> The statement of your sentiments . . . do you the greatest honor, my son . . . for by them I see well that integrity and filial love overruled all your youthful and natural feelings. . . .
> I have gained my main object in parting with you, my beloved son, which was not so much to fix you with affluent friends, or in a tide of fortune, as to give you time to know yourself a little, and to overcome your first ardent propensity for the Navy—which I know is even now the passion of your heart. . . .

She was not so carried away, of course, as immediately to summon William home. Such action would have belied her usual prudence. In the same packet with her reply to William went an eminently sensible letter to Antonio Filicchi, asking him to settle the matter with candor and dispatch:

> I must hope, dear Antonio, that William writes from a sense of duty, he being now in his twenty-first year, and we have so long been on your hands; besides that, at that age, he ought, as he says, to be earning his bread.
> If you see that William has not the requisite qualifications for a merchant —which he always doubted himself—will you not speak to him about it, and let him take up the course of life he is eventually to follow? Or if it should be a misjudging disposition on his part, you will point it out to him.
> If William should not be fit for a commercial life, I dread the attraction of the Navy, so powerful to our young Americans; but you, with God, are the fathers of the fatherless, and will direct my William for the best.

The greatest pain I have in this new trial is the fear that you may not be pleased; yet you will be the first to see my difficulty. Our God is pleased to hammer me like a truly poor sinner. My comfort is that we must have already added a good lustre to your Filippo's eternity, and we will surely brighten your crown *there*, though we are but rust to you here.

But her great love and gratitude would not permit Elizabeth to close without crying out wistfully to Antonio: "Oh, if my son could have taken off the least part of your heavy burden and daily care, it would have been too great an honor and happiness to me!"

She well knew what the outcome would be, for scarcely a week later, on April 10, she was telling Julia Scott: "I hear many little whispers that William is going to surprise us with a visit." What a brave way of putting the hard truth that her hopes had been dashed!

Kit was unwell, with the dry, hacking little cough that had boded the end of her sisters. It did not disturb Elizabeth, or even Kit, for both had long expected that she would go the way of all the Setons. The mother would have been vastly amused, had she known this remaining daughter would live to the age of ninety! With the coming of fine weather Madame Chatard appeared and carried Kit off to Baltimore "to consult her physician and change air, diet, etc."

As for Elizabeth herself, the years and the trials, and particularly the long hardship of Bec's illness, had taken their toll. She described herself gaily for Julia as a "poor creature, lame of one leg and blind of an eye, a poor old bit of broken furniture, good only to frighten the crows away." She exaggerated, of course. Even time and trouble had not been able to efface her essential beauty, the fine bones and planes of her face; especially was that beauty still in the large, dark eyes, "blind" or not. When her body was first exhumed in 1846, and her successor, Mother Xavier, who had been one of Elizabeth's pupils at St. Joseph's, saw it crumble to dust as the air touched it, the Reverend Mother had but one lamentation: "Oh, those lovely eyes!"

May brought visitors to the Valley, the faithful Mary Post, her husband, and their eldest daughter Catherine; and, as a special surprise, Mary Bayley, Elizabeth's half-sister, who had been a girl of fourteen when Elizabeth left New York. Mrs. Seton was overjoyed to see them. Mary Post had said as early as January that they might come; but when

Elizabeth's heart had leaped up at the thought, Mary had tried to temper her excited anticipation, for fear of disappointment. But they came, and all was well.

That same month the Sisters extended their holdings, agreeing to purchase part of "Mrs. Knouff's farm" and three hundred acres of woodland from Mrs. Elder. They also hired a "man for two months at ten dollars per month, to see if a quarry can be found near the stone house." Purchases and plans such as these showed how settled the Sisterhood was now, and how confident of the future.

The practice and interpretation of the rule was being solidified, too, as can be seen from decisions recorded in the *Council Minutes;* permissions granted, for example, were always qualified, so as not to set precedents. Thus, there are such entries as the following:

> Sister Joanna permitted to visit her dying parent to fulfill a promise made by Archbishop Carroll and our Reverend Superior.

> The candidate Mary Wagner permitted to visit her dying Mother for special reasons.

> Biddy Jordan admitted as candidate—her mother invited to remain with us the remainder of her days—many reasons for this proceeding.

There are innumerable such examples, demonstrating the foresight and noncommittal prudence of the woman who sat at the head of the council table.

Like so many of God's works the community had come into full flower as something quite different from the original intention of the founders. As Elizabeth told Antonio Filicchi in the letter of introduction Samuel Cooper carried to Leghorn that summer, Cooper's "meaning and my hopes" were that the establishment in Emmitsburg "was to have been a nursery only for Our Savior's poor country children; but it seems it is to be the forming of city girls to faith and piety as wives and mothers." But she hastened to add that it enjoyed that "blessing and success which is the work of God alone."

Elizabeth had not complained when God's plans proved to be different than hers, and He rewarded her by granting an early fulfillment of her hopes for the poor. The orphanage in Philadelphia had been one such fulfillment, outside all human prevision—even Archbishop Carroll, with his hard-earned knowledge of what the Church might expect in the mission land of America, had predicted that the Sisters would not be able to turn their hands to the sick and the destitute for at least a century. Now God had a further reward for the docility of His servant Mrs. Seton. In a letter written on July 14, 1817, Bishop John Connolly of New York invited the Sisters to staff an orphanage there.

The Roman Catholic Benevolent Society to provide for Catholic orphans had been founded by a group of laymen in 1816, and incorporated on April 15, 1817. Foremost among the Society's members were Francis Cooper, first Catholic member of the New York State Legislature, Cornelius Heeney, erstwhile partners of John Jacob Astor, and Robert Fox, whose three little daughters were pupils at Emmitsburg. It was quite evident from Bishop Connolly's letter that the gentlemen of the Benevolent Society were the prime movers in attempting to establish a permanent Catholic orphanage in the City. They had already purchased and renovated a house on Prince Street, the Bishop told Elizabeth, when they called on him and "prayed me to request that you will please to send them three Sisters of your Society to regulate and instruct said orphans." Not that the laymen were overstepping their bounds: they were devoting their money and their energies to the advancement of the Church in the accepted manner of that time, and the Bishop not only heartily approved, but was grateful. "I sincerely wish," he wrote Mrs. Seton, "it may be in your power to immediately grant the laudable request of the said gentlemen, as the object of it would be productive of a great deal of good here."

Francis Cooper had visited the Philadelphia orphanage earlier that summer, and told Sister Rose that Mother Seton had promised Sisters for New York. Be that as it may, the Council took prompt action on receipt of the Bishop's letter; and the following week Elizabeth wrote Robert Fox that the Benevolent Society's request had been granted, and that he and his friends might send an escort for the Sisters. Father Dubois and she did not see fit, however, to grant the gentlemen's further request for Sister Margaret George to be Sister Servant. "Was your institution a high-styled grammar school, Sister Margaret would suit better than any," Dubois wrote Bishop Connolly, "and great as the loss would be to this house, we would freely part with her; but for such an asylum as that of Philadelphia the main object is to have a zealous, prudent, economical Mother to govern it. . . . We contemplate to send, at least for a time, the excellent Sister Rose, who is now in Philadelphia—having acquired experience in Philadelphia, she will be better calculated to guide the beginners of New York."

There was also another reason for sending Sister Rose, Elizabeth admitted to Bruté: "So much must depend, as says the good gentlemen who write about it, on who is sent to my 'native city,' they say, not knowing that I am a citizen of the world." But, she finished, the basic reason for choosing Rose was that "she will keep so well the dignity of rules and pure intentions."

Rose set out with Sister Cecilia O'Conway and Sister Felicita Brady on August 13, 1817, arriving in New York on August 20. They had to stay with the Foxes for several weeks because, despite the assurance of the Bishop's letter of a month before, the house on Prince Street was not ready. Even when the Sisters moved into the dilapidated building, they had only five orphans to care for; but by the end of the first year there were twenty-eight. Arrangements were made for the trustees of the asylum to handle its finances—which were supplemented by the charitable activities of a Ladies' Auxiliary, as in Philadelphia—and for the Sisters to be paid thirty-six dollars each per year for their personal needs.

While Elizabeth was corresponding with Robert Fox, concerning the New York orphanage, she was also soliciting his help in a more personal matter.

She had not heard from William for a month. "February your last date, and here 25th [of] July," she wrote him urgently. "Eyes fill and heart aches; but God is God, and the hardest penance I can pay in this life is separation from you, and I must bear it. Oh, if but at last to be *forever united!*" Her panic increased when she considered how unsettled he had been when she last heard from him, and she cried out to him in an agony:

> I see you receiving my letters and carrying them to Mr. Filicchi, saying: 'Sir, my mother puts no obstacle to my pursuing the life of my own choice.' And you enter some ship or cruiser, and my William, my soul's William is gone. How often imagination has pictured you even in the chains of slavery! I shed my tears over you continually, appealing to Him,

Who alone knows and pities the whole of a mother's heart, and sees also such thoughts are not willfully indulged but at the worst are always mixed with bright hope and confidence in His goodness.

She had not heard either from Antonio, nor had any answer to her pressing question of what should be decided for William. She could not know, of course, that the decision had been made and that her son was on his way home. To add to her troubles, Dick was back from Baltimore, "displaced" and "unsettled, and not the least prospect before him." He had an idea of turning to farming, but Elizabeth was opposed, believing it was "only to preserve himself from the destruction of bad company."

William appeared before his mother's startled eyes in the middle of August, bearing a letter of explanation from Antonio, the first Elizabeth had received from her "dear brother" in two years. He was quite frank in his appraisal:

> Your good son William, whom I have closely watched since his arrival in Leghorn—and but little known him in his great reservedness—tho' of perfect character and most mild disposition, has thoroughly disappointed my expectation in point of rendering him useful to my counting house— both by a physical weakness and trembling in his right hand, which prevents him to write with care, and by his own moral indifference if not aversion to trade in general.

Antonio had worried, too, about William's moral and religious life. The young man had been "left necessarily unemployed almost all the day," Antonio told Elizabeth, and was "naturally inclined to join in preference his own young countrymen, travelers or settled here," a tendency which "would not much improve his Catholicism, though in a Catholic country"; nor did Antonio spare his own less fervent countrymen who "too frequent" gave William "bad example of ir- religion." The upshot of all this was, Antonio concluded, that "I thought it at last my indispensable duty to come to some resolution; and on Monday last, for result of a friendly explanation I had with him on the subject, his return to America was agreed and he will be the bearer of this, if it pleases to God, in good health, dutiful and affectionate son, of unspoiled character, and still I hope firm Catholic Christian."

Filicchi proffered no advice on the question of a naval career for William, but Elizabeth soon discovered that her son had made up his mind to enlist, and resignedly set about trying to get him an officer's berth through the influence of Robert Fox and Francis Cooper. Fox wrote on September 8 that he and Cooper had applied to Captain Stewart of Philadelphia, and were soliciting Daniel Tompkins, Vice President of the United States, for a letter of recommendation; they were also attempting to procure a like letter from John Quincy Adams. William left immediately for Philadelphia, where he had an interview with Stewart, and Elizabeth proudly informed Julia Scott of the result:

> William is a solid old gentleman, and has so prepossessing an appearance and manner that he has obtained the most effectual recommendations for his dear Navy; and his name, it seems, is at the head of a list of fourteen hundred who applied before him with state recommendations.

Actually, she was putting on a brave front for the world to see. Only Simon Bruté knew how she really felt. On August 1 she had poured out her heart to him:

> May you be spared the agony of heart to see the poor, good *Lipp,* who once adorned your sanctuary in Baltimore where I had last seen him, now with wife and child. I burst in tears at the sad reverse, and now, three hours after, the tears to Our Jesus redoubled. Oh, His Kingdom! Laborers for His vineyard! My poor, poor, poor Richard, William—My God, oh if the bleeding of a mother's heart can obtain! Poor, poor, poor blind ones! Such a Lord! Such a Master! Such a divine and glorious service!—but blind, blind, and lost to love and duty, groping along through the bright, heavenly light which shines so lovely to the happy ones who *comprehend.* Blessed, blessed G., most blessed, you are *His!* And in that, at least, [the] grateful soul of your own Mother rejoices. And, oh, remember those who are not.

Despite his own disappointment in William, Antonio Filicchi's friendship for Elizabeth was fathomless and, for her sake, he stretched out a hand to the drifting Richard: "I would be satisfied of a good will and a good handwriting, and I shall be ready to provide for him as I have for William," this truly great friend told the heartsick mother. "Let him make the trial."

Elizabeth sighed with relief, even though she sent Richard off with misgivings. He was far more immature than William; and could scarcely be trusted as far from home as Baltimore, let alone Italy. Elizabeth had proof of this unhappy fact at the end of September when he was preparing to sail, and it came out that he had squandered every possible penny over the past year. She wrote Julia Scott sorrowfully that he

> left me a thorn in the heart, poor fellow, which now, no doubt, he feels more than ever, though his tears and sobs in his acknowledgments to me were enough to move a stronger mother than I am. For we find, when too late, that the good and most respectable Mr. Tiernan, with whose family he made his home, made no account of his expenses; and poor Dick, not having fortitude or good sense to keep himself in the character of son of a poor widow, spent not only the two hundred dollars Mr. Filicchi allowed for his regular wants, but all that poor Kit had saved by her piano lessons and your constant remittances. Indeed, her loving heart wanted it only for her brothers, but we are hurt and mortified enough that he should have been playing the fool in that way.

Like a true mother, however, she was quick to seize forlornly on an excuse for her nineteen-year-old giant: "We find he has been imposed on, just like the poor countryman in the fable—for a more innocent, simple young man can scarcely be met with, and we must hope he will do well in the event with a little more experience and judgment."

XXII

"All Things Are Prepared . . . Come"

With the start of the year 1818 Elizabeth's life was entering its final phase. The three years remaining would be left to "making her soul," not in the elementary sense of saving it, but in the ultimate sense of refining it to the most exquisite perfection. In the hurly-burly years behind she had acted upon persons and events; now, in what might be termed the quiet years, she would be acted upon. Not that all action, all suffering, was past, but rather that such action and suffering flowed from sources already existing.

The community was flourishing: Elizabeth would welcome more daughters before she died, but it had expanded as far as she would see it expand, with houses at Philadelphia, Mount St. Mary's and New York. Nearly all who had influenced its establishment and growth were gone: Carroll and Nagot were dead; Dubourg was in New Orleans; Flaget and David in Bardstown; Babade remained in Baltimore. Dubois would stay on at the head of the community; and Bruté would soon return to Emmitsburg—appropriately, for he was above all others the architect of Elizabeth's lovely cathedral of a soul, and would be needed for the final glorious ornamentation.

The patterns of her children's lives were set also. Annina and Rebecca, of course, she had already delivered into the hands of God. She had helped William to the attainment of his naval career—his appointment had come in November, and he was but waiting a specific assignment. Richard was safe and settled for the time, in Leghorn. Kit had started on the round of extended visits that would keep her from her mother much of the time. Elizabeth could do little more for them now; "pray and dote, dote and pray, is poor mother's all for her darlings," was the way she put it.

And Elizabeth herself sat quietly in Emmitsburg, devoting all her time, all her ebbing strength, to the work God had given her—the government of her spiritual family, the encouragement and support of her children. As she told William: "Mrs. Patience, it seems, must be my companion the remainder of my fine life until . . . I back out of it."

She began the New Year sadly enough by parting with William and Kit. On January 19 she wrote Julia Scott, asking whether she would welcome Kit as a companion for a few months. "Every month of April and May the poor darling has been sick . . ." she explained, "and we think it may be owing to her want of exercise here, as the roads of a country place like this are almost impassible in the spring."

It was only a partial reason: Kit had had a taste of the world in Baltimore the previous summer and would never again be wholly satisfied with the quiet life of the Valley; her understanding and self-sacrificing mother, therefore, wisely determined to let her spread her wings under the prudent direction of trusted friends. Elizabeth's letter reached Julia at a propitious time, for the Philadelphia matron was living alone since her son's marriage, and was "sick half the time, afraid to stir from the house, and too blind and suffering too much cold to do anything in it." It was, therefore, with obvious delight that she sent back immediately for Kit to come.

William's orders to report to Commodore Bainbridge, commander of the historic *Independence*, at Boston, arrived early in February. After a delay of some days, due to bad weather, he set off by way of Lancaster and Philadelphia, leaving Kit there while he continued on to New York. The parting was hard on both William and his mother, but it was softened for her by the knowledge that he had matured since their parting of three years before. "Poor fellow—the agony of his heart leaving me!" she exclaimed to Ellen Wiseman. "But mine is full of confidence that Our God will protect so pure a soul, even in the flames he must pass through. I could not have believed there was such a young man in the world, if six months daily experience of his beautiful sentiments and conduct had not proved it. He is considered here as a model for those even in the sanctuary." He was scarcely gone when Elizabeth sent letter upon letter after him. The first, written on February 16, was one of her memorable essays of advice:

> My soul's darling—You go, so adieu once more. With how much more courage I say it now than in 1815. You must fill a station and take a part in our life of trial, and all your own Mother can beg is that you keep well with your Good Pilot and, as says old Burns, the correspondence fixed with heaven will be your noble anchor. To go when you can to the sacraments as a child to his Father will be a main point for that, and the next best is to look to your Mother's old rule of *intentions*, the comfort of my life.
>
> You and I are too softhearted about our friendships and condescensions to circumstances of the moment. Mind well the consequence, my beloved —in your situation they will go very far. But we have talked that over.
>
> Mind your promise to tell me all you can. Don't refuse that only *comfit* in my bitter draught of separation.
>
> Mind your health; be prudent in exposing it when you cannot say duty is in question. . . .
>
> Dearest, dearest child of my soul, mind we MUST be one day where we will part no more.

A week later she was writing again, using nautical terms to keep the tone light and conceal her heartache: "Now, my love, I must hope that you are safe in your berth. Your little ship left behind has had cloudy weather and dragged scarcely three knots an hour." She could not forbear, however, to let William know that he held first place in her heart: "Last night I had you close where you used to lie so snug and warm when you drew the *life stream* twenty years ago, and where the heart still beats to love you dearly, dearly till its last sigh, *which even then* loved you *best of all*." And she finished by offering to "kiss your Commodore's toe, if he will but be good to you."

Elizabeth breathed easier when she had her first word from Richard at the end of February. Antonio enclosed a few lines, too, and she hastened to assure William that the faithful Filicchi was "much pleased" with Dick and "will do everything to advance him for *Richard's* sake, for *his own* advantage in [the] counting house and *for my comfort*. These are his words." There had not been time for letters from William himself yet, and Elizabeth lamented:

> I feel your absence till I hear from you, and hum my little song:
>
> > Who cares if it rains or shines?
> > There is no Willy.
> > Dust or no dust—
> > There is no Willy.
> > Fish or flesh—
> > There is no Willy.
> > Sing this or that—
> > There is no Willy.
>
> Let the world go round, if only my Willy is happy and remembers me in all his dangers—since he cannot remember me, but the first wish of my soul will be remembered, too.

Kit had stepped into an enchanted world at Aunt Scott's in Philadelphia. She wrote long, excited letters to her mother, filled with wonder at the "great style and elegance" in which Mrs. Scott lived, and reflecting the struggle in her own heart between the quiet life she had known and the new, glittering world that attracted her strongly.

> Dearest Mother [she wrote on the 24th of February], what a grand temptation I had last night to go to a splendid military ball given on Washington's birth night. A ticket was given me and many proposed it, but I told Aunt Scott it was against our rules in Lent to go. Mrs. Cox said, if I thought you would disapprove of it, I was perfectly in the right to stay. I told her I thought you would rather I would not go. However, they persuaded me to go to the Washington Hall to look at the decorations, which were splendid. We went in the gallery, dressed as I am now (common dress), where we were separate from the company who attended the ball. I saw two or three cotillions danced and came away. All was like a fairy scene to me. Such a collection of beauty and dress astonished me. I hope I was not wrong to go. I did not dress, or join the company, but was merely a spectator for about an hour or an hour and a half.

This same sideward glancing at the newfound dazzle of the world while striving to hold fast to her mother's wishes and her conscience—which were often the same thing—is evident in Kit's concession to fashion: "As for my dress, it is plain. Aunt Scott asked me how I wished to dress. I told her plain, but not singular—as others did. I let her please herself in it. I wear a good many curls, a white velvet bonnet and a silk dress. She has procured me rather a stylish one, from material called poplin, but I will only wear it in company." And she added rather lamely: "You know I am not fond of style."

The conflict was starkly revealed in the matter of reading. "I shall lay a penance on myself to read no novels, except one which she [Mrs. Scott] says has so many good morals in it," she told her mother, and then added suddenly and piteously, "I am afraid to trust myself. I have not you, beloved, to guide me."

Elizabeth could understand her daughter's dilemmas: they were a reincarnation of her own. She had loved balls and dancing and dress—and though she had recognized their essential innocence, they had troubled her conscience. She had loved the pleasures of reading, too, and had delved into novels of "many good morals," novels like *Charlotte Temple* and *Pamela* which, too often, to soothe the sensibilities of upright young ladies, justified their themes of seduction and betrayal by presenting them as pious warnings to foolish young maidens.

It was precisely because she understood the joy of life and her child's awakening temperament that Elizabeth had sent her to school, as it were, under the prudent tutelage of Julia Scott. Elizabeth had often twitted Julia for her worldliness, but she knew her for a good and wise woman. Elizabeth knew also that Kit was not like Annina or Rebecca, both of whom had wanted to stay with their mother, even though for a time Annina had not known what she wanted—Kit had written, in fact, that "Mrs. Scott says I am so extremely like you, only I do not laugh so much as you once did."

Elizabeth must indeed have laughed now at Kit's attempts to explain her strange new reactions to her mother, knowing well that the girl was actually laboring to explain them to herself. Her capitulation came swiftly enough, for she was scarcely in Philadelphia four weeks when she was writing her mother eagerly that her Aunt Helen Bayley Craig, of New York, "presses me to come and pass some time with her," and "no doubt, I shall soon receive a similar [invitation] from Aunt Post," and a Colonel Barrack wanted her and Aunt Scott to visit at *his* house; and she salted the exciting reports with a request for more money because, she told her mother gravely, "you can't think what trifles cost in this great city!"

On April 4 Elizabeth wrote resignedly to Julia:

> I can see plainly my Kit wishes much to go to New York, as I should in her place. . . . If she went with you, I would be quite happy about it; but as it is, I can only leave the whole decision respecting the affair to you. . . . And as I well know her submission and wish to do for the best, I beg you, my Julia, to judge *that best* for her, since you now hold my place for my darling. Whatever is done, I shall be contented.

Elizabeth was feeling very unwell, and a great weariness lay on her. She compared herself, for Julia, to "good Mammy Sainte Croix I used to tell you about, whose chin and nose grew so near each other. I feel mine to see how they stand, and would like to kiss yours if I could. My head is as empty as a drum (not my heart) and has nothing to tell you."

Her heart was far from empty, and thoughts of her children crowded much of it. This was not surprising, for, as she had always stoutly insisted, she was first of all a mother; and now she was a mother who could see the ultimate horizon of her days. She, therefore, fretted over her children—worrying whether Richard was applying himself, whether Kit was keeping her feet dry, whether William was withstanding the damp chill of his night watches. Ever mindful of their strange, institutional childhood, she did little kindnesses for them to remember her by. Defending the cost of Kit's travels, she told Eliza Sadler: "She had been so little expense in any way since she has been born, I would not make it a matter of conscience."

On March 13 Robert Barry sent Mrs. Seton $46.75 in insurance stock dividends, after deducting $8.25 owed him by Dick. She sent back $28.00 to Baltimore to pay off William's tailor, and mailed $10.00 to Kit for her trip to New York, prudently holding $10.00 in reserve should the girl need more. She importuned William to tell her whether his money held out and whether "Aunt Post added anything." She directed him to apply to Bishop Cheverus if he was low in funds: "Fear not, I will clear it somehow or other. I write him that I am so afraid you should want, that I have charged you to apply to him if necessary." She even remembered the sailors under her son's command: "Be good to your poor Jacks, and give them tobacco. I will make up for it, and save all I can."

Some have maintained that Elizabeth was overindulgent with her children, that she was blind to their faults, to their ingratitude and thoughtlessness and selfish ways. Not so. She was too alert, too honest, to miss such flagrant shortcomings. But they were grown now—William was in his twenty-second year, Richard nearly twenty, and Catherine just short of eighteen—and there was no point, either psychologically or spiritually, in Elizabeth's assuming the role of martyred mother. There was only, indeed, one essential point—their soul's salvation; and on this point Elizabeth gave them no peace.

And so, she hid her pain deep inside herself, only occasionally revealing it to the closest of her friends as when she wrote Julia with candor to "excuse poor Kit to you where really there is not much excuse, poor darling. She will have many a pinch, if she lives, for her fruitless early days. So have I. And here I jog on to the grave, patting my own back, and hushing up poor pride and sorrow till both will go off with me bye and bye." However, until death claimed her, she must do what she could, as she wrote William on April 6: "It seems to me that I am more in the grave than out of it already. . . . I sometimes feel a transport when pain or weakness comes over me. Then one look at you dear children, and I see it is wrong, for I yet may comfort you in this world, if even at a distance."

The dust raised by the turmoil and anxiety of settling her children in life could easily obscure the larger, quieter part of Mrs. Seton's duty, the Sisterhood and the school. It could easily be forgotten that, despite the voluminous correspondence with her children at this period, the whole of her day was given to her spiritual daughters and beloved pupils. Only in the night watches when the constant, dry cough and the pain in the side would not let her sleep, as she told William, would she "draw up the little basket of chips you so well remember, make up a small blaze in your stove," and by the flaring light of a candle stump begin to write those long, loving letters to her distant children.

But, with the call of the rising bell, she began her long, active day: presiding at community prayers; directing the Sisters; assigning them to this task or that, listening with kind sympathy to their troubles, admonishing them for infractions of the rule; encouraging the novices and postulants, hearing the confession of their faults, praising their enthusiasms; hobbling from classroom to classroom, to sit with closed eyes while the children droned the list of the world's capitals or recited their singsong multiplication tables—then the conferences with Father Dubois and her council, the meetings with merchants, the endless correspondence of administration.

Remote as was the Valley, Mrs. Seton had a surprising number of callers who came for her comfort and advice. Many, indeed, were from the neighboring villages, but there were others from Baltimore and even intrepid souls like Mrs. Montgomery who made the hard, long journey from Philadelphia. On one occasion Mrs. Montgomery brought a prospective convert with her who, Elizabeth told Bruté bluntly, had a heart "the most completely blind of any I yet saw. Not her faith, indeed, since she has rather enough to condemn her, but the absolute ignorance of common principle of 'forgive as we forgive.' Such obstacles to grace in one who values herself on piety! Oh, Our God!—incredible, if she did not herself speak it!"

On other occasions the visitors were candidates for the community. One such was "the so well-meaning Miss Cocheran, sister of the wealthy man and all wealth herself, [who] insists to tread out all and be a Sister. I laugh at her as if she would build a tower to the skies, but she persists all things are possible with God, and with such a gravity that I can but bid her wait the return of the Pope [Father Dubois]." There were also, Elizabeth told Bruté with high amusement, "two most blessed souls from Philadelphia, one an accomplished musician—which sets Mrs. Séguin quite wild. In vain I assure her no one can rival her in affection of St. Joseph's family and my devoted heart; she is fairly sick and in the infirmary. So, so, so. Enough recreation for a sinner!"

When the troubled and perplexed could not come in person, they applied to Elizabeth by post. Former pupils particularly consulted her on every new encounter with life: should they accept tickets to balls? should they allow themselves to be escorted to the theatre? did Mrs. Seton think a young man to have serious intentions if he called more than twice? Elizabeth described one of these "consultations" in mock horror: "My Ellen Hamilton's distress in pages about an offer of marriage, alas!"

Not that Elizabeth ever took these problems of youth lightly. She had worked hard to train her charges to behave as proper young ladies, and she was proud to have them confide in her for many years after they had left St. Joseph's. Every letter brought a response and an invitation to write again; and the responses were always practical and to the point. Thus she answered Sarah Caufmann, of Philadelphia, who was troubled about a letter left by an admiring young man:

> Is it not more simple and consistent to hear and answer its contents with the respect and gratitude due to an amiable being who gives us an unmerited preference, than to play the part of a proud woman receiving an homage she thinks her due? If you must *reject*, my precious child, do it with reason, and a candid statement of your reasons. Then, if they are approved or condemned, you will have acted like a Christian and your mind will be at peace, however painful the exertion—and reject you will, unless there is a fund of uncommon virtue in the person in question.
>
> Your poor little Mother can only pray for you, my beloved.

Mother Seton's interest in youth was not confined to the girls of St. Joseph's; she was also the confidante of the boys and young men of Mount St. Mary's, many of whom she had instructed for their First Holy Communion. There is extant a touching interchange of notes between her and the lonely little Jerome Bonaparte, a great-grandson of old Charles Carroll and nephew to Napoleon; the boy had been left behind when his parents went to the Imperial Court at Paris, where his father, the King of Westphalia, allowed his marriage to the boy's mother to be annulled by order of the Emperor.

> My dear Mother [the child wrote], I am very anxious to get an Agnus Dei before I go home, in order to preserve me in the vacations from the dangers that will surround me. . . . I will keep it as a memorial of kindness and love for your little child, who always thinks of you with respect and love and who will think of you with gratitude also—especially if I shall have an Agnus Dei from you as a present.

Sending the little sacramental back across the Valley, Elizabeth wrote on the back of the boy's note:

> Dear Jerome: It is a great pleasure to me to send you the Agnus Dei. I wish I had one handsomely covered; but you will mind only the virtues of the prayers Our Holy Father has said over it. I earnestly beg Our Lord to preserve you in the graces He has so tenderly bestowed on you: take care yourself not to lose them. Pray for me, and I will for you. Your true friend, E.A.S.

There was more than the separation from her children to make Elizabeth's heart sore that cold spring. Word came from Mary Post of the death of William Bayley, their sea captain brother, at Batavia in the Dutch East Indies; he had been the kindest of men, and Elizabeth had counted on him to help advance William's career. Then, Kit had no sooner reached Philadelphia than she sent back the sad report of the death of John Wilkes, who had been a friend to Elizabeth when she needed friends badly.

But, despite her earlier protestations, the greatest pain of her heart remained the pain of her separation from William. She had dissembled well at first, but as time went on and sickness racked her she could dissemble no longer. On March 24 she cried out to him across the miles:

> I never was so overpowered as by this sad parting. Reasoning is in vain, or even religion. I look up a hundred times at the dear crucifix and *resign*, but too often with such agony of heart that nothing stops it but the fear that it will break before your return, or that my death will make you unhappy. But this will not strengthen you whom I wish to strengthen.
>
> I should say, my son: go on as you have begun; our *love* will not settle you in life, will not give you independence. Your Mother ought to say many things, but can say nothing.
>
> Look up to the pure heavens in your night watch, my soul's beloved, and you will hear what that soul would say to you, what our beloved ones gone would say, too. That night watch is more in my mind at night than my sleep. Could you know the blessings invoked upon you!
>
> But it is too much indulgence to say so much of my poor heart, dearest one.

Elizabeth's affection for this first-born son was truly a mystery of love. "I often ask," she confessed in a letter to him written on April 5, 1818, "but what is this dear rover to me so much more than all the world? Why do the heart strings all wind round him so? *That I cannot tell.* Let it pass, for it depends not on me." She may have been very close to the truth, for this overriding parental love gave her more pain than pleasure; and it may well be that God fanned its fires for her complete purification. Certainly it is ascetically sound to expect the whitest heat of refining flames to attack the fiercest emotion, and Elizabeth's love for William was at the very center of her burning heart.

Nor, weighing the infinite price of a soul, can it be discounted that

William's ultimate salvation may have depended on his mother's suffering the pangs of separation from him and the anxiety for his spiritual welfare that was a constant sword in her heart. There was a sense of this in the words she wrote: "You seem, indeed, my own William, to be more present to me than my own soul, and yours and its dear futurities are truly its very *passion*."

At all events, it was one of the greatest tragedies of Elizabeth's life that her maternal love was largely unrequited. William was frankly not worth the love she lavished on him. Not that he was bad in any profound sense; he was not, in fact, profound at all; but a shallow, self-centered seeker after his own.

His mother had been wrong to presume that he had matured in Italy; perhaps she had sought to lessen the pain of parting by such a presumption. He was only a few weeks at Boston, in an honorable position which Elizabeth had humbled herself to obtain for him through the influence of her highly placed friends, when he grew bored with shore and harbor duty; and without even a word to her, applied directly to Washington for transfer to some frigate bound for the Mediterranean. Nothing shows so clearly his utter lack of feeling. Commodore Bainbridge had been his father's friend; and General Harper and Captain Stewart had spoken for the young man at Elizabeth's instance. Her embarrassment was equaled only by her son's classic disregard of the amenities.

Elizabeth could only remind him that it might be to his disadvantage to leave so distinguished a commander, who had shown him special regard, and tell him that General Harper was of the same opinion.

In the meantime, the eager Kate had set off for New York. The town, and her relatives, took her by storm. She had never known the warmth and excitement of a large family, and the bewildering array of aunts and cousins captivated her. Surprisingly, those who had most injured her mother now exerted all their charm and cordiality on the guileless Miss and she, too young to remember their venom, succumbed completely. Using her Aunt Post's house as a base of operations, Kit began a perpetual round of social calls, parties and protracted visits.

She saw, of course, her mother's people; her Aunt Helen Bayley Craig and old Aunt Charlton; and Eliza Sadler and Dué and the Sisters at the orphanage. But she gave special attention to the "dear Setons" and Ogdens and Hoffmans, to say nothing of Bishop Hobart and Mrs. Startin and the Wilkes family—so much so that Sad was nettled, and wrote Elizabeth on April 16, asking that Kit "pass some little time with us," and adding pointedly: "You only . . . can regulate the end of her visit anywhere (she would find it difficult to say no to any), and perhaps may put some restraint on her inclinations." Helen Craig, too, was disappointed at seeing so little of her niece, and wrote Elizabeth a "quite painful" letter.

If her family and true friends were pained, Elizabeth herself was deeply disturbed. "You have no idea how Kit is taken with the Setons," she told William and she admitted candidly that her heart was "soured" at the thought: "You know, dearest, my bitter experience," she reminded him. It was not, however, past injuries long forgiven but hardly forgotten that upset Elizabeth; it was rather the influence these militantly anti-Catholic relatives might have on Kit, particularly after Elizabeth herself was gone. She had no wish to see Kit so enamored of them as, perhaps, to jeopardize her Faith. For this reason she took her cue from Sad's letter to summon Kit home. She wrote the girl, therefore, on May 5:

> The more I think of it at our bench in the choir, the more I see that your way to secure a more welcome reception among our friends when you have no Mother (and you must look for that, my darling) [is] by being a shorter time with them now. Your return will be a great change to you from what you have been enjoying, but you will take it in the Providence of God, my beloved, that we are so circumstanced. It might be a great deal worse, that you well know. It will be better for you to go again next winter. (We will not mind the expense in comparison with being again together this summer.) Fruit, milk, etc., will be plenty. Your health will not suffer and your Mother's, I promise you, will be enough better.

Elizabeth had not been entirely prompted by motives of courtesy when she reminded Kit not to overstay her welcome—she had indeed considered that, after her own death, Kit might have to live permanently, not with the Setons, but with the Posts; but after Kit's return to Emmitsburg she grew fearful of even such an arrangement as this—for she told William in August that General and Mrs. Harper would return from Europe in November, "which I wish much for themselves and for us.

The more I see of Kit since the habits and ideas she acquired abroad, the more I would wish her to be with them."

Five days after she had sent for Kit, Elizabeth had further upsetting news from William. He had been in some kind of accident and had lost all his money. Within the hour she set frantically about securing him more:

> I hasten to ease your dear heart. Mine is far from troubled at the loss of our pennies, but so grateful to Our God for your escape of instant and (alas, perhaps) unprovided death. Oh, my love, not a word must I say on that point, that only point to my soul. I write Mr. Barry pressingly to send you speedily as possible the 100; and if I am so happy as to get it, surely it will be your own and not for return. For to whom should it return, or who has had so small a share as your dear self of what has been going? I pray and trust that he will advance it; there is not now as high as a five dollar bill in the house, and Mr. Grover is pressing for the debt it owes him for spring goods, so I have no resource for the moment in either, but cannot think Mr. Barry will hesitate. If *he* does, I will surely get it *some-where*. Mr. Dubois is sick in Baltimore and they are overrun with demands, so I cannot apply there.

No matter how often Elizabeth tried to persuade herself and her friends of William's innate courtesy and gentleness, there is much evidence that he could be callous and obtuse. Having agitated his poor, ill mother by the tale of the accident and the urgent request for money, he then neglected entirely to inform her as to whether he had received it, and threw her into the undignified role of importuning him for news.

"I know not why I cannot get it out of my head to write you by this post, my beloved," she wrote on May 27, "altho' neither hearing of any obstacle on the part of Mr. *Barry* for sending you the one hundred dollars, nor from you that you have not received it, I ought to hope that all is well, and your anxiety about it over. Yet mine cannot be, till I hear from you; and I entreat you, my William, if you have it not, call on Mr. Cheverus and tell him how it is and he will take the money on credit for you. . . . DO, DO LET ME HEAR FROM YOU."

There was no answer to this plea but another request, this time that she use her influence to hasten his transfer by writing on his behalf to Daniel Brent of the State Department. Again she pressed him on June 15 to let her know whether he had the money:

I wrote you the last week to say the money had been sent [by] Mr. Barry, so I hope it is safe with you before any further application. You are tired of hearing about it, but that cannot be helped until you can tell me the welcome news that you have it. We must not mind these things, dear one, but I well remember when I was young how I hated them. Your letter of 3rd [of] June was immediately attended to. I had been bled at both arms for a slight inflammatory attack of the breast, and I got Mr. Dubois to write the very hour I received your letter. So I hope Mr. Brent has the petition long before this, and you will either get in the *Geurriere* or *Macedonian*. . . ."

Elizabeth must have had at least some grudging word about the money, for she never mentioned it afterward.

Kit had arrived home at just the critical moment when it seemed that her mother might die; but the bloodletting they had subjected her to had snatched Elizabeth temporarily from the grave. On July 12 Kit, with the easy optimism of youth, wrote Julia Scott: "I have from week to week delayed writing to you, hoping I might be able to give you more favorable accounts of my dear Mother's health, which I am most happy to say I can now do. Although the cough still continues, the inflammation in her breast has subsided, and we trust the former will gradually wear away."

Elizabeth allowed Kit her optimism, but neither she, nor the Sisters, nor her clerical friends were fooled; death was certainly in sight. Babade wrote from Baltimore, begging her to allow her biography to be written and published for the edification of others, but she made him promise to respect her desire for obscurity. On the same day that Kit had written her sunny report to Philadelphia Elizabeth's "blessed patriarch" wrote her the kind of letter he knew would comfort her most:

Ten years are passed; your work is consolidated. I desire nothing more for you but a happy death. . . . I would like very much to see you before you die, but I foresee that the Superior will not allow me to go to Emmitsburg in the present state of things. . . . As soon as I hear of your death I will say Mass for the repose of your dear soul. . . . If you find mercy, as I hope you will, do not forget above this one who has thought so much of you here below.

All July, while she languished, Elizabeth heard nothing from Boston, and the worst imaginings oppressed her. On July 21 she was at length forced to give them voice: "Dearest, dear, dear, dear William. . . . Now indeed some fears that you are giving up all to human views etc., yet all I judge from is the entire silence of Bishop Cheverus, who has never written me once since you are at Boston; and I have had so many full proofs of the kindness of his heart that I am sure if he could have said a word of your approach to Our God, he would have taken time from sleep to tell me. But that, and everything, I give up; and still hope and pray—all a poor little Mother can do." Through her darkest nights this intrepid woman's faith and spirit of abandonment to "The Will" never stumbled.

When William wrote at last on August 1 that he had received his transfer to the *Macedonian*, he was full of the adventure it promised: the ship was to go around Cape Horn and cruise in the Pacific for two years, visiting all the western ports of North and South America. There was no mistaking his jubilation, but the news sank like a stone to the bottom of Elizabeth's heart. He needed more money and clothes before he sailed, and the heartbroken mother set pathetically about trying to supply both. "I have taken measures for your receiving at least a poor, poor 50 dollars, my beloved," she wrote. "Tears are ready to start that they may be all you will have for your voyage, and I hope Mrs. J. Seton will get for you every comfort you may want in clothes. I shall be sure to repay her. That's understood! I wrote her and enclosed to the good Bishop, who will know if she is the kind of person who would meet the wish of a mother's heart on such an occasion. Take my intention and doting love, dearest, if I plague you by applying to her. I know not what else to do, as none but a woman can do it."

This Mrs. Seton was the second wife of Elizabeth's brother-in-law, Jack, and was a convert of Dr. Matignon's. Although Elizabeth had never met her, she felt that family ties allowed her to make the request about William's clothes; but Bishop Cheverus did not pass on the request: he told Elizabeth that Mrs. John Seton was ill and that, besides, William hardly knew her; he himself would give William the money to buy shirts and small-clothes, and someone could easily be found to do his sewing.

One sentence of William's letter had terrified Elizabeth. "I long to hear that you have perfectly recovered from your late illness," he had written. "If not, do, dearest Mother, let me know it, and I will use every endeavor to come to you. It would be a great satisfaction indeed to pass a little time with you before so long a voyage." That William should discover how truly sick she was and then have the pain of being forced to embark was the last thing Elizabeth wanted. "You must not think of coming, my beloved. . . ." she wrote in agitation. "One only thing I cannot stand in this world, that is *taking leave of you*. . . . Don't be uneasy about my health. . . . The sickness I had (inflammation of lungs) leaves a long weakness, but there is nothing alarming, my love, I assure you, as to immediate consequence. I may live to welcome your happy, joyful return from many a cruise."

She fired off an immediate note to Cheverus, too, begging him to help her keep the truth from William, and he agreed. "Dear child!" the kindly prelate exclaimed. "He is then to see you no more in this world. But I have confidence that he will one day be with you in heaven. 'The child of so many tears and prayers cannot perish.' "

As for Elizabeth herself, Cheverus told her:

> I do not pity you. I envy your situation, running now to the embrace of Him Who is love. . . . You are most frequently remembered at the Altar and will be as long as I shall celebrate the Holy Mysteries. Pray for me here and in heaven.

Elizabeth talked freely about her death to Antonio Filicchi when she wrote him on August 8:

> It is rather suspected that I, your poor little sister, am about to go and meet your Filippo, but nothing of health can be certain and calculated at my age, 45. I may recover and crack nuts yet with my nose and chin, as they say; *I know not*. All I know is, we must all be ready for this dear, dearest Thief who is to come when least expected. I go almost every day to Communion (as my good confessor and superior says, thro' *condescension to my weakness*), so if you good people are not *very* good over the water, it is no fault of my prayers; and I hope I shall not be forgotten in yours, *to which I so well owe all that I possess: my blessed Faith*.

And she was just as frank with her "soul's dear Ellen" (Wiseman), to whom she wrote condolingly:

> I know your uneasiness for me, but that should not be. Why uneasy at the fulfillment of the merciful designs of so dear a Providence Who left me to take care of my *Bec*, to bring Jos to an age to take care of herself and

our dearest boys to enter the way of life they were to choose . . .? What would you have, darling? Why be anxious if your poor, tired friend goes to rest?—*I HOPE!*

Elizabeth tried, however, to conceal her condition from her sister Mary, as she had from William, and to this purpose enlisted the aid of Wright Post; but he refused to keep the solemn news from his wife, feeling that she had a right to know. He wrote Elizabeth a long letter which must have warmed her heart for, stilted and constrained as it was, it showed unmistakably his admiration and love:

> My dear sister . . . how sincerely I am grieved to hear that your health is so much impaired, I need not tell you. Although it has pleased Providence to cast your lot at a distance from me, and thereby to deprive me of the happiness of that frequent intercourse which was once so delightful, yet no separation or circumstance can ever diminish my affection for you, or lessen the interest I have always had in your welfare.
>
> Perhaps you have conceived your situation more critical than it really is. . . . It may yet please God to restore you to that usefulness which has always marked the sphere in which you moved. That this may be His Will is my most fervent prayer.
>
> But should it be otherwise, should He in His wise and righteous Providence deem it proper to remove you from this world of care and disquietude, what shall I say, my dear Sister? Nothing. Nothing is necessary to a mind already familiarized to the prospect of a change which sooner or later must be realized, and which is so well disciplined in the way which leads to that place of blessedness where the anxieties of this life cease from troubling, and the weary are at rest.

Elizabeth was content, insofar as her life's work was concerned, if death should come. St. Joseph's House, she told Ellen Wiseman, was "well established," and she described her pupils for Antonio: "About one hundred precious souls which we cherish and prepare in silence and under a rather common look of no pretension to go over our cities like a good leaven. . . . Our orphan asylums in New York and Philadelphia promise more than we could have hoped."

And in September, after Archbishop Maréchal had paid her a visit, she informed Antonio that "All goes pretty well . . . for religion. The Archbishop says he could never have believed the increase of the true Faith to be half what it is, if he had not verified it in his tour; and I assure you, if I had another house as large as the one we are in, we could fill it with Sisters and children. We are obliged to refuse continually for want of room."

It seemed almost a signal to depart when Elizabeth finally heard from Richard after months of careless silence. After the first long wait for news of him, she had reprimanded him sharply for his laziness, and then wrote "him in all directions to soothe any pain my first letters may have given." The volatile young man had formed a close friendship with a certain Rosetti, and Elizabeth reported to Bill that "Dick is wild with the desire of Rosetti's coming to the Mountain as Italian or French teacher. Mr. Dubois says, 'Let him try it.'" The plan was short-lived, for Samuel Cooper, who had been touring Europe, brought home a second letter from Richard soon after in which, Elizabeth told Bill, "he mentions the death of his dearest friend by a dagger, and I much fear it is poor Rosetti. He says: 'As he gave his last gasp, he said, "Seton, do not revenge me in any way, but take care of my sister; show you loved me by protecting her." And at this moment, as he expired, Paulina entered the room,' says Dick, 'and judge what my feelings were.' It seems it was for some defense of his sister the poor fellow died, and his assassin is now in the galleys. What scrapes our Daddy must often be in, and"—she added wickedly, knowing her Richard—"what a scrape this Paulina may be in!"

Actually, Elizabeth confessed to William, she did not mind Richard's failure to write half so much as not hearing from her elder son. Dick's letters were often essays in nonsense and, as his mother put it, "one day he is so happy, the next so doubtful. He will be of a firmer mind bye and bye, I hope." She must have known the forlornness of such a hope.

Elizabeth was still worrying for fear William should have to sail with little or no money, and she returned to the subject in a letter of August 24:

> I would send you forty dollars I have safe, if I knew it would be sure to reach you by the mail. Tell me in your next if it would, that we may not apply to the merchants if we can help it. Oh, that I had enough to get you every comfort for such a long voyage! But I charge you, my love, not to want anything essential through unwillingness to apply to the Bishop, whom you know I can safely repay from our little share in Barry's hands. I charge you, beloved child, by all that is dear to us, do not hesitate—or if

you do not go before [the] last of September you will have time to tell me, and I will borrow it from the House, at all events, and never fear but we will clear our way very quietly; if it is three, four, five hundred, dearest, do not mind, but look at my poor heart whenever you hesitate. The forty I have without borrowing, and it is yours if I could but get it safe to you.

William's ship sailed from Boston on September 18, 1818. Elizabeth retailed the news ruefully to Julia Scott on October 2: "William is gone [on] his three years' voyage in the *Macedonian* frigate, [as] far as Cape Horn, perhaps. *Oh, my!* as Kit says, he will pay dear for his glory." Both mother and son had prepared themselves for a long separation—she, indeed, thought to see him again only in the next world—but an act of God intervened to unite them for a last parting. The ship ran into storms off the coast of Virginia and had to put into Norfolk for repairs. Elizabeth described the mishap for Ellen Wiseman:

> Think of poor *Will* the night of the so dreadful storm of the *Macedonian*, being asleep after a long watch and dreaming that I stood by him, with all the agony of heart asking: *"Are you prepared, my William?"* At that moment they came to tell him the masts were going over and the gale tremendous, so that when he sprang from his hammock he was to the knees in water.

And so William came, and the dying little mother, wrapped in "old shawls and flannels," had him to herself for a wonderful eight days. "Our William has been—we have enjoyed!!!" she wrote fervently to Ellen Wiseman. He had no sooner departed than she began to keep one of her *Journals* for his amusement, playfully entitling it *Extract from Log Book of the Shady Retreat.* She told him how she and Kit had followed him in imagination on his journey back to the ship, through Gettysburg, in Baltimore, to his arrival at Norfolk. She included the "droll story of Andeuse [a friend of William's] pretending to be a fool going to Baltimore, emptying a plate of eggs in his lap, pocketing the landlord's dollar, lighting his cigar with his bill-of-fare—still honestly leaving his friend to make their settlement for expenses." She closed by assuring William that she had received his "dear note from Gettysburg, which I took to bed with me; our sympathy in the arms of sleep amuses me so much. Oh do, my love, write all your hopes and fears about going!"

Kit hoped to distract her brother from the pain of departure by quoting him tidbits from Richard's lastest letters: "I have spent three or four days with the F.'s at the Baths. I saw there many full-blooded sheep, but as I am an *American* I pay very little attention to *titled beings.*"—and Kit's acid comment was: "You know we agreed we could not trust him if a *title* was offered him." She continued: "He tells mother in another letter: 'To be a good fellow, I know, suffices to make you happy, but as for Kit and I, though it adds to her happiness, it is not all we want. There is a certain something called riches which, at college, I was learned to despise; but bye-the-bye I find them requisite in a high degree in this world. It shall be my care to accumulate them, and have no doubt (though they are a cause of unhappiness to many) but that Kitty and myself will enjoy them with a true spirit'—hear his comparison!—'just as a poor man would a pot of sweetmeats (not devour it like a child in an instant) but takes it spoonful at a time to sweeten the hard crust which he had been so long gnawing.' He really does surpass everything I ever heard for *invention!*"

The following February Elizabeth had a tale of Providence for Julia concerning William's embarkation:

> I could make you laugh by telling you that I sent William a fifty dollars of pressing necessity after making the sign of the cross on it and entreating our good angel it might reach him. Well, all hands had been called, sailing orders given, and poor Will going off without any stores but his rations, when the purser came on board with the letter containing our sacred note. The wind happened to change at that very time for three hours, and my *darling* had time to go on shore and get some warm clothes and little stores for this formidable two-years' voyage—the greatest consolation I could have for the bitter moment.

While Elizabeth was experiencing the constant agony of William's departure, the Sisterhood in Philadelphia was taking on new work. The *Council Minutes* of September 4, 1818, recorded that the Vicar General, Father Louis de Barth, had requested an additional Sister "to keep a school." The school was the already established German Free School attached to Trinity Church. In its usual and laconic way the *Minute Book* reported the Council's action on the request: "Assented to. Sr. Susan sent to Phila. for school or to take Sr. Fanny's place & have her keep school—whatever V.G. wanted." Sister Fanny had taken Sister

Rose's place as Sister Servant when Rose went to New York; but now Fanny took over the German school, and Elizabeth's dear "Sus" was appointed Sister Servant on October 23.

On November 11 both Elizabeth and Antonio sat down, half a world apart, to write to each other, although neither would have the other's letter until February. Elizabeth's big news was sorrowful: that Dr. Matignon had died (on September 19), and that Bishop Cheverus was in "extreme distress" at the death of one who had been not only his faithful companion of twenty-five years in the American ministry, but also the closest friend of his heart. Death, she told Antonio, was drawing closer every day to her, too, but "I show him his master." The words were a sort of joyous battle cry, for they recur in an ecstatic letter written at the same time to Bruté:

> Mind not my health. Death grins broader in the pot every morning, and I grin at him and I show him his master. Oh, be blessed, blessed, blessed. I see nothing in this world but blue sky and our altars. All the rest is so plainly not to be looked at, but all left to Him, with tears only for sin. We talk now all day long of my death and how it will be just like the rest of the housework. What is it else? What came in the world for? Why in it so long? But this last great eternal end—it seems to me so simple, when I look up at the crucifix simpler still; so that I went to sleep before I made any thanksgiving but *Te Deum* and *Magnificat* after Communion. . . .
>
> This morning, Our *Adored Harp* pressed close on the aching breast, we swept every sacred chord of praise and thanksgiving. Then, weeping under the willows of that horrid Babylon whose waters are drunk so greedily while our heavenly streams pass by unheeded, the silent heart is pressed closer and closer.
>
> G. Blessed, mind not my follies. I see the everlasting hills so near and the door of my eternity so wide open that I turn too wild sometimes.
>
> Oh, if all goes well for me what will I not do for you! You will see. But, alas, yet if I am not one of His elect, it is only I to be blamed, and when *going down* I must still lift the hands to the very last look in praise and gratitude for what He has done to save me. What more could He have done? That thought stops all.

Bruté always struck sparks from Elizabeth's soul, and the language with which she expressed to him the unbearable heat of divine love within her had the excitement and extravagance of fireworks. In the spring of 1818, restless with apostolic zeal, he had talked of going to China as a missionary. Elizabeth had dissuaded him, because Dubois needed him so badly. When Samuel Cooper was ordained in August and came to assume the pastorate of Emmitsburg, Bruté revived his apostolic desires and looked longingly to Canada and the salvation of the Indians. The erratic Cooper had much of Bruté's zeal, and Elizabeth did him the honor of coupling his ardor with that of her "Blessed G's":

> Blessed, your poor little Bête-Mother is lost these days past in your Canada letters. Oh my! To see man a wild savage, a polished savage, man in any state what a savage!—unless he be in Christ. Oh, Blessed, I gasp with the desires to Him whom you are now carrying in and on your breast for full, whole accomplishment of His blessed Will. I glance a fearful look at you and Mr. Cooper and say secretly: if I was one or the other! Then adore and think.
>
> I know nothing about it; only it seems to me that those who have light and grace already might be trusted to keep it: and I would not stop night or day until I reached the dry and dark wilderness where neither can be found, where such horrid crimes go on for want of them, and where there is such a glorious death to be gained by carrying them. O G., if I was light and life as you are, I would shout like a madman alone to my God, and roar and groan and sigh and be silent all together until I had baptized a thousand and snatched these poor victims from hell.
>
> And pray, Madame Bête, say you, why does not your zeal make its flame through your own little hemisphere? True—but rules, prudence, subjections, opinions, etc.—dreadful walls to a burning soul wild as mine and Somebody's. . . . I am like a fiery horse I had when a girl, whom they tried to break by making him drag a heavy cart; and the poor beast was so humbled that he could never more be inspired by whips or caresses, and wasted to a skeleton until he died. But you and Mr. Cooper might waste to skeletons to some purpose, and after wasting be sent still living to the glories of the kingdom.
>
> In the meantime, that kingdom come. Every day I ask my bête-soul what I do for it in my little part assigned, and can see nothing but the smile, caress, be patient, write, pray and WAIT before Him.
>
> O G., G., G., my blessed God, that kingdom come!

Was ever zeal for the missions given more fervent tongue, or necessity for mission labors a truer *apologia*? This single, passionate letter, penned in some secret chamber of her heart, places Elizabeth Seton firmly by the side of Xavier, even as Thérèse of Lisieux made her way there from the quiet of her cloister.

Elizabeth knew, however, that zeal run wild was often worse than no zeal at all, and she did not hesitate to tighten the reins even on her beloved Bruté when he had overstepped himself. Thus, finding him sulking over some fancied wrong done him by the Sisterhood, she put him firmly in his place, at the same time teaching him by her own way of acting a lesson in prudent government:

> My Blessed, all is a true mystery to me in your disposition, much greater mystery than any of *Faith*. A man of your particular principle *on paper*, who has evidently the most dear and special graces—not given drop by drop as to other souls, but poured over your head in a daily torrent—yet I seldom see you but in such wild enthusiasm of your own impression of the moment that you can see nothing, hear nothing, but that one object; or else quite *reserved, hurt* and *anxious* because you have not been consulted in things *which spoke for themselves*, or others which we would not dare take your advice about without knowing the Superior's will, or others again which, like the poor German smiths, we go over in our blind ignorance and I never even guess I have not done well till someone points it out.
>
> How troubled, too, because Mr. Dubois don't come, and what responsibility have you? Is it your zeal and desire of the good you imagine he will do? You ought to know our Reverend Superior by this time and see that he is not to be pushed anywhere; and your urging him cannot but keep him away.
>
> When anything *essential* happens, I always inform him of it; and if the thing is not essential, his absence often hinders a fuss about nothing, and suffers little pets and passions to drop in silence.
>
> You speak as if your Mother's confidence is deficient, but it is surely not at this time I am to open your eyes to my situation in this community.

During the months that Elizabeth had been awaiting death so eagerly in the Valley, a storm that had long rumbled on the Mountain was finally dissipated, adding greatly to the contentment of her soul. The Sulpicians in Baltimore had for some time been dissatisfied with the state of things at Mount St. Mary's, especially the sizable debt, and were of a strong mind to close it. Dubois and Bruté, who loved the college as their lives, were of just as strong a mind to keep it open, even to the point of threatening to defy the will of their superior, Father Tessier, in the matter. They were not as contumacious as it would appear for, as has already been noted concerning the vague lines of authority of Archbishop Carroll and the Sulpicians in regard to the Sisterhood, the authority of

the Sulpician Superior in Baltimore over Mount St. Mary's was not at all
clearcut. Dubois, in fact, was to write to Father Garnier in Paris on
February 19, 1819: "It must appear evident to you that *Saint Sulpice* has
not yet any government in America, that, indeed, we need a constitution
adopted to our local situation and to our distance from the central government."

The crisis at the Mount came to a head in June when Tessier delivered
the decision of the Sulpician *Directeurs* that the college was to shut
down, and recalled Father John Hickey to Baltimore. The day was saved
in a most unexpected manner by the people of Emmitsburg, as Elizabeth
told William in her letter of July 1:

> A most interesting scene took place here last week. The Sulpicians of
> Baltimore (except poor Mr. Bruté) solicited Dr. Dubois' suppression of the
> Seminary, thinking he was rather getting in debt and that the masters he
> employed would be more useful in Baltimore. And ten [of] our good
> Emmitsburgers came forward [and] offered Mr. Dubois 8 or 10,000 in
> hand to buy the Seminary for him if he chose, if only he would not leave
> them. The Archbishop, seeing how hard it would go, has directed all to
> be left as it was before. So much for the good "country peeps," as Mr.
> Duhamel called them.

Elizabeth and the Sisters were vastly relieved, for they depended on the
Mount, not only for priestly service, but for much of their buying and
farm work.

It was also consoling for Elizabeth in the face of death to witness the
complete healing of old personal wounds. Her family in New York accepted her now more wholeheartedly than they ever had. It was but a
few years since a letter from her half-sister Helen had set up a longing
within her, and Eliza Sadler had warned her against the attempt to renew old ties; but now, on November 17, 1818, Helen could write easily
and familiarly to "my own beloved sister," and recount how her little
Henry, riding his uncle's cane, "often goes to Emmitsburg to see Aunt
Seton"—and Elizabeth could as easily and familiarly reply. It was typical
of the new family warmth that Elizabeth's name should have become
a household word to her sisters' and brother's children.

Dué wrote that fall—she had, she said, written often, but the evil star under which she lived had seen to it that her letters were lost. Poor Dué was as full as ever of the complaints that had become a habit of speech:

> Could I have the happiness of hearing from you regularly once a week, or even once a month [she pressed Elizabeth], I should deem myself happy under all my trials—and rest assured I have my share. . . . I must say that for one day I was so great a baby on finding my name not even mentioned in your letter to dear Helen Craig; I own it was a great pain to my heart, to appear to be so perfectly forgotten by my soul's friend and sister. . . .

She did not fail to detail her sufferings—which were not imaginary—or to lament her loneliness:

> I own to you that I did expect frequent visits from them [Elizabeth's sisters] during my last illness, which was considered by the doctor as very dangerous. 'Tis best, no doubt, to be alone. And since I lost my most dear Reverend friend Mr. Kohlmann and the three dear blessed nuns that were here, I may say I have been alone as to religious friendship, at least in New York—and so best, I think my soul's friend will say. I wish much to write to my beloved child Kitty, not less loved by me than if she had showed me every mark of former love when here.

The good soul could no more help her lamentations than she could stop breathing, and Elizabeth, who knew her loyal, loving heart, understood. Dué did have one piece of good news: that "my dear husband . . . at last seems to think a *little* on religion. He went to church with me last Sunday, and was delighted with the sermon and promises to go again." Helen had equally good news about the marital situation of Captain Dupleix and his wife. "You would be pleased," she told Elizabeth, "to see how much the hand of time has smoothed their sometimes rugged road. All is now peace and happiness."

It was remarkable how many of the exterior cares and anxieties that had lain sadly in the corners of Elizabeth's heart over the years were disappearing one by one. She would yet have her pangs, of course, but they would be passing. Now, as the autumn of 1818 blazed and died, her whole being was washed in the quiet mellowness that lay over her peaceful Valley.

XXIII

The World of Realities

It became obvious when winter had gone and Elizabeth continued to hold her own that she was not to die yet. By April she was able to reassure Ellen Wiseman that "I am quite well *in comparison*"; and Eliza Sadler that "I am pretty well, have laughed at Mr. Blustery March and really find no word stronger than Mr. [James] Thomson's 'Echo the mountains, round the forest smiles, and every sense and every heart is joy.'"

She was cheered by her first word from William since he had sailed. His letter was dated December 12, and had been written below the equator. He was, of course, constantly in his mother's thoughts, and she told Ellen Wiseman, "I look for him always in both worlds, so uncertain is every possible calculation." Mary Post was intensely interested in William's voyage, which was in the interests of American shipping, but appears also to have been one more attempt to find the elusive "Northwest Passage."

> Do you not long to know how far your William has progressed in his voyage? [she asked Elizabeth in a letter of March 12]. Has any lucky chance given you that pleasure? While we are surrounded by ice and snow, he may be melting in a West India climate or enjoying a temperate one. I should think, as William likes the water, that he—not excepting one on board the

ship—would be most likely to enjoy a voyage of the kind he is engaged in, owing to the interest he takes in views of nature. . . . Should they, by investigating the navigation of that part of our country, discover the wished-for facility to that of others, they will no doubt be highly gratified by succeeding in accomplishing a discovery of so much importance to this country that others have failed in accomplishing. I think they will be much more deserving of the thanks of the citizens of New York than General Jackson was, who received them here lately in the square fronting the new Hall, surrounded by military and music.

Welcome news concerning Richard, also, came in a letter written by Antonio on March 8:

Your giant Richard is very well. He gives me perfect satisfaction in his moral and religious conduct. Little by little he will be himself, I hope—daily better pleased with his lot with me, as well as I shall be myself with him, as he will try to be and become useful in my counting house. He is good enough now to give some part of his time and patience in reading the English language to my little ones, Maria and Julia. My two elder sons, Patrick and George, will return from college next September, and he may have a similar employment with them, too. I shall take a fatherly and friendly care of him, as I promised you.

The kind Antonio was apparently making his news as comfortable as possible for Elizabeth, since it was fairly obvious that Dick was not bounding forward in great leaps if, after a year, Antonio was still looking for him to "be himself" and to "become useful in my counting house." Although Elizabeth must surely have perceived the truth, she passed on only the happier news of Richard to her friends.

Antonio was quite aware of Elizabeth's condition through letters from herself and from Father Whitfield and Father Cooper, and he offered her spiritual consolation:

God will be your immense reward for eternity, if you persevere faithful to His Will. To your prayers, I doubt not, I owe the uninterrupted prosperity of all my concerns in this world; and I am confident that when you will be in heaven you will not let the door shut against your own true brother and friend, who has fortunately contributed to open it for you.

Antonio's affection had not wavered since that first week Elizabeth had spent in his house at Leghorn. "Be perfectly at ease in the steadiness of my friendship for you," he told her tenderly. "In spite of my stubborn silence, you are constantly in my mind, you have my warmest wishes. I love, I esteem, I venerate you. I boast of your benevolence towards me, and for you I shall always be ready to fight men and devils."

Kit was suffering her usual spring decline in weight and health, and Elizabeth sent her off to visit friends, the Smiths, at Carroll Manor on the Monocacy River near Frederick. Kit wrote back a charming description of Catholic rural life:

> Mr. Smith, as well as his brother, are plain country people; but possess, I assure you, solid good sense and are very religious. Today is Sunday. We have no Mass, but the good old gentleman assembles all his family in the room, black as well as white, and while the former stand respectfully (both young and old), he, seated in the midst like an old patriarch, reads them an instruction out of some good book. They all kneel down and say the Litany of Jesus and that of St. Joseph, etc.
>
> How far happier is this mode of life than that of those who live in style and elegance, seldom thinking of the life to come and but seldom really enjoying the present one.

Even at a distance Kit could not forget that she was her mother's official nurse, and lectured her earnestly about her health: "Take good care of yourself, particularly this damp kind of weather. Don't expose yourself to cold, particularly by going down to the refectory; and your knee, dearest, if you go too often down those steps, might become as it once was." She knew the way to secure her mother's cooperation. "Do, for the sake of the three who so dearly love you," she entreated, "do, for the sake of all around you, be careful of yourself."

Elizabeth's health had improved further, as she assured Julia Scott on May 26: "My poor old health you ask about, dearest, is so renewed that it hardly can be better; and the cheerfulness you think assumed is, believe me, from the heart." To John Hickey, whom she had literally hammered by her repeated scoldings into the good priest he was fast becoming, she said:

> I cannot die one way, it seems, so I try to die the other, and keep the straight path to God alone. The little daily lesson: to keep soberly and quietly in His Presence, trying to turn every little action on His Will; and to praise and love through cloud as sunshine is all my care and study. *Sam* offers his battle from time to time, but Our Beloved stands behind the wall

and keeps the wretch his distance. So much for your Mother's little nothing part; but oh, mind your own, so great and glorious, for whether in action or at rest you are forever *His priest.*

With better health Elizabeth's vigor returned, so that she began to practice something of her old industry with the pen, soothing, cajoling, advising, strengthening family and friends alike. She wrote with dismay to Ellen Wiseman that she had a recent note which read: "Pray for your Philadelphia children, Mother; they want it. *Kitty* Wiseman and R. Mallon alone resist the tide"; and she added fearfully:

> Much as to say my Ellen goes with it. Oh, my God! What a hard world to steer through with innocence! My Ellen, chosen, beloved child of my heart, I must leave you to Our God. You are as far out of my reach as my soul's William is. What is all I can say? How can I even guess your trials, circumstances, affairs of the heart, temptations of all kinds? But my God will protect and save my beloved ones, I trust.

Like so many lazy, careless people who have reformed, John Hickey was hard on others with the same faults, and Elizabeth now found herself scolding him for exactly opposite reasons than before. Hickey's sister Eleanor was a pupil at St. Joseph's, and his brother William a pupil at the Mount; and he was plaguing them with his newfound severity. Elizabeth promptly remonstrated with him in a letter that showed forth her keen knowledge of youth:

> I do not like . . . some things you wrote Ellen lately. You and I speak all through eternity; but take advice from your old Mother—I am a hundred to your thirty in *experience,* that cruel friend of our earthly journey.
> When you ask too much at first, you often gain nothing at last. *And if the heart is lost, all is lost.* If you use such language to your family, they cannot love you, since they have not our microscopes to see things as they are. Your austere, hard language was not understood by Ellen, who, dear soul, considers your letters as mere curiosity. She loves and venerates you, but do not push her away. . . . Gently, gently, my father in God and son in heart. Do you drive so in the tribunal? I hope not.
> The faults of young people, especially such faults as Eleanor's, must be moved by prayer and tears, because they are *constitutional* and cannot be frightened out. I have said much harder things to her than you do, but turning the tune in her own heart, and not her poor, dear family quite as respectable even—as to the point you press on so valiantly—as half our Legislature, Senate, etc. How can you, in such a country as ours, dwell

on such a motive of humility? A much stronger one, I think, is in a little
secret I will carry to the grave.

At this point Elizabeth broke off, like St. Paul, into a transport that
was entirely personal and intimate:

> I once told you how I wished to do as you have done, and I will tell you
> *in return*, that all the illusion and spider web of *earthly weaving* is broken,
> and nothing now more bright and steady than the *divine lamp* He feeds
> and trims Himself, because, as I suppose, I *stayed in obedience*. Oh, this
> *Master and Father!* . . . How can we be happy enough in His service?

And in another letter, she did not hesitate to hold up the younger
brother who Father Hickey was so intent on reprimanding as an ex-
emplar for the priest himself!

> William is surely one of the most estimable young men of the world.
> What a precious diamond, to be so covered with the cares of this world!
> But how can he help it? Be you gentle and considerate to him, you
> blessed man of God, feeding on sweetmeats every morning and rejoicing
> your heart with the choicest wine. Had his disposition to virtue and reli-
> gion been cultivated as yours has been, he would be already your equal,
> I believe—

and she added with sudden diffidence, "but [I am] not sure."

Elizabeth saw the last of her faithful friend Samuel Cooper that
June of 1819. The eccentric clergyman had painted himself into a corner,
as it were, and had no course but to stalk off, leaving the marks of his
imprudent zeal upon the fine work he had done. Without question
Cooper had aroused the congregation of Emmitsburg and brought it
closer to God: people flocked to hear his fiery sermons, and at Eastertime
there had been a substantial increase in the number of Communions. But
his very ardor had eventually spoiled everything.

Cooper had made up his mind to root out the vice of drunkenness
from among his congregation. The vice was probably real enough, for
Bruté has left the following picture of Emmitsburg's drinking facilities
at the time:

> The town numbers about seven hundred inhabitants. There are four
> principal taverns and perhaps seven or eight tippling shops under the

sign: "Liquors and fruits." But besides these, the principal groceries and dry goods stores, of which there are six quite considerable, sell drams and whiskey to any one coming, particularly to their customers.

Cooper's approach to the problem, however, was completely high-handed: he decided upon the extreme measure of public penance, of making ignominious examples of the chief offenders, despite the fact that Archbishop Maréchal and Father Dubois both looked with dim eye on his proposal. It seemed at first that his plan might succeed, for when he announced it to a shocked congregation, only Mr. Radford, himself a candidate for the role of public penitent, left the church indignantly. When, however, Cooper started to put his plan into effect by barring Radford from the church and asking Dubois to do the same at St. Mary's and St. Joseph's, the congregation protested so vehemently that the Archbishop had to order Cooper to desist. His action and authority thus repudiated, the defeated pastor could but resign, which he did on June 15, going to Baltimore and from thence to Augusta, Georgia, and Norfolk, Virginia, and eventually to France, where he had the happiness of assisting Cardinal Cheverus on his deathbed at Bordeaux in 1836.

Elizabeth, Dubois and Bruté were all unhappy at Cooper's departure, not that they had approved of his extremism, but because of the great good he had accomplished and the promise for the future could he have but disciplined his fervor. With Elizabeth, too, there was the personal debt she owed him; and it must have wrenched her heart to see one so estimable, generous and well-meaning depart under a cloud.

Kit had written again to her mother from Carroll Manor on June 8. She was obviously enjoying herself, learning to ride horseback and making the acquaintance of all the Smiths' friends and neighbors; she did not think that she would be able to return until after the midsummer harvest. Kit was particularly amused at a question of Aunt Scott's as to her "matrimonial prospects" which Elizabeth had passed on to her: "You gave her a right answer, dearest. I assure you I am in no hurry to take on the more serious cares of life, more especially while I have my Mother. I think I shall be a baby longer than twenty-one. Twenty-eighth of this month I shall be nineteen. Remember me."

Elizabeth was too much the mother to forget so important a date, and Kit had her birthday note:

Whose birthday is this, my dear Savior? It is my darling one's, my child's, my friend's, my only dear companion left of all You once gave with a bounteous hand, the little relic of all my earthly bliss. . . .

Elizabeth regaled her birthday girl with the homey bits of news that would most delight her: "What true fun here. Sister J. cleaning, white-washing our nest—the good Superior gone—the Brother must stay at the Mountain tomorrow, so we are to have a long sleep—I in the sacristy, since I am a relic." Lest Kit take her jesting too seriously, Elizabeth hastened to assure her that she was "so well, and put butter on my bread even in the morning, for your sake; and if it does not go down, for a second piece sprinkle sugar on it, too." She charged Kit, when she returned, to "bring me at least a half-dollar's worth of camphor —in a bottle or box, or the air will dissolve it—it helps my digestion so much."

Elizabeth enclosed for Kit's perusal a letter, "as sweet . . . as can be penned," from her half-sister Mary Bayley Bunch. Since her marriage a year and a half before, Mary had known troubles enough. She had gone to live with her husband, Robert, in Nassau, and from there traveled with him to England where he had business and also meant to lay rather tenuous claim to the Earldom of Rivers, which was about to revert to the Crown for lack of an heir. The very possibility of Mary's becoming a countess had caused delicious excitement in the family circle for a while, but nothing seems to have come of it. The young wife, who was pregnant, had nearly died of seasickness on the long crossing, and her baby died at birth soon after she landed.

Elizabeth and Kit had been intrigued all winter at Mary's bravery in proposing to take another voyage back to New York despite the tragic consequences of the first: and Elizabeth was pleased and touched when Mary wrote immediately upon her arrival to say she was safe. "I lift my heart to Him who united us by so tender a tie to beg Him to convey to yours some idea at least of my gratitude and delight on reading your letter," she replied on June 26. "To find you safe and well over this most anxious voyage is the greatest relief to me."

Elizabeth had a true family heart and, as has been said, it gave her great satisfaction to be allowed in her last days to give full vent to the sisterly affection she had never lost. She mingled her tears with Mary's over the remembrance of their dead brothers, and asserted earnestly that "although it is so long since I have seen our William, we had such a particular turn of heart for him that, next to seeing Uncle Craig, my children longed most to know him of all our family. I can see you when you take his darlings in your arms. What would I not give to embrace and pour my tears over them and dear Richard's, to embrace the two lonely, dear mothers!"

Leo Post was failing from some rheumatic ailment, and Elizabeth wrote Dué urgently in August to "beg and entreat . . . a word about poor Leo, as I cannot hear from him or of him, and suppose by the word in Sister Margaret's letter he is perhaps at the last extremity."

Margaret George had replaced Rose White as Sister Servant in New York on May 26, and it gratified Elizabeth that Dué was at once smitten with the charm of "my little Margaret." "If you cannot write at any time, my dearest Dué," she instructed her friend, "make her your clerk; she is swift with her pen and always delights to help." It pleased Elizabeth, too, that Sister Cecilia called Dué "the refuge of the miserable, and is never weary telling me of your tender love and care for the poor."

Kit had just returned to the Valley, and on August 19 the girl dispatched a letter to Julia Scott to assure her that "Mama . . . looks well and is well, her mind quiet and cheerful, especially since we have the delightful news of William's safety as far as the 13th of March." Elizabeth took the pen from Kit's hand to tack on a postscript, and the pitiful scribble—so marked a change from her usual writing—was mute evidence, despite Kit's protestations to the contrary, that her mother had traveled far and swiftly on the road to death. But Elizabeth made no complaint. Rather, she sang out, "How happy, happy I am!"

> I meant this to have gone by a private hand [she told Julia], but on consideration I hurry it to beg you, my dearest friend, not to put yourself to the least inconvenience in sending the usual bounty in this trouble of banks and general distress, in which many want a thousand times more than we do; for unless William is again shipwrecked or some quite unforeseen distress occurs, there can be no necessity for you continuing your unwearied patience of so many years, as the dear objects of my and your care are now pushed through for themselves. . . .

How do I pray that your and Filicchi's family may reap the fruits of that support which has enabled a poor, brokenhearted, broken-constitutioned creature like me . . . clear their way!

The "trouble of banks and general distress" Elizabeth referred to was in the wake of the national depression of 1819 which had been brought about, like the Great Depression of the 1930's, by an extravagant postwar boom that finally burst like the bubble it was. The Sisters had planned a new building to accommodate the growing number of day students, but the depression caused them to put off the start of construction indefinitely. The financial distress of the nation was accompanied by increasing talk of war with Spain over Andrew Jackson's peremptory invasion of Florida; the war scare eventually subsided when Spain, in surrender, sold the invaded territory to the United States for five million dollars before she should lose it by force.

But when Elizabeth wrote William on November 7 she could inform him that "we hear of nothing but war, war on all sides, so our dear prospect of a reunion is faint indeed." If that faint prospect should be realized, however, she promised him that he would find "everything . . . just as you left it. Losses plenty in the money way, by our crazy merchants, but we push along. No new buildings in such hard times, so you will yet come to the dear little old nest, your shady, blessed retreat of summer and always my dear corner of peace." Her talk of reunion was surely for William's benefit, that he might not guess how weak she was, for Elizabeth herself must surely have known that she could not last until his return.

The doors of other human affections were closing with finality, too. Mary Bunch wrote on October 26 that she was taking ship the next day for Nassau to join her husband. Leo Post was going with her in an attempt to regain his health but, as it turned out, he died on the way or soon after their arrival in the Bahamas. Mary had, besides, really startling news: that "Aunt Sad . . . sails an hour hence for France." This meant, of course, that Elizabeth would never see Sad again this side of eternity, but she never mentioned the melancholy fact when she sent a letter hurriedly after her departing friend; rather, she aired her vast amusement that Sad had so taken everyone by surprise. "I cannot get over it," she exclaimed. "What a droll thing, to give the slip with your matron gravity, I suppose!" And she confessed with a momentary wistfulness, "I think I should have been a traveler, too, if I had had no bairns to nail me."

It seemed that heaven meant to deprive her of yet another friend when the news came at the end of November that Pierre Chatard was critically ill. Elizabeth sat down at once to comfort his good wife. "All our community unite to beg for the most precious life of our dear doctor," she wrote. "With your dear heart mine pours its gratitude for the blessed preparations of His beautiful Providence who waited till he was ready; yet he may still be restored to you and the thousand poor whom he is father to. My nerves are so shaken, what must yours be!" She had not time to get the letter off, however, before she was able to add the happy lines, under the date of December 1: "Oh, the good and joyful news that he is better! Your dear Chatard is still with you. . . ."

Elizabeth was truly delighted beyond the bounds of courtesy and good will, for the Chatards had an exceptional place in her heart. Only two weeks before, she had written prophetically to Madame Chatard: "Indeed, dear friend, it is a great part of my devotion to pray for your dear family for, quite independent of my thousand reasons for gratitude and natural attractions, I think that your children's rise or fall in our Church of America will be more noticed than any; so that I can truly say that my heart hovers over them for many reasons." Her words found fulfillment in the brilliant career of Francis Silas Chatard as rector of the North American College in Rome and later as a successor of Simon Gabriel Bruté in the See of Vincennes; another son, F. E. Chatard, served the Church faithfully as a prominent and devoted Catholic layman; and a daughter, too young for Mother Seton to have known, spent a long life as a Sister of Charity, dying only in 1917.

Christmas came, and Elizabeth knew again the special joy the holy night brought always to St. Joseph's, the union of yet another class of dear pupils with their Lord in the Blessed Sacrament. She had in these fifteen First Communicants, she told Madame Chatard, a fullness of "peace and simplicity of delight I never enjoyed with the children before." It may well have been because she had drawn so close to heaven that even her New Year's greetings to the good doctor's wife were: "Eternal years to my friend!"

All winter long Elizabeth sat by the fire in contentment, the whole busy life of community and school revolving about, emanating from, the stronger blaze in her soul. Even though no word came from either William or Richard and Elizabeth still suffered for them agonies of apprehension in her soul, she rarely gave them voice, and only then to reassert her wholehearted trust in God. She was awaiting as quietly as she could the divine summons, trying, as she told Antonio on April 18, 1820, "to make my very breathing a continual thanksgiving."

As soon as the snow was gone Kit left for Baltimore to visit the Tiernans and the Harpers. Mrs. Harper took her to Annapolis where, Kit told her mother excitedly, she "was cordially received by old Mr. Carroll," the Signer of the Declaration of Independence, and where she saw Mrs. Stephen Decatur, widow of the naval hero who had died recently. "She keeps her room almost constantly," Kit told her mother, "and seems *truly to feel her loss*." On the 8th of May Elizabeth wrote with earnest entreaty to Richard:

> You can have no idea of our anxiety to hear from you. Six, seven, eight months pass without one line. . . . What a heartful consolation, my soul's Richard, it would be to me if you could write me in full sincerity before the Searcher of Hearts and not merely to comfort mine: "Mother, I preserve my Faith amidst all the dangers and scandals I meet—your Faith, Mother, the one so dear to you."

She assured him, however, with what must have cost her a great effort merely to form the words, that "if you have lost it, my beloved, think not you will be less wrapt round my soul, for I know well what your trials must be." Then, most uncharacteristically, she made a strange, tentative gesture at matchmaking:

> I have two dear little Harpers with me who are really like a part of ourselves. I often look with a loving eye on the eldest and think, while her beautiful mind is unfolded by me, that I am doing it for you; for they [General and Mrs. Harper] love our family so much I would not be surprised if the affection was reciprocal in our children. Mrs. H. says she would be so happy to see Josephine the choice of her son. He is expected in the summer, and by his letters seems a promising young man."

She broke off, as if routing a daydream, and exclaimed, "Oh, may you but be happy, and whoever you love, my son, I shall dearly love —that is poz [positive]"; then went on to give him the news:

Mr. Dubois like a prince on his Mountain—full school—debts paid—improvements in all directions. Egan, Mullen, Jamison, Wiseman, etc., still there. They are cutting the mountain in terraces to bring the garden up to Mr. Duhamel's house. . . .

I have now a great friend of Carolina, the eloquent Congressman Gaston. His two daughters are with me and, like good Mr. Harper, they puff us out handsomely. All for the good of the cause, or I should not like such puffings. . . .

Aunt Charlton is gone to the Land of Souls, but if she left us any shiners we cannot learn. All in time, I suppose.

On June 29 Elizabeth was worried again over Ellen Wiseman's spiritual difficulties, this time, apparently, a shyness about confession.

Think how I would beg you, supplicate you, this day [she began], to keep you near to Him by the *only means*, and not let the wall of partition be raised again in your dearest heart as it was before our last happy meeting. Wake up your faith. You know Our Lord never meant us to mind whom we go to, if they do but take us to Him. And the longer you stay back you well know the harder it is for you to go forward. And, alas, what does it end in? Dearest, to go through double trouble, pain and examens, which will not be pains of grace and merit, but of your own weakness and want of courage in delaying. Oh, do, dearest, write me you have been. . . .

She could tell Ellen that she had "at last long letters from Richard"; but, she added despondently, they were

full of schemes about settling on the Black River—black indeed will it be to him if he carries it through. He says, "Commerce is a dead loss of time at present." Poor fellow, I fear his faith is dead by the whole tenor of his letters; yet he puts change aside till another year. So, we will see. Nothing from William. You hear my sighs, and they go to your dear heart, I know; but never mind, my Ellen, Our God will pity.

How deeply she was sunk in gloom over her sons was evident in a letter of July 2 to John Hickey. "You pray, I hope, for my poor, very poor, dear boys," she wrote. "My tears for them smart more and more day and night." And on July 23 a mighty cry escaped to her William, a cry that was a paragon of beauty and pathos:

William, William, William, is it possible the cry of my heart don't reach yours? I carry your beloved name before the tabernacle and repeat it there as my prayers in torrents of tears which Our God alone understands.

Childish weakness, fond partiality, you would say half-pained, if you could see from your present scene the agonized heart of your Mother. But its agony is not for our present separation, my beloved one; it is on long, eternal years, which press on it beyond all expression. To lose you here a few years of so embittered a life is but the common lot; but to love as I love you, and lose you forever—oh, unutterable anguish!

A whole Eternity miserable, a whole Eternity the enemy of God, and such a God as He is to us—!

Reading so much, your faith is quite lost, having everything to extinguish and nothing to nourish it. My William, William, William, if I did not see your doting Bec and Nina above, what would save my heart from breaking?

Despite the maternal agonies which God willed she should suffer to the end, Elizabeth's thoughts were now wholly of heaven; and it was with increasing effort that she turned from God to deal with the problems of earth. Sister Jane Frances Gartland was "going home" faster than she, and it filled her with envious longing. She told John Hickey:

Poor, dying, good Sister Jane was present [when his most recent letter and some scapulars arrived] and I let her share the kiss of peace, which she did with starting tears, feeling so well her condition to be hopeless in the senseless language of this world. Oh, my father, friend, could I hear my last stage of cough and feel my last stage of pain and the tearing away of my prison walls, how would I bear my joy? *The thought of going home,* called out by *His Will*—what a transport!

But they say: "Don't you fear to die?" Such a sinner must fear, but I fear much more to live and know what I do: that every evening examen finds my account but lengthened and enlarged. I don't fear death half so much as my hateful, vile self.

She had always cultivated that hatred of self which is the true mark of the saints, and had written on one occasion:

I am atom! You are God! Misery all my plea! So few saved! If we are lost, are you less justified? the patience so long waiting, less adorable? And the soul, burying itself in the chaos of mystery, always rested in stupidity within; but without, played with children, amused with the Sisters, yielding to all minutiae, attentive to all necessities. . . . Not one spark of grace can the soul discern in it all, but rather a continuation of the original fault, of desire to do, to be loved, to please! And so far from the simplicity of grace which would turn every instant to gold, it felt ashamed when [it] returned to the tabernacle, as if it had played the fool, or acted like those women who try to please company and show all their ill humors at home. . . .

She had, nevertheless, the honesty of true humility, the candor to recognize her own good striving:

> Yet it might be a grace, for as often He saw, it was no more in choice to hinder these evaporations than to stop the giddiness of my head in a fever. And they [the Sisters] are so loving, so fixed on Mother's every look, clouds or sunshine, so depending, sometimes I would shudder at the danger of such a situation if it was not clear as light that it is a part of the materials He takes for His work; and so little did He prepare the composition that He knows, if nature was listened to, I would take a blister, a scourging, any bodily pain, with a real delight, rather than speak to a human being—that heavy sloth which, hating exertion, would be willing to be an animal and die like a brute in unconsciousness! O, my Father, all in my power is to abandon and adore. How good He is to let me do that!"

And again she admitted, while owning up to her weakness, that "it is not the soul that is guilty of all this: the evil spirit is most active, it is true; but the good one sits in anguish at the foot of the cross, looking over all this desolation, adoring, subjecting, abandoning all to Him, seeing only Him, annihilating itself and all creatures before Him, saying amen to the resounding alleluias, and willing any moment to go into hell rather than add one more offense to the mountain it has already laid upon Him."

She understood well the Pauline doctrine of the warfare between flesh and spirit, and expressed it only less admirably than he:

> Poor, poor *poverina*, obliged to preach [she exclaimed.] . . .! If you knew only one half my reluctance to give an instruction or a catechism (formerly the heart's delight), it seems to me even yourself would be tempted to turn away with disgust from the ungrateful culprit; but the Dearest says, "You shall, you must, only because I will it; trust your weak breast and turning head to Me; I will do all." And *Sam* is so cruel, whenever there is an evident success he pushes and says, "See how they are affected, how silent and attentive; what respect, what look of love!"—and tries to make distractions in every way. The poor, poor soul don't even look to-

wards him, but keeps direct forward with Our Dearest, but with such a heavy, heavy heart at this vile mixture.

So, in the refectory sometimes, the tears start and the weakness of a baby comes over me, but Our Dearest again says, "Look up, if you had your little morsel alone, of another quality, no pains of body or reluctance to eat, what part would I have in your meal? But here is your place, to keep order, direct the reader, give example, and eating cheerfully the little you can take—in the spirit of love, as if before My tabernacle. I will do the rest. Abandon all." Abandon all! All is abandoned. But pray, pray for your poor one continually.

She understood, too, and accepted with bent head, the salutary hopelessness, the virtuous dryness, the "dark night" which God allows to engulf the soul willing to suffer this discord between flesh and spirit, to strive toward that total, blind abandonment to the divine Will in which lies the only chance of victory. She thus described it once to her spiritual father:

Writing on a table opposite the door of the chapel, looking at the tabernacle, the soul appeals to Him, if this is not a daily martyrdom. I love and live, and love and live, in a state of separation indescribable. My being and existence, it is true, are real, because I meditate, pray, commune, conduct the community, etc., and all this with regularity, resignation and singleness of heart; but yet, this is not I, it is a sort of machinery, no doubt acceptable to the compassionate Father, but it is a different being from that in which the soul acts. In meditation, prayer, Communion, I find no soul; in the beings around me, dearly as I love them, I find no soul; in that tabernacle I know He is, but I see not, feel not: a thousand deaths might hang òver me to compel me to deny His Presence there, and I would embrace them all rather than deny it an instant; yet it seems that He is not there for me—and yesterday, while for a few minutes I felt His Presence, it was only to make me know that hell was gaping under me, and how awful His judgment would be.

She once summed up in a luminous sentence what was in effect the story of her heroic life: "I am sick, but not dying; troubled on every side, but not distressed; perplexed but not despairing; afflicted, but not forsaken; cast down, but not destroyed; knowing the affliction of this life is but for a moment, while the glory in the life to come will be eternal." That she had found her exalted salvation in such a formula was attested to by the director of her soul, the blessed Bruté, in handing her, some weeks before she died, the following note—almost as if he were bestowing a sacred diploma, or giving her a ticket to present at the gate of heaven:

> My good Mother, your poor physician of the soul does not see you much, as he does not wish to fatigue you. He has no cause to fear, knowing that the heavenly Physician, the Beloved, the Spouse, the Only Desire of your heart, is continually present: present in the love, confidence, abandon, which He inspires, abandon the most tender and most unreserved—present in the continual acts of penance, humility, dependence and resignation to suffer everything in union with Him, with His cross—present in the peace, the tranquil joy which He imparts; in the total disengagement which He teaches; in the grace of every moment, pain or comfort which He dispenses.

And, after her death, Bruté exclaimed in rapture over "her magnanimous faith on her deathbed! My Lord, I have seen it, felt it. Express it I cannot, and I suffer immensely in not being able to do so, for it would be a source of so much edification if it could be communicated such as I FELT it."

Some measure of Elizabeth's preparation for death can be taken from the consideration of the thoroughness with which she, who had such warm capacity for love and friendship, now set about eradicating every last trace of human affection and comfort from her heart. Speaking of her "Blessed G.," she told Father Hickey: "We have broken our old bonds. I seldom speak to him but in the tribunal. What a lofty grace for this low earth!—but it is to be nearer in heaven, I hope." This final and absolute rejection of even the highest of human loves was so uppermost in her thoughts these last months that she even, in another letter, urged it upon Hickey himself, who had been wanting to return to Mount St. Mary's:

> My heart and soul this week past has been under the press of the Beatitude: "Blessed are the pure of heart—they shall see God." . . . Happy, happy are you to live all for Him. Every bent of your heart's affection, every power of your soul, turned wholly to Him without even the mixture of the innocent sojourning with your old father [Dubois] and dear brother [Bruté]. How much purer is your service where you are above the midst of earthly attraction. One thing I hope you are convinced of (I as a wretched sinner know it well), that wherever we meet a little prop of human comfort, there is always some subtraction of divine comfort. For my part, I

am so afraid to cause any such subtraction, that I feel a reserve and fear in every human consolation that makes them more my pains than my pleasure. Yet the liberty of the children of God I hope in all. I only mean to say we should be too happy when the Providence of God keeps us wholly to Himself.

Elizabeth made the last retreat of her life with her Sisters that August of 1820, under the direction of Father Bruté. He wrote out in his own hand the resolutions he wished her to keep: to reread the advices of Madame de Chantal to superiors—to remember that she, also, was especially accountable to God as a foundress—to remember that the Superior was the voice of God speaking to her—to abandon herself to the grace of each moment—to strive for the spirit of St. Francis de Sales and of Madame de Chantal. Their spirit, he said, was the same as that of St. Vincent de Paul, who belonged to Elizabeth in a special way since he and his co-worker, Louise de Marillac, were the soul of the community she had founded. He cautioned her to "keep a good exterior and to flee from harsh words; and in exercising authority to have a certain modesty and goodness, because this will inspire confidence and love." And he reminded her that "God gives you this . . . naturally."

Despite increasing weakness accompanied by pain, nausea and a choking cough, Elizabeth continued to fulfill as many of her duties as she could. She told Madame Chatard on August 24, 1820, that she was "pushing to the last extent of my strength for His dear family here, and never with such courage and contentment as now."

Think of my delight, dear friend [she went on] to have Sister Xavier "MOTHER'S ASSISTANT" by the votes of the community. She will, with her zeal, judgment and charity, be the support and blessing of us all. Sister Margaret will come for the school, as our Superior has given up the Lancastrian school in New York, so uncertain as to the purposed good and so great a distance in so distracted a place, while we see so great a prospect of schools among our best friends and much nearer to us.

Dubois had apparently given serious consideration to opening a school in Manhattan which would employ the educational theories of Joseph Lancaster, an Englishman who had educated great masses of the poor by using student monitors to teach the basic elements of reading, writing and arithmetic. Plans were going forward, however, for schools like the one in Philadelphia to be opened in New York and Baltimore, but Mother Seton would not live to see the establishment of either. The energetic Dubois thought it prudent to resume work on the new building at St. Joseph's that summer, and the usual Valley quiet was invaded by sound of saw and hammer. Elizabeth seems to have been less than enthusiastic about the project, for it must have been at this time she confided to Bruté: "The building is a bad business, but our endless obligations to the Superior, the very formation of the house all his—what can we say now? I would rather trust Our God to draw us out of the danger than dare oppose or aggravate him in our relative position."

Ironically, it was this new construction that touched off Elizabeth's long last illness, as she told Sister Elizabeth Boyle: "Our good Superior sent for me among the carpenters. I had to climb the pile of boards, as he insisted. Not being well, and the wind very sharp, I was in a strong fever . . . in a few days."

The fever had seized on her toward the end of August, and Bruté later described for Antonio Filicchi the weeks that followed:

Her situation soon became alarming. . . . Her tranquillity was perfect; she manifested it in her answers to the questions concerning her state, which she wished they should occupy themselves with as little as possible.

"How are you, Mother?"

"Quiet," she replied—sometimes, "Very quiet."

She continued to follow as closely as possible the exercises and rules of the house, being assisted in doing so by a Sister who read and prayed with her. This she did until her death, with great fidelity and perseverance—manifested her uneasiness when some point of rule could not be fulfilled and supplying it as soon as there was an opportunity. Being obliged to make use of mitigations and necessary exemptions, she avoided them as much as she could without affectation. Sometimes she made excuses to her Sisters for what she termed her weakness, and she reproached herself for paying attention to it; and she endeavored as much as possible to repair what she considered a fault by mortifying herself the more.

On one occasion she sent for me and lamented so earnestly, with tears that elicited mine, the relief that she experienced and the comparative comfort she enjoyed in the use of a mattress that had been provided for Rebecca when she suffered too much to bear the hardness of the ordinary bed—and this mattress they had given to her.

By the middle of September Elizabeth was so weak that Father Dubois thought it advisable to anoint her and give her Viaticum. On Sunday, September 24, feast of Our Lady of Mercy, Bruté was hearing the confession of a poor immigrant in St. Joseph's Church at Emmitsburg when a Sister knocked urgently at the door of the confessional to tell him: "Come, our Mother is dying." He took the first horse at hand and raced for the White House, passing the Sister and her companions on the road. He found Elizabeth calm and serene and not, to his way of thinking, on the point of death; but as he had to return to the village to sing the High Mass, he decided, in his own words to "do everything."

> The sign of whole piety and consent. "Confess all, in general, my Mother, to receive once more absolution." She does aloud. I . . . announce her the last indulgence. I dress, and some Sisters come in and Josephine, her daughter, comes in, too. Mother so calm, so recollected and so wholly united to her Blessed Lord. Her eyes so expressive, the look that pierces heaven and the soul visible in it; her hand expressive, her very breathing; and when I require her "yes," pronounced so willingly to her best. I require her to renew her vows and she does, "with all my heart." To bless her Sisters as being the present Mother, and ask their prayers, and she does in the simple words, "Yes, I bless them and ask their prayers." To bless her daughter Josephine, and her two sons, absent, and she does with such a look to heaven. Ah, dear children, her look to heaven and their God, her Whole and their Whole!

When Bruté and the Sisters came to the recitation of the Litany and the prayers for the dying, poor Kit could not bear it, and wept uncontrollably. Bruté stopped to comfort the girl and entreat her "to spare for best love the Mother's heart that has need of such a sacred peace and union." Kit did her best, but broke down again as the priest began "Depart, Christian soul."

Bruté returned again that evening, and suggested that Elizabeth might like him to write in her name to friends and former co-workers. The suggestion pleased her, and together they made a list: Antonio Filicchi, of course, and Cheverus; Archbishop Maréchal, Sibourd, Hickey, who was himself at death's door; Dubourg, Flaget, David—at this name she began to sob: "Mr. David—" she repeated, "to ask him pardon for all pains I gave him." She asked Bruté to stay the night, close by in the sacristy, in case she should need him. "I knew her faith for the presence of the priest and, indeed, the wish of the rituals that he might remain by the dying souls," he wrote later, adding in evident admiration, "but on my observing, "Better not; besides, I trust you do not die this night,' she did not insist one word."

After this crucial Sunday Elizabeth slowly regained a part of her strength, to the point where she could sit up and attend to at least some of her duties. Kit seized on this illusion of well-being and wrote eagerly to Julia Scott on October 4 that her mother, "though she has been exceedingly ill from what she calls the change of life . . . is now happily recovering, and we trust soon to have her perfectly restored to us." Elizabeth's fever, however, hung stubbornly on, and was the occasion of an heroic act of love. Holy Communion was, as it had been all her life, her strongest prop in her illness. October 6 was one of the regular days appointed for the Sisters to receive; but the night before, Elizabeth was seized with a raging thirst. She fought it all night, time and again refusing the water that would have brought her relief but at the same time would have prevented the union with her Lord which she desired more ardently with each tick of the clock. When morning finally came, and Bruté entered the room carrying the ciborium,

> her joy was so uncommon [he wrote in awe] that when I approached, and as I placed the ciborium upon the little table, she burst into tears, and, sobbing aloud, covered her face with her two hands. I thought first it was some fear of sin and, approaching her, I asked,
> "Be still, Mother! Peace, peace be to you! Here is the Lord of Peace! Have you any pain? Do you wish to confess?"
> "No, no! Only give Him to me!" . . . she said with an ardor, a kind of exclamation, and her whole face so inflamed that I was much affected. . . .

At just the point when Elizabeth had climbed painfully back to a degree of strength, her maternal heart suffered a last blow that might have killed outright a less spiritual mother—and it was the irresponsible Richard who struck it. Elizabeth had long had some expectation that William would be home in January, but Richard she had resigned, thinking him safe and happy in Leghorn. She was literally blasted to the roots of her being, then, to receive a letter from him, written on October 1, and informing her that "he was in Norfolk in some difficulty with a protested bill." Immediately the thought of her boy in a debtor's prison loomed up to terrify her, and she wrote frantically to General Harper to help him.

Hard on Richard's letter came one from Antonio, explaining why her son had left Leghorn: he was of no use in the counting house, was unwilling to learn to be of use and—how this must have turned the knife in Elizabeth's heart—was morally unsatisfactory; so Antonio had sent him home. Sick as she was, the heartbroken mother answered at once in such a dreadful scrawl and words large and shaky with weakness as to testify in a way language could not, to the terrible pathos of her situation. "This, then, is the earthly fruits of your goodness and patience with us," she began, beaten, as it were, to the ground, "but happily, all is written in heaven." And she continued:

> I have not seen the poor boy yet. He wrote us he was in Norfolk in some difficulty with a protested bill. And as I did not know what your dear letter informed me since, thinking he might be arrested or anything else, I wrote General Harper to have the kindness to see about him—not, dearest Antonio, for his relief, but for a mother's duty. For many years I have had no prayer for my children but that Our Blessed God would do everything to them and in them in the way of affliction and adversity, if only—He will save their soul(s)!

It was indicative of how upset she was that Elizabeth could not even put the words down in order: she placed the verb "would" between "Blessed" and "God" and was too weary to notice or change it.

There was, however, "another side," she told Antonio, even wounding humility in her desperate effort to console this good, faithful friend who had been betrayed by her own blood:

> Could you but know what has happened in consequence of the little, dirty grain of mustard seed you planted by God's hand in America! The number [of] orphans fed and clothed, public and private, etc. Our Archbishop is going to take a company of us to Baltimore in the house where our Bishop Carroll of happy memory lived. At Conewago, a Dutch settlement, they now prepare us an extensive establishment. We take Dutch or any, trusting to God and educating them with as much care and daily regularity as our paid boarders, so as to extend their usefulness wherever our sweet Providence may call.

And the letter ended brokenly: "Soon as [I] see my unhappy Richard —I will write again, please God. The reason of this writing I received the last Sacraments three weeks ago. . . ." She was nevermore to write to Antonio, and it was on this note of heartbreak that the story of one of the world's greatest, most beautiful, friendships terminated, so far as earth is concerned.

Richard was not in prison, but he did not hurry home, perhaps from some remaining shred of shame. On November 23, he sent an arrogant, lying letter to General Harper:

> To pretend, Sir, to give an account of my reasons for leaving Leghorn to you would be useless—suffice it to say that religious matters were the principal causes of it. That I have been in the wrong and acted imprudently I candidly confess—and to pretend, glazing my faults with excuses, would be but to destroy the merit of confessing them.
>
> Mr. Filicchi gave me $180 when I left; but having one half a year's expenses to pay, I had a surplus of $80—a messbill of 3 Doubloons to Gibraltar left me $30. With $30 I got stores to come to America—and on arrival I went to a miserable place to live, where my expenses have been $22 for two months.
>
> I am now trying to get on board some vessel; I have not written mama for money, as I know her situation. I would give half my life to see her, but fear I never shall again. For three weeks I was very sick, or I should have walked there.

Elizabeth never allowed her personal sorrows to obtrude on the lives of her Sisters, and just a week after the crushing news about Richard, she was writing a cheerful "community" letter to Sister Elizabeth Boyle, whom she called fondly, "dearest old partner of my cares and bearer of my burdens." This letter was apparently the last of the thousands Elizabeth had written in nearly forty years, and it took her, she said, "near a day to write . . . blowing, puffing, all the time." After telling her "dear Betsy" of the critical days in September, she continued:

> Slow the getting well—but not slow to sin, my dearest—turning to life. When I used to hear of their sending children's bills to Superior or paying out money, in the lowest moments when I could not turn on the pillow without hartshorn, I would stop them; for as Jane and I only had known, they were all in the dark. It soon pleased God I could answer and see to those things without letting them go out of their own old track. . . .

She could not forbear telling Sister Elizabeth the latest exploit of Father Dubois:

It seems the Superior went the other day to the infirmary unexpected, heard some talking, and asked Sister Benedicta, I believe, . . . if silence was not observed there; and he wrote—in large letters—"Silence here at all times as below, when not in recreation." . . . Also, no one to go to the infirmary without permission.

And she commented with her old mischievous gaiety: "You never saw such a change as that made!"

With the chill winds of November there was a sharp decline in Elizabeth's condition, and the news Kit wrote Julia Scott on the 18th was more somber than that of the month before. "My dear Mother is far from recovered," she wrote worriedly. "An abscess on her breast, as was the case two or three years ago, keeps her very, very weak. I have every hope that all will be well, though she may still for some time be kept suffering." To complicate matters, Elizabeth wasn't eating, port wine being almost her only nourishment.

Cecilia O'Conway was one of Elizabeth's nurses, and she seized the opportunity of being constantly by her to continue a task she had unaccountably taken on herself: the industrious scouring of Elizabeth's soul. She asked the dying woman, one day, whether she would not like a crucifix or picture before her eyes, to keep her thoughts on God.

"No, dear," Elizabeth answered, "I have a crucifix I keep on my breast" —and then, not being able to resist teasing the earnest woman—"besides, my eyes are generally closed." Next day, thinking she might have offended Cecilia or given her scandal, she said gently:

"Cessy dear, you are uneasy that I don't have something to remind me more of Our Dearest. Don't be afraid, my dear one, I do try to keep as close as I can in His Presence."

And on another day she spoke more at length to this first spiritual daughter of hers concerning the divine union she now enjoyed uninterruptedly:

"If this be the way of death, nothing can be more peaceful and happy; and if I am to recover, still how sweet to rest in the arms of Our Lord! I never felt more sensibly the Presence of Our Dearest than since I have been sick. It seems as if Our Lord stood continuously by me in a corporeal form, to comfort, cheer and encourage me in the different weary and

tedious hours of pain. Sometimes sweet Mary, also, gently coaxing me
—but you will laugh at my imagination."

Elizabeth loved to lie still through the long afternoons, listening to
the children—her "dear little pusses"—shouting and laughing at their
play. She would have the youngest brought in to see her and, dividing
among them whatever fruit she had, would say that the very sight of
their quick movements and sparkling eyes gave her new life. Another
favorite entertainment was to hear the Sisters tell of their work, especially of their visits to the poor of the nearby villages.

When the short, dull days of December began to file slowly by, even
the most stubborn optimist in the house knew that her Mother's end
was not far off. The coming of Richard brought a sudden brightness to
Elizabeth's room, even though he came in disgrace. There is no record
of what passed between the mother and son, but the time for fruitless
recriminations was long since past. It is a matter of record, however,
that the unfeeling youth went off in a matter of days, despite the fact
that it was close on Christmas and that his mother was soon to die.
Sister Cecilia's remark that Elizabeth's "poor heart . . . keenly felt the
pain of a last separation" was rather a pallid description of how bitter
that moment must have been. It was beyond doubt his mother's prayers
that gained for Richard Seton a brave and honorable death. He died
at sea on June 26, 1823, of a fever contracted while nursing back to life
an Episcopalian minister, Jehudi Ashmun.

Richard's going had conjured up for Elizabeth the many separations
and farewells she had known, and one night, as she talked with Cecilia
of "departed friends, present suffering compared to the . . . suffering of
Purgatory, of souls dying in misery without the sacraments," she suddenly began to cry.

"I am ashamed to complain when I remember those dear ones who
have gone," she sobbed. "What agonies they must have suffered—! Their
poor, bleeding bones—! That sweet, lovely Rebecca that I told you of,
though not a Catholic, who suffered such bitter pain with such happy
disposition!"

Cecilia took her hand and kissed it, trying to soothe her.

"O my soul's Mother," she said tenderly, "Our Lord Who knows your
desires perhaps will realize your wish of suffering a long time on this bed

of sickness. May He grant you your Purgatory in this life, and in death you may fly to His bosom of peace and rest."

"My blessed God," breathed Elizabeth, looking to heaven, "how far from that thought am I, of going straight to heaven—such a miserable creature as I am!"

It was not an emotion of the moment. Elizabeth had never been pleased to "hear the dead so eagerly sanctified or canonized," for fear that the praise, which meant nothing to them, would deprive them of prayers they might desperately need. As for herself, Bruté has testified that "a soul who felt so sacredly, with such light, the holiness of her God, had no doubt of Purgatory, had no presumption that it would not be for her."

Even Kit had lost hope of Elizabeth's recovery when she wrote to Julia Scott on the day after Christmas: "If any change has taken place since you last heard from me, it is that (my Mother) is still weaker. The abscess discharges itself so slowly that she is reduced to almost a skeleton." It was characteristic of Elizabeth that, dying herself, she should yet direct Kit to ask earnestly after Mrs. Scott's health, which had not been good; and to implore her Philadelphia friend to write an account of it at once, by her son's hand if she herself was not able. Pathetically enough, Julia complied on the 9th of January, unaware that Elizabeth was already dead and buried.

It was one of life's constant oddities that Elizabeth Bayley Seton, who had lived so tumultuous a life in so short a span of years, should now lay dying in calm and silence—she who had danced, rode horseback, attended the theatre, read the latest novels, in fashionable New York; who had married wealth and social position only to find poverty and neglect; who had crossed the ocean twice, won a titanic battle for her own soul, raised five orphaned children, and taught school to support them; who had fed and clothed so many widows, nursed so many sick, assisted so many to die; who had founded the first native American religious community, opened the first American parish school, established the first American Catholic orphanage—thus stirring the waters of grace and setting in motion circles of salvation which move still in ever-widening sweep, to break only on the shores of eternity.

Her own house was in order, her work done, her soul ready. Her last maternal obligation was fulfilled: Kit was to live with the good, devout Harpers as their own daughter; nothing more could be done for William and Richard that she had not already done.

On Saturday, the 30th of December, Elizabeth received Viaticum from the hands of her beloved Bruté. On the next day she shared the usual Sunday Communion with her Sisters. The New Year of 1821 had scarcely come in when Sister Anastasia Nabbs, who was on watch, urged her medicine on her; but she pushed it aside with the remark: "Never mind the drink. One Communion more—and then eternity." And she fasted for the peace of her last Communion on earth.

The morning of the 2nd of January Elizabeth was so low that Bruté again absolved her, gave her the Last Blessing and recited with her the prayers for the dying; but she grew so fatigued that he did not finish. Dubois decided that she could be anointed again, and when Bruté told her the good news at noon, she managed to whisper, "Very thankful" —it was becoming very hard for her now to speak in sentences. The whole community assembled at one o'clock, the hour appointed by the Superior, and the solemn ceremony began. Dubois' first words gave the scene its character, for this was more than the Church's farewell to a departing soul; it was a community's farewell to its holy foundress. Turning to the Sisters, Dubois said:

> Mother, being too weak, gives me charge to recommend you at this sacred moment in her place: first, to be united together as true Sisters of Charity; secondly, to stand most faithfully by your rules; thirdly, she requests that I ask you pardon of all the scandals she may have given you. I obey her desire. You know she gave none by the indulgences she was allowed—she means particularly in what she had to eat, or other allowances for her situation—in which she did but follow my express prescriptions and those of the physician.

Dubois then took up his ritual and began the anointing prayers, but Elizabeth interrupted, making a great effort to leave her dear daughters a last word:

"I am thankful, Sisters, for your kindness to be present at this trial," she gasped. "Be children of the Church, be children of the Church." And then, heaving a great sigh—"Oh, thankful!"

Next day Bruté began a retreat for the children who were to make their First Communion on the 6th of January. Stopping by Elizabeth's bed before he entered the chapel, he suggested that God might spare her "to have one Communion more with them on the day of Epiphany," and told her he was going to start his first conference with "the joy the angels declared to the shepherds and that which the good magi felt seeing the Star." How dearly Elizabeth would have loved such a Communion!—for she herself had known the joy of the magi, just sixteen years before, when the light of the Star broke upon her from the pages of Bourdelou. But it was not to be. She died that night, or rather in the small hours of the morning of Thursday, January 4, 1821.

Sister Anastasia summoned the Assistant, Sister Mary Xavier, shortly before one o'clock. She came hurriedly, and Elizabeth greeted her with the words:

"Well, Xavier, how do you do, dear?"

Kit came, and Sister Cecilia and Sister Joanna and Sister Sally and Elizabeth's dear Sus. Elizabeth herself began the prayer of Pius VII, which she had said every day for the past four months: "May the most just, the most high and the most amiable Will of God be in all things fulfilled, praised and exalted above all forever." Sister Xavier, knowing how Elizabeth had loved to say her prayers in French, repeated by her ear in that soft tongue the *Gloria in Excelsis* and the *Magnificat*. Close on two o'clock, Elizabeth was gone.

Sister Xavier wrote later:

> I do not know if you will give . . . the name of superstition to that which I felt at this moment. It seemed to me that Our Lord was there, near to her, very close, awaiting this good soul. I do not know when His Presence made a livelier impression upon me. Finally, she ceased to breathe, without convulsions nor extraordinary movement. I remained with her, with the other Sisters, all in prayer in the great silence.

Bruté arrived fifteen minutes after Elizabeth died. Sister Xavier, in the excitement, had forgotten to summon him until too late.

On May 5, 1821, long after the spring grass had appeared on her grave, Bruté wrote, in a letter to Antonio Filicchi, the perfect epitaph for Mother Elizabeth Seton:

> Near home we deposited her precious remains on the day following that of her death. In this little wood she reposes with about fifteen Sisters and

novices who had come to join her. She leaves more than fifty Sisters to survive her, to regret her and to follow in her footsteps—forty of them at St. Joseph's, the others at the Mountain, in Philadelphia and New York. She lived only for her Sisters and for the performance of her holy duties. She translated for their benefit our best French works, and copied whatever might be useful to the community.

How profound her faith and how tender her piety! How sincere her humility, combined with so great intelligence! How great her goodness and kindness for all!

Her distinguishing characteristic was compassion and indulgence for poor sinners. Her charity made her watchful never to speak evil of others, always to find excuses or to keep silence. Her other special virtues were her attachment to her friends and her gratitude; her religious respect for the ministers of the Lord and for everything pertaining to religion. Her heart was compassionate, religious, lavish of every good in her possession, disinterested in regard to all things.

O Mother, excellent Mother, I trust you are now in the enjoyment of bliss!

Sources

Key

AB	— Archives of the Archdiocese of Baltimore, Baltimore, Md.
DCWP	— Archives of the Daughters of Charity, Western Province, St. Louis, Mo.
FDLC	— Archives of Les Filles de la Charité, Paris, France.
GU	— Archives of Georgetown University, Washington, D.C.
MIS	— Archives of Mary Immaculate Seminary, Northampton, Pa.
MSM	Archives of Mount St. Mary's College, Emmitsburg, Md.
MSSCG	— Archives of the Mother Seton Sisters of Charity of Greensburg, Greensburg, Pa.
MSV	— Archives of the Sisters of Charity of St. Vincent de Paul, Mount St. Vincent-on-Hudson, N.Y.
NDU	— Archives of Notre Dame University, Notre Dame, Ind.
PG	— Archives of the Postulator General, Rome, Italy.
SCC	— Archives of the Sisters of Charity of Cincinnati, Ohio.
SCH	— Archives of the Sisters of Charity of Halifax, Nova Scotia.
SCSE	— Archives of the Sisters of Charity of St. Elizabeth, Convent, N.J.
S-F	— Seton-Filicchi Collection: letters of Mother Seton to Antonio and Filippo Filicchi, formerly in possession of the Filicchi family, Leghorn, Italy; now in possession of the Sisters of Charity of Cincinnati, Ohio.
S-J	— Seton-Jevons Collection: family letters, formerly in possession of the Jevons Family, Mother Seton's great grandchildren; then in possession of the Mother Seton Guild, Emmitsburg, Md.; now in possession of various communities of Sisters of Charity.
SJCH	— Archives of the Daughters of Charity, Eastern Province, St. Joseph's Central House, Emmitsburg, Md.
	N.B. *All references cited merely by number (e.g., XI, 2) pertain to these archives.*
WHITE	— *Life of Mrs. Eliza A. Seton* by Rev. Charles I. White, New York, 1853, first biography of Mother Seton, called "The Bible of the Cause" by the Sacred Congregation of Rites.

CHAPTER I

Page

6. MSSCG, E. A. Seton's *Following of Christ.*
7. James Thacher, *American Medical Biography,* Vol. II.
9. *New York Genealogical and Biographical Record.*

CHAPTER II

11. SJCH, *Dear Remembrances.*
13. ibid.; ibid.; ibid.
14. ibid.
16. ibid.; ibid.
17. ibid.

CHAPTER III

18. SJCH, *Dear Remembrances.*
21. ibid.
23. ibid.; ibid.
25. ibid.

CHAPTER IV

27. XI, 18.
28. VI, 19.
29. IX, 82; ibid., 98.
30. IX, 105; ibid., 88; ibid., 105; ibid., 80.
31. ibid., 86; VII, 2.
33. IX, 102; Robert Seton, *Memoir, Letters and Journal of Elizabeth Seton,* Vol. I.
34. NDU, Seton to Seton, Pimlico, Eton St., Dec. 21.
35. NDU, Seton to Seton, copy in Robert Seton's hand.
36. ibid.; ibid.; ibid.
38. NDU, Memorandum of William Seton, July, 1791.
40. SJCH, C. J. Seton's *Red Notebook.*
41. SJCH, *Dear Remembrances;* S-J Coll., Seton to Seton, Feb. 19, 1811, (SCH).
42. IX, 66; ibid., 67; ibid., 68.

CHAPTER V

44. S-J Coll., Seton to Seton, Feb. 28, 1796, (SJCH).

Page

45. ibid., Seton to Seton, July 27, 1794, (SCC).
46. SJCH, *Dear Remembrances;* ibid.
47. VII, 1; ibid.
48. ibid.
49. *New York Genealogical and Biographical Record;* Arthur C. Jacobson, *Medical Times,* 1923.
50. VII, 2.
51. IX, 78; ibid., 79; VI, 20; IX, 98.
52. ibid.; ibid., 79; ibid.
53. VII, 3; ibid.; ibid., 4.
54. ibid., 3; ibid., 4; ibid.
56. ibid., 5.
57. VI, 2; ibid., 3; ibid., 4.
58. ibid., 43; ibid., 6; ibid.; NDU, William Seton Obituary, Copy in woman's hand; S-J Coll., Seton to Cayley, July 6, 1798, (SCC), (copy: original lost).

CHAPTER VI

60. VI, 7.
61. ibid.; ibid.
62. VI, 10; ibid., 11.
63. ibid., 12; ibid., 14; ibid., 16.
64. S-J Coll., Seton to Cayley, n.d., (MSV); ibid.
65. ibid.; ibid.
66. IX, 100; VI, 21; ibid., 19; ibid., 21.
67. IX, 71; VI, 27; ibid., 23.
68. S-J Coll., Seton to Seton, June 8, 1799, (SCC).
69. VII, 19; ibid., 18; ibid., 13.
70. VIII, 145.

CHAPTER VII

71. S-J Coll., Seton to Seton, Oct. 2, 1799, (SCSE).
72. VII, 16; VIII, 1.
73. S-J Coll., Seton to Seton, Jan. 3, 1800, (SCSE); VIII, 2.
74. VI, 32; ibid.
75. S-J Coll., Seton to Seton, March 20, 1800, (MSSCG); ibid., Aug. 14, 1800.

76. IX, 101.
77. ibid., 102; VI, 34.
78. VII, 62; VI, 34.
79. VIII, 33; VII, 21.
80. VI, 37; ibid., 35; ibid., 34.
81. ibid., 36.

CHAPTER VIII

82. VI, 39.
83. ibid.
85. VIII, 15.
86. ibid., 25; VII, 30.
87. XV, 12.
88. VIII, 19.
89. ibid., 20; IX, 69; S-J Coll., Seton
    to Seton, June 10, 1801, (SCSE).
90. ibid.; ibid., June 18, 1801, (MSV);
    VI, 40; ibid., 41.
91. VIII, 52; VII, 24.
92. S-J Coll., Seton to Seton, June 7,
    1801, (MSSCG); VII, 26; VIII,
    35.
93. ibid., 47; ibid., 9; S-J Coll., Seton
    to Seton, n.d., (SCSE); VIII, 11.
95. VI, 42.
96. ibid.; ibid.; VIII, 21.
97. VI, 42; VII, 73.
98. VIII, 56.

CHAPTER IX

99. VI, 42; VIII, 56; ibid.
100. ibid., 37; VI, 42; ibid., 43; VIII,
     50.
101. VI, 43; ibid., 44; ibid., 45; ibid.
102. ibid., 44; VIII, 37.
103. VI, 45; ibid.; III, 6.
104. VIII, 57; ibid., 32; ibid., 8; ibid.
105. VI, 46; III, 8; ibid.; ibid.
106. VIII, 87; VI, 47.
107. ibid.; VIII, 28; ibid., 5; ibid., 54.
108. SJCH, Uncatalogued, Seton to
     Seton, Aug. 23, 1803; VII, 27;
     VI, 51; VIII, 61.
109. ibid., 20; ibid., 88; VII, 27.
110. IX, 64.
111. VII, 27.

CHAPTER X

Page

113. III, 14a; ibid., 14c; ibid., 14d;
     ibid., 14g.
114. XVII, 14.
124. ibid.; ibid.
125. ibid.
126. ibid.

CHAPTER XI

127. VIII, 60.
128. ibid.
129. X, 1; S-J Coll., Seton to Seton,
     Jan. 3, 1804, (MIS).
130. XI, 70; X, 1.
131. III, 15.
132. ibid.; ibid.
133. ibid.; ibid.; ibid.
134. ibid.; VIII, 60; ibid.
135. ibid.; ibid.
136. ibid.
137. ibid.; ibid.; ibid.
138. ibid.
140. White, 107; X, 3; White, 106;
     VIII, 60.
141. X, 3a; SJCH, *Dear Remem-
     brances*; X, 3a; VIII, 60.
142. ibid.; SJCH, *Dear Remembrances*.
143. White, 107.

CHAPTER XII

144. White, 110.
145. ibid., 108.
146. III, 16, 3.
147. X, 3; ibid., 3a.
148. ibid.
149. VI, 53; III, 39; VI, 53; X, 3;
     White, 122.
150. X, 3; III, 4; VI, 53.
151. III, 39; X, 3.
153. SJCH, S-F, 4.
154. X, 3; SJCH, S-F, 6; X, 9; ibid.
155. ibid.; ibid., 14.
156. ibid., 13; ibid.; SJCH, S-F, 6.
157. X, 14; I, 38.
159. X, 10; ibid., 9; ibid., 11; ibid.
160. SJCH, S-F, 3; X, 16; ibid., 20.
161. ibid., 10.

162. ibid., 3a.
163. Footnote: John A. Hardon, *The Protestant Churches in America*.
164. SJCH, S-F, Filicchi to Cheverus, Feb. 19, 1805; X, 3a.
165. XI, 8; XII, 80.
166. MSV, Cheverus to Seton, March 4, 1805; XII, 80; X, 14.
167. ibid., 3a.
168. ibid.; ibid.; ibid.
169. ibid.; ibid.

CHAPTER XIII

170. XII, 80.
171. SJCH, S-F, 20; VI, 56; SJCH, S-F, 24.
172. ibid.; ibid., 25; ibid., 23; II, 95.
173. ibid.; X, 3a; ibid.; VI, 56.
174. SJCH, S-F, 17; ibid., 32.
175. ibid.; ibid., 35.
176. ibid., 38; ibid., 32; ibid., 29.
177. ibid.; X, 22; SJCH, S-F, 26.
178. ibid., 50.
179. ibid., 53; ibid., 50; ibid., 46; ibid.; VI, 60; I, 2.
180. ibid., 20; XI, 1.
181. SJCH, Uncatalogued, Seton to Seton, Oct. 7, 1805.
182. VIII, 103.
183. VI, 59; ibid., 57; X, 28.
184. SJCH, S-F, 50; X, 29; SJCH, S-F, 52; X, 27.
185. SJCH, S-F, 53; VI, 60.

CHAPTER XIV

186. I, 4.
187. VI, 61.
189. I, 22; ibid.
190. SJCH, S-F, 57; X, 29; VI, 61.
191. SJCH, S-F, 23, 59; ibid., n.n., (May 2, 1806).
192. ibid., 64.
193. IV, 168.
195. SJCH, S-F, 26; X, 33; I, 121; IX, 28.
196. ibid.; X, 34.
197. SJCH, S-F, 27; ibid., 28.
198. X, 26.

199. I, 34; ibid.
200. ibid., 39; VI, 64; SJCH, S-F, 28.
201. VI, 65.
202. ibid.; ibid., 66; ibid., 67; ibid.
203. VII, 32.
204. IV, 190; VIII, 145; ibid.
205. ibid.; ibid.; X, 36; ibid.
207. SJCH, S-F, 29.
208. VI, 71; I, 9; VI, 68.
209. ibid., 72.
210. VII, 35.

CHAPTER XV

211. VIII, 154; ibid.
212. ibid.; ibid.; ibid.; ibid.
213. ibid.; VI, 73; VII, 35; VIII, 154.
214. ibid.
215. XI, 33; ibid., 34.
216. VI, 77; VIII, 152; ibid., 151.
217. VII, 63; VI, 73; ibid., 74.
218. ibid.; AB, 7-M-4, Aug. 6, 1809.
219. VIII, 154; VII, 63; MSV, Dubourg to Seton, May 27, 1808; SJCH, S-F, 76.
220. ibid.; VI, 74; VIII, 157; VI, 75; ibid.; ibid., 74.
221. ibid.; SJCH, S-F, 30; VIII, 153.
222. XI, 6; ibid.
223. VI, 74; ibid., 75; ibid.
225. IV, 208; VIII, 154; VI, 75.
226. X, 39; SJCH, S-F, 32; ibid.; ibid., 33.
227. ibid.; SJCH, Annals, 1882, II, 71.
229. SJCH, S-F, 34.
230. VII, 37; VI, 67.
231. XI, 24; VI, 76.
232. ibid.; VII, 37; ibid., 64; II, 103.
233. VI, 76; XI, 24.
234. ibid.; VI, 77.
235. VIII, 154; ibid.; ibid.; II, 17.
236. VIII, 154; I, 10.
237. IV, 209; ibid.
238. White, 252.

CHAPTER XVI

240. VI, 78.
241. II, 5.
243. XIX, 2.

Sources   461

Page

245. VI, 79; MSV, *Red Diary*.
246. *Mother Rose White*, Emmitsburg, 1936.
247. SJCH, *Mother Rose's Journal*, 4.
251. ibid., 6.
253. AB, 7-M-4, Aug. 6, 1809.
254. ibid.; ibid.; MSV, I, 14, Dubourg to Seton, Oct. 29, 1817; IV, 9.
256. AB, 7-M-5, Sept. 8, 1809.
257. AB, 7-M-4, Aug. 6, 1809; II, 6.
258. XII, 102.
259. MSV, I, 8, Dubourg to Seton, Sept. 13, 1809.
260. VI, 79; ibid.; ibid.
261. ibid.

CHAPTER XVII

263. AB, 7-M-6, Nov. 2, 1809; ibid.; II, 7.
264. AB, 7-M-7, Nov. 14, 1809; XVI, 35.
265. ibid.
266. VIII, 83.
267. VI, 80.
268. MSM, *Ledger*, Dec. 24, 1809; MSV, I, 10, Dubourg to Seton, Dec. 28, 1809.
269. MSV, I, 23; AB, 7-M-7, Jan. 25, 1810.
270. I, 42; ibid.
271. ibid.; MSV, Seton to Stubbs, n.d.
272. VII, 36; MSV, Seton to Stubbs, n.d.
273. AB, 7-N-13, Sept. 5, 1811; ibid.; VII, 36.
274. IV, 112; IX, 48a.
275. II, Suppl., 4.
276. XVI, 35.
277. MSV, I, 23, Dubourg to Seton, Dec. 28, 1809; White, 275; SJCH, *Mother Rose's Journal*, 19.
278. VI, 81; SJCH, *Mother Rose's Journal*, 13–14; ibid.
279. VII, 39; ibid., 64.
280. VI, 81; ibid.
282. ibid., 82; VII, 38; VI, 82.
283. IX, 34; VI, 83; IX, 37; II, Seton to David, n.d.

Page

284. AB, 7-N-10, March 16, 1811; VII, 64.
285. XIX, 5; I, 44.
286. VI, 83.
287. VII, 43; XII, 102; ibid.
288. II, 13.
289. VI, 84.
291. V, 17; VII, 40; XI, 12; AB, 20-L.

CHAPTER XVIII

293. II, 19.
294. VI, 85; VII, 65.
295. XI, 26; VI, 86; ibid.
296. VII, 41; VI, 85; ibid., 86; VII, 41; VI, 85; XI, 26.
297. II, 68; VII, 83; II, Suppl., 2; AB, 7-N-10, March 16, 1811.
298. ibid.; I, 43.
299. II, 12; ibid.; AB, 7-N-11, May 13, 1811.
300. ibid.; VI, 87.
301. ibid.; ibid., 84; ibid., 87; SJCH, *Dear Remembrances*; ibid.
302. White, 323.
304. VII, 65; AB, 7-N-11, May 13, 1811; SJCH, *Annals*, 1882, II, 71.
305. II, 60.
306. SJCH, *Council Minutes*; FDLC, *Labouré Papers*.
307. MSV, I, 2; MSV, Dubois to Garnier, Apr. 8, 1816; NDU, Flaget to Bruté, Oct. 17, 1811.
308. I, 45; AB, 8-A-F.
309. SJCH, *Mother Rose's Journal*, 22.
310. I, 45; ibid.; ibid.

CHAPTER XIX

312. VII, 65; IV, 86.
313. XI, 12; VI, 89; VII, 44; ibid.
314. XI, 12; ibid., 35; I, 56; III, 18.
315. ibid.
316. ibid.; VII, 45; III, 18; ibid.; ibid., 21.
317. ibid., 18; XI, 27.
318. VI, 89; XI, 27; ibid., 9.
319. III, 18; IX, 40b; VII, 46.
320. MSM, Dubois to Bruté, May 7, 1812; XII, 102; VI, 91; VII, 47.

Page

321. ibid., 49.
322. XI, 16.
323. AB, Seton to Harper, Jan. 2, 1812; MSV, I, 2; AB, Seton to Harper, Dec. 28, 1811; ibid.
324. MSV, I, 3, Cheverus to Seton, Jan. 20, 1812.
326. SJCH, *Recollections of Old Sisters*, 1886.
327. III, 48b; White, 362; ibid., 363–364.
328. ibid., 364.
329. IV, 93.
330. ibid., 95; ibid., 94; MSV, Dubois to Bruté, May 7, 1812.
331. XII, 34b; James Roosevelt Bayley, *Memoirs of Bishop Bruté*, 40; VII, 91, 93.
332. XIII, 11; VI, 95; ibid.
333. VII, 47; ibid., 46; ibid., 49; ibid., 50; NDU, Seton to Seton, 1823.
334. VII, 50; ibid.; ibid.; VI, 96.
335. XII, 33; VI, 96.

CHAPTER XX

336. VI, 97.
337. SJCH, *Dear Remembrances*; ibid.
338. XII, 36; ibid., 38; ibid., 47; ibid., 57.
339. ibid., 41; White, 340.
340. ibid.; ibid., 341; ibid., 344.
341. ibid.; ibid., 345; ibid., 342.
342. XII, 17b; White, 347; XII, 13; III, 26.
343. XII, 40; ibid., 41; ibid., 76; ibid., 41.
344. IV, 119; III, 26.
345. VII, 45; XI, 18; VII, 51; ibid.; XI, 28.
346. VI, 100; XI, 38; ibid.
347. VII, 54; XI, 15; IX, 49a.
348. ibid., 42a; ibid., 42b.
349. SJCH, *Council Minutes*.
350. ibid.
351. ibid.; ibid.
352. SJCH, *Mother Rose's Journal*, 25; White, 352–353.
353. IV, 73; SJCH, *Mother Rose's Journal*, 25.

Page

354. ibid.; ibid., 26–27; VI, 104.
355. ibid.; IX, 1; ibid.
356. SJCH, S-F, 89; XII, 69.
357. IX, 2; III, 26; X, 41; ibid., 42.
358. SJCH, S-F, 93; XI, 19.
359. IX, 3; XII, 18.
360. III, 26.
361. ibid.; ibid.
362. ibid.; VI, 105; S-J Coll., Seton to Seton, May 10, 1815; III, 26.
363. XII, 70; III, 26.
364. ibid.; NDU, Preudhomme to Bruté, July 17, 1815; X, 44.
365. ibid.; SJCH, S-F, 93; ibid., 95; X, 44; IX, 6; ibid.
366. ibid.; ibid.
367. ibid., 10; XI, 3; IX, 43.
368. ibid.; ibid., 46; ibid., 45.
369. SJCH, S-F, 97; ibid.; XI, 6.
370. XII, 50.
371. ibid., 51; VI, 109.

CHAPTER XXI

373. XI, 28.
374. XII, 56.
375. VII, 66; VI, 110; S-J Coll., Seton to Seton, Feb. 23, 1816, (SCC).
376. IX, 15; VI, 111; IX, 16.
377. S-J Coll., Seton to Seton, Apr. 25, 1816, (SCSE); ibid.; XI, 18.
378. ibid., 15; S-J Coll., Seton to Seton, July 2, 1816, (DCWP).
379. XII, 55; III, 18; XII, 62; III, 18; ibid.
380. ibid., 93, 2; VII, 67; S-J Coll., Seton to Seton, 1816 (SJCH).
381. XI, b51; XII, 55; XI, 30.
382. III, 18; ibid.; ibid.; ibid.
383. XII, 81; V, 25; IX, 21; XI, 23.
384. III, 18; XII, 80.
385. XI, b19.
386. XII, 68; VII, 68.
387. I, 16; S-J Coll., Seton to Seton, 1817, (MSV).
388. ibid.; SJCH, S-F, 103.
389. S-J Coll., Seton to Seton, Feb. 14, 1817; SJCH, *Act of Incorporation*.
391. III, 42; VII, 57.

392. ibid.; XII, 71; XI, 14.
393. ibid.; XI, 71; XII, 85; White, 471–472.
394. IX, 52; ibid.; XII, 86; SJCH, S-F, 107.
395. NDU, Seton to Seton, Apr. 4, 1817; SJCH, S-F, 107.
396. VI, 115; ibid., 116; XII, 19.
397. SJCH, *Council Minutes;* ibid.; SJCH, S-F, 109.
398. IV, 61; SJCH, *Foundations,* II, Dubois to Connolly, July 24, 1817.
399. XII, 73; S-J Coll., Seton to Seton, July 25, 1817, (SCSE); ibid.
400. ibid.; X, 46.
401. VI, 118; XII, 73; X, 46.
402. VI, 118.

CHAPTER XXII

404. S-J Coll., Seton to Seton, Feb. 25, 1818, (MSV); VI, 119; XI, 31; XII, 12.
405. S-J Coll., Seton to Seton, Feb. 16, 1818, (MSSCG); NDU, Seton to Seton, Feb. 25, 1818; S-J Coll., Seton to Seton, 1818; ibid.
406. IX, 53; ibid.
407. ibid.; ibid.; ibid.
408. ibid., 54; VI, 121; ibid., 122; VII, 59; S-J Coll., Seton to Seton, March 24, 1818, (MSV).
409. VI, 122; S-J Coll., Seton to Seton, Apr. 6, 1818, (SCC); ibid., March 24, 1818, (MSV).
410. XII, 67; ibid., 74; ibid.
411. III, 22; IV, 100; ibid.
412. S-J Coll., Seton to Seton, March 24, 1818, (MSV); ibid., Seton to Seton, Aug. 6, 1818, (SCSE).
413. ibid.
414. XI, 20; S-J Coll., Seton to Seton, May 9, 1818, (MSV); ibid., Seton to Seton, May 5, 1818, (SJCH); ibid., Seton to Seton, Aug. 24, 1818, (DCWP).

415. ibid., Seton to Seton, May 10, 1818, (SCH), (original destroyed by fire; copy at SJCH); ibid., Seton to Seton, May 27, 1818, (MSSCG).
416. ibid., Seton to Seton, June 15, 1818, (DCWP); XI, b54; I, 71.
417. S-J Coll., Seton to Seton, July 21, 1818, (SCSE); ibid., Seton to Seton, Aug. 1, 1818, (SCC); ibid., Seton to Seton, Boston, July 21, 1818, (DCWP); ibid.; Aug. 1, 1818, (SCC).
418. MSV, Cheverus to Seton, Aug. 11, 1818; SJCH, S-F, 114; XII, 14.
419. XI, 25; SJCH, S-F, 114; ibid., 50.
420. S-J Coll., Seton to Seton, Aug., 1818, (SCSE); ibid., Seton to Seton, Aug. 24, 1818, (DCWP).
421. VI, 123; XII, 11; ibid., 1; S-J Coll., Seton to Seton, Oct. 24, 1818, (MSSCG).
422. ibid., Seton to Seton, Oct. 20, 1818, (MSSCG); VI, 126; SJCH, *Council Minutes.*
423. SJCH, S-F, Nov. 11, 1818; XII, 78.
424. ibid., 66.
425. ibid., 76.
426. MSM, Dubois to Garnier, Feb. 17, 1819, (copy; original in Paris Archives); S-J Coll., Seton to Seton, July 1, 1818, (SJCH); SJCH, Craig to Seton, Nov. 17, 1818.
427. SJCH, Dupleix to Seton, fall, 1818; ibid.; ibid.; SJCII, Craig to Seton, Nov. 17, 1818.

CHAPTER XXIII

428. XII, 16; VII, 61; XI, 24.
429. X, 48; ibid.; ibid.
430. IX, 57; ibid.; VI, 128; GU, 240: 7, Seton to Hickey, June 10, 1819.
431. XII, 15.
432. *Rev. Simon Gabriel Bruté in His Connection with the Community,* 306.

Page

433. IX, 58.
434. MSV, Seton to Seton, June, 1819; VII, 88.
435. ibid.; ibid., 69; ibid.; XI, 54; ibid.
436. S-J Coll., Seton to Seton, Nov. 7, 1819, (SCSE); VII, 60.
437. IV, 88; ibid., 87.
438. IX, 59; ibid., 61; S-J Coll., Seton to Seton, May 8, 1820, (DCWP); ibid.
439. ibid.; XII, 8; ibid.; GU, 240: 7, Seton to Hickey, July 2, 1820.
440. NDU, Seton to Seton, July 23, 1820; GU, 240: 7, Seton to Hickey, July 2, 1820; White, 417.
441. ibid.; ibid., 418; ibid., 425.
442. ibid., 416–417; ibid., 419.

Page

443. XII, 2; ibid., 12b; GU, 240, 7: Seton to Hickey, July 2, 1820; ibid., n.d.
444. XII, 16; IV, 92.
445. XII, 49; MSV, Seton to Boyle, Oct. 8, 1820; XII, 108.
446. ibid., 1; ibid.; ibid.; ibid.
447. XI, 56; XII, 2.
448. SJCH, S-F, 128; ibid.
449. AB, 20-N-20, Seton to Harper, Nov. 23, 1820; MSV, Seton to Boyle, Oct. 8, 1820.
450. ibid.; XI, 57; XII, 6; ibid.
451. ibid.; ibid.
452. ibid., 17; ibid., 13; XI, 58.
453. XII, 108; ibid., 3; ibid.
454. ibid.; ibid., 5; ibid., 108.

Bibliography

ARCHIVES OF SAINT JOSEPH'S CENTRAL HOUSE, EMMITSBURG, MARYLAND

Original Letters and Papers: Elizabeth Bayley Seton Letters and Papers; William Magee Seton Letters; Seton Children Letters and Papers; Seton Family Letters; Bayley Family Letters; Post Letters; Dupleix Letters; Sadler Letters; Scott Letters; Babade Letters and Papers; Bruté Letters and Papers; Dubois Letters and Papers; Sibourd Letters; Hurley Letters; Chatard Letters; Barry Letters; Weis Letters; Wiseman Letters; Miscellaneous Letters and Papers.

Council Minutes; Minutes of the Corporation; Mother Rose's Journal; Mother Seton Notebooks and Journals; Seton Children Notebooks; Community Annals; Recollections of Contemporaries of Mother Seton.

Photostats of Original Letters and Papers in the Archives of:
    The Sisters of Charity of Mount Saint Vincent-on-Hudson, New York
    The Sisters of Charity of Cincinnati, Ohio
    The Mother Seton Sisters of Charity of Greensburg, Pennsylvania
Elizabeth Bayley Seton Letters; Seton Children Letters; Seton Family Letters; Cheverus Letters; Carroll Letters; Dubourg Letters; David Letters; Filicchi Letters; Miscellaneous Letters and Papers.

Copies of Letters and Papers in the Archives of:
    The Archdiocese of Baltimore, Baltimore, Maryland
    The Catholic University of America, Washington, District of Columbia
    Georgetown University, Washington, District of Columbia
    Mount Saint Mary's College, Emmitsburg, Maryland
    Saint Mary's Seminary, Roland Park, Baltimore, Maryland
    The Sisters of Charity of St. Elizabeth, Convent, New Jersey
Elizabeth Bayley Seton Letters and Papers; Seton Family Letters; Bruté Letters and Papers; Dubois Letters and Papers; Cooper Letters; Hickey Letters; Dubourg Letters; David Letters; Cheverus Letters; Carroll Letters; Filicchi Letters.

ARCHIVES OF THE UNIVERSITY OF NOTRE DAME, NOTRE DAME, INDIANA

Original Letters and Papers: Elizabeth Bayley Seton Letters and Papers; Seton Family
Letters; Seton Children Letters; Bayley Family Letters and Papers; David Letters;
Dubourg Letters; Bruté Letters; Flaget Letters; Cheverus Letters; Carroll Letters;
Coóper Letters.

Mother Seton's Prayerbook.

ARCHIVES OF THE POSTULATOR GENERAL, ROME, ITALY

Sacra Rituum Congregatione; Sectio Historica. *Baltimoren. Beatificationis et Canon-
izationis Servae Dei Elizabeth Annae Bayley Viduae Seton Fundatricis Congrega-
tionis Sororum a Caritate Sancti Josephi in America:* Roma, Positio Super Virtutibus
Ex Officio Disposita, 1957; Nova Positio, 1958; Novissima Positio, 1959.

Copies of Original Letters and Papers: Miscellaneous Letters and Papers.

ARCHIVES OF THE DAUGHTERS OF CHARITY, PARIS, FRANCE

Labouré Papers

Angle, Paul M. *The American Reader,* New York, 1958.
Anglin, Thomas Francis. "The Eucharistic Fast," *The Catholic University of America
Canon Law Studies,* No. 124, Washington, 1941.
Bardi, Giuseppe. *De Anglicana a Cattolica, Elisabetta Seton,* Torino, 1939.
Bargellini, Piero. *Florence, An Appreciation of Her Beauty,* Firenze, 1960.
Bayley, James Roosevelt. *Memoirs of the Rt. Rev. Simon Wm. Gabriel Bruté, D.D.,
First Bishop of Vincennes,* New York, 1861.
Bridgeman, Charles. "Mother Seton," *Trinity Parish Herald,* Vol. III (March 1949).
Brooks, Van Wyck. *The World of Washington Irving,* New York, 1944.
———. *The Times of Melville and Whitman,* New York, 1953.
Calvet, Jean. *St. Vincent de Paul,* tr. by Lancelot C. Sheppard, New York, 1948.
———. *Louise de Marillac,* tr. by G. F. Pullen, New York, 1959.
Caulfield, Sister Marie Louise. *Our Union With France,* Emmitsburg, 1855.
Cicognani, Amleto Giovanni. *Sanctity in America,* Paterson, 1945.
Code, Joseph B. *Letters of Mother Seton to Mrs. Julianna Scott,* Emmitsburg, 1935.
Coste, Pierre. *Life of St. Vincent de Paul,* tr. by Joseph Leonard, 3 Vol., West-
minster, 1952.
de Barberey, Helen Bailly, *Elizabeth Seton,* tr. and adapted from the Sixth French
Edition with a brief sketch of the Community of the Sisters of Charity since the
death of Mother Seton by Joseph B. Code, New York, 1927.
de Caussade. *Abandonment to Divine Providence,* St. Louis, 1921.
Deering, Arthur. *Notes on the Early American Theatre,* unpublished manuscript in
the possession of the author of this biography.
De Lehen. *The Way of Interior Peace,* tr. by James Brucker, New York, 1888.
de Paul, Vincent. *The Conferences of St. Vincent de Paul to the Daughters of
Charity,* tr. by Joseph Leonard, London, 1939.
———. *Conferences and Select Letters of St. Vincent and Some Conferences of M.
Alméras, His Immediate Successor,* Dublin, 1888, ms. copy, Philadelphia, 1942.
de Sales, Francis. *Introduction to the Devout Life,* tr. by John K. Ryan, New York,
1949.
Dillon, Dorothy Rita. *The New York Triumvirate: A Study of the Legal and Political*

Careers of William Livingston, John Morin Scott, William Smith, Jr., Columbia University, New York, 1949.
Dirvin, Joseph I. *St. Catherine Labouré of the Miraculous Medal,* New York, 1958.
Dooley, Roger B. *Notes on the Early American Novel,* unpublished manuscript in the possession of the author of this biography.
Easterly, Frederick J. *The Life of Rt. Rev. Joseph Rosati, C.M., First Bishop of St. Louis, 1789–1843,* Washington, 1942.
Feeney, Leonard. *Mother Seton, An American Woman,* New York, 1947.
Godecker, Sister Mary Salesia. *Simon Bruté de Rémur, First Bishop of Vincennes,* St. Meinrad, Indiana.
Gross, Alexander. *Five Borough Atlas of New York City,* New York, 1954.
Grou, J. N. *Spiritual Maxims,* tr. by Theodore Baker, London, 1922.
Guardini, Romano. *The Lord,* tr. by Elinor Castendyk Briefs, Chicago, 1954.
Hardon, John A. *The Protestant Churches of America,* Westminster, 1956.
Hoare, Sister Mary Regis. *Virgin Soil,* Boston, 1942.
Jenkins, Stephen. *The Greatest Street in the World—Broadway,* New York, 1911.
Keller, Helen Rex. *The Reader's Digest of Books,* New York, 1933.
Kenrick, Francis Patrick. *Theologiae Moralis,* Vol. III, Philadelphia, 1843.
Laverty, Sister Rose Maria. *Loom of Many Threads: The English and French Influences on the Character of Elizabeth Ann Bayley Seton,* New York, 1958.
Leen, Edward. *In the Likeness of Christ,* New York, 1940.
Leen, James. *By Jacob's Well, A Planned Retreat,* tr. by Edward Leen, New York, 1940.
Maréchal, Ambrose. *Diary,* manuscript at Notre Dame University, Notre Dame, Indiana.
Marmion, Columba. *Christ the Ideal of the Monk,* tr. by a Nun of Tyburn Convent, London, 1926.
———. *Christ the Life of the Soul,* tr. by a Nun of Tyburn Convent, St. Louis, 1925.
Maturin, B. *Self-Knowledge and Self-Discipline,* New York, 1922.
Maynard, Theodore. *The Reed and the Rock,* New York, 1942.
McCann, Sister Mary Agnes. *The History of Mother Seton's Daughters, The Sisters of Charity of Cincinnati, Ohio, 1809–1923,* 3 Vol., New York, 1923.
Melville, Annabelle M. *Elizabeth Bayley Seton, 1774–1821,* New York, 1951.
———. *John Carroll of Baltimore,* New York, 1955.
Miller, William. *A New History of the United States,* New York, 1958.
Noldin, H. *Summa Theologiae Moralis,* recognovit et emendavit A. Schmitt, 3 Vol., New York, 1940.
Paine, Thomas. "Common Sense," *The Oxford Anthology of American Literature,* ed. by William Rose Bénet and Norman Holmes Pearson, Vol. I, New York, 1954.
Pecci, Giuseppe. *Elogio Funebre del Cav. Antonio Filicchi da Gubbio detto da Sua Reverendissima Mons. Giuseppe de' Conti Pecci, Patrizio e Vescovo di detta citta in occasione de' solenni funerali che si celebravano in patria nella Ven. Chiesa di S. Francesco, Gubbio,* 1847.
Pomerantz, Sidney I. *New York, An American City, 1783–1803,* New York, 1938.
Ruddy, James. *The Apostolic Constitution "Christus Dominus,"* The Catholic University of America, Washington, 1957.
Schroeder, H. J. *Canons and Decrees of the Council of Trent,* St. Louis, 1955.
Seaton, Oren Andrew. *The Seaton Family with Genealogy and Biographies.* Topeka, 1906.
Seton, Robert. *Memoir, Letters and Journal of Elizabeth Seton,* 2 Vol., New York, 1869.
———. *Memories of Many Years (1839–1922),* New York, 1923.

————. *An Old Family*, New York, 1899.

————. *Record of the Bayley Family in America*, manuscript at Notre Dame University, Notre Dame, Indiana.

Seton, Samuel Waddington. *Family Notes*, manuscript at Notre Dame University, Notre Dame, Indiana.

Seton, William. *Memoirs*, manuscript at Notre Dame University, Notre Dame, Indiana, 1898.

Sharkey, Sister Mary Agnes. *The New Jersey Sisters of Charity*, 3 Vol.

Souvay, Charles L. "Questions Anent Mother Seton's Conversion," *The Catholic Historical Review*, Vol. V (July–October 1919), p. 223 ff.

Tanquerey, Adolphe. *The Spiritual Life, A Treatise on Ascetical and Mystical Theology*, tr. by Herman Branderis, Tournai, 1930.

————. *Synopsis Theologiae Dogmaticae*, recognovit et de novo redegit J. B. Bord, Tournai, 1937.

Thacher, James. *American Medical Biography*, Vol. II, Boston, 1828.

Teresa of Avila. *The Life of St. Teresa of Jesus of the Order of Our Lady of Carmel Written by Herself*, tr. by David Lewis, ed. by Benedict Zimmerman, Westminster, 1933.

Walsh, Sister Marie de Lourdes. *The Sisters of Charity of New York*, New York, 1960.

————. *Mother Elizabeth Boyle, Mother of Charity*, New York, 1955.

White, Charles I. *Life of Mrs. Eliza A. Seton*, Baltimore, 1853.

————. *Mother Seton, Mother of Many Daughters*, revised and edited by the Sisters of Charity of Mount Saint Vincent-on-Hudson, New York, Emmitsburg, 1953.

Albany Tercentenary 1624–1924, Albany, 1924.

"Biographical Notice of Mrs. Seton Foundress and First Superior of the Sisters of Charity in the United States," *The Metropolitan Catholic Almanac and Laity's Directory for the Year of Our Lord 1842*, Baltimore, 1842.

The Catholic Encyclopedia, New York, 1907.

Codicis Juris Canonicis Fontes, cura Patri Card. Gasparri editi, 9 Vol., Rome, 1923–1939.

Common Rules of the Daughters of Charity, Paris, 1658, 1954.

Concilia Provincialia Baltimori habita ab anno 1829 usque ad annum 1849, "Diocesan Synod of Baltimore of 1791," Editio Altera, Baltimore, 1851.

Constitution of the Sisters of Charity of St. Joseph of Cincinnati, Ohio, United States of America, 1851.

Constitution of the Sisters of Charity of St. Joseph's Convent, Greensburg, Pennsylvania, United States of America, 1870.

The Constitutions and The Directory of the Sisters of Charity of Saint Vincent de Paul of New York, New York, 1948.

Constitution of the Sisters of Charity of St. Vincent de Paul, Halifax, New York, 1933.

Constitutions of the Sisters of Charity, Convent Station, New Jersey, 1948.

Course of Meditations for all the Days of the Year for the Use of the Congregation of the Mission by a Priest of the Same Congregation, Paris, 1889, manuscript copy, Perryville, 1941.

De Synodo Diocesano, Vol. I, Rome, 1806.

Dictionnaire de Theologie Catholique, "Baptême dans L'Église Anglicane," Vol. II, Paris, 1923.

Elogio Storico de Cav. Antonio Filicchi da Gubbio, scritto da un suo concittadino, Gubbio, 1847.

Encyclopedia Brittanica, Chicago, 1897.

Encyclopedia of American History, ed. by Richard B. Morris, New York, 1953.
History of the State of New York, ed. by Alexander C. Flick, Norwood, 1933–1937.
A Guide to Trinity Church in the City of New York.
The Independence Square Neighborhood, Philadelphia, 1926.
Juris Pontificii De Propaganda Fide, Pars Secunda, coll. Raphaelis De Martinis, Num. CLXXXVI, Roma, 1909.
Letters of Horace Walpole, ed. by Anna B. McMahan, Chicago, 1890.
Lives of Our Deceased Mothers, Emmitsburg, n.d.
Lives of Our Deceased Sisters, Emmitsburg, n.d.
Mother Augustine Decount, Emmitsburg, 1938.
Mother Rose White, Emmitsburg, 1936.
National Cyclopedia of American Biography, New York, 1897.
The New York Genealogical and Biographical Record, New York, 1900–1959.
"A Patriotic Mother," Mother Seton Guild Bulletin, No. 4 (September 1942).
Regulations for the Society of the Sisters of Charity in the United States of America, Mount St. Vincent-on-Hudson, New York, n.d.
Report of the Sixth Conference of Mother Seton's Daughters, Convent, New Jersey, 1950.
Rev. Simon Gabriel Bruté in His Connection with the Community, Emmitsburg, 1886.
Sisters of Charity, 1849–1949, Halifax, 1949.
The Soul of Elizabeth Seton: A Spiritual Autobiography, New York, 1936.

Index

Adams, John, friend of Filippo Filicchi, 128.

Adams, John Quincy, influence sought for William Seton, 401.

André, Major John, friend of William Seton, 37.

Arnold, Benedict, and meeting with Major André, 37.

Astor, John Jacob, fur store in New York, 40; partner of Cornelius Heeney, 398.

Babade, Father Pierre, S.S., Mrs. Seton's spiritual director, 218; religion instructor at Paca St. school, 220; secures first recruits for Mrs. Seton, 221; instructs First Communicants, 225; on Du-Pavillon, 232; at establishment of Sisterhood, 238; friendship for Harriet Seton, 244 ff; offers Mass for Harriet Seton, 245; on missionary tour, 246; Sisters forbidden to consult, 252; qualifications as spiritual director, 254-255; receives Harriet Seton into Church, 258-259; refuses Dubois' offer of assistantship, 259; on plan to transfer Mrs. Seton to Baltimore, 294; predicts DuPavillon's faithlessness,

294; learns of Mother Seton's happiness at Christmas, 314; prays for spirit of St. Vincent upon community, 343-344; wishes happy death for Mother Seton, 416.

Bainbridge, Commodore William, at Tripoli, 110; commander of *Independence*, 404.

Baltimore, visited by William Magee Seton, 68, 89–90; only American see, 152; St. Mary's College in, 183; Antonio Filicchi visits, 187 ff; Dubourg suggests Mrs. Seton establish school in, 199; Mrs. Seton arrives in, 212; consecration of St. Mary's Chapel in, 212-213; Paca St. school in, 219; raised to archdiocese, 224; beginnings of Sisterhood in, 235; Mrs. Seton leaves, 240; David's plan to establish separate community in, 275 ff; Cecilia Seton dies in, 281; Mrs. Seton proposes begging tour of, 425; war riots in, 329; Rebecca Seton visits, 329 ff; 348; under siege, 352; William Seton visits, 358 ff; Carroll dies in, 370; Bruté President of St. Mary's College in, 370 ff; Richard Seton visits, 375: Rich-